Writings on Britain

Writings on Britain

Leon Trotsky

Introduction by Rob Sewell

Wellred Books
London

Writings on Britain
Leon Trotsky

First edition
Wellred Books, March 2023
Edited by Wellred Books

First published in 1974 by New Park Publications
Edited by R. Chappell and Alan Clinton

UK distribution: Wellred Books, wellred-books.com
152-160 Kemp House, City Road
London
EC1V 2NX
books@wellred-books.com

USA distribution: Marxist Books, marxistbooks.com
WR Books
250 44th Street #208
Brooklyn
New York
NY 11232
sales@marxistbooks.com

DK distribution: Forlaget Marx, forlagetmarx.dk
Degnestavnen 19, st. tv.
2400 København NV
forlag@forlagetmarx.dk

Cover design by Nye Shaw and Jesse Murray-Dean

Front cover image: *A Demonstration of Workers in Crewe During the
1926 General Strike*, 10 May 1926
Vintage_Space / Alamy Stock Photo, ID: 2A12MYA

Back cover image: *Leon Trotsky*, from the David King Collection.
Purchased from David King by Tate Archive 2016.

Layout by Wellred Books

ISBN: 978 1 913026 82 0

Contents

III

The Labour Movement

VOLUME TWO

IV

Where is Britain Going?

V

Problems of the British Labour Movement

VI
The Lessons of the General Strike

Appendices

VOLUME THREE

VII
From World Slump to World War

VIII
Trotsky Versus Centrism in Britain

IX
British Imperialism and National Liberation Struggles

Introduction by Rob Sewell

Given the deepening crisis of world capitalism; the catastrophic position of British capitalism in particular; and the reawakening of the British working class, the republication of Leon Trotsky's *Writings on Britain* could not have come at a more opportune moment.

Leon Trotsky was not only the outstanding leader, along with Lenin, of the October Revolution in Russia – he was also one of the greatest Marxist theoreticians of the twentieth century. His voluminous writings cover a wide range of topics and constitute a rich treasure house for those who want to understand the Marxist method and how it can be applied concretely. Today, his extensive writings on Britain are of particular interest to a growing audience, politically awakened by the convulsions taking place in Britain and internationally.

While not all of Trotsky's prognoses worked out as predicted, his general analysis of British capitalism, and the revolutionary conclusions he drew from this analysis, are clearly more timely and relevant than ever, given today's prolonged crisis and decline. History tends to repeat itself, and when it does, it does so on a higher level. All the contradictions of capitalism mentioned by Trotsky nearly 100 years ago have come to the fore at the present time, in the most graphic and aggravated fashion. Britain has once again entered a pre-revolutionary period, in which the crisis of the capitalist system is being brought home ever more sharply, and with it the need for revolutionary leadership.

Of course, for the 'Left' cynics and sceptics, who wallow in their own self-pity, and who accept the 'market economy' in practice, these writings are worthless. For them, the very idea of the socialist revolution is a utopian dream. Instead, they look to Keynesianism and the discredited ideas of the past. Such useless pessimists, mostly disillusioned intellectuals, make up a modern-day 'League of Abandoned Hopes'. In fact, they constitute an additional barrier in the fight for the emancipation of the working class, and are of no interest to us in the slightest. We concur with the advice of the Bible: "Let the dead bury the dead."

For the class-conscious worker and the revolutionary youth awakened by the capitalist crisis, on the contrary, Trotsky's writings offer a veritable gold mine of ideas, which will greatly assist them in raising their political level, broadening their horizons, and equipping them for the struggles that lie ahead.

For our part, we are proud to republish this collection of Trotsky's writings on Britain, which was first published by New Park Publications nearly fifty years ago, but which has long been out of print. These writings cover an array of subjects, which reveal the encyclopaedic scope of Trotsky's knowledge and his grasp of the material. In his short work, *Where is Britain Going?* (1925), which can be found in this collection,[1] Trotsky predicted revolutionary upheavals that were inherent in the situation. His prognosis was confirmed in the 1926 General Strike. The book was translated and promoted by the British Communist Party, which at that time was a young revolutionary party, unaffected by Stalinism. Trotsky explained:

> … whatever the partial fluctuations in the economic and political conjuncture, everything points to a further aggravation and deepening of those difficulties which Britain is currently undergoing and thereby to a further acceleration of the tempo of revolutionary development.[2]

He showed how this would affect the Labour Party, which was in the grip of the reformists and opportunists. The coming to power of a Labour government under crisis conditions would, he believed, lead to divisions and splits:

> But in these conditions it seems highly likely that the Labour Party will come to power at one of the subsequent stages, and then a conflict between the working class and the Fabian top layer now standing at its head will be wholly unavoidable.[3]

In fact, such a crisis Labour government came to power in 1929, and under the impact of the world slump, ended in the betrayal of Ramsay MacDonald and a split in 1931. This pushed the Independent Labour Party (ILP), which was affiliated to the Labour Party, to split away in the following year. This

---

1   See p. 213 of the present edition.
2   Ibid., p. 334.
3   Ibid.

propelled the ILP far to the left, towards centrism – a tendency standing between reformism and Marxism. Sadly, the revolutionary opportunities that arose were squandered by the centrist leaders of the ILP, as well as by the Communist Party, which by now had succumbed to Stalinism.

Given that it had been the first capitalist country in the world, and the pre-eminent world power of the time, Britain had always been of great interest to Marx and Engels, theoretically and politically. Engels' book *The Conditions of the Working Class in England in 1844* – a product of his stay in Manchester – remains a classic text and essential reading for activists to this day. Marx, like Engels, lived in exile in London, where he studied the writings of the English classical economists and the workings of British capitalism first hand. These studies laid the basis for his discovery of surplus value and later for the production of *Capital*. Both Marx and Engels were involved in the struggles of their day, and they collaborated with the leaders of revolutionary Chartism in an attempt to rearm the movement with a scientific programme.

With the demise of Chartism, British capitalism enjoyed a spectacular growth and a monopoly over world trade, whilst its empire grew to cover a quarter of the globe. On this basis, the British ruling class could share its plunder with a privileged layer of the working class, an *aristocracy of labour*. These concessions provided a certain social stability, which permitted an extended period of relative peace between the classes. This period was described by Engels as a "forty year slumber" of the British working class, lasting until the late 1880s. But Britain's monopoly over world trade was broken by the rise of Germany and the United States, leading to a new period of social upheaval and the emergence of New Unionism and the creation of the Labour Party.

Lenin also followed the fortunes of British capitalism and the development of the working-class movement. While the workers had shown class militancy, its leaders were thoroughly imbued with opportunism and reformism, priding themselves on their 'pragmatic' outlook and displaying an open contempt for theory. In *What Is to Be Done?*, Lenin quoted Engels, who, while praising the strength of organisation of the British labour movement, believed that it crawled on its belly in the domain of theory.

However, the First World War and the victorious Russian Revolution transformed the entire world situation, shaking British imperialism to its foundation. The loss of its dominant position on the world arena further undermined its position at home. Trotsky also paid a great deal of attention to the fortunes of British imperialism, especially in his role in the new Soviet government as Commissar of Foreign Affairs, then as Commissar for War. At this time, Britain was in the forefront of a campaign of military intervention to overthrow the young workers' state, and Trotsky's immediate attention was absorbed in the struggle against counter-revolutionary intervention. But his interest and profound grasp of Britain's history and its working-class traditions extended far wider.

A simple glance at Trotsky's writings on Britain is sufficient to see what a host of questions he tackled, covering a wide range of historical, social, diplomatic, philosophical, and cultural questions, as well as questions of tactics and strategy facing the revolutionary movement in Britain. He analysed the origins of Britain's meteoric ascent, in the course of which her ruling class would become the most confident and far-sighted rulers in the world. "Not for nothing has it been said of the British imperialists that they do their thinking in terms of centuries and continents", explained Trotsky.[4] The philosophy of the British bourgeoisie was based upon empiricism, guided by decades of experience. On Britain's road to becoming a world power, this practical instinct and 'rule of thumb' served them well. They had little regard for theoretical generalisations, for the simple reason that their forebears had achieved success without the aid of such abstract understanding.

The rise of the British working-class movement, the first of its kind in history, posed a whole host of challenges before the capitalist class. All attempts to subjugate and crush the early workers' organisations, with the use of class laws and state repression, had failed. They sprang up like mushrooms after a storm. The bourgeoisie thus opted instead for a policy of repression *and* concessions. Part of this flexible approach entailed schemes to buy off and corrupt the leaders of the labour movement – a method that, in most cases, proved very effective.

Nevertheless, such bribery could not prevent the class struggle in Britain from continuing to break through the surface, as it did with the awakening of the working class towards the end of the nineteenth century. The growing rivalries between the imperialist powers eventually led to an attempt to redivide the world in the form of world war. Revolution was its by-product, epitomised by the Russian Revolution. This opened up a new and dangerous situation for the British ruling class, reflected in the outlook of its political representatives. At this time, Trotsky noted that Winston Churchill represented the extreme, rabid wing of the British imperialists, while Lloyd George, the sly old fox, had a more sober and cunning feel for the situation. It was precisely these latter skills that were needed to navigate and defuse the post-war revolutionary crisis. His clever engagement with the trade union leaders disarmed them.

---

4 Ibid., p. 39.

The same period also witnessed the rise of the Labour Party as the mass party of the British working class. The parliamentary leadership of the party, however, represented by Ramsay MacDonald and Co., championed Fabianism, gradualism, and a rejection of the class struggle. "The leaders of the Labour Party represent essentially the bourgeoisie's political agents",[5] remarked Trotsky, whose aim was to forestall revolution.

He continued to elaborate their role:

> These pompous authorities, pedants, and haughty, high-falutin' cowards are systematically poisoning the labour movement, clouding the consciousness of the proletariat, and paralysing its will. It is only thanks to them that Toryism, Liberalism, the Church, the monarchy, the aristocracy, and the bourgeoisie continue to survive and even suppose themselves to be firmly in the saddle.

He concluded by saying:

> The Fabians, the ILPers, and the conservative trade union bureaucrats today represent the most counter-revolutionary force in Great Britain, and possibly in the present stage of development, in the whole world.[6]

Trotsky's writings cover one of the stormiest periods of British history: the period of the 1920s, which saw the General Strike and its aftermath; as well as the development of Trotskyism in Britain in the 1930s – all of which contain a wealth of analysis that remains startlingly relevant today. This is especially true of *Where is Britain Going?*, which applies the Marxist method concretely to the British context, and outlines the challenges facing the working class. In doing so, he explained:

> *There is no abstract yardstick applicable to all spheres of life.* It is necessary to take living facts in their living, historical interaction. If we master this dialectical approach to the question, the latter becomes much clearer to us.[7]

We are republishing this material in order to bring this method, together with this wealth of knowledge, to the attention of the new generation of workers and youth, to arm and enrich them and prepare them for the tasks of the coming period. The present is pregnant with revolutionary possibilities and challenges, foremost among which is the challenge of forming a revolutionary leadership. Of course, there will be defeats as well as victories. There will be

---

5 Ibid., p. 186.

6 Ibid., p. 273.

7 Ibid., p. 25 (emphasis in original).

periods of retreat and of passivity. But they will give way to further advances in the class struggle. The republication of these writings forms part of the continuation of Trotsky's struggle to build a revolutionary leadership capable of putting an end to capitalism. This historic task is, once again, posed point blank before the new generation.

The ruling class of Britain today is utterly degenerate, and has become the complete inverse of what it once was. It was once a great revolutionary class, which, under the leadership of Oliver Cromwell in the English Revolution, did away with the absolute monarchy of Charles I, and that cleared the way for capitalist development. Although, if truth be told, it was the shock troops of the revolutionary petty bourgeoisie, rather than the big bourgeoisie, that carried things through to the end. In fact, the latter, after the destruction of royal absolutism, came to a compromise with the landed classes, which was consummated in the so-called 'Glorious Revolution' of 1688. From then on, the new bourgeois class used the squirearchy, monarchy, House of Lords, and state church to cement its rule, although this was not fully consummated until the Reform Act of 1832 and the Repeal of the Corn Laws in 1846.

> Thanks to this exclusive historic privilege of development possessed by bourgeois England, conservatism combined with elasticity passed over from her institutions into her moral fibre.[8]

Britain's colossal wealth and privileged position allowed the bourgeoisie to, in turn, create a labour aristocracy, imbued with the prejudices of conservatism. These prejudices were based on 'tradition', monarchy, greed, religiosity, servility and class rule, built up over centuries. Such qualities were relayed into the upper strata of the working class by the petty-bourgeois moralists and 'educators'. Through the agency of the petty bourgeoisie, this effluent seeped down, through the top layers of the working class, and even into the class as a whole. "Official morality", explained Trotsky, "is a bridle to restrain the oppressed."[9] This reflected the posterior of the working class. But there is another side of the working class, namely its face. There is a different tradition, which comes to life in times of crisis and turmoil. These are the revolutionary traditions of the proletariat, as represented by early revolutionary trade unionism and, above all, by the rise of physical force Chartism – the world's first ever independent working-class political party.

---

8 Ibid., p. 8.
9 Ibid., p. 29.

Today, British capitalism has suffered a reversal of fortunes. The once-mighty power of British imperialism has collapsed. The Empire has gone. Britain has been reduced to a second-rate power on the fringes of Europe, in fact, it has become the 'sick man of Europe'. All the contradictions, accumulated over decades, have come to the fore, creating one crisis after another. As a result, Britain has been transformed from one of the most stable countries to one of the most profoundly unstable. No longer far-sighted, the representatives of the bourgeoisie are now decrepit and degenerate, a product of capitalist decline. They have become narrow 'Little Englanders', or Brexiteers, eaten up with their baseless self-importance. They are caught in a vice. Everything they do is wrong. An old proverb aptly fits: "Those whom the gods wish to destroy they first make mad."

As an aside, Trotsky drew attention to the extreme ruthlessness of the British bourgeoisie, and the cold cruelty it displayed towards the colonial peoples under its domination. With this cruelty came the racial arrogance that it displayed towards those it considered racially inferior. It sought, and still seeks, to inject this chauvinist poison into the more politically backward layers of British society, creating divisions, setting one group against another, all the better to rule over them.

In the past, Trotsky noted that the religion of 'capitalist progress' had sunk deeper roots in Britain than anywhere else. This was certainly the case for quite a long period. While this idea was undermined in the interwar crisis, it was revived in the period of the post-war upswing, during which capitalism was able to grant reforms and was seen to be 'delivering the goods'. This period, roughly from 1945 to the slump of 1974, was the heyday of reformism. It was the era of Keynesianism, of 'managed capitalism', and of the granting of important reforms, such as the health service. As living standards improved, there was a certain optimism in the future. For the most part, this was a period of widespread illusions in capitalist progress. But the world economic upswing only served to mask the long-term decline of British capitalism. Britain's exports as a percentage of world trade fell from almost 12 per cent in 1948 to around 4 per cent in 1974. The UK's trade deficit rose from £200 million in 1948, to £4.1 billion in 1974.[10] But for a whole period, this decline was to a large extent disguised by the fact that the world market, in which Britain took a diminished share, had grown and was far larger.

---

10 M. Ward, *UK trade, 1948-2019: statistics*, December 2020, House of Commons Library Briefing, CBP 8261, p. 8.

By now, the optimism of the past has completely evaporated. In fact, it has turned to widespread despair and anxiety for the future. The period of upswing has turned into a period of downswing, representing an epoch of capitalist decline. A report by the Resolution Foundation revealed that Britain has seen weaker GDP per capita growth in the years 2004 to 2019 than at any time since the period 1919 to 1934[11] – precisely the period covered by Trotsky in these writings. The failure to invest and modernise industry meant that British capitalism has now based itself on a low-wage, low-skill service economy. The ruling class has become completely parasitic, a class of rentiers and speculators. By the mid-2000s £1 in every £12 of British economic output was generated by financial services: i.e., by the moneylenders. The British capitalist class has long forgotten the fact that real wealth is material, and is the product of manufacturing.

The collapse of industry was accompanied by massive attacks on the working class, in the hope of restoring the declining rate of profit. The failing capitalist system could no longer afford the reforms of the past. An epoch of counter-reforms and austerity has therefore opened up, and with it a crisis of reformism. Now we have reformism without reforms, and even 'reformists' carrying out counter-reforms and austerity.

The deep slump of 2008 marked a watershed moment, and it affected British capitalism far worse than other major capitalist economies. Overproduction was universal. The recovery that followed was weak and drawn out. In 2020, the new slump, aggravated and deepened by the COVID-19 pandemic, resulted in the biggest collapse in UK output in 300 years. Only massive bailouts by the capitalist state prevented another Great Depression, but the consequences were a mountain of debt.

The idea of a recovery was short-lived. The dislocation of supply chains, the disruption of the world market, the costly war in the Ukraine, the resulting energy crisis, and spiralling inflation are pushing capitalism into a new deep slump. Now, as always, the working class is being asked to pay the bill. But this situation has served to reignite the class struggle, starting in Britain, on a scale not seen in generations. "Class War", screamed the front page of the Murdoch papers, as Britain was hit with a rash of strikes. Even the idea of a general strike has become inherent in the situation. As I write today, there is wave after wave of strikes involving new layers who have never been on strike before. This represents a qualitative change and the reawakening of the British working class.

---

11 A. Corlett, F. Odamtten and L. Try, *The Living Standards Audit 2022*, Resolution Foundation, July 2022, p. 5.

For decades, consciousness was shaped by the idea that today is better than yesterday and tomorrow will be better than today. This was the basis of reformism. But, as Marx explained, social being determines social consciousness. That period has come to an end. For millions, tomorrow will no longer be better than today. Everything has been turned on its head. Living standards are falling as never before. Millions are being thrown into poverty and must rely on food banks. Many have to work two or three jobs just to survive. Life is going from bad to worse. As a result, consciousness is being transformed under the hammer blows of events. We are in a period of sharp and sudden changes. Events, events, events are creating enormous instability and shaking people up. Millions are discussing politics at the bus stop, in the supermarkets, at the hairdressers, on the street corners, which they never did before. Even the middle class are affected. In the words of Trotsky, this is nothing less than the "molecular process of revolution in the minds of the masses".

Of course, while it is true that every epoch is different, nevertheless, experience is demonstrating that the knot of history is being retied, but on a higher level. The 1920s in Britain was a period of deep crisis, especially in the coal industry, which was the key industry at the time. Britain was being undermined by stiff competition from Germany. The ruling class came to the conclusion that the working class must be prepared to shoulder the burden of the crisis to "put industry back on its feet". This was the message of Stanley Baldwin, the Tory prime minister. This meant savage wage cuts across the board. The showdown began in the coal industry, where the coal owners were demanding big wage cuts. In 1925 the Conservative government granted a subsidy for nine months, whilst forming a Royal Commission to look into the plight of the industry. The labour movement heralded this as a tremendous victory and called it 'Red Friday'. But the ruling class were simply buying time to better prepare an all-out offensive against the working class. The labour leaders, meanwhile, did nothing but lull the working class to sleep and made no preparations for the inevitable showdown.

It was at this time that Trotsky wrote *Where is Britain Going?* In it, he analysed the position of British capitalism and the challenges faced by the working class. It is a brilliant Marxist analysis, which has many lessons for today, not least the crucial role of leadership. It was written as guidance for the young British Communist Party, which at that stage was struggling to assert itself.

It was also the time when, in the wake of Lenin's death, the triumvirate of Stalin, Zinoviev and Kamenev had taken over the leadership of the Russian Communist Party so as to exclude Trotsky. They then created the myth of

'Trotskyism', which they contrasted to 'Leninism' and launched a campaign against him.

The isolation of the Russian Revolution in such terrible backwardness resulted in the growth of a mighty bureaucracy within the state and the party. Stalin became the figurehead of this bureaucratic caste, which now yearned for peace and stability so as to enjoy its privilege. The Stalinists therefore adopted the anti-Marxist theory of 'socialism in one country', which meant the rejection of world revolution. In 1928 Trotsky brilliantly predicted that the adoption of this theory would lead to the nationalist and reformist degeneration of the Comintern.

In early 1925, Trotsky was dismissed from his post as Commissar of War, and was gradually removed from all positions of authority. The Communist International was being transformed from an instrument of world revolution into a mere border guard for the Soviet regime.

However, by 1926 the triumvirate broke up and Stalin entered a bloc with Bukharin. This served to push the Communist International in an opportunist direction. In China, the Communists were directed to enter the nationalist Kuomintang and to subordinate themselves to the 'progressive' bourgeoisie, which led to the bloody suppression of the Communists in 1927 at the hands of Chiang Kai-shek, while in Britain, the Communists were pushed to align themselves with the left reformist trade union leaders, such as Purcell, Hicks and Swales.

The idea had been raised in Moscow – firstly by Zinoviev, who was always on the lookout for shortcuts – that the socialist revolution in Britain might come 'through a different door', namely through the agency of the 'lefts' of the Trades Union Congress (TUC). This was clearly falsified by the betrayal of these same 'lefts' in the General Strike of 1926. Trotsky's book was an attempt to counter this idea of a 'different door', posing instead the need for the British Communist Party to fight to become a mass party that could lead the working class to power.

In *Where is Britain Going?* Trotsky brilliantly analysed the situation in Britain, the objective conditions preparing the way for revolution, and the real traditions of the working class, contrasting its revolutionary and conservative sides. He also gave a description of the character of the bourgeois leaders and the leaders of the workers' movement. While he dealt with the ruthlessness of the British bourgeoisie, Trotsky displayed nothing but contempt for its agents within the labour movement: the MacDonalds and other carpetbaggers. He also accurately described the shortcomings of the official 'lefts' in the movement.

Within the Labour Party, "there took shape the so-called left wing, formless, spineless, and devoid of any independent future", wrote Trotsky,[12] referring to their ideological weakness and confusion.

In contrast, the right wing drew its strength from the fact that:

> ... with them stands tradition, experience and routine and, most important, with them stands bourgeois society as a whole which slips them ready-made solutions. For MacDonald has only to translate Baldwin's and Lloyd George's suggestions into Fabian language. [...]

> The weakness of the lefts arises from their disorder and their disorder from their ideological formlessness.[13]

And:

> It would be a monstrous illusion to think that these left elements of the old school are capable of heading the revolutionary movement of the British proletariat and its struggle for power.[14]

He outlined the historic challenges before the working class, and explained how these would be overcome:

> The ideas and prejudices which have been handed down from generation to generation become a factor of great historical force... But material facts are nevertheless stronger than their reflection in ideas and traditions... Living facts are more powerful than dead ideas.[15] [...]

> All her national traditions will undergo a test. What was shaped by centuries will be destroyed in the course of years.[16]

The greatest test to confront the British working class came with the General Strike of May 1926. It was called in defence of the miners, but it posed the question of workers' power point-blank. In such a situation there was no room for prevarication or compromise. The strike would usher in either the greatest of defeats or the greatest of victories. The right wing, naturally, worked to betray the strike from the very beginning. But the 'lefts', lacking any perspective of taking power, simply capitulated to the right.

---

12 See the present edition, p. 334.

13 Ibid., p. 351.

14 Ibid., p. 335.

15 Ibid., p. 379.

16 Ibid., p. 384.

Where is Britain Going? was published by the British Communist Party in 1925, and Trotsky's analysis was defended by the party's theoreticians, despite the beginning of the campaign against Trotsky emanating from Moscow. This was reflected in Palme Dutt's favourable review, and his criticisms of the TUC 'lefts'.[17]

The Anglo-Russian Trade Union Committee had been established by the leaders of the Russian and British trade unions following a visit to Russia by members of the TUC in 1924. The supposed aim of the Committee was to fight against the threat of imperialist war. This agreement served to provide the TUC leaders with a certain revolutionary 'aura', which they certainly did not deserve. The British Communist Party leaders, for their part – under pressure from Moscow, emanating initially from the Stalin-Zinoviev faction, and later from the Stalin-Bukharin faction – took at face value the pronouncements of the TUC 'lefts'. This attempt to trail after these 'lefts', who subsequently betrayed the General Strike, prompted the Communist Party leaders to issue such disastrous slogans as "All power to the General Council". This recognition of the General Council as the real representative of the working class only served to disorientate the ranks of the party and the advanced workers that looked to it for guidance.

Following the betrayal of the General Strike, the Russian Left Opposition led by Trotsky, which had been formed in 1923, argued for the breaking off of relations with the TUC leaders. The Russian party leaders of course refused.

> The attempt to cling to the bloc with the General Council after the open betrayal of the General Strike, and even after the betrayal of the miners' strike, was one of the greatest mistakes in the history of the workers' movement.

> […] the Anglo-Russian Committee merely shielded and covered over the base and treacherous work of the General Council.[18]

In fact, the initiative to break with the Anglo-Russian Committee was taken by the General Council itself in 1927 – by both the right and 'left' trade union leaders alike.

> The masses knew as the leaders of the movement only Purcell, Hicks and Cook, whom, moreover, Moscow vouched for. These 'left' friends, in a serious test, shamefully betrayed the proletariat. The revolutionary workers were thrown into

---

17 Included in the present edition from p. 483.
18 See the present edition p. 415.

confusion, sank into apathy, and naturally extended their disappointment to the Communist Party itself which had only been the passive part of this whole mechanism of betrayal and perfidy.[19]

Of course, this does not take anything away from the heroism displayed by the ordinary members of the Communist Party on a local level, who made colossal sacrifices, many of whom were beaten, persecuted, victimised, and imprisoned.

The criticism raised by Trotsky of the Party was intended as a means of drawing vital lessons, of reorienting the Party, and of preparing it for the revolutionary leadership of the British working class. However, the growing bureaucratic reaction within the Soviet Union under Stalin destroyed this potential and served to wreck this promising young movement.

Under Stalin, the Communist International lurched from opportunism between 1926-27, to the criminal policies of the so-called 'Third Period', characterised by an insane ultra-left policy between 1928-33. This resulted in a debacle in Germany with the victory of Hitler in 1933, which stemmed from the Stalinist theory of 'social-fascism', which fatally split and demoralised the German working class. And yet, the Stalinist heralded this policy of 'social-fascism' as correct and talked of, "after Hitler, our turn"! Having burned their fingers, they then made a 180-degree *volte face* to the strike-breaking policy of the Popular Front in the 1930s.

The Left Opposition was banned in the Soviet Union and its members expelled. Trotsky was exiled and deprived of Soviet citizenship. In Britain, a small group of oppositionists, known as the Balham group, was expelled from the Communist Party, and entered into contact with Trotsky. To overcome the group's isolation, he urged these supporters to enter the Independent Labour Party (ILP), which was at that time moving in a centrist direction, and to make contact with the party's rank and file with the aim of winning them to Bolshevism. However, Trotsky stressed that it was important to be flexible in relation to tactics and organisation, while being firm on principles.

> If you enter the ILP to work for the Bolshevik transformation of the party (that is, of its revolutionary kernel), the workers will look upon you as upon fellow workers, comrades, and not as upon adversaries who want to split the party from outside.[20]

However, he advised these comrades to avoid, at all costs, sectarianism and opportunism.

---

19 Ibid., p. 472.
20 Ibid., p. 599.

Nevertheless, the leaders of the group opposed the turn to the ILP, which led to a split, with only about a dozen inexperienced comrades entering the party. Ted Grant, who had arrived from South Africa, was involved in this group that entered the ILP. His experiences were published in his *History of British Trotskyism*.

Trotsky paid close attention to developments in Britain, which were moving in a revolutionary direction. Unfortunately, the forces of Trotskyism were too small and inexperienced to influence events at this stage. Trotsky pointed to the fact that "not all our comrades entered the ILP and they developed an opportunistic policy so far as I could observe, and that is why their experience in the ILP was not so good."[21]

The centrist leaders of the ILP displayed a complete inability to understand the political situation or to draw the necessary revolutionary conclusions. They made one mistake after another, in particular in trailing after the 'Third Period' Stalinists. They therefore remained mired in the fog of centrism, which led to the demise of the ILP.

Trotsky produced a wealth of writings dealing with tactics and approach, particularly of Marxists towards the mass organisations.

> The policy of a united front with reformists is obligatory but it is of necessity limited to partial tasks, especially to defensive struggles. There can be no thought of making the socialist revolution in a united front with reformist organisations. The principal task of a revolutionary party consists in freeing the working class from the influence of reformism.[22]

Eventually, Trotsky advised his supporters to leave the ILP and enter the Labour Party, which had recovered from the betrayal of 1931, and which was shifting to the left. He urged them, above all, to concentrate on the youth. As with the previous proposed entry into the ILP, this turn once again led to resistance within the group, leading to a further split.

This period can be regarded as the early pre-history of British Trotskyism, which was plagued with organisational weaknesses and political confusion. Only with the emergence of the Workers' International League in 1938, and the launch of the Revolutionary Communist Party in 1944, did a genuine Trotskyist current develop in Britain, in which Ted Grant played a crucial role. His work, in particular, kept the flame of revolutionary Marxism alive and it is from these roots that our present tendency emerged.

---

21 Ibid., p. 654.
22 Ibid., p. 577.

In answering his critics, Trotsky did not rule out that the working class could come to power by parliamentary means, but not in the utopian reformist fashion advocated by those who simply worship bourgeois democracy. There must be no illusions on this score.

> The conclusion to be drawn from all this is that the British proletariat must not reckon on any historic privileges. It will have to struggle for power by the road of revolution and keep it in its hands by crushing the fierce resistance of the exploiters. There is no other way leading to socialism.[23]

This, in turn, required the building of a revolutionary party that was prepared to take the necessary measures to overthrow capitalism. In 1938, given the bankruptcy of the Second and Third Internationals, Trotsky launched the Fourth International as the party of world revolution. This was in a period of defeats for the working class, above all in Spain. However, the prospect of world war would inevitably provoke revolution. The Marxist movement needed to prepare itself for that perspective, politically and organisationally. The founding conference of the Fourth International adopted as its programme, *The Death Agony of Capitalism and the Tasks of the Fourth International*, drafted by Trotsky, known as *The Transitional Programme*.

Unfortunately, following the assassination of Trotsky by a Stalinist agent in 1940, the leaders of the Fourth International proved incapable of rising to the challenge, leading to its demise. They were incapable of understanding Trotsky's method, and instead simply repeated his words when the situation had fundamentally changed following the war. This, together with prestige politics, destroyed the movement.

A revolutionary party is first and foremost its ideas, programme, tradition, and method. Only lastly is it an organisation. Despite the destruction of the Fourth International, these ideas and traditions were preserved by the tenacious work of Ted Grant in the post-war period, and today they constitute the theoretical heritage of the International Marxist Tendency.

We have no illusions as to the immensity of the task before us, given the weakness of the forces of Marxism in Britain and on a world scale. However, the objective basis is being prepared for revolution in one country after another. This will be a protracted period, extending over many years, given the weakness of the bourgeoisie in imposing its own 'solution' on the one hand; and on the other the strength of the working class internationally, which is nevertheless hampered by the weakness of the forces of Marxism

---

23 Ibid., p. 533.

that are too small to lead the working class out of this impasse. Nonetheless, despite all the ups and downs and the many detours to come, the general line of march remains. In the process, the consciousness of the working class, and indeed of all classes, will be transformed again and again, posing ever more sharply the need to change society.

As Trotsky explained:

> Today in Britain the question is not one of assigning a 'day' for the revolution – we are a long way from this! – but in clearly understanding that the whole objective situation is bringing this 'day' closer and into the ambit of the educational and preparatory work of the party of the proletariat, and at the same time creating conditions for its rapid revolutionary formation.[24]

The question of questions, raised by Trotsky throughout these writings, is the crisis of proletarian leadership. As he pointed out in *Where is Britain Going?*,

> The contradictions undermining British society will inevitably intensify. We do not intend to predict the exact tempo of this process, but it will be measurable in terms of years, or in terms of five years at the most; certainly not in decades. This general prospect requires us to ask above all the question: will a Communist Party be built in Britain in time with the strength and the links with the masses to be able to thaw out at the right moment all the necessary practical conclusions from the sharpening crisis? It is in this question that Great Britain's fate is today contained.[25]

This question still remains the task of the hour, but now, given the increased tempo of events, it is posed with even more urgency. We believe the republication of Trotsky's *Writings on Britain* will greatly assist in this endeavour, educating the future cadres, and laying the basis for a successful socialist revolution in Britain and elsewhere.

Rob Sewell,
London,
February 2023

---

24 Ibid., p. 374.
25 Ibid., p. 230.

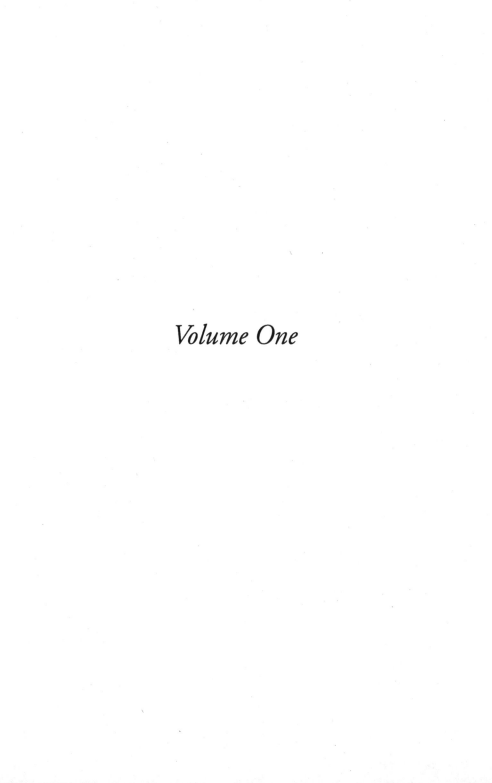

Volume One

Volume One

I

History and Culture

The Seventeenth-Century Revolution

From Chapter 3 of *The History of the Russian Revolution* (1931).

In England serfdom had disappeared in actual fact by the end of the fourteenth century – that is, two centuries before it arose in Russia and four and a half centuries before it was abolished. The expropriation of the landed property of the peasants dragged along in England through one Reformation and two revolutions to the nineteenth century. The capitalist development, not forced from the outside, thus had sufficient time to liquidate the independent peasant long before the proletariat awoke to political life.

* * *

From Chapter 11 of *The History of the Russian Revolution* (1931).

The English revolution of the seventeenth century, exactly because it was a great revolution shattering the nation to the bottom, affords a clear example of this alternating dual power, with sharp transitions in the form of civil war.

At first the royal power, resting upon the privileged classes or the upper circles of these classes – the aristocrats and bishops – is opposed by the bourgeoisie and the circles of the squirearchy that are close to it. The government of the bourgeoisie is the Presbyterian Parliament supported by the City of London. The protracted conflict between these two regimes is finally settled in open civil war. The two governmental centres – London and Oxford – create their own armies. Here the dual power takes a territorial form, although, as always in civil war, the boundaries are very shifting. Parliament conquers. The king is captured and awaits his fate.

It would seem that the conditions are now created for the single rule of the Presbyterian bourgeoisie. But before the royal power could be broken, the parliamentary army has converted itself into an independent political force. It has concentrated in its ranks the Independents, the pious and resolute petty bourgeoisie, the craftsmen and farmers. This army powerfully interferes in social life, not merely as an armed force, but as a Praetorian Guard, and as the political representative of a new class opposing the prosperous and rich bourgeoisie. Correspondingly the army creates a new state organ rising above the military command: a council of soldiers' and officers' deputies ('agitators'). A new period of double sovereignty has thus arrived: that of the Presbyterian Parliament and the Independents' army. This leads to open conflicts. The bourgeoisie proves powerless to oppose with its own army the 'model army' of Cromwell – that is, the armed plebeians. The conflict ends with a purgation of the Presbyterian Parliament by the sword of the Independents. There remains but the rump of a parliament; the dictatorship of Cromwell is established. The lower ranks of the army, under the leadership of the Levellers – the extreme left wing of the revolution – try to oppose to the rule of the upper military levels, the patricians of the army, their own veritably plebeian regime.

But this new two-power system does not succeed in developing: the Levellers, the lowest depths of the petty bourgeoisie have not yet, nor can have, their own historic path. Cromwell soon settles accounts with his enemies. A new political equilibrium, and still by no means a stable one, is established for a period of years.

* * *

From Chapter 1 of *The History of the Russian Revolution* (1931).

In the middle of the seventeenth century the bourgeois revolution in England developed under the guise of a religious reformation. A struggle for the right to pray according to one's own prayer book was identified with the struggle against the king, the aristocracy, the princes of the church, and Rome. The Presbyterians and puritans were deeply convinced that they were placing their earthly interests under the unshakeable Protection of divine providence. The goals for which the new classes were struggling commingled inseparably in their consciousness with the texts from the Bible and the forms of churchly ritual. Emigrants carried with them across the ocean this tradition sealed with blood. Hence the extraordinary virility of the Anglo-Saxon interpretation of Christianity. We see even today how the minister 'socialists' of Great Britain back up their cowardice with these same magic texts with which the people of the seventeenth century sought to justify their courage.

* * *

From Chapter 4 of *Terrorism and Communism* (1920).

Let us first look at the religious Reformation, which proved the watershed between the Middle Ages and modern history; the deeper were the interests of the masses that it involved, the wider was its sweep, the more fiercely did civil war develop under the religious banner, and the more merciless did the terror become on the other side.

In the seventeenth century England carried out two revolutions. The first, which brought forth great social upheavals and wars, brought amongst other things the execution of King Charles I, while the second ended happily with the accession of a new dynasty.[1] The British bourgeoisie and its historians maintain quite different attitudes to these two revolutions: the first is for them a rising of the mob – the 'Great Rebellion'; the second has been handed down under the title of the 'Glorious Revolution'. The reason for this difference in estimates was explained by the French historian, Augustin Thierry. In the first English revolution, in the 'Great Rebellion', the active force was the people; while in the second it was almost 'silent'. Hence, it follows that, in surroundings of class slavery, it is difficult to teach the oppressed masses good manners. When provoked to fury they use clubs, stones, fire and the rope. The court historians of the exploiters are offended at this. But the great event in modern 'bourgeois' history is, none the less, not the 'Glorious Revolution' but the 'Great Rebellion'.

* * *

From Chapter 6 of *The History of the Russian Revolution* (1931).

But was parliamentarism born on the Thames by a peaceful evolution? Was it the fruit of the 'free' foresight of a single monarch? No, it was deposited as the result of a struggle that lasted for ages, and in which one of the kings left his head at the crossroads.

The historic-psychological contrast mentioned above between the Romanovs and the Capets can, by the way, be aptly extended to the British royal pair of the epoch of the first revolution. Charles I revealed fundamentally the same combination of traits with which memorists and historians have endowed Louis XVI and Nikolai II. "Charles, therefore, remained passive", writes Montague, "yielded where he could not resist, betrayed how unwillingly

---

1 The accession of William III (William of Orange) in 1688.

he did so, and reaped no popularity, no confidence." "He was not a stupid man", says another historian of Charles Stuart, but he lacked firmness of character... His evil fate was his wife, Henrietta, a Frenchwoman, sister of Louis XIII, saturated even more than Charles with the idea of absolutism." We will not detail the characteristics of this third – chronologically first – royal pair to be crushed by a national revolution. We will merely observe that in England the hatred was concentrated above all on the queen, as a Frenchwoman and a papist, whom they accused of plotting with Rome, secret connections with the Irish rebels, and intrigues at the French court.

But England had, at any rate, ages at her disposal. She was the pioneer of bourgeois civilisation; she was not under the yoke of other nations, but on the contrary held them more and more under her yoke. She exploited the whole world. This softened the inner contradictions, accumulated conservatism, promoted an abundance and stability of fatty deposits in the form of a parasitic caste, in the form of a squirearchy, a monarchy, House of Lords, and the state church. Thanks to this exclusive historic privilege of development possessed by bourgeois England, conservatism combined with elasticity passed over from her institutions into her moral fibre. Various continental philistines, like the Russian professor Milyukov, or the Austro-Marxist Otto Bauer, have not to this day ceased going into ecstasies over this fact. But exactly at the present moment, when Britain, hard pressed throughout the world, is squandering the last resources of her former privileged position, her conservatism is losing its elasticity, and even in the person of the Labourites is turning into stark reaction. In the face of the Indian revolution the 'socialist' MacDonald will find no other methods but those with which Nikolai II opposed the Russian revolution. Only a blind man could fail to see that Great Britain is headed for gigantic revolutionary earthquake shocks, in which the last fragments of her conservatism, her world domination, her present state machine, will go down without a trace. MacDonald is preparing these shocks no less successfully than did Nikolai II in his time, and no less blindly. So here too, as we see, is no poor illustration of the problem of the role of the 'free' personality in history.

Britain and Military Strategy

From *It Happened in Spain*, written in November and December 1916 and first published in *Krasnaya Nov*, July 1922 and January 1926.

The old British historian of Spain, Adam, relates in four volumes, which have been particularly well gnawed by bookworms, the history of the Pyrenean peninsula from the time of its discovery by the Phoenicians until the death of Charles III.[1] Great Britain's role in destroying Spanish might emerges from under Adam's pen in an instructive light. Over the course of a century Britain played upon the antagonism between France and Spain, striving to weaken them both, but once having weakened Spain began to defend her as well as plundering her colonies. In the so-called 'War of Spanish Succession', Britain led a European coalition made up of the Dutch, the Austrians and the Portuguese against the Bourbons who had unified France and Spain. The war was conducted supposedly in the name of the right of succession of the Austrian ruling house to the Spanish throne. In passing, Britain seized Gibraltar (1704), and at a cheap price: a detachment of sailors clambered on to a rock, which was undefended on account of its 'impregnability', from where Britain was to hold sway over the entrance and exit to the Mediterranean Sea. In the War of Spanish Succession British methods of international banditry found their classic expression:

1. The alliance against the Bourbons, who unified France with Spain, was an alliance against *the chief continental power*;

---

1 John Adams, *Histoire d'Espagne depuis la découverte qui en a été faite par les phéniciens jusqu'à la mort de Charles III*, Paris, 1808.

2. Once this alliance was created Britain took its leadership;

3. She suffered less and gained more from the war than her allies, not only by seizing Gibraltar but also by securing in the Treaty of Utrecht first-class trading privileges in Spain and her colonies;

4. Having weakened the unified Spain-France, thereby achieving her main aim, Britain was quick to betray the Austrian pretender to the Spanish throne by recognising Philippe Bourbon, Louis XIV's grandson, as King of Spain on condition that he renounce any claim to the French throne.

The analogies with the present war speak for themselves. Incidentally we can let the philosophers of social-patriotism determine who was the aggressor and who was on the defensive in the Anglo-Spanish War.

At the end of the 1750's Pitt the Elder considered it necessary to declare war on Spain because of the secret "family pact", directed against Britain, which had been concluded by the Madrid and Versailles courts. The British government hesitated, and the worthy historian, Adam, tells of the reasons for this hesitation in epic fashion. "The details of the family pact were still not known. Britain was burdened with debts; Spain had done nothing that could provoke Britain to war; she was obliged to respect international law and, more particularly, the great interests of commerce and moreover the solid strength of the Spanish navy." These words might appear ironic when applied to Great Britain were not the author himself a devout Englishman. We can see that, long before Lloyd George, British rulers knew how to turn their back on international law when it was convenient.

* * *

From *Military Doctrine or Pseudo-Military Doctrinairism* (dated 5 December 1921), *Kommunisticheskii International,* 17 December 1921.

[For example] what is the military doctrine of Britain? Into its composition there evidently enters (or used to enter): the recognition of the urgent need for naval hegemony; a negative attitude towards a regular land army and towards military conscription; or, still more precisely, the recognition of Britain's need to possess a fleet stronger than the combined fleets of any two other countries and, flowing from this, Britain's being enabled to maintain a small army on a volunteer basis. Combined with this was the maintenance of such an order in Europe as would not allow a single land power to obtain a decisive preponderance on the continent.

It is incontestable that this British 'doctrine' used to be the most stable of military doctrines. Its stability and definitive form were determined by the prolonged, planful, uninterrupted growth of Great Britain's power in the absence of events and shocks that would have radically altered the relationship of forces in the world (or in Europe, which used to signify the selfsame thing *in the past*). At the present time, however, this situation has been completely disrupted. Britain dealt her 'doctrine' the biggest blow when during the war she was compelled to build her army on the basis of compulsory military service. On the continent of Europe, the 'equilibrium' has been disrupted. Nobody has confidence in the stability of the new relationship of forces. The power of the United States excludes the possibility for any longer maintaining automatically the rule of the British fleet. It is too early now to forecast the outcome of the Washington Conference?[2]

But it is quite self-evident that after the imperialist war Great Britain's 'military doctrine' has become inadequate, impotent and utterly worthless. It has not yet been replaced by a new one. And it is very doubtful that there will ever be a new one, for the epoch of military and revolutionary convulsions and of radical regroupment of world forces leaves very narrow limits for military doctrine in the sense in which we have defined it above with respect to Britain: *A military 'doctrine' presupposes a relative stability of the domestic and foreign situation.*

* * *

From a speech to the All-Russian Conference of Sailors, 1 April 1922.

… At the same time we have to bear in mind that our navy could take on a great and wide role with a change in international conditions. Here it must be noted that there is something in our navy, that weak, at the moment so very weak organism, that forms our superiority and advantage by comparison with even the British Navy: for we have left our deepest crisis behind us, whereas they still have all of their crisis to come. They have a powerful organism, yet their crisis will also be very powerful – this crisis will paralyse the forces of the British Navy for a long while.

The British revolution will to an enormous extent depend on the behaviour of the British Navy; the latter will likewise predetermine the fate of the British colonies. How the process of decomposition in the British Navy will take place, with its inner struggle and uprisings, possibly of one section against another, we do not nor cannot tell; but we do know that it is inevitable and

---

2 The Washington Conference (12 November 1921 to 6 February 1922) drafted a Naval Convention which pledged the nine powers participating not to build capital ships for ten years and fixed a ratio between Britain, USA and Japan of 5:5:3 for capital ships.

by that critical and sharp period we must have a Red Navy which, even if small, is firmly cohesive and absolutely conscious.

* * *

From a speech to a conference of military delegates to the
11th Party Congress, 1 April 1922.

For the sake of illustration let us take Britain and let us try to imagine what will be, or more correctly, may be the character of a civil war in the British Isles. Naturally, we cannot prophesy. Naturally, events may unfold in an altogether different way, but it is nevertheless profitable to try to imagine the march of revolutionary events under the peculiar conditions of a highly developed capitalist country in an insular position.

The proletariat constitutes the overwhelming majority of the population in Britain. It has many conservative tendencies. It is hard to budge. But in return, once it starts moving and after it overcomes the first organised opposition of internal enemies, its ascendancy on the islands will prove to be overwhelming owing to its overwhelming numbers. Does this mean that the bourgeoisie of Great Britain will not make the attempt with the assistance of Australia, Canada, the United States and others to overthrow the British proletariat? Of course it will. For this, it will attempt to retain the Navy in its hands. The bourgeoisie will require the navy not only to institute a famine blockade but also for purposes of invasion raids. The French bourgeoisie will not refuse black regiments. The same fleet that now serves for the defence of the British Isles and for keeping them supplied uninterruptedly with necessities will become the instrument of attack upon these islands. Proletarian Great Britain will thus turn out to be a beleaguered naval fortress. There is no way of retreat from it, unless into the sea. And we have presupposed that the sea will remain in enemy hands. The civil war will consequently assume the character of the defence of an island against warships and invasion raids. I repeat this is no prophecy: events may unfold in a different way. But who will be so bold as to insist that the scheme of civil war outlined by me is impossible? It is quite possible and even probable. It would be a good thing for our strategists to ponder over this, they would then become completely convinced how unfounded it is to deduce manoeuvrability from the revolutionary nature of the proletariat. For all anyone knows, the British proletariat may find itself compelled to cover the shores of its islands with trenches, deep ribbons of barbed wire defences and positional artillery.

The Working Class in the Nineteenth Century

From *War and the International, Golos*,
20 and 21 November and 13 December 1914.

In Britain the stormy era of Chartism, of the revolutionary awakening of the British proletariat, had entirely exhausted itself a full ten years before the emergence of the First International. The repeal of the Corn Laws (1846), the industrial flowering of the country consequent upon this which turned Britain into the workshop of the world, the introduction of the ten-hour working day (1847), the increase in emigration from Ireland to America and finally the extension of suffrage to the urban workers (1867) were all conditions which significantly improved the position of the upper layers of the proletariat and led its class movement along the peaceful course of trade unionism and to the liberal-labour politics that complemented it. The era of possibilism, that is of the conscious and steady adaptation to the economic, judicial and state forms of national capitalism, had for the British working class, as the oldest of its kind, already opened up before the rise of the International, two decades earlier than for the continental proletariat. If more British trade unionists joined the International in the beginning, then it was purely because they considered that in this way they would have a possibility of defending themselves better against the import of continental blacklegs during strike struggles.

* * *

From *War and the International, Golos*,
20 and 21 November and 13 December 1914.

Britain had far earlier based her capitalist development upon imperialist plunder. She gave the upper layer of the proletariat an economic interest in her dominion over the world. In upholding its interests the British working class confined itself to pressure upon the bourgeois parties which had in turn accustomed it to the idea of the capitalist exploitation of the backward countries. It began to start upon the path of an independent policy only as Britain began to lose her positions on the world market, being squeezed out in the process by her main rival, Germany...

* * *

Thoughts on the Progress of the Proletarian Revolution: En Route, Izvestia,
29 April and 1 May 1919.

The oldest capitalist country in Europe and the world is Britain. Britain, especially during the last half-century, has been from the standpoint of the proletarian revolution the most conservative country. The consistent social-reformists, i.e., those who try to make both ends meet, hence drew all the conclusions they needed, asserting that it was precisely Britain that indicated to other countries the possible paths of political development and that in the future the entire European proletariat would renounce the programme of social revolution. For the Marxists, however, the 'incongruity' between Britain's capitalist development and her socialist movement, as conditioned by a temporary combination of historical forces, did not contain anything disheartening. It was Britain's early entry onto the path of capitalist development and world robbery that created a privileged position not only for her bourgeoisie but also for a section of her working class. Britain's insular position spared her the direct burden of maintaining militarism on land. Her mighty naval militarism, although requiring huge expenditures, rested nevertheless on numerically small cadres of hirelings and did not require a transition to universal military service. The British bourgeoisie skilfully utilised these conditions in order to separate the top labour layer from the bottom strata, creating an aristocracy of 'skilled' labour and instilling into it a trade union caste spirit. Flexible despite all its conservatism, the parliamentary machinery of Great Britain, the incessant rivalry between two historical parties – the Liberals and the Tories – a rivalry which at times assumed rather tense form although remaining quite hollow in content, invariably created when the need arose an artificial political safety-valve for the discontent of the working masses. This was supplemented by the fiendish dexterity of the ruling bourgeois clique in the business of spiritually crippling and bribing, quite 'exquisitely' at times, the leaders of the working class. Thus, thanks to Britain's early capitalist development her bourgeoisie disposed of resources that enabled them systematically to counteract the proletarian revolution. Within the proletariat itself, or more correctly, within its upper layer, the same conditions gave shape to the most extreme conservative tendencies which manifested themselves in the course of decades prior to the World War... While Marxism teaches that class relations arise in the process of production and that these relations correspond to a certain level of productive forces; while Marxism further teaches that all forms of ideology and, first and foremost, politics correspond to class relations, this does not at all mean that between politics, class groupings and production there exist simple mechanical relations, calculable by the four rules of arithmetic. On the contrary, the reciprocal relations are extremely complex. It is possible to interpret dialectically the course of a country's development, including its revolutionary development, only by proceeding from the action, reaction and interaction of all the material and superstructural factors, national and world-wide alike, and not through superficial juxtapositions, nor through formal analogies.

* * *

From Chapter 8 of *Between Red and White* (1921).

History on the whole knows of no revolution that was accomplished in a democratic way. For revolution is a very serious contest, which is always settled, not according to form, but according to substance. It happens quite frequently that individuals lose their fortunes and even their 'honour' when playing cards according to the rules of the game; but classes never consent to lose possessions, power and 'honour' by observing the rules of the game of 'democratic' parliamentarism. They always decide this question in grim earnest, i.e., in accordance with the real correlation of the material forces, and not with the phantom shadows of these forces.

No doubt even in countries like Britain with an absolute majority of proletarians, the representative institution called into being by a working-class revolution will reflect, not only the first needs of the revolution, but also the monstrous conservative traditions of this country. The mentality of a present-day British trade union leader is a mixture of the religious and social prejudices of the period of the restoration of St. Paul's Cathedral, the practical skill of a trade union official at the height of capitalist development, the snobbishness of a petty bourgeois fighting to be respectable, and the uneasy conscience of a labour politician who has repeatedly betrayed the workers. To this must be added the influences of intellectuals, of professors and Fabians; of the Socialist moralisings of Sunday preachers, the rationalist schemes of pacifists, the dilettantism of 'Guild Socialists',[1] and the stubborn and haughty Fabian narrow-mindedness. Although the present social relations in Britain are quite revolutionary, her mighty historical past has deposited a conservative crust on the consciousness of not only the labour bureaucracy but also the upper strata of the more skilled mechanics. The obstacles to social revolution in Russia are *objective*: the predominance of petty peasant farming, and technical backwardness in industry; in England these obstacles are *subjective*: the ossified consciousness of a collective Henderson and a hydra-headed Mrs. Snowden. The proletarian revolution will dispose of these obstacles by methods of elimination and self-purification. But it cannot hope to dispose of them in a democratic way. Mr. MacDonald himself will prevent such a consummation, not by his programme but by the mere fact of his conservative existence.

* * *

From a speech to the Communist University for Toilers of the East, 21 April 1924 (*Perspectives and Tasks in the East*).

The whole present-day political and cultural movement rests upon capitalism, out of which it is growing, has grown and has outgrown. But capitalism has, schematically speaking, two different facets: the capitalism of the metropolis and the capitalism of the colonies. The classic model of a metropolis is Britain. At the present time it is crowned by the so-called 'Labour' government of MacDonald. As for the colonies, I would hesitate to say which one of them is most typical as a colony: this would either be India, a colony in the normal sense, or China, which preserves the semblance of independence yet in her world position and the course of her development belongs to the colonial type. Classic capitalism is in Britain. Marx wrote his *Capital* in London by directly observing the development of the most advanced country – you will know this, though I do not remember which year you cover this in... In the colonies capitalism develops not out of its own fragments but as an intrusion of foreign capital. This is what creates the two different types. Why is MacDonald, to put it not very scientifically but in quite precise terms just the same, why is MacDonald so conservative, so limited and so stupid?

---

1 Guild Socialism – A political movement advocating workers' control of industry through trade-related guilds; its most prominent exponent was G. D. H. Cole.

Because Britain is the classic land of capitalism, because capitalism there organically developed from handicrafts through manufacture into modern industry, step by step, by an 'evolutionary' road so that yesterday's prejudices and those of the day before, the prejudices of the past and the previous centuries, all the ideological garbage of the ages can be discovered under MacDonald's skull. [*Applause.*] At first glance there is here some historical contradiction: why did Marx appear in backward Germany, in the most backward of the great countries of Europe in the first half of the nineteenth century, not counting Russia of course? Why did Marx appear in Germany and why did Lenin appear in Russia on the borders of the nineteenth and twentieth centuries? A clear contradiction! But what is its nature? One that can be explained by the so-called dialectic of historical development. In the shape of British machinery and in the shape of British cotton cloth, history created the most revolutionary factor of development. But this machinery and this cloth were processed and created by way of a prolonged and slow historical transition, one step at a time, while human consciousness remained, in general, frightfully conservative.

When economic development proceeds slowly and systematically it tends to find it hard to break through human skulls. Subjectivists and idealists in general say that human consciousness, critical thought and so on and so forth draw history forward like a tug towing a barge behind it. This is untrue. You and I are Marxists and we know that the motive power of history consists of the productive forces which have up till now taken shape behind man's back and with which it tends to be very difficult to smash through man's conservative skull in order to produce there the spark of a new political idea, and especially, let me repeat, if the development takes place slowly, organically and imperceptibly. But when the productive forces of a metropolis, of a classic land of capitalism, like Britain, encroach upon a more backward country, as with Germany in the first half of the nineteenth century, and with ourselves on the watershed of the nineteenth and the twentieth centuries, and at the present time with Asia; when economic factors intrude in a revolutionary way cracking the old regime, when development takes place not gradually, not 'organically' but by means of terrible shocks, and abrupt shifts in the old social layers, then critical thought finds its revolutionary expression incomparably more easily and rapidly, providing there is of course the necessary theoretical prerequisite for this. That is why Marx appeared in Germany in the first half of the nineteenth century and that is why Lenin appeared here and that is why we can observe at first sight the paradoxical fact that in the land of the highest, oldest and most revered European capitalism, Britain, we have the most conservative 'Labour' party. While on the other hand in our Soviet Union, an extremely backward country economically and culturally speaking, we have – and I say this unashamedly for it is a fact – the best communist party in the world. [*Applause.*]

* * *

From a speech to the 5th All-Russian Congress of
Medical and Veterinary Workers, 21 June 1924
(*Through What Stage Are We Passing?*).

... What in reality explains the fact that in such a powerful, cultured, educated, civilised, etc., country as Britain, the Communist Party still exists as a mere propagandist society, not yet possessing the power to play an active part in politics? In order to answer in a radical way the explanation – at first glance so simple and fitting – that Communism is directly proportionate to backwardness and barbarism, an explanation which expresses the whole wisdom of Menshevism, I will recall a few other phenomena and institutions in the life of Great Britain. In Britain, there is – and I ask you not to forget it – a monarchy, whereas there is none here or in France or in Germany. Now a monarchy cannot be depicted from any point of view as an expression of the highest culture, as one of the highest attainments of mankind – even MacDonald doesn't do that, he keeps quiet about it, politely and diplomatically holds his tongue, and doesn't say that a sign of the high cultural level of Britain is that there, in contrast to barbarous Russia, they have a monarchy. In Britain there is still to this day an aristocracy enjoying distinctions of rank. There is a House of Lords. In Britain, finally, the church, or rather the churches, wield tremendous influence in all spheres of life. There is no country in Europe where church influence in political, social and family life is so great as in Great Britain. Over there, for a man to say that he does not belong to a church, does not go to church, and even more, that he does not believe in God, requires quite exceptional personal courage. So it is difficult there, in each separate case, to break through the old, dense web of hypocrisy and clerical prejudices and the worldly customs which are based on this hypocrisy and these prejudices. None of you will say, I hope, that the influence of the church or of the churches on social consciousness is an expression of human progress. Thus it turns out that in Britain, alongside of the fact that the Communist Party is exceptionally weak, there are to be found such other facts, not matters of indifference for us, as the existence of a monarchy, an aristocracy, a House of Lords and a tremendous influence of religion in politics, in social life, and in everyday affairs. And if you approach Britain one-sidedly from this aspect, that is, from the aspect of the monarchy, the House of Lords, the aristocracy, landlordism and church influence, then you would doubtless say that the most barbarous and backward country in Europe is Britain. That would be as true as the statement of the Mensheviks that communism is a product of backwardness; that is to say, it would be as untrue, as one-sided, as false. Can one really agree that Britain is the most backward country in Europe? No, this idea cannot at all be fitted into the framework of our general picture of Britain. In Britain technique is at a very high level, and technique is decisive in human life. America, true, has outstripped Britain in the field of technique: the daughter of British culture has raced ahead of her mother along the line of technique. Before the war Germany was rivalling Britain more and more sharply, threatening to outstrip and in certain branches of industry actually outstripping Britain. But today, after the defeat of Germany, Britain leads Europe economically, British science, literature and art have played and are playing a role of the first order in the development of human thought and human creative achievement. How can one find one's way out of this contradiction? For a contradiction stares us in the face: on the one hand, high technique, science, etc.; on the other, monarchy, aristocracy, House of Lords, power of religious prejudices over people's minds. What conclusion can be drawn? This conclusion: that there is no single yardstick with which one can measure the development of a country in every sphere, and on the basis of that measurement make a uniform evaluation covering all aspects of social life. Development is contradictory. In certain spheres a country achieves tremendous successes, but it happens quite often that by these very successes that country holds back its own development in other spheres. Let me speak concretely about this matter. Britain was the first country to take the road of capitalist development and won, thanks to that fact, the hegemony of the world market in the nineteenth century. The British bourgeoisie became, again thanks to this fact, the richest, strongest, and most enlightened of the bourgeoisies. These conditions enabled it, as we know, to create a privileged position for the upper strata of the British working class and thereby to blunt class antagonisms. The British working class is becoming conscious of itself as an independent class hostile to the bourgeoisie much more slowly than the working class of other countries with less powerful bourgeoisies. Thus it turns out that the growth of the British bourgeoisie, the most advanced bourgeoisie in Europe, having taken place in exceptionally favourable conditions, has for a long time held back the development of the British proletariat. The slow and 'organic' growth of technique in England, and the fact that the Reformation and the bourgeois revolution happened close together in time, held back the work of critical thought in relation to the church. The British bourgeoisie developed under the protection of ancient institutions, on the one hand adapting itself to them and on the other subjecting them to itself, gradually, organically, 'in an evolutionary way'. The revolutionary upheavals of the seventeenth century were profoundly forgotten. In this consists what is called the British tradition. Its basic feature is conservatism. More than anything else the British bourgeoisie is proud that it has not destroyed old buildings and old beliefs, but has gradually adapted the old royal and noble castle to the requirements of the business firm. In this castle, in the corners of it, there were its icons, its symbols, its fetishes, and the bourgeoisie did not remove them. It made use of them to consecrate its own rule. And it laid down from above upon its proletariat the heavy lid of cultural conservatism.

The British working class has developed quite differently from ours. Our young proletariat was formed in a period of some fifty years, mainly from peasants and handicraftsmen who had lived in the countryside, along with their fathers and grandfathers, in ancient surroundings, in economic backwardness, amid ignorance and religious prejudices. Capital ruthlessly seized the peasant lad or youth by the scruff of the neck and at once flung him into the cauldron of factory life. The change in his conditions took place catastrophically. When the young peasant felt the blast of the factory's steam he at once began to think about who he was and where he was. At that stage the revolutionary party caught up with him and began to explain to him what and where he was. It gained ascendancy over him all the more easily because he had no conservative ideas: the old village notions did not fit at all; he needed a complete and radical change in his whole outlook on the world.

With the British worker things went quite differently. His father and his grandfather were workers, and his great-grandfathers and remoter ancestors were small artisans. The British worker has a family tree, he knows who his ancestors were, he has a family tradition. This is also a kind of 'culture', but it is expressed in the fact that in his consciousness he drags around with him many of the prejudices of his ancestors. For him, the British worker, there was not this sudden, sharp, catastrophic transition from the closed little world of the village to modern industry; he has developed organically from his remote ancestors into gradually changing conditions of factory life and urban culture. In his mind there still to this day sit old, medieval craft ideas and prejudices, only modified in form and adapted to the conditions of capitalism. The life of the crafts and the craft festivals – celebration of the birth of a son, his entry into apprenticeship, graduation to the independent position of master-craftsman, and so on – were shot through and through with religiosity, and this religiosity passed over into trade unionism, which has a heavy conservative tail stretching back into the Middle Ages...

British technique is a fundamentally capitalist technique. It was not brought in from outside, destroying national economic forms, but has developed on the basis of these national forms. The consciousness of the working class reflects this 'organic' growth of technique, while lagging very much behind it. It must not be forgotten that human consciousness, taken on the scale of society, is fearfully conservative and slow-moving. Only idealists imagine that the world is moved forward through the free initiative of human thought. In actual fact the thought of society or of a class does not take a single step forward except when there is extreme need to do so. Where it is at all possible, old familiar ideas are adapted to new facts. We speak frankly if we say that classes and peoples have hitherto not shown decisive initiative except when history has thrashed them with its heavy crop. Had things been different, would people have allowed the imperialist war to happen? After all, the war drew nearer under the eyes of everyone, like two trains hurtling towards each other along a single track. But the peoples remained silent, watched, waited and went on living their familiar, everyday, conservative lives. The fearful upheavals of the imperialist war were needed for certain changes to be introduced into consciousness and into social life. The working people of Russia overthrew Romanov, drove out the bourgeoisie and took power. In Germany they got rid of Hohenzollern but stopped half-way... The war was needed for these changes to take place, the war with its tens of millions of dead, wounded and maimed... What a clear proof this is of how conservative and slow to move is human thought, how stubbornly it clings to the past, to everything that is known, familiar, ancestral – until the next blow of the scourge.

Such blows have occurred in Britain too, of course. Thus, after the rapid industrialisation there developed in the second third of last century the stormy movement of the working class which is known as Chartism. But bourgeois society stood sufficiently firm and the Chartist movement came to nothing. The strength of the British bourgeoisie lay in its maturity, its wealth, its world power, the crumbs which it shared with the upper strata of the working class, thereby demoralising also the weakened masses.

Think over this process to the extent necessary to understand the profound difference from our development, which was extremely delayed and therefore extremely contradictory. Take our metalworking and coal-mining South: boundless expanses of steppe, thinly populated, steppe settlements with deep mud around them in spring and autumn… and suddenly huge metalworking enterprises arise in these steppes. They did not, of course, develop out of our own economy but broke in upon us thanks to foreign capital. From the backward and scattered villages European (and sometimes American) capital assembled fresh cadres of workers, tearing them from the conditions which Marx once called "the idiocy of rural life".[2] And there you had these fresh proletarians of the Donets Basin, of Krivoi Rog and so on, not bringing with them into the pits and the factories any hereditary traditions, any craft conservativism, any fixed and firm beliefs. On the contrary, it was in these new, unfamiliar and stern conditions that they only for the first time properly felt the need for firm beliefs, which would give them moral support. To their aid came Social-Democracy, which taught them to break with all their old prejudices and so gave a revolutionary consciousness to this class which had been born in a revolutionary way. This, in broad outline, is the answer to the question which was put to me and which I, in my turn, have set before you.

It is possible to put the matter like this: the richer, stronger, mightier, cleverer, firmer a bourgeoisie has proved to be, the more it has succeeded in holding back the ideological and consequently the revolutionary development of the proletariat. Here is another expression of the same idea. The British bourgeoisie has got used to the servility of the so-called workers' leaders whom it has educated. Let me interrupt myself to introduce a very interesting quotation from the British newspaper, *The Sunday Times*. The newspaper complains because in Britain today, under the MacDonald Government, stormy strikes are taking place, and it says: "We have in Great Britain the finest body of Labour leaders in the world, men of experience and patriotism, with a real sense of responsibility and a wide knowledge of economics. But they are rapidly being thrust aside by the avowed revolutionaries, whose influence is increased every time the Government capitulates to them."[3] That's what it says, word for word. As to the statement that they are being "thrust aside by the avowed revolutionaries", that, alas, is as yet an exaggeration. Of course, revolutionaries are increasing in number in Britain too, but unfortunately they

---

2   K. Marx and F. Engels, *The Communist Manifesto*, *The Classics of Marxism*, Vol. 1, Wellred Books, 2013, p. 7.

3   *The Sunday Times*, 8 June 1924.

have still far from sufficiently "thrust aside" those leaders whom *The Sunday Times* calls wise politicians, filled to the brim with wisdom and patriotism.

How has this come about? In our country there have never been leaders who won such praise from the bourgeoisie, even if we bear in mind that at a certain period the Socialist-Revolutionaries and the Mensheviks played a considerable role, because our bourgeoisie – discounting the sharpest and most decisive moments, when things were at their most critical – was dissatisfied even with the Socialist-Revolutionaries and the Mensheviks. What is the cause of such satisfaction with the workers' leaders on the part of the bourgeoisie over there in Britain? It is due to the fact that the British bourgeoisie themselves have trained these leaders. How did they get the opportunity of training 'labour' leaders? This was due to the circumstance that they were powerful and cultured, being the ruling class of an advanced capitalist country. As fast as the working class advanced young leaders from its ranks, all sorts of political 'specialists' in the service of the British bourgeoisie at once settled on them, won them over, brought to bear on them all that could be imagined by a powerful bourgeois culture. Among us the average petty-bourgeois, the philistine, the member of the intelligentsia of liberal and even radical views, has considered from time immemorial that since Britain is a highly civilised country therefore everything which exists in Britain or which comes from Britain is superior, good, progressive, and so on. In this we see expressed the petty-bourgeois incapacity for thinking dialectically, analysing phenomena, grasping a problem in its historical concreteness. There is something which is really good, British technique, and that we are trying to transfer to our country in exchange for grain, timber and other valuable commodities. The British monarchy, hypocritical British conservatism, religiosity, servility, sanctimoniousness – all this is old rags, rubbish, the refuse of centuries which we have no need for whatsoever. [*Applause.*]

If British culture has affected our average philistine in this way from afar off, by correspondence, so to speak, evoking in him a blind infatuation, how much more strongly, directly and concretely does it affect the British petty-bourgeois and the semi-petty bourgeois representative of the British working class. What the British bourgeoisie has been able to achieve is a sort of hypnotic fascination for its culture, its world-historical importance. By means of this skilfully organised hypnosis it has influenced the workers' leaders, whom it has known how to keep always surrounded by its reporters, photographers, sportsmen, clergymen, lecturers and so forth, all cunningly turned on to each newcomer among the workers' leaders. The newcomer in this way finds himself in a bourgeois milieu. They praise him to the skies if he nibbles at the bait, and they give him a good brushing the wrong way if he takes the slightest step against the bourgeoisie. And this does not just happen once, but day by day, week by week, and year in and year out. And the young leader going out into society begins to feel ashamed because his Sunday suit is not sufficiently well-cut; he dreams of a top-hat to wear when he goes out on a Sunday, so as not to be any different from a real gentleman. These may seem trifles but, after all, they make up a man's life. And in this hypnosis of a way of life lies the art of a ruling class, a powerful, cultured, hypocritical, base, greedy class – an art which consists in exercising an everyday influence whereby to work upon and subject to itself everyone who comes forward from among the working class, everyone who stands a head taller than the others in every factory, in every ward and borough, in every town and throughout the country.

Probably a lot of you have seen *The Times*. It comes out every day in dozens of pages of splendid fine print, with a variety of illustrations and an endless range of sections, so that everything has its place in the paper, from questions of high politics to all kinds of sport, and including the affairs of the churches and of the world of fashion. And from what point of view is everything presented? Naturally, from the point of view of the interests of the bourgeoisie.

Other British bourgeois newspapers are not so solid as *The Times*, but they are built on the same model, so as to capture the reader's attention from every direction and lead him to genuflect before the British national tradition, that is, before the bourgeoisie. And the workers' press is very weak; besides which, with the exception of the Communist publications, it is permeated through and through with the same hypnosis of bourgeois culture. This hypnosis is supplemented by direct terrorism. To belong to a church is in Britain the same as covering your nakedness with clothes, or paying what you owe in a shop. May one walk down the street naked? May one not belong to a church? To declare that one does not belong to a church, and still more than one does not believe in God, requires in Britain the same sort of extraordinary courage as to go naked in public. The so-called Labour government headed by MacDonald is also a product of the age-long education of the workers' leaders in this way. That is the reason, in the last analysis, why British Menshevism is so strong and communism weak.

Now let us repeat our question: is the weakness of communism in Britain a symptom of the country's high level of civilisation, or is it a symptom of backwardness? After our analysis we have no grounds for failing into the trap of such a mechanical presentation of the question. We say: it is at one and the same time a symptom of very early development and of great backwardness, because history operates not mechanically, but dialectically: it combines during long periods advanced tendencies in one sphere with monstrous backwardness in another. If we compare, from the standpoint of world-historical development, the 'Labour' government of MacDonald and the bourgeois-nationalist government of Turkey (about which I spoke in my speech at Tbilisi) the conclusion we draw is not in MacDonald's favour. You recall that the 'great' Liberal leader Gladstone – in reality he was a liberal philistine, and Marx had a most highly concentrated hatred of him – the 'great' Gladstone once delivered a tremendous speech against the bloodstained Sultan, the representative of fanatical, barbarous Islam, and so on. If you take the average philistine and say to him: Britain and Turkey – well, of course, Britain means civilisation and progress, Turkey means backwardness and barbarism. But see what is happening. There is now in Britain a government of Mensheviks and in Turkey a bourgeois-nationalist government. And this bourgeois-nationalist government of Turkey has found it necessary to abolish the Caliphate. The Caliphate is the central institution of Pan-Islamism, that is, one of the most reactionary trends in the entire world. But the Menshevik government of Britain has re-established the Caliphate of Hejaz, in order to uphold the rule of the bourgeoisie over its Moslem slaves. History's conclusion is that the Menshevik government of Britain, in spite of British civilisation, etc., is playing in this conjuncture of forces a reactionary role, whereas the bourgeois-nationalist government of backward Turkey, as of a nationally oppressed country, is playing a progressive role. Such is the dialectic of history! Of course, from the standpoint of the development of technique, science and art, Britain is immeasurably superior to Turkey. The accumulated wealth of Britain is beyond comparison with what Turkey possesses in this respect. But we see that it turns out that, precisely in order to protect this wealth and its whole national 'civilisation' in general, the British bourgeoisie has been obliged to follow an ultra-conservative policy, so that a Labour government becomes in its hands an instrument for re-establishing the Caliphate. *There is no abstract yardstick applicable to all spheres of life.* It is necessary to take living facts in their living, historical interaction. If we master this dialectical approach to the question, the latter becomes much clearer to us. Germany, for example, is placed not by accident, as regards this question of the relationship between the forces of the Communist Party and of Social-Democracy, between Russia and Britain. This is to be understood by the course of development of capitalism in Germany. It is necessary, of course, to investigate concretely the history of each separate country, in order to discover more exactly the causes of the delayed or hastened growth of the Communist Party. In a general way, however, we can draw the following conclusion: the conquest of power by the proletariat in countries which have entered the path of capitalism very late in the day, like our country, is easier than in countries with an extensive previous bourgeois history and a higher level of culture. But this is only one side of the matter. A second conclusion, no less important, states: socialist construction after the conquest of power will be easier in countries with a higher capitalist civilisation than in countries which are economically backward like ours. This means that for the British working class to break through to real proletarian power, to dictatorship, will be incomparably harder than it was for us. But once having broken through to power, it will advance to socialism much quicker and much more easily than ourselves. And it is even uncertain, history has spoken with a double tongue on this question, who will build socialism earlier, we or the British. If the British working class takes power in the next ten years – I speak approximately, and give this figure not in order to prophesy but merely as an arithmetical example – it will then within another ten years have a real socialist economy, very highly developed, while we in twenty years' time will probably still have, not only somewhere in Yakutia but also nearer here, very many survivals of peasant backwardness…

Decades will be needed to transform our North and our South into a centralised socialist economy, based on a high level of technique, with our great expanses of territory still only thinly populated. And I think that in twenty-or twenty-five-years' time the British worker, turning to us, will say: "Don't be annoyed, but I've got a bit ahead of you." Naturally, we shan't be annoyed – those of us, that is, who survive till then. Get ahead, comrade British workers, do us the favour of getting ahead, please, we beg you, we've been waiting a long time for this. [*Laughter.*] Such is the dialectic of history. Politics has held the British worker back, has for a long time, so to speak, hobbled him, and he is advancing with such timid, pitiful, MacDonaldite little steps. But when he frees himself from his political trammels, the British racehorse will outstrip our peasant nag.

To generalise theoretically what I have said, in the Marxist terminology which is familiar to us, I should say that the question itself boils down to the inter-relation between the basis and the superstructure and to the inter-relation of bases and superstructures of different countries one with another. We know that superstructures – state, law, politics, parties and so on – arise on an economic basis, are nourished and determined by this basis. Consequently, basis and superstructure have to correspond. And this happens in fact, only not simply but in a very complicated way. A powerful development of one superstructure (the bourgeois state, bourgeois parties, bourgeois culture) sometimes holds back for a long time the development of other superstructures (the revolutionary proletarian party), but in the last analysis – in the *last* analysis, not immediately – the basis reveals itself nevertheless as the decisive force. We have shown this by the example of Britain. If we approach the problem in a formal way, it may appear that the weakness of the British Communist Party *contradicts* the Marxist law of the relationship between basis and superstructure. But this is certainly not the case. Dialectically, the basis, as we have seen, will, in spite of everything, secure its victory. In other words: a high level of technique, even through the barrier of ultraconservative politics, will nevertheless manifest its preponderance and will lead to socialism sooner than in countries with a low level of technique.

That, comrades, is what I conceive the fundamental answer to be to the question which was put to me at Sokolniki.

British Bourgeois 'Morality'

From Chapter 4 of *Between Red and White* (1921).

We have a strong suspicion that Mrs. Snowden is burning with curiosity to know what we, who deny God and His commandments, understand by 'honesty'. We even suspect that Mr. Henderson puts this question to us not without irony, that is if irony can be at all compatible with piety.

We confess that we are not acquainted with the Absolute Morality of the Popes, either of the Church or of the University, of the Vatican or of the PSA.[1] The Categorical Imperative of Kant, the Transubstantiation of Christ, and the artistic virtues of a religious myth are as unknown to us as the old, hard and cunning Moses who found the treasure of eternal morality on Mount Sinai. Morality is a function of living human society. There is nothing absolute in its character, for it changes with the progress of that society, and serves as an expression of the interests of its classes, and chiefly of the governing classes. Official morality is a bridle to restrain the oppressed. In the course of the struggle the working class has elaborated its own revolutionary morality, which began by dethroning God and all absolute standards. But we understand by honesty *a conformity of words and deeds before the working class*, checked by the supreme end of the movement and of our struggle: the liberation of humanity through the social revolution. For instance, we do not say that one must not deceive and be cunning, that one must love one's enemies, etc., for such exalted morality is evidently only accessible to such deeply religious statesmen as Lord Curzon, Lord Northcliffe, and Mr.

---

1 Pleasant Sunday Afternoon – Societies formed in the 1880s by non-conformist sects to bring unreligious workers around the church through social activities.

Henderson. We hate or despise our enemies, according to their deserts; we beat them and deceive according to circumstances, and, even when we come to an understanding with them, we are not swept off our feet by a wave of forgiving love. But we firmly believe that one must not lie to the masses and that one must not deceive them with regard to the aims and methods of their own struggle. The social revolution is entirely based upon the growth of proletarian consciousness and on the faith of the proletariat in its own strength and in the party which is leading it. One may play a double game with the enemies of the proletariat, but not with the proletariat itself. Our party has made mistakes, together with the masses which it was leading. We have always quite openly acknowledged these mistakes to the masses, and, together with them we have made the necessary changes. What the devotees of legality are pleased to call demagogy is merely truth, too plainly and too loudly expressed. That, Mrs. Snowden, is our conception of honesty.

* * *

From Chapter 10 of *Between Red and White* (1921).

We Russian Marxists, owing to the belated development of Russia, were not weighed down by a powerful bourgeois culture. We became allied to European spiritual culture not through the medium of our miserable national bourgeoisie, but independently: we assimilated the most revolutionary conclusions of European experience and European thought, and developed them to their highest pitch. This has given some advantages to our generation. Let us declare frankly: the sincere and profound enthusiasm with which we contemplate the products of the British genius in the most varied spheres of human creative endeavour, only the more sharply and pitilessly accentuates the sincere and profound contempt with which we regard the spiritual narrow-mindedness, the theoretical banality and the lack of revolutionary dignity, which characterise the authorised leaders of British socialism. They are not the heralds of a new world; they are but the surviving relics of an old culture, which in their person expresses anxiety for its further fate. And the spiritual barrenness of these relics seems to be a sort of retribution for the profligate lavish past of bourgeois culture. [...]

The bourgeois mind has imbibed some of the great cultural achievements of mankind. Yet at the present time it is the chief obstacle to the development of human culture.

One of the leading virtues of our party, which makes it the mightiest lever of development of the epoch, consists of its complete and absolute independence of bourgeois public opinion. These words signify much more than they at first sight seem. They need to be explained. Particularly if we bear in mind such a thankless section of the audience as the Second International. Every revolutionary thought, even the simplest truth, must be nailed down here with extreme care.

Bourgeois public opinion is a close psychological web which envelops on all sides the tools and instruments of bourgeois violence, protecting them against any incidental shocks, as well as against the fatal revolutionary shock, which, however, in the last resort is inevitable. Active bourgeois public opinion is composed of two parts: first, of inherited views, actions, and prejudices which represent the fossilised experience of the past, a thick layer of irrational banality and useful stupidity; and second, of the intricate machinery and clever management necessary for the mobilisation of patriotic feeling and moral indignation, of national enthusiasm, altruist sentiment, and other kinds of lies and deceptions.

Such is the general formula. But some explanatory examples are necessary. When in famine-stricken Russia, a Cadet lawyer, who with funds supplied by Britain or by France, helped in making a noose for the neck of the working class, dies of typhus in a prison, the wireless and cables of bourgeois public opinion produce a sufficiently great number of vibrations to arouse a wave of indignation in the receptive conscience of the collective Mssrs. Snowdens. It is quite obvious that all the devilish work of the capitalist wireless and cables would have been useless if the skull of the petty-bourgeois did not serve as a gramophone box.

Let us take another instance: the famine on the Volga. In its present form of unprecedented calamity, this famine, at least half of it, is a result of the civil war raised on the Volga by the Czechoslovaks[2] and Kolchak, that is by the Anglo-American and French capital which organised and sustained it. This drought fell upon a soil that had been already exhausted and ruined, denuded of working cattle, machinery and other stock. We, on the other hand, have cast into gaol some officers and lawyers (which we by no means hold up as an example of humanitarianism), and bourgeois Europe and America attempted

---

2 The Czechoslovak Corps was a force made up of Czech and Slovak prisoners of war in Russian captivity in order to fight against the Central Powers in the First World War. After the Russian revolution it was arranged that they should be transferred via the Trans-Siberian Railway to Vladivostock for transport to the Western Front. En route in May 1918 they were incited by French agents to seize the Trans-Siberian Railway as part of an attempt to overthrow the revolutionary government. They were eventually evacuated in 1920.

then to picture the whole of Russia, with its hundred million inhabitants, as a vast hunger-prison. They encircled us with a wall of blockade, while their hired White Guard agents applied the bomb and torch to the destruction of our scant supplies. If there is anyone who handles the scales of pure morality, let him weigh up the severe measures that we are compelled to adopt in our life and death struggle against the whole world, against the calamities which world capitalism, in quest of unpaid interests on loans, showered upon the heads of the Volga mothers. Yet the machine of bourgeois public opinion works so systematically, and with such arrogant self-righteousness, the cretinism of the middle-class represents such a valuable gramophone box, that as a result, Mrs. Snowden pours her surplus human pity out upon... the poor down-trodden agents of imperialism in our land.

Reverence of bourgeois public opinion is a more impassable barrier to the activity of social reformers than even the bourgeois laws. It may be put down as a law of modern capitalist governments, that the more 'democratic', the more 'liberal' and 'free' is their regime, the more respectable are their national socialists, and the more stupid the obeisance of the national Labour Party before the public opinion of the bourgeoisie. Why have an outward policeman over Mr. MacDonald when there is an inward one within his soul?

Here we must not shirk the question, the very mention of which is a menace to respectability. I speak of religion. It was not so very long ago that Lloyd George called the Church the central power station of all parties and currents, i.e., of bourgeois public opinion as a whole. This is particularly true in reference to Britain. Not in the sense, of course, that Lloyd George derives the real inspiration for his politics from religion, or that the hatred of Churchill for Soviet Russia is due to his burning desire to enter the Kingdom of Heaven, or that the Notes of Lord Curzon are copied directly from the Sermon on the Mount. Oh no! The driving force of their politics are the very mundane interests of the bourgeoisie which put them in power. But that 'public opinion' which alone makes possible the smooth working of the mechanism of governmental compulsion, finds its chief resources in religion. The legal restraint that has been put over men, over classes, and over society as a whole, as a sort of ideological whip, is merely the unadorned application of religious restraint – that heavenly whip which is held over the head of exploited humanity. After all is said and done, it is a hopeless matter to impose upon an unemployed Dockers a faith in the sacredness of democratic legality by the force of formal arguments. The first essential thing here is material argument – a policeman with a heavy club on earth, and above him

– the Supreme Policeman, armed with the thunder in Heaven. But when even in the minds of 'socialists' the fetishism of bourgeois legality is coupled with the fetishism of the epoch of the Druids, we get as a result that ideal inner policeman, with whose aid the bourgeoisie (at least for a time) can allow itself the luxury of approximate observance of democratic ritual.

When speaking of the treasons and betrayals of the social reformers, we by no means desire to assert that they are all, or a majority of them, merely bought. If so, they would never do for the serious role set to them by bourgeois society. It is even unimportant to guess the extent to which the vanity of a middle-class man might feel flattered by becoming an MP in a loyal opposition, or even a member of the Imperial Cabinet, although there is a good deal of that sentiment, of course.

Suffice it to say that the same bourgeois public opinion which in days of quietude permits them to be in the Opposition, at a decisive moment, when the life or death of bourgeois society is at stake, or at least its most important interests – in a war, a rebellion in Ireland or in India, the great coal lock-out, or the Soviet Republic in Russia – proved capable of forcing them to take the political position which was necessary to the capitalist order. Without wishing in any way to attribute to the personality of Mr. Henderson any titanic features that it does not possess, we may confidently assume that Mr. Henderson as the head of the 'Labour Party' is a supremely important asset to bourgeois society in Britain. For in the heads of the Hendersons the fundamental elements of bourgeois education and the fragmentary scraps of socialism are welded into one by the traditional cement of religion. The question of the economic emancipation of the British proletariat cannot be seriously put as long as the labour movement is not purged of such leaders, organisations, and moods, which are the embodiment of the timid, cringing, cowardly and base submission of the exploited to the public opinion of the exploiters. The inward policeman must be cast out before the outward policeman can be overthrown.

* * *

From a draft of a Soviet government reply to a protest
by a number of British church leaders dated
3 June 1922 and first published in *Izvestia*, 8 June.

The protest of a number of the clergy of Great Britain against the preferment of charges against the former patriarch Tikhon, addressed to the Soviet Government, makes it necessary to give the following clarifications.

1. Notwithstanding the words of protest, there is no attack on the church, but there is the preferment of charges against individual representatives

of the church, including the former patriarch of it, of organising resistance to measures taken by the Soviet regime, which were carried out with the object of saving the lives of tens of millions of human beings, children among them.

2. The overwhelming majority of the priesthood in the conflict between the former patriarch Tikhon and the Soviet regime, are on the side of the Soviet regime and of the toiling masses represented by it. Only some elements of the church, not numerous ones, the most privileged and debauched by their connection with the tsarist aristocracy and with capital, constitute the group of the former Patriarch Tikhon. Public opinion in Russia will note the fact that the protecting British ecclesiastical hierarchy is identifying itself not with the hungry, toiling masses of Russia, not even with the majority of the priesthood, but with a numerically insignificant church hierarchy, which has always gone hand in hand with the tsars, the bureaucracy, the nobility, and has now entered upon an outright struggle against the regime of the workers and peasants.

3. Public opinion in Russia also affirms that in the most brutal periods of the blockade, in which the British Government also participated, the authors of the protest did not raise their voice against the throttling of Russian workers and peasants and their children. The population of Russia has equally not heard of any protest by the Protestants against the attempt to strangle the toiling Russian people in the noose of usury.

4. This is why both the Soviet regime and the toiling people regard the above mentioned protest of the princes of the various churches in Great Britain as having been dictated by narrow caste solidarity, wholly directed against the real interests of the people and the elementary requirements of humanity.

* * *

From a speech to the All-Union Conference of
Agricultural Workers, 28 May 1926
(*For Quality, Against Bureaucratism, For Socialism!*).

For comparison I've brought along one British and one American newspaper. Many of you have probably seen them. [*Voices:* "We haven't."]

Here's *The Times* newspaper, a big paper, curse it. [*Laughter, applause.*] It is the main organ of the British press, a Conservative newspaper which supports any government on matters of foreign policy, whether Liberal, Conservative or MacDonald's so-called Labour government which however has conducted a conservative foreign policy and domestic policy. This is the issue for just one day with thirty-two pages and the paper is printed in brevier and nonpareil.[3]

Today I asked a comrade to count up how much this would come to if transferred into our *Pravda*. On six pages in *Pravda*, there are 270,000 printed characters, but here on thirty-two pages there are 2,300,000 i.e., 8.75 times more. What a lot of lies that makes! [*Applause.*] You will ask: where do they find such an amount of material every day? How many '*Burkors*',[4] must they have? [*Laughter.*]

So allow me to show you: the first, second and third pages are set in the smallest type, here the advertisements are printed, without screaming headlines or wasting unnecessary space, yet a model of order with a strict plan so that it's very easy to find any advertisement.

Then comes a page devoted to the law report. On various occasions I've spoken and written that public education must also include attentive coverage of what goes on in the courts because the court shows the seamy side of society. In the courts we have a reflection both of our day-to-day life and our whole process of construction but an inverted reflection as it were. However, coverage of the courts is done badly in our press: we have neither enough space nor the necessary know-how.

Next, on two pages of *The Times* comes the sport – of every kind: who spilt whose blood at boxing; football takes up a huge space; and finally every vixen hunted by a lord will find its biography here. [*Laughter, applause.*] Next comes parliament, again in very small type, nonpareil, two pages, receiving about the same attention as football and boxing, then home affairs compact and packed in tightly.

Next comes what we call 'miscellany'. Next, commerce, here's that page, theatre, a page, foreign news – just a page, but in the number of characters these pages count for two of *Pravda's*.

This middle sheet here forms what we would call simply a newspaper. Here you have foreign affairs, here the main news of the previous day and here features, leaders and anything else. Next a continuation of the most important news. These four pages form the core of the paper. But there are twenty-eight pages besides them!

Let's go on. Here again are 'various' reports from all over the world. I will not describe them in any more detail. Here are the pages of illustrations,

3 Brevier and nonpareil – Names for the typecasting font sizes 8pt and 6pt respectively.
4 *Burkors* – Bourgeois correspondent.

photographs and so on, sharp and far better than in our weeklies and monthlies, yet this is a daily printed by the rotary method. Here is finance and the Stock Exchange, company reports, business, share prices, commodity markets, then shipping and so on, and then the last pages with advertisements.

That's what a daily issue of *The Times* is like. If you think that this is a record-breaking paper in size, then you're wrong. In this respect America leaves Britain far behind at least in quantity. [*Voice:* "what about quality?"]

In the quality of the technique *The Times* is superior to all papers. In respect of vulgarity, sensations, and playing upon the basest feelings, the Americans probably hold the record, though it is difficult to decide this exactly. During the recent General Strike in Britain the government's paper was printed on just four pages, I will show it to you, but what a vast quantity of compressed lies it contained! [...]

You must not forget that in Britain, where there are dozens of bourgeois newspapers with wider circulations than *The Times*, there's only one daily 'Labour' paper and that's a MacDonaldite one, that is, if not belonging to the bourgeoisie itself then to its political henchman.

This alone fully explains why it so happens that the bourgeoisie can manage without censorship and have a 'free' press, at least in normal times when there is no General Strike, no civil war and no international war.

Why have censorship if you have the printing works, the writers and the paper wholly and completely in your hands? In 'peace' time this is more than enough, for the property-owners' press is an organised conspiracy to safeguard the interests of the landlords and capitalists. This press has its internal censorship. Every bourgeois journalist has a gendarme sitting inside him so that an external one is unnecessary...

This same *Times* and all the rest of the British press experienced a few difficult days not so long ago. That was during the General Strike, which by its very fact showed that the 'freedom' of the press, like all other freedoms apart from the press itself, rests upon a specific industrial basis, upon the continuity of the proletariat's labour and turns to dust with the interruption of this continuity.

All the bourgeois papers were replaced by one government paper. It came out like this, in four pages. The government requisitioned all the paper for itself, thereby demonstrating that 'freedom' of the press is not a paragraph of the constitution but a matter of possessing the material resources. An instructive lesson for the British proletariat!

Here now is the *News of the General Council* – four little pages. It wasn't however, because they had only four little pages that they suffered such a defeat. On four small pages you can say a lot. In 1917 *Pravda* was ever so small, but what a revolution it produced, first in minds, then in relationships. It's all a question of what you say!

So here in the paper of the strike there reigned the spirit of conciliation, kowtowing, submissiveness and cowardice and therefore the strike suffered such a defeat.

During the strike there was one incident which must be of interest not only to printers but also to our reporters. The compositors on the *Daily Mail*, one of the most villainous papers in the world (and that's saying something!), suddenly refused to set a leading article aimed against the strike and written in a mad dog's saliva.[6] The greatest excitement and indignation throughout public opinion up to and including MacDonald! "What, interference with editorial business, an infringement of the freedom of the press!"

So what then is their freedom of the press? The freedom of the press is the undisputed right of the bourgeoisie to print with workers' hands in 'their' printing works on 'their' paper everything that is directed against the interests of the people, whereby the attempt by the workers to intervene in the matter and declare that today, on the day of the General Strike, we typographical slaves refuse to print your slander against the proletariat, is condemned and assailed as an attack on the freedom of the press!

The strike was quite big enough, despite its defeat, to lay bare to the bones the whole fraud of British democracy.

It would be a fine thing if in every workers' club in Britain and in every trade union premises there was on the wall this issue here of the *Daily Mail* published in Paris on the day of the start of the strike.

Here is the leader printed under the headline 'For King and Country'. After it, a second article 'For the Freedom of the Press'. A pompous, emotive, patriotic, militant tone. "Days of great ordeals are beginning. Moscow is raising up the working class against Britain, the King, the country and the freedom of the press." (This, comrades, is the same *Daily Mail* that accuses our trade unions of sending not their own money but that of the Soviet government to the British miners in order to wreck the British economy.)

---

5   The newspaper issued by the General Council of the TUC was in fact called *British Worker*.

6   It was the machine operators and not the compositors who refused to work on the leading article.

But here is what is particularly remarkable. This most profoundly moral newspaper which intervenes on behalf of the King, the country and the freedom of the press prints just in front of this very regal article, here in these two columns, right under the nose of King and country, dozens of bawling advertisements for houses of ill-repute in Paris which exist for the delight of the noble public with fat wallets.

Just imagine, in this newspaper on the day of great 'national ordeal' when this paper utters especially rabid abuse at Moscow and the working class, right here on the first page are these enticing advertisements for night entertainments, fleshpots for the lords who have fled to Paris in a jitter.

This patriotic newspaper gathers its sinless revenue both from the defence of King, country and the freedom of the Press and from houses of ill-repute. [*Applause.*]

The Philosophy of British Capitalism

From *Military Doctrine or Pseudo-Military Doctrinairism*
(dated 5 December 1921), *Kommunisticheskii Internatsional*,
17 December 1921.

If the advanced bourgeoisie has banished inertia, routinism and superstition
from the domain of productive technology, and has sought to build each
enterprise on the precise foundations of scientific methods, then in the field
of social orientation the bourgeoisie has proved impotent, because of its class
position, to rise to the heights of scientific method. Our class enemies are
empiricists, that is, they operate from one occasion to the next, guided not by
the analysis of historical development, but by practical experience, routinism,
rule of thumb, and instinct.

Assuredly, on the basis of empiricism the British imperialist caste has set
an example of wide-flung predatory usurpation, provided us with a model
of triumphant far-sightedness and class firmness. Not for nothing has it
been said of the British imperialists that they do their thinking in terms of
centuries and continents. This habit of weighing and appraising practically
the most important factors and forces has been acquired by the ruling British
clique thanks to the superiority of its position, from its insular vantage point
and under the conditions of a relatively gradual and planned accumulation
of capitalist power.

Parliamentary methods of personal combinations, of bribery, eloquence
and deception, and colonial methods of sanguinary oppression and hypocrisy,
along with every other form of vileness, have entered equally into the rich

arsenal of the ruling clique of the world's greatest empire. The experience of the struggle of British reaction against the French Revolution has given the greatest subtlety to the methods of British imperialism, endowed it with utmost flexibility, armed it most diversely, and, in consequence, rendered it more secure against historical surprises.

Nevertheless the exceedingly potent class dexterity of the world-ruling British bourgeoisie is proving inadequate – more and more so with each passing year – in the epoch of the present volcanic convulsions of the bourgeois regime. While they continue to tack and veer with great skill, the British empiricists of the period of decline – whose finished expression is Lloyd George – will inescapably break their necks.

* * *

From *A 'Declaration of Rights' and a 'Velvet Book'*,
Vostnochnoe Obozrenie, 13 and 14 March 1901.

Buckle,[1] the son of a progressive merchant, sincerely believed that the rule of 'enlightened businessmen' would finally make war – as a form of zoological struggle and not as the social rivalry of man against man – the property of the murky past, yet today the omnipotent organ of the bigoted British bourgeoisie, in its Christmas editorial, *The Times*, resounds with brazen hypocrisy: "It is the business of combatants to kill each other but… they ought to kill each other 'as Christians should'…"

And today in connection with the behaviour of Britain in South Africa and the activity of the 'enlightened businessmen' like Cecil Rhodes, Chamberlain and Co., and their protectors like Roberts and Kitchener, what murderous irony echoes in the following words of John Stuart Mill:

> The British state comprehends the meaning of freedom more than others and whatever might have been its mistakes in the past it has reached in its dealings with other states an honesty and frankness that other great nations consider impossible or even undesirable.

The evolution of the bourgeoisie with its glorious beginning and its grievous end is present before us. While the bourgeoisie fought against feudalism, absolutism, Catholicism, guild restrictions and so on it embodied progress and movement forward, it was the bearer of advanced ideals and it carried society along with it.

---

1   Henry Buckle (1821-1862) – English historian, whose chief work was *History of Civilisation in England*.

But when having captured the field it tried to entrench itself in this position for good and preparing to retreat backwards rather than move forward, history condemned it for lack of ideals and for moral and political decomposition. Life is merciless: it strikes those who, like Lot's wife, look back, with a fearful punishment.

Feeling the real soil under its feet shaking, the bourgeoisie ever gradually renounces its free-thinking and begins to seek support from supernatural powers. Mysticism becomes its spiritual diet. Brunetière[2] more and more often goes to Rome to kiss the Pope's slipper.

* * *

Fragment written in 1940 and first published in
Fourth International, January 1942.

The entire philosophy of British utilitarianism is derived in the last analysis from a cookery book. In order to make people happy it is necessary to introduce such and such reforms, such and such improvements. In order to prepare a pudding for twelve it is necessary to take two pounds of flour, so many eggs, so much sugar, plums, and so on. In its specifications the cookery book presupposes that flour, plums, etc., are always available in necessary amounts and ready to hand. Similarly, the empiricists-utilitarians from Jeremy Bentham down to the latter-day pragmatists consider it sufficient to issue 'practical' prescriptions in order to assure the salvation of society. So far as the organic laws of society itself are concerned, they prefer not to bother their heads about them. These gentlemen have not become accustomed to thinking about the organic laws which govern the development of society, for the simple reason that their forefathers had achieved uninterrupted progress without understanding either its sources or its laws. It is noteworthy that British methods have found their greatest flowering on American soil.

* * *

From *Their Morals and Ours* (dated 16 February 1938),
New International, June 1938.

It is remarkable that the common sense of the Anglo-Saxon philistine has managed to wax indignant at the 'Jesuit' principle and simultaneously to find inspiration in the utilitarian morality, so characteristic of British philosophy. Yet, the criterion of Bentham-John Mill, "the greatest possible happiness of

---

2 Ferdinand Brunetière – Leading French literary critic and editor of the *Revue des deux Mondes* who held an evolutionary theory of literary development and opposed naturalism in fiction.

the greatest possible number", signifies that those means are moral which lead to the common welfare as the highest end. In its general philosophical formulations Anglo-Saxon utilitarianism thus fully coincides with the 'Jesuit' principle, "the end justifies the means". Empiricism, we see, exists in the world only to free us from the necessity of making both ends meet.

Herbert Spencer,[3] into whose empiricism Darwin inculcated the idea of 'evolution' as a special vaccine, taught that in the moral sphere evolution proceeds from 'sensations' to 'ideas'. Sensations impose the criterion of immediate pleasure, whereas ideas permit one to be guided by the criterion of *future, lasting and higher pleasure*. Thus the moral criterion here too is 'pleasure' and 'happiness'. But the content of this criterion acquires breadth and depth depending upon the level of 'evolution'. In this way Herbert Spencer too, through the methods of his own 'evolutionary' utilitarianism, showed that the principle "the end justifies the means", does not embrace anything immoral.

It is naive, however, to expect from this abstract 'principle' an answer to the practical question "what may we, and what may we not do?" Moreover, the principle, the end justifies the means, naturally raise the question "and what justifies the end?" In practical life as in the historical movement the end and the means constantly change places. A machine under construction is an 'end' of production only that upon entering the factory it may become the 'means'. Democracy in certain periods is the 'end' of the class struggle only that later it may be transformed into its 'means'. Not embracing anything immoral, the so-called 'Jesuit' principle fails, however, to resolve the moral problem.

The 'evolutionary' utilitarianism of Spencer likewise abandons us half-way without an answer since, following Darwin, it tries to dissolve the concrete historical morality in the biological needs or in the 'social instincts' characteristic of gregarious animals, and this at a time when the very understanding of morality arises only in an antagonistic milieu, that is, in a society divided into classes.

Bourgeois evolutionism halts impotently at the threshold of historical society because it does not wish to acknowledge the driving force in the evolution of social forms: *the class struggle*. Morality is one of the ideological functions in this struggle. The ruling class forces *its* ends upon society and habituates it into considering all those means which contradict its ends as immoral. That is the chief function of official morality. It pursues the idea of the "greatest possible happiness" not for the majority but for a small and

---

3 Herbert Spencer (1820-1903) – English philosopher and political theorist, best known as the founder of Social Darwinism.

ever-diminishing minority. Such a regime could not have endured for even a week through force alone. It needs the cement of morality. The production of this cement constitutes the profession of the petty-bourgeois theoreticians and moralists. They radiate all the colours of the rainbow but in the final analysis remain apostles of slavery and submission.

* * *

The first paragraph is from *A Petty-Bourgeois Opposition in the Socialist Workers Party of the United States* (dated 15 December 1939) *Byulleten Oppozitsii*, February-April 1940.

The subsequent passages are fragments most probably originally intended for inclusion in the above article but omitted from the published version. These fragments were first published in 1972, *The Writings of Leon Trotsky 1939-1940* (Second Edition).

Last year I was visited by a young British professor of political economy, a sympathiser of the Fourth International. During our conversation on the ways and means of realising socialism, he suddenly expressed the tendencies of British utilitarianism in the spirit of Keynes and others: "It is necessary to determine a clear economic end, to choose the most reasonable means for its realisation" etc. I remarked: "I see that you are an adversary of dialectics". He replied, somewhat astonished: "Yes, I don't see any use in it." "However", I replied to him, "the dialectic enabled me on the basis of a few of your observations upon economic problems to determine what category of philosophical thought you belong to – this alone shows that there is an appreciable value in the dialectic." Although I have received no word about my visitor since then, I have no doubt that this anti-dialectic professor maintains the opinion that the USSR is not a workers' state, that unconditional defence of the USSR is an 'outmoded' opinion, that our organisational methods are bad, etc.[4] If it is possible to place a given person's general type of thought on the basis of his relation to concrete practical problems, it is also possible to predict approximately, knowing his general type of thought, how a given individual will approach one or another practical question. That is the incomparable educational value of the dialectical method of thought…

In the same conversation the young British scholar said:

I understand the weight of the proposition that everything undergoes change and that, given these conditions, the immutability of the syllogism is

---

4   See Trotsky's *In Defence of Marxism* for a full treatment of the polemic with the group in the Socialist Workers' Party led by Burnham and Schachtman in 1938-9.

incomprehensible; but I think that the syllogism is simply an agreement among people to understand specific concepts in one and the same sense, something like a rule in a game...

I replied to him that in the sphere of logic he had arrived at Rousseau's social contract in sociology. He took my remark as a joke. As a matter of fact it is quite precise and perhaps even too indulgent an appraisal of the logical method of my opponent. If one thinks the matter through as one should, it is difficult to believe that any man in the twentieth century with a knowledge of science, with a knowledge of evolution, could talk about the syllogism as being the product of agreement among people. Precisely in this is revealed the entire hopeless backwardness of the "scientific" method of this anti-dialectician. To say that people have come to an agreement about the syllogism is almost like saying, or more correctly it is exactly the same as saying, that people came to an agreement to have nostrils in their noses. The syllogism is no less an objective product of organic development, i.e., the biological, anthropological, and social development of humanity, than are our various organs, among them our organ of smell.

American, or, generally, Anglo-Saxon empiricism contains both formal logic and dialectical logic within itself in undeveloped form, and does not distinguish between them. Pragmatism insofar as I understand it, is precisely the philosophy of this undifferentiated combination of formal logic with the dialectic. But in all those cases where a representative of this empirical school of thought is compelled to leave his place of refuge, whenever he is compelled to bring his thoughts to a conclusion, he falls into the most trivial rationalism, that is, whenever he proves himself incapable of rising to the dialectic. This is what happened with my British opponent on the question of the dialectic.

On the question of the syllogism, let us take up the following argument as to why the syllogism, taken apart from all that exists, remains immutable: because the syllogism is simply an agreement arrived at between people that every concept should remain unchanged during a discussion, and so on. Here rationalism reveals to us its Achilles' heel. Being absolutely incapable of penetrating into the objective historical nature of society, Rousseau thought of society as the product of a contract between people; in the same way, the fetishists of formal logic arrive at Rousseau's theory (of the social contract) in the sphere of knowledge. However, the elements of the syllogism do obtain among animals; the chicken knows that grain is in general useful, necessary, and tasty. It recognises a given piece of grain as that grain – of wheat – with which it is acquainted and hence draws a logical conclusion by means of its beak. The syllogism of Aristotle is only an articulated expression of those elementary mental conclusions which we observe at every step among animals. To speak therefore of the syllogism as the product of a contract is absolutely ludicrous. It is doubly ludicrous in relation to the past because it rationalises our entire previous history, and furthermore it is especially ludicrous in relation to the future. It turns out that our biblical and pre-biblical ancestors were capable of arriving at an agreement concerning such forms of thought as preserve their compulsory and imperishable force for all time to come.

Logical thinking, formal logical thinking in general, is constructed on the basis of the deductive method, proceeding from a more general syllogism through a number of premises to the necessary conclusion. Such a chain of syllogisms is called a 'sorites'. It is well known with what case Anglo-Saxon thought breaks the chain of syllogisms and, under the influence of purely empirical data and considerations, arrives at conclusions which have no connection whatever with the previous logical chain. We see this especially clearly in the sphere of politics, as well as in other spheres. Thus the cult of the syllogism is not at all characteristic of Anglo-Saxon thought. On the contrary, it is possible to say that this school of thought is distinguished by a sovereign-empirical contempt for the pure syllogism, which did not prevent the English from making colossal conquests in many spheres of scientific investigation. If one really thinks this through as one should, then it is impossible not to arrive at the conclusion that the empirical disregard for the syllogism is a primitive form of dialectical thinking; with the aim of purely empirical corrections, the English save themselves from the formal-logical emptiness of the syllogism, i.e., to a certain extent they attain that which can more fully, much better, on a much broader scale, and more systematically be attained through dialectical thinking.

Anglo-Saxon thinking, and to a large extent that of the French, submits to the dialectic with difficulty because of historical factors. France is the land of the syllogism. The entire struggle against the dialectic is conducted in the name of the sovereign rights of the syllogism. The syllogism is looked upon not as an instrument of our consciousness in the process of its adaptation to nature and the growing knowledge of nature – in short, not as a psychological formation that has a relative, logical, i.e., conscious value – but rather as a distinct, super-historical absolute which determines and controls all our cognitive processes and thereby our consciousness as well. The fetishists of formal-logical thinking represent a form of logical idealism...

Human thought has assimilated the cosmogony of Kant and Laplace, the geology of Lyell, the biology of Darwin, the sociology of Marx, which analyses every existing thing in the process of its uninterrupted change, evolution, development, catastrophes, etc. But for formal logic the syllogism remains immutable; it does not appear as an instrument, a historical lever of our consciousness in the process of its adaptation to external nature with the aim of learning about nature – in a word, not a concrete historical formation conditioned by the circumstances of time and place, including the structure of our consciousness, the scope of its experience, etc. On the contrary, the syllogism appears as a once-and-for-all-given form of comprehending external events. The syllogism stands above these events, above humanity itself and its consciousness, above matter, and is the eternal beginning, immutable and all-powerful, for it controls all our activity; in other words the syllogism is invested with all the attributes of God.

Dr. John Dewey writes that my world outlook partakes of teleology. I place before myself certain social goals (socialism) and at the same time deduce from this that the objective development of my consciousness has prepared all the necessary conditions for the realisation of these goals. The dialectic in this sense appears to Dewey to be akin to religion, which views the historical process as the fulfilment of divine prescriptions.

In no case is it permissible to accuse Anglo-Saxons of excessive worship of the syllogism. On the contrary, their thought is permeated with a spirit of compromise in the form of empiricism, or in the form of pragmatism which is a partial expression of this same empiricism. A Britisher easily departs from his democratic syllogism in order to put on abbreviated court knickers and bow before His Majesty. An English scholar readily breaks the thread of the syllogism in order to bow before religion. This tradition has been wholly borrowed by the United States.

But if the Anglo-Saxon does not consider himself, in contrast to the Latin peoples, bound by the compulsory force of the syllogism, then he attempts to defend himself before the highest form of logical thought, namely, before the dialectic. In the struggle against the dialectic or in self-defence against the dialectic our empirical or pragmatic Anglo-Saxon turns out to be the captive of the syllogism, as the highest, and sole immutable, form of human thought. In the struggle against the revolutionary dialectic the syllogism still remains a better or a less compromised weapon than the empirical compromise of religion. Similarly, in defence of the interests of British imperialism, an appeal to democracy appears more convincing than an appeal to the rights of the British monarch.

"We do not know anything about the world except what is provided through experience." This is correct if one does not understand experience in the sense of the direct testimony of our individual five senses. If we reduce the matter to experience in the narrow empirical sense, then it is impossible for us to arrive at any judgement concerning either the origin of the species or, still less, the formation of the earth's crust. To say that the basis for everything is experience is to say too much or to say nothing at all. Experience is the active interrelationship between subject and object. To analyse experience outside this category, i.e., outside the objective material milieu of the investigator who is counter-posed to it and who from another standpoint is a part of this milieu – to do this is to dissolve experience in a formless unity where there is neither object nor subject but only the mystical formula of experience. 'Experiment' or 'experience' of this kind is peculiar only to a baby in its mother's womb, but unfortunately the baby is deprived of the opportunity to share the scientific conclusions of its experiment.

In order to deal me a blow in the most vital spot Burnham informs me that in the university textbooks on logic that he deals with, the dialectic is not mentioned at all. He should have added that in the university courses on political economy Marx's labour theory of value is not mentioned either, or it is mentioned only under the sign of condemnation. And the main thing that should have been mentioned is that in the university textbook there is no mention, or only a condemnation, of historical materialism. In the courses in civil law there is no exposition, or only a condemnation, of the socialist attitude toward property forms, etc., etc... From the fact that the dialectic is not mentioned in the university textbooks, it is essential to draw some conclusions about the class nature of official scholarship – its fear of revolution, the inability of bourgeois thought to go beyond the limits of empirical tasks, etc. For Burnham and his ilk the banning of Marxism from official scholarship suffices to disprove the scientific nature of Marxism.

Common sense opposed to religion is progressive. But common sense opposed to science is reactionary and stupid.

The aphorism of His Majesty's Opposition, "The State is created for and not man for the state" represents a circular model of nationalistic rationalistic thinking. As a matter of fact this aphorism expresses merely the demands of the bourgeois that the state trouble him as little as possible. From the scientific point of view this aphorism does not in the slightest way express a correct relationship between the individual and the state. The individual in the modern world to a far greater measure is created by the state than the state by the individual. That is why it is an outright rationalisation to assign to the creation of the state a definite goal dictated by individual personal interests.

* * *

From *The Revolution and the War in China*, foreword to
The Tragedy of the Chinese Revolution (1938) by Harold Isaacs.

Despite all the indisputable greatness of Anglo-Saxon genius one cannot help observing that it is precisely in the Anglo-Saxon countries that the laws of revolution are least understood. This can be explained on the one hand by the fact that the phenomenon of revolution itself in these countries relates to a far distant past and evokes from the official "sociologists" the condescending smile intended for a naughty child. On the other hand the pragmatism so characteristic of Anglo-Saxon thinking is of least avail for the understanding of revolutionary crises.

The English Revolution of the seventeenth century, like the French Revolution of the eighteenth century, had the object of rationalising the structure of society, i.e., clearing out feudal stalactites and stalagmites and subordinating it to the laws of free competition, which in that era seemed to be the laws of 'common sense'. To this end the puritan revolution clad itself in biblical garb, thereby displaying an infantile inability to comprehend its real meaning. The French revolution, which exerted a considerable influence on progressive thought in the United States, was guided by the formulas of a pure rationalism. Common sense, which was still afraid of itself, and resorted to the mask of biblical prophets or secularised common sense which regarded society as the product of a reasonable 'contract', to this day forms the basic outline of Anglo-Saxon thinking in the field of philosophy and sociology.

Meanwhile real historical society has been built neither according to Rousseau, upon a reasonable 'contract', nor according to Bentham upon the principle of the 'common good', but has taken shape 'irrationally' through contradictions and antagonisms. For a revolution to become inevitable, class contradictions must reach an ultimate degree of tension. It is this very historical fatalism of a collision, which does not depend on good or bad will but on the objective interrelations of classes, that makes revolution, along with war, the most dramatic expression of the 'irrational' basis of the historical process.

'Irrational' does not, however, mean arbitrary. On the contrary, in the molecular preparation of a revolution, its outbreak, its upsurge and its decline, there lies a profound inner pattern, which can be established and broadly foreseen in advance. Revolutions, as has been said more than once, have their own logic. But this is not Aristotelian logic or even less the pragmatic semi-logic of 'common sense'. It is a higher function of thought: the logic of development and its contradictions, i.e., dialectics.

The persistence of Anglo-Saxon pragmatism and its hostility to dialectical thinking have therefore their material causes. Just as a poet cannot grasp the dialectic of feelings from books and without his own experiences, so a secure society which has lost the habit of upheavals and has grown used to uninterrupted 'progress' is incapable of understanding the dialectic of its own development. However, it is only too obvious that this privilege of the Anglo-Saxon world is a thing of the past. History is about to give Great Britain and the United States some sharp lessons in dialectics.

II

The Decline of British Imperialism

II

Imperialist Diplomacy in the Middle East

From *The Balkans, Capitalist Europe and Tsarism*
(dated 14 October 1908), *Proletarii*, 1 November 1908.

Gritting its teeth, the Berlin government has stepped aside and decided to wait. The more it is forced to seek a rapprochement with the Young Turks[1] the firmer their positions will grow. But there is no doubt that capitalist Germany is just as genuinely prepared to welcome the downfall of constitutional Turkey as she has up till now hypocritically welcomed its victory. On the other hand the more Turkey weakened Germany's position in the Balkans, the more noisily Britain demonstrated her friendship towards the new order. In this interminable struggle between the two mighty European states the Young Turks naturally sought support and 'friends' on the Thames. But the sore point in Anglo-Turkish relations is Egypt. There can of course be no thought of her voluntary evacuation by Britain: she has too great an interest in ruling the Suez Canal to do this. Would Britain support Turkey in event of military

---

1 The 'Young Turks' – Exiled Turkish liberals who in 1907 joined with young army officers, led by Enver Pasha, who staged a rising in Macedonia in July 1908 to demand the restoration of the constitution by the Sultan, Abdul Hamid II. In the face of the wide support that this movement attracted the Sultan quickly gave way, and a parliament was called in December. 'Young Turks' dominated the Turkish government from then on, building an alliance with Germany while continuing to oppress the non-Turkish peoples of the Ottoman Empire. The Sultan dismissed the 'Young Turks' from the government upon Turkey's defeat in October 1918.

difficulties? Or would she stab her in the back and declare Egypt to be her property? One is as likely as the other depending on circumstances. But in either case it is not sentimental love for liberal Turkey but cold and merciless imperialist calculation that guides the actions of the British government.

* * *

From *The Balkans, Capitalist Europe and Tsarism*
(dated 14 October 1908), *Proletarii*, 1 November 1908.

Russian diplomacy wishes to gain for its navy a free exit from the Black Sea into the Mediterranean from where it has been barred for over half a century. The Bosphorus and the Dardanelles, two sea gateways fortified with artillery, are in the hands of the Turks, the custodians of the straits by virtue of a European mandate. But if Russian warships cannot leave the Black Sea neither can foreign ships enter it. Tsarist diplomacy wants the ban to be lifted only for its own ships. Britain can hardly agree to this. The disarming of the straits is acceptable to her only if it gives her the opportunity of sending her fleet into the Sea of Marmara or the Black Sea. But then Russia with her insignificant naval forces would not gain but lose. And Turkey would lose in either case. Her Navy is worthless and the master of Constantinople would be the state that could place its battleships under its walls. *Novoe Vremya*[2] lashes out at Britain who denies the tsarist government this right, which has, in view of the weakness of the Black Sea Fleet, a "purely theoretical nature" and yet persuades the Shah's government to open the gates before Russia while promising in exchange to safeguard Turkey's rule over the straits from foreign encroachment. While protesting in the name of the Treaty of Berlin against the private agreement between Turkey and Austria, Russia herself wants by means of a private agreement with Turkey to break her European mandate. If she had succeeded in achieving her aim this would present a danger not only to the peaceful development of Turkey but also to the peace of all Europe. While Izvolsky[3] ties up the knots of diplomatic intrigues in Europe, Colonel Lyakhov[4] shares his work and sets off for Asia to cut some diplomatic knots

---

2   *Novoe Vremya* – Extreme reactionary St. Petersburg newspaper published from 1868 until 1917. After 1905 it openly supported the ultra-right terrorist bands known as the Black Hundreds.

3   Alexander Izvolsky (1856-1919) – Russian Foreign Minister from 1905 to 1909.

4   Colonel Lyakhov (1869-1919) – Commander of a Cossack Brigade in Iran staffed by Russian officers. In June 1908 he bombarded the Iranian parliament in support of a counter-revolutionary coup d'état.

with a sword. Behind the noise of the Balkan events[5] and behind the patriotic shrieks of the loyalist press, tsarism is preparing a second offensive of the Cossack boot against the heart of revolutionary Persia.[6] And this is being accomplished not only with the silent complicity of Europe but with the active collaboration of 'liberal' Britain too.

The victory of Tabriz, the most considerable city of Persia, over the Shah's troops, threatened to upset the plans of St. Petersburg and London diplomacy completely. Besides the fact that the final victory of the revolution was pregnant with Persia's economic and political rebirth, the protracted civil war inflicted immediate damage upon the interests of Russian and British capital… sentence on Persia had been pronounced.[7] Reporting on the most recent talks between Izvolsky and Grey, the London Foreign Office demonstratively emphasised the complete solidarity of both governments as a guarantee of their "harmonious cooperation" in solving Central Asian problems. And as early as 11 October six Russian infantry battalions, supported by a corresponding force of artillery and cavalry, crossed the Persian frontier to occupy revolutionary Tabriz. Telegraphic links with the city have been cut for a long time now so that the humane peoples of Europe are spared the necessity of following step by step how tsarism's brazen rabble realises the "harmonious cooperation" of two 'Christian' nations amid the smoking ruins of Tabriz…

---

5 Bosnia-Herzegovina was annexed by Austria-Hungary in October 1908. This consolidation of Austro-Hungarian power in the Balkans was opposed by tsarist Russia.

6 The Persian Revolution of 1905-8 was led by petty-bourgeois democrats with the support of the peasantry and workers to win democratic reforms from the Shah's feudal regime. Local revolutionary councils (*enjumens*) were set up with their main centre at Tabriz. In September 1906 Shah Mohammed Ali was forced to convene the Majlis (parliament) with a restricted franchise. Further minor reforms were insufficient to stem an upsurge of strikes and land seizures, and in June 1908, with the backing of British and Russian imperialism, the Shah staged a coup dissolving the Majlis and the Tehran *enjumen*. Tabriz then rose up in arms and the *enjumen* took power only to be overthrown by tsarist forces in October 1908.

7 The "sentence" was the Anglo-Russian Entente of August 1907 which defined the two imperial powers' interests in Central Asia, Tibet, Afghanistan and Persia, where a northern zone (including Tehran and Tabriz) and an eastern zone were assigned respectively to Russia and Britain as "spheres of influence".

The First World War

From *War and the International*, *Golos*,
20 and 21 November and 13 December 1914.

... By upsetting the European *status quo* which had been so carefully maintained over the course of four and a half decades, imperialism has once again raised all the old questions which the bourgeois revolution proved powerless to solve. But in the present era these questions lack an independent character. The creation of normal conditions of national life and economic development in the Balkan peninsula is inconceivable alongside the preservation of tsarism and Austria-Hungary. Tsarism at the present time forms a vital military reserve for the financial imperialism of France and the conservative colonial might of Britain. Austria-Hungary serves as the chief support for Germany's offensive imperialism. Beginning as a domestic squabble between Serbian nationalist terrorists and the Habsburg political police,[1] the present war rapidly unfolded its fundamental content: a life-and-death struggle between Germany and Britain. While simpletons and hypocrites prate about the defence of national liberty and independence, the Anglo-German war is actually being waged in the name of the liberty of imperialist exploitation of India and Egypt on the one hand, and a new imperialist division of the world's peoples on the other. Germany, once awakened to capitalist development on a national base, began with the

---

1 The political police of Austria-Hungary which ruled Bosnia-Herzegovina, a mainly Slav-inhabited territory. Serbian-backed nationalist terrorists active in the region assassinated the Austrian heir, Franz-Ferdinand, in July 1914, causing Austria to declare war on Serbia.

destruction of France's continental hegemony in 1870-71. Now, when the
flowering of German industry on her national base has made Germany the
primary capitalist force in the world, her continued development collides
with Britain's world hegemony.

* * *

From *Kievskaya Mysl*, 13 January 1915.

Sir John French

French soldiers often make the most flattering comments about the British
army. Every British soldier taken individually is in himself an officer. They are
self-reliant, courageous, resourceful, and unbeatable in defence.

At the head of this army formed by a nation free from conscription, a
nation of ancient liberties and a nation of sportsmen, stands Sir John
Denton Pinkston French. As with some other prominent British admirals
and generals, French comes from Ireland.[2] He was born into an eminent
family from County Galway in the province of Connaught whose head is at
present Sir Arthur French. In Ireland, where landlords loom over the land
like demigods, there reigns in the ruling layers a most favourable atmosphere
for bringing up military leaders of the old 'heroic' type. Yet he was to develop
his abilities wholly in colonial wars. For over two human generations now
Britain has not sent its forces on to the continent of Europe.

The Frenches were a naval family by tradition. The father of today's field-
marshal was a naval officer but he soon resigned the service and went to
settle with his family on his inherited estate. Sir John was born there on 28
September 1852. Consequently French is an almost exact contemporary of
Joffre.[3] Family traditions urged the young French along the path of a naval
career. After leaving preparatory school at the age of thirteen he entered a
naval academy at Portsmouth and, while not distinguishing himself especially
with brilliant success, he did complete a training voyage as a midshipman
on the *HMS Britannia* in 1866. Four years later he decided on the spur of
the moment to abandon serving in the navy and at the age of nineteen he
joined the army. He was appointed an officer in the Suffolk Artillery Militia
and only in 1874 did he exchange into the regular army as an officer in a
Hussar regiment. His biographer says: "It would be a sheer exaggeration
to imagine that in this period the young French hankered after books; he

---

2 French was born at Ripple, Kent.

3 Joseph Joffre (1852-1931) – Commander-in-chief of the French Army 1911-1916.

preferred foxhunting and steeplechasing far more than the study of strategy and tactics". At that time his superiors would have trusted him far more readily with breaking in a foursome of the most untameable horses than with an expeditionary force.

Promoted to the rank of captain in 1880 French married an aristocratic lady, having occupied the post of adjutant for a few months, with some territorial forces. In 1882 the Hussar regiment in which French had served was transferred to Egypt and two years later Sir John was sent out to rejoin it at his own request. Neither the young officer nor the regiment to which he belonged had at that time any military past behind them. He was now to create for himself a reputation of invincibility in the conditions most favourable to this: those of colonial war. "Napoleon sought officers who had been born under a lucky star" says the same biographer, "and French was always lucky in the critical moments of his life". For this reason he became known in the army as "Lucky French". In Egypt he served under the command of Colonel Percy Barrow and took part in the ill-fated Nile expedition under his leadership. A detachment of the 19th Hussars under Barrow's command and with French as second-in-command formed part of a flying column of a thousand men and two thousand camels under the leadership of General Sir Herbert Stewart. Ten cavalry detachments served as cover while this column was on the move. After a two week march an engagement with the natives took place at Abu Klea which continued with great ferocity for two days. General Stewart was mortally wounded. The campaign ended in failure and the column was forced to commence a difficult retreat during which French's unit acted as rearguard cover. "These were not soldiers but heroes", Count Moltke is reputed to have said (not the nephew but the uncle)[4] of the participants in this desert retreat. Here French received his baptism in combat and it was from this point that his interest in military questions and especially those of the cavalry can be dated. In the rank of lieutenant-colonel of the Hussars he returned to Britain and devoted himself to reforms in the 19th Hussars which soon became a model. French received a command in India where he is on close terms with his immediate superior, the cavalry general George Luck, who admired his

---

4   Helmuth von Moltke (1800-1891) – Chief of Prussian and, later, German General Staff from 1857 to 1888, responsible for re-organising the Prussian Army and the strategic planning of the Danish, Austrian and French campaigns between 1864 and 1870. His nephew, also Helmuth von Moltke (1848-1916), was Chief of the German General Staff from 1906 to September 1914 when he was asked to resign over the failure to take Paris and the setback on the Marne.

brilliant colonel's views on reforms. Together they organised manoeuvres along the lines of the new 'principles' which aroused strong opposition from the army routinists and conservatives. In 1893 Colonel French was placed on half pay. Now French devoted all his spare time to a study of all questions related to the branch of arms he was familiar with. After cavalry manoeuvres in Berkshire, French made serious criticisms of the numerous defects in the organisation and training of British cavalry. By this time, General Luck had returned to Britain from India and in earnest set about the reforming work whose basis had already been laid in India. Despite stubborn opposition from the routinist party, Luck instructs Colonel French to prepare the draft of a new *Cavalry Drill Book* which was to mark a complete 'revolution' in cavalry thinking. In 1895 French entered the War Office as assistant adjutant-general of cavalry to direct the implementation of his new methods in the field. He soon left the War Office to lead the 2nd Cavalry Brigade and to demonstrate during manoeuvres all the advantages of his tactical principles over the obsolete methods of his antagonists. French sustained a victory. His opponents declared it to have been a matter of chance and predicted the innovator's total rout in a war. A heated polemic broke out in the professional press, which of course did not go beyond a narrow circle of devotees. After all, French's name was at that time quite unknown to broad circles of the public, and when British imperialist policy took him to South Africa for a war with the Boers, French's name was not among those canvassed in the press for the post of senior cavalry commander. "Lucky" Sir John had still to arm himself with patience if only for a little while longer. Buller, the British commander-in-chief, valued him from the days of the Sudan campaign, and thanks to his vote French was appointed cavalry commander in Natal. From this moment his ascent began. Ten days after the ultimatum was handed by President Kruger[5] to the British envoy in Pretoria (10 October 1899) French entered Ladysmith.[6] The same day he found himself leading a column which had been instructed to seize a railway station where a British supply train had been halted and captured by the Boers. The success of this engagement, which lasted two days, was, according to French's biographer, wholly guaranteed by the cavalry general's tactical dispositions. He threw back the enemy, took the station, freed the prisoners and cleared the railway line. After this success the

5 Paul Kruger (1825-1904) – President of the Boer Transvaal Republic from 1883-1900.
6 Ladysmith, site of a battle (29 October 1899), which the Boers won, and an unsuccessful siege (2 November – 27 February 1900) by the Boers at the beginning of the Second Boer War (1899-1902).

British press decorated the name of French with a halo of such qualities as firmness, bravery and *sang-froid*.

An American correspondent accompanying the British army reported in passing the following episode. Under the Boers' shells and bullets but without batting an eyelid, French discussed the bad light which prevented the war correspondent from taking photographs. In the general's coquettish bravado the military leader lay concealed behind the dashing huntsman and daredevil who trusted in his star. And the nickname of "lucky" indeed stuck to him among soldiers now more than ever. After General White's[7] unfortunate venture at Ladysmith French put his card down *va banque* and... he won. The Boers were besieging the town and no one knew whether they had cut the railway line. If they had not it could only have been through inexperience. In spite of the station commander's warnings French and his staff commandeered a train and steamed off down the track at full speed. The Boers greeted them with rifle fire but the train broke through and arrived safely at Pietermaritzburg. At the end of November the position of the British army was becoming very tough and only French's cavalry operations along a sixty-mile front finally stopped the Boers from holding all the positions in the Cape Colony. Lord Roberts was appointed commander-in-chief. He ordered French to relieve beleaguered Kimberley at the head of a cavalry division of 8,500 sabres. To this assignment French replied: "I promise you faithfully that I shall relieve Kimberley at 6 o'clock in the evening of the 15th [of February] if I am still alive". This reply was highly typical of "lucky" John – here one seemed to hear a fiery steeplechaser or Denisov,[8] the dashing partisan. Instead of the promised division French received only 4,800 men. Against him was a considerably stronger enemy but French nevertheless decided to win his bet, i.e., to fulfil the military assignment he had received. He entered Kimberley victoriously on 15 February at seven o'clock in the evening – French was one hour late. But it must also be said that he had been given little more than half the sabres that were stated in the conditions. French's subsequent role in the Boer War had the same character: one of courage and risk.

In 1902 French returned triumphant to Britain. Soon after his return he was appointed commander-in-chief at Aldershot. Here for the first time in peace he commanded an army unit with all its branches. But, as before, the

---

7   Sir George Stuart White (1835-1912) – British general, commander of the garrison during the siege of Ladysmith.

8   A character in Tolstoy's *War and Peace* who leads daring guerrilla raids on Napoleon's retreating armies in Russia in 1812.

cavalry attracted his main attention: to this day he preserves a particular affection for this, the most primitive arm. Notwithstanding the enormous technical changes in military science and the strategic and tactical changes that have followed in their wake, the aristocratic huntsman has remained a convinced advocate of the horse, the sabre, the lance and the gallop – in short, of 'the cavalry spirit'. In December 1907 French was appointed inspector-general of the forces and in 1912 he was made Chief of Staff, now newly re-organised on the German pattern.

French never adopted clear-cut positions on politics, at least not publicly, for he considered that the army must remain outside politics. He did however become for a short time a 'victim' of politics. When, in connection with the unrest of Ulster Protestants which led to Colonel Seely's[9] resignation, ferment began in the British officer caste. General French, as Chief of General Staff, left his post in solidarity. He was to spend all of four months in retirement. The war broke out and French, now a Field-Marshal, was placed in command of the British Expeditionary Force with Joffre as his commander-in-chief.

* * *

From *From Pontius to Pilate*, dated 16 January 1915
and first published in 1927 in *Works*, Vol. 9.

In our last letter we attempted to explain once more that the plan to "starve out" Germany would be at least as exhausting for France as for her enemy. The "supreme effort" which is due in the spring, promises to counterpose approximately equal forces on either side and this will not open any paths to a solution. The only possibility of breaking the enemy lies in achieving a decisive numerical superiority over him by adding a million fresh soldiers to the French army. But where can she get them from? I have already written of France's dissatisfaction with Britain. Here in France it has become even more well-defined now that the limited effect of the naval blockade has become evident. Why doesn't Britain give us more forces? Because she wants at the moment of the war's liquidation to preserve her old army intact as far as possible: herein lies the old 'national egoism' of the island power. The other day, an official explanation of the position was given by British ruling circles. Dissatisfaction with Britain's tardiness, says the statement, can be explained only by a fundamental lack of information with regard to what is happening in Britain. To date over a million men have shown their willingness to fight in the ranks of the allied army. But this figure in itself has for the moment only a

_____

9   J. E. B. Seely (1868-1947) – British War Secretary from 1912 to 1914.

secondary character. The main task now consists of military training, arming and the overall provision of supplies for Kitchener's first army. Until the present war nobody in Britain had entertained the possibility of organising a colossal expeditionary army at a minimum of notice. Neither the military apparatus nor the state of British industry was prepared for such a task. It is necessary to produce from scratch the entire equipment for an army of 500,000 men: rifles, artillery, ammunition, clothing, etc., etc. She has to supplement the extremely inadequate equipment of the territorial army. She has to guarantee everything necessary to those troops already fighting not only in France but also in Egypt and Mesopotamia. Finally, she has to supply the allies with everything that their industry, half-paralysed by the mobilisation, cannot provide at the present moment. To be equal to these tasks, working day and night in existing plants is insufficient: new plants have to be built, new machines installed, and thousands of fresh workers brought together. Many of the plants now under construction will only be in operation in early spring. Consequently: the allies have to *wait*. Only upon the foundation of such a systematic preparation is it possible to assure a decisive intervention by a new British army in the course of a continental war. Impatience must not prevent one taking account of the actual state of affairs. Forming an army of a million and a half men in under a year when the standing army does not exceed 300,000 is a task that Britain alone can set herself and solve.

* * *

From *From Pontius to Pilate* dated 16 January 1915
and first published in 1927 in *Works*, Vol. 9.

In this war Britain is fighting for the preservation of her colonial domains. Meanwhile, if she goes too far to meet Japanese claims she will undermine her own position in *Australia* and *Canada*. The readiness with which these two colonies have come to the aid of the metropolis with ships, material and men was for them dictated in the first instance by their urgent desire to reduce Japan's role in this war to a minimum. The Japanese would not be satisfied with compensation in the form of favourable tariff agreements, territorial concessions or loans but will demand above all the right to free settlement and equal citizenship rights in all the British colonies: this would threaten to make them masters of the situation on the shores of the Pacific and Indian Oceans. There is no need to mention how hostilely the United States would treat a plan for the solemn inclusion of Japan into the so-called 'family' of civilised great powers now destroying each other. The spectre of Japanese intervention alarms the Dutch to the extreme who fear for the fate of their colonial possessions. "Java was lost the moment Japan landed on the Marshall Islands".[10] The Dutch, as is well known, justify the tendency of their neutrality in favour of the USA by the Japanese danger.

Britain's viewpoint in this matter is more flexible and qualified than that of her colonies. If the Japanese in case of necessity had to take over the discharge of order in India, and if they defended the Suez Canal from the Turks, this would be permissible from the British standpoint. She could even reconcile herself to Japanese intervention over Constantinople. But thus far and no further. If the yellow armies encroached upon the soil of Germany this would at once produce a decisive shift in the public opinion of the neutral states of Europe and even more in the United States. The direct danger of Japanese expansion would be aggravated by the final collapse of the prestige of the great powers in the Asiatic and African colonies. All these preoccupations and fears find their expression in the question of compensation. Who will pay the Japanese? Obviously, the country which needs Japanese aid most but which can gain the least in the event of a victorious outcome to the war – France. As we have already reported, half-veiled agitation was earlier conducted in the press with the object of softening public opinion to the idea that Indo-China will have to be given to the Japanese. This qualified suggestion not only met a natural opposition in France but ran into stubborn resistance from Britain. With control of Indo-China the Japanese would be able directly to threaten Southern China, the chief sphere of British 'influence' in the Far East, just as today their rule over Kiaochow[11] makes them masters in Northern China. "The main objections" insists *L'Éclair*,[12] "come, as before, from London whence there comes distrust, almost ill-will tantamount to an unwillingness to act".

* * *

From *A "Guarantee" of Peace*, *Nashe Slovo*, 1 and 2 September 1916.

British pacifists, and especially the International Defence League, have in recent days drafted a number of schemes aimed at putting an end to wars. There always lies at the bottom of these projects the idea of a Court of Arbitration or a supreme "Council of Nations" whose decisions have a mandatory force. But how do you enforce them? Some propose to place an

---

10 The Marshall Islands lie 3,500 miles east of Java and were a German colony until they were seized by Japan in 1914.

11 A territory and naval base in northern China adjacent to Shantung province; occupied by Germany in 1897 but captured by the Japanese in November 1914.

12 Right-wing daily newspaper published in Paris from 1888 to 1924.

"international" army and navy at the disposal of the Court of Arbitration so that it can enforce the observance of the international rulings. But others more modestly allow each nation its own national army as before but "on the condition" that this army is employed only against those who transgress the international law and the rulings of the Court of Arbitration. Thus to guarantee an eternal peace we can see that 'just' wars will be necessary from time to time.[13]

An international military force, says Cromer,[14] formed as an instrument for the enforcement of the rulings of the Court of Arbitration "almost necessarily connotes the whole or partial disappearance of purely national military or naval forces".[15] But Britain, according to the author, would never agree to weaken her Navy in which she sees her chief defence, i.e., the defence of her imperialist rule over the seas and colonies. If Britain argues like this over the navy then it would be hard to imagine, says *L'Éclair*, that continental powers would argue any differently over their armies. Moreover, how is the Court of Arbitration to be constituted? Surely every nation would have an equal voting right? Cromer feels sure that mighty Britain would never agree to that. Can one suppose that vessels contributed by Britain would execute a sentence against the same Britain? And if Britain refused to abide by a decision of the Court of Arbitration, do you think that British soldiers incorporated in an international army would take up arms to compel their own country to submit? Cromer doubts so. In justification of his doubts he quotes one very lucid historical example: Britain's war against the Boers. "It is highly probable", he says, "that a decision of an International Court would be adverse to Great Britain". But, he says that Britain would most probably… not recognise the Court of Arbitration.

* * *

From Chapter 10 of Between Red and White (1921).

… On 13 November 1914, Sir George Buchanan (according to Paléologue)[16] declared to Sazonov:[17] "The Government of his Britannic Majesty has

---

13 The scheme referred to here was published in *The Mutual Defence of Nations* by O. F. Maclagan.

14 Evelyn Baring, 1st Earl of Cromer (1841-1917) – British diplomat and colonial administrator.

15 *Thinking Internationally, Nineteenth Century*, July 1916.

16 Maurice Paléologue (1859-1944) – French diplomat and historian, ambassador to Russia 1914.

17 Sergei Sazonov (1860-1927) – Russian Foreign Minister from 1909 to 1916.

recognised that the question of the Straits and Constantinople must be settled according to Russian aspirations. It gives me pleasure to announce this to you". Thus was laid down the programme of the war of right, justice, and national self-determination.

Four days later, Buchanan declared to Sazonov: "The British government will be compelled to annex Egypt. It trusts that the Russian government will not offer any opposition to this". Sazonov was not slow in giving his consent. Three days after that Paléologue 'reminded' Nikolai II that Syria and Palestine were bound to France by a wealth of historic recollections and also by *moral* and material interests. He, Paléologue, hoped that His Majesty would approve of the measures which the government of the republic (the same democratic republic) deemed it necessary to take, in order to safeguard these interests.

"*Oui certes*", ("Yes, certainly"), was His Majesty's reply. Finally, on 12 March 1915, Buchanan demanded that in return for Constantinople and the Straits, Russia should cede to Great Britain the neutral part of Persia (that part as yet un-partitioned). Sazonov answered "*C'est entendu*" ("That is understood").

So two democracies in conjunction with tsarism, which at that period shone with the reflected democratic light emanating from the Entente, settled the fate of Constantinople, Syria, Palestine, Egypt, and Persia. Sir George Buchanan was as worthy a representative of the British democracy as Paléologue of the French. Buchanan remained at his post after the downfall of Nikolai II. Henderson, a minister of His Majesty, and, if we are not mistaken, a British socialist, came to Petrograd during the Kerensky regime, in order to take Buchanan's place (should this be necessary), because someone in the British government had imagined that they should speak in a different tone to Kerensky than to Rasputin. Buchanan was the right man in the right place as the representative of British democracy. Buchanan undoubtedly held the same opinion of Henderson, the socialist.

Paléologue exhibited 'his' Socialists as an example to the restive tsarist dignitaries. In connection with the Court 'agitation' of Count Witte[18] for the speedy conclusion of the war, Paléologue declared to Sazonov: "Look at our Socialists and their correct attitude". This summing up by Paléologue of Messrs. Renaudel, Longuet, Vandervelde, and all their followers, is rather

---

18 Sergei Witte (1849-1915) – Russian Prime Minister in 1905-6. At the outbreak of the
    First World War, he opposed Russian war policy and favoured alliance with France
    and Germany against Britain.

startling even now, after all we have gone through. Paléologue, having received and respectfully acknowledged Rasputin's admonitions, in his turn expressed to the tsarist minister his patronising appreciation of the French socialists, and recognised the correctness of their attitude. These words: "*voyez mes socialistes – ils sont impeccables*" ("Look at my socialists – they are beyond reproach") should form a device for the banner of the Second International, from which the words: "Workers of the world unite" should have been removed long ago. This latter device suits Henderson as much as the Phrygian cap suits Paléologue.

The Hendersons consider the domination of the Anglo-Saxon race over the other races as a natural fact ensuring the spread of civilisation. For them the question of national self-determination begins only beyond the confines of the British Empire. This national arrogance is the chief link between the western social-patriots and their bourgeoisie, *viz.*, it makes them the slaves of their bourgeoisie.

* * *

From *What the Secret Treaties State*, *Pravda*, 25 November 1917.

Only an insignificant part of the documents which contain the secret treaties of the capitalists have yet been published. Much, much more of the secrets will become public as we proceed with the dismantling of the archives of the Ministry of Foreign Affairs where damning evidence against imperialist diplomacy, which of course never anticipated its publication nor conceived the possibility of the victory of the proletarian revolution, is preserved.

The plan for the seizure of territories laid down by the Russian bourgeoisie and its "allies" has been unmasked in its main features. "Britain" and "France" have reserved themselves the right "freely" i.e., at their own discretion, to determine the western frontiers of Germany and Austria, conceding the same right to "Russia" in exchange for these seizures by leaving to her discretion the fixing of the eastern frontiers of Austria and Germany. "You scratch my back and I'll scratch yours" is the first principle of the politics of imperialist piracy.

The project of annexations in Europe did not stop here. "Russia" i.e., the Sazonovs and Tereshchenkos[19] had been assured, as is well known, the annexation of Constantinople. But it emerges from the treaties that the Russian bourgeoisie was to gain not only Constantinople but all of European Turkey. The agreement on the Balkans has not yet been published, but from the "notes" on Russo-Rumanian relations published today both the

---

19 Mikhail Tereshchenko (1886-1956) – Russian Foreign Minister from May to October 1917.

fraudulent policy of the Rumanian government which is seizing territories with a purely Slav population, and the policy of deceit which Russian diplomacy intended to implement at a convenient moment by breaking the treaty with Romania, become abundantly clear. But the most far-reaching plans of seizure relate to Asiatic Turkey. To a considerable degree the whole of the present war is a war for the partition of the "Turkish Legacy", for the "re-partition" of Turkish lands between the banks, industrialists, and merchants of the strongest capitalist powers. According to the agreement which we publish today, Asiatic Turkey would be subject to a share-out among all the "allies".

Only a "rump" of Turkey would remain – a region of small dimensions surrounded on all sides by the possessions of the lucky men who have prospered at her expense. Italy and Greece will receive comparatively little. France will receive a solid prize in the form of the Syrian coast and the lands north of the Mediterranean coast. This zone allocated to France will border on a zone which will be given to Russia and will include part of the Black Sea coast (as far as a point west of Trabzon) and the lands lying to the south of it. Meeting the Russian and French zones from the east will be a British zone, running in a tapering strip to the Persian Gulf and embracing all Mesopotamia, including Baghdad. Besides these three major slices of the Turkish pie to be handed out openly to the "powers", the agreement envisaged in addition the formation of an "independent" Arab federation, subject, however, to demarcation into "spheres of influence".

"Spheres of influence" is a diplomatic term which in everyday language means "areas of domination". The Arab "independent" federation divided in advance into "areas of domination" would in point of fact be "independent" only of the Arabs and wholly dependent upon the bosses of international capital.

* * *

From a speech to a workers' meeting, 14 April 1918
(*A Word to Russian Workers and Peasants on Our Friends and Enemies and How to Preserve and Strengthen the Soviet Republic*).

America joined the war over a year ago and promised to finish it within the next few months. What did America seek by her intervention? At first she patiently observed Germany over there across the ocean fighting against Britain. And then she intervened. Why? What does America need? America needs Germany to exhaust Britain and Britain to exhaust Germany. And then American capital will appear as the heir who will plunder the world.

When America noticed that Britain was bowed down and bent to the ground while Germany was standing upright she said: "No, I must support Britain – like the rope supporting a hanging man – just so that they will exhaust each other completely and so that European capital will be completely deprived of the possibility of ever getting to its feet again".

* * *

From a lecture read in the Sergiev People's House, Voronezh, 16 June 1918 (*The International Situation and Organisation of the Red Army*).

The major roles in this war belong, as you know, to the two dominant countries in Europe. Germany and Britain. Britain has always played first fiddle in the world market and the British bourgeoisie and the British capitalists have grown used to treating all the other weaker nations as people who are summoned to enrich Britain. That was how Britain treated India, whose population lay under the yoke of British capital; that was how she thought about Egypt and the countries of America; she maintained that British capitalism and only British capitalism had the right to exploit all the remaining countries. The younger and highly powerful German capitalism came in the opposite direction to meet British capitalism. In Britain with its older culture and industry, old methods, old devices, and old technique are retained. German industry is younger and more revolutionary; operating with the last word in science and technology, it has started to produce more cheaply than British industry; it has thrown its products out onto the world market, including the British colonies, and pushed out British ones. Here is the soil and basis for the war. British capitalism is guarding its purse and so is German capitalism; the Germans say: it is time to give British rule in India a push. The British say: it is time to contain Germany which is squeezing all of Europe. That is the basis of the struggle between two mighty profiteers and plunderers who cannot share their profits from their exploitation of the world.

Many fine words have been said about all this, and many ideas and schemes have been drawn up: some assure us that Germany is fighting for the freedom of peoples, while others say that Britain is fighting for the weak and oppressed – thus speak the journalists, professors, and priests in every country. Each at his own post, whether in the churches, the universities or the schools, and each in his own language justified his master and his national capitalism. In the first period of the war it was said that this war would be unlike all other wars: it would not be a destructive war but a liberating war. The Germans were to liberate all the colonies. Britain promised to liberate Egypt. Thus each country strove to 'liberate' the slaves from the rule of others so as to turn them into its own slaves; and there were dozens, thousands, and millions among workers who sincerely believed this deception; Russian workers believed that the Russian Tsar wanted to give freedom to Serbia; German workers believed that the Kaiser was only defending himself, tsarism was attacking from one side, the British capitalists pressing down on the other side and so on. But this blindness was only temporary.

* * *

From the *Manifesto of the Communist International: To the Workers of the World*, drafted by Trotsky and adopted at the First World Congress of the Communist International, 6 March 1919.

British diplomacy did not lift its visor of secrecy up to the very outbreak of war. The government of the City obviously feared to reveal its intention of entering the war on the side of the Entente lest the Berlin government take fright and be compelled to eschew war. In London they wanted war. That is why they conducted themselves in such a way as to raise hopes in Berlin and Vienna that Britain would remain neutral, while Paris and Petrograd firmly counted on Britain's intervention.

Prepared by the entire course of development over a number of decades, the war was unleashed through the direct and conscious provocation of Great Britain. The British government thereby calculated on extending just enough aid to Russia and France, while they became exhausted, to exhaust Britain's mortal enemy, Germany. But the might of German militarism proved far too formidable, and demanded of Britain not token but actual intervention in the war. The role of a gleeful third partner to which Great Britain, following her ancient tradition, aspired, fell to the lot of the United States.

The Washington government became all the more easily reconciled to the British blockade, which one-sidedly restricted American stock market speculation in European blood, because the countries of the Entente reimbursed the American bourgeoisie with lush profits for violations of 'international law'. However, the Washington government was likewise constrained by the enormous military superiority of Germany to drop its fictitious neutrality. In relation to Europe as a whole, the United States assumed the role which Britain had taken in previous wars and which she tried to take in the last war in relation to the continent, namely: weakening one camp by playing it against another, intervening in military operations only to such an extent as to guarantee her all the advantages of the situation. According to American standards of gambling, Wilson's stake was not very high, but it was the final stake, and consequently assured his winning the prize.

Against the Russian Revolution

From *Captive of the British* (1917).

The publication of the documents relating to my month-long captivity by the British now appears to me to be a matter of political necessity. The bourgeois press, the very same which spread the most Black Hundred slanders against the political exiles who found themselves compelled to return through Germany, has acted dumb as soon as it came up against Britain's piratical raid on Russian exiles returning home across the Atlantic Ocean. The social-patriotic press, and today the government press – which is at their service – operates little more honestly: it too has no interest in explaining the embarrassing fact that the socialist ministers, fresh off the peg and who still for the moment address themselves with the deepest respect to the exiled 'teachers', prove to be the closest and most immediate allies of Lloyd George, who seizes these same 'teachers' by the collar on the Atlantic highway. In this tragi-comic episode we have a sufficiently convincing revelation of the attitude of ruling Britain towards the Russian revolution, as well as the general meaning of that holy alliance whose service Citizens Tsereteli, Chernov, and Skobelev[1] have now entered.

For, whatever statements the 'left' government parties and groups make, the socialist ministers bear entire responsibility for the government of which

---

1 Irakli Tsereteli (1881-1960), Victor Chernov (1873-1952), and Matvey Skobelev (1885-1938) were Menshevik and Socialist-Revolutionary ministers in the Russian Provisional Government of May-August 1917.

they form a part. The government of Lvovs[2] and Tereshchenkos[3] maintains an alliance not with British revolutionary socialists like Maclean, Askew,[4] and others, but with their jailers Lloyd George and Henderson.

* * *

From Chapter 23 of *My Life* (1930).

On 25 March [1917] I called at the office of the Russian Consul-General in New York. By that time the portrait of Tsar Nikolai had been removed from the wall, but the heavy atmosphere of a Russian police station under the old regime still hung about the place. After the usual delays and arguments, the Consul-General ordered that papers be issued to me for the passage to Russia. In the British consulate, as well, they told me, when I filled out the questionnaire, that the British authorities would put no obstacles in the way of my return to Russia. Everything was in good order.

I sailed with my family and a few other Russians on the Norwegian boat *Christianiafjord* on 27 March. We had been sent off in a deluge of flowers and speeches, for we were going to the country of the revolution. We had passports and visas. Revolution, flowers, and visas were balm to our nomad souls. At Halifax the British naval authorities inspected the steamer, and police officers made a perfunctory examination of the papers of the American, Norwegian, and Dutch passengers. They subjected the Russians, however, to a downright cross-examination, asking us about our convictions, our political plans, and so forth. I absolutely refused to enter into a discussion of such matters with them. "You may have all the information you want as to my identity, but nothing else". Russian politics were not yet under the control of the British naval police. But that did not prevent the detectives, Machen and Westwood, from making inquiries about me among the other passengers after the double attempt to cross-examine me had proved futile. They insisted that I was a dangerous socialist.

The whole business was so offensive, so clearly a discrimination against the Russian revolutionaries, in contrast to the treatment accorded other passengers not so unfortunate as to belong to a nation allied to England, that

---

2   Prince Georgi Lvov (1861-1925) – head of Provisional Government from 23 March to 7 July 1917.

3   Mikhail Tereshchenko (1886-1956) – Russian Foreign Minister from 5 May to 25 October 1917.

4   John Bertram Askew (1869-1929) – British Social Democrat with close connections with German Social Democracy, translator of many SPD documents and texts.

some of the Russians sent a violent protest to the British authorities. I did not join with them because I saw little use in complaining to Beelzebub about Satan. But at the time we did not foresee the future.

On 3 April, British officers, accompanied by bluejackets, came aboard the *Christianiafjord* and demanded, in the name of the local admiral, that I, my family, and five other passengers leave the boat. We were assured that the whole incident would be cleared up in Halifax. We declared that the order was illegal and refused to obey, whereupon armed bluejackets pounced on us, and amid shouts of "shame" from a large part of the passengers, carried us bodily to a naval cutter, which delivered us in Halifax under the convoy of a cruiser. While a group of sailors were holding me fast, my older boy ran to help me and struck an officer with his little fist. "Shall I hit him again, papa?", he shouted. He was eleven then, and it was his first lesson in British democracy.

The police left my wife and children in Halifax; the rest of us were taken by train to Amherst, a camp for German prisoners. And there, in the office, we were put through an examination the like of which I had never before experienced, even in the Peter-Paul fortress. For in the Tsar's fortress the police stripped me and searched me in privacy, whereas here our democratic allies subjected us to this shameful humiliation before a dozen men. I still remember Sergeant Olsen, a Swedish-Canadian with a red head of the criminal-police type, who was the leader of the search. The *canaille* who had arranged all this from a distance knew well enough that we were irreproachable Russian revolutionaries returning to our country, liberated by the revolution.

Not until the next morning did the camp commander, Colonel Morris, in answer to our repeated demands and protests, tell us the official reason for the arrest. "You are dangerous to the present Russian government", he said briefly. The colonel, obviously not a man of eloquence, had worn an air of rather suspicious excitement since early morning. "But the New York agents of the Russian government issued us passports into Russia", we protested, "and after all the Russian government should be allowed to take care of itself." Colonel Morris thought for a while, moving his jaws, then added, "You are dangerous to the Allies in general".

No written orders for our arrest were ever produced. But, speaking for himself, the colonel explained that since we were political emigrants who obviously had left the country for good reason, we ought not to be surprised at what had happened. For him the Russian revolution simply did not exist. We tried to explain that the Tsar's ministers, who in their day had made us political emigrants, were themselves now in prison, excepting those who had escaped to other countries. But this was too complicated for the colonel, who had made his career in the British colonies and in the Boer war. I did not show proper respect when I spoke to him, which made him growl behind my back, "If I only had him on the South African coast." That was his pet expression. [...]

The relations between the rank-and-file and the officers, some of whom, even in prison, were still keeping a sort of conduct book for their men, were hostile. The officers ended by complaining to the camp commander, Colonel Morris, about my anti-patriotic propaganda. The British colonel instantly sided with the Hohenzollern patriots and forbade me to make any more public speeches. But this did not happen until the last few days of our stay at the camp, and served only to cement my friendship with the sailors and workers, who responded to the colonel's order by a written protest bearing 530 signatures. A plebiscite like this, carried out in the very face of Sergeant Olsen's heavy-handed supervision, was more than ample compensation for all the hardships of the Amherst imprisonment.

All the time we were confined in the camp, the authorities steadfastly refused us the right to communicate with the Russian government. Our telegrams to Petrograd were not forwarded. We made an attempt to cable Lloyd George, the British Prime Minister, protesting against this prohibition, but the cable was held up. Colonel Morris had become accustomed to a simplified form of *habeas corpus* in the colonies. The war gave him still more protection. He went so far as to stipulate that I refrain from trying to communicate through my wife with the Russian consul before he would let me meet her again. That may sound incredible, but it is true. On such a condition, I declined to meet my wife. Of course, the consul was in no hurry to help us, either. He was waiting for instructions, and the instructions, it seemed, were slow in coming.

I must admit that even today the secret machinery of our arrest and our release is not clear to me. The British government must have put me on its black-list when I was still active in France. It did everything it could to help the Tsar's government oust me from Europe, and it must have been on the strength of this blacklist, supported by reports of my anti-patriotic activities in America, that the British arrested me in Halifax. When the news of my arrest found its way into the revolutionary Russian press, the British embassy in Petrograd, which apparently was not expecting my early return, issued an official statement to the Petrograd press that the Russians who had been arrested in Canada were travelling "under a subsidy from the German embassy, to overthrow the Russian Provisional government". This, at least, was plain speaking. The *Pravda*, which was published under Lenin's direction, answered Buchanan on 16 April, doubtless by Lenin's own hand:

> Can one even for a moment believe the trustworthiness of the statement that Trotsky, the chairman of the Soviet of Workers' Deputies in St. Petersburg in 1905 – a revolutionary who has sacrificed years to a disinterested service of revolution – that this man had anything to do with a scheme subsidised by the German government? This is a patent, unheard-of, and malicious slander of a revolutionary. From whom did you get your information, Mr. Buchanan? Why don't you disclose that? Six men dragged Comrade Trotsky away by his legs and arms, all in the name of friendship for the Russian Provisional government!

[...] Buchanan in his memoirs says that "Trotsky and other Russian refugees were being detained at Halifax until the wishes of the Provisional Government with regard to them had been ascertained". According to the British ambassador, Milyukov was immediately informed of our arrest. As early as 8 April the British ambassador claims he conveyed Milyukov's request for our release to his government. Two days later, however, the same Milyukov withdrew his request and expressed the hope that our stay in Halifax would be prolonged. "It was the Provisional government, therefore", concludes Buchanan, "that was responsible for their further detention". This all sounds very much like the truth. The only thing that Buchanan forgot to explain in his memoirs is: What became of the German subsidy that I was supposed to have accepted to overthrow the Provisional government? And no wonder – for as soon as I arrived in Petrograd, Buchanan was forced to state in the press that he knew nothing at all about the subsidy. Never before did people lie as much as they did during the "great war for liberty". If lies could explode, our planet would have been blown to dust long before the treaty of Versailles.

* * *

From a report on the work of the
Workers' and Peasants' Government, 3 December 1917.

... By publishing the secret treaties we would win enemies for ourselves in the shape of heads of state, but the support of their peoples will be with us. It is not a diplomatic peace we will conclude but a people's peace, a soldiers' peace, a trench peace! [*Stormy applause.*] And the results of this frank policy have shown themselves: Judson[5] appeared in the Smolny Institute and declared on behalf of America that its protest to Dukhonin's[6] staff against the new authorities was a misunderstanding and that America does not at all wish to interfere in Russia's internal affairs. Thus the question of America has been settled.

Another conflict is as yet unsettled and I wish to give you a report on it. In their struggle for peace, the British government has arrested and holds in its concentration camp Georgi Chicherin, who has contributed his wealth and knowledge to the peoples of Russia, Britain, Germany, and France, and the bold agitator among British workers, the exile Petrov.[7] I sent a letter to the British embassy where I pointed out that, as Russia is tolerating the presence of many rich British people who are in conspiracy with the counter-revolutionary bourgeoisie, we can even less allow Russian citizens to be imprisoned in British jails, and consequently those against whom no criminal charges have been made must be immediately released. Non-compliance with this demand will entail the refusal of passports to British citizens wishing to leave Russia. People's Soviet power is responsible for the interests of all its citizens; wherever each one may find himself he is under its protection. Kerensky may have addressed the allies like a steward to his master, but we have to show them that we can live with them only on an equal footing. We are here stating once and for all that whoever wishes to count on the support and friendship of the free and independent Russian people must treat its human dignity with respect.

* * *

From a speech to the 3rd All-Russian Congress of Soviets, 23 January 1918.

The German imperialists have in words renounced claims to indemnities but they have presented a whole number of demands whose satisfaction would on our reckoning require 4-8,000 million from us. German imperialism's Shylockian account has not yet been presented to us, but we feel convinced that they will not stint themselves an assessment of all the losses from

---

5   William Judson (1865-1923) – United States military attaché in Petrograd (1917-18).

6   Nikolai Dukhonin (1876-1917) – Chief of Russian Staff until November 1917, when he was killed by his own troops.

7   Peter Petrov (1884-1947) – Russian revolutionary, veteran of the 1905 Revolution who sought asylum Britain, close collaborator of John Maclean, arrested in 1916 along with his wife Irma under the Defence of the Realm Act (DORA) and subsequently deported to Russia.

confiscations and requisitions and so on, crimes of the war period which had been committed by the tsarist government and Kerensky government. In our firm conviction, the account as well as the terms to be put by the German annexationists have been tacitly approved in London. British imperialism well knows that it is in no state to beat Germany, and thus allow her the compensation at Russia's expense which German imperialism needs to be given to make it more amenable at negotiations with its British and French colleagues. This diabolical plan emerges from a very superficial analysis of one of Lloyd George's speeches, where he could not conceal this common account of world imperialism for the Russian revolution. Similarly pointing in this direction is the whole of world imperialism's policy in the Ukraine, Romania, and all the regions where imperialism borders on the Russian revolution.

Fighting Soviet Russia

From an interview given to Vyacheslav Neubert,
a representative of the Czechoslovak Corps, 31 May 1918.

At the beginning of April, the Japanese made a landing at Vladivostok. The subsequent intentions of the Japanese were not known. Consequently, it could not be known whether the Czechoslovaks would be able to embark at Vladivostok.[1] In accordance with instructions from the government I held up the movement of the Czechoslovak echelons, and I explained to the representatives of the French military mission and also to representatives of the Czechoslovak National Council who had come to me, that the halting of the movement of the Czechoslovak echelons in no way represented a measure hostile to the Czechoslovaks but was motivated solely by the new political and strategic situation in the Far East. I proposed moreover to the representatives of the National Council,[2] Messrs. Max and Cermak, to urge the British and French governments to officially declare their readiness to take the Czechoslovaks on their vessels at Archangel and Murmansk. For my part I committed myself to a definite date, to be established by means of negotiations, by which to transport the Czechoslovaks there. In

---

1 The Czechoslovaks were prisoners of war from the Austro-Hungarian Army who were being formed into a legion to fight on the Allied side. The officers were bourgeois nationalists hostile to Austrian rule but also to Bolshevism. The terms of the Brest-Litovsk Treaty required the legion to be disbanded.

2 The Czechoslovak National Council was set up in 1916 to propagate the idea of the break-up of the Austria-Hungarian Empire and the establishment of an independent Czechoslovak state. In 1918 it was officially recognised by the Allies.

spite of the fact that Messrs. Max and Cermak promised me they would obtain an official statement to this effect from the interested governments of Britain and France in the next few days, I received no such notification. In the course of a private exchange of views with Mr. Lockhart, the British plenipotentiary, I indicated to him the need for the British and French governments to make a specific decision with regard to the Czechoslovaks, as it was absolutely impossible to keep men in echelons for a period of months especially during summer time. Mr. Lockhart could give no reply and merely pointed out that the problem of available tonnage was very acute and he did not know whether the British government considered it feasible to send the necessary number of ships. Thus the question was left quite undefined not through any fault of the Soviet government but entirely as a result of, on the one hand, the Japanese landing in Vladivostok and, on the other, the absence of any definite statements on the part of the governments of Britain and France.

* * *

From a speech in the Kazan theatre, 12 September 1918
(The Significance of the Capture of Kazan for the Course of the Civil War).

The capture of Kazan![3] How should we assess this gladdening event?

The internal class struggle in the Soviet Republic has become complicated and taken on the form of a drawn out and just war, owing to the fact that the resistance of the Russian bourgeoisie has been combined with the military intervention, invasion, and incursion of foreign imperialism in the shape of the European-American landing and a network of conspiracies. For a start, having landed an expeditionary force of 2-3 thousand British and French at Murmansk and Archangel, the imperialist raiders had reckoned that broad masses of the people would start rallying to them.[4] They did not at all count upon the resistance of the revolution when they saw the harsh conditions of Russian workers. But the carrier of the revolution, the hungry proletariat of Moscow and Petrograd, said to them: "I've got two ounces

---

3 The recapture of Kazan from the Whites and Czechoslovaks on 19 September 1918 was the first victory of the newly formed Red Army and marked a turning point in the Civil War. Kazan is some 600 miles east of Moscow.

4 British forces landed at Murmansk on the Arctic Sea at the end of June 1918, ostensibly to forestall a German advance from Finland to the coast. A combined Anglo-French landing took place at Archangel at the beginning of August, while American reinforcements arrived at both ports.

to eat today and nothing tomorrow, but I can tighten my belt a bit more and say openly: I have taken power and I will never give that power up!" So that no sooner had the imperialists encountered their first rebuff after their unexpected onslaught on Archangel, than cries went up throughout the bourgeois press of Britain and France that the whole undertaking in the North was an adventure.

* * *

From Chapter 2 of *Between Red and White* (1921).

The revolution was not only temporarily deprived of Baku, but it also lost for ever many of its best sons. In September 1918, almost at the very time when Gegechkori[5] was negotiating with Denikin, twenty-six Bolsheviks, the leaders of the Baku proletariat, headed by Comrade Shaumyan, a member of the Central Committee of our party, and by Alexei Japaridze,[6] were shot at a lonely Transcaspian station.[7]

You can get full information on this matter, Mr. Henderson, from your own General Thompson, the commander in this war of liberation: his agents acted as the executioners.

Thus neither Shaumyan nor Japaridze were in a position to hear about the jubilation of Zhordania on the fall of Soviet Baku. But nevertheless, they took with them into the grave a burning hatred towards the Menshevik abettors of the executioners.

The manuscript of this book had been completed, when I received a new book by Vadim Chaikin, a Socialist-Revolutionary and member of the Constituent Assembly, entitled: *A Contribution to the History of the Russian Revolution: The Execution of Twenty-six Baku Commissars*, and published by Grzebin, Moscow. This book, consisting mostly of documents of which the more important ones are reproduced in facsimile, narrates the story of the murder of twenty-six Baku Commissars by order of the British military authorities, without the least pretence of a public trial. The direct practical

---

5   Evgeni Gegechkori (1881-1954) – Georgian Foreign Minister from May 1918 to February 1921; Menshevik.

6   Prokopius Japaridze (1880-1918) – Georgian Bolshevik, candidate member of the Bolshevik Central Committee, one of the leaders of the Baku Commune and one of the twenty-six Baku Bolsheviks executed without trial by the British occupation forces in September 1918.

7   This is a reference to twenty-six leaders of the Baku Commune executed without trial by the British occupation forces on 20 September 1918.

organiser of the massacre was the chief of the British Military Mission at Ashkhabad, Reginald Teague-Jones. General Thompson was cognisant of the whole case, and Teague-Jones, as the evidence shows, acted with the consent of the gallant general. After the consummation of the slaying of twenty-six unarmed men at a station, where they had been taken under the pretence of exiling them to India, General Thompson aided the escape of one of the leading perpetrators of the crime, the hired scoundrel Druzhkin. The appeals of Vadim Chaikin, by no means a Bolshevik, but a Socialist-Revolutionary and a member of the Constituent Assembly, to the British General Malcolm and to the British General Milne were left unheeded. On the contrary, all these gentlemen demonstrated their solidarity in aiding and abetting the crime and the criminals and in the fabrication of false statements.

This book shows with documentary evidence that Gegechkori, at the insistence of Chaikin, promised to prevent the escape of the criminal scoundrel Druzhkin from Georgia. Yet, in collusion with the British General Thompson, he gave Druzhkin every facility to escape from trial and justice. While the committees of Russian and Georgian Socialist-Revolutionaries and of the Russian Transcaspian Mensheviks, after an investigation of all the facts of the case, signed a declaration testifying to the criminal manner in which the British military authorities had acted, the committee of the Georgian Mensheviks, although as the other Committees arriving at the same conclusion, refused to sign the document for fear of displeasing the British authorities. The telegraph officer of the Menshevik Georgian government refused to accept for transmission the telegrams of Vadim Chaikin which exposed the murderous activities of the British authorities. If nothing more were known about the Georgian Mensheviks except what is established by indisputable and irrefutable documents in Chaikin's book, it would be quite sufficient to imprint for all time the brand of shame and dishonour upon these gentlemen, upon their 'democracy', their protectors and apologists.

We do not entertain the least hope that after the direct, exact, and irrefutable evidence furnished by Chaikin's book, either Mr. Henderson, or Mr. MacDonald, or Mr. J. R. Clynes, Mr. Jimmy Sexton, or Mr. William Adamson, Mr. John Hodge, Mr. Frank Rose, Mr. C. W. Bowerman, Mr. Robert Young, or Mr. Benjamin Spoor will – as Labour MPs – deem it now their duty to investigate the case frankly and honestly and make these representatives of Great Britain, who in Transcaucasia were so gloriously defending democracy, civilisation, justice, religion, and morality against Bolshevik barbarism, answerable for their conduct.

The international Messrs. Snowdens have denied the cooperation of the Georgian Mensheviks with the counter-revolutionary organisations and armies, basing this on the two following circumstances. First, that the Mensheviks themselves complained to the British socialists about the Entente, which had, so to speak, forced them to support the counter-revolution; second, that there was friction between Georgia and the Whites, which at that time assumed the character of armed conflict.

The British General Walker shook his fist in the face of the premier Zhordania, and threatened to close down immediately the central Menshevik organ if it dared to publish a paragraph which might give umbrage to the Entente. A British lieutenant violently struck the table of the Georgian Attorney-General with his sword and demanded the immediate release of all those arrested people whom he, lieutenant by the grace of God, designated. Generally speaking, the British military authorities, according to the documents, conducted themselves even more insolently than the German. Of course, in such cases, Zhordania most respectfully mentioned Georgia's semi-independence, and complained to MacDonald about the violation of Georgia's semi-neutrality. This was necessitated by ordinary caution. When Denikin was robbing Georgia of the Sukhumi area, the Mensheviks complained about Denikin to General Walker. Now they complained about General Walker to Henderson – in both instances with the same success.

If these complaints and frictions had not occurred it would have simply meant that the Mensheviks did not differ in the least from Denikin. But this would be as erroneous as to say that Henderson did not differ in the least from Churchill. The range of petty-bourgeois vacillations during the revolutionary period extends from supporting the proletariat to a formal union with the landlord's counter-revolution. The less the petty-bourgeois politicians are independent, the louder they talk of their complete independence and of their absolute neutrality. From this viewpoint it is very difficult to follow the history of the Mensheviks and the Right and Left Socialist-Revolutionaries in the course of the revolution. They have never been neutral or independent. Their 'neutrality' has always been a critical point in the movement from the right to the left, or from the left to the right. In supporting the Bolsheviks (as did the Left Socialist-Revolutionaries and the anarchists), or in supporting the tsarist generals (as did the Right

Socialist-Revolutionaries and the Mensheviks), the petty-bourgeois parties frequently took fright at the decisive moment of the impending victory of their ally, and even more frequently deserted him in the moment of his greatest peril. One must certainly admit that if, during the revolutionary period, the petty-bourgeois parties bear their share of all the drawbacks of defeat, they seldom benefit by the advantages of victory. After having consolidated its power with the help of 'democracy', the monarchist counter-revolution in the East (in the person of Kolchak), in the North and West (in the person of Yudenich, Miller and the British generals), and in the South (in the person of Denikin) always treated its aiders and abettors with the utmost arrogance and severity.

* * *

From a report in the Hall of Columns,
Moscow, 24 February 1919 (*At the Fronts*).

Lloyd George not long ago stated that it was dangerous to take the offensive against our country for, as a result of an offensive, peasant millions would rally around Soviet power to safeguard their country with all their might. The American President Wilson according to newspaper reports now considers the offensive of Messrs. 'Allies' against Archangel was a mistake. After our capture of Shenkursk there followed the demoralisation of British and American soldiers who abandoned their positions by withdrawing into Archangel. There was open unrest in Murmansk.[8] On the Odessa Front, according to available information, French troops are demanding to be sent home and the black colonial troops cannot endure the climate and have already been withdrawn to their country.[9] Wilson and Lloyd George are beginning to realise that they have made a mistake…

* * *

From Chapter 3 of *Between Red and White* (1921).

The commander of the British troops in Western Transcaucasia, General Forester Walker, on 4 January 1919 explained to Zhordania, both orally and

---

8 During February and March 1919, a number of British, French, American and Canadian companies refused to go up to the line on the Northern Front.

9 Some 40,000 French troops landed at Odessa and other Black Sea ports between December 1918 and April 1919. The operations were coordinated with those of Denikin's Volunteer Army and at first clashed with the forces of the Ukrainian nationalists (the Directorate). Serious mutinies occurred in both the French Army and Navy in the early part of 1919.

in writing, that the enemy of the Entente in the Caucasus is "Bolshevism, which the Great Powers have resolved to destroy wherever and whenever it should make its appearance". In connection with this, a fortnight afterwards, Zhordania declared to the British General Milne: "General Walker... proved to be the first person that understood the state of affairs in our country." General Milne himself summarised his agreement with Zhordania in the following manner: "You and we have common foes – they are the Germans and the Bolsheviks." All these circumstances together furnished of course, the most favourable conditions for the "fullest liberty of action" for the Bolsheviks.

On 18 February General Walker gives the following order, No. 99/6, to the Georgian government: "All Bolsheviks entering Georgia must be imprisoned only in the Mskhet (the jail of Tbilisi), and put under a strong guard." The reference is to those Bolsheviks who were seeking refuge from Denikin. But, already, on 25 February, in Order No. 99/9, Walker wrote: "Arising out of the conversation I had on the 20th inst., with his Excellency M. Zhordania, I have come to the conclusion that it will be necessary in the future to prevent the entrance of Bolsheviks into Georgia by the main road."[10] The imprisonment of the Bolshevik refugees in the Mskhet at least preserved their lives for a time. Walker had "come to the conclusion" that it was best to bar their way of escape, thus throwing them back into the hands of Denikin's executioners. If Arthur Henderson has a few moments to spare from his labours in exposing the cruelties of the Soviet Government, and from his Brotherhood services,[11] he should have an exchange of views with Forester Walker upon this subject.

* * *

From a speech to the Samara Provincial Executive Committee of the RCP and trade union representatives, 6 April 1919 (*The Eastern Front*).

We were menaced by the claws of Anglo-French imperialism and there was a moment when these claws seemed to threaten to crush us in a deadly embrace. After their victory over Germany there was no limit to the omnipotence of the British and the French. Moreover, the German bourgeoisie itself, including

---

10 British forces entered Georgia in December 1918 following the collapse of the Turkish and then German forces. They withdrew towards the end of 1919. The Georgian republic became in this period an involuntary agency of British imperialist policy in Transcaucasia.

11 Henderson was a Methodist and not in fact a member of the Brotherhood Church.

Hindenburg, readily entered the service of France and Britain to put down the Bolsheviks. I have here some recent German papers where it is openly stated in a number of leading articles:

> In the West (i.e., on the frontier between Germany and France) iron and concrete walls and fortresses are being erected – the walls of the old national hatred between France and Germany are being put up. But all this is insignificant compared to the abyss that separates us in the East. We must somehow or other come to an agreement with France, but with the Bolsheviks and Soviet power – never. Theirs is a different world order, they deny – and they say this openly – they deny the whole basis of economic life and private property.

And let us add ourselves, the order on which most holy profits are based. The struggle against Britain and France, the old forts of Belfort and Verdun, is insignificant compared to the hatred we inspire in unified European capital. Such is the admission of the German bourgeoisie, crushed down, humiliated, plundered, but which even now, while reeling under the boot of the French and British bourgeoisie, says: "but all the same you are closer and more kindred to me than that horrible Soviet communist republic." That's the feeling they harbour towards us in Germany, France, Britain, and everywhere else.

You can of course say that when Britain and France proposed a trip to the Prinkipo Islands, Soviet power agreed to such a trip and it agreed then as it had done at Brest-Litovsk because we were ready to seize any opportunity to stand down our front, win an armistice and a respite, and lighten the burden on our Red Army and all the working people.[12] It stands to reason that we would have gone to the Prinkipo Islands as we went to Brest-Litovsk, not out of sympathy, respect, or trust for Clemenceau, Lloyd George, and that old transatlantic Tartuffian hypocrite Wilson, no comrades, on that score Clemenceau, Lloyd George, and Wilson, like the Hohenzollerns and Habsburgs before them, are not for a single minute mistaken, for they know that we harbour the same feelings for them as they do for us. We are joined to them by an intimate hatred, an intimate mortal enmity, and any agreement with them will only be dictated by cold calculation and form by its very nature a temporary armistice, after which the struggle will inevitably break out again with renewed force.

---

12 On 22 January 1919 United States President Wilson invited the belligerent parties in Russia to a conference on the Prinkipo Islands near Constantinople. The Soviet government agreed to attend but the various White Guard regimes declined.

It had seemed before that they were strangling us; then they offered us the Prinkipo Islands and then they stopped talking about them. Why? Because Kolchak, Denikin, Krasnov,[13] and Mannerheim[14] in Finland declared to the imperialist stock exchange, "give us a time limit, give us two or three more spring months: Soviet power will be strangled and you will not need to negotiate with it on the Prinkipo Islands." To this Lloyd George replied: "you made that promise a long time ago. First of all Milyukov did, then Kerensky, Skoropadsky[15] in the Ukraine, and then Krasnov; now Krasnov has fled from Rostov and Bogaevsky[16] has replaced him, you all made that promise. Kolchak promised America long ago. We shall no longer give you assistance with troops; our position in the north and the south is becoming worse and worse." Then Kolchak, Denikin and the others answered: "We ask you and beg you to give us just a little while longer to finish off Soviet power. But don't have talks with them, don't strengthen their position. We are preparing a wide offensive for the spring."

And so they had their offensive – that spring offensive – and we are now surviving it. Throughout the winter the allies gave money and shells. They did not give manpower as they were afraid of getting too mixed up in our affairs and getting bogged down in our Soviet plain, for they realised from Germany's experience that the imperialists' troops enter our Russia under the tricolour of imperialism and violence, but the same troops leave Soviet Russia under the red banner of communism.

---

13 Pyotr Krasnov (1869-1947) – Tsarist general, commanded a Cossack brigade during the First World War; appointed by Kerensky in October 1917 as commander of the army sent against Petrograd; defeated and taken prisoner by the revolutionary forces; released after promising not to take up arms against the revolution; fled to the Don region, where he was elected Ataman of the Don Cossacks; led counter-revolutionary White forces armed by the Germans in southern Russia but was eventually defeated in late 1918.

14 Gustaf Mannerheim (1867-1951) – Finnish aristocrat and tsarist officer; after October Revolution formed a White army in Finland and bloodily suppressed the revolutionary forces in May 1918; led the Finnish forces during the Russo-Finnish War (1939-40 and 1941-1944); president of Finland 1944-1946.

15 Pavlo Skoropadsky (1873-1945) – Tsarist general, seized power in Ukraine with German support in April 1918; ousted by Symon Petliura in November 1918; went into exile in Germany where he was active in anti-Soviet organisations and maintained close contacts with the German military.

16 Afrikan Petrovich Bogaevsky – Cossack general who was elected to replace Krasnov and placed the Don Cossacks under the supreme command of Denikin.

They agreed to provide arms, money, rifles, and pieces of silver, but they withdrew their soldiers.

In France the leading newspaper, *Le Temps*, and the paper of the same name, *The Times*, in Britain, openly say that the French troops are being withdrawn from Odessa because "since the occupation of Nikolaev and Kherson"… the position of the expeditionary force in Odessa has been "critical". They talk about this quite frankly in the European press. I have a telegram here, received today or yesterday, dealing with the position of the allied armies in the north of Russia – I do not know whether it was published in the press:

> America, radio from Paris for Canada. The involuntary anxiety gripping British circles concerning the grave risk of destruction threatening the Archangel expedition only confirms the opinion of the American military expressed many months ago. Stark new facts have been added namely: the mutiny of Finnish troops in Archangel.

The Americans and British had mobilised, or rather attracted round themselves, Finnish forces when German forces were occupying Finland, as the British presented themselves as Finnish liberators from German imperialism. Now the American wireless reports publicly from Paris on the mutiny of Finnish soldiers incorporated in the Anglo-American army on our northern shore:

> The mutiny of Finnish troops threatens to cut off the only road for our soldiers, and the Bolsheviks' concentration of warships on the Dvina and the Vaga indicates their readiness for an attack… Men from Canada form the main part of the detachment in this area. Official figures admit that there is not the slightest hope of reinforcing their effectives before a Bolshevik assault.

The London *Daily Mail* says in a leading article: "responsibility for this danger… rests upon the Allies… The eyes of the whole world are upon them. If they should fall into the hands of that enemy their fate baffles description", and so on and so forth. This of course is a blatant lie. If they fall into our hands we shall treat them as we treated those hundreds and now possibly thousands of French, British, and Americans who were captured by us in the Ukraine and the north. We sat them on school benches and gave them teachers, French and English communists, and they were most successful.

Not long ago, a bourgeois MP asked the Naval Minister whether it was true that some Englishman called Price was conducting criminal Bolshevik agitation on the Murmansk coast, and whether it was true that there had been an uprising in a British battalion which then had to be withdrawn. The British Naval Minister was forced to confirm that yes, this Price had previously been a correspondent of the *Manchester Guardian*, a British democratic newspaper, became a communist at a school here, set out from Moscow for the north and there conducted agitation with great success, and that there was an uprising of more than one battalion there and that these troops had to be brought back home...[17]

* * *

From 'The Brest Stage', foreword (dated 1 August 1919) to
Protocols of the Brest-Litovsk Peace Talks, Vol. 1 (1920).

... Anglo-French imperialism is still not only alive but dangerous.

For our part we are ready to repeat Brest-Litovsk negotiations with new Anglo-French partners; history has shown that we did not emerge the loser from the first Brest. But for precisely this reason the bourgeois classes of the Entente, after all their hesitations, waverings, and pondering, finally rejected negotiations with the government of the Bolsheviks. In this refusal there is an extremely valuable historical admission, both of the correctness of our policy at Brest-Litovsk and of our increased strength. German imperialism had entered negotiations with us because it hoped to settle us with ease. Anglo-French imperialism does not trust itself and thus fears us. Although history required a Brest stage in order to overthrow Austro-German imperialism, this does not in any way mean that the Anglo-French plunderers will, by avoiding a Brest, avoid their downfall. History is resourceful and it has at its disposal many methods and means, while we are not dogmatic and will gladly accept the downfall of our enemies, irrespective of the form in which it crashes down on their heads.

* * *

An interview dated 29 August 1919,
first published in 1926 in *Works*, Vol. 17, Part 2.

Churchill Threatens But We Are Not Afraid

Churchill does not rank among those politicians whose words should be taken for the genuine article. But for the impolite and numbskulled petty-

---

17 In the House of Commons on 20 February 1919, a British Foreign Office spokesman confirmed that M. Phillips Price had been editing a Bolshevik newspaper, *The Call*, which was spread among British troops in the Murman territory (North Russia) and incited them to revolt.

bourgeois rabble to which Churchill speaks, the figure of "fourteen states" entering the battle against Russia must make a big impression. Critically-thinking workers of Great Britain will say that it appears that the affairs of victorious British imperialism cannot be in a very brilliant state, if the champion of capitalist violence has to boast noisily about the number of his small – militarily speaking, insignificant – allies in the struggle against the Red Army. Kolchak would be immeasurably more pleased with fourteen divisions than fourteen geographical terms.

That the artificially installed bourgeois governments of Finland, Estonia, Latvia, Lithuania, Poland, Hungary and so on are hostile to Soviet Power we had no doubt, as we have had no doubt that sooner or later the working class of these countries will settle accounts with their bourgeoisie as soon as the proletariat of Britain and France put a rein on the violence of Entente imperialism against small and weak nations.

Ambitions of conquest are wholly and totally alien to Soviet policy, which is clear to any sane person who is informed as to the objects and tasks of Soviet power and the whole past of the party that guides the life of our country. That is why the order was given to our forces operating on our Western Front not to cross the frontiers of the little states which had announced their secession from the former tsarist empire. But this does not of course mean that subsequent attempts by Finland and Estonia upon Petrograd will go unpunished.

If you believe Churchill (and that is not obligatory), then the hesitations of the Finnish and Estonian bourgeoisies have been now resolved in favour of a military invasion. Without doubt such a decision (if it was made) would have been aided by our retreat on the Western Front and Denikin's temporary successes.

As you know, we had regarded the Western Front as of third-rate importance in comparison with the Eastern and Southern Fronts. Now, after we have moved our Kolchak Front some 600 miles eastwards and are advancing further every day, and when we have halted Denikin's onslaught and gone over to a victorious offensive along the whole Southern Front, we are in a position to pay adequate attention to the Western Front. All the necessary measures have been taken so that even without any kind warning from Churchill we would not have been caught off guard.

As previously we have no motives for launching hostile operations against Finland and Estonia. But we do know full well that the lines which have been laid down by Churchill and others for an offensive against Petrograd lead in the opposite direction to Helsinki and Tallin. You can rest assured that our Red soldiers can find that road.

With regard to Churchill's generous promise: in the event of the failure of the offensive by fourteen states against Soviet power, we for our part have not the slightest doubt that, following the inevitable collapse of a new onslaught on Soviet Russia, absolutely friendly relations will be established between the latter on the one hand, and Britain, France and their allies on the other. One can, however, assume that such a lesson will not pass without effect on Great Britain's internal life. By that time, the British proletariat will have given Churchill and his friends and allies sufficient free time to draw a comparison between his current policy and the behaviour of the Dickensian character who tried to keep back the waves with a broom.

* * *

A letter to the Central Committee of the RCP dated 20 September 1919.[18]

Further to my report of August, I consider it essential to raise the following points.

The Truce between Afghanistan and Britain may, according to certain evidence, wholly rebound against us.[19] According to reports from our people in Turkestan, Britain is actively at work uniting Persia, Bukhara, Khiva, and Afghanistan against Soviet Turkestan. It would be incredible if she were not to do so. Britain is now attempting to form a chain of States to the East just as she did on our Western Borders. The above work offers in turn far fewer difficulties than there are in the West. The whole question now is who will be first in the race.

Our successful advance on Turkestan and the destruction of Kolchak's Southern Army create conditions in which we can come first in the race. But from this it follows that while conducting an entirely correct policy of biding our time, tactical adjustment, avoiding engagement, and concession in the West, we must switch to a policy of resolute and dynamic action in the East.

We can forthwith thwart Britain's efforts to rally the Asian States against us by setting up a major military base in Turkestan, for which there are already adequate elements. A feasible line of direction for a thrust needs to be immediately selected, and one out of the chain of States which Britain is ranging against us confronted with immediate attack, presented with an

---

18 First published in The Trotsky Papers edited by J. Meijer and published by the International Institute for Social History

19 The truce was signed on 8 August 1919 following fighting on the Indian border from May of that year. As a result, Britain conceded recognition of Afghanistan's independence.

ultimatum to conclude a peace treaty, and made to comply with our bidding or subjected to attack.

From this there follows:

1. The need to send someone to Turkestan armed with exceptionally broad powers and furnished with instructions that would provide a guarantee that the comrade in question would not take to sidestepping the issue in the East with the already traditional defensive evasiveness that is forced on us in the West.

2. That the Military Revolutionary Council of the Republic should be instructed to concentrate in Turkestan the material wherewithal and personnel for our launching a possible offensive from Turkestan southwards.

* * *

From a speech to the all-city conference
of the Moscow organisations of the RCP, 24 September 1919.

For us the most secure position has been created on the Northern Front, where there are now no large-scale military operations but only minor and partial clashes. This can be explained by the international situation that has developed, the internal difficulties of British imperialism, and the British command's withdrawal of forces from Archangel and Baku which can be considered as final.[20]

Churchill, who not so long ago spoke of fourteen powers preparing an offensive against Soviet Russia, speaks now not only of the withdrawal of British forces from the Russian North, but also that Britain must grant asylum to the Archangel White Guard 'Chaikovskyites' whom she had led into temptation.[21]

On this front two roads are possible: either the enemy will reinforce themselves along a narrower front and replace regular British units by volunteer White Guard units, or Archangel will be evacuated even before the onset of winter. But these are essentially two stages of one and the same path.

* * *

---

20 British forces finally evacuated North Russia in October 1919 and Baku in November 1919.

21 The British occupying forces had installed Nikolai Vasilyevich Chaikovsky (1850-1926), formerly a Socialist-Revolutionary, as head of a puppet 'National Government of the North' at Archangel in 1918.

Order No. 159, published in *Pravda* and *Izvestia*, 25 October 1919.

ORDER
Of the Chairman of the Revolutionary War Council of the
Republic and the People's Commissar for War and Naval Affairs
to the Red Army and the Red Navy

24 October 1919, No. 159, Detskoe Selo (formerly Tsarskoye)

The Two Britains

Red Warriors! On all fronts you are encountering the hostile machinations
of Britain. Counter-revolutionary forces are firing on you from British
artillery. In the dumps at Shenkursk and Onega[22] and on the Southern
and Western Fronts you are finding supplies of British manufacture.
Prisoners that you have taken wear British uniforms. Women and
children of Archangel and Astrakhan are being killed by British pilots
using British dynamite. British vessels bombard our coastline. British
gold sows depravity by corrupting dishonest elements on the front and in
the rear. The British wireless lies and slanders our workers' and peasants'
Russia day in and day out, and attempts to poison the whole world with
its lies.

Soldiers! Sailors! Your hearts have on many occasions overflowed with
hate for predatory, lying, hypocritical, bloody Britain. And your hate is just
and sacred. It will multiply your energies in the struggle against the enemy
tenfold.

Yet even now at the moment of our ferocious battles against Britain's
hireling Yudenich, I demand of you: *never forget that two Britains exist.
Alongside the Britain of profit, violence, corruption and bloodthirstiness there
exists the Britain of labour, intellectual might, and great ideals of international
solidarity.* Against us fights arrogant and dishonest stock-exchange Britain.
Labouring people's Britain is behind us. We firmly believe that the latter will
soon raise itself to its full height and put a strait-jacket on the criminals who
are currently leading plots against the toiling masses of Russia. Driven on by
this unshakeable confidence let us shout in the fire and smoke of the struggle:
Death to the plunderers of imperialism! Long live workers' and labouring
people's Britain!

---

22 Towns recaptured from the British and White forces on the Northern Front during
1919.

* * *

From a report to the Central Executive Committee, 7 November 1919.

The advantages that the bourgeois counter-revolution had in the struggle against us came down to the fact that they were guaranteed absolutely everything necessary, and of course on the technical side they had greater possibilities than we had. Who transported those legions from Archangel? The British Navy of course. Tanks came into Yudenich's hands. Who brought these tanks? Britain. Who drove these tanks? British specialists trained in military science. Who bombarded Krasnaya Gorka[23] with heavy artillery? British vessels and monitors armed with fifteen-inch guns – the last word in naval artillery technique, only introduced in 1916. Our sailors defended Krasnaya Gorka under fire from those terrible shells. I have in my hands a wireless communiqué stating that Krasnaya Gorka must be taken today or tomorrow, and there is a communiqué stating that Kronstadt had fallen under the blows from British monitors. They thought that our sailors could not withstand bombardment from fifteen-inch artillery, but our sailors held out, and Krasnaya Gorka and Kronstadt are more firmly in our hands than ever before.

Let me repeat: they had prepared for this campaign, they had awaited this decisive moment. In the first days of October, even before Yudenich's thrust against Yamburg,[24] one of the bourgeois papers wrote that Yudenich's offensive against Petrograd was imminent in a few days and it would be decisive – this did not reach us at the time for we received the newspaper late. Obviously the British newspaper had given away a military secret, but they were so impatient to promise and propose the toppling of Soviet power that they did this even when it meant damaging their own military interests. British imperialists of the Churchill type had tied their fate too closely to the fate of intervention, and the desperate bourgeoisie put pressure on Churchill and said: "You have squandered over 2,000 million francs on the campaigns of the Russian bourgeoisie – and that is merely the military expenditure of British imperialism – this expenditure has brought us nothing except the strengthening of the military might of the Russian Red Army." He, Churchill answered: "Just wait a bit, another week or two or three and General Yudenich will do what that deceitful Kolchak didn't do and Denikin couldn't manage. He will take Petrograd, and in Petrograd his first job will be to form a mighty army for an offensive deep into Russia." A Swedish paper

---

23 Fortress on the southern shore of the Gulf of Finland west of Petrograd.

24 Yamburg – Now Kingisepp, near the Russian-Estonian border.

had spoken of this plan before the start of the campaign: a short decisive blow at Petrograd, the seizure of Petrograd, securing bases, regrouping, and then a thrust from Petrograd to Moscow. Everything had been carefully planned.

Certainly Britain had wanted the thrust to come simultaneously from two sides, from Estonia and from Finland. And throughout October the whole British Press was goading on Finland: for example, the British newspaper *The Times* wrote in its leading article about "the moral duty" of Finland to take part in a robber campaign and that this would raise her international prestige.[25] Mighty Britain, in whose hands lie all favours and all retribution, applied the whole force of concrete threats and bribes in order to involve Finland in an adventure in support of Yudenich. Finland all the while hesitated and wavered, and she has not to date made up her mind, and the explanation of this indecision we find in the Finnish bourgeois press. I have here the most interesting evidence of the growth and rebirth of the communist movement in Finland. This is what the paper *Karjala* says:

> Until recently, Bolshevik newspapers have been distributed here underground, the publications coming from Petrograd, but over the last months our own workers' press has taken on a purely Bolshevik tone. There are a whole number of legal publications which would directly and openly threaten us with revolution in the event of an offensive against Soviet Russia.

* * *

From a speech in Yekaterinburg, 28 February 1920
(*The General Position of the Republic and the Tasks of the First Labour Army*).

This evening's radio brought us a document which we have long awaited, a document which expresses the attitude of the Entente imperialists towards the Soviet government. You will know that over the last weeks and even months the governments of the Entente countries have been discussing the question of their attitude towards the Soviet government. They came to the conclusion that this attitude must be changed and that Soviet Russia could not be squashed by the military force of Kolchak, Yudenich, and Denikin. Millerand, a one-time socialist, the successor to the French Prime Minister Clemenceau and an advocate of a ruthless armed struggle against Soviet Russia, appeared to tend towards the viewpoint of the British Prime Minister Lloyd George who has come to the conclusion that a deal with the Soviet government is necessary... I shall read you this literary work written

---

25 'Finland and the Bolsheviks', *The Times*, 24 October 1919.

in the intricate language of bourgeois diplomacy which, it was said long ago, possesses language designed to conceal or distort its original thoughts. This what the memorandum says:

> The Allied powers have come to an agreement regarding the following points: If the states which hay been formed on the frontiers of Soviet Russia – i.e., Finland, Estonia, Latvia, Poland, Georgia, Armenia, and Azerbaijan, whose independence is recognised *de facto* (i.e., in practice) by the Allied powers – ask the latter (i.e., Britain and France) what their policy should be in relation to Soviet Russia, then the Allied governments will reply that they cannot take on the responsibility of advising them to continue a war whose outcome could damage their vital interests in the extreme.

That is the intricate beginning to an intricate document. Lloyd George, Clemenceau, Nitti[26] and other, lesser ones who are with them, say: if Poland, if Latvia, and if Finland ask us how they should act with regard to Soviet Russia, then we Britain, France, Italy now are unable to give the advice: go to war! No, now we will say to them: don't go to war, for a war will threaten your vital interests.

What a turnabout, in the name of heaven! Britain and France did not make war on us, they gave 'advice' to Denikin, Kolchak, Yudenich, the Estonians, White Latvia, the White Finns and the White Romanians, saying to them: we advise you to rob Soviet Russia of Bessarabia; they said to Yudenich, Denikin, and Kolchak: we advise you to put down the workers and peasants. And in order that the advice was not too 'lean' they spiced it up with money, artillery, machine-guns, and all the necessary war supplies. It was no secret to any of us – the British minister Churchill spoke about this for all to hear – that Britain was mobilising fourteen nations against us. He stated as much: "fourteen nations under Britain's leadership are at present in action against Soviet Russia." Now not a trace of this talk is left. Of course, Britain neither mobilised, armed, nor incited anyone against us, but merely gave advice. Now she gives different advice: she says that war against Soviet Russia can damage their vital interests – i.e., the Red Army has become sufficiently powerful for the stock merchants of all countries to realise that a war by Poland against us would mark the death of the Polish landlord, the death of the Polish bourgeoisie, and consequently great damage to the interests of the ruling class.

---

26 Francesco Saverio Nitti (1868-1953) – Italian economist and Radical Party politician, Italian Prime Minister from June 1919 to June 1920.

Thus, the Anglo-French stock exchange says: don't make war! We all try to approach the matter from another angle. Which angle? The document states further on:

> The Allied powers cannot, in view of [their] past experiences, enter into diplomatic relations with the government of the Soviets until they can be certain that the Bolshevik outrages have ended and the Moscow government feels prepared to make its conduct conform to the conduct of all civilised governments.

Isn't that good? They are telling us: We will not enter diplomatic relations with the Soviet government because it has bad manners, a bad character and a bad education. But if it was like us, diplomats of Britain and France, if it corrected itself in that direction and drew closer to the methods of the governments of the 'civilised' nations, we would enter diplomatic relations with it. Thus they are looking at us both ways: at present we won't enter into relations with you, but if you correct yourself in the course of time, have a wash and comb your hair, then we will enter into relations with you.

We are grateful for the kindness. So, they recommend that we make our conduct conform to the conduct of all civilised governments. Here it should be said that the experiences that Britain and France had here in Russia were very unpleasant. Many of you have probably forgotten these experiences. We had a British representative here. I must admit I've forgotten his name, although in his time he often visited the Commissariat for War.[27] This gentleman, (we cannot say 'character' for we must be polite, as they demand of us), this gentleman organised nothing less than a conspiracy (in which the former SR Savinkov played first fiddle) which had the aim of destroying bridges, cutting railway lines, staging an insurrection in the Kremlin, and killing Lenin and other officials of Soviet power. They were acting in accordance with the methods of civilised nations, but we were acting like barbarians: we caught them red-handed with all their papers giving precise and detailed documentary evidence. In Petrograd, one of the agents of this criminal band (I beg you not to record the phrase "criminal band" for Lloyd George might be offended) – at the moment of arrest one of the agents of this band put up armed resistance and was killed in the hotel where he was living...

They have suggested that the British and Swiss governments found themselves compelled to expel the representatives of the Soviet government from their

---

27 See L. Trotsky, 'A Letter to Our French Comrades' in *The First Five Years of the Communist International*, Wellred Books, 2020, pp. 97-100.

territory because they abused their privileges. Thus Litvinov,[28] who was in London as a semi-official envoy of the Soviet government, maintained open contact with revolutionary working-class organisations, for which he was deported.

But let me repeat: these gentlemen are silent about the fact that their own representatives here in our country tossed out gold right and left to organisers of counter-revolutionary mutinies.

But we can reconcile ourselves to that. It is still not so long ago that first the German and then the Anglo-French imperialists promised, not only promised but actually prepared, to crush us. This was a little more serious than Churchill's chatter about fourteen armies being mobilised against us or Britain's intention to crown Kolchak. This was a little more serious than the phrase about us having "bad manners". Of course, they would have come to like us more if we were nice and black. But we are red. Won't you deign to prefer us nice and red? For we are not going to change our colour.

* * *

From a report to the 16th Moscow Provincial Conference of the Russian Communist Party, 25 March 1920 (*The Party Faced with New Economic Tasks*).

The Western Front forms a passive front. Standing against us there are little states which had split off from the former tsarist empire. They now form vassals of the Entente: Britain and France. At the present moment they reflect all the fluctuations in our military successes on the one hand, and the policies of Britain, France, and to some extent America on the other. You all recall how Estonia offered us peace talks, and while our peace delegation was preparing to set out (that was at the beginning of October), Estonian forces made a thrust for Petrograd. Now, after they have been thrown back and we are drawing close to Narva, they are holding armistice negotiations. Latvia, Poland, and Finland are conducting basically the same policy with slight variations. We are, of course, as ready today as we were at the beginning of October to meet them in any negotiations. You will know that Comrade Litvinov has just left for negotiations which could take on a very great importance. In Copenhagen he met a British trade unionist, O'Grady[29] by name. This British social-

---

28 Maxim Litvinov (1876-1951) – Russian revolutionary and Soviet diplomat; Bolshevik since 1903. Arrested in 1918 and exchanged for Bruce Lockhart, a British diplomat and secret agent arrested in Russia; worked as roving ambassador of the Soviet government for the next decade; Commissar for Foreign Affairs from 1930 to 1939.

29 James O'Grady (1866-1934) – British trade unionist and Labour politician; president of the TUC in 1898; staunch supporter of British participation in the First World War;

chauvinist, who is playing the role of an agent of the imperialist government, is at the same time a trade unionist, the leader of a workers' organisation. He is thus a most suitable man for the British government, for on the one hand he is an agent of the government, and on the other a workers' leader whose words can be disowned on the grounds that he did not say them as a representative of the British government. So Britain has found a suitable person. The talks must deal only with the question of hostages and prisoners of war, i.e., not a matter of primary political importance. It is clear however that in embarking on these negotiations Britain is pursuing some other object, for she has so far regarded the fate of the hostages quite calmly, yet now she suddenly begins to be interested in this question. Lloyd George's statement, now familiar to you, replaced Churchill's statement.

Churchill represents the extreme, rabid wing of the British imperialists. He spoke of the fourteen countries that Britain was mobilising against us and predicted the inevitable fall of Petrograd in a week or two. After Yudenich had faltered, he also stated that a new factor would soon appear which would upset the balance at Petrograd. This factor remains as yet a secret of Churchill, but his speech was highly typical in the period of our tough military position. Now Churchill seems to have fallen silent while the sly old fox Lloyd George takes over, making two or three extremely expressive statements to the effect that he maintains his old opinion or conviction that Soviet power cannot be crushed by force of arms. We shall not inquire how this ties up with the whole past policy of the government headed by Lloyd George, but he has now put it before the British parliament. Moreover, in the last statement to reach us, he said that Denikin had seized tens of thousands of square miles but was still unable to create a proper state administration. This is, as it were, an open dethronement, not only of Kolchak but also of Denikin, a refusal to place a stake on his card. Lloyd George's statement has for us, of course, a colossal importance. The watershed in British imperialism's policy is at this moment reflected in the behaviour of the little states which live on our western fringe. To be sure they intend no good towards us, but they are in themselves incapable of great ill.

---

organised an exchange of prisoners between Britain and revolutionary Russia in 1919.

The Soviet-Polish War

From *Izvestia*, 13 June 1920.

On a Speech by Bonar Law

In his speech in the House of Commons on 29 May, Bonar Law justified the aid that Britain is giving to Poland by referring in passing to a message from Comrade Trotsky to French soldiers which said: "We can watch this temporary advance of the feeble Polish troops without being too alarmed; when we have finished with Denikin and the day is near we will throw ourselves on that front with overwhelming reserves." Seeing in these words a threat to Poland's independence, the government of Great Britain bound itself by a commitment to assist her and is now fulfilling that commitment.

I have not written any letters to French soldiers, but a phrase similar to one quoted by Mr. Bonar Law was contained in my letter to Comrade Loriot, a leader of the French communists. The letter was written on 1 September last year during the period of Denikin's closest approach to Moscow. The threat from Yudenich's quarter was no reason for the unhindered movement of White Guard Polish forces into areas which in no way could be allocated to Poland. French comrades, like honest workers throughout the world, were at that time anxiously watching the development of military operations on our west and south-west. In my letter I explained that the operations by the Polish forces could not have a decisive importance, that the main enemy was Denikin and that after his rout we could switch sufficient reserves to the western front to safeguard the Soviet Republic from an onslaught by White Guard Poland. To see in those words the proclamation of a future offensive by us against Poland is trebly absurd. First, these sort of intentions are not being announced in the press, yet my letter had been printed in *Kommunisticheskii Internatsional* No. 5 on page 511; secondly a statement of this kind would in no event be addressed to French communists; thirdly it would run counter to the whole policy of Soviet power.

Mr. Bonar Law would very likely have been clear about this had he taken the trouble to think, but there is no cause for him to take such an exercise. Like all countries, Britain is today divided into two parts: the honest majority of the people which wants peace with Russia, wants to understand the whole dishonesty and villainy of Poland's assault upon her and the support given by the Entente, and a predatory minority which approves and supports any ill caused to the Russian people dictated by whatever motives. As the policy of intervention rests upon this minority, Mr. Bonar Law has no need to be over-scrupulous in his choice of arguments.

* * *

From a letter to members of the Politburo dated 13 July 1920.[1]

1. It seems to me that it would be essential to find out at once whether Curzon's[2] ultimatum is known in Britain and what the reaction of the press is to it. In general to sound out, so far as this is possible through Klyshko, Rothstein[3] and others, the attitude to the ultimatum in government and opposition circles.

2. *Qua* answer we might adopt, as it seems to me, the following fundamentals:

---

1 First published in The Trotsky Papers edited by J. Meijer and published by the International Institute for Social History

2 This refers to Curzon's note of 11 July 1920 which was discussed by the Central Committee on 16 July. Chicherin's reply, which was dated 17 July, largely embodied Trotsky's suggestions. See the appeal from page 108 of the present edition for details of the Curzon note. The 1920 Curzon note, loosely referred to as an "ultimatum" by Trotsky, should not be confused with the 1923 Curzon Ultimatum dealt with from pages 128 to 136.

3 Klyshko and Rothstein were Russian communists who had emigrated to Britain in 1907 and 1891 respectively. In 1920 Klyshko was a member of a Soviet trade delegation to Britain. Theodore Rothstein (1871-1953) was a founder member of the British Communist Party.

a. Poland is an independent state, whose inviolability we have never encroached on. We agree to accept the mediation of Britain and to guarantee the inviolability of the frontier of Poland as it is projected by the Allies, without finally predetermining the question of these frontiers, since this is a question of the self-determination of nations.

b. As for the Crimea: we reject the intervention of Great Britain on the basis of the fundamental premises put forward by the government of Lloyd George and accepted by us: obligatory non-intervention in internal affairs. The Crimea is not an independent state. We could permit the intervention of Britain in questions of the Crimea only on a basis of reciprocity: that is on the basis of our putting forward demands in relation to Ireland. To this question must be added the fact that Ireland represents a nation, while in no case do Wrangel's White Guards constitute any specific nationality.

c. The week that we have at our disposal must be used to give effect to the old decree of the Politburo of the Central Committee on the subject of acquainting the working masses with the policy of Great Britain in relation to the Crimea. Even people like Rosmer,[4] for instance, who know what the rule of Britain is like, are greatly impressed by a straightforward account of the facts of British policy in relation to the Crimea.

d. It must be stipulated, in one form or another, that we do accept the mediation of Britain: of Britain, that is, and not of the League of Nations; that we agree to negotiations in London, but demand for our delegates the same rights as the delegates of all free, independent countries have: that is, the right to give interviews, to contact whoever they choose, etc., etc.

e. It seems to me that a refusal on our part to accept British intervention in our internal affairs is an absolute must. This refusal cannot give rise to major complications, since there is virtually no chalice of rousing up anyone or anything against us on this score, especially so provided that we agree at the same time to accept mediation with regard to Poland.

f. It is essential to commence negotiations with Romania at the same time.

---

4 Alfred Rosmer (1877-1964) – Leading supporter of the Communist International in the French trade unions, and a founder of the French Communist Party.

g. In view of the fact that it may prove inconvenient to modify or revoke the decision of the Council of People's Commissars on questions of the ultimatum, it seems essential to call an emergency session of the Central Executive Committee, or even a Congress of Soviets.

* * *

An appeal issued by the Council of People's Commissars, first published in *Pravda* and *Izvestia* 21 July 1920.

To all workers, peasants and all honest citizens of Soviet Russia and Soviet Ukraine,

On 11 July the British government approached us with a proposal for ending the war with Poland, and sending our representatives to London for peace talks with Poland and other border states. In addition, Lord Curzon, the British Foreign Secretary, reported that in the event of an armistice being concluded, the Polish forces will retreat to the frontier which was laid down for Poland at the peace conference in December of last year. In the same note it proposed that we do not touch Wrangel in his Crimean "sanctuary".

To this offer of mediation by the British government we, the Council of People's Commissars, replied in the negative. And in explaining this action of ours to the Russian and Ukrainian peoples may we express our firm conviction that our words will also reach the Polish people.

The People's Commissariat for Foreign Affairs has issued a *Red Book* in Russian and foreign languages on Russo-Polish relations, where specific documents reveal day by day on the one hand the energetic, sincere, and honest efforts of Soviet power to secure peace with Poland even at the price of big concessions, and on the other the stubborn, malicious, and predatory ambitions of bourgeois-landlord Poland to inflict at the Entente's instigation a mortal blow on Soviet Russia. If Britain had not wanted the war, she could easily have prevented it. It would have been sufficient to refuse Poland war supplies and money. But Britain wanted the war. While holding talks with us in order to lull the working masses, she was at the same time continuously sending war material to Piłsudski and Wrangel against the Russian workers and peasants. Britain caused the Polish War and Britain is responsible for it.

Lord Curzon refers to the League of Nations on whose behalf he is presenting his proposal. But Poland, who has launched a campaign of robbery and plunder against us, is a member of this League of Nations. Another member of that League of Nations is rapacious imperial Japan, which is currently conducting monstrous outrages in the Far Eastern Republic under the cover of her allies. If the task of the League of Nations was to assist the cause of peace, then it ought to have prevented Poland from starting the war, and demanded that Japan evacuate Eastern Siberia. But there was none of that. All the members of the League of Nations, and especially France, Britain and America, are linked by a collective guarantee in the matter of provoking a war by Poland against the Ukraine and Russia. The most powerful League of Nations members have been and are helping Poland as much as they can. They did not even reply to us when we approached them in April with an appeal to restrain the hand of the Piłsudski government, which was already poised to strike. Yet now, when cruel blows have been dealt to the White Guard Polish forces by the Red Army, the League of Nations which is responsible for this comes forward with an olive branch in its hands – or rather, Britain, under the cover of the League over which she rules, offers us her mediation in reconciling us with Poland and the other border states and invites us to send peace delegates for this purpose to London: the very centre where all the snares are set against the Soviet Republic, and from where the order was given to Poland to launch her offensive against the Ukraine and Russia.

No, Britain has not been called upon to act as intermediary and peacemaker in the bloody struggle which her criminal bourgeoisie conceived and feeds.

But the British government, as we have seen, already does not confine itself to the question of Poland. Lord Curzon, in his same note of 11 July, proposes to us nothing more or less than ending the war with Baron Wrangel if, in exchange, he promises to withdraw his bands south of the isthmus in order to establish himself within the limits of the Crimean Peninsula which Britain has placed at his disposal. Just a few days ago, the same Lord Curzon stated on behalf of the British government that the pre-condition for commercial relations was the mutual obligation of Russia and Great Britain to non-interference in each other's internal affairs; but hardly had the British government time to acknowledge the receipt of Soviet Russia's agreement to this condition than Lord Curzon considered himself called upon not only to interfere in Russia's internal affairs, but also to donate a part of federal Soviet territory to private bandits acting in the service of British imperialism.

It is not the first time that the British government has manifested an interest in Baron Wrangel in the Crimea. When the Red forces which had routed Denikin were preparing to step over the Crimean threshold in order to mop up Wrangel's remnants of Denikin's army, Lord Curzon came forward with the same olive branch in hand and offered us the complete capitulation of Wrangel and his forces on condition of an amnesty. We agreed, and upon the insistence of the British government we halted the offensive immediately. Whereupon Lord Curzon at once changed the conditions and began to talk, instead of Wrangel's capitulation, of our non-incursion over the boundaries of the Crimea. At the same time, the War and Naval departments of Great Britain were vigorously working to arm and supply Wrangel's forces. The outcome of this coordinated collaboration of Curzon, Churchill, and Wrangel was a new offensive by the White Guard forces northwards from the Crimea at the beginning of June. It was quite evident that the offensive by Baron Wrangel, for whom Lord Curzon had previously requested the amnesty, was mapped and planned to supplement White Guard Poland's offensive and consequently was dictated from the same London centre. Yet now the British Foreign Secretary again proposes that we abandon the offensive action against Wrangel, and prepares to set up his hireling on Russian territory just as if nothing had happened before.

No, neither Lord Curzon, the British government as a whole, nor the League of Nations which it commands are called upon to interfere in the internal affairs of the Russian Soviet Federation and to act as peacemakers over a civil war which they themselves have caused and inflamed.

All the previous work of the British government, its allies and helpmates bear witness to the fact that their mediation pursues at the present time a single goal: to save Piłsudski and Wrangel, whom they had set against us, from their deserved rout, and to gain for them an opportunity to recover, re-form, re-equip, and re-arm, and to commence a fresh campaign against workers' and peasants' Russia.

We have rejected League of Nations mediation in our war against White Poland and her accomplice Wrangel. But this does not of course mean that we are refusing to continue our negotiations with Britain and other countries, whether members of the League of Nations or not. Our policy of peace remains unaltered. While turning down Lord Curzon's mediation, we are ready at any moment to enter into trading relations with British industrialists and merchants as well as with the capitalists of other countries. In justification of his policy, Lloyd George recently explained to the House of Commons that in Africa, Britain had frequently to trade with cannibals. On this question we have common ground with Lloyd George and his government, inasmuch as we consider that until Europe and America become communist, Soviet Russia must, in the interests of economic development, enter into trading relations with capitalist cannibals. We merely deny them the right to come forward as the saviours of small nations and the peacemakers of civil war. We know them too well to trust them. Let us warn the toiling masses of France, Britain, Poland, and all countries against trusting the incorrigibly greedy, incurably base, and indefatigably criminal bourgeois governments…

* * *

From a report to the Moscow Soviet, 17 August 1920
(*On the Wrangel Front*).

According to all the information we have from various sources, Great Britain has possibly not since the age of Chartism lived through such a period of working-class re-awakening of interests and strivings to action as she does now in connection with the Russo-Polish War and the Russo-Polish peace negotiations. For the notes that are sent us by British diplomacy form but a reflection, a caricatured shadow, a faint image of the profound events and realities which are now taking place in British life. This is first and foremost the influence of the British working class. However much Lloyd George and Curzon might chatter, had there not been a congress in London to which 2,000 delegates from throughout the country had come, not a letter of our replies would have been read.[5]

Given such a serious factor as the will of the awakening British working class, we can say that our diplomatic work has now a great point of support in Great Britain. Some reports say that in France also, where the situation is less promising as regards the state of the labour movement, an upsurge is observable and that the federation of metalworkers' and masons' unions has already backed the British Council of Action, and has proclaimed the necessity for a general strike should France not go to the peace talks. Thus our

---

5   The Trades Union Congress and the Labour Party held a special conference on 9 August which called for the whole industrial power of the working class to be used in the event of a war against the Soviet Union, and for the formation of local Councils of Action. The national Council of Action held a national meeting on 13 August attended by 1,044 delegates from trade unions, local Labour Parties and trades councils.

diplomatic position, which is a result of our military position, has improved because our Red forces stand twelve miles from Warsaw. It is for this reason that Comrade Kamenev's and Comrade Krasin's[6] work in London has turned out so favourably.

* * *

From 'Personal Notes on the Proletariat and Peasantry in the Revolution and the Soviet-Polish War', written in 1920 and first published in *Works*, Vol. 17, Part 2.

Of all the villainies of world imperialism whose full measure has been displayed over recent years, Poland's invasion of our country is still a fact which is exceptional in its enormity.

It is essential that every Russian peasant man and woman knows of all the steps which we have undertaken to avoid the war (report the basic facts). France's role:

1. Her publication of a telegram in March of a purported offensive by us against Poland.
2. The stubborn repetition of these lies until the present time.

Britain's conduct:

1. Supplying ammunition to Poland through an agreement concluded last autumn.
2. Bonar Law's reference in parliament to my letter to French soldiers as grounds for concluding this treaty.

Britain's conduct in relation to Wrangel.

1. Curzon's first note in April.
2. Our immediate agreement.
3. Curzon's prolonged silence and then threat.
4. Alteration of the conditions in the note.
5. A fresh pause.
6. Proposal to send a mediator.

---

6   Lev Kamenev (1883-1936) was the head of the Soviet peace delegation that arrived in London at the beginning of August 1920. He was accompanied by Krasin (1870-1926) and Klyshko. Kamenev, a member of the Politburo, advised Lloyd George of Soviet peace terms for an end to the Polish war. On 11 August Lloyd George sent a telegram to the Polish government urging acceptance of the Soviet terms. But on 16 August the Poles counter-attacked the Red Army outside Warsaw and drove them back, securing more favourable terms.

7. We were all the while constrained.
8. Wrangel's blow.
9. The responsibility for it lies with Curzon.
10. Lloyd George's statement to Krasin.

The bourgeois press had prepared for Poland's offensive by means of lies about an offensive by us. By means of false references to a preparation by us for an offensive, Bonar Law deceives public opinion to justify military aid to Poland.

By means of diplomatic mediation, Curzon is assisting Wrangel to concentrate his forces for a thrust against us.

The Post-War Crisis

From the report to the Third World Congress of the
Communist International on *The World Economic Crisis and the
New Tasks of the Third International*, 23 June 1921.

Let us pass now to Great Britain, the richest and most powerful country
in Europe. During the war we grew accustomed to saying that Britain was
getting rich from the war, that the British bourgeoisie had plunged Europe
into war and was feathering its nest. This was true, but only within certain
limits. Britain made profits in the initial period of the war, but began to
suffer losses in the second period. The impoverishment of Europe, especially
of Central Europe, acted to disrupt trade relations between Britain and the
rest of the continent. In the last analysis, this had to hurt and did hurt
Britain's industry and finances. Moreover, Britain herself was compelled
to shoulder enormous war expenditures. Today Britain is in a state of
decline, and this decline is becoming more and more precipitous. This
fact may be illustrated by industrial and commercial indices which I shall
presently cite, but the fact itself is incontestable and is corroborated by a
whole series of public and wholly official declarations by the most eminent
British bankers and industrialists. During the months of March, April,
and May, the respective British publications carried the annual reports of
corporations, banks, and so on. These authoritative gatherings, where the
leaders of the various enterprises make their reports, assessing the general
state of affairs in the country or in their own particular branch of industry,
provide exceptionally instructive material. I have gathered a whole file of
such reports. All of them bear out one and the same thing: Britain's national

income, i.e., the aggregate income of all her citizens and the state, has
dropped considerably below the pre-war total.

Britain is poorer. The productivity of labour has fallen. Her world trade
for 1920 has, in comparison to the last year before the war, declined by at
least one-third, and in some of the most important branches, even more.
Especially sudden is the change undergone by the coal industry, which used
to be the main branch of the British economy, or more precisely, the root
and trunk on which Britain's entire world economic system rested. For the
coal monopoly was the root of the power, vigour, and prosperity of all other
branches of British industry. Not a trace of this monopoly remains today.
Here are the basic factual data on the state of the British economy. In 1913
Britain's coal industry supplied 287 million tons of coal; in 1920 – 233
million tons, i.e., 20 per cent less. In 1913, the production of iron amounted
to 10.4 million tons; in 1920 – a little more than 8 million tons, i.e., again
20 per cent less. The export of coal in 1913 amounted to 73 million tons; in
1920 – all told only 25 million tons, i.e., one-third of the pre-war total. But
during the current year, 1921, the slump in the coal industry and coal exports
took on absolutely abnormal proportions. In January the coal output was 19
million tons (i.e., below the 1920 monthly average); in February – 17; in
March – 16. And then the general strike erupted and the coal output verged
on nil. For the first five months of 1921 the exports are six times below what
they were for the same period in 1913. Expressed in prices, Britain's entire
export for May of this year is three times below that of May of last year. As
of 1 August 1914, Britain's national debt was £700 million: on 4 June of this
year – £7,709 million, i.e., an elevenfold increase. The budget has swelled
threefold.

If you thumb through the reports of the directories of banks and industrial
enterprises for March and April, you will find that Britain's national income
has declined one-third or one-quarter as against the pre-war period. That is
how matters stand in Britain, the richest country in Europe, a country which
suffered the least from military operations and gained the most from the war
in its initial period.

The most graphic proof of the decline of British economic life lies in the
fact that the British pound sterling is no longer a pound sterling; that is,
it is no longer equivalent to the set of figures which once exercised their
sway everywhere and which are still imprinted on it. Today it is only 76
per cent of what it pretends to be. As against the incumbent sovereign of
the money market – the US dollar – the pound has lost 24 per cent of its

nominal magnitude. What could better characterise the instability of our epoch than the fact that the most stable, absolute, and incontestable thing in the whole world – the British sovereign (in English this word signifies both "pound sterling" and "ruler") – has lost its former position and has become transfigured into a relative magnitude! Considering nowadays in Germany the sphere of philosophy has become activated over relativity – and I refer here to Einstein's philosophy – one ought perhaps to interpret German philosophy as an act of revenge against British economics, inasmuch as the British pound sterling has finally become – relative. Incidentally, it has always been the custom in Germany to reply to economic poverty by exacting revenge in the field of philosophy.

* * *

From the report to the Third World Congress of the Communist International on *The World Economic Crisis and the New Tasks of the Communist International*, 23 June 1921.

The growth of France's influence in Europe, and partly in the world as well, during the past year, is due not to the strengthening of France but to the patent progressive weakening of Britain.

Great Britain has conquered Germany. This was the chief issue settled by the last war. And in essence the war was not a world war but a European war, even though the struggle between the two mightiest European states – Britain and Germany – was resolved with the participation of the forces and resources of the entire world. Britain has conquered Germany. But today, Britain is much weaker in the world market, and generally in the world situation, than she was before the war. The United States has grown at Britain's expense much more than Britain has at the expense of Germany.

America is battering Britain down, first of all by the more rationalised and more progressive character of its industry. The productivity of an American worker is 150 per cent above the productivity of a British worker. In other words, two American workers produce, thanks to a more perfectly equipped industry, as much as five British workers. This fact alone, established by British statistical researches, testifies that Britain is doomed in a struggle with America; and this alone suffices to push Britain towards a war with America, so long as the British fleet maintains its preponderance on the oceans.

American coal is crowding out British coal throughout the world and even in Europe. Yet, Britain's world trade has been based primarily on her export of coal. In addition, oil is now of decisive significance for industry and defence; oil not only runs motor cars, tractors, submarines, aeroplanes, but is greatly superior to coal even for the big ocean liners. Up to 70 per cent of the world's oil is produced within the boundaries of the United States. Consequently, in the event of war, all this oil would be in the hands of Washington. In addition, America holds in her hands Mexican oil, which supplies up to 12 per cent of the world output. True, Americans are accusing Britain of having cornered, outside the United States borders, up to 90 per cent of the world oil sources and of shutting off the Americans from access to them, while American oil fields face exhaustion within the next few years. But all these geological and statistical computations are quite dubious and arbitrary. They are compiled in order so as to justify American pretensions to the oil of Mexico, Mesopotamia, and so on. But were the danger of exhaustion of American oil fields actually to prove real, it would constitute one more reason for speeding up the war between the United States and Britain.

Europe's indebtedness to America is a touchy question. The debts on the whole amount to $18 billion. The United States always has the opportunity of creating the greatest difficulties in the British money market by presenting its demands for payment. As is well known, Britain has even proposed that America cancel British debts, promising in turn to cancel Europe's debt to Britain. Since Britain owes America much more than the continental countries of the Entente owe her, she stands to profit from such a transaction. America has refused. The capitalist Yankees showed no inclination to finance with their own funds Great Britain's preparations for war with the United States.

The alliance between Britain and Japan, which is fighting America for preponderance on the Asiatic continent, has likewise aggravated in the extreme the relations between the United States and Britain.

But most acute in character, in view of all the indicated circumstances, is the question of the Navy. Wilson's Government, upon running up against Britain's opposition in world affairs, launched a gigantic programme of naval construction. Harding's government has taken this programme over from its predecessor, and this programme is being rushed through at top speed. By 1924 the US Navy will not only be far more powerful than that of Britain, but also superior to the British and Japanese fleets put together, if not in tonnage, then in firing power.

What does this mean from the British point of view? It means that by 1924 Britain must either accept the challenge and try to destroy the military, naval, and economic might of the United States by taking advantage of her present superiority, or she must passively become converted into a power of the second or third order, surrendering once and for all domination of the oceans and seas to the United States. Thus the last slaughter of the peoples, which 'settled' in its own way the European question, has for this very reason raised in all its scope the world question, namely: Will Britain or the United States rule the world? The preparations for the new world war are proceeding full speed ahead. The expenditures for the army and the Navy have grown extraordinarily as compared with pre-war times. The British military budget has increased threefold, the American – three and a half times.

The contradictions between Britain and America are being transformed into a process of automatic proliferation, an automatic approach closer and closer to tomorrow's sanguinary conflict. Here we actually are dealing with automatism.

* * *

From *The Theses on the International Situation and the Tasks of the Communist International*, drafted by Trotsky and adopted by the Third World Congress of the Communist International, 4 July 1921.

Economically, the strongest country and the one least damaged by the war in Europe is Britain. Nevertheless, even with regard to this country one cannot say that capitalist equilibrium has been restored after the war. True, thanks to her world organisation and her position as victor, Britain has attained certain *commercial and financial* successes after the war: she has improved her trade balance and has raised the exchange rate of the pound and has recorded a fictitious surplus in her budget. But in the sphere of *industry* Britain has since the war moved backwards not forwards. Both the productivity of labour in Britain and her national income are far below the pre-war levels. The situation of the basic branch of her industry, the coal industry, is getting worse and worse, pulling down all other branches of her economy. The incessant paroxysms caused by strikes are not the cause but the consequence of the decline of the British economy...

The British Empire is today at the peak of its power. It has retained all its old dominions and has acquired new ones. But it is precisely the present moment that reveals that Britain's dominant world position stands in contradiction to her actual economic decline. Germany, with her capitalism incomparably more progressive in respect to technology and organisation, has been crushed by force of arms. But in the person of the United States, which economically subjected both Americas, there has now arisen a triumphant rival, even more menacing than Germany. Thanks to its superior organisation and technology, the productivity of labour in US industry is far above that of Britain. Within the territories of the United States 65-70 per cent of the world's petroleum is being produced, upon which depends the motor industry, tractor production, the Navy, and the air force. Britain's age-old monopoly in the coal market has been completely undermined; America has taken first place; her exports to Europe are increasing ominously. In the field of the merchant navy, America has almost caught up with Britain. The United States is no longer content to put up with Britain's world overseas cable monopoly. In the field of industry Great Britain has gone over to the defensive, and under the pretext of combatting 'unwholesome' German competition is now arming herself with protectionist measures against the United States. Finally, while Britain's Navy, comprising a large number of outdated units, has come to a standstill in its development, the Harding administration has taken over from Wilson's administration the programme of naval construction intended to secure the preponderance of the American flag on the high seas within the next two or three years.

The situation is such that either Britain will be automatically pushed back and, despite her victory over Germany, become a second-rate power, or she will be constrained in the near future to stake in mortal combat with the United States her entire power gained in former years.

That is just the reason why Britain is maintaining her alliance with Japan and is making concessions to France, in order to secure the latter's assistance or at least neutrality. The growth of the international role of the latter country – within the confines of the European continent – during the last year has been caused not by a strengthening of France but by the international weakening of Britain.

Germany's capitulation in May on the question of indemnities signifies, however, a temporary victory for Britain and is the warrant of the further economic disintegration of Central Europe, without at all excluding the occupation of the Ruhr and Upper Silesian basins by France in the immediate future.

* * *

From a speech to the Moscow Soviet, 16 January 1922.

Briand left for Washington hoping for success in a diplomatic game resembling one he had played more than once in the French Parliament. To the proposal to limit land armies, Briand replied in the negative. He pointed out that the Versailles Peace required not the reduction but the strengthening of French armaments. That is correct. France was maintaining with an armed hand the system of slavery and the conjunction of contradictions and ruthless hostility which over the last three years we have been in the habit of calling the Versailles Peace. When it came to the question of naval armaments and their possible limitation, the decomposition of the old Entente became clearly revealed, even to the uninitiated.

France miscalculated, and she miscalculated in that Britain proved more realistic than she expected. Britain had also added up her gold balance, her Navy, shipyards, and so on, and compared them with the United States. She became only too clearly aware that the British pound sterling, which was accustomed to being the ruler of the world money market, had long ago been forced to make a big leap downwards – to a quarter of its pre-war value by comparison with the American dollar. As a result of her calculations, Britain agreed to accept the balancing of her Navy with that of the United States. Thus, after her struggle with Germany for world power and the rule of the universe, and after Versailles, we are now witnesses to Washington. The United States refused to join the so-called League of Nations, which is nothing other than a decorative cloak for Britain's domination over Europe exercised through the intermediary of France's military and political rule on the continent. The United States refused to sign the Versailles Peace or enter the League of Nations. Conscious of the preponderance of her industry and her gold reserve, America appeared at Washington to remake or finish off what in her opinion had not been sufficiently well and sufficiently firmly finished at Versailles. The centre of gravity of the capitalist world edifice was moved from Versailles to Washington. Washington made first and foremost an attempt to calm and pacify the so-called Pacific Ocean, which, however, is fraught with major international storms. There an attempt was made to reach an international agreement based on progressive international disarmament. France, intoxicated with her supposedly unlimited power, was sure that at Washington she would be able to turn the world antagonism between Great Britain and the United States to her advantage and secure a majority for the solution for which she would vote and thus strengthen her domination.

After her struggle and her victory, Britain was no longer the first naval power that she was before the war, and now does not even dare to contemplate her Navy equalling the navies of the two next largest naval powers. At present, the United States Navy is not yet equal to the British, but it will catch up in the near future.

—

Before the work had time to be finished a new location for the same work appeared. This place is beautiful Genoa, and it is supposed that the equilibrium necessary to Europe will be found here.[1] We have been invited there and we may possibly take part in the work of the conference. However, here things are not quite so simple. The great disorder in inter-state relations will come to the surface. Some states will not be too ready to participate in a conference to which Soviet Russia has been invited. And we must state that it will be the hardest of all to turn France on to this new path. It has to be said that Lloyd George has taken up this problem as strenuously and energetically as he had formerly set the counter-revolutionaries against us. It took him a lot of trouble to bend Briand to accept participation in the negotiations, and in reply to Briand's objections he delivered a speech which our ROSTA[2] reported in full. He said in this speech: "France, by holding talks with Turkey in the person of Bouillon, is shaking the eastern robber by the hand; now she turns up her nose (I don't know exactly what word Lloyd George used but the meaning was just that) and refuses to shake the northern robber by the hand." By "northern robbers" Lloyd George means of course you and me. As we do not make a particular issue over etiquette, leaving that to the mandarins of the bourgeois delegations, we are prepared to accept his not very flattering definition. He also said: "When you go to international negotiations then be prepared for the worst and take a bar of disinfected soap with you, because you will have to shake all sorts of hands". He meant the hands of the robbers of the North and East, but, let me add, every other sort too. We have always born this circumstance in mind in our international relations, and we too carry disinfected soap in our pockets on such occasions. How Lloyd George finally convinced Briand is hard to know, but the fact is that the Washington fiasco knocked a large part of France's conceit away, and Briand, on returning to Paris, sensed that France's international position had become much more difficult.

---

1   The Economic and Financial Conference was held in Genoa from 10 April to 11 May 1922. It was attended by all European countries with the object of regularising economic and political relations between Europe and Soviet Russia. It aimed to work out a plan for international economic and political relations between Europe and Soviet Russia and come up with a plan for international economic reconstruction. It had little practical result since the attempts by France with other capitalist powers to penetrate the Soviet economy and obtain repayment of debts incurred under tsarism were unsuccessful.

2   Russian Telegraph Agency, forerunner of TASS.

Anglo-Soviet Relations
1921-1923

From a speech to secretaries of Moscow party cells, 26 November 1920
(*There are No More Fronts*).

The international revolution has not come as soon as we wished; there
remain, if not decades, then more than weeks. It is hard to say how long it
will be before the world revolution comes. Therefore, it cannot be said with
any certainty that no one else will make an attempt to start a war with us.
The place from where a new danger could threaten us is Batumi.[1] A year and
a half ago, negotiations were held with the British over the leasing of Batumi.
It was not leased to her, but Britain could attempt to take it by force. If such
an attempt proved successful, Georgia would turn into a bridgehead where
the remnants of Wrangel's army could be thrown and we would thus have
an abscess in the Caucasus. With all our love of peace we must be prepared
for war. Batumi is not important to us but the Caucasian Front is, and our
diplomacy has stated this clearly; when in turn it inquired of Lord Curzon as
to Britain's intentions with regard to Batumi, he answered with the question
whether we intended to occupy it. What does Curzon's reply mean? The

---

1 Batumi – The principal Black Sea port of Georgia, which was occupied by a British
   force from November 1918 to June 1920, during which time Britain had sought to
   lease it on a long-term basis from Georgia. The British had withdrawn from the rest
   of Transcaucasia (Georgia, Armenia and Azerbaijan) by the end of 1919 and Soviet
   power was established in Baku and Azerbaijan in April 1920, Armenia in November
   1920 and in Georgia in February 1921.

world bourgeoisie was amazed at Wrangel's rapid rout, but after a brief respite found a new slogan for agitation and launched it by spreading rumours about an alleged new assault by us on Georgia.

In the Caucasus generally our position is not altogether favourable. Venizelos'[2] Greece was a tool of the Entente against Turkey; now at the elections Venizelos' party has received a minority and the Germanophile party has come forward. This is more advantageous to us as it will move – even if shyly and uncertainly – against the Entente. Britain and France cannot rely on Turkey in present conditions, but they can promise her Baku; that is, they can settle with her from our account. Thus, it is clear that we have dangers ahead of us in the Caucasus. But we can prepare this front with a small concentration of forces and reinsure ourselves with regard to Batumi and Baku.

* * *

From a speech to the Moscow Soviet, 30 August 1921
(*The Famine and the World Situation*).

What, however, are the possible chances of intervention, and above all what are the possible forms that intervention might take? Independent military action by any of the major European powers is not counted on even by the Russian émigrés. But they do expect of the capitalist governments, and the French especially, active assistance for Russia's lesser adversaries on the one hand, and the presentation of definite demands with regard to aid for the famine on the other.[3]

Let us begin with the latter idea. Its absurdity is quite apparent. Conditions – and in the form of an ultimatum at that – have already been put to us. They were rejected. Then followed the period of interventions and blockades. We stood firm. The capitalist states were compelled by the logic of the situation to open negotiations with us. We went to meet them. A trade agreement with Britain was signed by both sides, in which Lloyd George drew the conclusions from past experience and did not dream of presenting any conditions

---

2   Eleftherios Venizelos (1864-1936) – Greek Prime Minister, 1910-1915, 1917-1920 and 1928-1932; leader of the pro-Entente and anti-German section of the Greek bourgeoisie, who led Greece into the First World War in 1917, having already set up a rival government and forced the King to abdicate.

3   The famine struck in the spring of 1921 as a result of two successive years of drought, aggravated by the devastation wrought by the Civil War. It centred on the important grain-producing Volga region, and inflicted hardship and starvation on some 20 million peasants and workers, as well as severely disrupting the economy.

whatsoever relating to Russia's internal regime.[4] One surely cannot believe that this same Lloyd George would decide to put forward political demands over the question of philanthropic aid? A crazy idea! Even if one were to allow for a moment the impossible, namely that a rabid supporter of Milyukov, Burtsev,[5] and Kuskova[6] took over from Lloyd George and presented political conditions to us, it is quite obvious that this could only end in the greatest discomfiture for him. It is self-evident that we would turn down any talks on such a basis...

* * *

From a speech to the Zhitomir Soviet, 5 September 1921.

The fact that in such a devastated, exhausted, and deeply shaken country as Russia, a famine which gripped tens of millions of people has not brought the Soviet apparatus to a state of complete helplessness; that Soviet power has from the very start begun to make vigorous efforts to ensure the winter sowing of the Volga lands, already achieving the first successes in this direction; that the apparatus continues to work even under such extremely arduous conditions – all this demonstrates to the bourgeoisie, part of which was beginning to realise this even before the famine, that Soviet power is not a passing or temporary phenomenon but a factor to be reckoned with for a definite number of years to come. The British bourgeoisie has evidently understood this fully enough. The British bourgeoisie is, broadly speaking, the most perceptive: it has been said long ago that it thinks in centuries and continents. The British bourgeoisie has forged its might over centuries and grown used to looking a long way ahead, and is led by politicians who concentrate the whole past experience of their class in their consciousness.

Lloyd George said: "It is not a matter of philanthropy but a matter of returning Russia to a state of economic equilibrium and this can be done by establishing a regular economic alliance with Soviet Russia." Lloyd George hopes that regular economic commercial relations will lead us to restore our

---

4   The Anglo-Soviet Trade Agreement had been signed on 16 March 1921 by Krasin and Horne, the Chancellor of the Exchequer. It established official commercial relations between the two countries for the first time.

5   Vladimir Lvovich Burtsev (1862-1942) – Russian revolutionary and journalist; member of Narodnaya Volya in the 1880s; opposed the Bolsheviks in 1917; during the Civil War he supported Kolchak and Denikin.

6   Yekaterina Dmitriyevna Kuskova (1869-1958) – Author of the *Credo*, a manifesto of the revisionist current in the Russian Marxist movement known as Economism; opponent of the Bolsheviks; deported from Russia in 1922.

economy and believes that it is as little possible to bring us down by famine as it was by military intervention. Thus, we have here a seeming paradox. The famine, a profoundly negative fact, has not weakened us internationally but rather strengthened us. The bourgeois newspapers write: "Yes, this power must have living roots, it has withstood the scourge of the famine, we will have to reckon with it, there is no one else who can replace it.'

* * *

From a speech to the 4th All-Russian Congress of the
Russian Communist League of Youth, 21 September 1921.

The European bourgeoisie has at once begun to weigh things up this way and that, in order to determine its orientation. Britain wondered whether she had made a mistake by entering economic relations with us, at a time when the famine could perhaps have laid bare our insolvency and approaching collapse.

Those elements in the ranks of the French bourgeoisie who have had enough of awaiting the long-promised downfall of Soviet power have now obtained a preponderance and have started to insist upon the inevitability of our collapse more stubbornly, together with the need to assist this collapse by military intervention. It has finally emerged that the public opinion of the European bourgeoisie has split into two basic groupings. I do not want to talk about the feelings of the western proletariat and its pressing desire to help us (the proletariat of Europe and America has shown its sympathy as far as its strength permits, by raising money, agitation and so on), because from the standpoint of the international situation it is the policy of the ruling bourgeoisie that has an immediate significance for the moment. So, the orientation of the bourgeoisie has followed two lines. On the one hand, the bourgeoisie – that of Britain, for instance, which Lloyd George represents – has come to realise what has come about and said to itself. "No, this regime is stronger than we thought. If it could endure such a terrible disaster as the famine which struck tens of millions of human beings in such a weakened and exhausted country, and if the state machine did not split at the seams – if Soviet power did not lose its head but concentrated its attention on the very vital tasks of sowing the Volga lands; if it managed in the very first days to gather millions of poods[7] of seed so as to save the Volga peasant economy for the following year, then this regime must have firm roots." The British bourgeoisie is of course hostile to us, but it is perceptive and said to itself that there is in Soviet

---

7   A Russian unit of weight equal to about 16.38 kilograms.

Russia no other force apart from the Communist Party and the working class organised into the state capable of maintaining law and order and assuming the functions of government.

* * *

From a speech to the Moscow Soviet commemorating the
5th anniversary of the February Revolution, 12 March 1922.

Today the telegraph has brought news that the British government has taken a decision not to give aid to our famine-stricken people. This telegram evidently strictly reflects reality: not because Lloyd George had reckoned seriously on the collapse of Soviet power, but because the decision itself was very symptomatic. It means that pre-Genoa hesitations are being experienced and Lloyd George, whose position has become somewhat less stable, in order to insure himself with that section of bourgeois public opinion which opposes an agreement with us, has tossed a bone to those irreconcilable capitalists by a decision which is in itself of course quite 'legal': one cannot force the British government to give relief to the Volga famine.

But on the other hand, this decision when taken in conjunction with commentaries in several semi-official British newspapers, acquires a semi-demonstrative character. One of the papers, the *Daily Chronicle*, says that, I quote, "the refusal of the British government to give relief is caused by the fact that Soviet power still maintains the Red Army..." So, is the British government intending to propose at Genoa disarmament or the reduction of armies? As far as we are concerned, then of course no obstacles need be expected to any measures which will relieve the peoples of the military burden. While preparations go ahead all along the line for new blows against us in the spring, and while the French general staff has presented the Petlyura-ites through its military mission such an 'innocuous' gift as a tank, the British government, to judge from the *Daily Chronicle*, is astonished that we are maintaining the Red Army! Yes, we shall maintain it simply because we well remember (and I started with this) the experience of the conference on the Prinkipo Islands: after the conference on the Prinkipo Islands which was never held, we lived through a dark and hard year.

* * *

From a speech to the 5th All-Russian Congress of the
Russian Communist League of Youth, 11 October 1922
(*The Position of the Republic and the Tasks of Young Workers*).

Today the European bourgeoisie has no certainty as to how events will take shape tomorrow or the day after. It lives from one day to the next.

The economic soil is exhausted while the crisis passes from convulsions to a temporary recovery which gives way to new convulsions. International relations are shaky. Yesterday's allies and the chief ones, Britain and France, more and more oppose each other hostilely on all levels of capitalist relations, and that is why not a single European government is today capable of conducting a policy even to the extent that it could before the last imperialist war, calculated for fifteen, ten, or even five years ahead. All the bourgeois governments live by the impulses of the given moment. They try to plug up and patch up the most crying contradictions, but that is all. And so – from contradiction to contradiction, from conflict to conflict, and moving on from one diplomatic resort to another, they attempt to put off the most acute question. Hence their diplomatic impotence, akin to their previous military impotence. They have mighty armies – and yet they cannot smash us. They have a diplomacy with age-old experience – and yet they are incapable of carrying through to the end with us a single piece of business.

We talk about our retreats. Of course, we have retreated a great deal, but compare our diplomatic platform in February and April of 1919 (I have just read it out to you) with the platform which we came to Genoa with and left there with. At Genoa we said: "Russia will not give herself up, nor sell herself off, Russia is not capitulating to the ultimatum of European world imperialism." And what then? A short time afterwards there turns to us Urquhart,[8] a representative of the leading lights of the stock exchange of Great Britain, a representative of enterprises worth billions in different parts of the world (he used to own many undertakings both in the Urals and in Siberia), and signs a preliminary conditional agreement with Comrade Krasin for a period of ninety-nine years. A long period! I think that few of the youngest comrades here now will see the end of this period.

You might say: if the bourgeoisie is at present unable to look even five or ten years ahead, how is it that Urquhart is looking ninety-nine years ahead? Herein lies the fact that the bourgeoisie, ruling as a class, as a state, must have a plan – who to conclude an alliance with, who is the greater and who the lesser enemy, and it has to foresee how relations will shape in five, ten or

---

8 Leslie Urquhart (1874-1933) – British businessman with extensive interests in the Russian oil and mining industry; expropriated by the Bolsheviks, he threw his weight behind British efforts to overthrow the revolutionary government; when this failed, he reached a compromise with the Soviet government.

fifteen-years' time. But Urquhart is acting as an individual proprietor and nothing more, and his calculations are very simple and very correct in their simplicity. He says: "If we, the Urquharts, i.e., capital, hold on in Britain, in France, and throughout the world, then sooner or later we shall stifle Soviet Russia." And he is right. But if – reasons Urquhart – we capitalists are overthrown both in Britain and in France we shall of course lose our property in the Urals and Siberia too. But the man who loses his head is not going to weep over his hairs. If capital is to be expropriated throughout the world then of course Mr. Urquhart's concession will expire in a shorter period than ninety-nine years. That is why his reckoning is entirely realistic and entirely correct. I do not know whether Comrade Krasin said this to him: "As long as you are a force throughout the world we will not of course expropriate you individually. But if the British worker expropriates you and takes your property into his hands then somehow or other we will come to an agreement with the British worker about this concession." [*Laughter.*] But you will say that nevertheless the Soviet government has renounced this agreement.

Yes, it has unconditionally. Britain's policy does not provide a minimal guarantee for concluding a responsible and major agreement of a type which presupposes the possibility of normal relations between countries. Britain seeks to prevent Turkey establishing an opportunity for her existence within the natural frontiers of the Turkish state. Britain is in effect waging a war against France: Britain acts under the pseudonym of Greece while France in fact provides support for Turkey. The war has brought victory to Turkey with whom we have complete sympathy, for Turkey was fighting for her independence while Greece was carrying out Great Britain's rapacious imperialist plans.

There arose the question of the Black Sea and the Straits. On the Black Sea exist states which form part of our federation, in addition Turkey, Bulgaria and Romania. Yet Britain wants to settle the question of the Black Sea jointly with France and Italy, but without the participation of the countries for whom the Black Sea forms an internal sea and its shores the doorstep of their house. In these conditions, where Britain tramples on the elementary rights and interests of the peoples of our federation, the Soviet government did not consider it possible to sign an agreement with a British citizen: fulfilling an agreement, let me repeat, presupposes a minimum of loyal relations between countries and governments.

* * *

From the report to the Fourth World Congress of the
Communist International on *The New Economic Policy and the
Perspectives for World Revolution*, 14 November 1922.

So far as concessions are concerned today, Comrade Lenin has here remarked: "Discussions are plentiful, concessions are scarce." [*Laughter.*] How to explain this? Precisely by the fact that there is not, and there will not be, any capitulation to capitalism on our part. To be sure, those who favour the resumption of relations with Soviet Russia have more than once contended and written that world capitalism, in the throes of its greatest crisis, is in need of Soviet Russia; Britain needs an outlet for her goods in Russia, Germany needs Russian grain, and so forth and so on. This seems perfectly true, if one surveys the world through pacifist spectacles, that is, from the standpoint of "plain horse sense" which is invariably quite pacifistic. [*Laughter.*] And that is why it is invariably bamboozled. One would then imagine that the British capitalists would try with might and main to invest their funds in Russia; one would then imagine that the French bourgeoisie would orient German technology in this same direction so as to create new sources whereby German reparations could be paid. But we see nothing of the sort. Why not? Because we are living in an epoch when the capitalist equilibrium has been completely upset; because we live in an epoch when economic, political, and military crises instantly criss-cross; an epoch of instability, uncertainty, and unremitting alarm. This militates against the bourgeoisie conducting any long-range policy, because such a policy immediately becomes transformed into an equation with too many unknowns. We finally succeeded in concluding a trade agreement with Britain. But this happened a year and half ago. In reality, all our transactions with Britain are still on a cash-and-carry basis – we pay with gold, and the question of concessions is still in the phase of discussion.

If the European bourgeoisie and above all the British bourgeoisie believed that large-scale collaboration with Russia would bring about *immediately* a serious improvement in Europe's economic situation, then Lloyd George and Co. would undoubtedly have brought matters in Genoa to a different conclusion. But they are aware that collaboration with Russia cannot *immediately* bring any major and drastic changes. The Russian market will not eliminate British unemployment within a few weeks or even months. Russia can be integrated only gradually, as a constantly increasing factor, into Europe's and the world's economic life. Because of her vast extent, her natural resources, her large population, and especially because of the stimulus imparted by her Revolution, Russia can become the most important economic force in Europe and in the world, but not instantaneously, not overnight, but only over a period of years. Russia could become a major buyer and supplier provided she were given credits today and, consequently, enabled to accelerate her economic growth. Within five or ten years she could become a major market for Britain. But in the latter event, the British government would have to believe that it could last ten years and that British capitalism would be strong enough ten years hence to retain the Russian market. In other words, a policy of genuine economic collaboration with Russia can only be a policy based on very broad foundations. But the whole point is that the post-war bourgeoisie is no longer capable of conducting long-range policies. It doesn't know what the next day will bring and, still less, what will happen on the day after tomorrow. This is one of the symptoms of the bourgeoisie's historical demise.

To be sure, this seems to be in contradiction with Leslie Urquhart's attempt to conclude an agreement with us for not less than ninety-nine years. But this contradiction is truly only an apparent one. Urquhart's motivation is quite simple and, in its own way, unassailable; should capitalism survive in Britain and throughout the world for the next ninety-nine years then Urquhart will keep his concessions in Russia too! But what if the proletarian revolution erupts not ninety-nine years or even nine years from now but much earlier? What then? In that case, naturally, Russia would be the last place where the expropriated proprietors of the world could retain their property. But a man who is about to lose his head, has little cause to shed tears over his mop of hair.

* * *

From a speech at the Red Square Parade, Moscow, 1 May 1923.

Take a look at Britain. The conservative wing of capital is triumphant there. Having suppressed Ireland and stained her with blood while pursuing her age-old oppression in India, Britain is at this moment in Lausanne, attempting for a second time to bend and bring our friend Turkey to her knees.[9] Under the pretext of a bogus freedom of the seas, Britain is demanding access to the

---

9 The Turkish Provisional Government, established at Ankara in 1920 under the leadership of Mustapha Kemal (1881-1938), refused to accept the Sèvres peace treaty between Ottoman Turkey and the Entente, and negotiated the less harsh Lausanne Treaty of July 1923. This allowed Kemal's Turkish Republic to retain Eastern Thrace (European Turkey), Izmir and Armenia, which were to be surrendered under the terms of Sèvres. Nevertheless, Britain still secured the 'demilitarisation' of the Bosporus and the Dardanelles as stipulated by the Sèvres Treaty.

shores of the Black Sea so as to keep them under the threat of her long-range artillery. What is more, Britain is busy fishing off our shores but depicts our attempt to protect our country's vital economic interests as an assault on her interests. If that were not enough, Britain is also attempting to interfere in our internal life. She has the audacity to dictate to us on whom we should pass judgement and whom we should pardon. But let us who are gathered here on this May Day with our ranks closed say to everyone: hands off! We workers and peasants, and working and peasant women, are the masters here and we well know on whom to pass judgement and whom to pardon.

* * *

From a report to the Moscow Provincial Congress of Metalworkers,
5 June 1923.

At the Hague, several weeks after Genoa, respect towards our diplomacy had already diminished somewhat. After Genoa (which as you remember finished with nothing) our international situation (I am speaking all the while about the official situation, that is, about relations with bourgeois governments) began increasingly to deteriorate. Lord Curzon was by this time already counting on a new period of economic growth in Britain and throughout the world. By the laws of natural development, an economic crisis is usually succeeded by economic growth. At present economic advance in Europe has by no means reached pre-war levels, but the number of unemployed in Britain has nevertheless dropped sharply. In France it had not been great in the first place, while in America after an enormous crisis we can observe a general boom. During the past year, very many major American trusts have on their own initiative raised wages so as to paralyse any strike movement in advance.

You will probably ask how our gracious correspondence with Lord Curzon will end.[10] Comrades, I must admit in all conscience that I do not know and I am greatly afraid that at this moment Lord Curzon does not know either. He began at a time when, as I have said, it seemed that one push would be enough to bring us down. Seven weeks passed and nothing came down. He gave us a ten-day time limit then he added a few more days until Wednesday, and finally by the Wednesday, on the thirteenth or fourteenth day, he wrote

---

10 On 8 May 1923 the British Foreign Secretary, Curzon, sent an ultimatum to the Soviet government threatening to break off economic and diplomatic relations unless the Soviet Union relinquished its twelve-mile fishing limit; ceased anti-imperialist propaganda in Persia, Afghanistan and India; and paid compensation for two British agents captured in Russia sometime previously.

a new note, and in this latter note he asked us to reply as soon as possible and once and for all, but this time he did not set a time limit. It is to be hoped that our diplomacy will not abuse the patience of the very good Lord Curzon and reply at the first opportunity. But what will Lord Curzon answer to that? He was a minister in the Bonar Law government, and the attempts to topple the Soviet government began under Bonar Law. But Bonar Law himself toppled first: between the two notes a change of government took place. It is said that the new one has a more conciliatory attitude towards us – I cannot take any responsibility for this report – that is what they say.[11] So that the situation is that we are, as it were, sitting in a lottery and the number to be drawn is unknown: this best typifies the international situation and diplomatic activity and also the policy of the bourgeoisie, for it can pursue no consistent line and cannot predict the next day as it does not follow logically from the present. If we presume the worst, then a break in relations would of course be a serious blow to us, yet a blow we could survive.

* * *

From a report to the 6th All-Russian Congress of Metalworkers,
16 June 1923.

The ultimatum of ten days (by Lord Curzon's calendar) is an ultimatum which was presented on 8 May. Today is 16 June, I believe; that is, the same amount of time has passed that the flood lasted according to the Bible, and the matter has still not been finally settled.

What, however, is the explanation for this ultimatum – which is a little imprecise with its time-limits – and what explains the great compliance shown by us in our reply to this ultimatum?

Here is has to be said clearly and distinctly: Britain – and of course I am speaking of ruling, bourgeois Britain – is remaining true to her traditional policy in this ultimatum. She regards her present struggle against us as in a certain sense the continuation of an overall struggle against Russia as a whole.

But what forms the fundamental line of British policy today? One should not forget that leading Great Britain is the most experienced bourgeoisie. Not that every one of its Curzons is a Solomon – that cannot be said at all – but all the Curzons have together accumulated over the centuries the collective wisdom, the collective experience and the collective treachery of the British

---

11 Bonar Law had resigned through ill health on 20 May 1923 and was succeeded
   by Baldwin rather than Curzon, who led the extreme right anti-Soviet wing of the
   Conservative Party.

ruling classes. The essence of Britain's policy has always consisted of setting one stronger state against another weaker one and then staying on one side, and offering up prayers to the Lord of imperialism. This has been Britain's traditional policy over a period of centuries.

Britain was likewise deeply hostile to tsarist Russia. Britain is an ocean of water while Russia is an ocean of land which joins Europe to Asia. Britain strove to encircle every continent with the necklace of its ocean, but in Asia she always came into conflict with the rapacious imperialist ambitions of Russian tsarism. During the Crimean War in 1855, Britain rallied to the side of Russia's enemies. During the Russo-Turkish War in 1878, Britain was again on the side of Russia's enemies. During the Russo-Japanese War Britain was on Japan's side. Only in 1907, after the first Russian Revolution, did Britain's policy change. Considering Russia to have been sufficiently weakened by her unsuccessful war with Japan, by the Revolution, and by internal disorder and so on, Britain concluded the Anglo-Russian agreement on the Persian question which formed the prelude to an Anglo-Russian alliance.

On the eve of the imperialist war Britain hesitated. Comrades, when the British proletariat opens all the steel archives of British diplomacy (if those sly devils don't destroy them) it will find conclusive proof that Great Britain wanted the imperialist war more than all the other states. If on 1 August Britain had said that she would go to war, then neither Germany nor Austria-Hungary would have been dragged into the war but would have given way. If Britain had said that she would not go to war, then neither Russia nor France would have begun to fight but would have come to an agreement. On the eve of the war Britain took a provocative stance, and thus brought the war down on to the European continent. The same thing in relation to the Ruhr.[12] If Britain had not wanted France to get bogged down in the Ruhr, thereby weakening herself and exhausting Germany, then there would not have been a Ruhr story. Britain provoked it, Britain wanted it, and now she stands on the side and watches, awaiting the moment for her intervention. Remaining aside and having the fire banked with the hands of others: that is the essence of the policy of the British bourgeoisie, the most treacherous in the world.

Remember the policy of Britain during the period of the interventions and blockades. All these facts are so fresh in our memories that I shall not

---

12 On 11 January 1923 French and Belgian troops marched into Germany's Ruhr industrial region when the latter failed to maintain her reparation payments to France. No other Entente country supported this action.

enumerate them, although I will not conceal from you that as soon as I received the ultimatum, I instructed our war department here to compile a short list of what official Britain did to us during the first three years of interventions and blockades. In particular let me recall that during the imperialist war Russia lost 3,080,000 men but Britain lost 455,000 – that is, six times less than Russia. In order that Lord Curzon might at the present moment consider himself powerful enough to present us with a ten-day ultimatum, the blood of over three million Russian workers and peasants had to be spilt for the glory of British imperialism. We shall present this account one day to the British bourgeoisie. After Britain's victory had been assured by the death of over three million Russian peasants and workers, Britain inaugurated an era of interventions and blockades. The same policy both on a large and a small scale. Britain was not at war with us, but she did have her expeditionary units at Archangel and Murmansk. For what purpose? To mobilise Russian peasants and workers there in support of the White Guards, and to force them to fight the Red peasants and workers. In the North, in the Archangel-Murmansk region, during the occupation Britain lost no more than ten to fifteen men, but she shot hundreds. British counter-intelligence there had its own favourite method: those whom it had any suspicion of being unsympathetic to the Russian bourgeoisie it simply dropped through the ice.

Now Britain is demanding compensation from us for two British citizens – a male and a female. They were occupied here on the most innocent matters: engaging in espionage, helping to blow up railways, assassinate Soviet public figures and so on. One of them suffered for it – he was shot (but this is a spy's occupational hazard) while the other was put in prison. Now we have to pay out 30,000 [roubles] in gold for the lady and 70,000 as a pension to the dependants of the worthy gentleman. We must acknowledge Lord Curzon's extreme moderation, for he is not demanding pensions in the case of the fifteen or thirty British who died in our North.

Two words about Britain's role in the Caucasus. We still remember the story of the shooting down at a remote station of the twenty-six Bolsheviks who had been brought from Baku (they have gone down in history as the twenty-six Baku Commissars):[13] this was carried out in accordance with the instructions of the British officer Teague-Jones and with the agreement of the British General Thompson. One day we shall

---

13 This is a reference to twenty-six leaders of the Baku Commune executed without trial by the British occupation forces on 20 September 1918.

demand pensions and damages for our twenty-six Baku comrades, of whom Comrade Shaumyan was an old revolutionary and a member of the Central Committee of our party.

There you have a schematic picture of Great Britain's role in the imperialist and civil wars. Then a turn followed and we had a trade agreement with them. Why? Under the pressure of a most severe crisis and the search for a solution to it. 3 million unemployed put a colossal burden on the British budget, and Lloyd George had hoped first to aid the unemployed, and secondly to be the first to go into Russia and reorganise her with the aid of British capital – that is, economically shackle her and convert her into a colony. About two years of this trading policy have passed. What have they revealed? Above all that, economically speaking, we are developing more slowly than the impatient profiteers of the City would have liked, and not along the line they had imagined. They had reckoned that the NEP was a capitulation by the Russian proletariat in the field of economic construction, but in actual fact it was not. On the other hand, Britain's economic situation has improved and Anglo-Russian economic relations are at the present moment not such a major factor in Great Britain's general balance of trade…

Nor have the Conservatives in Britain been elected for all time. The Labour Party – that is, British Menshevism – the British Liberals, and the Independents, in short everything needed to produce a British Kerenskyism or Milyukovism, all this has to replace the Conservatives whose right wing is formed by Lord Curzon's group. This will be in a year or two. There can be no doubt that a victory of the Left Bloc[14] in France will automatically bring about a strengthening of the reformist, Menshevik position in Britain.

In the year that remains before such changes, the extreme Conservative wing of the bourgeoisie will make an attempt to exploit a fascist war against Soviet Russia, which even today presents of course a fundamental danger in the eyes of the world bourgeoisie – and especially that of Britain. What did Lord Curzon's task consist of when he presented us with an ultimatum? He hoped that in reply we would make a move which could be interpreted as a slap in the eye for the British government, and which would offend the public opinion of all the British philistines and narrow-minded petty-bourgeois, including both the philistines and the narrow-minded people of the British Labour Party – and their proportion is said to be pretty high. But we spotted this artless trap.

---

14 The Left Bloc or *Cartel des Gauches* was an electoral alliance between the French Radical Socialists (liberals) under Herriot and the Socialists under Blum. It came to power at the 1924 elections and formed a coalition government.

We had to force the philistines to understand how we saw things here, and because their skulls are made of a material which takes a long time to penetrate, the ten-day time limit which Lord Curzon gave us was insufficient. That, comrades, is the explanation of our policy. Our job was to say: Lord Curzon is displaying magnanimity but we will display even more magnanimity; Lord Curzon is peaceably disposed but we are disposed even more peaceably; he does not want war but we trebly do not want it. That is the meaning of our reply.

Thus, we engaged in diplomatic preparation, explained our position, and managed to hammer something into them. The first formal result lies in the fact there will apparently be no rupture of relations; but I regard this result as minor because, given the nature of Lord Curzon – and his nature merely reflects the nature of the ruling groups of the British bourgeoisie – there can be no stability in our relations with Great Britain. Judge for yourself: during the intervention we shot a British spy and forgot about it long ago. The trade agreement was signed after this. Now they declare to us: pay up the cash or we shall break off trade relations with you. Well, comrades, this is monstrous evidence of the fact that this clever, experienced British bourgeoisie has bad nerves, threatening us now with every kind of extortion and demand. It will go on doing so in the future. Therefore, the current situation for us does not contain any great guarantees as regards stability.

The caution which we manifested on this question had good educational effects. It thwarted the schemes of the bourgeoisie for the present. But in no event can we have a complete peace, primarily because, as I have said, there remains an unstable situation in Europe, and moreover a gigantic revolutionary process in the East which worries Britain particularly.

Of course, the main point of the ultimatum was, in Curzon's own definition, the so-called propaganda in the East. Curzon's demand for ending propaganda in the East is, according to analyses by the more perceptive bourgeois journalists, an empty demand by its very nature, for it is not a question of this or that Soviet citizen turning up there or even occupying an official position and in this or that statement violating Britain's right to exploit and plunder the peoples of the East, but of our country, as long as it behaves correctly on the national question, presenting the greatest mortal threat to any colonial might and especially the British.

That is why Britain most of all is disturbed by the resolutions of our 12th Party Congress on the national question. We developed and refined our national policy and are adopting serious measures to implement all aspects of it, and especially in such countries of the Soviet Union as Turkestan and Azerbaijan where it has a great demonstrative importance for the East…

* * *

From a speech to party, trade union,
Young Communist, and other organisations of the
Krasnaya Presnya district (Moscow), 25 June 1923.

Comrades! Our most recent history begins with Lord Curzon's ultimatum, so allow me to start with this historic fact.

Comrades, you will remember the contents of the ultimatum and you will remember that the history dragged on not for ten days but forty-one or forty-two days, and you will remember than on some very substantial points we gave way, but on some other likewise very substantial ones we did not give way. In order to draw a balance, let us recall what exactly we conceded to Lord Curzon. In the first place we withdrew Comrade Weinstein's letter[15] which had not been written quite in total accordance with the textbook of etiquette. Secondly, on the question of fishing in the three or twelve-mile limit, we paid a due of respect to the long-range naval artillery of Great Britain and recognised her right to catch fish in the murky water beyond the three-mile limit. We paid out 100,000 roubles cash down. On the question of propaganda, we undertook with a clear conscience to do against Britain nothing worse than what she might do against us on the principle of the complete equality of the parties and I have no doubt, and nor will you, that our word is firm – we may not answer for tsarist treaties but we fulfil our own in earnest.

On the question of recalling our two representatives, Comrade Raskolnikov[16] from Afghanistan and Comrade Shumyatsky[17] from Persia, we answered with a refusal. In his last note, or memorandum, Lord Curzon portrays matters as though we would still recall Raskolnikov for reasons of internal business or something of that nature. This was an obscure passage. Anyway, we have not given anyone any commitments to this effect. If it is a matter of internal business it is of concern only to the Soviet government and no one else. As regards Shumyatsky, Lord Curzon proposed to leave him

---

15 As head of the Foreign Commissariat's Anglo-American section, Gregory Weinstein formulated a rather undiplomatic reply to a British protest note in 1923, which prompted Curzon to issue the so-called 'Curzon ultimatum'.

16 Fedor Raskolnikov (1892-1939) – Russian revolutionary, joined the Bolsheviks in 1910; leader of the Kronstadt sailors in 1917.

17 Boris Shumyatsky (1886-1938) – Russian revolutionary active since 1903; represented Soviet interests in Iran 1923-25.

in Persia after having given him a severe reprimand. We accept this on the condition that a similar reprimand be given to the representative of Great Britain over there, and I can assure you, comrades, that he does need a little reprimanding.

That is the formal balance. On some substantial points we gave way, without any joy on our part, and on others we refused and the agreement was preserved. But if you try to draw up not a formal, diplomatic balance but a political balance, and ask yourself: as a result of this attempt to seize us by the throat with a ten-day ultimatum, did we become weaker or stronger? Then I believe, comrades, that without bragging we can say we have become stronger. Not because we showed any finesse or diplomatic wisdom, but simply because the ten-day ultimatum not only failed to produce a capitulation from our side, but turned into just over forty days of negotiations which led to concessions, and it all boiled down to a rotten compromise between mighty Great Britain and the Soviet Union...

The British and French bourgeoisies are today ruling through their extreme right wing, but they feel it necessary to reform and reconstruct themselves. In France a shift towards the Left Bloc, and in Britain to the Labour Party, would almost inevitably signify recognition of the Soviet Union, and consequently the liquidation of our revolution recedes into the misty distance. But if this is so, the Fascists and Fochists (after our friend, General Foch), i.e., two parties which have identical feelings towards us, will argue: why, in the period still remaining, while imperialism has not yet spent all its energies (in Italy the Fascists have just triumphed and a coup has taken place in Bulgaria), why can't we have a go at overthrowing Soviet Russia?

There, comrades, is the basic reason for Lord Curzon's attempt to put us on our knees (and if possible, to lay us out on the floor), by his ultimatum. We know of course that today, Lord Curzon cannot send a single expeditionary corps or a single British regiment to Archangel, the Murmansk, or Odessa. Such an act would provoke the deepest indignation of the proletarian masses in Britain, and the Labour Party on coming to power would be forced to respond to such indignation. Lord Curzon was banking on his ultimatum inciting some other country against us. He was counting on our close neighbours. Let us name them: Romania and Poland...

That, comrades, is what explains the Curzon ultimatum and the failure of the ultimatum. But if we digress from diplomacy – from the withdrawal of the letters, and from the 100,000 pieces of silver, which is after all a sum which even our modest budget can manage somehow – if we digress and weigh up the political result then you get this picture: the most powerful imperialist state in Europe had tolerated us, but finally presented us with an ultimatum hoping thereby to bring matters to a decisive conclusion. During the course of this ultimatum the government in Britain changed, while even within the government there was a conflict over it. The business dragged on and ended up with us paying 100,000 roubles for two agents and we forwent what in the language of bourgeois diplomacy is called 'prestige', but as our concept of prestige does not quite coincide with Lord Curzon's we set a different price on this imponderable quantity. We have become stronger and more powerful, and this is emphasised most sharply by the fact that we have undertaken negotiations, for the time being of a preliminary nature, with Japan, that mighty imperialist power in the Far East which, though linked with the Entente and linked with Great Britain, agreed to negotiations in the very same period as the Curzon ultimatum...

The Revolutionary Crisis in Germany

From a report to the 8th All-Russian Congress of the
Communications Union, 20 October 1923.

I said that Britain might intervene. But on this score, one must at once clearly
understand Britain's impotence on the continent of Europe. It is important
to understand this not only for the German revolution[1] but also for ourselves:
Britain is impotent on the continent of Europe. The more clearly we understand
this and the more forcefully and distinctly we repeat it, the more useful it will

---

1 On 12 October 1923, amid economic collapse and revolutionary upsurge by the
working class throughout Germany, the Communist Party joined the social-
democratic governments of the states of Saxony and Thuringia, partly in order to
have access to state arsenals to arm the workers. On 21 October a conference of
workers' organisations was called at Chemnitz to organise a general strike against
the impending invasion of Saxony by the Reichswehr. The proposal was defeated by
the social-democrats and Brandler, the leader of the Communists, called off hastily
made plans for a workers' insurrection by armed detachments throughout Germany.
On 24 October, Reichswehr units under General Müller entered Dresden, the
capital of Saxony, and deposed the state government and disarmed the communist
workers' detachments. The fatal nature of the vacillation and indecisiveness of the
immature Communist Party, the responsibility of the Comintern leadership, and
the need to draw the lessons of the Russian Revolution, are discussed by Trotsky in
Lessons of October, which effectively opened the battle with Stalin through the 'literary
discussion' it initiated.

be for our international policy, in the sense that Britain will brandish her threats and ultimatums around less. In point of fact Britain is a purely maritime state. She has played an enormous role in Europe. But how and when? Whenever there were two countries in Europe fighting each other for mastery. When France was fighting Germany with approximately equal forces, Britain stood behind their back, supporting over a long period first one, and then the other. This had been so even earlier when Spain was strong; she would in this way first assist her and then weaken her. Britain has been playing such a role for many centuries now. She uses the struggle between the two major European states and supports the slightly weaker one with money, technical assistance, and materials against the stronger one. And the European balance depends on Britain. She, as it were, gets a lot of fun for little cost. That is her age-old policy. Why did Britain intervene in the war in 1914? Because Germany had become too strong. Germany had here become so strong that Britain could not achieve a balance just by giving assistance to France. So Britain had to depart from her traditional policy. Now she had to roll up her sleeves and get involved in a war and a struggle. She managed this by mobilising quite a large number of British workers and throwing them onto the European continent. Consequently, she supported France so strongly that the latter finally crushed Germany. So now the hegemony in bourgeois Europe belongs exclusively to France. Germany is prostrate at France's feet and France does not wish even to talk to Germany about the terms of Germany's capitulation. But from the very moment that France had obtained complete hegemony and complete mastery, Britain was rendered completely impotent. France declared: "I will take the Ruhr." Britain replied: "That is not to my benefit." They had a big row which went on a long time. Why was it not to Britain's benefit? Because she needed to raise Germany up a little against France so as to restore the equilibrium. So what did France do? Curzon's protests notwithstanding, France went into the Ruhr and took the Ruhr. And what did terrible Britain do? She resigned herself. Terrible Britain threatened Turkey, and the Turks who enjoy good-neighbourly relations with us organised an army, and not without our assistance.

What did Britain do? She counterposed the Greeks to them. She had absolutely no forces of her own. What did the Turks do? They smashed the Greeks and marched to Constantinople against the terrible Britain who had packed up and left Constantinople.

Comrades, from the standpoint of international relations this is a most important fact of the epoch in which we are living. On the European continent Britain is impotent. Of course, we are not complaining about this.

What can Britain do to the German revolution? Deliver an ultimatum? But this would be inadequate. In fact, the question can be reduced to France's conduct, not Britain's. Thus, if France decides to intervene then Britain could be useful to France by assisting her with the money that she needs, by blockading German ports and shipping and so on. Britain's role has been one of a quartermaster and pirate. But the decisive role in an occupation of Germany would belong to France and her land-based vassals Belgium, Poland, and Czechoslovakia...

* * *

From a report to a conference of political workers in the
Red Army and Navy, 21 October 1923.

But the German revolution will not be decided by the inner relation of forces alone. Germany is situated in a capitalist encirclement and a victorious German revolution would have to leap out of it. This encirclement is formed principally out of France, Belgium, across the Channel Britain, Poland, and Czechoslovakia. These are the decisive states. There are in addition Austria, Switzerland, Holland. They will not play an active part, but of course if the big neighbours decide to follow a policy of suffocation then the little ones will be able to help by pulling the ends of the rope. But we must take account of the conduct of the chief imperialist states. Let us start with Britain. Yesterday, I was speaking to the metalworkers about this, and let me say again now that Britain is today powerless on the continent. Britain delivered an ultimatum to us and we made this or that concession not because she could have routed us, but because we were interested in maintaining our economic relations. This powerlessness of Britain appears to contradict the conception of her as an extremely rich country, a strong maritime power with her Stock Exchange, her City, and her Navy, although in this latter respect she has a great rival in the shape of the United States. But Britain was strong on the continent only so long as there were two equally matched land powers fighting in Europe. Britain always supported the weaker against the stronger. If the weaker outgrew the stronger then Britain would change her sympathies. By adding her weight to the scale pan of Europe's destiny she would thereby decide it. By intervening directly in the 1914 war she broke violently with her own traditions and put a big army on the continent because Germany had too far outgrown France. You know that the patriotic British trade unions have always maintained pacifist ideas, at least with regard to land wars, for their leaders were more inclined to live off their fatherland than to die for it. These pacifists only supported their government with great reluctance.

During the war, Britain helped France too energetically and France emerged the hegemon (the master of the situation) in Europe. Now whenever Britain attempts to intervene in European affairs, France doesn't give a damn. We can see this in the case of the Ruhr. British diplomacy first protested, and then gave in. An even more striking case was her policy in relation to Turkey. Britain declared Turkey to be an enemy of the human race. So what resulted? When Turkey (I mean Ankara) began to get to her feet, what could Britain do? She counterposed Greece to her. Turkey smashed Greece. In the end, Britain left Constantinople and the Turks entered. Britain's impotence on the continent was obvious.

Naturally, the most avowed enemy of the German revolution will be none other than the British bourgeoisie. She has more than once previously formed a coalition against revolution, as for instance at the end of the eighteenth century and the beginning of the nineteenth century. But Britain's arms are short. She is not a land power. She could only support France, if the latter took the path of intervention, by blockading German ports and delivering supplies and so on to the occupying armies.

The Foreign Policy of the First Labour Government

From a speech to the Baku Soviet, 14 April 1924.

Of course we cannot demand much from MacDonald: he is not a Bolshevik, he cannot take the bourgeoisie by the throat, he cannot take its banks. But in Britain, in democratic, advanced, cultured Britain, there exists to this day a monarchy. Couldn't we at least demand from MacDonald as a leader of the Second International and a most influential Menshevik, that on coming to power he would take a broom and sweep the cobwebs out of his monarchy? But it seems that the Second International wages a struggle for democracy only as long as this struggle is directed against the dictatorship of the working class. But when it is a matter of sweeping out the old medieval trash and garbage, democracy ceases to be important.

In spite of his repeated declarations against war and his accusations that we are resorting to violence, upon taking power in his hands MacDonald embarked on the construction of five new cruisers. A tank-building programme is in full swing. The air force is developing rapidly. Yet if MacDonald had devoted himself to abolishing the monarchy, abolishing the House of Lords, and halting the construction of cruisers, he would make a great saving of millions of pounds which could be used for schools, workers' housing, unemployment benefit, and so on...

Imagine, comrades, the talks that are to be held in London. What will our representatives say? Obviously, they will talk about the riches of the USSR, the surplus of raw materials that we have, raw materials so vital to the British people. In Britain there is technical equipment and enormous capital funds. Our delegates will therefore propose the following agreement to the British: "Give us capital and we will pay for this with our raw materials, our natural resources – in ten years we shall both be ten to twenty times richer."

Of course, we would be able to come to an agreement with the British workers if there were people in the British government with backbone, character and will, who were not afraid of the bellowing of the British bourgeoisie. Given these conditions we could conclude an excellent agreement with a British Labour government, and British workers would have good cheap bread, and the peasants of Russia, Transcaucasia, and Azerbaijan would have British machinery, manufactures, and technical resources for the development of our handicrafts, industry, and so on. Such an alliance would not be in any way unrealistic, but is hampered by the fact that there is not a strong Communist Party in Britain.

Under the sway of the British Labour government are millions of oppressed Indians and Egyptians. The duty of an honest revolutionary party is to give the oppressed the right to self-determination. Does MacDonald do so? No. Through his administrators he is conducting a struggle against revolutionaries in India and thus his name has become one of the most hated to the colonial working masses.

What demands will MacDonald present? Curzon stated in the House of Lords that Britain's recognition of the USSR would be a mistake unless Britain received her old debts from us. But these debts are £130 million for pre-war debts, £500 million for war debts and I think £150 or £180 million due to individual British citizens who suffered during the October revolution. I managed somehow to add up these figures and they come to about 10,000 million gold roubles.

We will completely refuse the demands of the British moneylenders for the settlement of old debts by the USSR. A business-like economic link with Great Britain must begin with a clean slate and the past has to be buried. If Britain demands compensation for the murder of the two spies, then we should present a counter-claim for the murder of the twenty-six Baku Commissars and for the destruction of our towns and villages carried out with the aid of British gold. We will not repay old debts, incurred before us. As early as 1905 we warned through the St. Petersburg Soviet of Workers' Deputies that we would not repay tsarist debts. But if we received a loan from Britain signed by representatives of the trade unions of the USSR, then of course we shall repay these loans in full, for the prestige and honour of our workers' and peasants' country is very dear to us.

We need not speak about the firmness of MacDonald's position, for his party has compromised itself sufficiently in the eyes of the British workers: this will provide a powerful impulse to the development and growth of the Communist Party in Britain.

* * *

From an interview with a representative of the
International News Service, 18 April 1924.

You ask whether the British press is correct to regard my Tbilisi speech[1] as an attack on Britain, or rather on MacDonald. I do not know what you mean by an attack. MacDonald has repeatedly attacked the Soviet system and the tactics of the Communist Party. Only recently MacDonald stated as one of the leaders of the Second International that he had fought Moscow and had beaten Moscow. We reserve the same right of criticism of MacDonald's policy as he reserves in regard to us.

It is well known that MacDonald and his party made bitter accusations against us over our policy in regard to Georgia. I have just returned from that country and I greatly regret that MacDonald is, in view of his past, deprived of the opportunity of visiting Georgia to be convinced on the spot of the mood of the workers and peasants. I doubt whether the mood of the workers and peasants of India or Egypt can be set alongside that reigning in Georgia and Azerbaijan. I permitted myself to express this view in Tbilisi and in Baku.[2]

MacDonald has on various occasions sharply censured us for violating the methods of formal democracy. As a matter of fact, we set the rule of the working class above formal democracy. But it did seem that we were right to expect that MacDonald and his party would set precisely such a democracy above all else. In our conception, the existence of a monarchy and a House of Lords contradicts democracy. Although the real rule of the toilers is for us higher than formal democracy, we do consider formal democracy a step forward in comparison with the monarchy and the aristocracy. This too I permitted myself to observe in both speeches, in Tbilisi and Baku.

Allow me to put another question: does MacDonald's criticism of the Soviet system and communist policy signify hostility to our Union?

---

1 See p. 196 of the present edition.

2 Ibid., p. 141.

The tempo and the forms in which the conflict between the Third and the Second Internationals will be resolved is a great historical question. I think that Mr. MacDonald is somewhat mistaken to say that he has beaten Moscow. He has beaten a great deal if he has beaten this last-born child. But I do not at all see why extremely serious and long-standing disagreements over the Soviet system, the revolutionary dictatorship, the British monarchy and the Church need prevent us establishing broad economic links of equal benefit to either side.

* * *

From a speech on the 5th anniversary of
The Communist Young Workers Home, 29 April 1924
(*Young People, Study Politics!*).

Certainly, our situation would be ten times, 100 times easier if in Britain there was a revolutionary workers' government. It would grant us, on the basis of a comradely business-like agreement, a very substantial credit. We should be immediately able to increase our production, flood the market with all kinds of goods for the peasants' use, and in five years raise the level of our agriculture. What would that mean for Britain? It would mean abundant and cheap grain, timber, hides, flax, and all kinds of raw material. The British people, the working people – that is to say nine-tenths of the total population of Britain – as also the people of the Soviet Union, would benefit to an extraordinary degree from such business-like cooperation, and we, comrades, would be able in a few years to rise to the summit of economic well-being, to a height from which we are still very, very distant. Alas, I do not believe that the present government of Britain, a Menshevik government, is capable of taking such a bold, decisive step.

No, we shall have to learn, for several years yet before the coming to real victory of the proletariat, in the main to stand on our own feet. This means that we shall advance, but slowly. We shall be frank with ourselves about this. And when the bourgeois newspapers ask us, and me in particular: "Suppose our ruling classes don't grant you a loan – what will that mean? The collapse of Russia? The collapse of the Soviet power?" – we shall answer them: "How can a gigantic country of 130 million people, who have been awakened for the first time by the revolution, where the young are learning to think critically – how can such a country collapse? A country with inexhaustible natural resources like ours cannot collapse and will not collapse."

The bourgeois press of London, we are told by the latest news telegrams, quotes our speeches, in particular my own, as evidence that by our sharp criticism we wish to break off negotiations. That is a slander. An agreement with the British people will be a good thing for us and for the British people. But if the British bourgeoisie think that we shall say: "Help, we are collapsing!" – if the British bourgeoisie think we shall agree to any conditions they care to impose, then the British bourgeoisie are wrong.

We have already raised ourselves the two or three first steps and have already shown ourselves and others that we are able to work, to advance the economy and culture of our country. And, if I could, I would say to the City, that centre of London, to its banks and bankers, to the MacDonald government, to all the ruling circles of Britain: here, take a look at these, our young generation, the flower of the working class. They are learning to work and to think. Our young generation has passed through the furnace of October, it has grown up in the great school of Lenin. We and our country, so rich in natural wealth, will not perish. With your aid we shall go forward faster, and that will be a great gain for you. Without you we shall go forward slower, but go forward we will, and the reign of labour will come to triumph in our country.

* * *

From a speech to the Moscow Soviet, 29 April 1924
(*May Day in the East and West*).

We can now see a further example – that of the government of the British trade unions, the government of the Labour Party, that is a government of the Amsterdam and the Second Internationals. And the 'Amsterdam' military budget of the British government? – I have worked it out, not a difficult job, since you only have to put together three parts: the army budget, the naval budget, and the air force budget. In all it comes to £115 million which, translated into roubles, comes to 1,150 million gold roubles. Not a scrap less it would appear, but in fact 10 to 15 million gold roubles more than last year, that is, more than the budget of the Conservative government of Britain, and some four if not five times more than our Soviet budget! When this budget was placed before the British parliament, there happened to be present some naive MPs of this same Labour Party who threw up their hands and asked how this could be linked with the puritan pacifism of the Labour Party? And there was a member of this same party, one Mr. Guest – I have not heard this surname before – who at that very moment nodding in the direction of Moscow, said (I have quoted this once already) "and what about Moscow's militarism?" Comrades, permit me to give you a quotation from an old speech of Vladimir Ilyich [Lenin]. He made it on just this very same question against our Mensheviks on 13 March 1919: "A certain Prussian monarch in the eighteenth century made a very wise remark: 'If our soldiers understood what we are fighting for, then we would not be able to wage a single war more.' The old Prussian monarch was no fool." But we are now in a position to say in comparing our situation with that of this monarch: "We can wage a war because the masses know what they are fighting for." And moreover:

> There are some stupid people who howl about red militarism. Really, what a ghastly crime! The imperialists of the whole world fling themselves upon the Russian Republic to strangle it, and we set about creating an army which for the first time in history knows what it is fighting for and what it is making sacrifices for, and which is successfully resisting a numerically superior enemy, while each month brings nearer the resistance of the world revolution on a hitherto unseen scale. And they condemn this as red militarism! I repeat: either they are idiots not standing up to political analysis, or they are political knaves.

And further on a few lines lower down, he says again still more sharply and bluntly: "We have a position where only the filthiest and lowest political crooks can utter strong words and accuse us of red militarism." Vladimir Ilyich liked to express himself simply, clearly, and sharply. And so in London, we find a so-called Labour MP, who knows that it was not the Red Army which made a landing on the Thames but British forces which landed on the banks of the Northern Pechora and other rivers; who knows that British officers took part in the Yaroslavl uprising and in other bloody acts; we find a so-called Labour MP who, in answer to the reproach that it is you who are building five new cruisers and new minesweepers, and it is you who are expanding the Curzon programme for light tanks and are enlarging your air force and navy endlessly, says: "But look, over there in Moscow, isn't there some militarism being started up?" It is not surprising if after these words you go to the quotation from Ilyich where it is said that only the dirtiest and lowest of political crooks can make this sort of accusation of red militarism.

Anglo-American Rivalry and the Growth of Militarism

From a speech to the Society of Friends of the
Physics and Mathematics Faculties, 28 July 1924
(*Perspectives of World Development*).

The basic world antagonism occurs along the line of the conflict of interests between the United States and Britain. Why? Because Britain is still the wealthiest and most powerful country, second only to the United States. It is America's chief rival, the main obstacle on its path. If Britain should be squeezed, or undermined, or, all the more so, battered down, what would then remain? The United States will, of course, dispose easily of Japan. America holds all the trumps: finances and iron and oil, political advantages in relations with China, which is, after all, being 'liberated' from Japan. America is always liberating somebody, that's her profession. [*Laughter, applause.*]

The main antagonism is between the United States and Britain. It is growing and approaching ever closer. The British bourgeoisie has not been feeling so well since the first years of Versailles. They know the value of ringing coin; they have had great experience in this connection. And they cannot have failed to notice that the dollar now outweighs the pound sterling. They know that this preponderance inescapably finds its expression in politics. The British bourgeoisie has completely demonstrated the power of the pound sterling in international politics, and it now senses that the era of the dollar is dawning. It seeks consolation, and tries to console itself with illusions. The most serious British newspapers say: "Yes, the Americans are very rich, but they remain, in the last analysis, provincials. They do not know the paths of world politics. We British have had far more experience. The Yankees need our advice and our leadership. And we British will guide these provincial relatives of ours, who have suddenly grown so rich on the paths of world politics; and naturally we shall retain the corresponding position, while collecting a fee in the bargain."

There is, of course, a modicum of truth in this. I have already mentioned my doubts about the senatorial knowledge of European geography. I am sincerely uncertain about it. Yet in order to do big things in Europe, it does not hurt to possess a knowledge of European geography. But how difficult is it for a possessing class to learn the sciences? We know that it is not at all difficult for the bourgeoisie, grown quickly rich, to learn the sciences. The sons of the *lapti*-wearing Morozovs and Mamontovs[1] bear a striking resemblance to hereditary nobles. It is the oppressed class, the proletariat, that finds it difficult to rise, develop, and conquer all the elements of culture. But for a possessing class, especially one so fabulously rich as the American bourgeoisie, this is not at all hard. They will find, train, or buy specialists in all fields. The American is just beginning to take stock of his world importance, but is not yet fully cognisant of it. His American 'consciousness' still lags behind his American and world 'being'. The whole question must be approached not from the standpoint of a cross section of the present-day situation but in its proper perspective. And this is a perspective not in terms of many long decades but rather in terms of a few brief years.

This Babylonian tower of American economic might must find its expression in everything, and it is already expressing itself, but not yet fully by far. What capitalist Europe has now at its disposal in world politics is the heritage of its former economic power, its old international influence which no longer corresponds to today's material conditions. America has not yet learned to realise her power in life. That is true. But she is learning quickly, on the bones and flesh of Europe. America still needs Britain as a guide on the paths of world politics. But not for long.

We know how swiftly a possessing class, in its ascent, alters its character, its appearance, and its methods of operation. Let us take, for example, the German bourgeoisie. Was it so long ago that the Germans were considered shy, blue-eyed dreamers, a people of 'poets and thinkers'? A few decades of capitalist development transfigured the German bourgeoisie into the most aggressive armour-clad imperialist class. True, the settlement came

---

1   Morozovs and Mamontovs – Rich Russian merchant families of peasant origin.

very quickly. And the character of the German bourgeois again underwent a change. Today on the European arena, they are rapidly assimilating all the customs and usages of beaten curs.

The British bourgeoisie is more serious. Their character has been moulded in the course of centuries. Class self-esteem has entered into their blood and marrow, their nerves and bones. It will be much harder to knock the self-confidence of world rulers out of them. But the American will knock it out just the same, when he gets seriously down to business.

In vain does the British bourgeois console himself that he will serve as guide for the inexperienced American. Yes, there will be a transitional period. But the crux of the matter does not lie in the habits of diplomatic leadership but in actual power, existing capital and industry. And the United States, if we take its economy, from oats to big battleships of the latest type, occupies the first place. They product all the living necessities to the extent of one-half to two-thirds of what is produced by all mankind.

Oil, which now plays such an exceptional military and industrial role, totals in the United States two-thirds of the world output, and in 1923 it had even reached approximately 72 per cent. To be sure, they complain a lot about the threats of the exhaustion of their oil resources. In the initial post-war years, I confess I thought that these plaints were merely a pious cover for coming encroachments on foreign oil. But geologists actually do affirm that American oil at the current rate of consumption will, according to some, last twenty-five years, according to others, forty years. But in twenty-five or forty years, America with her industry and fleet will be able to take away oil from all the others ten times over again. [*Laughter.*] There is hardly any need for us, comrades, to spend sleepless nights over it. [*Applause.*]

The world position of the United States is expressed in figures which are irrefutable. Let me mention a few of the most important ones. The United States produces one-fourth of the world wheat crop; more than one-third of the oats; approximately three-fourths of the world maize crop; one-half of the world coal output; about one-half of the world's iron ore; about 60 per cent of its pig iron; 60 per cent of the steel; 60 per cent of the copper; 47 per cent of the zinc. American railways constitute 36 per cent of the world railway network; its merchant navy, virtually non-existent prior to the war, now comprises more than 25 per cent of the world tonnage; and, finally, the numbers of motor cars operating in the trans-Atlantic republic amounts to 84.4 per cent of the world total! While in the production of gold the United States occupies a relatively modest place (14 per cent), thanks to its favourable trade balance, 44.2 per cent of the world's gold reserve has collected in its vaults. The national income of the United States is two and a half times greater than the combined national incomes of Britain, France, Germany and Japan. These figures decide everything. They will cut a road for themselves on land, on sea, and in the air.

What do these figures presage for Great Britain? Nothing good. They signify one thing: Britain will not escape the common lot of capitalist countries. America will place her on rations. Whether Lord Curzon likes it or not, he will have to accept rations. This is our 'ultimatistic' message to him from here. But we must also add: When Britain's position becomes such as to compel her openly to accept rations, this will not be performed directly by Lord Curzon – he will not be suitable, he is too unruly. No, this will be entrusted to a MacDonald. [*Applause.*] The self-esteem of the politicians of the British bourgeoisie is not such as to make them amenable to the transference of the greatest empire in the world to the meagre foundations of American rations. Required here will be the benign eloquence of MacDonald, Henderson and the Fabians in order to exert pressure on the British bourgeoisie and to convince the British workers: "Are we, then, actually to engage in war with America? No, we stand for peace, for agreements." And what does agreement with Uncle Sam mean? The foregoing figures speak eloquently enough on this score. Accept rations. That's the only agreement for you, there is no other. If you refuse, get ready for war.

Britain has up to now retreated step by step before America. Before our very eyes, it is still fresh in our memory, President Harding invited Britain, France and Japan to Washington and in the calmest way offered Britain – what? That Britain limit her fleet. No more, no less.

Yet before the war, it was Britain's doctrine that her Navy must be more powerful than the combined fleets of the next two strongest naval powers. The United States has put an end to this, once and for all. In Washington, Harding began, as is customary, by invoking the "awakened consciousness of civilisation," and he ended by telling Britain that she must accept rations. You will take five units; I will take (meanwhile) five units; France, three units; Japan, three units. Whence these proportions? Before the war the American fleet was much weaker than Britain's. In the course of the war, it grew enormously. And therewith, whenever the British write with alarm concerning the American Navy, the American naval writers reply by demanding: "What did we build our Navy for? Why, it was to defend your British Isles from the German submarines."

That is why, mind you, they built their fleet. But it is useful for other purposes too. But why did the United States resort to this naval limitation programme at Washington? Not because they are unable to build warships fast enough, and the biggest battleships, at that. No, in this respect no one can match them. But it is not possible to create, train, and educate the necessary cadres of sailors in a brief period. For this, time is required. Here is the source of the ten-year breathing space projected in Washington. In defending the programme limiting the construction of battleships, the American naval journals wrote: "If you so much as dare to baulk at an agreement, we shall turn out warships like so many pancakes." The reply of the leading British naval periodical was approximately as follows: "We are ourselves in favour of pacifist agreements. Why do you keep threatening us?'

This already expresses the new psychology of ruling Britain. It is growing accustomed to the fact that it is necessary to submit to America, and that the most important thing is to demand... polite treatment. This is the most that the European bourgeoisie can expect from America on the morrow.

In the competition between Britain and the United States, only retreats are possible for Britain. At the price of these retreats, British capitalism buys the right to participate in the deals of American capitalism. Thus a coalition of Anglo-American capitalism seemingly arises. Britain saves face, and does so not unprofitably, for Britain derives substantial profits from it. But it receives them at the price of retreating and clearing the way for America. The United States is strengthening her world positions; Britain's are growing weaker.

Only the other day, Britain renounced the previously adopted plan of reinforcing Singapore. It is too bad we have no map here. Singapore and Hong Kong mark the most important highways of imperialism. Singapore is the key between the Indian Ocean and the Pacific. It represents one of the most important bases of British policy in the Far East. But in the Pacific, Britain can conduct her policy either with Japan against America, or with America against Japan. Huge sums were appropriated for the fortification of Singapore. And MacDonald had to decide: with America against Japan or with Japan against America? And so, he renounced the fortification of Singapore.

This is not, of course, the last word of British imperialist policy. The question can come up again for a new decision. But at the given moment it is the beginning of Britain's renunciation of an independent policy – or an alliance with Japan – in the Pacific. And who ordered Britain (yes, ordered!) to break the alliance with Japan? America. A formal ultimatum was issued:

break the alliance with Japan. And Britain broke. Meanwhile, Britain is conceding and retreating.

But does this mean that this is how matters will proceed to the very end, and that war between them is excluded? In no case. On the contrary, at the cost of concessions today Britain is buying only redoubled difficulties on the morrow. Under the cover of collaboration, contradictions of unprecedented explosive power are accumulating. Things not only can but also must come to war, because it will be extremely difficult for Britain to move to a secondary position and to roll up her empire. At a certain point, she will be compelled to mobilise all her forces in order to resist with arms in hand. But in an open struggle, too, so far as it is possible to foresee, all the odds are on America's side.

Britain is an island and America is likewise an island of a sort, but much larger. Britain is completely dependent in her day-to-day existence on countries beyond the ocean. But the American 'insular' continent contains everything that is necessary for existence and for the conduct of war. Britain has colonial possessions on many seas and America will 'liberate' them. Having begun the war with Britain, America will summon hundreds of millions of Indians to rise in defence of their inalienable national rights. The same summons will be issued to Egypt and Ireland – there is no lack of those who can be called upon to free themselves from the yoke of British capitalism. Just as today America, in order to drain the living juices from Europe, comes to the fore draped in the toga of pacifism, so in the war with Britain she will step out as the great emancipator of the colonial peoples.

Mother history has made things easy for American capitalism: for every act of plunder, there is a liberating slogan ready at hand. With regard to China, it is the 'Open Door' policy! Japan seeks to dismember China and to subjugate certain provinces by military force, because there is no iron in Japan, no coal, no oil. These constitute three colossal minuses in Japan's struggle with the United States. For this reason, Japan seeks through seizure to assure herself of the riches of China. But the United States? It says: "Open Door in China."

With regard to oceans, what does America have to say? "Freedom of the seas!" This rings superbly. But what does it mean in action? It means: Get over to one side, Britain's Navy, make room for me! "Open Door in China" means: Stand aside, Japan, and let me pass! It is essentially a question of economic seizures, of robberies. But because of the specific conditions of US development, this travail appears at one time under the guise of pacifism, and at another, it almost assumes a liberating aspect.

Naturally, Britain, too, possesses great advantages which derive from her entire past history. First and foremost, she disposes of powerful bases of support and the strongest naval bases in the world. America doesn't have that. But, in the first place, it is possible to create all this; secondly, it is possible to take all this away, piecemeal and by force; and thirdly, and lastly, Britain's bases are bound up with her colonial rule and are vulnerable for just this reason. America will find allies and helpers all over the world – the strongest power always finds them – and together with these allies, America will find the necessary bases.

If, at the present time, the United States binds Canada and Australia to herself through the slogan of defending the white race against the yellow – and in this way justifies her right to naval supremacy – then, on the next stage, which may come very soon, these virtuous Presbyterians may announce that, in the last analysis, the yellow-skinned peoples are likewise created in God's image and are consequently entitled to replace the colonial rule of Britain by the economic domination of America. In a war against Britain the United States would be in a highly favourable position, since it could from the very first day issue a summons to the Indians, the Egyptians, and other colonial peoples to rise up, and could assist them with arms and supplies.

Britain will have to think ten times before deciding on war. But, in avoiding war, she will be compelled to retreat step by step under the pressure of American capitalism. The conduct of war requires the Lloyd Georges and the Churchills; the MacDonalds are required for the conduct of retreats without a battle.

What has been said about the interrelations of the United States and Britain also applies, with corresponding changes and, so to speak, in miniature, to Japan, and on a truly minute scale to France and other second-rate European powers. What is at stake in Europe? Alsace-Lorraine, the Ruhr, the Saar territory, Silesia, that is, some tiny area of land, some petty strips. In the meantime, America is drafting a plan to place everybody on rations.

In contrast to Britain, America is not preparing to create an American army, and American administration for the colonies including Europe. It will 'allow' them to preserve at home a reformist, pacifist, toothless order, with the assistance of the Social Democracy, with the help of the (French) Radicals and other middle-class parties, and at the expense of their respective peoples. And it will extort from them blessings (up to a certain time) for not having violated their 'independence'. This is the plan of American capitalism and this is the programme on the basis of which the Second International is being resuscitated.

This American 'pacifist' programme of putting the whole world under her control is not at all a programme of peace. On the contrary, it is pregnant with wars and the greatest revolutionary paroxysms. Not for nothing does America continue to expand her fleet. She is busily engaged in building light and fast cruisers. And when Britain protests in a whisper, America replies: You must bear in mind that I not only have a five to five relationship with you, but also a five to three relationship with Japan, and the latter possesses an inordinate number of light cruisers which makes it necessary for me to restore a balance.

America chooses the largest multiplicand and then multiplies it by her Washington coefficient. And the others cannot vie with her, because, as the Americans themselves say, they can turn out warships like so many pancakes.

The perspective this offers is one of preparation for the greatest international dogfight, with both the Atlantic and the Pacific as the arena, provided, of course, the bourgeoisie is able to retain its world rule for any considerable length of time. For it is hard to conceive that the bourgeoisie of all countries will docilely withdraw to the background, and become converted into America's vassals without putting up a fight; no, this is hardly likely. The contradictions are far too great; the appetites are far too insatiable; the urge to perpetuate ancient rule is far too potent; Britain's habits of world rule are far too ingrained. There will inevitably be military collisions. The era of 'pacifist' Americanism that seems to be opening up at this time is only laying the groundwork for new wars on an unprecedented scale and of unimaginable monstrosity.

* * *

From a speech to supply units of the Red Army, 25 October 1924
(*The Growth of World Militarism and Our Military Tasks*).

If we were to look for some elements of stability in the present unstable, shaky era of historical development, then possibly the only stable element is the uninterrupted, automatic growth of militarism. In Europe today we are observing a change of parliamentary regimes. Elections in Britain and forthcoming elections in Germany. MacDonald's government was the first so-called Labour government in Britain. Who will replace it? Most likely the Conservatives, far less probably MacDonald will return. Let us not make guesses – that is not the object of the report I wish to make today – but one thing we can say without fear of error: whoever returns to power over the British Empire, the automatic growth of militarism is assured...

The United States was a non-militarist country until recently. An abrupt turning point came with the imperialist war. The United States intervened at the end of the war and they achieved what they needed in that war, i.e., they routed Germany at the end, which Britain, the chief obstacle in the USA's path to world dominion did not desire. Britain needed a weakened but not a routed Germany – against France, but the United States needed a powerful France against Britain...

Thus, let me say there are processes of two kinds: basic and secondary; from the standpoint of policy we cannot avoid taking temporary processes into account too.

MacDonald appeared. It was no accident that he appeared either! We attempted to conclude a treaty with him but did not complete it – complications in MacDonald's own career impeded that. Curzon has come back and we shall hold talks with Curzon as well. All these are processes of a secondary and tertiary nature, but the basic one is the growth of contradictions, the frantic growth of militarism, the desperate situation of the productive forces, and the preparation for a world bloodbath.

* * *

From a speech to the Kislovodsk Soviet, 9 November 1925
(*Eight Years: Results and Prospects*).

They have concluded an international 'pact' under which Britain has now become something of a Justice of the Peace for Europe. Britain must see that France does not upset Germany but so as Germany does not upset France. Britain represents a guarantor – again just a word like 'pact' – for the inviolability of frontiers. However, less cautious diplomats now and again add that though this is a pact for peace, it is for a peace only for civilised, democratic, pious states, and that this pact has an edge which is directed against that impious, undemocratic, un-peace-loving state which is called the Soviet Union. When recently our press began with its characteristic impoliteness to denounce them, saying: you, Messrs. diplomats, are all hypocrites, for all your pact is a criminal deal in order, in the first place, to plunder the colonies, in the second to obtain American capital, and in the third to oppose the Soviet Union, leading diplomats replied that it was in no way against the Soviet Union; for if she comes to her senses, takes a proper attitude to us, and is so good as to complain to the League of Nations, we will have a seat ready for her there, and so on.

But these gentlemen cannot add two and two together. For only just recently, ministers of the Britain who was appointed to act as Europe's Justice of the Peace expressed their opinion about us very sharply. I have with me here some newspaper cuttings to this effect. Joynson-Hicks, the British Home Secretary, stated: "I cannot believe that British people (that is British workers) will let themselves be fooled by a foreign power whose only objective is the destruction of Great Britain." They unite with each other for peace and scream that there is a power whose *only* objective – just think! – is to destroy Great Britain. "In Moscow they are gunning for Britain", Joynson-Hicks goes on, "as they have realised there that Britain is defending the freedom of the world". Britain defending the freedom of the world! Let's see, if we were to commission our State Publishing House to issue a twelve-page booklet, one copy for every literate person, we would catalogue how Britain over the centuries has defended the freedom of the world, how she ruined Spain and Portugal; how she made war on China because the Chinese did not want to be poisoned with British opium; how she subdued and strangled India; how for centuries she forced Ireland to shed blood; how she strangled Egypt; how she supported the most reactionary Chinese Marshal, Chang Tso-lin against Chinese democracy; how in China at present she is forming with the aid of sterling a force for the Russian monarchist Nechaev to support Chinese monarchist reaction; how in Turkey she supports the reactionary Old Turks against national Turkish democracy and detaches Mosul where the large oil deposits are situated; and finally, how she has been and still is operating in our country. Only a few days ago we read how our GPU uncovered an Anglo-Estonian spy plot, led by the ex-tsarist officer Frank, with the participation of the Russian monarchists and a central organisation in Tallin, and branches in Leningrad and other places. Ruling-class Britain, defending the freedom of the world! She has attracted and amassed the fierce hatred of the popular masses of both hemispheres. Yet this British bourgeoisie, dyed through and through and reared on the traditions of slave ownership, plunder, and strangulation of whole peoples, in the words of one of its most die-hard operators, Hicks, the Home Secretary, states that a plot is being hatched in *Moscow* against Britain, the defender of peace!

Another minister whose name we know a little better, Churchill, stated that "world history entered a new period when the gang of inhuman plotters moved into the Kremlin". That history has entered a new period, we agree. But as regards the gang of plotters we shall remind Churchill about this at a suitable moment. We have good and firm memories. "In relation to Britain", continues the minister, "these dark forces exhibit a special malevolence". Let us say without equivocation: ruling-class Britain has organised a pact which by design must represent a gang of imperialist plotters against the freedom of the whole world, for this is just what their 'pact' is when translated into straight language. They merely heap the blame on the Soviet Union for what the imperialists are guilty of. However, Churchill suddenly spoke up with a wild tongue on the second day after the October revolution when both foreign and our own capitalists had not had time to bandage their wounds. We would have thought that eight years was long enough to get used to the fact, gentlemen! But no, their wounds are apparently still smarting today. A gang of plotters! The destruction of Great Britain! The British imperialists scream this not through strength but out of fear and hatred, gnashing their teeth and expressing themselves in virtual obscenities. But fortunately, the devil's bark is worse... sorry, I mean Churchill's, bark is worse than his bite. [*Laughter.*]

* * *

A speech delivered on 15 February 1926 and
first published in *Ekonomicheskaya Zhizn*, 16 February 1926
(*Two Poles of the Workers Movement*).

The unexampled economic superiority of the United States, even independently of a conscious policy on the part of the American bourgeoisie, will no longer permit European capitalism to raise itself. American capitalism, in driving Europe more and more into a blind alley, will automatically drive her onto the road of revolution. In this is the most important key to the world situation.

This is revealed most graphically and incontestably in Britain's situation. Britain's trans-oceanic exports are cut into by America, Canada, Japan, and by the industrial development of her own colonies. Suffice it to point out that on the textile market of India, a British colony, Japan is squeezing out Britain. And on the European market, every increase of sales of British merchandise cuts into the sales of Germany, France and vice versa. Most often it is *vice versa*. The exports of Germany and France hit those of Great Britain. The European market is not expanding. Within its narrow limits, shifts occur now to one side, now to another. To hope that the situation will change radically in favour of Europe is to hope for miracles. Just as under the conditions of the domestic market, the bigger and more advanced enterprise is assured victory over the small or backward enterprise, so, in the conditions of the world market, the victory of the United States over Europe, that is first and foremost over Britain, is inevitable.

In 1925, Britain's imports and exports reached respectively 111 per cent and 76 per cent of their pre-war levels. This implies an adverse trade balance of unprecedented proportions. The reduction in exports signifies an industrial crisis which strikes not at the secondary but at the basic branches of industry: coal, steel, shipbuilding, woollens, etc. Temporary and even considerable improvements are possible and even inevitable, but the basic line of decline is predetermined.

One becomes filled with justifiable contempt for the 'statesmen' of Britain who have retained all their old conformities so incompatible with the new conditions, and who lack the most elementary understanding of the world situation and the inevitable consequences inherent in it. The reigning British politicians, Baldwin and Churchill, have recently favoured us again with their candour. At the end of last year, Churchill announced that he had twelve reasons (yes, he said that) for being in an optimistic mood. In the first place, a stabilised national currency. The British economist Keynes has called Churchill's attention to the fact that this stabilisation meant a maximum reduction of 10 per cent in the prices of merchandise exported, and consequently a corresponding increase in the adverse trade balance.

The second reason for being optimistic was the excellent price of rubber. Sad to say, Mr. Hoover's twenty-nine questions have considerably reduced the rubberised optimism of Churchill. Thirdly, there was the decrease in the number of strikes. But let us wait on this score until the end of April when the collective contract of the miners comes up for consideration. Fourth reason for optimism – Locarno.[2] From one hour to the next, there is no improvement. The Anglo-French conflict, far from diminishing, has intensified since Locarno. As touches Locarno let us wait, too; one counts one's chickens when they are hatched. We refrain from enumerating the remaining reasons for optimism; on Wall Street the price they fetch is still dropping. It is interesting to note that *The Times* of London published an editorial on this same subject entitled 'Two Rays of Hope'. *The Times* is more modest than Churchill, it has not twelve but only two rays of hope, and these too are x-rays, that is, rather problematical rays.

---

2   The 'pact' was signed at the Locarno Conference in October 1925 by France, Belgium and Germany, and guaranteed by Britain and Italy. It confirmed Germany's western frontiers and laid down the complete de-militarisation of the Rhineland which had been occupied by Britain and France since the German surrender in 1918.

To the professional light-mindedness of Churchill, one can counterpose the more serious opinions of the Americans who make an appraisal of the British economy from their own standpoint, and also the opinion of British industrialists themselves. Upon returning from Europe, Klein, the director of the US Department of Commerce, made a report to industrialists which, notwithstanding its purely conventional tone of reassurance, lets the truth break through.

> From the economic point of view [he said] the only gloomy spot, [abstraction evidently made from the situation of France and Italy as well as the relatively slow restoration of Germany] – the only gloomy spot, I say, is the United Kingdom. It seems to me that Britain is in a doubtful commercial position. I would not want to be too pessimistic because Britain is our best customer, but a number of factors are developing in that country, which, it seems to me, must give rise to serious consideration. There exist in Britain formidable taxes, the reason for which, according to certain people, must be found in our thirst for money, not to say more. Still, it is not entirely correct… The stock of tools of the coal industry is the same as a few dozen years ago, with the result that the cost of manual labour per ton is three or four times more than in the United States.

And so forth and so on in the same vein.

Now, here is another comment. J. Harvey, American ex-ambassador in Europe, considered by the British as a "friend and well-wisher" – which is in a sense true for he speaks, as a rule, sentimentally of the need of coming to Britain's aid – this same J. Harvey recently published an article entitled: 'The End of England' (the title alone is priceless!), in which he comes to the conclusion that "British production has had its day. Hereafter the lot of Britain is to be an intermediate agent", that is to say, the sales clerk and bank teller of the United States. Such is the conclusion of a friend and well-wisher.

Let us now see what George Hunter, a great British shipbuilder, whose note to the government made a stir in the entire British press, has to say:

> Has the Government [and the government, after all, is Churchill with his twelve reasons for optimism] a clear idea of the disastrous condition of British industry? Does it know that this condition, far from improving, is worsening progressively? The number of our unemployed and of our partially unemployed represents at the minimum 12.5 per cent of the employed workers. Our trade balance is unfavourable. Our railroads and a large part of our industrial enterprises pay dividends out of their reserves or pay none at all. If that continues it is bankruptcy and ruin. There is no improvement in prospect.

The coal industry is the keystone of British capitalism. At present it is completely dependent upon government subsidies. "We can", says Hunter, "subsidise the coal industry as much as we like; that will not prevent our industry generally from waning." But if subsidies stop, British industrialists could not continue to pay the wages they now pay; and that would provoke, beginning with the next May Day, a grandiose economic conflict.[3] It is not hard to imagine what would be implied by a strike embracing not less than a million railwaymen and transport workers. Britain would enter into a period of great economic shocks. One must either continue to grant ruinous and hopeless subsidies, or resign oneself to a profound social conflict.

Churchill has twelve reasons for optimism, but the social statistics of Britain testify that the number of employed workers is decreasing, that the number of miners is decreasing, but that there is an increase in the number of restaurant employees, cabaret personnel, and elements of the lumpenproletarian type. At the expense of producers, the number of lackeys increases, and, by the way, these figures do not include the political lackeys and ministers who with servility implore the generosity of Americans.

Let us once again counterpose America and Britain. In America there is a growing aristocracy of labour which aids in the establishment of company unions; while in Britain, fallen from her supremacy of yesterday, there grow layers of lumpenproletariat below. Revealed best of all in this juxtaposition and counterposition is the displacement of the world economic axis. And this displacement will continue to operate until the *class* axis of society is itself displaced, that is, until the proletarian revolution.

Mr. Baldwin, of course, demurs to this. Though Mr. Baldwin carries more weight than Churchill, he understands as little. At a gathering of industrialists, he outlined a means of getting out of the predicament – a Conservative Prime Minister always has patent remedies for all ailments. "It sometimes seems to me", he said, "that some of us have slept for at least six or seven years." Much longer! Mr. Baldwin himself has been asleep for at least fifty years, while others stayed up. "We will do well", continued the Prime Minister, "to be guided by the progress realised during this period by the United States". It would indeed take a bit of trying to be guided by the "progress" of the United States. In that country they dispose of a national wealth of 320 billion, 60 billion in the banks, an annual accumulation of 7 billion, while in Britain there is a deficit. Let us be guided a little! Let us try!

---

3 Trotsky's prediction was accurate: the General Strike began on 4 May 1926.

"The two parties [capitalists and workers]", continues Baldwin, "can learn much more at the school of the United States than in the study of the situation in Moscow." Mr. Baldwin should refrain from spitting into the Moscow well. We could teach him a few things. We know how to orient ourselves among facts, analyse the world economy, forecast a thing or two, in particular the decline of capitalist Britain. But Mr. Baldwin cannot do it.

Churchill, the finance minister, also referred to Moscow. Without it, you can't make a good speech nowadays. Churchill, you see, had read that morning a horrible speech by Mr. Tomsky, who is not a member of the House of Lords. He happens to be, as Mr. Churchill truthfully asserts, a man who occupies an extremely important post in the Soviet Republic. Mr. Tomsky spent his youth not at Oxford or at Cambridge with Mr. Churchill but in the Butirky Prison, here at Moscow. Nevertheless, Mr. Churchill is obliged to speak of Mr. Tomsky. And, it must be admitted, he does not speak very kindly about Mr. Tomsky's speech at the Trades Unions Congress at Scarborough. Mr. Tomsky did indeed make a speech there, and apparently not a bad one, judging from the impression it made on Mr. Churchill. The latter cited extracts from the speech which he characterised as "ramblings of a barbarian".

"I estimate", he said, "that in this country we are capable of managing our own affairs without unwarrantable interference from outside." Mr. Churchill is a very proud man, but he is wrong. His patron Baldwin says that one must learn at the school of the United States.

"We do not want to have a freshly laid crocodile egg for breakfast", continues Mr. Churchill. It is Tomsky, it seems, who laid a crocodile egg in Britain. Mr. Churchill does not like it; he prefers the politics of the ostrich that hides its head in the sand, and, as you know, both the ostrich and the crocodile propagate themselves in the same tropical colonies of Britain. Then Mr. Churchill gets really cocky: "I am not afraid of the Bolshevik revolution in this country. I do not criticise personalities." And so forth and so on. That does not prevent him from delivering a wild speech against Tomsky. So he is afraid, after all. He does not criticise the personality of Tomsky. God forbid, he merely calls him a crocodile.

"Great Britain is not Russia." Very true. "What use is there in introducing to the British workers the dull doctrine of Karl Marx and in making them sing the *Internationale* out of tune?" It is true that the British workers sometimes sing the *Internationale* off-key with music supplied by MacDonald, but they will learn to sing it without any false notes precisely from Moscow. In our opinion, despite all the twelve reasons for optimism, the economic situation of Britain brings nearer that hour when the British working class will sing the *Internationale* at the top of their voices. Prepare your eardrums, Mr. Churchill! [...]

As touches the preparation of the disarmament conference, of exceptional interest is a semi-official article recently published in a British review and eloquently signed "Augur". Everything points to the fact that this Augur has close ties with the Ministry of Foreign Affairs, and is generally well acquainted with what goes on behind the scenes. Under the banner of preparing the disarmament conference, the British Augur threatens us "with measures which will not be pacific measures". This amounts to a direct threat of war.

Who is threatening? Britain, who is losing her foreign markets; Britain, where unemployment prevails; Britain, where the lumpenproletariat is growing; Britain, who has only a single optimist left, Winston Churchill – this Britain is threatening us with war in the present situation. Why? Under what pretext? Is it not because she wants to take it out on somebody else because of the affronts dealt her by America?

As for us, we do not want war. But if the British ruling classes wish to accelerate the birth pangs, if history wishes to deprive them of their reason before depriving them of power, it must, precisely now, push them over the steep slope of war. There will be incalculable suffering. But should the criminal madmen let loose a new war on Europe, those who will emerge victorious will not be Baldwin, nor Churchill, nor their American masters, but the revolutionary proletariat of Europe.

III

The Labour Movement

1906-24

The Revival of the Working Class

From *A Letter to Comrade Larin* (dated 1 December 1906),
published in *In Defence of the Party* (1907).

In offering us a dizzying leap into the unknown, you consider it necessary to
lean upon historical precedents. On the one hand you point to Britain, where
the proletariat has "given shape to the class struggle by the formation of a
broad party", and on the other to Belgium where a workers' party has been
formed by the coming together of social-democratic workers' organisations.
It is to Belgium – in fact, not to Belgium but to twenty lines of Vandervelde's
book – that Comrade Shcheglo, another supporter of the sudden broad party
like yourself, makes reference. Britain and Belgium; since when have these
two countries become models of political development for us?

You take as an example in Britain the Labour Representation Committee,
which, however, can in no instance lay claim to the role of the central
committee of a workers' party. It is a special organ, promoted for the most
part by the trade unions, with the object of independent labour representation
in parliament. The victory of the Committee at the last General Election[1]
has, without question, an enormous symptomatic meaning. The British
proletariat, which had fallen into lethargy after the defeat of Chartism,
awakens once again to political life. But from the Labour Representation
Committee, after whose model we are supposed to build our own, it is a very
long way to the party of the proletariat. This will be readily understood by
anyone who takes into account the fact that British Social-Democracy has
not entered this parliamentary organisation of workers' unions and groups. I
am frankly amazed that you, a social-democrat, have not mentioned a single

---

1 Of January 1906, where the Committee increased its seats from five to twenty-six.

word on this point in recommending to us this new British 'party' as an example. Of course, you are not obliged to agree with the tactic of the British social-democrats. But in any case, you are obliged to examine and consider it. We must accept that they are sufficiently competent in evaluating British conditions and sufficiently interested in creating a broad workers' party to have serious grounds for not joining the Representation Committee.

Besides trades unions, there belong to this committee: the Fabian Society with some 900 members, and the Independent Labour Party consisting of 16,000 members. The latter is doubtless the left wing of the parliamentary organisation of the British proletariat. And yet the Social-Democratic Federation at its last congress at Bradford (Easter 1906) rejected the idea of merging even with the Independent Labour Party, adopting Hyndman's resolution in this connection. It is clear that these 'details' do not interest you in the least. A party with some million members lends itself to your attention, but I must divert your glance towards Social-Democracy which numbers only some 20 thousand members. Let me nevertheless dare to assure you that the incipient political self-determination of the British working masses owes itself in great part to the tireless propaganda of the numerically small British Social-Democratic party. And now, when after years of partially fruitless efforts, broad horizons are obviously opening up before it, it has preferred not to tie itself by organisational discipline to the mass of trade unionists still imbued with bourgeois prejudices, but to preserve its independence in the interest of making criticism and propaganda. The fact of the entry of the thirty independent Labour MPs into the House of Commons is, as we have already said, very noteworthy; but the behaviour of these MPs far from always answers the requirements of a class policy. The central organ of British Social-Democracy, *Justice*, has had in various connections to ask: "Just when will the Labour Party understand that forming an inseparable part of the present-day parliamentary machine does not lie within its tasks?" One can be sure that the political development of the British proletariat will from now on proceed at a rapid pace – for the social-political conditions are extremely favourable – but British Social-Democracy will contribute far more to this process if it remains an independent vanguard, conscious and vigilant, than if it dissolves itself into a huge but infantilely helpless labour 'party'.

And so, provided you are not blinded by your preconceived notion, you must draw conclusions from your unexpected excursion to Great Britain, which completely destroy your metaphysical constructions:

1. In spite of the fact that the proletariat by the objective conditions of its existence directs itself towards the social revolution, the very example of Britain shows that the political development of the working class far from always forms a logical ascent towards socialism; 'pauses' sometimes last, as you see, for several decades. Consequently the 'destiny of history' can by no means serve as an immediate guarantee for our leaps into the unknown and the indeterminate.

2. Britain's example shows that Social-Democracy, while remaining by force of unfavourable historical conditions a narrow and almost sectarian organisation, can still carry out its work by training numerous teachers of socialism on the one hand, and on the other facilitating outside its ranks the dissociation of the organised working masses from the bourgeois parties.

3. Britain's example shows that even after the formation of an independent broad workers' party, Social-Democracy can prove to carry out the greatest service to this party by not dissolving into it and preserving its full freedom of action for criticism and propaganda.

That is the situation with regard to Britain. I am afraid that you will ask me the question: but are our own social-political conditions quite as unfavourable for the rapid drawing together of a mass social democratic party as Britain's? No, I would reply, of course not! But why then do you take as an example a country which cannot serve as an example to us and whose experience anyway proves the direct opposite to what you want to prove?

* * *

From *On May Day*, *Pravda* (Vienna), 23 April 1912.

In Britain, where the working masses have for long dragged along at the tail of the bourgeois parties, an acute sharpening of the class struggle is taking place at present. Colossal strikes of seamen, railwaymen, textile workers, and miners have over the past year shaken the whole economic life of the country, and at every stage the question is being posed point-blank: who should own and dispose of the means of production? A clique of exploiters, or all society as a whole, organised in a fraternal productive and consumer alliance? The British working masses, in the process of these titanic conflicts, are being fed with a revolutionary spirit and the ideas of socialism are making huge gains among them.

The British Proletariat and the War

From *May Day 1890-1915*, *Nashe Slovo*,
1 May 1915.

In the oldest capitalist country, Britain, May Day reflects in equal measure the national-possibilist nature of the class struggle of the British proletariat and the sectarian-propagandist nature of British socialism. Adopted by the trade unions, May Day has been assimilated as a conservative ritual of trade unionism, serving the cause of the propaganda of its immediate class tasks and scarcely rising to social-revolutionary generalisations. As a holiday of militant internationalism, May Day in Britain has remained not the act of a revolutionary working class but a demonstration by the numerically small revolutionary groups in the working class.

* * *

From *Unrest in Europe*, *Novy Mir* (New York),
15 March 1917.

There is unrest in Britain too. Lloyd George displayed great dexterity when it was a question of sticking a knife into his chief, Asquith. Idlers and simpletons had expected that as a result Lloyd George would smash the Germans at the earliest moment; but the unfrocked-priest minister who turned chieftain of the bandits of British imperialism proved incapable of performing the miracle. The population of Britain, like that of Germany, is becoming increasingly convinced that the war has got into a desperate blind alley. The agitation by opponents of the war is encountering an ever-greater response. The jails are overflowing with socialists.

The Irish are ever more insistently demanding the implementation of Home Rule from a government which replies with arrests of Irish revolutionaries.

* * *

From a speech to the Voronezh Soviet, 18 November 1918
(*On Guard Over the World Revolution*).

At present the situation is not very different in Britain. Admittedly, Britain is accustomed to stand aside from Europe. The bourgeoisie has brought the British people up to think of the continent as one thing and Britain another. The government of Great Britain used to intervene in the old European wars by supporting the weaker side with money, and sometimes part of the Navy, against the stronger, only until the moment that an equilibrium was established on the continent. The entire world policy of Britain has for centuries, comrades, consisted in this: dividing Europe into two camps, but not allowing one camp to grow strong at the expense of the other. Ruling class Britain supports its allies like a rope supports a hanging man: that is, by drawing a noose around their necks as tight as possible in the form of all sorts of obligations, so as thereby to exhaust the strength not only of her enemies but also of her "allies". But this time it did not turn out that way. Germany had developed far too powerfully and showed herself to be too mighty a country, and so Britain had herself to get mixed up and deeply involved, no longer just with money, but with meat and human blood. But it is said that "blood is a special juice". This intervention the British bourgeoisie will have to pay for... The privileged position of Britain, once fundamentally undermined by Germany's competition, has disappeared forever. The British trade unionist used to say: "Here we don't have militarism, I'm a free citizen on our island which is defended by the Navy. Here we have only a few dozen thousand volunteer sailors in the Navy and that's it."

Now, this 'free' proletarian of Britain has been seized by the scruff of his neck and thrown on to the territory of Europe, while the war has caused a fearful increase in taxation and fearfully high prices. All this has undermined the old 'privileged' economic position, even of the upper layer of the British working class, to the very roots.

The more privileged that the British proletariat had earlier felt itself to be and the more haughtily it regarded itself, the more terrible the awareness of the catastrophe will be for it. Great Britain's economy is devastated, ruined. A gigantic number of cripples and invalids – all these are consequences of the war. To think that after her victory over Germany Britain would be able to abandon her militarism or strictly limit it would be a grave mistake. Tomorrow Britain's most powerful enemy will be the United States. There is already today a deep *private* antagonism between them. For the British proletariat, there remain today only two possibilities: the degeneration of the economy and the working class or – social revolution.

To be sure, there exists a prejudice that the British working class supposedly lacks a revolutionary temperament. There is a subjectively nationalistic theory that the history of a nation is to be explained by national temperament. This is rubbish. That is what the superficial gossip-mongers of bourgeois origin who have only observed British people in the smart restaurants of Switzerland and France believe and write: they observe the so-called cream of British society, whose representatives have become corrupt and emaciated over the generations and lack both the energy and will to live, and set them up as representatives of the British nation.

But whoever knows the history of the British people and the British working class, the history of the English Revolution of the seventeenth century and then British Chartism of the nineteenth century, will know that the Englishman too has a "devil inside him". There have been repeated occasions when the Englishman has taken up the cudgel against his oppressor. And there is no doubt that the time is near when he will take up his cudgel against the King, against Lloyd George, against his lords and against the cruel, cunning, clever and perfidious British bourgeoisie. And the first thunderclaps of the great storm can already be heard from the island of Great Britain.

Labour Bureaucracy and the Post-War Class Struggle

From the preface (dated 29 May 1920) to
Terrorism and Communism (1920).

... In that country [Great Britain], the ruling class of which is oppressing and plundering the whole world more than ever before, the formulae of democracy have lost their meaning even as weapons of parliamentary swindling. The specialist best qualified in this sphere, Lloyd George, appeals now not to democracy, but to a union of Conservative and Liberal property holders against the working class. In his arguments, no trace remains of the vague democracy of the 'Marxist' Kautsky. Lloyd George stands on the ground of class realities, and for this very reason speaks in the language of civil war. The British working class, with that ponderous learning by experience which is its distinguishing feature, is approaching that stage of its struggle before which the most heroic pages of Chartism will fade, just as the Paris Commune will grow pale before the coming victorious revolt of the French proletariat.

Precisely because historical events have, in these last months, been developing their revolutionary logic with stern energy, the author of this present work asks himself: Does it still require to be published? Is it still necessary to confute Kautsky theoretically? Is there still a theoretical necessity to justify revolutionary terrorism?

Unfortunately, yes. Ideology, by its very essence, plays an enormous part in the socialist movement. Even for practical Britain the period has arrived when the working class must exhibit an ever-increasing demand for a theoretical statement of its experiences and its problems. On the other hand, even the proletarian psychology includes a terrible inertia of conservatism in itself – all the more so since in the present case, it is a question of nothing less than the traditional ideology of the parties of the Second International which first roused the proletariat, and recently were so powerful. After the collapse of official social-patriotism (Scheidemann, Victor Adler, Renaudel, Vandervelde, Henderson, Plekhanov, etc.), international Kautskyism (the staff of the German Independents, Friedrich Adler, Longuet, a considerable section of the Italians, the British Independent Labour Party, the Martov group, etc.) has become the chief political factor on which the unstable equilibrium of capitalist society depends.

* * *

From *The Manifesto of the Second World Congress*
drafted by Trotsky and adopted at the Second World Congress
of the Communist International, 7 August 1920.

Routinism among the summits of the labour movement in Britain is so ingrained that they have yet even to feel the need of rearming themselves. The leaders of the British Labour Party are stubbornly bent upon remaining within the framework of the Second International.

At a time when the march of events during recent years has undermined the stability of economic life in conservative Britain and has made her toiling masses most receptive to a revolutionary programme – at such a time, the official machinery of the bourgeois nation – the Royal House of Windsor, the House of Lords, the House of Commons, the Church, the trade unions, the Labour Party, George V, the Archbishop of Canterbury, and Henderson – remains intact as a mighty automatic brake upon progress. Only the Communist Party – a party free from routine and sectarianism, and closely bound up with the mass organisations – will be able to counterpose the proletarian rank and file to this official aristocracy.

* * *

From *On the Policy of the KAPD* (dated 5 November 1920)
Kommunisticheskii Internatsional, 7 June 1921.

It is quite probable that Britain will enter the epoch of proletarian revolution with a Communist Party still comparatively small. One can do nothing about it, because the propaganda of communist ideas is not the sole factor in history. The only conclusion that flows from this is: that the working class of Britain – if, through the criss-crossing of major historical causes, it finds itself in the near future already drawn into an unfolding proletarian revolution – will have to create, expand, and consolidate its mass party in the very course of the struggle for power, and in the period immediately following the conquest of power; while, during the initial phase of the revolution, the numerically small Communist Party will – without tearing itself away from the mainstream of the movement, and by taking into account the existing organisational level of the proletariat and its degree of class consciousness – seek to introduce the maximum of communist consciousness into the actually unfolding revolution.

* * *

From *Theses on the International Situation and the Tasks of the Communist International*, drafted by Trotsky and adopted by the Third World Congress of the Communist International, 4 July 1921.

The mighty strike movement in Britain was shattered again and again during the last year by the ruthless application of military force, which intimidated the trade union leaders. Had these leaders remained faithful to the cause of the working class, the machinery of the trade unions despite all its defects could have been used for revolutionary battles. The recent crisis of the Triple Alliance furnished the possibility of a revolutionary collision with the bourgeoisie, but this was frustrated by the conservatism, cowardice, and treachery of the trade union leaders.[1] Were the machinery of the British trade unions to develop today half the amount of energy in the interests of socialism it has been expending in the interests of capitalism, the British proletariat could conquer power with a minimum of sacrifice and could start a systematic reconstruction of the country's economic system.

---

1   The Triple Alliance of the Miners' Federation, the Transport Workers' Federation and the National Union of Railwaymen had been formed in 1914, but collapsed in April 1921 when the leaders of the transport workers and the railwaymen refused to call their members out in sympathy with the miners' strike against the coal owners' wage cuts.

The Growth of the Labour Party

From *A Necessary Discussion with Communist Syndicalists*,
Pravda, 21 March 1923.

What is the meaning of the quotations from Marx adduced by Comrade
Louzon?[1] It is a fact that Marx wrote in 1868 that the workers' party would
emerge from the trade unions. When writing this he was thinking mainly
of Britain, at that time the only developed capitalist country that already
possessed extensive labour organisations. Half a century has passed since
then. Historical experience has in general confirmed Marx's prophecies in so
far as Britain is concerned. The British Labour Party has actually been built
up on the foundations of the trade unions. But does Comrade Louzon really
think that the British Labour Party, as it is today, led by Henderson and
Clynes, can be looked upon as representative of the interests of the proletariat
as a whole? Most decidedly not. The British Labour Party betrays the cause
of the proletariat just as the trade union bureaucracy betrays it, although in
Britain the trade unions approach nearer to comprising the working class as a
whole than anywhere else. On the other hand, we cannot doubt but that our
Communist influence will grow in this British Labour Party which emerged
from the trade unions, and that this will contribute to sharpening the
struggle of masses and leaders within the trade unions until the treacherous
bureaucrats are ultimately driven out, and the party is completely reformed
and renewed. And we, like Comrade Louzon, belong to an International
which includes the little Communist Party of Britain, but which combats

---

1   Robert Louzon (1882-1976) – French communist who held the syndicalist idea of
    the 'unqualified independence' of the trade unions from political parties.

the Second International supported by the British Labour Party that had its origins in the trade unions.

In Russia – and in the logic of capitalist development Russia is exactly the opposite of Britain – the Communist Party, the former social democratic party, is older than the trade unions, and created the trade unions. Today, the trade unions and the workers' state in Russia are completely under the influence of the Communist Party, which is far from having its origins in the trade unions, but on the contrary created and trained them. Will Comrade Louzon contend that Russia has evolved in contradiction to Marxism? Is it not simpler to say that Marx's judgement on the origin of the party in the trade unions has been proved by experience to have been correct for Britain, and even there not 100 per cent correct, but that Marx never had the least intention of laying down what he himself once scornfully designated as a "supra-historical law"? All the other countries of Europe, including France, stand between Britain and Russia on this question. In some countries the trade unions are older than the party, in others the contrary has been the case; but nowhere except in Britain, and partially in Belgium, has a party of the proletariat emerged from the trade unions. In any case, no communist party has developed organically out of the trade unions. But are we to deduce from this that the Communist International has orginated wrongly?

When the British trade unions alternately supported the Conservatives and the Liberals, and represented to a certain extent a labour appendage to these parties, when the political organisation of the German workers was nothing more than a left wing of the democratic party, when the followers of Lassalle and Eisenach were quarrelling among themselves, Marx demanded the independence of the trade unions from all parties. This formula was dictated by the desire to oppose the labour organisations to all bourgeois parties, and to prevent their being too closely bound up with socialist sects. But Comrade Louzon may perhaps remember that it was also Marx who founded the First International, the object of which was to guide the labour movement in all countries, in every respect, and to render it fruitful. This was in 1864, and *the International created by Marx was a party.* Marx refused to wait until the international party of the working class formed itself in some way out of the trade unions. He did his utmost to strengthen the influence of scientific socialism in the trade unions – as first laid down in 1848 in the *Communist Manifesto.* When Marx demanded for the trade unions complete independence from the parties and sects of the bourgeoisie and the petty bourgeoisie, he did this in order to make it easier for scientific socialism to gain dominance in the trade unions. Marx never saw in the party of scientific socialism one of the ordinary parliamentary democratic political parties. For Marx, the International was the class-conscious working class, represented at that time by truly a very small vanguard.

* * *

A letter to the Politburo dated 9 February 1922.[2]

Comrade Bukharin has told me that the British Labour Party has addressed to their government a proposal that the question of Georgia be inscribed as the first item on the agenda of the Genoa Conference.[3] If this information has been verified, I recommend that the All-Russian Central Council of Trade Unions and individual trade unions pass a resolution along the following lines:

The British Labour Party has been pleased to inspire the British capitalist government to intervene in the internal affairs of the Soviet Workers' and Peasants' Republics. We are not going here into the question of why it is that the British Labour Party confines itself to Georgia. In Russia too, in the Ukraine, in Azerbaijan, and Turkestan and so on, the Mensheviks and their allies were expelled by the workers and peasants in the same way as they were in Georgia. We are, likewise, not going into the question of the motives and inducements which inspire the so-called British Labour Party in its attempts to facilitate the wrecking of the Genoa Conference for the benefit of the extreme interventionist wing of imperialism in Britain, France, and other countries. If, however, the British government were to attempt to follow the path towards which the British Labour Party is trying to draw it, we categorically insist that our delegation shall put down on the agenda of the Genoa Conference the question of the liberation of Egypt, India, and other colonies struggling heroically for their liberation. At the same time, we consider it the paramount duty of the Communist International to redouble its efforts for the exposure of the Socialist hypocrites in Great Britain, who neglect their elementary duty to conduct, hand in hand with the insurgent masses of its colonial slaves, a determined struggle against British imperialism, and at the same time

---

2 First published in *The Trotsky Papers* edited by J. Meijer and published by the International Institute for Social History

3 This proposal had been made by a conference representing the Labour Party, the TUC, and the Parliamentary Labour Party.

attempt to represent the overthrow of the Georgian bourgeoisie and its Menshevik agents as an act of military coercion.

This repulsive manoeuvre of the conciliators must be mercilessly exposed *vis-à-vis* the working masses of Britain.

I am giving here not the text of a resolution but only the approximate outline of one. I think that we need to get a move on with this. The resolutions of the various unions as adopted could vary in their working. The more of them there are, the better. We shall be able to transmit them every day by radio. I recommend that this should be discussed by telephone without delay in order to speed things up.[4]

* * *

A letter to the Politburo dated 10 February 1922.[5]

The following idea might also be included in the resolution of our trade unions about the proposal of the British Labour Party concerning Georgia:[6]

> In requiring the removal from Georgia of revolutionary troops, the British Labour Party is, by this token, leaving Georgia completely at the mercy of imperialism which, first in the shape of Turkish and German troops, and then in the shape of British troops, enjoyed unchallenged domination there prior to the Soviet revolution. In now requiring the withdrawal of the Red Army, is the Labour Party requiring the withdrawal of the British and French fleets from the Black Sea, from which the French and British fleets are undoubtedly threatening the independence and freedom of Georgia? Instead of curbing British imperialism the British Labour Party is striving to disarm, in the former's interests, the revolutionary maritime countries in relation to which this same imperialism announces its rapacious claims.

I am dictating by telephone only the main idea, not the text. I think that this idea will have importance as propaganda.

* * *

---

4   Lenin, and subsequently the Politburo, rejected Trotsky's proposal and recommended that the Soviet trade unions take no action but that *Izvestia* should publicly welcome Henderson's suggestion of expanding the Genoa agenda to include questions of national self-determination.

5   First published in The Trotsky Papers edited by J. Meijer and published by the International Institute for Social History,

6   See p. 179 of the present edition.

From a report on the 5th anniversary of the October Revolution
and the Fourth World Congress of the Communist International
to the active membership of the Moscow organisation of the RCP,
20 October 1922.

A few words on Britain. Here our Communist Party still remains a successfully functional educational and propaganda society, but not a party, capable of directly leading the masses.

In Britain, however, the situation is taking shape or tending in a direction favourable to us, outside of the Communist Party's framework – within the working class as a whole. Today we received a cable that Lloyd George's government has resigned.

This was the only government older than ours. [*Laughter.*] We were considered to be the least stable among all the governments. This is Lloyd George's polite gift to our jubilee, so as not to hurt our feelings. [*Laughter.*] It obviously means new elections in Britain. And new elections imply a struggle between the three basic groupings, which are: the Tories, the Unionists, and the Independent Liberals. What Lloyd George does personally is a subsidiary question. He may go either with the Tories or with the Independent Liberals, clasping the Labour Party's right hand. His personal career is all that is involved here. Essentially, the struggle will occur between the three groupings, and therewith chances are by no means excluded that a coalition of the Labour Party and the Independent Liberals may turn up in power. What this means hardly requires comment. The appearance of the working class in power will place the entire responsibility for the government's actions upon the Labour Party – and will give rise to an epoch of British Kerenskyism in the era of parliamentarism, providing a favourable environment without parallel for the Communist Party's political work. Should the Tories win (I hesitate to weigh the odds, but let us here assume they are favourable),[7] it would only signify a worsening of the country's domestic situation; it would tend to sharpen the Labour Party's opposition and would thereby bring about new elections very quickly, because elections in Britain can take place within a month or a few months, as has happened more than once in the past. In other words, the stability of the domestic political situation, which had been enhanced by the coalition headed by Lloyd George, is relegated to the museum with Lloyd George's departure; and Britain is experiencing shocks and oscillations which can play only into our hands.

* * *

7 The Conservatives won the 1922 General Election.

From the report to the Fourth World Congress of the
Communist International on *The New Economic Policy and the
Perspectives for World Revolution*, 14 November 1922.

In Britain, the general elections are now taking place. Because of the collapse
of Lloyd George's coalition government, they came sooner than expected.
The outcome is still unknown.

There is a likelihood that the previous ultra-imperialistic grouping will be
returned to power. But even if they do win, their reign will be short. A new
parliamentary orientation of the bourgeoisie is clearly being prepared both in
Britain and France. The openly imperialist aggressive methods, the methods
of the Versailles Treaty, of Foch, Poincaré, and Curzon, have obviously run
into a blind alley. France cannot extract from Germany what Germany hasn't
got. France in turn is unable to pay her debts. The rift between Britain and
France keeps widening. America refuses to renounce collecting payments of
the debts. And among the intermediate layers of the population, especially
among the petty bourgeoisie, reformist and pacifist moods are growing
stronger and stronger: an agreement ought to be reached with Germany,
and with Russia: the League of Nations should be expanded; the burden of
militarism should be lightened; a loan from America should be made, and
so forth and so on. The illusions of war and defencism, the ideas and slogans
of nationalism and chauvinism, together with the subsequent hopes in the
great fruits that victory would bring – in brief, the illusions which seized a
considerable section of the working class itself in the Entente countries, are
giving way to more sober reactions and disillusionment. Such is the soil for
the growth of the 'Left Bloc' in France, and of the so-called Labour Party
and the independent Liberals in England. Naturally, it would be false to
expect any serious change of policy consequent upon the reformist-pacifist
orientation of the bourgeoisie. The objective conditions of the capitalist world
today are least suited to reformism and pacifism. But it is quite probable that
the foundering of these illusions in practice will have to be experienced before
the victory of the revolution becomes possible.

* * *

From *Political Perspectives*, *Izvestia*, 30 November 1922.

In Britain the situation is no less instructive. The rule of the Liberal-Tory
coalition has been replaced, as a result of the recent elections, by a pure Tory
government. Clearly, a step 'to the right'! But on the other hand, the figures of
the last election precisely go to show that bourgeois-conciliationist Britain has
already fully prepared a new orientation – in the event of a further sharpening

of contradictions and growing difficulties (which are inevitable). The Tories obtained less than 5.5 million votes. The Labour Party, together with the independent Liberals, almost 7 million. Thus, the British electorate has, in its majority, already swung from the lush illusions of imperialist victory to the emaciated illusions of reformism and pacifism. It is noteworthy that the League for Democratic Control,[8] a radical-pacifist organisation, has had its entire committee elected to parliament. Are there serious grounds for believing that the incumbent Tory regime may bring Britain *directly* to the dictatorship of the proletariat? We see no such grounds. On the contrary, we assume that the insoluble economic, colonial and international contradictions of the present-day British Empire will tend more and more to swell the plebeian and petty-bourgeois opposition in the person of the so-called Labour Party. From all indications, in Britain more than in any other country on the globe, the working class will, before passing over to the dictatorship, have to pass through the stage of a Labour government in the person of the reformist-pacifist Labour Party which has already received in the last elections about 4.25 million votes…

It is by no means excluded that the German revolution may erupt before the present-day aggressive imperialist governments are replaced in France, Britain, and Italy. No one disputes that the victory of the German proletariat would give a mighty impetus to the revolutionary movement in every country in Europe. But just as the impact of the Russian revolution within a year brought Scheidemann and not Liebknecht to power in Germany, so the impact of the victorious proletarian revolution in Germany might bring Henderson or Clynes to power in Britain; and Caillaux[9] in an alliance with Blum and Jouhaux[10] in France. Such a Menshevik regime in France would, under the given historical conditions, be only a very brief interlude in the death-agony of the bourgeoisie. There is even a possibility that in such a case the communist proletariat in France might come to power directly over the heads of the (French) Mensheviks. In Britain this is less likely. In any case, such a perspective presupposes the victory of the revolution in Germany during the next few months. Is victory certain so soon? Scarcely anyone would seriously maintain this. At all events it would be the crassest blunder

---

8   In fact called the Union for Democratic Control.

9   Joseph Caillaux (1863-1944) – Leader of the French Radical Socialist Party (liberals).

10 Léon Jouhaux (1879-1954) – Syndicalist and general secretary of the CGT in 1906. A supporter of the war in 1914, he joined the government and became a Commissioner of the Nation gearing the working class to the war effort.

to restrict our prognosis to such a one-sided and conditional perspective. On the other hand, without a prognosis it is generally impossible to arrive at a far-reaching revolutionary policy. But our prognosis cannot be mechanistic – it must be dialectical. It must take into account the interaction of objective and subjective historical forces. And this opens up the possibility of several variants – depending on how the relation of forces shapes up in the course of living historical action.

And so there is hardly any ground for a categoric assertion that the proletarian revolution in Germany will triumph before the domestic and foreign difficulties plunge France into a governmental parliamentary crisis. This crisis would mean new elections and new elections would result in the victory of the 'Left Bloc'. This would deal a heavy blow to the Conservative government in Britain: it would strengthen the Labour Party opposition and, in all likelihood, produce a parliamentary crisis, new elections, and the victory of the Labour Party as such or in an alliance with independent Liberals. What would be the effect of such events upon Germany's internal situation? The German Social-Democrats would immediately drop their semi-oppositional status in order to offer 'the people' their services in restoring peaceful, normal, etc., relations with the 'great Western democracies'. This was the sense of my remarks to the effect that a shift in the domestic policy in France and Britain, should it occur prior to the victory of the Communists in Germany, could for a while lend wings to the German Social-Democracy. Scheidemann could once again come to power – but this would already signify the open prelude to the revolutionary culmination. For it is perfectly obvious that, under the existing European conditions, the impotence of the reformist-pacifist regime would be laid bare not over a number of years but in the course of a few months or weeks. In his speech on the draft programme [of the Comintern] Comrade Thalheimer[11] quite correctly reminded us once again about those basic causes which exclude the possibility of a turn in capitalist policy toward Manchesterism:[12] pacifist liberalism and reformism. In power, Clynes or Caillaux–Blum or Turati[13] would be unable to pursue a policy

---

11 August Thalheimer (1884-1948) – German Communist; joined the SPD before the First World War; opposed the war; founder member of the KPD.

12 Manchesterism – The economic policies of free trade and *laissez-faire* advocated by nineteenth century radicals who led the Anti-Corn Law League which was founded in Manchester in 1838.

13 Filippo Turati (1857-1932) – Italian sociologist and Socialist Party politician.

essentially different from the policy of Lloyd George, Bonar Law, Poincaré, and even Mussolini. But when they come to power, the position of the bourgeoisie will be rendered even more difficult, even more inextricable than it is today. Their complete political bankruptcy – provided, naturally, we pursue correct tactics, i.e., revolutionary, resolute, and at the same time flexible tactics – can become laid utterly bare in a very brief span of time. In a ruined and completely disorganised capitalist Europe after the illusions of war and of victory, the pacifist illusions and the reformist hopes can come only as the ephemeral illusions of the death agony of the bourgeoisie. Comrade Ravenstein[14] is apparently willing, with a reservation here and there, to recognise all this so far as the plebeian capitalists are concerned, but not as touches the capitalist aristocrats, i.e., the colonial powers. In his opinion, the perspective of a reformist-pacifist prologue to the proletarian revolution is as inappropriate for Great Britain, France, Belgium, and Holland as the slogan of a workers' government. Comrade Ravenstein is perfectly correct in linking up the slogan of a workers' government with the fact that the bourgeoisie still disposes of a reformist-pacifist resource, not a material but an ideological resource, in the shape of the influence still retained by the bourgeois-reformist and the social-democratic parties. But Comrade Ravenstein is absolutely wrong in offering exemptions to the colonial powers. Before bringing her armed might upon the Russian revolution, Britain sent her Henderson to assist Buchanan in steering the revolution on to a 'correct' path. And it must be said that during the war, Russia was one of Britain's colonies. The British bourgeoisie followed exactly the same course in relation to India: it first sent well-intentioned and liberal viceroys and then, on their heels, squadrons of bombing planes. The growth of the revolutionary movement in the colonies would doubtless accelerate the assumption of power by the British Labour Party, despite its invariable and repeated betrayals of the colonies to British capitalism. But it is equally unquestionable that the further growth of the revolutionary movement in the colonies, parallel with the growth of the proletarian movement at home, would once and for all topple petty-bourgeois reformism and its representative, the Labour Party, into the grave of history.

* * *

---

14 Ravenstein – Dutch communist who defended an ultra-left position at the Fourth World Congress (1922) opposing any parliamentary activity and participation in reformist trade unions.

From a speech to party, trade union, Young Communist,
and other organisations of the Krasnaya Presnya district
(Moscow), 25 June 1923.

What then does the general picture add up to? Extreme right-wing
Conservatives in Britain; extreme imperialists, the National Bloc,[15] in
France; the Fascists in Italy; the conservative rights in Poland; the counter-
revolutionary Liberal Party in Romania; and, one of the latest developments,
the counter-revolutionary coup in Bulgaria.[16] We seem to be observing the
swing of counter-revolutionary reaction flying forward to reach its highest
point. To understand this more clearly and concretely let us say two words
on the domestic situation in Britain and France.

In Britain, the Conservatives hold power. The Liberals have become
numerically the third party. The Labour Party forms the immediate
opposition. At the elections it won more votes than the Liberals. The whole
of British politics now stand under the sign of the inevitable coming to
power of the Labour Party. You know the Labour Party there: it is British
Menshevik reformism. The leaders of the Labour Party represent essentially
the bourgeoisie's political agents. For the fact is that there are periods when
the bourgeoisie rules through agents like Curzon (who was the British
Viceroy of India), but there are also moments when it is compelled to
move to the left and govern the masses through MacDonald, Henderson,
and others.

The influence of the Labour Party is growing continuously. You read
yesterday in the newspapers that Robert Smillie, one of the left leaders of
the Labour Party, won the Morpeth by-election, advocating moreover a
programme not only of maintaining the agreement with the Soviet Union
but also of full diplomatic recognition of Soviet Russia. He obtained a
very considerable majority of votes over a bloc of Conservatives and
Liberals. This fact is indicative. Comrades, anyone who follows the life of
Great Britain will tell you that the bourgeois parties there are counting
upon the Labour Party coming to power in a year or two's time as an

---

15 The right-wing coalition government formed by Millerand, the former socialist, in
   France in 1920.

16 A military coup d'état led by General Tsankov and backed by right wing parties
   overthrew Aleksandar Stamboliyski's Peasant Union government in June 1923. The
   Bulgarian Communists adopted a mistaken position of neutrality towards this seizure
   of power but were soon subjected to persecution and, following an abortive uprising
   in September, driven underground by Tsankov's regime of White terror.

unavoidable fact, and that the bourgeoisie are having to accommodate themselves to the fact that their interests will be represented not by their old acknowledged leaders but through the intermediary of the Mensheviks from the Labour Party.

The MacDonald Government

Around October, Pravda and Izvestia, April 1924.

A Philistine on a Revolutionary

In one of the many anthologies devoted to Lenin, I stumbled upon an article by the British author, Wells, entitled 'The Dreamer in the Kremlin'.[1] The editors of the anthology note in the preface that even such progressive people as Wells had not understood the meaning of the proletarian revolution which occurred in Russia. This would appear to be in itself insufficient reason for including Wells' article in an anthology devoted to the leader of that revolution. But it is not really worth quibbling over: I, for one, read Wells' few pages with some interest for which, however, their author is not responsible, as we shall see presently.

I can clearly visualise the time when Wells visited Moscow. It was the cold and hungry winter of 1920-21. In the air was an anxious presentiment of the troubles to come in the spring. Hungry Moscow lay under snow-drifts. The economic policy was on the eve of an abrupt turning-point. I remember very well the impression that Vladimir Ilyich [Lenin] brought back from his talk with Wells: "How middle class! How philistine!", he kept repeating, lifting his arms above the table and laughing and sighing, with a laugh and a sigh which indicated in him a certain inward shame for another person. "Oh dear, what a Philistine", he would repeat when he recalled the talk later. This exchange of ours took place just before a Politburo meeting and was essentially confined to a repetition of the brief description of Wells I have just

1 *Sunday Express*, 28 November 1920.

quoted. But this was more than sufficient. Certainly I have read little of Wells, nor have I ever met him. But the English drawing-room socialist, Fabian, and writer of Utopian and science fiction, who had travelled here to have a look at the communist experiments formed a picture I could imagine perfectly well. Lenin's exclamation, and the tone of that exclamation in particular, rounded it off neatly. So now Wells' article, which found its way into a Lenin anthology by some inscrutable path, not only revived Lenin's exclamation in my memory but also filled it with a living content. For if there is scarcely a trace of Lenin in Wells' article, then Wells himself is written all over it.

Let us start right away with Wells' introductory complaint: do you realise that he had to go to great pains and take some time to obtain an audience with Lenin which was "tedious and irritating" for him. But why so? Perhaps Lenin had sent for Wells? Maybe he was obliged to receive him? Or perhaps Lenin had so much time to spare? On the contrary, in those ultra-harsh days every minute of his time was full up; it was very hard for him to cut out an hour to see Wells. It would not be difficult for even a foreigner to realise that. But the whole trouble was that Wells, as a distinguished foreigner, and for all his 'socialism' a highly conservative Englishman of an imperialist cast, was thoroughly convinced that he was paying this barbarian country and its leader a great honour by his visit. Wells' entire article from the first to the last line reeks of this baseless conceit.

His description of Lenin starts, as you might imagine, with a revelation. Did you know that Lenin "is not a writer"? For who can in fact decide this question, if not Wells, a professional writer? "The shrill little pamphlets and papers issued from Moscow in his name, full of misconceptions of the labour psychology of the West... display hardly anything of the real Lenin mentality..." The worthy gentleman is not cognisant of the fact that Lenin has produced a number of basic works on the agrarian question, economic theory, sociology, and philosophy. Wells knows only the "shrill little pamphlets", and then he makes the remark that they were issued only "in his name", intimating that others wrote them. The true "Lenin mentality" reveals itself not in the dozens of volumes he wrote, but in the hour-long conversation which the most enlightened guest from Great Britain most magnanimously deigned to hold.

One might have at least expected an interesting sketch of Lenin's external appearance from Wells, and we would have been ready to forgive all his Fabian banalities for a single well-drawn feature. But in the article, there is not even this. "Lenin has a pleasant, quick-changing brownish face with a lively smile"… "Lenin's not very like the photographs you see of him"… "he gesticulated little with his hands during our conversation…" Beyond such trivialities in the style of a pen-pushing hack reporter of a capitalist newspaper, Wells did not go. He did, however, discover that Lenin's forehead reminded him of the "domed and slightly one-sided cranium" of Arthur Balfour,[2] and Lenin was generally "a little man: his feet scarcely touch the ground as he sits on the edge of his chair." With regard to Arthur Balfour's cranium, we are not able to say anything about that worthy object and we will willingly believe that it is domed. As for the rest – what an obscene mish-mash! Lenin had a reddish-blond colouring which in no way could be called brownish. He was of average height or possibly a little under; that he gave the impression of a "little man" and that he could scarcely reach the floor with his feet could only occur to Wells, who had arrived with the self-esteem of a civilised Gulliver in the land of northern communist Lilliputians. Wells also noticed that during pauses in the conversation Lenin was "pushing up his eyelids with his hand"; "this habit", the perceptive writer deduces, "is due perhaps to some defect in focussing." We know this gesture. It could be observed when Lenin had a strange and alien person in front of him and would cast a quick glance at him through his fingers resting against his forehead. The "defect" in Lenin's sight consisted in that he could in this way see right through his collocutor, see his pompous smugness, his narrow-mindedness, his civilised arrogance, and his civilised ignorance, and once having made a mental note of that picture he could long afterwards shake his head and keep repeating "What a Philistine! What a ghastly middle-class!"

During the conversation Comrade Rothstein[3] was present, and Wells made the discovery in passing that his presence was "characteristic of the present condition of Russian affairs". You see, Rothstein keeps a check on Lenin from the Commissariat for Foreign Affairs, in view of Lenin's excessive sincerity and his dreamer's imprudence. What can we say about such a priceless observation? When he went into the Kremlin, Wells brought along in his mind all the rubbish of the international bourgeois news media and with his penetrating eye – which of course lacks any "defect"! – discovered in Lenin's office what he had previously fished out of *The Times* or some other repository of pious and well-smarmed gossip.

---

2 Arthur Balfour (1848-1930) – British Conservative politician; Prime Minister from 1902 to 1905.

3 Theodore Rothstein (1871-1953) – Russian revolutionary active in the British socialist movement; played an important role in the founding of the CPGB.

Of what then did the conversation consist? On this score we can divine from Wells just a few hopeless commonplaces which prove how miserably and pathetically Lenin's ideas break into some other craniums which, by the way, we do have some grounds for describing as one-sided.

Wells arrived "expecting to struggle with a doctrinaire Marxist" but "in fact found nothing of the sort." This cannot surprise us. We know by now that "the real Lenin mentality" was revealed not in more than thirty years of his political and literary activity, but in the conversation with the citizen from Britain. "I had been told that Lenin lectured people; he certainly did not do so on this occasion", Wells continues. But how in all truth can one lecture a gentleman so overflowing with self-esteem? That Lenin liked to lecture was not at all true. It is true that Lenin could speak very instructively. But he did so only when he considered that his collocutor was capable of learning something. In such circumstances he would spare absolutely no time or effort. But with the marvellous Gulliver who, by the kindness of fate, had found himself in the "little man's" office, Lenin must have needed only two- or three-minute's conversation to gain an unshakeable conviction to the approximate effect of the notice over the entrance to Dante's *Inferno*. "Abandon hope forever…"

The conversation touched on big cities. In Russia, Wells declares, the idea occurred to him for the first time that the face of a city is determined by the trade in its shops and markets. He shared this discovery with his collocutor. Lenin "admitted" that under communism cities might diminish considerably in size. Wells "pointed out to Lenin that the renovation of the cities would require a colossal labour and that many of Petersburg's huge buildings would retain the significance of historical monuments." Lenin agreed also with this unparalleled commonplace of Wells. "I think", the latter added, "it warmed his heart to find someone who understood a necessary consequence of collectivism that many even of his own people fail to grasp." There's a ready-made yardstick of Wells' mental level! He regards as the fruit of his tremendous power of vision the discovery that under communism today's urban conglomerations will disappear and that many of today's capitalist architectural monstrosities will retain merely the significance of historical monuments (unless they merit the honour of being demolished). But, of course, how could the poor communists ("the tiresome class-war fanatics") reach such discoveries, which were, however, long ago elaborated in a popular commentary to the old programme of German Social-Democracy. This is not to mention the fact that the classic Utopians knew all about these things.

Now you will understand, I hope, why Wells "did not at all notice" during his conversation that laugh of Lenin's about which he had been told so much. Lenin was in no mood for laughing. In fact, I fear that his jaw may well have been convulsed by a reflex quite the reverse of laughter. But here a mobile and clever hand performed Ilyich a necessary service, for it always knew how to conceal the reflex of a discourteous yawn from a collocutor too much taken up with himself.

As we have already heard, Lenin did not lecture Wells, for reasons which we consider quite acceptable. In exchange, Wells lectured Lenin all the more persistently. He would keep impressing upon him the totally new idea that for socialism to succeed "it is necessary to reconstruct not only the material side of life but also the mentality of a whole people." He pointed out to Lenin that "Russians are by nature individualists and traders." He explained to him that communism was "in too much of a hurry" and destroying before it was ready to rebuild, and so on in that vein. "That brought us", relates Wells, "to our essential difference – the difference of the collectivist and the Marxist." By "evolutionary collectivism" one is to understand a Fabian concoction of liberalism, philanthropy, thrifty social legislation, and Sunday meditations on a brighter future. Wells himself formulates the essence of his evolutionary collectivism in this way: "I believe that through a vast sustained education campaign, the existing capitalist system could be civilised into a Collectivist world system. "Wells, does not make it clear by exactly who, and for exactly whom this "vast sustained educational campaign" will be carried out; will it be the lords with their domed craniums for the British proletariat, or conversely the proletariat carrying it out against the lords' craniums? Oh no, anything you like but not the latter. Why in the world do there exist the enlightened Fabians, people with altruistically conceived ideas, ladies and gentlemen like Mr. Wells and Mrs. Snowden, if not to civilise capitalist society and turn it into a collectivist one by means of a systematic and sustained excretion of everything concealed under their own craniums, and with such a sensible and happy gradualness that even the British royal dynasty will not notice the transition?

All this Wells expounded to Lenin, and all this Lenin listened through. "For me", Wells remarked graciously, "it was very refreshing" to have a talk with this "unusual little man". But for Lenin? Oh, poor long-suffering Ilyich! In private he would probably have uttered some highly expressive and juicy Russian words. He did not put them into English speech not only because his English vocabulary probably did not stretch that far, but also out of courtesy. Ilyich was very polite. But nor could he confine himself to a polite silence. "He had to argue", Wells tells us, "that modern capitalism is incurably predatory, wasteful, and unteachable." Lenin made reference to a number of points contained in Money's[4] new book amongst others: capitalism destroyed the British shipyards, hindered a rational exploitation of coal resources, and so on. Ilyich knew the language of facts and figures.

"I had, I will confess", Mr. Wells concludes unexpectedly, "a very uphill argument". What does this mean? Not the beginning of the capitulation of evolutionary collectivism in the face of the logic of Marxism? No, not by any means. "Abandon hope forever." This, at first sight unexpected, remark was in no way accidental – it forms part of a system, and had a consistently Fabian evolutionary didactic nature. It is directed at the British capitalists, bankers, lords, and their ministers. Wells is saying to them: "You see, you act so badly and destructively and selfishly that in my arguments with the dreamer in the Kremlin it tends to be difficult to defend the principles of my evolutionary collectivism. Be sensible, perform weekly Fabian ablutions, be civilised, and march along the path of progress." In this way, Wells' doleful confession was not a beginning of self-criticism but an extension of the educational work on the same capitalist society that had emerged from the imperialist war and the Versailles Peace so much improved, moralised, and Fabianised.

Wells remarks, not without a patronising sympathy, that Lenin "has an unlimited confidence in his work". We have no need to dispute this. Lenin did have a sufficient fund of confidence in his cause. What is true is true. This fund of confidence provided him, amongst other things, with the patience in those dark months of the blockade to talk to any foreigner whatever who could serve even as a crooked link between Russia and the West. Thus, Lenin's talk with Wells. He would talk in quite a different way with British workers who came to visit him. With them he would have a lively intercourse; he both learned and taught. But with Wells the conversation had essentially a half-forced, diplomatic character. "Our argumentation ended indecisively", the author concludes. In other words, the contest between evolutionary collectivism and Marxism ended in a draw. Wells went off to Great Britain, while Lenin stayed in the Kremlin. Wells wrote his pompous feature for the bourgeois public while Lenin shook his head and kept repeating: "How middle class! Dear, dear, what a Philistine!"

———

4   Leo Chiozza Money (1870-1944) – Italian-born economic theorist who moved to
    Britain in the 1890s.

Possibly I will be asked for what precise reason or purpose I have been dwelling here and now, almost four years later, on such an inconsequential article by Wells. The fact that his article had been reproduced in one of the anthologies commemorating Lenin's death is of course no justification. The fact that these lines of mine were written in Sukhumi while undergoing treatment is likewise insufficient reason. But I do have more serious motives. In Britain today, Wells' party stands in power, being guided by enlightened representatives of evolutionary collectivism. I thought, and perhaps not without reason, that Wells' lines on Lenin might unveil to us better than much else the spirit of the leading layer of the British Labour Party: after all, Wells is not the worst of them. How terribly backward these people are, burdened as they are with the heavy load of bourgeois prejudices! Their arrogance, a delayed reflex of the great historical role of the British bourgeoisie, does not permit them to interest themselves as they ought in the life of other nations, in new ideological phenomena and in the historical process which is rolling past over their heads. Narrow routinists, empiricists blinkered by bourgeois public opinion, these gentlemen betake themselves and their prejudices around the world and contrive to see nothing around them except themselves. Lenin had lived in every country of Europe, mastered foreign languages, read, studied, listened, investigated, compared, and generalised. While leading a great revolutionary country he would not waste any opportunity to learn, inquire and find out, attentively and conscientiously. He never wearied of following the life of the whole world. He could read and speak German, French and English, and read Italian with ease. In the last years of his life, when overburdened with work in the Politburo, he was learning Czech grammar on the quiet so as to have direct access to the labour movement of Czechoslovakia: we sometimes "caught him at it', and not without embarrassment he would laugh and try to justify himself. Yet face to face with him was Wells, the incarnation of that species of pseudo-educated, narrow middle-class people who look in order not to see, and consider that they have nothing to learn because they are safeguarded by their inherited store of prejudices. Mr. MacDonald, who represents a more stolid and grim variety of the same type, reassures bourgeois public opinion: "we fought Moscow and we beat Moscow." Did they beat Moscow? They are the real poor "little men", fully-grown as they might be! Today, after all that has happened, they know nothing about their own yesterday. The Liberal and Conservative businessmen can easily lay down the law to the 'evolutionary' socialist pedants now in power, compromise them, and consciously set about their political as well as ministerial downfall.

At the same time, however, they are preparing, albeit far less consciously, the coming to power of the British Marxists. Yes, that's right, Marxists, the "tiresome class-war fanatics". For even the British social revolution will take place according to laws established by Marx.

Wells once threatened with his peculiar stodgy pudding-like wit to crop Marx's "doctrinaire" head of hair and beard and anglicise, respectablise, and Fabianise Marx. But this scheme neither has nor will come to anything. Marx will remain Marx just as Lenin remained Lenin after Wells had subjected him to the agonising effect of a blunt razor for an hour. We will venture to predict that in the not-so-distant future two bronze figures will be erected side by side in London, say in Trafalgar Square: those of Karl Marx and Vladimir Lenin. The British proletarian will say to his children: "What a good thing the little men from the Labour Party did not manage to crop or shave those two giants!"

In anticipation of that day which I hope to live to see, I shut my eyes for an instant and I can clearly see Lenin's figure in the armchair, the same one in which he saw Wells, and I can hear, on the day after Wells' visit or perhaps the same day, those words uttered with a stifled groan: "How middle class! How Philistine!"

* * *

From a speech to the Tbilisi Soviet, 11 April 1924
(*On the Road to the European Revolution*).

We must say a few words at this point about Great Britain, with its new experience of a so-called Labour government on a parliamentary, 'democratic' basis, that is, the most ideal and sacred, so it would seem, for every right-thinking Menshevik.

What has this experience given us thus far? You know that the so-called Labour Party does not have an absolute majority in Parliament. Why? Because a significant section of the British workers to this day tag along at the tail of liberalism. These workers are not by any means the most obtuse; they simply don't see much difference between liberalism and MacDonald. They say: "What's the sense of changing our quarters and going to the expense of moving when the only difference is in the landlord's surname?"

So none of the parties in Parliament has an absolute majority. The Liberals and Conservatives have stepped back and said to the Labour Party. "Oh sirs, you are the most powerful party. Oh please, come rule and be master over us." The British are great humourists, as you know. This is testified to by Dickens, that great representative of British humour.

And MacDonald took the government. Now we ask: What next? How will the 'Labour' government proceed? If it does not have a majority in Parliament, that does not mean its situation is totally hopeless. There is a way out – one need only have the will to find it.

Suppose MacDonald said this: "To our shame, our country has to this day a kind of august dynasty that stands above democracy and for which we have no need." If he added that those sitting in the House of Lords and in other state institutions were all the titled heirs of bloodsuckers and robbers, and that it was necessary to take a broom and sweep them out – if he said that, wouldn't the hearts of British workers quicken with joy?

What if he added: "We are going to take their lands, mines, and railways, and nationalise their banks." And there's surely more to be found in the British banks than we found in ours! [*Stormy applause.*] If he added: "With the resources released by the abolition of the monarchy and the House of Lords we are going to undertake the construction of housing for the workers", he would unleash tremendous enthusiasm.

In Britain, three-quarters of the population is working class. It is a purely proletarian country. It has a small handful of landlords and capitalists – they are very rich and powerful, it is true, but still they are only a handful.

If MacDonald walked into Parliament, laid his programme on the table, rapped lightly with his knuckles, and said: "Accept it or I'll drive you all out" (saying it more politely than I've phrased it here) – if he did this, Britain would be unrecognisable in two weeks. MacDonald would receive an overwhelming majority in any election. The British working class would break out of the shell of conservatism with which it has been so cleverly surrounded; it would discard that slavish reverence for the law of the bourgeoisie, the propertied classes, and church, and the monarchy.

But MacDonald will not do that. He is conservative, in favour of the monarchy, private property, and the church. You know that the British bourgeoisie has created a variety of churches, religious associations, and sects for the people's needs. As in a big clothing store, everyone can find a church for his own size and shape. This is no accident; it is quite expedient from the ruling-class point of view. This splintering and varied adaptation of the church provides greater flexibility and, consequently, more successfully befuddles the consciousness of the oppressed class.

In our country, the dominant church was the embodiment of the most official bureaucratism. It did not concern itself overmuch with the soul. But in Britain, there are subtler methods and devices. In Britain there is an ultra-flexible, conciliatory, I might even say Menshevik, church. In addition, British Menshevism is thoroughly imbued with the priestly spirit. All this is merely the church's way of adapting to the different groups and layers of the proletariat – a complex division of labour in the service of the bourgeois order.

Comrades, there is no need to mention that even before the 'Labour' government, I did not have a high opinion either of the Second International or of MacDonald. But you know, and this is something I said earlier today in speaking with some friends, each time you encounter Menshevism in a new situation, you have to conclude that it is even more rotten and worthless than you had supposed.

This so-called Labour government is weighed down totally, to the very limit, with the worst petty-bourgeois prejudices and most disgraceful cowardice in relation to the big bourgeoisie. MacDonald's ministers reek of piety, and make a show of it in every possible way. MacDonald himself is a Puritan: he looks at political questions, if you can call it looking, through the glass of the religion that inspired the revolutionary petty-bourgeoisie of the seventeenth century. His colleague, Henderson, the Home Secretary, is the president or vice-president, or something of the sort, of the Christian evangelical societies. Every Sunday the Home Secretary in the Labour government pronounces a devout sermon.

This is not a joke, comrades, not something from the British equivalent of *Krokodil,*[5] this is a fact. And this fact is tied in the most intimate way with the whole British conservative tradition, the clever, skilful, sustained ideological work of the British bourgeoisie. It has created an unbelievable terrorism of public opinion against anyone who dares declare that he is a materialist or atheist. Britain has a glorious history in science. It gave us Darwin, the Marx of biology. But Darwin did not dare call himself an atheist.

The British big bourgeoisie is a handful, and police repressions would be of no avail if the political influence of the church did not exist. Lloyd George once said, not without reason, that the church was the central power station of all the parties. To clarify this for you more specifically, let me cite one example that I mentioned in speaking privately with some friends. In 1902, that is, twenty-two years ago, I was in England and, with Vladimir Ilyich, attended a social-democratic meeting in a church. The meeting proceeded in the following fashion: a worker in the printing trade who had returned from Australia gave a speech that for those times was fairly revolutionary, against

---

5   A satirical magazine published in the Soviet Union from 1922-92.

the ruling classes, for revolution, etc.; then everyone rose and sang a hymn or psalm on the theme: Merciful God, grant that there be neither rich nor kings nor oppressors. [*Laughter.*] All this is an important constituent feature of British political mores. The British bourgeoisie is the stronger for it, and the British proletariat weaker.

In recent days I read, I forget in which paper, a speech by MacDonald himself to an evangelical society. He spoke with indignation of the class struggle, preaching that society can save itself only through Christian morality, etc. Isn't it hard to imagine him speaking of the Soviet Republic with indignation? But what happened? This Puritan, pacifist preacher of Christian morality, no sooner entered the government than he confirmed a proposal to build five new cruisers. His colleague declared that in the field of military aircraft the plans of the preceding Conservative government would remain unchanged.

Moreover, even after the Labour government came to power in Britain, the production of light tanks continued apace. You see what Christian pacifism looks like in practice. And it is not surprising that the same MacDonald declares that in the field of politics, *continuity* is necessary, that is, anything the Conservatives can do, we can do too.

In a letter to Poincaré, he writes that the alliance between Britain and France is the basis of European peace and order. Why? How does this follow? Present-day France is the personification of militarism and reaction. Why should this Labour government of Britain find itself in alliance with the vile French plutocracy?

Why couldn't a Labour government, an *actual* Labour government, make an alliance with us? Would this be a bad alliance – one between the working class of Britain and the working class of the Soviet Republic? Between tsarist Russia and capitalist Britain, a long struggle went on. Tsarist Russia wanted to encroach on Britain's colonies – above all India – while Britain denied Russia access to the Dardanelles. Bismarck called this struggle between Russia and Britain the battle of the elephant and the whale.

But now, with the great new change in history, cannot the whale of Labour Britain conclude a friendly alliance with the Soviet elephant? Would not such an alliance represent the greatest advantage for both sides? British industry and the British people need our fields, our forests, our bread, our raw materials, and we need their capital and technology. The alliance of Labour Britain with us would be a strong check on bourgeois France; it would not dare commit further outrages and ravages in Europe.

Together with Britain, we would help Europe reduce the burden of armaments; we would draw closer to the creation of a workers and peasants United States of Europe, without which Europe is threatened with unavoidable economic and political decline.

But what does MacDonald do? This devout pacifist tells Poincaré, the most ferocious representative of stock-market France, that he wishes to remain in alliance with him, of all people, and consequently in opposition to us and the labouring masses of Europe. There you have real Menshevism, not the pocket edition, like you had here with Zhordania, but Menshevism of world proportions, placed in power in a country that encompasses hundreds of millions of colonial slaves.

In the few weeks of its rule, British Menshevism has become hated in the colonies, in both India and Egypt, where revolutionary nationalist aspirations have won out under the slogan of full separation from Britain. The Mensheviks will start complaining that British industry can't get along without Indian and Egyptian cotton and colonial raw materials in general. As if that were the question! If MacDonald tried to reach agreement with the Indians and Egyptians on the basis of their full independence, Britain would have cotton in exchange for machines, would have economic ties, and these ties would develop. But here too MacDonald acts as a Menshevik-steward for the British imperialists.

Finally, there is another fact that has a direct symbolic significance for history: it concerns Turkey. Turkey, as you know, has done away with the caliphate. This is a progressive liberal-bourgeois measure. Nationalist Turkey throws off the feudal vestments of the Caliph and Sultan and becomes a more or less bourgeois-democratic country. This is a step forward.

What does the MacDonald government do, this Menshevik 'Labour' government? It crowns a new Caliph in the Hejaz, the so-called 'sheikh of Mecca and Medina', in order to have, in his person, a weapon for colonial enslavement.

I read in *The Times* – although it is a Conservative organ, in foreign policy it always expresses the official line of the existing government, whether bourgeois, Liberal, or MacDonaldite – I read there that in Turkey, alas, the age-old sacred, majestic foundations are cracking, and that we have the profound misfortune to see it happening before our eyes. And MacDonald subsidises this very same newly cooked-up Caliph in Hejaz, because for majestic institutions a majestic establishment is necessary, and a corresponding budget.

In particular, the entourage of the Caliph is linked with a rather vast harem, which as we have read, was recently expelled from Constantinople. With the unemployment existing in Britain and the difficulties of the British budget, it is necessary, obviously, for MacDonald to cut unemployment benefit slightly in order to cover the additional expenses of the Caliph's new harem. This all seems like a humorous anecdote, but it is a fact that cannot be erased from history...

Just think! This 'humane' and 'civilised' Britain, in the person of Gladstone, threatened Turkey because of its backwardness and barbarity. And now, when Turkey has got on its feet and chased out Caliph and Sultan, parliamentary Britain establishes a Caliph under its protectorate. There you have the full measure of the decline of bourgeois democracy!

If in regard to all this you should ask what will be the fate of our further discussions with the new British government regarding possible loans, joint settlement of claims, etc., I would find it hard to give even an approximate answer. How can one know what MacDonald will decide to do, and what his Liberal and Conservative controllers will allow him to do?

And here I should correct the second inaccuracy in the interview published in *Zarya Vostoka*. It said there that Trotsky had indicated the possibility that these talks would serve as a lever to overthrow the so-called Labour government of MacDonald. No more, no less! Comrades, if I were to say something like that, Comrades Chicherin and Rakovsky would take stern measures against me, and they would be right.

Imagine the situation: we have sent a delegation for talks and at the same time I declare that we have sent this delegation in order to overthrow MacDonald, in passing. How? What for? To have Baldwin or Lloyd George in his place? Nonsense. I said nothing of the kind. On the contrary, our delegation is one of the levers that may immensely strengthen the British government. Under what conditions? Those of daring and decisive action by that government.

In Britain there is unemployment: it could be reduced by granting us credits, by increasing our purchasing power. The Soviet Union could serve as a truly vast market for British goods. No colonial plunder could give the British economy the advantages that a solid alliance with us could. Credit is not philanthropy. We pay the going interest rates. There are obvious mutual advantages in such an arrangement.

What are the obstacles? The capitalists demand, through MacDonald, that we repay the tsarist debts. Whenever did the victim, after breaking free of the ropes that had bound him, pay the robber for the ropes? Well, we broke out of the tsarist bonds. And do you think we are going to pay the British stock exchange for them? No, never!

Our own obligations we will rigorously fulfil. We openly and triumphantly avowed in the first Soviet, in 1905, that we would not pay the tsarist debts, and we shall fulfil that international obligation of ours. [*Stormy applause.*] If we now deem it necessary to enter into one or another business agreement with the bourgeoisie, we will fulfil our new obligations most rigorously.

Bankers of Britain, if you give us a loan, then as long as you remain the bankers of Britain, that is, as long as the British proletariat tolerates you, we will pay it back promptly and exactly. And when the British proletariat overthrows you, it will disinherit you of our debts as well. There you have a clean, business-like and irrefutable statement of the situation.

The surest guarantee of our fulfilling international obligations is our own self-interest! If MacDonald would make a broad agreement with us, he would strengthen himself. Of that I have not the slightest doubt. In general, he can win the hearts of millions of workers only by a courageous policy, and then no one could turn him out by parliamentary tricks. As you can see, this is not at all what was ascribed to me in the newspaper interview. It was a hasty conversation, in a railway carriage, before the train pulled out; the comrade was jotting things down quickly with his pencil. I am not trying to reproach him, but merely to *rehabilitate* myself. [*Laughter.*]

That MacDonald will, with all his strength, help to overthrow himself, is absolutely clear to me, as it is to all of you. The Liberals, as I gather from a quick glance at the paper today, left MacDonald in a minority in Parliament on the question of workers' housing, and he felt obliged to accept the Liberal bill. What does this mean? The worker will say, "Why get a Liberal bill via MacDonald when I can get it directly from a Liberal?" From this it is clear not only that the Liberal Party will remove MacDonald as Prime Minister whenever it wants to; it is also undermining the authority that the Labour Party has in the workers' ranks.

A section of the workers, the more aristocratic, better-off workers who voted in the last election for the Labour Party, will probably vote for the Liberals in the next election. They will say, "This is a solid, established firm; why fool around with the middleman?" But the broad mass of workers will make a turn to the left. At what rate I do not know, but there is no doubt that as a result of the temporary splendour of having even a Menshevik government, a very significant strengthening of the left wing in the working class will take place. MacDonald is working for the communists. Yes, from the viewpoint of the international revolution, he is working for us.

However, I certainly don't intend to send him a note of thanks for that. He is working in this direction not only unselfishly, but also unconsciously. Flushed by the Liberals and Conservatives, who intentionally compromise him, revealing that he is only a toy in their hands, MacDonald in turn pushes the British workers towards the revolutionary road. Such will be the final result of this historical experiment, the coming to power of the British Labour Party.

* * *

From a speech to the 7th Congress of Railwaymen, 19 April 1924.

The most acute question in our international position, at least on the plane of journalism, are our talks with Britain. Here, comrades, we still find ourselves in an extremely uncertain situation which reflects the political uncertainty of Europe as a whole and of Britain's Menshevik government in particular.

Yesterday I met journalists from the American and British press, and on behalf of their newspapers they demanded from me an explanation in connection with certain, supposedly impolite or sharp expressions about MacDonald's government which I used in my report in Tbilisi. To justify my alleged attacks against the British government, I asked the editors of *Pravda* to print the report in full. It is printed today, and if Mr. MacDonald is interested in what we think about him he can instruct his translator to translate what refers to him and interests him.

But comrades, it is quite remarkable how these gentlemen are arrogant on the one hand, yet touchy on the other. Over Georgia, which I visited the other day, MacDonald threatened us with an international democratic, or social-democratic tribunal. We are "not democrats". We "trample on" nationalities. We have "strangled' Georgia. He excommunicated us from all the Menshevik and puritan churches – he is both a Menshevik and a practising puritan – because we violated the principle of democracy. He declared when he was already Prime Minister: "I fought Moscow and I beat Moscow", not he personally but together with the whole Second International. Yet we are supposed to treat this as something legitimate. MacDonald, the representative of a great enlightened country, criticises us, excommunicates us, threatens us, and this must not impede the progress of peace negotiations or economic negotiations. I, a citizen of a backward country, in Tbilisi, a remote city in a similarly backward country in whose fate MacDonald had earlier shown interest, permitted myself to say:

"Well, good, you enlightened citizens of a greater democracy have come to power, yet you still keep human rubbish in the form of lords and an aristocracy and so forth, just when will you pick up a broom and do some sweeping?" – which is of course a very naive question from the standpoint of a representative of a backward country which is accused of violating all the principles and laws of democracy. It is true that we have always said that the power of the toilers, the dictatorship of the toilers is in fact our rule. The way it was constituted is entirely democratic, or if not entirely so, the rule of the toiling masses is in itself a hundred and a thousand times higher than formal democracy.

We have never denied formal democracy. We said: formal democracy is higher than Asiatic despotism, higher than the power of the Shah of Persia or the King of England. The dictatorship of the proletariat is higher than formal democracy. Formal democracy is higher than monarchic and aristocratic barbarism and any shameless titled oligarchy. This has always been our viewpoint, and those who accuse us of dictatorship have explained to us the advantages and sacred values of democracy. When they came to power it emerged that democracy was only opposed to the working class and not the power of the House of Lords and the British monarchy.

At the same time, I made the objection that MacDonald has not got a majority in parliament, but I advanced the suggestion that if he were to appear in the House of Commons, or in the House of Lords, and say: honourable members, we need to make economics in the budget to provide the unemployed with necessary means and therefore the House of Lords is to be abolished – nine-tenths of the people would be behind him. But then, over these business considerations, which could be called costing questions [*laughter*], over these the British press, the pro-government, semi-government, and conservative press beat a frantic alarm. This means that we are "breaking off negotiations" which MacDonald granted us.

Just note, what a narrow conceit! Where does MacDonald get it from? This is a reflection of the omnipotence of the London Stock Exchange. When we have self-confidence it reflects the strength of the working class which has taken power for the first time. [*Applause.*] With MacDonald it is a reflection of the omnipotence of the Stock Exchange whose authorised agent he effectively is when in power. How dare impoverished Soviet Russia tell the truth to the face of Britain or America, cultured, rich, enlightened countries, with a foreign trade turnover of many millions! That's their psychology. We shall wean them from this psychology! [*Applause.*] […]

We find ourselves living in an era of extreme instability. There can be a reaction of a directly contrary nature following recognition. For you know that when that MacDonald criticises us (he considers that in the order of things), and in criticising us makes this or that political remark, then he or his press rears up on its hind legs. What does this signify? This signifies that they have still not got away from the idea, and today's telegram from France is the best testimony to the fact, that when we go to negotiations we should go with our head bowed.

Today there is a telegram in the morning papers in which the official French telegraph agency states: "for our part we are following the negotiations between the Soviet Union and Britain, we are following them very attentively and we cannot here permit any deal at the expense of the first and oldest creditor". Britain, they say, is a second-rank creditor, but the old and the chief creditor of tsarist Russia was France, and the moment it comes to agreements then France will stretch out her claw: pay France first of all please.

Simultaneously with our delegation's negotiations, other negotiations, the so-called reparations negotiations between Germany and the Entente, are being held over Germany's repayment of the contributions imposed upon her. Here too the prospects for either side are hopeless. To lend to Germany would mean to create a powerful competitor for Britain. Britain to date exports only three-quarters the amount of goods she exported before the war while her population has increased. Industry and plant has grown. If Britain gives credit to Germany (German industry is now working at half its capacity), Germany will be able at once to turn out – and German technique is first-rate and German workers first-rate producers – 50-75 per cent more goods than at present. This means an industrial crisis for Britain. Likewise for France.

Britain can give credit to us. Why? Because we are an agricultural country, because we will give Britain raw materials, timber, agricultural produce in exchange for machinery, advanced technique and in part industrial products. But to do this we are once again faced with the question of the stability of the whole bourgeois world.

* * *

From a speech to the 5th All-Russian Congress of
Medical and Veterinary Workers, 21 June 1924
(Through What Stage Are We Passing?).

In Britain, the conservative-reformist and pacifist illusions of the working class, seriously undermined by the war, are now booming again, and more luxuriantly than before, under the sign of the Labour Government. The entire political past of the British working class, in so far as it is expressed in political moderation, conciliation, reformism, and complicity in the imperialist policy of the bourgeoisie, is now being subjected to its highest test, with the transfer of power to the Labour Party. The Labour Party itself is playing down the seriousness of this text by pointing to the fact that it has not an absolute majority in Parliament and therefore is not responsible for everything. But history has nevertheless mounted a full-scale experiment. The outcome of the MacDonald regime, however it may finish from the formal standpoint, will be a deepening of criticism and self-criticism in the ranks of the working class. And criticism and self-criticism means a growth of the left wing. For Britain the period of the formation of the Communist Party is only now really opening.

The MacDonald government has not only deepened the temporary democratic-pacifist illusions of the British working class, it has also increased its self-awareness. One cannot say that the British working class now feels itself master in the house, for if it had that feeling then it would already have become master. But the average British worker says to himself: "We do count for something, then, since the King has called our trade unionists to power." And this awareness, whatever conservative limitations it may bear within itself as a result of the entire past, itself gives a big stimulus to future development. The workers have become more demanding, less patient, and as a result the number of strikes has sharply increased in Britain. And it is not for nothing that the *Sunday Times* is complaining that though they have splendid Labour leaders in Britain these are being rapidly thrust aside by revolutionaries. Rapidly or not, they are being thrust aside and they will be thrust aside – thrust aside and thrust out. [*Applause.*]

* * *

From a speech to the Moscow Soviet, 29 April 1924
(*May Day in the West and East*).

We can see how the government of the same MacDonald quivers at the voice of its masters, the bourgeoisie, while restraining the British proletariat from making a bold step to confront it. If there were any elements of energy and courage in the British Labour government then it would make a broad treaty with us, and this treaty would make a new page in the history of the whole world. Just look how bank deposits have grown in Britain over the last years. British industry does not have its former outlets; it has scarcely won back three-quarters of its pre-war markets. If they do not make a treaty with us, they will be choked to death by the pressure of America. We, with our boundless spaces and our 130 million-strong population, represent for them the most enormous interest. Our country is rich in the natural resources which Britain lacks. Look at our agricultural lands which could feed Europe. Look at our subterranean wealth, our oilfields, and our forests with which we could furnish all of Europe, and all the world. All this cries out for British technique! Just let us unite and you will see how quickly you and we will be able to raise ourselves up. The British working class would have cheap wheat, bread, they would have meat and they would have sufficient raw materials and would grow richer – as we would ourselves. And an alliance of Labour Britain and the workers' and peasants' Soviet Union would be a mighty lever in the world, not a platonic demonstration on the third Sunday in September, but the opportunity for combining the most powerful naval force with the most powerful land-based armed forces. Along with the working class of Britain we could order Europe to disarm and Europe would not dare shove us off! [*Applause.*] And yet these gentlemen chide us for the fact that this or that sharp expression of ours is upsetting the progress of the negotiations in Britain. But isn't this a shameful and contemptible view? Surely the interests of two great nations, two states, cannot be determined by this or that sharp expression? But why are these expressions on the tips of our tongues? Because the programme which I have just sketched in rough outline, this programme of the pacification of Europe and its rapid advance will not be realised, for the working class of Britain does not have a government which could make this bold step which is vouchsafed by all history, of an alliance with us.

In London we have accepted a series of agreements and we shall quite sincerely accept new ones; we shall fulfil all our obligations and at the same time we will say – and no diplomatic considerations can prevent this – we will say to the British working class: "You do not have at your head a government which is worthy of you!" When I called the MacDonald government a government of stewards to the British bourgeoisie, the British press pounced upon this expression almost as if it offended the national dignity of Britain. Over there they translated it in various ways. They asserted that I said that MacDonald was a bank "clerk" and others said a "stock market shark". I have already explained that I didn't say that. A bank clerk is an employee, a bank proletarian, and among them are many fine revolutionaries. As far as I know, MacDonald has not worked in a bank, and if he had, then he has now radically changed his profession. [*Laughter.*] Nor did I call him a stock-market shark. This too is the profession, though a less laudable one, of the small speculator on the Stock Exchange. As far as I know, MacDonald has not had any relation to this category, or at any rate he has not now. But when I say that he is the political steward of the bourgeoisie, then this is the truth and on May Day we can repeat this truth with a clear conscience. [*Applause.*] When I said this, I did not know that I was committing a literary plagiarism on Lloyd George, for it was he (we must put this in!), who said on 24 April that the Liberals had put MacDonald in power and wished him well, but that in three months he had completely squandered the reserve of their benevolence. Whose voice is this? This is the voice of the master who has "put a steward in charge". "I put you in charge, I trusted you, but you have not fulfilled my trust." And are we not right to say that if MacDonald acknowledges this criticism and this voice of the master then can he blame us if we translate this into the language of our political terminology? It might seem that the British Labour government had been put in by the proletariat and bears responsibility to it. And it might seem that MacDonald should make an appeal to the proletariat in order to insert in his programme the policy of an alliance with the Soviet Union on a platform of fraternal cooperation. And had he presented such a programme and Lloyd George dared to raise his voice against it, then nine-tenths of the proletariat would have swept both the Liberals and the Conservatives clean out and then the new Labour government of Britain would be unshakable. But will this happen now? No, nor will it happen tomorrow. But this hour is nevertheless approaching. And who is bringing it nearer? MacDonald and his associates are bringing it nearer. They accuse us of propaganda. But surely not a single one of us, if we went off to Britain knowing the English language, customs, habits, and traditions to perfection, could have such an influence through his propaganda or produce such a shift in the consciousness of the working class as the fact that at the head of the country stands a government which considers itself to be the government of the working class but to which Lloyd George says: "I put you in charge but you did not fulfil my trust." There's an instructive dialogue! There's propaganda for you! This will embed itself for ever in the consciousness of the workers of Britain. We are not making propaganda but a prediction, for we do have a theory of political foresight and perception wrought by revolutionary experience. We predict that MacDonald and his government will play in Britain a very great preparatory role for the revolution, not because MacDonald wishes it so but, on the contrary, because he does not wish it so. MacDonald belongs to the Puritans. The Puritan church is the English branch of Calvinism. Calvinism is the Protestant doctrine at the base of which lies the law of pre-destination. This law states that man does not enjoy free will, but fulfils his destiny in accordance with the designs of divine providence. There is no free will. Every man is a tool in the hands of divine providence. This ideology of Calvinism closely resembles the politics, psychology, and objective role of democracy and Menshevism in the present epoch of imperialist autocracy. Calvinism says: your ideas and hopes are but subjective illusions, for actually you are a tool in the hands of providence. And the petty-bourgeois politician is indeed fed with illusions, each step he takes is dictated by subjective error, but in fact he is a tool, if not in the hands of providence then in the hands of Morgan, Rockefeller, and big capital in general. And while it is beyond doubt that in this sense MacDonald represents a tool in the hands of the City of London and of the British Stock Exchange, history has allotted him a still greater role in that he represents the unconscious tool not of divine providence – we have quite a serious difference with MacDonald on this score, for there is no place for divine providence in either our programme or our ideas – but of the laws of history. History has said to him: "MacDonald, guided by your subjective prejudices, show what you can do and show what you wish to do." And so MacDonald shows us that he wishes for little and is capable of even less. [*Laughter, applause.*] And it is this which is his enormous role – in the hands of the providence of history. As a result, MacDonald gives a mighty impulse to the revolutionary movement of the masses of Britain. Let me repeat once again: this is not propaganda – this is Marxist foresight made on the basis of the laws of history and all our political experience. We are conducting negotiations with MacDonald in good faith and I, like every one of you here, want these negotiations to yield practical results. These negotiations are on one plane, while the problems of the great contest of classes and of the struggle between the two Internationals are on another, higher plane, and embrace great masses of people and great periods. For we shall spend May Day in the profound certainty that in this great play of historical forces, in the struggle of the classes and in the working of the laws of history, MacDonald and the whole of European Menshevism form an instrument which is preparing, not according to the laws of Calvin but according to the laws of Marx, the ground for the advent of British Bolshevism.

Not so long ago, MacDonald said: "We fought against Moscow and we beat Moscow." This is presumably not propaganda! "We fought Moscow and we beat Moscow." He considers the fact that today, at the 35th anniversary of May Day, Europe, dismembered, bled white, led by Mensheviks and semi-Mensheviks (as far as the bourgeoisie permits them to lead), is still alive, he considers that this fact signifies our defeat. No, this is but one of the stages on the road to our forthcoming historic victory. You fought Moscow and you are fighting Moscow. And what of it? We are not afraid of waging this struggle alongside negotiations. But no, you haven't beaten Moscow. Not by a long shot!

What we are talking about is Red Moscow, that Moscow where we are here preparing to celebrate May Day in our own Soviet fashion. This Red Moscow is strong, a great and strong builder constructed it, and European Menshevism and British MacDonaldism shall not beat it! It is true that the great builder of Red Moscow will not be greeting May Day with us – he lies in the heart of Moscow in the mausoleum on Red Square; but if the great builder of Red Moscow has died then he who shall defeat our Red Moscow has yet to be born! [*Stormy applause, Internationale.*]

* * *

From a speech given to the Pyatigorsk Soviet, 14 October 1924

There has never been a more favourable moment in history to gain an absolute majority in parliament, but to do this MacDonald would need a different party from MacDonald's. It is difficult to predict today the results of the election.[6] If the Conservatives obtain a majority, Curzon will be in power. This will complicate the question of a treaty but will produce an explosion in the class struggle. The workers will press on with their old trade union demands and pose the question point-blank. British politics have reached a turning point and a sharpening of the class struggle.

---

6 The Conservatives won the 1924 General Election.

Volume Two

IV

Where is Britain Going?

(1925)

Preface to the American Edition

The present work is devoted to the future destiny of Britain. But it may also interest the American reader – firstly, because Britain occupies all too great a place in the world, and secondly, because the United States and Great Britain are twin stars, and the faster the one dies out, the more brightly the other flares up.

The conclusion which I reach in my study is that Britain is approaching, at full speed, an era of great revolutionary upheavals. Of course, British secret policemen and their American disciples will say that I am engaging in propaganda for a proletarian revolution – as if one could alter the direction of development of a great nation from outside, by means of a pamphlet! In fact, however, I am merely attempting, by analysing the leading factors in Britain's historical development, to elucidate the historical path down which she has been thrust by external and internal conditions. In this respect, to make accusations of revolutionary interference in other people's business is like accusing an astronomer of causing the solar eclipse that he had forecast.

Naturally I do not mean by this that astronomical events can be identified with social phenomena. The former occur outside of us and the latter through us. But this does not mean that historical events take place solely at our volition and can be steered by means of pamphlets. Books and newspapers which have as their task the defence and protection of capitalism, British capitalism included, have been and are being published on a far greater scale than ones directed against it. The matter is not, however, decided this way. This or that idea can exert an effect only in so far as it is rooted in the material conditions of social development. Britain is moving towards revolution because the epoch of capitalist decline has set in. And if culprits are to be sought, then in answer to the question who and what are propelling Britain along the road to revolution we must say: not Moscow but New York.

Such a reply might seem paradoxical. Nevertheless, it corresponds wholly to reality. The powerful and ever-growing world pressure of the United States makes the predicament of British industry, British trade, British finance, and British diplomacy increasingly insoluble and desperate.

The United States cannot help striving towards expansion on the world market, otherwise excess will threaten its own industry with a 'stroke'. The United States can only expand at the expense of Britain. Speeches on the revolutionary import of this or that 'Moscow' pamphlet can only produce an ironic smile when the economic life of a great nation is being choked in the steel vice of American dominance by Mr. Dawes'[1] patented system. Under the cloak of today's 'pacification' and 'recovery' of Europe, huge revolutionary and military upheavals and conflicts are being prepared for the future. Mr. Julius Barnes, who stands close to the Washington Department of Commerce, proposes that the European debtor countries be allocated those sectors of the world market where poor and debt-ridden European cousins will not hinder the expansion of their transatlantic creditor. By helping to restore the European monetary system the United States is merely bursting one inflationary illusion after another, and helping Europe to translate its poverty and dependence into the language of hard currency. By either pressurising or giving deferments to creditors, by granting or refusing credit to European countries, the United States is creating for them an increasingly constricted, economically dependent, but ultimately untenable position; which also provides the conditions for revolutionary social upheavals. The Communist International today is... almost a conservative institution by comparison with the New York Stock Exchange. Mr. Morgan, Mr. Dawes, and Mr. Julius Barnes are the busy artificers of the approaching European revolutions.

To a considerable degree the United States is carrying out its work, in Europe and throughout the world, with Britain's collaboration and through her agency. But for Britain this 'collaboration' is only the form of a growing dependence. Britain is, as it were, ushering the United States in only for

---

1   Drawn up in April 1924 by a committee headed by the American financier and general, Charles G. Dawes, later US Vice President in 1925-29. The plan provided for a scale of annual payments of German war reparations and reorganisation of the Reichsbank, and recommended a large foreign loan for Germany.

her to take possession. While surrendering their world domination, British diplomats and businessmen introduce the new ruler of the world to their former clients. The cooperation between America and Britain masks the deepest world-wide antagonism between the two powers and is preparing for fearful conflicts, perhaps in the none-too-distant future.

There is no space within the limits of a brief preface to discuss the destiny of America herself. It is clear that nowhere today does capital feel itself so secure as there. American capital has grown enormously, making itself strong first through the war in Europe, and now by means of 'pacification' and 'rehabilitation'. But for all its might, American capitalism is not a self-sufficient whole but a part of the world economy. Furthermore, the greater United States industry grows the deeper becomes its dependence on the world market. While driving Europe more and more into a blind alley, American capital is preparing wars and revolutionary upheavals which will then strike back at the economy of the United States with a terrible rebound. Such is the perspective for America herself. America occupies only the second place in the line of revolutionary development. The American bourgeoisie have still to watch the great collapse of their elder sister in Europe. But the inescapable hour will strike for American capitalism too. The magnates of the American trusts, the great plantation owners, oil tycoons and exporters, the billionaires of New York, Chicago, and San Francisco are irreversibly, if unconsciously, fulfilling their revolutionary function. And the American proletariat will ultimately fulfil theirs.

24 May 1925

Preface

Britain today stands at a point of crisis – perhaps more so than any other capitalist country. But Britain's crisis is to a large extent also a crisis for four of the world's continents, and at least the beginning of a shift for the fifth – and today the most powerful – America. At the same time the political development of Britain exhibits great peculiarities, flowing from the whole of her past, and in large measure blocking the path before her. Without cramming our account with facts and figures which the reader can easily find for himself in reference books and studies of Britain's economic situation, we have set ourselves to identify and characterise those historical factors and circumstances that will define Britain's development in the immediate period. We shall deal with Britain in particular and not the British Empire, with the metropolis and not the colonies and dominions. The latter have their own line of development which increasingly diverges from that followed by the metropolis.

Our account will be largely critical and polemical. History is made through men. An assessment of the vital forces making today's history cannot but be an active one. In order to understand what the classes, the parties, and their leaders are struggling for, and what awaits them tomorrow, we must cut through the dense mass of political conventions, lies and hypocrisy, the all-pervading parliamentary 'cant'.[1] Under these circumstances polemic becomes

---

1   Cant – A particular form of conventional falsehood, tacitly acknowledged by all as a type of social hypocrisy. According to Carlyle, cant is the art "whereby a man speaks openly what he does not mean". In Parliamentary-Protestant Britain this art-form has been carried to extraordinary heights – or depths. – *Trotsky*

an indispensable method of political analysis. Nonetheless, the question we have set ourselves, and to which we shall try to find the answer, has an objective character: "Where is Britain going?"

1. The Decline of Britain

Capitalist Britain was formed by the political revolution in the middle of the seventeenth century and the so-called 'industrial revolution' at the end of the eighteenth century. Britain emerged from her civil war and Cromwell's dictatorship as a small nation numbering hardly 1,500,000 families. She entered the 1914 imperialist war as an empire containing within its frontiers a fifth of humanity.

The English revolution of the seventeenth century, the school of puritanism, Cromwell's harsh school, prepared the British nation, and its middle classes in particular, for their subsequent world role. From the middle of the eighteenth-century Britain's world power was undisputed. Britain ruled the ocean and in the process created a world market.

In 1826 a British Conservative publicist depicted the age of industry in the following terms:

> The age which now discloses itself to our view promises to be the age of industry [...] By industry, alliances shall be dictated and national friendships shall be formed [...] The prospects which are now opening to England almost exceed the boundaries of thought; and can be measured by no standard found in history [...] The manufacturing industry of England may be fairly computed as four times greater than that of all the other continents taken collectively, and sixteen such continents as Europe could not manufacture so much cotton as England does [...][1]

---

1 Quoted in M. Beer, *A History of British Socialism*, Vol. 1, 1919, p. 283, from *Quarterly Review*, June-August 1826, pp. 92-9.

Great Britain's colossal industrial domination over the rest of Europe and the whole of the world laid the foundations of her wealth and her unequalled world position. The age of industry was at the same time the age of Britain's world hegemony.

From 1850 to 1880, Britain became the industrial school for Europe and America. But her own monopoly position was undermined by this very fact. From the 1880s Britain visibly began to weaken. Onto the world stage came new states, with Germany in the front rank. At the same time, the fact that Britain was the first-born of capitalist states began to reveal its pernicious, conservative aspects. The doctrine of free trade was dealt a heavy blow by German competition.

Still got a monarchy aristocracy

It became clear during the final quarter of the last century that Britain was being elbowed out of her position of world domination: and by the beginning of the present century this had produced an internal uncertainty and ferment among the upper classes, and a deep molecular process of an essentially revolutionary character in the working class. At the centre of these processes were mighty conflicts between labour and capital. It was not only the aristocratic status of British industry in the world, but also the privileged position of the 'aristocracy of labour' within Britain that was shaken. 1911 to 1913 were years of unparalleled class battles by miners, railwaymen and other transport workers. In August 1911 a national, in other words a general strike developed on the railways. During those days a dim spectre of revolution hung over Britain. The leaders made every effort to paralyse the movement. Their motive was 'patriotism': the strike was on at the time of the Agadir incident[2] which threatened to lead to war with Germany. Today it is well known that the Prime Minister invited the workers' leaders to a secret meeting, and called on them to "save the nation". And the leaders did all they could to strengthen the bourgeoisie, and thereby to prepare for the imperialist slaughter.

The 1914-1918 war seemed to cut the revolutionary process short. It put a stop to the development of the strike movements. By bringing about the break-up of Germany it had apparently restored Britain to her role of world hegemony. But it was soon to be revealed that Britain's decline, while temporarily checked, had in reality only been deepened by the war.

---

2 On 1 July 1911 a German warship visited the Moroccan port of Agadir allegedly to protect German interests against French expansion. The British government threatened action against a German presence so close to Gibraltar, and the threat of imperialist war was averted by a deal under which Germany was conceded part of French Congo to compensate for her withdrawal from Morocco.

In the years of 1917 to 1920 the British labour movement again passed through an extremely stormy period. Strikes took place on a broad scale. MacDonald signed manifestos from which, today, he would recoil in horror. Only after 1920 did the movement return within bounds; after 'Black Friday', when the Triple Alliance of miners', railwaymen's and transport workers' leaders betrayed the general strike. Paralysed in the sphere of economic action, the energy of the masses was directed on to the political plane. The Labour Party grew as if out of the earth itself.

In what does the change in the external and internal situation of Britain consist?

During the war, the gigantic economic domination of the United States had demonstrated itself wholly and completely. The United States' emergence from overseas provincialism at once shifted Britain into a secondary position.

The 'cooperation' between America and Britain is the momentarily peaceful form within which Britain's continuing retreat will proceed.

This 'cooperation' may at this or that moment be directed against a third power; nonetheless, the fundamental antagonism in the world is that between [Russia] Britain and America, and all the other antagonisms which seem more acute and more immediately threatening at a given moment can be understood and assessed only on the basis of this conflict of Britain with America.

Anglo-American cooperation is preparing the way for a war, just as a period of reforms prepares a revolution. The very fact that, by taking the path of 'reforms' (i.e., compulsory 'deals' with America) Britain will abandon one position after another, must force her in the end to resist. Great Britain's productive forces, and most of all her living productive forces, the proletariat, no longer correspond to her place in the world market. Hence the chronic unemployment. The commercial and industrial (and the military and naval) pre-eminence of Britain has, in the past, almost safeguarded the links between the parts of the empire. As early as the end of the last century, Reeves, the Prime Minister of New Zealand, wrote:

> Two things maintain the present relations between the colonies and Britain: 1) their belief that Britain's policy is in the main a policy of peace, and 2) their belief that Britain rules the waves.

The second condition was, of course, the main one. This loss of the "rule of the waves" goes hand-in-hand with the build-up of centrifugal forces within the empire. Imperial unity is increasingly threatened by the diverging interests of the dominions and the struggles of the colonies.

geographical, quantitative facilities combined + difference + uneven.

The development of military technique militates against Great Britain's security. Aviation and chemical warfare is reducing the tremendous historical advantages of an island position to zero. America, that gigantic 'island' walled off on both sides by oceans, remains invulnerable. But Britain's greatest centres of population, and London above all, can face a murderous air attack from the continent of Europe in the course of a few hours.

Having lost the advantages of inaccessibility, the British government is compelled to take an increasingly direct part in purely European matters and in European military pacts. Britain's overseas possessions, her dominions, have no interest in this policy. They are interested in the Pacific Ocean, the Indian Ocean, and to some extent in the Atlantic, but not in the slightest in the English Channel. At the first world clash this divergence of interests will turn into a gaping abyss in which imperial links will be buried. The political life of Great Britain is, in anticipation of this, paralysed by internal frictions and is doomed to be essentially a policy of passivity, with a consequent worsening of the empire's world position.

Meantime, military spending must form an ever-growing share of Great Britain's shrinking national income.

One of the conditions of Britain's 'cooperation' with America is the repayment of the gigantic British debt to America, without any hope of ever receiving repayment of the debt owed her by the continental states. The balance of economic power will thereby swing still further in America's favour.

On 5 March this year, the Bank of England raised the Bank Rate from 4 to 5 per cent following the example of the New York Federal Reserve Bank, which had raised its rate from 3 to 3.5 per cent. In the City of London this sharp reminder of financial dependence on their cousins from across the Atlantic was felt very painfully. But what were they to do? The American gold reserve is approximately $4,500 million, while the British is approximately $750 million, six times less. America *has* a gold currency, while Great Britain can only make desperate efforts to re-establish one. It is natural that, when the rate is raised from 3 to 3.5 per cent in America, Britain is compelled to reply by raising her rate from 4 to 5 per cent. Such a measure strikes at British industry and commerce by raising the cost of essential materials. In this way America at every step shows Britain her place: in one case by the methods of diplomatic pressure, in another by a banking decision, and always and everywhere by the pressure of her colossal economic domination.[3]

---

3 Since this was written the British government has taken a series of legislative measures in the fields of banking and finance to guarantee the change to the

At the same time the British press notes with alarm the "striking progress" of various branches of German industry, and of German shipbuilding in particular. Arising from the latter, *The Times* of 10 March wrote:

> Gold Standard. Here we seem to have a "great victory" for British capitalism. In actual fact Britain's decline is nowhere expressed more clearly than in this financial achievement. Britain was compelled to carry out this expensive operation through the pressure of the gold-backed American dollar, and the financial policy of her own dominions which were orientating themselves increasingly towards the dollar and turning their backs on the pound sterling. Britain could not have accomplished this recent step towards gold currency without extensive financial 'aid' from the United States. But that means that the fate of the pound sterling is becoming directly dependent on New York. The United States is taking into its own hands a mighty weapon of financial impression. Britain is being compelled to pay a high interest rate for this dependence. The dividends will be charged against an already ailing industry. In order to hinder the export of her own gold she is forced to cut back the export of her own goods. At the same time, she cannot refuse to transfer to gold currency without hastening her own decline in the world capital market. This fatal combination of circumstances brings on a feeling of severe malaise among the British ruling classes and gives rise to malevolent but impotent grumbling in the Conservative press itself. The *Daily Mail* writes:

> > By accepting the Gold Standard the British government is giving the Federal Reserve Bank (which is in practice in the power of the United States government) the *possibility of creating a monetary crisis in Britain at any moment it chooses*. The British government is bringing the whole financial policy of its own country into submission to a foreign nation [...] The British Empire is being mortgaged to the United States.

"Thanks to Churchill", writes the Conservative newspaper, the *Daily Express*, "Britain is falling under the heel of the American bankers". The *Daily Chronicle* expresses itself more decidedly: "Britain is in fact demoted to the position of being the forty-ninth state of America". It could not be put more clearly or vividly! To all these reproaches (which lack conclusions or perspectives) Churchill, the Chancellor of the Exchequer, replies to the effect that there is nothing else for Britain to do but to bring her financial system into conformity "with reality". Churchill's words signify: we have become immeasurably poorer, the United States immeasurably richer; we must either fight America or submit to her; in making the pound sterling dependent on American banks we simply translate our general economic decline into the language of currency; we cannot leap over our own heads; we must conform "with reality". – *Trotsky*

It is probable that one of the factors which makes for the ability of the German yards to compete is the complete 'trustification' of the material, from the mine to the fitted plate, from the financing bank to the sale of tickets. This system is not without its effects on wages and the cost of living. When all these forces are turned in the same direction the margin for reduction in costs becomes very considerable.

In other words, *The Times* here states that the organic superiority of the more up-to-date German industry will once again be fully demonstrated as soon as other countries give Germany the possibility of displaying signs of life.

There are indications, it is true, that the order for ships had been placed with the Hamburg yard with the object of frightening the trade unions, and thus preparing the ground for reducing wages and lengthening working hours. Needless to say, such a manoeuvre is more than likely. But that does not weaken the force of our general contention regarding the irrational organisation of British industry and the overheads resulting from it.

It is now four years since the number of officially registered unemployed in Britain fell below 1,135,000; it has fluctuated between 1.5 and 1.75 million. This chronic unemployment is the sharpest revelation of the system's insolvency; it is also its Achilles' heel. The Unemployed Insurance Act introduced in 1920 was designed to meet exceptional circumstances which, supposedly, would quickly pass. But meanwhile unemployment was becoming permanent, insurance ceased to be insurance, since spending on the unemployed was not covered by the payments of contributors. The British unemployed can no longer be regarded as a 'normal' reserve army, contracting and expanding and constantly changing its composition, but must be seen as a permanent social layer created by industry during the period of growth and discharged in a period of recession. It is a gouty growth on the social organism, stemming from a weak metabolism.

The President of the Federation of British Industries, Colonel Willey, declared at the beginning of April that the return on industrial capital had been so insignificant during the last two years that it could not stimulate businessmen to develop industry. Business enterprises do not yield any higher return than fixed-interest paper values (gilt-edged securities and so on). "Our national problem is not a problem of production but a market problem." But how do you resolve a market problem? It is necessary to produce more cheaply than others. Yet to do this it is necessary either radically to re-organise industry, to reduce taxes, to cut workers' wages, or to combine all three methods. Cutting wages, which can give only an insignificant result in terms of reducing production costs, will produce firm opposition since the workers are today fighting for wage rises. It is impossible to reduce taxes since it is necessary to pay off debts, to establish a gold-based currency, and to maintain the apparatus of empire and 1.5 million unemployed to boot.

All these items enter into the cost of production. Industry could only be reorganised by investing new capital; meanwhile low profits drive free capital towards state and other loans.

Stanley Machin, the President of the Association of British Chambers of Commerce, recently declared that the solution to unemployment was emigration. The benevolent fatherland tells a million or so workers who, together with their families, make up several million citizens: "Stuff yourselves in the hold and clear off somewhere overseas!" The utter bankruptcy of the capitalist regime is stated here without the least equivocation.

We must examine Britain's internal life from the standpoint of the abrupt and continuously declining world role of Great Britain which, while holding on to her possessions, and the apparatus and tradition of world domination, is in actual fact being relegated increasingly to a secondary position.

The break-up of the Liberal Party crowns a century of development of the capitalist economy and bourgeois society. The loss of world domination has brought whole branches of British industry to a dead end and has struck a lethal blow at self-sufficient medium-sized industrial and commercial capital – the basis of Liberalism. Free trade has reached an impasse.

In the past, the internal stability of the capitalist regime was in large measure assured by a division of labour and responsibility between Conservatism and Liberalism. The break-up of Liberalism exposes all the other contradictions in the world position of bourgeois Britain at the same time as it reveals the internal crisis of the regime. The upper circles of the Labour Party are politically very close to the Liberals; but they are incapable of restoring stability to British parliamentarism since the Labour Party, in its present form, itself expresses a temporary stage in the revolutionary development of the working class. MacDonald's seat is even shakier than Lloyd George's.

At the beginning of the 1850s, Marx thought that the Conservative Party would soon quit the scene and that political development would follow the line of a struggle between liberalism and socialism. This perspective presupposed a rapid revolutionary development in Britain and in Europe. Just as, for example, our own Cadet Party (Constitutional-Democrats) became, under the pressure of the revolution, the sole party of the landowners and the bourgeoisie, so British Liberalism would have absorbed the Conservative Party and become the sole party of property, if a revolutionary onslaught by the proletariat had developed in the course of the latter half of the nineteenth century. But Marx's prophecy was made on the very eve of a new period of rapid capitalist development (1851-1873). Chartism finally disappeared. The workers' movement took the path of trade unionism. The inner contradictions of the ruling class took on the appearance of a struggle between the Liberal and the Conservative Parties. By rocking the parliamentary swing from right to left and from left to right, the bourgeoisie found a vent for the opposition feelings of the working masses.

German competition was the first serious threat to British world hegemony, and dealt it the first serious blow. Free Trade ran up against the superiority of German productive technique and organisation. British Liberalism was only the political generalisation of Free Trade. The Manchester School had occupied a dominant position from the time of the bourgeois, property-qualified, electoral reforms of 1832,[4] and the repeal of the Corn Laws in 1846. Over the course of the next half-century, the doctrine of Free Trade seemed to be an immutable programme. Accordingly, the leading role belonged to the Liberals. The workers tailed behind them. From the beginning of the 1870s the pattern was upset: Free Trade was discredited; a protectionist movement set in; the bourgeoisie was increasingly seized by imperialist tendencies. Symptoms of the Liberal Party's decay appeared as early as Gladstone's time, when a group of Liberals and Radicals led by Chamberlain raised the banner of protectionism and joined with the Conservatives.[5] From the middle of the 1890s trade took a turn for the better. This delayed Britain's political transformation. But by the beginning of the twentieth century Liberalism, as the party of the middle classes, had cracked. Its leader, Lord Rosebery, placed himself openly behind the banner of imperialism. However, the Liberal Party was destined for one more upsurge before leaving the scene. Under the influence of the evident decline of British capital on the one hand, and of the mighty revolutionary movement in Russia on the other, there developed

---

4 The demand to put an end to the system whereby seats in Parliament could be bought and tiny groups could elect MPs came to a head with the election of a reforming Whig government in 1830. Under intense popular pressure, and the threat to flood the House of Lords with new peers, a measure was passed abolishing the worst of the 'rotten boroughs' and extending the franchise to some of the middle class.

5 The issue of Irish Home Rule and the support for it by the Liberal Party leadership, especially Gladstone, resulted in this break-away by the more pro-imperialist Liberals led by Joseph Chamberlain, who set up the Unionist Party and ultimately united with the Conservatives.

a political re-awakening of the working class which, in applying itself to the creation of a parliamentary Labour Party, also poured flood-water into the mill of the Liberal opposition. Liberalism came to power again in 1906. But this upsurge could not, by its very nature, last for long. The political movement of the proletariat led to the further growth of the Labour Party. Before 1906 the Labour Party's representation had grown more or less in step with the Liberals'; after 1906 the Labour Party was clearly growing at the expense of the Liberals.

It was formally the Liberal Party which, through Lloyd George, led the war. In fact, the imperialist war, from which even the sacred regime of Free Trade could not save Britain, inevitably strengthened the Conservatives as the most consistent party of imperialism. Thus, the conditions were finally prepared for the Labour Party's entrance onto the scene.

While impotently hovering over the question of unemployment, the Labour Party daily newspaper, the *Daily Herald*, draws from capitalist admissions such as we quoted above, the general conclusion that, since British capitalists prefer to give financial loans to foreign governments rather than for domestic industrial expansion, there is nothing left for the British workers to do but to produce without the capitalists. In a very general sense, this conclusion is perfectly correct, only here it is drawn not at all with the intention of arousing the workers to drive the capitalists out, but merely to urge the capitalists along the road of 'progressive efforts'. As we shall see, the whole of the Labour Party's policy turns on this. To this end the Webbs write a whole book, MacDonald delivers his speeches and the editors of the *Daily Herald* supply daily articles. Meanwhile, if this pathetic scaremongering has any effect at all on the capitalists, it is in the opposite direction. Every serious British bourgeois understands that behind the mock-heroic threats of the Labour Party leaders, there lies concealed a real danger from the deeply stirring proletarian masses. It is precisely because of this that the shrewd bourgeoisie concludes that it is better not to tie up fresh resources in industry.

The bourgeois fear of revolution is not always and under all circumstances a 'progressive' factor. For there can be no doubt that the British economy would derive great benefits from the cooperation of Britain and Russia. But this presupposes a comprehensive plan, large credits and adapting a considerable section of British industry to the needs of Russia. The obstacle to this is the bourgeoisie's dread of revolution, and their uncertainty about the future.

The fear of revolution drove the British capitalists along the path of concessions and re-organisation as long as the material opportunities for

British capitalism were, or seemed, limitless. The shocks of the European revolutions have always found a clear reflection in Britain's social development; they led to reforms as long as the British bourgeoisie, through their world position, retained in their own hands gigantic resources for manoeuvre. They could legalise trade unions, repeal the Corn Laws, increase wages, extend the franchise, institute social reforms, and so on. But in Britain's present radically altered position in the world the threat of revolution is no longer capable of pushing the bourgeoisie forward: on the contrary, it now paralyses the last remnants of their industrial initiative. What is necessary now is not threats of revolution but revolution itself.

The factors and circumstances set out above are not of a chance and transient character. They are developing in one and the same direction, systematically aggravating Britain's international and domestic situation, and making it historically intractable.

The contradictions undermining British society will inevitably intensify. We do not intend to predict the exact tempo of this process, but it will be measurable in terms of years, or in terms of five years at the most; certainly not in decades. This general prospect requires us to ask above all the question: will a Communist Party be built in Britain in time with the strength and the links with the masses to be able to thaw out at the right moment all the necessary practical conclusions from the sharpening crisis? It is in *this* question that Great Britain's fate is today contained.

2. Mr. Baldwin and…
Gradualness

On 12 March of this year [1925], Mr. Baldwin, the British Prime Minister and leader of the Conservative Party, delivered a long speech on Britain's future to a Conservative audience at Leeds. This speech, like many other of Mr. Baldwin's public utterances, was pervaded with anxiety. We consider that, from the point of view of Mr. Baldwin's party, such anxiety is entirely well-founded. We for our part shall approach these same questions from rather a different angle. Mr. Baldwin is afraid of socialism, and in his demonstrations of the dangers and difficulties attending the road to socialism Mr. Baldwin made a somewhat unexpected attempt to gain support from the author of this book. This gives us, we hope, a right to reply to Mr. Baldwin without risk of being accused of interfering in Great Britain's internal affairs.

Mr. Baldwin considers, and not without reason, that the greatest danger to the regime he supports is the growth of the Labour Party. He hopes, of course, for victory, since "our [the Conservatives] principles are in closer accord with the character and traditions of our people than any traditions or any principles of violent change." The Conservative leader nonetheless reminds his audience that the verdict of the last election was not the final one.

Mr. Baldwin is convinced, of course, that socialism is not practicable. But as he is in a rather confused state of mind and as, in addition, he is addressing an audience already convinced of the impracticability of socialism, Mr. Baldwin's arguments to this effect are not distinguished by great originality.

He reminds his Conservative audience that children are born neither free, nor equal, nor as brothers. He addresses this question to each mother at the meeting: were her children born equal? The self-satisfied laughter of his audience was his answer. To be sure, the mass of the British people had heard the same answer from the spiritual great-great-grandfathers of Baldwin, in reply to their demand for the right to freedom of belief and to be allowed to set up their church as they wished. The same arguments were later brought against equality before a court, and later, not at all so long ago, against universal suffrage.

People are not born equal, Mr. Baldwin; why then do they have to answer before one and the same court, according to the same law? One could have objected to Mr. Baldwin that although children are not born exactly alike, a mother normally feeds her dissimilar children alike at the table, and makes sure, if she can, that they all have a pair of shoes on their feet. A bad stepmother, of course, might well act differently.

One could have explained to Mr. Baldwin that socialism is concerned not with the creation of anatomical, physiological, and psychical equality, but tries only to guarantee all people similar material conditions of existence. But we shall not weary our readers with further exposition of these elementary ideas: Mr. Baldwin can himself, if he is interested, turn to the relevant sources; and as his world-outlook inclines him towards ancient and purely British authors we could recommend to him old Robert Owen who, it is true, had no understanding whatsoever of the class dynamics of capitalist society, but in whose works one may find most valuable observations regarding the advantages of socialism.

But the socialist aim, though reprehensible enough in itself, does not of course frighten Mr. Baldwin so much as a violent road towards it. Mr. Baldwin perceives two tendencies in the Labour Party. One of them is, in his words, represented by Mr. Sidney Webb who has recognised "the inevitability of gradualness". But there are leaders of another kind, like Cook, or Wheatley, especially since he left his ministerial post, who believe in force. According to Mr. Baldwin, the responsibility of government has in general had a salutary influence on the Labour Party leaders and has compelled them to recognise, along with Webb, the futile character of revolutionary methods and the advantages of gradualness. At this point Mr. Baldwin made a sort of god-like excursion into Russian affairs to enrich his meagre arsenal of arguments against British socialism.

Let us quote the report in *The Times*:

The Prime Minister quoted Trotsky, who, he said, had discovered in the last few years and written "that the more easily did the Russian proletariat pass through the revolutionary crisis, the harder becomes now its constructive work." Trotsky had also said what no leader of the extremists had yet said in Britain: "We must learn to work more efficiently." He wondered how many votes would be cast for a revolution in Britain if people were told that the only [? – *LT*] result would be that they would have to work more efficiently. [*Laughter, cheers.*] Trotsky said in his book: "In Russia before and after the revolution, there existed and exists unchanged Russian human nature [?! – *LT*]." Trotsky, the man of action, studied realities. He had slowly and reluctantly discovered what Mr. Webb discovered two years ago – the "inevitability of gradualness". [*Laughter, applause.*]

Of course, it is very flattering to be recommended to a Conservative audience at Leeds; a mortal can scarcely ask for more. It is nearly as flattering to fall into a direct association with Mr. Sidney Webb, the prophet of gradualness. But, before accepting this honour, there are one or two clarifications we should like from Mr. Baldwin.

It had never entered the heads of either our teachers or ourselves, even before the experience of "the last few years", to deny the fact of gradual development in either nature or in human society, in its economy, politics or morals. We would merely like to make some qualifications about the nature of this gradualness. Thus, to take an example close to Mr. Baldwin as a protectionist, let us consider the fact that Germany, which gradually emerged into the arena of world competition in the final quarter of the last century, became an extremely threatening rival to Britain. It is well known that it was along this path that matters came to war. Does Baldwin regard the war as a manifestation of gradualness? During the war, the Conservative Party demanded "the destruction of the Huns" and the toppling of the German Kaiser by the force of the British sword. From the standpoint of the theory of gradualness it might have been better to rely upon an improvement in German morality and a gradual improvement in her relations with Britain. However, in the period from 1914 to 1918 Mr. Baldwin, as far as we recall, categorically rejected the applicability of gradualness to Anglo-German relations and endeavoured to settle the matter by means of vast quantities of high explosive. We submit that dynamite and lyddite can scarcely be regarded as the proper instruments of an evolutionary-conservative style of operation.

Pre-war Germany, for her part, by no means emerged in shining armour one fine morning from the waves. No, she had developed gradually out of her former economic insignificance. However, there were one or two breaks in this gradual process; thus, we have the wars Prussia waged against Denmark in 1864, against Austria in 1866, and against France in 1870; these played a colossal role in increasing her might and provided her with the possibility of triumphantly starting out along the path of world competition with Britain.

Wealth, the result of human labour, is without doubt created with a certain gradualness. But Mr. Baldwin would agree that the years of the war caused a gigantic upward leap in the development of the United States. The gradualness of accumulation was abruptly upset by the catastrophe of a war that caused the impoverishment of Europe and the feverish enrichment of America.

A 'leap' in his own personal life was recounted by Mr. Baldwin himself in a parliamentary speech devoted to the trade unions. As a young man he managed a factory which had been handed down from generation to generation, where workers were born and died and where, in consequence, the principle of patriarchal 'gradualness' held complete sway.

But a miners' strike broke out, the factory could not operate owing to the shortage of coal, and Mr. Baldwin found himself forced to close it down and release "his" thousand workers to the four corners of the world. Certainly, Baldwin can plead the ill-will of the miners who compelled him to infringe a sacred Conservative principle. The miners could probably have cited in their defence the ill-will of their employers, who had compelled them to call a colossal strike that brought a break in the monotonous process of exploitation.

But subjective promptings are in the last resort immaterial: for us it is enough to know that gradualness in various spheres of life goes hand in hand with catastrophes, breaks and upward and downward leaps. The long process of competition between the two states *gradually* prepares the war, the discontent of exploited workers *gradually* prepares a strike, the bad management of a bank *gradually* prepares bankruptcy.

The honourable Conservative leader may reply, it is true, that such breaks in gradualness like war and bankruptcy, the impoverishment of Europe and the enrichment of America at her expense, are all most regrettable and that in general it would be better to avoid them. The only objection to this is that the history of nations is in considerable part a history of wars and the history of economic development is embellished with bankruptcy statistics. Mr. Baldwin would probably say that these are properties of human nature. We might concede this, but it still means that the 'nature' of man couples gradual development with catastrophic leaps.

However, the history of mankind is not only a history of wars but also a history of revolutions. The seignorial rights which grew up over centuries, and which economic development then took centuries to undermine, were swept away in France at one stroke on 4 August 1789. On 9 November 1918 the German revolution annihilated German absolutism, which had been undermined by the struggle of the proletariat and brought to heel by the victories of the Allies. We have already recalled that one of the war slogans of the British government of which Mr. Baldwin was a member was "War till the total destruction of German militarism!" Doesn't Mr. Baldwin think, then, that in so far as the catastrophe of the war – with a little assistance from Mr. Baldwin himself – prepared for a revolutionary catastrophe in Germany, all this took place with no little detriment to the principle of historical gradualness? Of course, one can object that German militarism, and the Kaiser's ill-will, were both also to blame here. We will gladly believe that had Mr. Baldwin created the world he would have populated it with the most benevolent Kaisers and the most kind-hearted forms of militarism. But such an opportunity did not present itself to the British Prime Minister; and what is more we have heard from him that people, including Kaisers, are born neither equal nor good nor as brothers. One has to take the world as it is. Moreover: if it is true that the rout of German imperialism was a good thing then it must be recognised that the German revolution which completed the work of the military defeat was also a good thing; that is to say, that a catastrophic overthrow of what had taken shape gradually, was a good thing.

Mr. Baldwin may, it is true, object that all this has no direct bearing on Britain and that only in that chosen country has the principle of gradualness found its legitimate expression. But if this is so then it was pointless for Mr. Baldwin to refer to my words, which referred to Russia, and thus to impart a universal, general, absolute character to the principle of gradualness. My political experience, at least, does not confirm this. If my memory serves me right, three revolutions have taken place in Russia: in 1905, in February 1917, and in October 1917. As regards the February revolution, a certain modest assistance was provided by Buchanan (a man not unknown to Mr. Baldwin), who evidently calculated then (with the knowledge of his government), that a little revolutionary catastrophe in Petrograd would be more useful to Great Britain than all Rasputin's gradualness.

But is it in the end true that "the character and history of the British people" is so decisively and unconditionally permeated with the Conservative traditions of gradualness? Is it true that the British people is so hostile to "violent changes"? The whole history of Britain is above all a history of violent changes that the British ruling classes have wrought in the lives of other peoples. For example, it would be interesting to know whether the seizures of India or Egypt can be interpreted in terms of the principle of gradualness? The policy of the British propertied classes in relation to India is most candidly expressed in Lord Salisbury's words: "India must be bled!" It is not out of place to recall that Salisbury was the leader of the same party that is today led by Mr. Baldwin. To this one must add in parenthesis that, as a result of the excellently organised conspiracy of the bourgeois press, the British people do not in fact know what is being done in India (and we are in what is called a democracy). Perhaps we may recall the history of ill-fated Ireland, which is particularly rich in examples of the *peaceful, evolutionary methods of operation of the British ruling classes?* As far as we remember, the subjugation of South Africa did not evoke protests from Mr. Baldwin, and when General Roberts' forces broke the defensive front of the Boer settlers, the latter could scarcely have found a very convincing demonstration of gradualness in that.

All this, to be sure, relates to Britain's external history. But it is nevertheless strange that the principle of evolutionary gradualness, which is recommended to us as a universal precept, ceases to operate beyond the confines of Great Britain – on the frontiers of China when she had to be forced by war to buy opium, on the frontiers of Turkey when Mosul had to be taken from her, and on the frontiers of Persia and Afghanistan when submission to Britain had to be imposed on them.

Is it not possible to draw from all this the conclusion that the greater the success with which Britain applied force to other peoples, the greater the degree of 'gradualness' she managed to realise within her own frontiers? Indeed it is! Britain, over three centuries, conducted an uninterrupted succession of wars directed at an extending her arena of exploitation, removing foreign riches, killing foreign commercial competition, and annihilating foreign naval forces, all by means of piracy and violence against other nations, and thereby enriching the British governing classes. A diligent investigation of the facts and their inner linkages leads to the inescapable conclusion that the British governing classes managed to avoid revolutionary shocks within their country in so far as they were successful at increasing their own material power by means of wars and shocks of all sorts in other countries. In this way did they gain the possibility of restraining the revolutionary indignation of the masses through timely, and always very niggardly, concessions. But such a conclusion, which is completely irrefutable in itself, proves the exact opposite of what Baldwin wanted to prove, for the very history of Britain testifies in practice that "peaceful development" can only be ensured by means of a succession of wars, colonial acts of violence and bloody shocks. This is a strange form of "gradualness"!

A fairly well-known populariser of British history, Gibbins, writes in his outline of modern British history:

> In general – though, of course, *there are exceptions to this* – the guiding principle of British foreign policy has been the support for political freedom and constitutional government.

This sentence is truly remarkable; at the same time as being deeply official, 'national', and traditional-sounding, it leaves no room for the hypocritical doctrine of non-interference in the affairs of other nations; at the same time, it testifies to the fact that Britain supported constitutional movements in other countries only in so far as they were advantageous to her commercial and other interests. But on the other hand, as the inimitable Gibbins says, "there are exceptions to this rule". The entire history of Britain is depicted for the edification of her people (the doctrine of non-intervention notwithstanding), as a glorious struggle of the British government for freedom throughout the world. Every single new act of perfidy and violence – the Opium War with China, the enslavement of Egypt, the Boer War, the intervention in support of tsarist generals – is interpreted as an exception to the rule.

Thus, there generally prove to be gaps in "gradualness" both on the part of "freedom" and the part of despotism.

One can, of course, go further and say that violence in international relations is permissible and even inevitable, but that in relations between social classes it is reprehensible. But then there is no point in speaking of a "natural law" of gradualness which supposedly governs the whole development of nature and society. Then one must simply say: an oppressed class is obliged to support the oppressor class of its own nation when the latter adopts violence for its own ends; but that the oppressed class has no right to use violence to ensure a better position for itself in a society based upon oppression. This will be no longer a "law of nature" but the law of the bourgeois criminal code.

However, even within the limits of Great Britain's own internal history the principle of gradual and peaceful development is by no means as prevalent as Conservative philosophers would have us believe. In the final analysis the whole of present-day Britain has come out of the revolution in the seventeenth century. In the great civil war of that era were born the Tories and Whigs who were to set their seals alternately on Britain's history for over three centuries. When Mr. Baldwin appeals to the conservative traditions of British history, we must permit ourselves to remind him that the tradition of the Conservative Party itself is based firmly in the revolution of the middle of the seventeenth century. Similarly, the reference to the "character of the British people" forces us to recall that this character was beaten into shape by the hammer of the civil war between the Roundheads and the Cavaliers.[1] The character of the Independents: petty bourgeois traders, artisans, free farmers, small landed gentry, business-like, devout, economical, hard-working, and enterprising, this character collided violently with the character of the idle, dissolute, and haughty governing classes of old England: the court aristocracy, the titled state bureaucracy, and the bishops.

And yet both the former and the latter were Englishmen! With a heavy military hammer, on the anvil of civil war, Oliver Cromwell forged that same national character which over two and a half centuries ensured gigantic advantages in the world for the British bourgeoisie. Only later, at the close of the nineteenth century, was it to reveal itself as too conservative, even from the standpoint of capitalist development. It is clear that the struggle of the Long Parliament against the tyranny of Charles I, and Cromwell's severe dictatorship, had been prepared by Britain's previous history. But this means, simply, that a revolution is not made to order but grows organically out of the conditions of social development, and forms at least as inevitable a stage in the development of relations between the classes of one and the same nation as does war in the development of relations between organised nations. Perhaps Mr. Baldwin can find theoretical consolation in this gradualness of preparation?

Conservative old ladies – including Mrs. Snowden, who has recently discovered that the Royal family is the most hard-working class in society – must shudder at nights when they remember the execution of Charles I. And yet even the reactionary Macaulay came close to an understanding of that event:

> Those who had him in their grip [he says – *LT*] were not midnight stabbers. What they did they did in order that it might be a spectacle to heaven and to

---

1   The popular titles given to the soldiers on the respective sides in the Civil War. 'Roundheads' was a term of abuse for the forces of Puritanism, Parliament, and bourgeois revolution, referring to the fact that they cut their hair short. 'Cavaliers' were the more fashionably dressed, but less efficient, forces who supported the King.

earth, and that it might be held in everlasting remembrance. They enjoyed keenly the very scandal which they gave. That the ancient constitution and the public opinion of England were directly opposed to regicide made regicide seem strangely fascinating to a party bent on effecting a complete political and social revolution. In order to accomplish their purpose, it was necessary that they should first break in pieces every part of the machinery of government; and this necessity was rather agreeable than painful to them [...] A revolutionary tribunal was created. That tribunal pronounced Charles a tyrant, a murderer, and a public enemy; and his head was severed from his shoulders before thousands of spectators in front of the Banqueting Hall of his own palace.[2]

From the standpoint of the Puritans to break up all sections of the old government machine, the fact that Charles Stuart was an extravagant, lying, and cowardly scoundrel is completely secondary. Not only Charles I, but royal absolutism itself was dealt a mortal blow by the Puritans, the fruits of which are enjoyed to this day by the preachers of parliamentary gradualness.

The role of revolution in the political and social development in general of Britain is not, however, limited to the seventeenth century. It could be said – although this might seem paradoxical – that *all Britain's subsequent development has taken place in the train of European revolutions.* We shall give here merely an overall summary of the main elements which may prove to be of some use not only to Mr. Baldwin.

The French Revolution gave a powerful thrust to the development of democratic tendencies in Britain and above all to the labour movement, which was driven underground by the Combination Laws of 1799.[3] The war against revolutionary France was 'popular' only among the governing classes; the popular masses sympathised with the French Revolution and expressed their indignation against the Pitt government. The creation of the British trade unions was to a large extent the result of the influence of the French revolution on the labouring masses of Britain. The triumph of reaction on the

---

2　Lord Macaulay, *History of England*, 1889, p. 63.

3　During the eighteenth century, a number of legislative measures were passed forbidding trade union organisation in different trades. The first general measure was passed in 1799 in the wake of other restrictions on the press and democratic rights, banning all trade unions and imposing fines and imprisonment. A further measure in 1800 slightly reduced the penalties. These laws were not repealed until 1824, and although trade unions were formed in this period and bargains were even made with employers, workers' organisations could be crushed at the will of the capitalists.

continent, which strengthened the position of the landlords, led in 1815 to the restoration of the Bourbons in France and the introduction of the Corn Laws in Britain.

The July Revolution of 1830[4] in France gave an impetus to the first electoral Reform Bill of 1831 in Britain: a bourgeois revolution on the continent produced a bourgeois reform in the British Isles.

The radical reorganisation of the administration of Canada, giving much greater autonomy, was carried out only after the rising in Canada of 1837-1838.[5]

The revolutionary movement of Chartism led in 1844-1847 to the introduction of the ten-hour working day, and in 1846 to the repeal of the Corn Laws. The defeat of the revolutionary movement on the continent in 1848 not only meant the decline of the Chartist movement but put a brake on the democratisation of the British parliament for a long time afterwards.

The electoral reform of 1867[6] was preceded by the Civil War in the United States. When, in 1861, war flared up in America between the North and the South, British workers demonstrated their sympathy with the Northern states, while the sympathies of the ruling classes were wholly on the side of

---

4   On 26 July 1830, French King Charles X dissolved the parliament – dominated by the liberal bourgeoisie – in order to remove opposition to his measures against democracy and in favour of the old aristocracy. For three days the workers of Paris fought on the barricades, while many soldiers refused to fire. The liberals, led by Thiers, took fright and proposed handing the throne to a nominee of the French people (i.e., the bourgeoisie). Louis-Philippe Orléans was installed, representing the interests of the financial bourgeoisie as opposed to the aristocracy.

5   In 1791 Canada had been partitioned at the Ottawa River into Lower Canada, chiefly French, and the British area of Upper Canada, which included 'loyalists' who had fled from the American Revolution. In 1837 there was a revolt of French Canadians in Lower Canada led by Louis Papineau to establish an independent French state and another revolt in Upper Canada against ruling officialdom. After these revolts were put down the Earl of Durham was sent to Canada and though he was dismissed for showing too much leniency to the rebels his report was the basis of the 1840 Act of Union which unified the two parts of Canada under more rigorous British imperial rule.

6   Carried out by the Tories under the leadership of Lord Derby and Benjamin Disraeli in an unsuccessful bid to defeat the Whigs in the face of rising pressure for an extension of the franchise, including enormous demonstrations in Hyde Park. They passed the Second Reform Act extending the franchise to prosperous urban workers and continuing the process of granting more parliamentary representation to urban centres.

the slave-owners. It is instructive to note that the Liberal Palmerston, the so-called 'Firebrand Palmerston', and many of his colleagues including the notorious Gladstone, were in sympathy with the South and were quick to recognise the Southern states as belligerents rather than insurgents. Warships were built for the Southerners in British yards. The North nevertheless won, and this revolutionary victory on American territory *gained the vote for a section of the British working class* (the 1867 Act). In Britain, incidentally, the reform was accompanied by a stormy movement which led to the "July Days" of 1866, when major disorders lasted for forty-eight hours.

The defeat of the 1848 revolution had weakened the British workers but the Russian Revolution of 1905 immediately strengthened them. As a result of the 1906 General Election, the Labour Party formed for the first time a strong parliamentary group of forty-two members. In this the influence of the 1905 revolution was clear!

In 1918, even before the end of the war, a new electoral reform was passed in Britain which considerably enlarged the ranks of working-class voters, and allowed women to participate in elections for the first time. Even Mr. Baldwin would probably not begin to deny that the Russian Revolution of 1917 was an important stimulus to this reform. The British bourgeois considered that a revolution could be avoided in this way. It follows that even for passing reforms, the principle of gradualness is insufficient and a real threat of revolution is necessary.

If we look back in this way over the history of Britain for the last century and a half in the context of the general European and world development it transpires that Britain exploited other countries not only economically but also politically, by cutting its own political 'costs' at the cost of the civil wars of the nations of Europe and America.

So what was the meaning of those two phrases that Mr. Baldwin extracted from my book in order to counterpose them to the policy of the revolutionary representatives of the British proletariat? It is not hard to show that the clear and simple meaning of my words was the exact opposite of what Mr. Baldwin was looking for. The more easily the Russian proletariat took power the greater were the obstacles it met on the path of socialist construction. Yes, I said this and I repeat it.

Our old governing classes were economically and politically insignificant. Our parliamentary and democratic traditions hardly existed. It was easier for us to tear the masses away from the bourgeoisie's influence and overturn their rule. But precisely because our bourgeoisie had appeared later and had done little, we received a small inheritance. We are now obliged to lay down roads, build bridges and schools, teach adults to read and write, and so forth – that is, to carry out the main bulk of the economic and cultural work which had been carried out by the bourgeois regime in the older capitalist countries. It was in exactly this sense that I said that the easier that it was for us to deal with the bourgeoisie the more difficult the business of socialist construction.

But this direct political theorem presupposes its converse: the richer and more cultured a country and the older its parliamentary-democratic traditions the harder it is for the communist party to take power; but *the faster and the more successfully will the work of socialist construction proceed after the conquest of power.* Put more concretely, the overturn of the British bourgeoisie is no easy task; it does require a necessary 'gradualness', i.e., serious preparation; but once having taken control of state power, the land, the industrial, commercial and banking apparatus, the proletariat of Britain will be able to carry out the reorganisation of the capitalist economy into a socialist one with far less sacrifices, far more success and at a much quicker pace. Such is the converse theorem, which I have more than once had occasion to set out and prove, and which has the most direct bearing on the question which concerns Mr. Baldwin.

That, however, is not all. When I spoke of the difficulties of socialist construction, I had in mind not only the backwardness of our own country but also the gigantic opposition from outside. Mr. Baldwin probably knows that the British government, of which he was a member, spent about £100 million on military intervention and the blockade of Soviet Russia. The object of these costly measures, let us recall in passing, was the overthrow of Soviet power: the British Conservatives, as also the British Liberals (at least at that time) firmly rejected the principle of "gradualness" in relation to the Workers' and Peasants' Republic and tried to settle a historical question by inflicting a catastrophe on it. It is sufficient to quote this one point to establish that the whole philosophy of gradualness has an extraordinary resemblance to the morality of those monks of Heine's who drink wine themselves, while recommending water to their flock.[7]

---

7 Not wishing to overstep the limits of decency, we shall refrain from enquiring, for example, how forged documents attributed to a foreign state and exploited for electoral purposes can be regarded as a tool of "gradualness" in the development of so-called Christian morality in a civilised society. But without posing this delicate question we still cannot refrain from recollecting that, even according to Napoleon, the falsification of diplomatic documents was nowhere so widely practised as by British diplomacy. And undoubtedly technique has much advanced since then! – *Trotsky*

Be that as it may, the Russian worker, who was the first to seize power, found against him first Germany and then all the countries of the Entente, led by Britain and France. The British proletariat when it takes power will have against it neither the Russian Tsar nor the Russian bourgeoisie. On the contrary, it will be able to find support from the gigantic material and human resources of our Soviet Union, for – and this we shall not conceal from Mr. Baldwin – the cause of the British proletariat is at least as much our cause as the cause of the Russian bourgeoisie was and remains the cause of the British Conservatives.

My remarks about the difficulties of our socialist construction are interpreted by the British Prime Minister as if I had meant: the game was not worth the candle. Yet my point had exactly the opposite sense: our difficulties flow from an international situation that is unfavourable to us, as the pioneers of socialism; by surmounting these difficulties we are changing the situation to the advantage of the proletariat of other countries. Thus, not a single one of our revolutionary efforts fails to have an effect on the international balance of forces.

There is no doubt that, as Mr. Baldwin points out, we are striving for a greater productivity of labour. Without this the upsurge in the welfare and culture of the people would be inconceivable, and in this lies the basic goal of communism. But the Russian worker is today working for himself. Having taken into their hands an economy that had been devastated – first by the imperialist war, then by the Civil War aggravated by intervention and blockade – the Russian workers have now managed to bring their industry, which was almost defunct in 1920-21, up to an average of 60 per cent of its pre-war productivity.

This achievement, however modest it might be when compared with our objectives, represents an undoubted and tangible success. If the £100 million expended by Britain in attempting a catastrophic overturn had been invested, as a loan or as concession capital, into the Soviet economy for its *gradual* uplift we should by now undoubtedly have surpassed the pre-war level, paid high interest rates to British capital and, what is most important, we would have provided a wide and ever-expanding market for it. It is not our fault that Mr. Baldwin has violated the principle of gradualness precisely where he should not have done so. But even given the present, still very low level of our industry the workers' position has considerably improved in comparison with recent years. When we reach the pre-war level – and this is the task of the next two to three years – the position of our workers will be incomparably better than it was before the war.

This is the reason, and the only reason, why we consider ourselves entitled to call upon the proletariat of Russia to raise the productivity of labour. It is one thing to work in plants, factories, shipyards, and mines belonging to capitalists but quite another to work in one's own. There's the big difference, Mr. Baldwin! And when British workers take control of the powerful means of production that have been created by themselves and their forefathers, *they* will try with every effort to raise the productivity of labour.

British industry greatly needs this since despite its lofty achievements, it is entangled in the mesh of its own past. Baldwin seemingly realises this; at any rate in his speech, he says:

> We owe our position and our place in the world largely to the fact that we were the first nation to endure the pangs which brought the industrial age into the world; but we are also paying the price of that privileged priority, and the price in part is our badly planned and congested towns, our back-to-back houses, our ugly factories, and our smoke-laden atmosphere.

Here one must also add the fragmentation of British industry, its technical conservatism, and its organisational rigidity. For precisely this reason British industry is succumbing to German and American industry.

For its salvation it needs a broad and bold reorganisation. It is necessary to look upon the soil and subsoil of Britain as the basis for a single economic system. Only in this way can the coal industry be reconstructed on a healthy footing. Britain's electrical industry is distinguished by its fragmented and backward character; attempts to reorganise it have at every step faced the opposition of private interests. Not only are British cities, by their historical origin, irrationally planned, but all British industry has "gradually" piled itself up, devoid of system or plan. New life can be poured into it only by tackling it as a single whole.

But this is inconceivable while private ownership of the means of production is preserved. The main aim of socialism is to raise the economic strength of the people. Only upon this basis is it possible to build a more cultured, a more harmonious and happier human society. If Mr. Baldwin has, despite his sympathies for old British industry, been compelled to recognise that the new capitalist forms – the trusts and syndicates – represent a step forward, then we consider that a single socialist combine of industry represents a gigantic step forward in comparison with capitalist trusts. But such a programme cannot be realised without the transfer of all the means of production into the hands of the working class, that is to say, without the expropriation of the bourgeoisie. Baldwin himself recalls the "titanic forces let loose by the industrial revolution of the eighteenth century, which changed the face of the country and all the features of our national life".

Why does Baldwin in this instance speak about revolution and not of gradual development? Because at the end of the eighteenth century there took place within a short space of time fundamental changes which led, in particular, to the expropriation of the petty industrialists. To all those who pay attention to the essential logic of the historical process, it should be clear that the industrial revolution of the eighteenth century, which regenerated Great Britain from top to bottom, would have been impossible without the political revolution of the seventeenth century. Without a revolution in the name of bourgeois rights and bourgeois enterprise, and against aristocratic privilege and genteel sloth, that great spirit of technical innovation would not have been aroused and there would have been nobody to apply it to economic ends. The political revolution of the seventeenth century, which had grown out of the entire previous development, prepared for the industrial revolution of the eighteenth century.

Now at this moment Britain, like all capitalist countries, needs an economic revolution far surpassing, in its historical significance, the industrial revolution of the eighteenth century. But this future economic revolution – the rebuilding of the whole economy according to a single socialist plan – cannot be achieved without a political revolution first. Private ownership of the means of production today presents a far greater obstacle on the path of economic development than the craft privileges, which were a form of petty bourgeois property, presented in their time. As the bourgeoisie under no circumstances will renounce its property rights voluntarily, it is necessary that a bold revolutionary force must be set to work. History has not yet thought up any other method. And there will be no exception in the case of Britain.

As for the second quotation ascribed to me by Mr. Baldwin, here I find myself in the greatest perplexity. I firmly deny that I could have said anywhere or at any time that there exists some unalterable "Russian nature" against which revolution was powerless. Where is this quotation from? I know from long experience that not all men, not even all Prime Ministers, quote with complete precision. By complete chance I came across a passage in my book *Problems of Cultural Work* which deals fully with the question which concerns us. I quote it in full:

What are the grounds for our hopes of victory?

The first is that criticism and initiative has been aroused in the popular masses. Through the revolution our people have opened themselves up a window on Europe – meaning by 'Europe' culture – just as two hundred or so years before, Peter's Russia opened not a window but a ventilator on Europe for the top layers of the noble and bureaucratic statesmen. Those passive qualities of humility and meekness which the official or voluntarily idiotic ideologues declared to be the specific, immutable, and sacred qualities of the Russian people but in practice were merely the expression of its slavish, downtrodden state and its isolation from culture – those wretched and shameful qualities received a mortal blow in October 1917. This does not, of course, mean that we no longer carry the heritage of the past with us. We do and shall continue to for a long time yet. But a great turning-point, not only materially, but also psychologically, has been passed. No one any longer dares to recommend the Russian people to build their destiny upon the precepts of humility, submissiveness, and long-suffering. No, the virtues that are henceforth entering ever more deeply into the people's consciousness are: criticism, initiative, and collective creativity. And upon this, the greatest conquest of the national character rests above all our hope of success in all our work.

This, as we see, has very little similarity to what Mr. Baldwin ascribes to me. It should be said in mitigation that the British Constitution does not oblige Prime Ministers to quote correctly. And as for the precedents that play such a major part in British life there is certainly no shortage of them – just how many false quotations is one William Pitt good for?

It may be objected – what is the point of discussing revolution with a Tory leader? What importance can the historical philosophy of a Conservative Prime Minister have for the working class? But the fact of the matter is this: the philosophy of MacDonald, Snowden, Webb, and the other Labour Party leaders is merely an echo of Baldwin's historical theories. And in due course we shall demonstrate this, with all appropriate… gradualness.

3. One or Two Peculiarities of English Labour Leaders

On the death of Lord Curzon, party leaders and others delivered eulogistic speeches. In the House of Commons the socialist MacDonald concluded: "He was a great public servant, a man who was a fine colleague, a man who had a very noble idea of public duty, which may well be emulated by his successors". *That* about Curzon! When workers protested against this speech, the *Daily Herald*, the Labour Party's daily paper, printed the protests under the modest headline 'Another Point of View'. The wise editors evidently wished in this way to indicate that besides the courtiers' Byzantine, bootlicking, lackeyish point of view, there was that of the workers as well.

At the beginning of April the not altogether unknown labour leader, Thomas, secretary of the National Union of Railwaymen and former Colonial Secretary, participated with the Prime Minister, Baldwin, in a banquet given by the directors of the Great Western Railway Company. Baldwin had once been a director of this company, and Thomas had worked for him as a fireman. Mr. Baldwin spoke with magnificent condescension about his friend Jimmy Thomas, while Thomas proposed a toast to the directors of the "Great Western" and their chairman, Lord Churchill. Thomas spoke with great fondness of Mr. Baldwin who – just think of it! – had walked all his life in the footsteps of his venerable father. He himself (Thomas) – said this absolutely unprecedented lackey – would of course be accused of being a traitor to his class for banqueting and mixing with Baldwin but he, Thomas, did not belong to any class, for truth is not the property of a particular class.

Arising out of the debates provoked by the 'left' Labour MPs over the voting of funds to the Prince of Wales for his overseas tour, the same *Daily Herald* came forth with a leading article on its attitude to royalty. Anybody who might have concluded from the debates that the Labour Party wishes to do away with royalty, says the newspaper, would have made a mistake. Yet, on the other hand, one cannot help noting that royalty is not improving its standing in the public opinion of sensible people: too much pomp and ceremonial, inspired possibly by "unintelligent advisers"; too much attention to horse-racing, with the inevitable totalisator; and what is more, in East Africa the Duke and Duchess of York have been hunting rhinoceroses and other creatures who really deserve a better fate. Of course, the paper argues, one cannot blame the Royal Family on its own; tradition ties them too tightly to the habits and members of a particular class. But an effort should be made to break with this tradition. In our opinion this is not only desirable but necessary. A post must be found for the heir to the throne that will make him a part of the government machine, and so on and so forth, all in the same singularly vulgar, stupid, and lackeyish vein. So in our country in the past – around 1905 and 1906 – might the organ of the Samara advocates of peaceful regeneration have written.

The ubiquitous Mrs. Snowden intervened in the Royal Family affair, and stated in a brief letter that only loudmouthed soap-box orators could fail to understand that royal families belong to the most hard-working elements of Europe. And since the Bible itself says: "Thou shalt not muzzle the mouth of the ox that treadeth out the corn", then Mrs. Snowden is, naturally enough, in favour of voting funds for the Prince of Wales' tour.

"I am a socialist, a democrat, and a Christian," this same lady once wrote, explaining why she was against Bolshevism. That, however, is not a complete list of Mrs. Snowden's virtues. Out of politeness we shall not name the rest.

The honourable Dr. Shiels, Labour MP for Edinburgh East, explained that the Prince of Wales' tour was useful for trade, and consequently also for the working class. He, therefore, was in favour of the voting of the funds.

Let us now take one or two of the 'left' or semi-left Labour MPs. Certain property rights of the Scottish Church were being discussed in parliament. A Scottish Labour MP, Johnston, invoked the Act of Union of 1707[1] to deny the

---

1   Under the Articles of Union drawn up in 1706 the Scots had abandoned their own parliament but retained independent legal and ecclesiastical institutions. The final settlement followed several years of negotiations during which the Scots held out for trading independence. England's initial refusal led to sharp retaliation in the form of

right of the British parliament to interfere with the solemnly acknowledged rights of the Scottish Church. Yet the Speaker refused to remove the matter from the order paper. Then Maclean, another Scottish MP, stated that if such a Bill went through, he and his friends would go back to Scotland and call for the Act of Union between England and Scotland to be revoked and the Scottish parliament restored, prompting laughter from the Conservatives and cheers from representatives of the Scottish Labour Party.

Everything is instructive here. The Scottish group, which stands on the left wing of the Parliamentary Labour Party, protests against ecclesiastical legislation, not starting out at all from the principle of the separation of church and state, or any practical considerations, but basing themselves on the sacred rights of the Scottish Church as guaranteed to it by a treaty which is now over two centuries old. In retaliation for the violation of the rights of the Scottish Church these same Labour MPs threaten to demand the restoration of the Scottish parliament, which would, of course, be quite useless to them.

George Lansbury, a left pacifist, relates in a leading article in the Labour Party's daily organ how working men and women at a meeting in Monmouthshire sang a religious hymn with great enthusiasm, and how this hymn "helped" him, Lansbury. Individual people may reject religion, he says, but the labour movement as a movement cannot reconcile itself to this. Our struggle needs enthusiasm, piety, and faith, and this cannot be achieved only by an appeal to personal interests. Thus, although our movement needs enthusiasm, it has according to Lansbury, no power to arouse it, but is compelled to borrow it from the priests.

John Wheatley, the former Minister of Health in MacDonald's cabinet, is regarded as a more or less extreme left. But Wheatley is not only a socialist, but a Catholic too. Or to put it better: he is first and foremost a Catholic and only then a socialist. Since the Pope has called for a struggle against communism and socialism, the editors of the *Daily Herald*, courteously not naming His Holiness, requested Wheatley to clarify how things stood over the mutual relations between Catholicism and socialism. We must not suppose that the newspaper asked how a socialist could be a Catholic or a believer generally; no, the question was posed as to whether it was permissible for a Catholic to become a socialist. The obligation for a man

---

the 1703 Security Act and trading agreements with France. The Scots accepted the Articles of Union only when they included the right to trade independently and on equal terms with England's colonies. The Church question was not even at this point the main contentious issue.

to be a believer remained beyond doubt; placed in question was only the right of a believer to be a socialist, while remaining a good Catholic. And it is on this ground that the 'left' Wheatley takes his stand in his reply. He considers that Catholicism does not directly intrude in politics, but determines "only" the general rules of moral conduct, and obliges a socialist to apply his political principles "with due regard to the moral rights of others". Wheatley maintains that the only correct policy on this question is that of the British party which, as distinct from continental socialism, has not adopted an "anti-Christian" slant. For this 'left', a socialist policy is guided by personal morality, and personal morality by religion. This is in no way distinguishable from the philosophy of Lloyd George who considers the church to be the central power station of all parties. Compromise receives here its religious sanctification.

With regard to the MP Kirkwood, who made a political attack on the Prince of Wales' travelling allowance, a socialist wrote in the *Daily Herald* that he, Kirkwood, had a drop of old Cromwell's blood in his veins, evidently meaning a drop of revolutionary determination. Whether or not this is the case we do not yet know. What Kirkwood has certainly inherited from Cromwell is piety. In his speech in Parliament, Kirkwood declared that he had no personal grudge against the Prince and did not envy him.

> The Prince can give me nothing. I am keeping excellent health, I enjoy independence as a man and there is only one before whom I bear responsibility for my actions and that is my creator.

From this speech we thus learn not only of the Scottish MP's excellent health, but also of the fact that this health cannot be explained by the laws of biology and physiology but by the intentions of a creator, with whom Mr. Kirkwood maintains quite definite relations, based upon personal favours on the one hand and sentiments of grateful obligation on the other.

The number of such examples could be multiplied indefinitely. Almost all the political activity of the top layers of the Labour Party could be resolved into episodes of this sort, which at first sight seem to be amusing and indecent curiosities, but on which the peculiarities of past history have been deposited rather as, for example, the complex metabolic processes of an organism are precipitated out as bladder stones. But we wish it to be remembered that the 'organic' nature of this or that peculiarity in no way precludes surgery to remove it.

The outlook of the leaders of the British Labour Party is a sort of amalgam of Conservatism and Liberalism, partly adapted to the requirements of the trade unions, or rather their top layers. All of them are ridden with the religion of 'gradualness'. In addition, they acknowledge the religion of the Old and New Testaments. They all consider themselves to be highly civilised people, yet they believe that the Heavenly Father created mankind only then, in his abundant love, to curse it, and subsequently to try, through the crucifixion his own son, to straighten out this highly knotty affair a little. Out of the spirit of Christianity there have grown such national institutions as the trade union bureaucracy, MacDonald's first ministry, and Mrs. Snowden.

Closely tied to the religion of gradualness and the Calvinist belief in predestination is the religion of national arrogance. MacDonald is convinced that since his bourgeoisie was once the foremost bourgeoisie in the world then he, MacDonald, has nothing whatsoever to learn from the barbarians and semi-barbarians on the continent of Europe. In this regard, as in all others, MacDonald is merely apeing bourgeois leaders like Canning who proclaimed – albeit with far greater justification – that it did not become parliamentary Britain to learn politics from the nations of Europe.

Baldwin, in monotonously appealing to the conservative traditions of Britain's political development, is doubtless hoping for support from the mighty buttress of bourgeois rule in the past. The bourgeoisie knew how to feed the top layers of the working class with conservatism. It was no accident that the most resolute fighters for Chartism came out of the artisan layers that had been proletarianised by the onslaught of capitalism within two generations.

Equally significant is the fact that the most radical elements in the modern British labour movement are most often natives of Ireland or Scotland (this rule does not of course extend to the Scotsman, MacDonald). The combination of social and national oppression in Ireland, given the sharp conflict between agricultural Ireland and capitalist England, facilitated abrupt leaps in consciousness. Scotland entered on the capitalist path later than England: a sharper turn in the life of the masses of the people gave rise to a sharper political reaction. If Messrs. British 'socialists' were capable of thinking over their own history, and the role of Ireland and Scotland in particular, they would possibly manage to understand how and why backward Russia, with its abrupt transition to capitalism, brought forward the most determined revolutionary party and was the first to take the path of a socialist overturn.

The basis of the conservatism of British life is, however, being irreversibly undermined today. The 'leaders' of the British working class imagined for decades that an independent workers' party was the gloomy privilege of continental Europe. Nowadays, nothing is left of that naive and ignorant conceit. The proletariat forced the trade unions to create an independent party. It will not stop at this, however.

The Liberal and semi-Liberal leaders of the Labour Party still think that a social revolution is the gloomy prerogative of continental Europe. But here again events will expose their backwardness. Much less time will be needed to turn the Labour Party into a revolutionary one than was necessary to create it.

The principal element in the conservatism of political development has been, and to some extent still is, the Protestant-based religious nature of the British people. Puritanism was a harsh school, the social disciplining of the middle classes. The masses of the people however always resisted it. The proletarian did not feel himself to be 'chosen' – Calvinist predestination was plainly not for him. From out of the Independents' movement there took shape English Liberalism, whose chief mission was to 'educate' the working masses – that is, to subordinate them to bourgeois society. Within certain limits and for a certain period, Liberalism fulfilled this mission, but in the end it as little succeeded in swallowing up the working class as Puritanism had.

The Labour Party took over from the Liberals, with the same Puritan and Liberal traditions. If one takes the Labour Party only on the level of MacDonald, Henderson and Co., then it has to be said that they have come to complete the uncompleted task of totally enslaving the working class within bourgeois society. But there is in fact, against their will, another process moving in the masses which must finally liquidate the Puritan-Liberal traditions, and in so doing liquidate MacDonald.

Catholicism, and likewise Anglicanism, were for the English middle classes an existing tradition bound up with the privileges of the nobility and the clergy. Against Catholicism and Anglicanism, the young English bourgeoisie created Protestantism as its form of belief and as the justification of its place in society.

Calvinism, with its iron doctrine of predestination, was a mystical form of approach to the law-governed character of history. The ascendant bourgeoisie felt that the laws of history were behind it, and this awareness they shrouded in the form of the doctrine of predestination. Calvin's denial of free will in no way paralysed the revolutionary energy of the Independents – on the contrary, it powerfully reinforced it. The Independents felt themselves to be summoned to accomplish a great historical act. An analogy can with some truth be drawn between the doctrine of predestination in the Puritans' revolution and the role of Marxism in the revolution of the proletariat. In both cases the highest level of political activity rests not upon subjective impulse but on an iron conformity with a law, only in the one case mystically distorted and in the other scientifically known.

The British proletariat received Protestantism as a tradition already formed, that is to say, just as the bourgeoisie prior to the seventeenth century had received Catholicism and Anglicanism. As the awakened bourgeoisie counterposed Protestantism to Catholicism, the revolutionary proletariat will counterpose materialism and atheism to Protestantism.

While for Cromwell and his comrades-in-arms, Calvinism was the spiritual weapon in the revolutionary transformation of society, for the MacDonalds it merely inspires bowing and scraping before anything that has been 'gradually' created. From Puritanism the MacDonalds have inherited – not its revolutionary strength but its religious prejudices. From the Owenites – not their communist enthusiasm but their reactionary Utopian hostility to the class struggle. From Britain's past political history the Fabians have borrowed only the spiritual dependence of the proletariat on the bourgeoisie. History has turned its backside on these gentlemen and the inscriptions they read there have become their programme.

An island position, wealth, success in world politics, all this cemented by Puritanism, the religion of the 'chosen people', has turned into an arrogant contempt for everything continental and generally un-British. Britain's middle classes have been long convinced that the language, science, technology, and culture of other nations do not merit study. All this has been completely taken over by the philistines currently heading the Labour Party.

It is curious that even Hyndman, who published while Marx was alive a book called *England For All*, refers in it to the author of *Capital* without naming either him or his work: the cause of this strange omission lay in the fact that Hyndman did not want to shock the British – is it really conceivable that a Briton could learn anything from a German!

The dialectic of history has in this respect played a cruel trick upon Britain, having converted the advantages of her forward development into the cause of her present backwardness. We can see this in the field of industry, in science, in the state system, and in political ideology. Britain developed without historical precedents. She could not seek and find a model for her own future in more advanced countries. She went forward gropingly and empirically, only generalising her experience and looking ahead insofar as was unavoidable. Empiricism is stamped on the traditional mode of thought of the British – that means above all of the British bourgeois; and this same intellectual tradition has passed over to the top layers of the working class. Empiricism became a tradition and a banner – that is, it was coupled with a disdainful attitude to the 'abstract' thought of the continent.

Germany for long philosophised about the true nature of the state, while the British bourgeoisie actually built the best state for the needs of its own rule. But with the passage of time it turned out that the German bourgeoisie which, being backward in practice tended towards theoretical speculation, turned its backwardness to advantage and created an industry far more scientifically organised and adapted to the struggle on the world market. The British socialist philistines took over from their bourgeoisie an arrogant attitude towards the continent in a period when Britain's earlier advantages were turning into their opposite.

MacDonald, in establishing the 'congenital' peculiarities of British socialism, states that to seek its ideological roots we "will have to pass by Marx to Godwin".[2] Godwin was a major figure for his time. But for a British person to go back to him is the same as for a German to seek roots in Weitling,[3] or for a Russian to go back to Chernyshevsky.[4] We do not mean by this that the British labour movement does not have 'peculiarities'. It is precisely the Marxist school which has always devoted the greatest attention to the idiosyncrasies of British development. But we explain these idiosyncrasies by objective conditions, the structure of society, and the changes in it. We Marxists can, thanks to this, understand far better the course of development of the British labour movement, and better foretell its future than can the present-day 'theoreticians' of the Labour Party. The old call of philosophy to "know thyself" has not sounded in their ears. They consider that they are

---

2 William Godwin (1756-1836) – Radical writer. Though trained as a minister of religion, under the influence of the French Revolution he became a republican and an atheist. He was an important influence on romantic writers, particularly Shelley, and agitated through his writings against social injustices such as the subjection of women.

3 Wilhelm Weitling (1808-1871) – Leading German utopian socialist and a tailor by trade. His conception of an ideal communist society was partly influenced by Fourier and widely known during Marx's early years.

4 Nikolay Gavrilovich Chernyshevsky (1828-1889) – Russian petty-bourgeois radical, utopian socialist writer, publicist, and literary critic.

summoned by destiny to reconstruct the old society from top to bottom. Yet at the same time they halt, prostrate, before a line chalked across the floor. How can they assault bourgeois property if they dare not refuse pocket money to the Prince of Wales?

Royalty, they declare, "does not hinder" the country's progress and works out cheaper than a president if you count all the expense of elections, and so on and so forth. Such speeches by Labour leaders typify a facet of their 'idiosyncrasies' which cannot be called anything other than conservative block-headedness. Royalty is weak as long as the bourgeois parliament is the instrument of bourgeois rule and as long as the bourgeoisie has no need of extra-parliamentary methods. But the bourgeoisie can if necessary use royalty as the focus of all extra-parliamentary, i.e., *real* forces directed against the working class. The British bourgeoisie itself has well understood the danger of even the most fictitious monarchy. Thus, in 1837 the British government abolished the title of the Great Mogul in India and deported its incumbent from the holy city of Delhi, in spite of the fact that his name had already begun to lose its prestige. The English bourgeoisie knew that under favourable circumstances the Great Mogul might concentrate in himself the forces of the independent upper classes directed against English rule.

To proclaim a socialist platform and at the same time to declare that royal power does not 'interfere' and is actually cheaper, is equivalent, for example, to a recognition of materialistic science combined with the use of magical incantations against toothache on the grounds that the witch comes cheaper. In such a 'trifle' the whole man is expressed, along with his spurious acknowledgement of materialist science and the complete falsity of his ideological system. For a socialist, the question of the monarchy is not decided by today's book-keeping, especially when the books are cooked. It is a matter of the complete overturn of society and of purging it of all elements of oppression. Such a task, both politically and psychologically, excludes any conciliation with the monarchy.

Messrs. MacDonald, Thomas and the rest are indignant with the workers who protested when their ministers arrayed themselves in clownish court dress. Of course this is not MacDonald's main crime: but it does perfectly symbolise all the rest. When the rising bourgeoisie fought the nobility, they renounced ringlets and silken doublets. The bourgeois revolutionaries wore the black dress of the Puritans. As against the Cavaliers they were nicknamed Roundheads. A new content finds itself a new form. Of course, the form of dress is only a convention, but the masses – rightly enough – do not have the patience to understand why the representatives of the working class have to adopt the buffoonish conventions of a court masquerade. And yet the masses *will* come to understand that he who is false in one small thing will be false in many things.

The characteristics of conservatism, religiosity, and national arrogance can be seen in varying degrees and combinations in all the official leaders of today, from the ultra-right Thomas to the 'left' Kirkwood. It would be the greatest error to underestimate the tenacity of these conservative 'peculiarities' of the top echelons of the British working-class movement. By this we do not mean, of course, that church-going and nationalistic conservatism is wholly absent from the masses. But while these traits have worked their way into the flesh and blood of the leaders, disciples of the Liberal Party that they are, they have a much less deep-seated and stable character in the working masses. We have already said that Puritanism, the religion of the money-making classes, never succeeded in penetrating deep into the consciousness of the working masses. The same also applies to Liberalism. Workers used to vote for the Liberals but in their majority they remained workers, and the Liberals always had to be on their guard. The very displacement of the Liberal Party by the Labour Party was a result of the pressure of the proletarian masses.

In other circumstances, if Britain were growing economically stronger, then a Labour Party of the present type might be able to continue and deepen the 'educational' work of Protestantism and Liberalism, that is to say, it would be able to bind the consciousness of broad circles of the working class more tightly to the national conservative traditions and discipline of the bourgeois order.

But under present-day conditions – with the evident economic decline of Britain and the lack of any perspective – the development can be expected to go in exactly the opposite direction. The war has already dealt a heavy blow to the traditional religiosity of the British masses. Not for nothing has Mr. Wells occupied himself with the creation of a new religion, attempting en route from Earth to Mars to make a career as a Fabian Calvin. We are doubtful of his success. The mole of revolution is digging too well this time! The masses will liberate themselves from the yoke of national conservatism, working out their own discipline of revolutionary action.

Under this pressure from below, the top layers of the Labour Party will quickly shed their skins. We do not in the least mean by this that MacDonald will change his spots to those of a revolutionary. No, he will be cast out. But those who will in all probability form the first substitutes, people of the ilk of

Lansbury, Wheatley, and Kirkwood, will inevitably reveal that they are but a left variant of the same basic Fabian type. Their radicalism is constrained by democracy and religion, and poisoned by the national arrogance that ties them spiritually to the British bourgeoisie. The working class will in all probability have to renew its leadership several times before it creates a party really answering the historical situation and the tasks of the British proletariat.

4. The Fabian 'Theory' of Socialism

Let us overcome our natural aversion and read over an article in which Ramsay MacDonald expounded his views a short time before leaving office. We warn the reader in advance that we shall have to enter a mental junk shop in which the suffocating odour of camphor has no effect on the work of the moths.

"In the field of feeling and conscience", MacDonald begins, "in the realm of spirit, socialism is the religion of service to the people." Behind these words there at once appears a benevolent bourgeois, a left Liberal who 'serves' the people by coming in from outside, or rather – from above. Such an approach has its roots wholly in the distant past, when radical intellectuals settled in working-class districts of London to undertake cultural and educational work. What a monstrously anachronistic sound these words have when applied to today's Labour Party, which rests directly upon the trade unions!

The word "religion" must be understood here not merely in an emotive sense. What is being discussed here is Christianity in its Anglo-Saxon interpretation. "Socialism is based upon the gospels", proclaims MacDonald. "It is an excellently conceived [*sic*] and resolute attempt to Christianise government and society." But are there not certain problems with this line of argument?

Firstly: the peoples who are statistically reckoned to be Christian comprise approximately 37 per cent of mankind. How about the non-Christian world?

Secondly: atheism is having no small success even among the Christian peoples and especially among the proletariat. This is so far less noticeable in the Anglo-Saxon countries. But mankind, even Christian mankind, is not exclusively composed of Anglo-Saxons. In the Soviet Union which has a population of 130 million, atheism is the officially proclaimed state doctrine.

Thirdly: Great Britain has held sway over India for centuries now. European nations with this same Britain at their head long ago cleared a path to China. Nevertheless, the number of atheists in Europe is growing faster than the number of Christians in India and China. Why? Because Christianity confronts the Chinese and Indians as the religion of oppressors, aggressors, slave-owners, plunderers breaking into someone else's house. The Chinese know that Christian missionaries are sent to clear the path for the warships. That's the real, historical Christianity! And this Christianity is to form the basis of socialism? For China and for India?

Fourthly: Christianity has, by the official reckoning, now been in existence for 1,925 years. Before becoming MacDonald's religion it was the religion of the Roman slaves, of the barbarian nomads who settled in Europe, the religion of crowned and uncrowned despots and feudal lords, the religion of Charles Stuart – and, in a transmuted form, the religion of Cromwell who cut off Charles Stuart's head.

Finally, today it is the religion of Lloyd George, Churchill, *The Times* and, we must assume, of the devout Christian who forged the 'Zinoviev Letter', to the greater glory of electing the Conservatives in the most Christian of democracies. But exactly how did the Christianity which took root in the consciousness of European peoples and became their official religion by means of sermons, schoolroom violence, threats of torments in the hereafter, hell-fire, and the sword of the police – exactly how in the twentieth century of its existence did it lead to the most bloody and the most evil of wars, when the remaining nineteen centuries of Christianity's history had already been centuries of bestiality and crime? And where precisely are there any reasonable grounds for hoping that 'divine teaching' will, in the twentieth, twenty-first, or even the twenty-fifth century of its history, establish equality and brotherhood where it has earlier sanctified violence and slavery?

It would be futile to expect an answer to these schoolboy questions from MacDonald. Our sage is an evolutionist, that is to say, he believes that everything is 'gradually' changing and, with God's help, for the better. MacDonald is an evolutionist, he does not believe in miracles, he does not believe in leaps apart from a single one that took place 1,925 years ago: at that time a wedge was driven into organic evolution by none other than the Son of God and He put into circulation a certain quantity of heavenly truths from which the clergy collect a substantial terrestrial income.

The Christian basis of socialism is given in two crucial sentences in his article: "Who can deny that poverty is not only a personal, but a social evil? *Who does not feel pity for poverty?*" Here, behind a theory of socialism, is betrayed the philosophy of a socially-minded philanthropic bourgeois who feels "pity" for poor folk and makes a "religion of his conscience" out of this pity without, however, upsetting his business habits unduly.

Who does not feel pity for poverty? All Britain's history is, as is well known, a history of the pity of the propertied classes for the poverty of the toiling masses. Without delving into the depths of time it is sufficient to trace this history merely, let's say, from the sixteenth century, from the time of the enclosures of the peasants' lands; the time, that is, of the conversion of the majority of the peasants into homeless vagrants, when pity for poverty expressed itself in the galleys, the gallows, the lopping-off of ears, and other such measures of Christian compassion. The Duchess of Sutherland completed the enclosures in the north of Scotland at the beginning of the last century, and the staggering tale of this butchery was given by Marx in immortal lines, in which we meet not snivelling 'compassion', but instead find the passion of revolutionary indignation.[1]

Who does not feel pity for poverty? Read through the history of Britain's industrial development and of the exploitation of child labour in particular. The pity shown by the rich for poverty has never protected the poor from degradation and misery. In Britain, no less than anywhere else, poverty has only gained anything in cases where it has managed to take wealth by the throat. Does this really have to be proved in a country with an age-long history of class struggle, which was at the same time a history of niggardly concessions and ruthless reprisals?

---

1 See K. Marx, *Capital*, Vol. 1, *Marx and Engels Collected Works*, Lawrence and Wishart, 1975, p. 720, which includes the following passage about the Duchess of Sutherland's tenants:

> From 1814 to 1820 these 15,000 inhabitants, about 3,000 families, were systematically, hunted and rooted out. All their villages were destroyed and burnt, all their fields turned into pasturage. British soldiers enforced this eviction, and came to blows with the inhabitants. One old woman was burnt to death in the flames of her the, which she refused to leave.

"Socialism does not believe in force", continues MacDonald, "Socialism is a state of mental health and not mental sickness [...] and therefore by its very nature it must repudiate force with horror [...] It fights only with mental and moral weapons." This is all very fine, though not entirely new; the same ideas were set forth in the Sermon on the Mount and, what is more, in considerably better style. We have recalled above what this led to. Why should MacDonald's prosaic re-hash of the Sermon on the Mount result in anything better? Tolstoy, who commanded rather more powerful resources of ideological conviction, did not manage to draw even members of his own landed family over to these evangelical precepts about the impermissibility of force. MacDonald gave us a lesson when he was in power. Let us remind our readers that during that period the police force was not disbanded, the courts were not abolished, the prisons were not demolished, and warships were not scuttled – on the contrary, new ones were built. And, insofar as I am any judge, the police, the courts, prisons, the army, and the navy are organs of force. The recognition of the truth that "socialism is a state of mental health and not mental sickness" in no way prevents MacDonald from strutting round India and Egypt in the sacred footsteps of the great Christian, Curzon. MacDonald as a Christian recoils from violence "with horror"; as Prime Minister he applies all the methods of capitalist oppression, and hands over the instruments of force to his Conservative successor intact.

So what does the renunciation of force in the final resort signify? Only that the oppressed must not adopt force against a capitalist state: neither workers against the bourgeoisie, nor farmers against landlords, nor Indians against the British administration and British capital. The state, constructed by the violence of the monarchy against the people, the bourgeoisie against the workers, the landlords against the farmers, by officers against soldiers, Anglo Saxon slave-owners against colonial peoples, 'Christians' against heathens – this bloodstained apparatus of centuries-long violence inspires MacDonald with pious reverence. He reacts "with horror" only to the force of liberation. And in this lies the sacred essence of his "religion of service to the people".

"There is an old and a new school of socialism", MacDonald says. "We belong to the new school." MacDonald's "ideal" (he does have an "ideal") he shares with the old school, but the new school has a "better plan" for realising this ideal. What does this plan consist of? MacDonald does not leave us without an answer. "We have no class consciousness [...] our opponents are the people with class consciousness [...] But in place of a class consciousness we want to evoke the consciousness of social solidarity." Beating the air,

MacDonald concludes: "The class struggle is not made by us. It is created by capitalism, and will always be its fruit just as thistles will always be the fruit of thistles."

That MacDonald lacks class consciousness, while the leaders of the bourgeoisie have such a consciousness, is absolutely beyond doubt, and it means that at present the British Labour Party is walking along without a head upon its shoulders, while the party of the British bourgeoisie does have such a head – and with a very thick skull and an equally solid neck at that. If MacDonald had confined himself to an admission that he is a little weak in the head as regards "consciousness" there would be no grounds for argument. But MacDonald wishes to construct a programme out of his head and its weak "consciousness". We cannot agree to that.

"The class war", says MacDonald, "is created by capitalism." That, of course, is false. Class war existed before capitalism. But it is true that the *modern* class war – between the proletariat and the bourgeoisie – was created by capitalism. It is also true that "it will always be its fruit", that is to say, that it will exist as long as capitalism exists. But in a war there are obviously two warring parties. One of them is composed of our enemies who, according to MacDonald, "stand for the privileged class and desire to preserve it." It might seem that, since we stand for the destruction of a privileged class that does not wish to leave the scene, it is precisely in this that the basic content of the class struggle lies. But no, MacDonald "wants to evoke" a consciousness of social solidarity. With whom? The solidarity of the working class is the expression of its internal unity in the struggle *against* the bourgeoisie. The social solidarity that MacDonald preaches is the solidarity of the exploited *with* the exploiters, that is, the maintenance of exploitation. MacDonald boasts moreover that his ideas differ from the ideas of our grandfathers: by which he means Karl Marx. In fact, MacDonald differs from this 'grandfather' in the sense that he more closely resembles our great-grandfathers. The ideological hash that MacDonald puts forward as a "new school" marks – on an entirely new historical base – a return to the petty-bourgeois, sentimental socialism that Marx subjected to a devastating criticism as early as 1847, and even before.

MacDonald counterposes to the class struggle the idea of the solidarity of all those charitable citizens who are trying to re-build society by democratic reforms. In this conception, the struggle of the class is replaced by the 'constructive' activity of a political party which is built, not on a class base, but on the basis of social solidarity. The excellent ideas of our great-grandfathers – Robert Owen, Weitling, and others – when completely emasculated and adapted for parliamentary use, sound particularly absurd in modern Britain with its numerically powerful Labour Party resting on the trade unions. There is no other country in the world where the class nature of socialism has been so objectively, plainly, incontestably, and empirically revealed by history as in Britain, for there the Labour Party has grown out of the parliamentary representation of the trade unions, i.e., purely class organisations of wage labour. When the Conservatives, and for that matter the Liberals, tried to prevent the trade unions raising political levies then, in so doing, they were not unsuccessfully counterposing MacDonald's idealist conception of the party to that empirically class character that the party has actually acquired in Britain. To be sure there are, in the top layers of the Labour Party, a certain number of Fabian intellectuals and liberals who have joined out of despair, but in the first place it is to be firmly hoped that workers will sooner or later sweep this dross out, and in the second place the 4.5 million votes which are cast for the Labour Party are already today (with minor exceptions) the votes of British workers. As yet, by no means *all* workers vote for their party. But it is almost solely workers who *do* vote for the Labour Party.

By this we do not at all mean that the Fabians, the ILPers, and the Liberal defectors exert no influence on the working class. On the contrary, their influence is very great but it is not fixed. The reformists who are fighting against a proletarian class consciousness are, in the final reckoning, a tool of the ruling class. Throughout the whole history of the British Labour movement there has been pressure by the bourgeoisie upon the proletariat through the agency of radicals, intellectuals, drawing-room and church socialists, and Owenites who reject the class struggle and advocate the principle of social solidarity, preach collaboration with the bourgeoisie, bridle, enfeeble, and politically debase the proletariat.

The programme of the Independent Labour Party in full accord with this 'tradition', points out that the party strives "at a union of all organised workers together with all persons of all classes who believe in socialism". This deliberately nebulous formula has the aim of slurring over the class character of socialism. No one, of course, is demanding that the party's doors be closed to tested entrants from other classes. However their number is already insignificant, if one does not look only at statistics of the leadership but takes the party as a whole; and in the future, when the party enters on the revolutionary road, it will be even less. But the ILPers need their formula about "people of all classes" to deceive the workers themselves as to the real, class source of their strength, by substituting for it the fiction of a supra-class solidarity.

We have mentioned that many workers still vote for bourgeois candidates. MacDonald contrives to interpret even this fact in the bourgeoisie's political interest. "We must consider the worker not as a worker, but as a man", he teaches, and he adds: "even Toryism has to some extent learnt [...] to treat people as people. Therefore many workers voted for Toryism." In other words: when the Conservatives, terrified by the pressure of the workers, have learnt to adapt to the most backward of them, to break them down, to deceive them, to play upon their prejudices and frighten them with forged documents – all this means that the Tories know how to treat people as people!

Those British labour organisations that are the most unalloyed in class composition, namely the trade unions, have lifted the Labour Party directly upon their own shoulders. This expresses the profound changes in Britain's situation: her weakening on the world market, the change in her economic structure, the falling out of the middle classes, and the break-up of Liberalism. The proletariat needs a class party, it is striving by every means to create it, it puts pressure on the trade unions, it pays political levies. But this mounting pressure from below, from the plants and the factories, from the docks and the mines, is opposed by a counter-pressure from above, from the sphere of official British politics with its national traditions of 'love of freedom', world supremacy, cultural primogeniture, democracy, and Protestant piety. And if (in order to weaken the class consciousness of the British proletariat) a political concoction is prepared from all these components – then you end up with the programme of Fabianism.

Since MacDonald declares that the Labour Party, which openly rests upon the trade unions, is an organisation above classes, then the 'democratic' state of British capital has, for him, an even more classless character. He admits that the present state, governed by landowners, bankers, shipowners, and coal magnates does not form a 'complete' democracy. There still remain one or two defects in it: "Democracy and, for example [!!], an industrial system not governed by the people are incompatible concepts." In other words, this democracy turns out to have one small snag: the wealth created by the nation belongs not to the nation but to a tiny minority of it.

Is this accidental? No, bourgeois democracy is the system of institutions and measures whereby the needs and demands of the working masses, who are striving upwards, are neutralised, distorted, rendered harmless, or purely and simply come to naught. Whoever says that in Britain, France, and the

United States private property is kept in being by the will of the people is lying. No one has asked the people about it. Labouring people are born and brought up in conditions not created by themselves. The state school and the state church inculcate them with concepts that are directed exclusively at maintaining the existing order. Parliamentary democracy is nothing but a resumé of this state of affairs. MacDonald's party enters into this system as an essential component.

When events – generally of a catastrophic nature like economic upheavals, crises and wars – make the social system intolerable for the workers, the latter find themselves with neither the opportunity nor the wish to express their revolutionary anger within the channels of capitalist democracy. In other words: when the masses grasp how long they have been deceived, they carry out a revolution. The successful revolution transfers power to them and their possession of power allows them to construct a state apparatus that serves their interests.

But it is precisely this that MacDonald does not accept. "The revolution in Russia", he says, "taught us a great lesson. It showed that a revolution means ruin and calamity and nothing else." Here the reactionary Fabian steps out before us in all his repulsive nakedness. Revolution leads only to calamities! Yet British democracy led to the imperialist war, not only in the sense that all capitalist states shared responsibility for the war, but also in the sense that British diplomacy had a direct responsibility, consciously and deliberately pushing Europe towards war. Had British 'democracy' declared that she would intervene on the side of the Entente, Germany and Austria-Hungary would most probably have retreated.

But the British government acted otherwise: it secretly promised support to the Entente, and deliberately deceived Germany with the possibility of neutrality. Thus British 'democracy' brought about a war whose devastation far exceeds the calamities of any revolution. Apart from that, what sort of ears and what sort of brains must one have to assert in the face of the revolution that toppled tsarism, the nobility and the bourgeoisie, shook the church and aroused a 150 million strong people, forming a whole family of peoples, to a new life, that revolution is a calamity and *nothing else*? Here MacDonald is only repeating Baldwin. He does not know or understand the Russian revolution or even British history.

We are compelled to remind him as we reminded the Conservative Prime Minister. If the initiative in the economic field up to the final quarter of the last century belonged to Britain, then in the political field Britain has developed over the last century and a half in the wake of the European and American revolutions. The French revolution, the July revolution of 1830, the revolution of 1848, the American Civil War of the 1860s, the Russian Revolution of 1905, and the Russian Revolution of 1917 – all pushed Britain's social development ahead and set the landmarks of major legislative reforms in her history. Without the Russian Revolution of 1917, MacDonald would never have been Prime Minister in 1924. Of course we do not mean by this that MacDonald's ministry was the highest conquest of October. But it was at all events largely its by-product.

And even children's picture-books teach us that if you want to have acorns you must not dig up the oak tree. Besides, how ridiculous is this Fabian conceit: since the Russian Revolution has taught "us" (who?) a lesson, then "we" (who?) shall settle things without revolution. But why then did the lessons of all previous wars not permit "you" to manage without the imperialist war? In the same way that the bourgeoisie calls every successive war the last war, so MacDonald wants to call the Russian Revolution the last revolution. But why exactly should the British bourgeoisie make concessions to the British proletariat and peacefully, without a fight, renounce its property – merely because it has received in advance from MacDonald a firm assurance that, following the experience of the Russian revolution, British socialists shall never take the path of violence? Where and when has the ruling class ever given up their power and property by a peaceful vote, least of all a class such as the British bourgeoisie, which has behind it centuries of world-wide plunder?

MacDonald is against revolution and for organic evolution: he carries over poorly digested biological concepts into society. For him revolution, as a sum of accumulated partial mutations, resembles the development of living organisms, the turning of a chrysalis into a butterfly and so forth; but in this latter process he ignores just those decisive, critical moments when the new creature bursts the old casing in a revolutionary way. Here though it turns out that MacDonald is "for a revolution similar to that which took place in the womb of feudalism, when the industrial revolution came to maturity". MacDonald in his ignorance evidently imagines that the industrial revolution took place molecularly, without upheavals, calamities, and devastation. He simply does not know Britain's history (let alone the history of other countries); and above all he does not understand that the industrial revolution, which was already maturing in the womb of feudalism in the form of merchant capital, brought about the Reformation, caused the

Stuarts to collide with parliament, gave birth to the Civil War, and ruined and devastated Britain – in order afterwards to enrich her.

It would be tedious here to interpret the conversion of a chrysalis into a butterfly so as to establish the necessary social analogies. It is simpler and shorter to recommend MacDonald to ponder over the old comparison between a revolution and childbirth. Can we not draw a "lesson" here – since births produce "nothing" except pains and torment (the infant does not come into it!), then in future the population is recommended to multiply by painless Fabian means, with recourse to the talents of Mrs. Snowden as midwife.

Let us warn, however, that this is by no means so simple. Even the chick which has taken shape in the egg has to apply force to the calcareous prison that shuts it in; if some Fabian chick decided out of Christian (or any other) considerations to refrain from acts of force the calcareous casing would inevitably suffocate it. British pigeon fanciers are producing a special variety with a shorter and shorter beak, by artificial selection. There comes a time, however, when the new offspring's beak is so short that the poor creature can no longer pierce the egg-shell: the young pigeon falls victim to compulsory restraint from violence; and the continued progress of the short-beaked variety comes to a halt. If our memory serves us right, MacDonald can read about this in Darwin.

Still pursuing these analogies with the organic world so beloved of MacDonald, we can say that the political art of the British bourgeoisie consists of shortening the proletariat's revolutionary beak, thereby preventing it from perforating the shell of the capitalist state. The beak of the proletariat is its party. If you take a glance at MacDonald, Thomas, and Mr. and Mrs. Snowden, then it must be admitted that the bourgeoisie's work of rearing the short-beaked and soft-beaked varieties has been crowned with striking success – for not only are these worthies unfit to break through the capitalist shell, they are really unfit to do anything at all.

Here, however, the analogy ends, revealing all the limitations of such cursory data from biology textbooks in place of a study of the conditions and routes of historical development. Human society, although growing out of the organic and inorganic world, represents such a complex and concentrated combination of them that it requires an independent study. A social organism is distinguished from a biological one by, amongst other things, a far greater flexibility and capacity for regrouping its elements, by a certain degree of conscious choice of its tools and devices, and by the conscious application (within certain limits) of the experience of the past, and so on. The pigeon chick in the egg cannot change its over-short beak and so it perishes. The working class when faced with the question of whether to be or not to be can sack MacDonald and Mrs. Snowden and arm itself with the 'beak' of a revolutionary party for the destruction of the capitalist system.

Especially curious in MacDonald is the coupling of a crudely biological theory of society with an idealist Christian abhorrence of materialism. "You talk about revolution and a catastrophic leap but take a look at nature and see how intelligently a caterpillar behaves when it is due to turn into a chrysalis, take a look at the worthy tortoise in its motion, you will find the natural rhythm of the transformation of society. Learn from nature!" And in this same vein MacDonald brands materialism "a banality, a nonsensical assertion, there is no spiritual or intellectual refinement in it". MacDonald and refinement! Isn't this indeed an astounding "refinement": seeking the model for man's collective social activity in a caterpillar, while at the same time demanding for his private use an immortal soul with a comfortable existence in the hereafter?

"Socialists are accused of being poets. That is correct", explains MacDonald, "we are poets. There cannot be good politics without poetry. And in general without poetry there can be nothing good." And so on and so forth in the same style. And in conclusion: "The world needs more than anything some political and social Shakespeare." This drivel about poetry may not be so obnoxious politically as lectures on the impermissibility of violence. But MacDonald's utter lack of intellectual talent is here expressed even more convincingly, if that is possible. A solemn, cowardly pedant, in whom there is as much poetry as in a square inch of carpet, attempts to impress the world with Shakespearian grimaces. Here is where the "monkey-tricks" that MacDonald ascribes to the Bolsheviks really begin. MacDonald, as the "poet" of Fabianism! The politics of Sidney Webb as an artistic creation! Thomas' ministry as the poetry of the colonies! And finally, Mr. Snowden's budget as the City of London's song of love triumphant!

While drivelling about a social Shakespeare, MacDonald has overlooked Lenin. What a good thing for MacDonald, if not for Shakespeare, that the greatest English poet worked over three centuries ago: MacDonald has had sufficient time to see the Shakespeare in Shakespeare. He would never have recognised him had he been his contemporary. For MacDonald has overlooked – fully and completely overlooked – Lenin. Philistine blindness finds a dual expression: aimlessly sighing for Shakespeare, and ignoring his greatest contemporary.

"Socialism is interested in art and the classics." It is amazing how this "poet" is able by his very touch to vulgarise an idea in which there is, in itself, nothing vulgar. To be convinced of this it is enough to read his conclusion: "Even where great poverty and great unemployment exist as, unfortunately, they do in our country, the public must not begrudge the acquisition of pictures and in general anything that evokes ecstasy and elevates the spirit of young and old." It is not, however, altogether clear from this excellent advice whether the acquisition of pictures is recommended to the unemployed themselves – this would presuppose an appropriate supplementary grant for their need – or whether MacDonald is advising the high-minded ladies and gentlemen to purchase pictures "despite the unemployment" and thereby to "elevate their spirit". We must assume that the second is closer to the truth. But surely in that case we only see in front of us the liberal, drawing-room, Protestant clergyman who speaks a few tearful words about poverty and the "religion of conscience", and then invites his worldly flock not to succumb completely to despondency but to continue their former way of life? After this let those who want to believe that materialism is vulgar, while MacDonald is a social poet yearning for Shakespeare. We consider that, if in the physical world there exists a degree of absolute cold, then in the spiritual world there must be a degree of absolute vulgarity which is equivalent to the ideological temperature of MacDonald.

—

Sidney and Beatrice Webb represent another variety of Fabianism. They are accustomed to assiduous work, they know the value of facts and figures, and this imposes a certain restriction on their diffuse thought. They are no less tedious than MacDonald, but they tend to be more instructive as long as they do not go beyond the bounds of factual research. In the sphere of generalisations they stand a little higher than MacDonald. At the Labour Party Conference in 1923, Sidney Webb recalled that the founder of British socialism was not Karl Marx but Robert Owen, who preached not the class struggle but the time-hallowed doctrine of the brotherhood of all mankind. To this day, Sidney Webb regards John Stuart Mill as the classic figure of political economy and he accordingly teaches that a struggle must be waged not between capital and labour but between the overwhelming majority of the population and the appropriators of rent. This typifies the theoretical level of the Labour Party's leading economist well enough.

As is well known, the historical process, even in Britain, does not move as Webb dictates. The trade unions represent the organisation of wage labour against capital. On the basis of the trade unions there grew up the Labour Party, which even made Webb a minister. He implemented his programme only in the sense that he did not conduct a struggle against the expropriators of surplus value. But he did not conduct one against the appropriators of rent either.

In 1923 the Webbs published a book, *The Decay of Capitalist Civilisation*. The book represents in essence a partly diluted and partly renovated paraphrase of Kautsky's old commentaries on the Erfurt Programme.[2] Yet in *The Decay of Capitalist Civilisation*, the political tendency of Fabianism is expressed in its full hopelessness, and in this case semi-consciously. That the capitalist system must be changed, say the Webbs, there can be no doubt (to whom?). But the whole question is how it shall be changed. "It may by considerate adaptation be made to pass gradually and peacefully into a new form…" For this just one small thing is needed: good will from both sides. "Unfortunately", our honourable authors relate, agreement cannot be reached with regard to how to change the capitalist system for "many" consider that the destruction of private property is tantamount to halting the rotation of the earth about its axis, "but they misunderstand the position". There now, how unfortunate! Everything could be settled to the satisfaction of all by means of "considerate adaptation" if only workers and capitalists alike understood what needs to be done and how.

But since "so far" this has not been achieved, the capitalists are voting for the Conservatives. And the conclusion? Here the poor Fabians come unstuck altogether, and even *The Decay of Capitalist Civilisation* turns into a doleful 'Decay of Fabian Civilisation'. "Before the great war there seemed to be a substantial measure of consent", the book recounts, "that the present-day social order had to be gradually changed, in the direction of greater equality", and so on.

Whose consent? Where was this consent? – these people take their tiny Fabian anthill for the world. "We thought, perhaps wrongly [!] that this characteristic [!] British acquiescence [!] on the part of a limited governing class in the rising claims" of the people "would continue and be extended" towards a peaceful transformation of society. "But after the War everything

---

2 The *Erfurt Programme* of the German Social-Democratic Party was drafted by Kautsky in 1891 and, revised according to Engels' criticism, was adopted as the official programme of the party and formed the model for the programme of the Russian and other Social-Democratic parties.

fell into desuetude: the conditions of existence worsened for the workers, we are threatened with the re-establishment of the *veto* power of the House of Lords, with the particular object of resisting further concessions to the workers", and so on.

What follows from all this? In the hopeless quest for a conclusion, the Webbs have written their little book. Its closing lines are as follows: "In an attempt, *possibly vain*, to make the parties understand their problems and each other better [...] we offer this little book."

This is excellent: "a little book" as a means of reconciling the proletariat with the bourgeoisie! To sum up... before the war there "seemed" to be consent that the existing system should be changed for the better; however, there was not complete agreement on the nature of the change: the capitalists stood for private property, the workers against it; after the war the objective situation worsened and the political differences sharpened yet more: *therefore,* the Webbs write a little book in the hope of bending both sides towards a reconciliation; but this hope is "possibly vain". Yes, it possibly, very possibly is vain. These honourable Webbs who believe so much in the force of persuasion ought in our view, in the interests of 'gradualness', to have set themselves a simpler task, like, for example, that of persuading certain highly-placed Christian scoundrels to renounce their monopoly of the opium trade and their poisoning of millions of people in the East.

Poor, wretched, feeble-minded Fabianism – how disgusting its mental contortions are!

To attempt to turn over other philosophical varieties of Fabianism would be a futile task, since for these people "freedom of opinion" reigns only in the sense that each of the leaders has his own philosophy – which ultimately consists of the same reactionary elements of Conservatism, Liberalism, and Protestantism but in differing combinations.

We were all surprised when, not so long ago, Bernard Shaw – such a witty writer! – informed us that Marx had long ago been superseded by Wells' great work on universal history.[3] Such discoveries, so surprising to all mankind,

---

3   I must confess that until Bernard Shaw's letter I had not even known of the existence of this book. Afterwards I acquainted myself with it – I cannot in good conscience say I read it because an acquaintance with two or three chapters was quite enough to stop me wasting any more time. Imagine a complete absence of method, of historical perspective, of understanding of the interdependence of the different facets of social life, and of scientific discipline in general, and then imagine a 'historian' burdened with these qualities roaming far and wide over the history of a few millennia with the

can be explained by the fact that the Fabians form, in a theoretical respect, an exceedingly cloistered little world, deeply provincial, despite the fact that they live in London. Their philosophical inventions are necessary neither to the Conservatives nor to the Liberals. Even less are they necessary to the working class, for whom they provide nothing and explain nothing. These works in the final reckoning serve merely to explain to the Fabians themselves why Fabianism exists in the world. Along with theological literature this is possibly the most useless, and certainly the most boring, type of literary activity.

In various spheres of life in Britain today the men of the 'Victorian era' (i.e., public figures of the time of Queen Victoria) are spoken of with a certain contempt. Everything in Britain has moved on since that time, but possibly the Fabian type has been the best preserved. The vulgarly optimistic Victorian epoch, when it seemed that tomorrow would be a little bit better than today and the day after that a bit better than tomorrow, has found its most finished expression in the Webbs, Snowden, MacDonald, and the other Fabians. That is why they seem to be such clumsy and unnecessary survivals from an epoch that has suffered a final and irrevocable collapse. It can without exaggeration be said that the Fabian Society, which was founded in 1884 with the object of "arousing the social conscience", is nowadays the most reactionary grouping in Great Britain. Neither the Conservative clubs, nor Oxford University, nor the English bishops and other priestly institutions can stand comparison with the Fabians. For all these are institutions of the enemy classes and the revolutionary movement of the proletariat will inevitably burst the dam they form. But the proletariat itself is restrained by precisely its own top leading layer, i.e., the Fabian politicians and their yes-men.

These pompous authorities, pedants, and haughty, high-falutin' cowards are systematically poisoning the labour movement, clouding the consciousness of the proletariat, and paralysing its will. It is only thanks to them that Toryism, Liberalism, the Church, the monarchy, the aristocracy, and the bourgeoisie continue to survive and even suppose themselves to be firmly in the saddle. The Fabians, the ILPers, and the conservative trade union bureaucrats today represent the most counter-revolutionary force in Great Britain, and possibly in the present stage of development, in the whole world. Overthrowing the Fabians means liberating the revolutionary energy of the British proletariat, winning the British stronghold of reaction for socialism, liberating India and

---

carefree air of a man taking his Sunday stroll. Then you will have Wells' book, which is to replace the Marxist school. – *Trotsky*

Egypt, and giving a powerful impetus to the movement and development of the peoples of the East.

Renouncing violence, the Fabians believe only in the power of the 'idea'. If a wholesome grain can be sifted out of this trivial and hypocritical philosophy then it lies in the fact that no regime can maintain itself by violence alone. This applies equally to the regime of British imperialism. In a country where the overwhelming majority of the population consists of proletarians, the governing Conservative-Liberal imperialist clique would not be able to last a single day if it were not for the fact that the means of violence in its hands are reinforced, supplemented, and disguised by pseudo-socialist ideas that ensnare and break up the proletariat.

The French 'enlighteners' of the eighteenth century[4] saw their main enemy as Catholicism, clericalism, and the priesthood, and considered that they had to strangle this reptile before they could move forward. They were right in the sense that it was this very priesthood, an organised regime of superstition, the Catholic spiritual police apparatus, that stood in the way of bourgeois society, retarding the development of science, art, political ideas, and economics. Fabianism, MacDonaldism, and pacifism today play the same role in relation to the historical movement of the proletariat. They are the main prop of British imperialism and of the European, if not the world bourgeoisie. Workers must at all costs be shown these self-satisfied pedants, drivelling eclectics, sentimental careerists, and liveried footmen of the bourgeoisie in their true colours. To show them up for what they are means to discredit them beyond repair. To discredit them means rendering a supreme service to historical progress. The day that the British proletariat cleanses itself of the spiritual abomination of Fabianism, mankind, especially in Europe, will increase its stature by a head.

---

4   The eighteenth century philosophers and writers like Voltaire, Diderot, Montesquieu, and Rousseau. They anticipated the French bourgeois revolution in their ideological opposition to superstition and prejudice. Propounding a materialist view of man, they had an idealist conception of the history of society.

5. The Question of
Revolutionary Force

We have acquainted ourselves with MacDonald's views on revolutionary force. They proved to be a development of Mr. Baldwin's Conservative theory of gradualness. The rejection of the use of force by the 'left' Lansbury has a more curious, although more sincere, character. The latter, you see, purely and simply "does not believe" in force. He "does not believe" either in capitalist armies or armed uprisings. Had he believed in force he would not, he says, have voted for the British Navy but would have joined the communists. What a plucky devil! The fact that Lansbury, while not believing in force, does believe in the hereafter, of course casts doubt on his realism.

Nonetheless, one or two events on earth have, by leave of Mr. Lansbury, taken place by means of force. Whether Lansbury does or does not believe in the British Navy, the Indians know that this Navy exists. In April 1919, General Dyer gave orders to fire without previous warning on an unarmed gathering of Indians at Amritsar – as a result of which 450 persons were killed and 1,500 wounded. While we may leave the dead in peace, it must be said of the wounded that they at any rate could not "not believe" in force. But even as a believing Christian, Lansbury ought to have realised that if the rogues of the Jewish priesthood, in conjunction with the cowardly Roman proconsul Pilate, the political ancestor of MacDonald, had not in their day adopted the use of force against Christ there would have been neither crown of thorns, nor resurrection nor ascension, and Mr. Lansbury himself would not have had the opportunity of being born a devout Christian and becoming an inferior socialist.

Not believing in force is the same as not believing in gravity. All of life is built upon different forms of force, and the opposition of one force to another; so that to renounce liberating force amounts to supporting the oppressors' force, which today governs the world.

We feel, however, that cursory comments are of no avail here. The question of force and its 'denial' by Messrs. Pacifists, Christian socialists, and other such hypocrites, occupies such a big place in British politics that a particular and detailed examination, specially adapted to the political level of the present-day 'leaders' of the British Labour Party is required. At the same time, we apologise in advance to the rest of our readers for this level of exposition.

What does denying any use of force really mean? If, say, a thief broke into Mr. Lansbury's flat we very much fear that this pious gentleman (we are here speaking of the householder), would adopt force or invite the nearest policeman to do so. Even if out of his Christian mercy Lansbury let the thief go in peace – of which we are not altogether certain – then it would only be on the clear understanding that he immediately left the flat. What is more, the honourable gentleman could only permit himself the luxury of such a Christian gesture because his flat lies under the protection of the British law of property (and its numerous Arguses), with the result that on the whole, nocturnal visits by thieves constitute the exception rather than the rule. Perhaps Lansbury will venture to reply that an intrusion into an honourable private Christian flat is an act of force, and thus calls for retaliation. We say to him that such an argument is an abandonment of the renunciation of force in general. It is, on the contrary, its admission, in principle and in practice, and can be wholly translated into the class struggle, where the intrusion day in and day out by the thief, capital, into the life and labour of the proletariat, and its plundering of surplus value fully justifies retaliation. Maybe Lansbury will reply to us that he understands by force not all the means of coercion in general, without which our marvellous social arrangements could not function, but only the violation of the Sixth Commandment: "Thou shalt not kill".

To substantiate such a view many high-flown phrases about the sanctity of human life can be quoted. But here too we must ask, in the language of the Gospel parables which best suits the leaders of British socialism, how Mr. Lansbury would behave if a robber brandished a club at children before his very eyes, and if there was no other means of saving them than an immediate and accurate revolver shot. If he does not wish to resort to wholly crude sophisms he will reply, and possibly to his own relief, that our example has too exceptional a character.

But this reply would merely signify once more that Lansbury had entrusted his right to resort to homicide in such circumstances to the police, that specialised organisation of force which in the majority of cases relieves him of the need to use a revolver, or even to ponder its practical purpose.

But, let us ask, what happens when armed strike-breakers beat up and kill strikers? Such incidents are quite usual in America, and not exceptional in other countries. Workers cannot entrust their right to resist strike-breakers to the police, because in all countries the police defend the right of strike-breakers to beat up and kill strikers – to whom, as is well known, the law of the sanctity of human life does not extend. We ask: have strikers the right to use sticks, stones, revolvers and bombs against fascists, Ku Klux Klan gangs and other such hired scoundrels of capital? There's a nice little poser to which we would request a clear, precise, and in no way evasive, hypocritical answer.

If Lansbury tells us that the task of socialism is to give the masses of the people such an education that would make fascists not fascists, scoundrels not scoundrels and so forth, then this is the purest humbug. That the aim of socialism is the elimination of force, first in its crudest and bloodiest forms, and then in other more covert ones, is indisputable. But here we are dealing not with the manners and morals of a future communist society, but with the concrete paths and methods of struggle against capitalist force.

When fascists disrupt a strike, seize a newspaper's editorial offices and its safe, and beat up and kill workers' deputies while the police encircle the thugs with a protective ring, then only the most corrupt hypocrite would advise workers not to reply blow for blow, on the pretext that force would have no place in a communist system. Obviously in each particular case it is necessary to decide, with respect to the whole situation *how* to answer the enemy's force and *just how far* to go in one's retaliation. But that is a matter of tactical expediency which has nothing to do with the acknowledgement or denial of force in principle.

What really is force? Where does it start from? Where do permissible and expedient collective actions by the masses become acts of force? We greatly doubt that Lansbury or any other pacifist is capable of giving a reply to this question unless he confines himself to a simple reference to the criminal code, where what can be tolerated and what cannot is set out. The class struggle forms a continuous chain of open or masked acts of force which are 'regulated' to this or that degree by the state, which in turn represents the organised the most powerful of adversaries, namely the ruling class.

Is a strike an act of force? There was a time when strikes were banned and every strike was almost inevitably linked with physical conflicts. Then, as a result of the development of the strike struggle, that is to say, as a result of the masses' acts of force against the law, or more exactly as a result of the continual blows by the masses against force used by the law, strikes were legalised. Does this mean that Lansbury considers only peaceful, 'legal' strikes, i.e., those allowed by the bourgeoisie, to be a permissible means of struggle? But if workers had not conducted strikes at the beginning of the nineteenth century the British bourgeoisie would not have legalised them in 1824. But if one allows the application of force or violence in the form of a strike then one has to accept all the consequences, including the defence of strikes from strike-breakers by means of appropriate measures of counter-force.

Moreover, if strikes by workers against the capitalists, or particular groups of capitalists, are permissible then would Lansbury venture to say that it was impermissible for workers to organise a general strike against a fascist government that was suppressing the workers' unions, smashing the workers' press, and flooding the workers' ranks with provocateurs and murderers?

Once again, a general strike can be adopted not at any hour on any day but only under specific concrete conditions. But this is a matter of strategic expediency, not of a general 'moral' assessment. As for the general strike, as one of the most decisive means of struggle, Lansbury and all his fellow-thinkers taken together have hardly devised any other means that the proletariat could adopt for achieving a decisive end. Lansbury would surely not fall so low as to recommend workers to wait until the spirit of brotherly love takes command of the hearts of let us say, the Italian fascists who are, by the way, to a large extent extremely devout Catholics. But if you recognise that the proletariat not only has the right, but is duty-bound to prepare for a general strike against a fascist regime you must draw all the conclusions that follow from such a recognition.

A general strike, if it is not to be a mere protest, signifies an extreme upheaval of society and in any event places at stake the fate of the political regime and the reputation of the strength of the revolutionary class. A general strike can only be undertaken when the working class, and above all its vanguard, is ready to carry the struggle through to the end. But fascism will not of course begin to surrender to a peaceful protest strike. In the event of a real and immediate danger the fascists will set all their forces in motion, they will launch provocations, assassinations, and arson on an unprecedented scale. One may ask: is it permissible for the leaders of a general strike to form their own militias for the defence of the strikers against acts of force and for disarming and dispersing the fascist bands? And as no one has succeeded, at least in our memory, in disarming furious enemies by means of religious hymns, then the revolutionary detachments must obviously be armed with revolvers and hand grenades until such time as they can lay hold of rifles, machine-guns, and cannon. Or is it perhaps only at this point that the domain of impermissible force begins?

But then we should become completely entangled in absurd and shameful contradictions. A general strike that does not safeguard itself from acts of force and rout is a demonstration of cowardice and doomed to defeat. Only a lunatic or a traitor could call for a struggle under such conditions. By the logic of relations that do not depend on Lansbury, an 'unarmed' strike struggle produces armed clashes. This happens quite often in economic strikes and in a revolutionary political strike it is absolutely unavoidable, for the strike has the task of toppling the existing state power. Whoever renounces force must renounce struggle as a whole, that is to say, he must in practice join the ranks of the supporters of ruling class victory.

But the question is not limited to this. The general strike under consideration has the object of overthrowing a fascist regime. This can only be achieved by gaining the upper hand over its armed forces. Here again there are two possibilities: a straight military victory over the forces of reaction or the winning of these forces over to the side of the revolution. Neither is practicable in a pure form. A revolutionary uprising can hold on to victory only where it succeeds in cracking the firmest, most resolute, and reliable detachments of reaction and attracting the remaining armed forces of the regime over to its side. Once again this can only be achieved in a situation where the wavering government forces are convinced that the working masses are not simply demonstrating their discontent but have this time firmly made their mind up to overthrow the government at all costs, not baulking at the most ruthless means of struggle. Only this sort of impression will be capable of swinging the wavering forces over to the side of the people. The more procrastinatory, hesitant, and evasive the policy of the leaders of the general strike, the less will be the waverings in the soldiers' ranks, the more resolutely they will support the existing power, and the more chances the latter will have of emerging the victor from the crisis so as then to loose all the scorpions of bloody repression on to the heads of the working class.

In other words, since the working class is compelled to resort to a general political strike to gain its freedom, it must take warning that the strike will inevitably give rise to partial and general, armed and semi-armed conflicts; it must take warning that the only way for the strike to avoid defeat is if it immediately deals the necessary rebuff to strike-breakers, provocateurs, and fascists. It must foresee that the government whose fate is in question will inevitably bring its armed force out onto the streets at some point in the struggle, and that on the outcome of the clash between the revolutionary masses and this armed force hangs the fate of the existing regime and consequently of the proletariat. Workers must take all measures in advance to attract soldiers to the side of the people by preliminary agitation; and at the same time they must foresee that the government will always be left with a sufficient number of dependable or semi-dependable soldiers whom it will bring out to quell the uprising; so that in the last analysis the question has to be settled by an armed clash which must be prepared with thorough planning and waged with total revolutionary determination.

Only the highest resoluteness in the revolutionary struggle is capable of striking the arms out of the hands of reaction, shortening the duration of civil war, and minimising the number of its victims. Whoever does not take this road should not take to arms at all; and without taking to arms a general strike cannot be organised. And if the general strike is rejected there can be no thought of serious struggle. The only thing that then remains is to educate workers in the spirit of total prostration which is already the concern of official education, governing parties, the priests of every church, and… the socialist preachers of the impermissibility of force.

But this is what is remarkable: rather as idealist philosophers in their practical life feed on bread, meat, and contemptible matter in general and try to avoid being run down by cars instead of relying on the immortality of the soul, so also Messrs. Pacifists, the impotent opponents of force, moral 'idealists' on all those occasions where it comes within the ambit of their immediate interests, appeal to political force and make use of it directly or obliquely. Thus, as Mr. Lansbury is evidently not devoid of something akin to temperament, such adventures happen to him more than others. In the parliamentary debates in connection with the unemployed (the House of Commons sitting of 9 March 1925), Lansbury recalled that the Unemployed

Insurance Act was passed in its present form in 1920 "not so much to safeguard the lives of men and their families but, as Lord Derby had recently told them, to forestall a revolution". In 1920, Lansbury continued, all the workers who were serving in the army were included among those insured because the government was at the time not quite sure whether they would turn their rifles in the direction desirable to the government.[1] After these words the parliamentary report records: "cheers from Opposition benches", that is from the Labour Party, and cries of "Oh!", on the government benches.

Lansbury does not believe in revolutionary force. But he nevertheless recognises, following Lord Derby, that a fear of revolutionary force brought about a law on state insurance for the unemployed. Lansbury is conducting a struggle against attempts to repeal this law; consequently, he believes that a law brought about through fear of revolutionary force is bringing a certain benefit to the working class. So, the benefit of revolutionary force is hereby proved virtually mathematically. For, with respect to Mr. Lansbury, if there were not acts of force there would be no fear of it. If there were not a real possibility (and necessity) of turning rifles against the government in certain circumstances then the government would have no grounds to fear it. Consequently, Lansbury's so-called disbelief in force is the purest delusion. In practice he makes use of this force, in the form of an argument, at least every day. Even more does he enjoy in practice the conquests of the revolutionary force of past decades and centuries. He merely refuses to draw the threads of his ideas together. He rejects revolutionary force for the seizure of power, that is to say for the complete liberation of the proletariat. But in struggles that do not transcend the bounds of bourgeois society he is perfectly amenable to force and makes use of it. Mr. Lansbury is for retail but against wholesale force. He resembles the vegetarian who accepts duck or rabbit meat with equanimity but rejects the slaughter of larger animals with righteous indignation.

—

We can foresee, however, that Mr. Lansbury or his more diplomatic and more hypocritical fellow-thinkers will object: yes, against a fascist regime or any sort of despotic government, perhaps we won't argue: well, in the end a certain degree of force might be permissible; but it is quite impermissible under a regime of democracy. We for our part would right away register this objection as a surrender of a position of principle, for we were originally

---

1 *The Times*, 10 March 1925.

talking not about under what conditions force is permissible, or expedient, but whether it is ever permissible taken from an abstract, Humanitarian-Christian-socialist point of view.

When we are told that revolutionary force is impermissible only under a regime of political democracy then the question is thereby transferred to another plane. This does not, however, mean that democratic opponents of force are more profound and cleverer than the Christian-humanitarian ones. Here we can without difficulty be convinced that this is not so.

Is it indeed true that the question of the expediency and permissibility of revolutionary force is decided by reference to the greater or lesser 'democraticness' of the *forms* of the rule of the bourgeoisie? Such a formula is wholly refuted by historical experience. The struggle between the revolutionary and the peaceful legalistic reformist tendency within the workers' movement did not at all begin from the moment a republic was established or universal suffrage introduced. In the era of Chartism and right up to 1868 workers in Britain were utterly deprived of the vote, that is, of the basic implement of 'peaceful' development. Nonetheless, the Chartist movement was split between the supporters of physical force whom the masses followed, and the supporters of moral force, predominantly petty-bourgeois intellectuals and labour aristocrats.

In Hohenzollern Germany[2] with its impotent parliament, a struggle within social democracy took place between the supporters of parliamentary reforms and the proponents of a revolutionary general strike. And finally, even in tsarist Russia under the 3 June regime[3] the Mensheviks liquidated revolutionary methods of struggle under the slogan of a struggle for legality.

Thus, to invoke the bourgeois republic or universal suffrage as the basic reformist and legalist argument is a product of theoretical narrowness, a short memory, or pure hypocrisy. Legalistic reformism in its true essence signifies the subservience of slaves to the laws and institutions of the slave-owners. Whether universal suffrage forms one of these institutions or not, and whether they are crowned by a king or a president, are for the opportunist

---

2 The ruling family of the Kingdom of Prussia from 1701 to 1871 and of the German Empire from 1871 until 1918 when the monarchy was overthrown in the November Revolution.

3 On 3 June 1907 the Russian Tsar dissolved the State Duma, arrested the Social-Democratic deputies and set up the Third Duma with a more restricted franchise excluding the peasantry. This day marked the beginning of the period of harshest repression and reaction in Russia.

questions of a secondary nature. He always goes on his knees before the idol of the bourgeois state and agrees to proceed towards his 'ideal' by no other way than through the asses' gate built for him by the bourgeoisie. But the gate is built so that it is impossible to pass through it.

What is political democracy and where does it start from? In other words, where, which countries, does the ban on force cover? Can for example a state be called a democracy where there is a monarchy and an aristocratic chamber? Is it permissible to adopt revolutionary methods to topple these institutions? To this the answer may be made that the British House of Commons has sufficient power to abolish royalty and the House of Lords should it find this necessary, so that the working class has a peaceful way of completing a democratic regime in its country. Let us allow this for the moment. But what is the position with the House of Commons itself? Can this institution really be called democratic, even from a formal point of view?

Not in the slightest. Considerable groups of the population are deprived of the franchise. Women have the vote only from the age of thirty and men only from twenty-one.[4] The lowering of the age qualification is from the standpoint of the working class, where working life starts early, an elementary demand of democracy. Besides, parliamentary constituencies are divided up in such a perfidious fashion that one Labour member must win twice as many votes as one Conservative.

By keeping the age qualification up, the British parliament exiles active youth of both sexes and charges the destiny of the country to primarily the older generations which, wearying of life, look more under their feet than out in front. Here lies the point of the high age qualification. The cynical geometry of the constituencies gives a Conservative vote as much weight as two Labour votes. Thus the present-day British Parliament represents the most flagrant mockery of the will of the people even taken in the bourgeois-democratic sense.

Has the working class the right, even while remaining on the ground of the principles of democracy, to demand that the present privileged and basically usurping House of Commons introduce a really democratic franchise? But if parliament answers that with a refusal – which, we contend, would be inevitable, for only the other day Baldwin's government refused to make women the equal of men in respect of the age qualification – would the proletariat in such an event have the 'right' to win from the usurper

---

4 Women from the ages of twenty-one to twenty-nine obtained the vote only in April 1928, three years after Trotsky wrote this book.

parliament the introduction of a democratic franchise by means of, let's say, a general strike?

If we further suppose that either the present, usurping House of Commons, or a more democratic one, resolved to abolish royalty and the House of Lords – of which there is not a hope – this would still not mean that the reactionary classes which had proved to be in the minority in parliament would submit unreservedly to such a decision. Not so very long ago we saw the Ulster reactionaries under the leadership of Lord Carson taking the path of open civil war when they had a difference of opinion with the British parliament over the question of the system of administration for Ireland, in which the British Conservatives openly supported the Ulster rebels. But, we shall be told, such a case amounts to an open rising on the part of the privileged classes against a democratic parliament and obviously such a rebellion would have to be quelled with the aid of state force. Let us record this admission but demand here that one or two practical conclusions be drawn from it.

Let us allow for the minute that a Labour majority in parliament results from the next elections and that as a start it resolves in the most legal fashion to hand over the landlords' land to the farmers and the chronically unemployed without compensation, to introduce a high tax on capital and to abolish the monarchy, the House of Lords, and a few other obscene institutions. There cannot be the least doubt that the possessing classes would not give in without a fight, and all the less so since the entire police, judicial, and military apparatus is wholly in their hands. In the history of Britain there has already been one instance of civil war when the King rested upon a minority in the Commons and a majority in the Lords against the majority of the Commons and a minority in the Lords. That affair was in the 1640s. Only an idiot, let us repeat, only a wretched idiot, can seriously imagine that a repetition of a civil war of that kind (albeit on new class bases) can be prevented in the twentieth century by the evident success of the last three centuries of a Christian world-outlook, humanitarian feelings, democratic tendencies, and all the other excellent things. The same example of Ulster shows that the possessing classes do not play around when parliament, their own institution, finds itself compelled to squeeze their privileged position.

In preparing to take state power, it is thus necessary to prepare for all the consequences that flow from the inevitable resistance of the possessing classes. It must be firmly understood: if a truly workers' government came to power in Britain even in an ultra-democratic way, civil war would become unavoidable. The workers' government would be forced to suppress the resistance of the privileged classes. To do this by means of the old state apparatus, the old police, the old courts, the old army would be impossible. A workers' government created by parliamentary means would be forced to construct new revolutionary organs for itself, resting upon the trade unions and working-class organisations in general. This would lead to an exceptional growth in the activity and initiative of the working masses. On the basis of a direct struggle against the exploiting classes the trade unions would actively draw closer together not only in their top layers, but at the bottom levels as well, and would arrive at the necessity of creating local delegate meetings, i.e., councils (Soviets) of workers' deputies. A truly Labour government, that is to say, a government dedicated to the end to the interests of the proletariat, would find itself in this way compelled to smash the old state apparatus as the instrument of the possessing classes and oppose it with workers' councils. That means that the democratic origin of the Labour government – even had this proved possible – would lead to the necessity of counterposing revolutionary class force to the reactionary opposition.

We have shown above that the present British parliament forms a monstrous distortion of the principles of bourgeois democracy and that without adopting revolutionary force one can hardly obtain in Britain even an honest division of parliamentary constituencies or the abolition of the monarchy and the House of Lords. But let us allow for the minute that these demands have been realised in one way or another. Does that mean that we would then have a really democratic parliament in London? Not by any means. The London parliament is a parliament of slave-owners. Even were it to represent a nation of 40 million in the most ideal and formally democratic manner, the British parliament would still pass laws for the 300 million population of India and have financial resources at its disposal that it had acquired by force of Britain's rule over the colonies. India's population does not take part in the passing of laws that determine its own fate.

British democracy is similar to that of Athens in the sense that equality of democratic rights (which in fact does not exist) affects only the 'free-born' and rests upon the lack of rights of the 'lower' nations. For each inhabitant of the British Isles there are some nine colonial slaves. Even if you consider that revolutionary force is impermissible in a democracy, this principle can in no case be extended to the peoples of India who are rising up not against democracy but against the despotism that oppresses them. But in this event, even a British person if he is really a democrat cannot recognise a binding democratic force for British laws passed for India, Egypt, and elsewhere.

And as the whole social life of Britain herself as the colonial power rests upon these laws then it is obvious that all the activity of the Westminster parliament as the focal point of a predatory colonial power is anti-democratic to its very roots. From the point of view of consistent democracy it has to be said: as long as the Indians, Egyptians, and others are not permitted full freedom of self-determination i.e., the freedom of secession, or the Indians, Egyptians, and others cannot send their representatives to an imperial parliament with the same rights as the British representatives, then not only the Indians, Egyptians, and others, but also British democrats have the right to rise up against the predatory government formed by a parliament representing an insignificant minority of the population of the British Empire. Consequently, that is how matters stand with Britain if we judge the question of the use of force merely by the criterion of democracy but carrying through to its conclusion.

The British social-reformists' denial of the right of the oppressed masses to use force is a shameful rejection of democracy and forms a contemptible support for the imperialist dictatorship of an insignificant minority over hundreds of millions of enslaved people. Before lecturing the communists on the sanctity of democracy and denouncing Soviet power, Mr. MacDonald would do well to give his own nose a good blow!

—

First we examined the question of force from a 'humanitarian', Christian, priestly point of view, and were persuaded that the social-pacifists in seeking a way out of insoluble contradictions were in fact forced to concede their position and admit that revolutionary force is permissible once outside the pale of democracy. We further showed that it is as hard for those who deny force to base themselves on a democratic standpoint as it is on a Christian one. In other words, we have revealed the complete inconsistency, fraudulence, and hypocrisy of social-pacifism even by its own standards.

But this does not at all mean that we are prepared to recognise these standards. In resolving the question of revolutionary force, the parliamentary-democratic principle for us by no means forms the highest criterion. Not mankind for democracy but democracy as one of the auxiliary instruments on the road of mankind's development. Where bourgeois democracy has turned into an obstacle it has to be torn down. The transition from capitalism to socialism derives not at all from formal democratic principles elevated above society, but from the material conditions of the development of society itself: from the growth of the productive forces, from insoluble capitalist contradictions, domestic and international, and from a sharpening of the struggle between the proletariat and the bourgeoisie. A scientific analysis of the whole historical process and of our generation's own political experience, including the imperialist war, all alike testify that without a transition to socialism all our culture is threatened with decay and decomposition. The transition to socialism can only be accomplished by the proletariat led by its revolutionary vanguard and leading behind it all the toiling and oppressed masses of the metropolitan country and the colonies.

In all our work and all our political decisions our highest criterion is the interests of the revolutionary struggle of the proletariat to take power and to reconstruct society. We consider that to judge the movement of the proletariat from the standpoint of the abstract principles and legal clauses of democracy is reactionary pedantry. We consider the only correct way to judge democracy is from the standpoint of the historical interests of the proletariat. It is not a matter of the nutshell but the kernel. The discussions of Messrs. Fabians about the impermissibility of a 'narrow class' viewpoint is the purest blockheadedness. They want to subordinate the basic tasks of social development to be effected by the proletariat to the schoolroom pedants. By the name of the solidarity of all mankind they mean an eclectic jumble that corresponds to *the narrow class horizon of the petty bourgeois*. Between their property and the revolutionary proletariat, the bourgeoisie sets up the screens of democracy. The socialist pedants say to the workers: you must take control of the means of production but as a preliminary you must see that the necessary holes and channels are made through these screens by means of legislation. But cannot the screens be pulled down? Not under any circumstances. Why not? Because even if we did save society in this way, we would still have upset that complex system of state force and fraud that the bourgeoisie has taught us to regard as sacred democracy.

The opponents of force, dislodged from their first two positions, may occupy a third line of trenches. They may agree to cast Christian mysticism and democratic metaphysics right out and attempt to defend the reformist, pacifist, peaceful, parliamentary road on the grounds of bare political expediency. Some of them may say roughly the following: of course, Christ's teaching does not make provision for solving the contradictions of British capitalism; democracy is likewise not a sacred institution but merely a temporary, and subsidiary product of historical development; but why on earth should the working class not avail themselves of a democratic parliament with its methods, devices, and legislative machinery for the effective taking of power and the re-building of society? For this would be quite natural and by all indications a more economical way of carrying out the socialist revolution.

We communists are in no event inclined to advise the British proletariat to turn its back on parliament. On the contrary, when individual British communists did reveal such a tendency, they met with a rebuff from us at the international congresses.[5] Thus, the question is not whether the parliamentary road should be made use of, but what place parliament occupies in the development of society and where the class forces lie, inside or outside parliament; in what form and on what ground these forces will collide, and whether a parliament created by capitalism for its own development and protection can be made into a lever for the overthrow of capitalism.

To answer this question an attempt has to be made to imagine with a certain degree of concreteness what path the future political development of Britain will take. Clearly, any attempted forecast of this sort can only be of a conditional, tentative nature. But without such attempts we would be doomed to wander in the dark.

The present government has a firm majority in parliament. Consequently, it is not excluded that it will survive in power for another three or four years, although its term of office could prove shorter. In the course of this period the Conservative government which began with 'conciliatory' speeches by Baldwin will reveal that it has been in the last resort summoned to conserve all the contradictions and ulcers of post-war Britain. With regard to the most terrible of these ulcers, chronic unemployment, the Conservative party itself has no illusions. No substantial expansion of exports can be hoped for. Competition from America and Japan is mounting and German industry is reviving. France is exporting with the aid of a falling currency. Baldwin declares that politicians cannot bring relief to industry; it must find it within itself. The fresh efforts to re-establish the Gold Standard signify new sacrifices on the part of the population and consequently of industry, which foreshadow a further rise in discontent and alarm. The radicalisation of the British working class will proceed apace.

All this will prepare the coming to power of the Labour Party. But we have every reason to fear, or rather, to hope, that this process will cause much displeasure not only to Baldwin but to MacDonald too. Above all, a growth in the number of industrial conflicts can be expected and along with this

---

5 The main polemic on which these attacks were based is to be found in Lenin's *Left-Wing Communism: An Infantile Disorder*.

an increase in the pressure of the working masses upon their parliamentary representatives. Neither the former nor the latter can be to the taste of leaders who applaud Baldwin's conciliatory speeches and express their grief over the dead Curzon. The inner life of the Parliamentary Party as well as its position in Parliament will thereby become the more difficult.

On the other hand, there can be no doubt that the capitalist tiger will soon stop purring about gradualness and start to show its claws. Under such conditions will MacDonald manage to retain his leadership until the next election? This question does not of course have a decisive importance and an answer to it can have only a conjectural nature. In any event, a further sharpening of relations between the right and the so-called 'left' wings of the Labour Party and, what is far more important, a strengthening of revolutionary tendencies in the masses can be expected.

The possessing classes will begin to follow what is taking place in the ranks of the working class with mounting alarm and begin to prepare for the election well in advance. In such conditions the election campaign will acquire an exceedingly tense character. The last election, in which there figured a forged document,[6] put out through all the bourgeois press and at all meetings on a signal from the centre, was only a pale shadow of elections to come.

The election, always assuming that it does not develop directly into a civil war (and generally speaking that is not excluded), will have three possible outcomes: either the Conservatives will return to power but with a sharply reduced majority; or else none of the parties will have a clear majority and the parliamentary position of last year will be reverted to, only in political conditions far less favourable to compromise; or finally an absolute majority will pass to the Labour Party.

In the event of a new victory for the Conservatives, the indignation and impatience of the workers will inevitably sharpen. The question of the electoral mechanism and its swindling of constituencies will inevitably come to the fore with all its sharpness. The demand for a new, more democratic parliament will resound with greater force. This may for a while hold back the internal struggle inside the Labour Party to a certain extent, but it will create more favourable conditions for the revolutionary elements.

Will the Conservatives make a peaceful concession over a question which may become for them a question of fate? Highly unlikely. On the contrary,

6 The 'Zinoviev Letter' – A fake document published by the *Daily Mail* before the 1924 general election purported to be a directive from Zinoviev to the CPGB ordering it to engage in seditious activities.

once the question of power becomes sharply posed the Conservatives will attempt to split the workers, finding support from the Thomases at the top and the trade unionists who refuse to pay the political levy at the bottom. By no means excluded is an attempt by a Conservative government to produce isolated clashes, crush them by force, terrify the liberal philistines leading the Labour Party and thrust the movement back.

Could this plan succeed? Such a possibility cannot be ruled out. In so far as the leaders of the Labour Party lead it with their eyes shut, without perspectives, and without any understanding of social realities, they make it easier for the Conservatives to strike a blow at the movement at the next and higher stage. Such a variant would contain a more or less serious temporary defeat for the working class but it would, of course, have nothing in common with that peaceful, parliamentary road that the compromisers imagine. On the contrary, a defeat of this sort would prepare for a resumption of the class struggle at the next stage in more decisive revolutionary forms and consequently under new leadership.

If after the next election neither of the parties has a majority, parliament will be prostrated. A repetition of the Labour-Liberal coalition could hardly take place after the experience gained and in a situation of new and sharpened inter-class and inter-party relations at that. A Conservative-Liberal government would be more probable. But this would in essence coincide with the first variant, that of a Conservative majority, that we have just been examining. In the event of their failure to reach an agreement, the only parliamentary solution would be a revision of the electoral system. The question of constituencies, second ballots, and so forth would become a question of the direct struggle of the two main parties for power. Would a parliament divided between parties, neither of which is in a position to take power, be capable of passing a new electoral act? That is more than doubtful. It would in any case require powerful pressure from outside. The weakness of a parliament without a secure majority would create a favourable circumstance for such a pressure. But this once again opens up a revolutionary perspective.

However, this intermediate variant does not have for us an intrinsic importance as it is obvious that an unstable parliamentary position must be resolved in one direction or the other, that is to say leading either to a Conservative or to a Labour government. We have examined the first case. As regards the second case, this is precisely the one that presents for us the basic interest from the standpoint of the subject concerning us. The question consequently is: can it be assumed that the Labour Party, having made sure of an overall parliamentary majority at the election and put forward its own government, will carry out by a peaceful road the nationalisation of the principal branches of industry, and develop socialist construction within the framework and methods of the present parliamentary system?

So as not to complicate the question at the start, we shall assume that MacDonald's grouping of compromise with the Liberals will retain the party's official leadership in its hands even during the next election, so that a Labour Party victory will lead to the formation of a MacDonald government. It will no longer, however, be a simple repetition of the first experience: first, it will have behind it, according to our supposition, a safe majority; secondly, inter-party relations must inevitably sharpen in the coming period, especially in event of a Labour Party victory. Today when the Conservatives have a firm majority in their hands, they tend to treat MacDonald, Thomas, and Co. with a patronising condescension. But as the Conservatives are made of more serious stuff than the mock-socialists they will, when left in a minority, certainly show their claws and teeth. There can be no doubt therefore that even if the Conservatives could not prevent the formation of a stable government by the Labour Party by this or that parliamentary or extra-parliamentary method, the minority Conservatives would even in such an event, which might seem to be the most favourable from the standpoint of a peaceful development, do everything in their power to sabotage all the measures of the Labour government by means of the Civil Service, the judiciary, the military, the House of Lords, and the courts.

Facing the Conservatives, as well as the remnants of the Liberals, would be the task of discrediting at all costs the first stable government of the working class. For here it is a question of life or death. It is not at all the old struggle between the Liberals and the Conservatives where disagreements never went beyond the bounds of the 'family' of the possessing classes. Any serious reforms by a Labour government in the field of taxation, nationalisation, and a general democratisation of government would evoke a mighty flood of enthusiasm from the labouring masses, and – as appetite grows with the eating – successful *moderate* reforms would inevitably push towards the path of increasingly *radical* reforms.

In other words, each additional day would further remove the possibility of the Conservatives' return to power. The Conservatives could not fail to realise very clearly that this was no longer a routine change of government, but the beginning of a socialist revolution by parliamentary means. The resources of filibustering, legislative, and administrative sabotage that the possessing classes have in their hands are very great for, whatever the parliamentary majority, the whole state apparatus is from top to bottom inextricably tied to the bourgeoisie. Belonging to it are: the whole of the press, the principal organs of local government, the universities, schools, the churches, and innumerable clubs and voluntary associations in general. In its hands are the banks, the whole system of public credit, and finally, the transport and trading apparatus, so that the day-to-day food supply of London, including that of its Labour government, depends upon the big capitalist corporations. It is absolutely self-evident that all these gigantic means will be brought into motion with furious violence in order to put a brake on the activity of the Labour government, paralyse its efforts, intimidate it, introduce a split in its parliamentary majority, and finally to create a financial panic, dislocation of the food supply, lock-outs, to terrorise the top layers of the labour organisations, and render the proletariat powerless. Only an utter fool can fail to understand that the bourgeoisie will move heaven, earth, and the nether regions in the event of the actual coming to power of a Labour government.

Today's so-called British fascism is for the time being more of a curiosity than anything else, but this curiosity is nonetheless symptomatic. The Conservatives are today still sitting too firmly in the saddle to need the aid of the fascists. But a sharpening of inter-party relations, the growth of the persistence and militancy of the working masses, and the perspective of a Labour Party victory will inevitably cause the development of fascist tendencies on the right wing of the Conservatives. In a country that has become poorer in recent years, where the position of the small and middle bourgeois has worsened in the extreme and there is chronic unemployment, there will be no shortage of elements for the formation of fascist detachments.

There can therefore be no doubt that at the moment of an election victory for the Labour Party the Conservatives will have behind them not only the official state apparatus but also the unofficial gangs of fascism. They will begin the bloody work of the provocateur before the parliament has even had time to proceed to the first reading of a bill for the nationalisation of the coal mines. What is there left for a Labour government to do? Either shamefully capitulate or crush the opposition. The latter decision will, however, by no means prove so simple. The experience of Ireland bears witness that a solid material force and a tough state apparatus is indispensable to crush this sort of opposition. A Labour government will find itself with neither the former nor the latter. The police, the courts, the army, and the territorial forces will always be on the side of the disruptors, saboteurs, and fascists. The administrative machinery will have to be broken up and the reactionaries replaced by Labour Party members. There will be no other road. But it is quite obvious that such abrupt state measures, although wholly 'legal', will sharpen the legal and illegal opposition of unified bourgeois reaction in the extreme. In other words: this will also be a path of civil war.

But can the Labour Party when once in power go about the business so cautiously, so tactfully, and so skilfully that the bourgeoisie will – how shall we put it? – not feel the need for active resistance? Such an assumption is in itself of course laughable. It must nevertheless be recognised that just such is the basic hope of MacDonald and Co. When today's mock-leader of the ILP says that the Labour Party will carry out only those reforms whose realisation can be "proved scientifically" (MacDonald's "science" is already known to us), then he means that a Labour government would look inquiringly into the bourgeoisie's eyes before every one of its reformist steps. Of course, if everything depended upon MacDonald's good will and his "scientifically" justified reforms things would never come to a civil war – owing to the lack of any ground for one on the part of the bourgeoisie. If a second MacDonald government was like the first one then there would be no cause to raise even the question of the feasibility of socialism by the parliamentary road, for the budget of the City has nothing in common with the budget of socialism.

But even if a Labour government retained its former composition its policy would necessarily undergo a few changes. It is ridiculous to think that the same mighty Labour wave that raises MacDonald to power will immediately afterwards flood deferentially back. No, the demanding mood of the working class will grow in the extreme. Now there will be no longer any place for excuses of dependence on Liberal votes. The opposition of the Conservatives, the House of Lords, the bureaucracy, and the monarchy will redouble the energy, impatience, and indignation of the workers. The slanders and calumnies of the capitalist press will goad them on. If their own government in these conditions displayed even the most unfeigned energy it would still seem to be too sluggish to the working masses. But there is about as much ground for expecting revolutionary energy from MacDonald, Clynes, and Snowden as there is to expect perfume to rise from a rotten beetroot. Between a revolutionary onslaught by the masses and the fierce resistance of the bourgeoisie, a MacDonald government would rush about from one side to the other, irritating some, not satisfying others, provoking the bourgeoisie by its inertia, exacerbating the revolutionary impatience of the workers, kindling a civil war, and striving at the same time to deprive it of the necessary leadership on the side of the proletariat.

Meanwhile, the revolutionary wing would inevitably grow and the most far-sighted resolute and revolutionary elements of the working class would come to the top. On this path a MacDonald government would, sooner or later, depending upon the balance of forces outside parliament, have to surrender its position either to a Conservative government with fascist and not conciliatory tendencies, or to a revolutionary government that was really capable of carrying the job through to the finish. In both the one and the other event a new explosion of civil war is inevitable, a sharp collision between the classes all along the line. In the event of the Conservatives' victory – the ruthless smashing of workers' organisations; in the event of the victory of the proletariat – the shattering of the resistance of the exploiters by means of the revolutionary dictatorship. Is this not to your liking, my Lords? We cannot help it. The fundamental springs of motion depend as little upon us as they do upon you. We can 'decree' nothing. We can only analyse.

Among MacDonald's 'left' self-supporters and half-opponents who, like him, assume a democratic stance, there are some who will probably say: obviously if the bourgeois classes attempt to put up resistance to a democratically-elected Labour government, the latter will not baulk at methods of the most severe coercion – but this will be not a class dictatorship, rather the power of a democratic state… and so on and so forth.

It is quite futile to put the argument on this plane. To think in fact that the fate of society can be determined by whether there are elected to parliament 307 Labour MPs i.e., a minority, or 308, i.e., a majority, and not by the effective balance of class forces at the moment of the sharp clash of classes over the basic questions of their existence – to think in that way would mean to be completely captive to the fetish of parliamentary arithmetic.

And let us ask, what happens if the Conservatives, faced with a mounting revolutionary flood and the danger of a Labour government, not only refuse to democratise the electoral system but on the contrary introduce new restrictions? Unlikely! – some ninny will object who does not understand that where it is a matter of the life and death of classes anything is likely.

But already in top circles in Britain a great deal of preparatory to-ing and fro-ing is going on over the reorganisation and strengthening of the House of Lords. MacDonald recently stated in connection with this that he could understand the concern of some Conservative lords but "why Liberals should make endeavours in the same direction I cannot understand". The sage cannot understand why the Liberals are reinforcing a second line of trenches against the offensive of the working class. He does not understand this because he himself is a liberal, and a profoundly provincial, petty, and limited one at that. He does not understand that the bourgeoisie has serious intentions, that it is preparing for a mortal struggle, and that the crown and the House of Lords will occupy a prominent place in that struggle. Having curtailed the rights of the House of Commons, that is to say, carrying out a legal coup d'état, the Conservatives will, despite all the difficulties of such an undertaking, still emerge in a more advantageous situation than if they had had to organise opposition to a Labour government that had successfully reinforced itself.

But obviously in such an event, some 'left' phrasemonger will exclaim, we should call upon the masses to resist. To use revolutionary force, does he mean? So does it turn out that revolutionary force is not only permissible but in fact inevitable in a case where the Conservatives carry out a pre-emptive coup d'état, by the most legal parliamentary means? But in that case is it not simpler to say that revolutionary force is expedient when and where it strengthens the position of the proletariat, weakens or repulses the enemy, and accelerates the socialist development of society?

But heroic promises to put up lightning resistance in the event the Conservatives should 'dare' and so forth are not worth a rotten egg. One cannot lull the masses day in and day out with claptrap about a peaceful, painless transition to socialism and then at the first solid punch on the nose summon the masses to an armed response. This is the surest way of assisting reaction in the rout of the proletariat. To prove equal to a revolutionary repulse, the masses must be ideologically, organisationally, and materially prepared for it. They must understand the inevitability of a sharpening of the class struggle and of its turning at a certain stage into a civil war. The political education of the working class and the selection of its leading personnel must be adjusted to such a perspective. The illusions of compromise must be fought day in and day out, that is to say, war to the death must be declared on MacDonaldism. Thus and only thus does the question stand today.

Leaving aside the concrete conditions, what can now be said is that MacDonald did have a chance in the past of greatly easing the transition to socialism and reducing the upheavals of civil war to a minimum. That was during the first coming to power of the Labour Party. If MacDonald had immediately placed parliament face to face with a decisive programme (the liquidation of the monarchy and the House of Lords, a heavy tax on capital, the nationalisation of the principal means of production and so forth), and had, having dissolved parliament, appealed to the country with a revolutionary determination, he could have hoped to catch the possessing classes to some extent off guard, not letting them gather their forces, shattering them with the pressure of the working masses and seizing and renewing the state apparatus before British fascism had time to form itself – and thus take the revolution through the gate of parliament, 'legalise' it and lead it to a complete victory with a firm hand.

But it is absolutely obvious that such a possibility is a purely theoretical one. It would require another party with other leaders, and that would in turn presuppose other circumstances. If we construe this possibility in relation to the past then it is only in order to reveal the more sharply its impossibility in the future. The first experience of a Labour government, for all its cowardly incompetence, formed, however, an important historical warning for the ruling classes. They will no longer be caught off guard, now they follow the life of the working class and all the processes taking place within it with ten times more vigilance. "Not under any circumstances shall we fire first", the most humane, devout and Christian Baldwin stated, apparently quite unexpectedly, in his speech in parliament on 5 March. And on the Labour benches there were fools who applauded these words. But Baldwin does not for a minute doubt that he will have to fire. He merely wants in the forthcoming civil war to put the responsibility, at least in the eyes of the intermediate classes, on to the enemy, that is, the workers. In exactly the same way, the diplomacy of each country strives in advance to transfer the blame for a coming war on to the other side.

Of course, the proletarian party also has an interest in throwing responsibility for a civil war back on to the capitalist bosses, and in the final count the Labour Party has and will have far greater political and moral grounds for this. Admittedly, an assault upon the House of Commons by the Conservatives would form a most 'noble' motive for agitation, but such a circumstance has in the end but a third – or fifth – rate importance. Here we are examining not the question of the causes of a revolutionary conflict but the question of how to take control of the state with the object of a transition to socialism. Parliament cannot in the slightest degree guarantee a peaceful transition: revolutionary class force is indispensable and unavoidable. This must be prepared for and trained for. The masses must be educated and tempered in a revolutionary way. The first condition for this is an intransigent struggle against the corrupting spirit of MacDonaldism.

———

On 25 March, a House of Lords committee solemnly resolved that the title of the Duke of Somerset must pass to a certain Mr. Seymour who would thus henceforth acquire the right to legislate in the House of Lords, and this decision in favour of Seymour depended upon the settlement of another preliminary circumstance: when a certain Colonel Seymour was married in 1787 to give Britain a few generations later a new lord, was his wife's first husband at that time alive or dead in Calcutta?

This question is, as we can see, one of prime importance to the fate of British democracy. In the same issue of the *Daily Herald* with this instructive episode of the first husband of the wife of the forefather of the legislator, Seymour, the editors defend themselves from accusations of desiring to establish Soviet methods in Britain: no, no, we are only for trade with the Soviets but in no case for a Soviet regime in Britain.

But what is so bad, we permit ourselves to ask, about Soviet methods applied to British technique, British industry, and the cultural habits of the British working class? Let the *Daily Herald* ponder a little the consequences that would flow from the introduction of the Soviet system in Great Britain.

In the first place, royalty would be abolished and Mrs. Snowden would be spared the necessity of grieving over the excessive labour of members of the Royal Family. In the second place, the House of Lords, where Messrs. Seymours legislate by force of a mandate given them by the timely death of the first husband of their great-great grandmother in Calcutta, would be abolished. In the third place there would be abolition of the present parliament, whose falsity and impotence are recorded even in the *Daily Herald* nearly every day. The land parasitism of the landlords would be done away with forever. The basic branches of industry would pass into the hands of the working class which in Britain comprises the overwhelming majority of the people. The mighty apparatuses of the Conservative and Liberal newspapers and publishers could be used for the education of the working class. "Give me a dictatorship over Fleet Street for only a month and I shall destroy the hypnosis!", exclaimed Robert Williams in 1920. Williams himself has defected and Fleet Street as before awaits a proletarian hand.

Workers would elect their representatives not within the framework of those fraudulent parliamentary constituencies that Britain is split up into today, but according to factory and plant. Councils of workers' deputies would renew the government apparatus from bottom to top. Privileges of birth and wealth would disappear along with the falsified democracy based upon financial support from the banks. A genuine workers' democracy would come to power that combined management of the economy with the political government of the country. Such a government that for the first time in history really had its support in the people would inaugurate free, equal, and brotherly relations with India, Egypt, and the other present colonies. It would immediately conclude a powerful political and military alliance with workers' and peasants' Russia. Such an alliance would be designed for many years ahead. The economic plans of both countries would in their corresponding sectors be coordinated for a number of years. The exchange of goods, products, and services between these two complementary countries would raise the material and spiritual well-being of the labouring masses of Britain as also of Russia.

Surely this would not be too bad a thing? So why is it necessary to try to vindicate oneself from accusations of striving to introduce a Soviet order into Britain? By terrorising the public opinion of workers, the bourgeoisie wants to instil them with a salutary fear of an assault upon the present British regime while the labour press, instead of ruthlessly exposing this policy of reactionary hypnosis, adapts in cowardly fashion to it and thus supports it. This too is MacDonaldism.

The British opportunists like those in Europe have repeatedly said that the Bolsheviks had arrived at a dictatorship only by the logic of their position and counter to all their principles. In this connection it would be highly instructive to examine the evolution of Marxist and revolutionary thought in general on the question of democracy. Here we are forced to confine ourselves to just two brief testimonies. As early as 1887 Lafargue, a close pupil of Marx and linked to him by close personal bonds, sketched the general course of revolution in France in these lines:

The working class will rule in the industrial cities, which will all become revolutionary centres and form a federation in order to attract the countryside over to the side of the revolution and overcome the resistance that will be organised in such trading and maritime cities as Havre, Bordeaux, Marseilles, and so on. In the industrial cities the socialists will have to seize power in local institutions, arm the workers and organise them militarily: "He who has arms has bread", said Blanqui. They will open the gates of the prisons to let out the petty thieves and put under lock and key the big thieves like the bankers, capitalists, big industrialists, the big property owners, and so on. Nothing worse will be done to them but they will be regarded as hostages answerable for the good behaviour of the of their class. The revolutionary power will be formed by means of a simple seizure and only when the new power is fully in control of the situation, will the socialists seek confirmation for their actions by 'universal' suffrage. The bourgeoisie have for so long refused the ballot box to the propertyless classes that they must not be surprised if all the former capitalists are deprived of the franchise until the revolutionary party triumphs.

For Lafargue the fate of the revolution is not decided by an appeal to some constituent assembly but by the revolutionary organisation of the masses in the process of the struggle against the enemy:

"When local revolutionary institutions are established, the latter will have to organise by means of delegations, or otherwise the central power upon which will be placed the obligation to take overall measures in the interests of the revolution and of impeding the formation of a reactionary party."

It is self-evident that there is not yet in these lines even a slightly formed characterisation of the Soviet system which by and large forms not an *a priori* principle but the outcome of revolutionary experience. However, the construction of a central revolutionary power by means of delegation from local revolutionary organs, conducting a struggle against reaction, comes very close to the Soviet system in idea. And at any rate, as regards formal democracy then Lafargue's attitude to it is characterised with a remarkable clarity. The power can only be obtained by the working class by means of a revolutionary *seizure*. "'Universal' suffrage", as Lafargue ironically puts it, "can be introduced only after the proletariat has taken control of the apparatus of the state". But even then the bourgeois must be deprived of the right to vote and the big capitalists must be transformed into the status of hostages.

Anyone with the least conception of the nature of the relations between Lafargue and Marx can be in absolutely no doubt that Lafargue had developed his conceptions on the dictatorship of the proletariat on the basis of frequent conversations with Marx. If Marx himself had not dwelt in detail on the elucidation of these questions then it is only because, of course, he considered the character of the revolutionary dictatorship of the class to be self-evident. In any case what was said by Marx on this score, not only in 1848 and 1849, but also in 1871 with regard to the Paris Commune, leaves no doubt that Lafargue was only developing Marx's idea.

However, not only Lafargue stood for class dictatorship as opposed to democracy. This idea had been already advanced with adequate precision back in the time of Chartism. In the organ *The Poor Man's Guardian* the following "sole true reform" was advanced in connection with the sought-for extension of the franchise: "It is but common justice that people that make the goods should have the sole privilege of making the laws." The significance of Chartism lies in the fact that the whole subsequent history of the class struggle was as if summarised in advance, during that decade. Afterwards the movement turned backwards in many respects. It broadened its base and amassed experience. On a new and higher basis it will inevitably return to many of the ideas and methods of Chartism.

6. Two Traditions: The Seventeenth-Century Revolution and Chartism

The editor of the *Daily Herald* recently expressed his doubts as to whether Oliver Cromwell could be called a "pioneer of the labour movement". One of the newspaper's collaborators supported the editor's doubts and referred to the severe repressions that Cromwell conducted against the Levellers, the sect of equalitarians of that time (communists). These reflections and questions are extremely typical of the historical thinking of the leaders of the Labour Party. That Oliver Cromwell was a pioneer of *bourgeois* and not *socialist* society there would appear to be no need to waste more than two words in proving. The great revolutionary bourgeois was against universal suffrage for he saw in it a danger to private property. It is relevant to note that the Webbs draw from this the conclusion of the "incompatibility" of democracy and capitalism while closing their eyes to the fact that capitalism has learnt to live on the best possible terms with democracy and to have taken control of the instrument of universal suffrage as an instrument of the stock exchange.[1] Nevertheless, British workers can learn incomparably more from Cromwell than from MacDonald, Snowden, Webb, and other such compromising brethren. Cromwell was a great revolutionary of his time, who knew how to uphold the interests of the new, bourgeois social system

---

1   It is curious that, two centuries later, in 1842 in fact, the historian Macaulay as an MP protested against universal suffrage for the very same reasons as Cromwell. – *Trotsky*

against the old aristocratic one *without holding back at anything*. This must be learnt from him, and the dead lion of the seventeenth century is in this sense immeasurably greater than many living dogs.

Following at the tails of those living non-lions who write leading articles in the *Manchester Guardian* and other Liberal organs, the Labour Party leaders generally counterpose democracy to any sort of despotic government whether "the dictatorship of Lenin" or "the dictatorship of Mussolini". The historical mumbo-jumbo of these gentlemen is nowhere expressed more clearly than in this juxtaposition. Not because we are in hindsight inclined to deny the "dictatorship of Lenin" – his power was, through its effective influence on the whole course of events in an enormous state, exceptional.

But how can one speak of dictatorship while passing over its social and historical content? History has known the dictatorship of Cromwell, the dictatorship of Robespierre, the dictatorship of Arakcheev, the dictatorship of Napoleon I, and the dictatorship of Mussolini. It is impossible to discuss anything with a crackpot who puts Robespierre and Arakcheev on a par. Different classes in different conditions and for different tasks find themselves compelled in particular and indeed, the most acute and critical, periods in their history, to vest an extraordinary power and authority in such of their leaders as can carry forward their fundamental interests most sharply and fully. When we speak of dictatorship we must in the first place be clear as to what interest of what particular classes find their historical expression through the dictatorship. For one era Oliver Cromwell, and for another, Robespierre expressed the historically progressive tendencies of development of bourgeois society. William Pitt, likewise extremely close to a personal dictatorship, defended the interests of the monarchy, the privileged classes, and the top bourgeois against a revolution of the petty bourgeoisie that found its highest expression in the dictatorship of Robespierre.

The liberal vulgarians customarily say that they are against a dictatorship from the left just as much as from the right, although in practice they do not let slip any opportunity of supporting a dictatorship of the right. But for us the question is determined by the fact that one dictatorship moves society forward while another drags it back. Mussolini's dictatorship is a dictatorship of the prematurely decayed, impotent, thoroughly contaminated Italian bourgeoisie: it is a dictatorship with a broken nose. The "dictatorship of Lenin" expresses the mighty pressure of the new historical class and its superhuman struggle against all the forces of the old society. If Lenin can be juxtaposed to anyone then it is not to Napoleon, nor even less to Mussolini, but to Cromwell and Robespierre.

It can be with some justice said that Lenin is the proletarian twentieth-century Cromwell. Such a definition would at the same time be the highest compliment to the petty-bourgeois seventeenth-century Cromwell.

The French bourgeoisie, having falsified the revolution, adopted it and, changing it into small coinage, put it into daily circulation. The British bourgeoisie has erased the very memory of the seventeenth century revolution by dissolving its past in 'gradualness'. The advanced British workers will have to rediscover the English revolution and find within its ecclesiastical shell the mighty struggle of social forces. Cromwell was in no case a 'pioneer of labour'. But in the seventeenth-century drama, the British proletariat can find great precedents for revolutionary action. This is equally a national tradition, and a thoroughly legitimate one that is wholly in place in the arsenal of the working class.

The proletarian movement has another great national tradition in Chartism. A familiarity with both these periods is vital to every conscious British worker. The clarification of the historical significance of the seventeenth-century revolution and the revolutionary content of Chartism is one of the most important obligations for British Marxists.

—

A study of the revolutionary era in Britain's development, which lasted approximately from the enforced summoning of parliament by Charles Stuart until the death of Oliver Cromwell, is necessary above all in order to understand the place of parliamentarism and of 'law' in general in a living and not an imaginary history. The 'great' national historian Macaulay vulgarised the social drama of the seventeenth century by obscuring the inner struggle of forces with platitudes that are sometimes interesting but always superficial. The French conservative Guizot approaches events more profoundly. But either way, whichever account is taken, the man who knows how to read and is capable of discovering under the shadows of history real living bodies, classes, and factions will be convinced from this very experience of the English revolution how subsidiary, subordinate, and qualified a role is played by law in the mechanics of social struggle and especially in a revolutionary era, that is to say, when the *basic* interests of the *basic* classes in society come to the fore.

In the England of the 1640s we see a parliament based upon the most whimsical franchise, which at the same time regarded itself as the representative organ of the people. The lower house represented the nation in that it represented the bourgeoisie and thereby national wealth. In the reign of Charles I it was found, and not without amazement, that the House of Commons was three times richer than the House of Lords. The king now dissolved this parliament and now recalled it according to the pressure of financial need. Parliament created an army for its defence. The army gradually concentrated in its ranks all the most active, courageous, and resolute elements. As a direct consequence of this, parliament capitulated to this army. We say "*as a direct consequence*", but by this we wish to say that Parliament capitulated not simply to armed force (it did not capitulate to the King's army) but to the Puritan army of Cromwell which expressed the requirements of the revolution more boldly, more resolutely, and more consistently than did Parliament.

The adherents of the Episcopal or Anglican, semi-Catholic Church were the party of the court, the nobility, and of course the higher clergy. The Presbyterians were the party of the bourgeoisie, the party of wealth and enlightenment. The Independents, and the Puritans especially, were the party of the petty bourgeoisie, the plebeians. Wrapped up in ecclesiastical controversies, in the form of a struggle over the religious structure of the church, there took place a social self-determination of classes and their regrouping along new, bourgeois lines. Politically the Presbyterian party stood for a limited monarchy; the Independents, who then were called "root and branch men" or, in the language of our day, radicals, stood for a republic. The half-way position of the Presbyterians fully corresponded to the contradictory interests of the bourgeoisie – between the nobility and the plebeians. The Independents' party, which dared to carry its ideas and slogans through to their conclusion, naturally displaced the Presbyterians among the awakening petty-bourgeois masses in the towns and the countryside that formed the main force of the revolution.

Events unfolded empirically. In their struggle for power and property interests, both the former and the latter side hid themselves behind a cloak of legitimacy. This is put quite well by Guizot:

> Then commenced between the Parliament and the King, a conflict previously unexampled in Europe [...] Negotiations were still continued, but neither party expected any result from them, or even had any intention to treat. It was no longer to one another that they addressed their declarations and messages; both appealed to the whole nation, to public opinion; to this new power both seemed to look for strength and success. The origin and extent of the royal authority, the privileges of the Houses of Parliament, the limits of the obligations due from subjects, the militia, the petitions for the redress of grievances, and the distribution of

public employments, became the subjects of an official controversy, in which the general principles of social order, the various nature of governments, the primitive rights of liberty, history, laws, and customs of England, were alternately quoted, explained and commented upon. In the interval between the dispute of the two parties in parliament and their armed encounter on the field of battle, reason and learning interposed, as it were, for several months, to suspend the course of events, and to put forth their ablest efforts to obtain the free concurrence of the people, by stamping either cause with the impress of legitimacy [...] When the time came for drawing the sword, all were astonished and deeply moved [...]

Now, however, both parties mutually accused each other of illegality and innovation, and both were justified in making the charge: for the one had violated the ancient rights of the country, and had not abjured the maxims of tyranny; and the other demanded, in the name of principles still confused and chaotic, liberties and a power which had until then been unknown.[2]

As the storm of the Civil War began to break, the most active Royalists left the House of Commons and the House of Lords at Westminster and fled over to Charles' headquarters at York: parliament split as in all great revolutionary periods. Whether the 'legitimate' majority was in this or that event on the side of revolution or on the side of reaction does not in such situations decide the question.

At a certain moment in political history, the fate of 'democracy' hung not upon parliament but – however terrible this might be to scrofulous pacifists! – upon the cavalry. In the first stage of the war the king's cavalry, at that time the most considerable section of the army, filled the horsemen of Parliament with terror. It is worthy of note that we encounter the same phenomenon in later revolutions, especially during the American Civil War where the Southern horse had in the first phase an indisputable superiority over the horse of the Northerners; and most recently in our own revolution, in the first period of which the White cavalrymen dealt us a series of cruel blows before the workers could be taught to sit firmly in the saddle.

The horse is by its origin the most aristocratic branch of arms. The royal cavalry was far more cohesive and resolute than the hastily and haphazardly recruited parliamentary riders. The horse of the Southern states was the innate branch of arms for the planter and plainsman whereas the commercial and industrial North had to learn the horse from scratch. Finally, with us the very hearth and home of the cavalry was in the steppes of the South-East,

---

2   F. Guizot, *History of the English Revolution, from the Accession of Charles I.*

the Cossack Vendée.[3] Cromwell very quickly realised that the fate of his class would be decided by cavalry. He said to Hampden: "I will raise such men as have the fear of God before them and make some conscience of what they do; and I warrant you they will not be beaten."[4]

The words that Cromwell addressed to the free landowners and artisans that he had enlisted are in the highest degree interesting:

> I will not cozen you by perplexed expressions in my commission about fighting for King and Parliament. If the King chanced to be in the body of the enemy, I would as soon discharge my pistol upon him as upon any private man; and if your conscience will not let you do the like, I advise you not to enlist yourselves under me.[5]

In this way Cromwell built not merely an army but also a party – his army was to some extent an armed party and herein precisely lay its strength. In 1644 Cromwell's 'holy' squadrons won a brilliant victory over the King's horsemen and won the nickname of 'Ironsides'. It is always useful for a revolution to have iron sides! On this score British workers can learn much from Cromwell.

The observations on the Puritans' army made by the historian Macaulay are here not without interest:

> A force thus composed might, without injury to its efficiency, be indulged in some liberties which, if allowed to any other troops, would have proved subversive of all discipline. In general, soldiers who should form themselves into political clubs, elect delegates, and pass resolutions on high questions of state, would soon break loose from all control, would cease to form an army, and would become the worst and most dangerous of mobs. Nor would it be safe, in our time, to tolerate in any regiment religious meetings at which a corporal versed in scripture should lead the devotions of his less gifted colonel, and admonish a back-sliding major. But such was *the intelligence, the gravity, and the self-command of the warriors whom Cromwell had trained that in their camp a political organisation and a religious organisation could exist without destroying military organisation*. The same men who, off duty, were noted as demagogues[6] and field preachers, were distinguished by steadiness, by the spirit of order, and by prompt obedience on watch, on will and on the field of battle.

---

3   Vendée – A region of Western France which during the French Revolution was economically backward and dominated by the clergy. It became the basis of two counter-revolutionary revolts, backed by royalist agents.

4   F. Guizot, *History of the English Revolution*.

5   Ibid.

6   Macaulay means revolutionary agitators. – *Trotsky*

And further:

> But in his camp alone the most rigid discipline was found in company with the
> fiercest enthusiasm. His troops moved to victory with the precision of machines,
> while burning with the wildest fanaticism of Crusaders.[7]

Any historical analogies demand the greatest caution especially when we are
dealing with the seventeenth and the twentieth centuries; yet nonetheless one
cannot help being struck by some distinct features that bring the regime and
character of Cromwell's army and the character of the Red Army close together.
Admittedly, then everything was founded upon faith in predestination and
upon a strict religious morality; now with us militant atheism reigns supreme.
But running beneath the religious form of puritanism there was the preaching
of the historical mission of a new class, and the teaching on predestination
was a religious approach to an historical pattern.

Cromwell's fighters felt themselves to be in the first place puritans and only
in the second place soldiers, just as our fighters acknowledge themselves to
be above all revolutionaries and communists and only then soldiers. But the
points of divergence are even greater than the points of similarity.

The Red Army formed by the party of the proletariat remains its armed
organ. Cromwell's army, which also embodied his party, became itself the
decisive force. We can see how the puritan army began to adapt parliament
to itself and to revolution. The army obtained the expulsion of the eleven
Presbyterians, that is, the representatives of the right-wing, from parliament.
The Presbyterians, the Girondists[8] of the English revolution, attempted to
raise a rebellion against parliament. A truncated parliament sought salvation
in the army and thus all the more subordinated itself to it. Under the pressure
of the army, and particularly of its left and more resolute wing, Cromwell was
compelled to execute Charles I. The axe of revolution was bizarrely intertwined
with psalms. But the axe was more persuasive. Then Cromwell's Colonel
Pride surrounded parliament and ejected eighty-one Presbyterian members.
Of parliament there remained but a rump. It consisted of Independents,

---

7 Lord Macaulay, *History of England*, 1889, p. 60.

8 Girondists – A group of deputies in the French Legislative Assembly of 1791, most of
whom came from the Gironde district around Bordeaux. Led by Brissot, Roland, and
Vergniaud they opposed the revolutionary methods of rule imposed by the Jacobins.
They represented the reformist elements of the middle class and were hostile to the
Jacobins' appeals to the masses. They were overthrown by the Jacobins on 2 June 1793,
and on 31 October all the leaders of the Gironde were executed.

that is, of supporters of Cromwell and his army; but for just this reason Parliament, which had waged a colossal struggle against the monarchy, at the moment of victory ceased to be a source of any independent thinking and force whatsoever.

Cromwell was the focal point of both the former and the latter, and he rested directly upon the army, but in the final analysis drew his strength from his bold solution of the fundamental tasks of the revolution. A fool, an ignoramus, or a Fabian can see in Cromwell *only* a personal dictatorship. But in fact here, in the conditions of a deep social rupture, a personal dictatorship was the form taken on by the dictatorship of a class which was, moreover, the only one capable of liberating the kernel of the nation from the old shells and husks. The British social crisis of the seventeenth-century combined in itself features of the German Reformation of the sixteenth century with features of the French Revolution of the eighteenth century. In Cromwell, Luther joins hands with Robespierre.

The Puritans did not mind calling their enemies philistines, but the matter was nonetheless one of class struggle. Cromwell's task consisted of inflicting as shattering a blow as possible upon the absolutist monarchy, the court nobility, and the semi-Catholic Church which had been adjusted to the needs of the monarchy and the nobility. For such a blow, Cromwell, the true representative of the new class, needed the forces and passions of the masses of people. Under Cromwell's leadership the revolution acquired all the breadth vital for it. In such cases as that of the Levellers, where it exceeded the bounds of the requirements of the regenerate bourgeois society, Cromwell ruthlessly put down the 'Lunatics'. Once victorious, Cromwell began to construct a new state law that coupled biblical texts with the lances of the 'holy' soldiers, under which the deciding word always belonged to the pikes.

On 19 April 1653 Cromwell broke up the rump of the Long Parliament. In recognition of his historical mission the Puritan dictator saw dispersed members on the way with biblical denunciations: "Thou drunkard!", he cried to one; "Thou adulterer!", he reminded another. After this Cromwell forms a parliament out of representatives of God-fearing people, that is, an essentially class parliament; the God-fearers were the middle class who completed the work of accumulation with the aid of a strict morality and set about the plunder of the whole world with the Holy Scriptures on their lips. But this cumbersome Barebone's Parliament[9] also hampered the dictator by

---

9 This assembly of 1653, named after one of its members, was one of Cromwell's
    attempts to establish an alternative form of political rule after he had executed the King

depriving him of the necessary freedom of manoeuvre in a difficult domestic and international situation. At the end of 1653 Cromwell once again purged the House of Commons with the aid of soldiers.

If the rump of the Long Parliament dispersed in April had been guilty of deviating to the right, towards deals with the Presbyterians – then Barebone's Parliament was on a number of questions inclined to follow too closely along the straight road of Puritan virtue and thus made it difficult for Cromwell to establish a new social equilibrium. The revolutionary realist, Cromwell, was building a new society. Parliament does not form an end in itself, law does not form an end in itself, and although Cromwell himself and his 'holy' men regarded the fulfilment of divine behests to be ends in themselves, these latter were merely the ideological material for the building of a bourgeois society. In dispersing parliament after parliament, Cromwell displayed as little reverence towards the fetish of 'national' representation as in the execution of Charles I he had displayed insufficient respect for a monarchy by the grace of God.

Nonetheless, it was this same Cromwell who paved the way for the parliamentarism and democracy of the two subsequent centuries. In revenge for Cromwell's execution of Charles I, Charles II swung Cromwell's corpse up on the gallows. But pre-Cromwellian society could not be re-established by any restoration. The works of Cromwell could not be liquidated by the thievish legislation of the Restoration because what has been written with the sword cannot be wiped out by the pen. This, the converse of the proverb, is far truer, at least so far as the sword of revolution is concerned.

As an illustration of the inter-relations between 'law' and 'force' in an era of social overturns, the Long Parliament will always retain an especial interest, undergoing as it did for twenty years all the vicissitudes of the course of events, reflecting in itself the shocks of class forces, truncated from the right and the left, first rising up against the King, then receiving a slap in the eye from its own armed servants, twice dispersed and twice recalled, now commanding and now demeaning itself, before finally obtaining the opportunity of passing the act of its own dissolution.

Whether the proletarian revolution will have its own 'long' parliament we do not know. It is highly likely that it will confine itself to a *short* parliament. However, it will the more surely achieve this the better it masters the lessons of Cromwell's era.

---

and driven most of his opponents from Parliament. Most of its members represented various Puritan religious groups and as a result had little contact with political realities, so it was soon dissolved by Cromwell.

—

On the second and genuinely proletarian revolutionary tradition we shall here say but a few words.

The era of Chartism is immortal in that over the course of a decade it gives us in condensed and diagrammatic form the whole gamut of proletarian struggle – from petitions in parliament to armed insurrection. All the fundamental problems of the class movement of the proletariat – the inter-relation between parliamentary and extra-parliamentary activity, the role of universal suffrage, trade unions and cooperation, the significance of the general strike and its relation to armed insurrection, even the inter-relation between the proletariat and the peasantry – were not only crystallised out of the progress of the Chartist mass movement but found out their principled answer. Theoretically this answer was far from always irreproachable in its basis, the conclusions were not always fully drawn, and in the movement as a whole and in its theoretical expression there was much that was immature and unfinished. Nonetheless, the revolutionary slogans and methods of Chartism are even today, if critically dissected, infinitely higher than the sickly-sweet eclecticism of the MacDonalds and the economic obtuseness of the Webbs.

To use a hazardous comparison then, it can be said that the Chartist movement resembles a prelude which contains in an undeveloped form the musical theme of the whole opera. In this sense the British working class can and must see in Chartism not only its past but also its future. As the Chartists tossed the sentimental preachers of 'moral force' aside and gathered the masses behind the banner of revolution, so the British proletariat is faced with ejecting reformists, democrats, and pacifists from its midst and rallying to the banner of a revolutionary overturn.

Chartism did not win a victory not because its methods were incorrect but because it appeared too soon. It was only an historical anticipation. The 1905 revolution also suffered defeat. But its tradition lived on for twelve years, and its methods were victorious in October 1917. Chartism is not at all liquidated. History is liquidating Liberalism and prepares to liquidate the pseudo-Labour pacifism precisely so as to give a second birth to Chartism on new, immeasurably broader historical foundations. That is where you have the real national tradition of the British labour movement!

7. Trade Unions and Bolshevism

That the fundamental tasks of the labour movement cannot be assessed and defined from the formal and, ultimately, purely legalistic, standpoint of democracy is especially clearly evident from the recent history of Britain herself, and particularly graphically so from the question of the trade unions' political levies. This question, at first sight purely practical, has as a matter of fact a huge importance in principle which, we fear, is not understood by Messrs. Labour Party leaders.

The trade unions have as their object the struggle for the improvement of the working and living conditions of wage earners. To this end union members make certain financial contributions. As for political activity, the trade unions used to be formally regarded as neutral while in practice they most often followed at the tail of the Liberal Party. It goes without saying that the Liberals who, like the Conservatives, sell all sorts of honours to the rich bourgeois in return for a substantial contribution to the party's funds, needed not the financial assistance of the trade unions but only their votes. The position changed from the moment that the workers, through the medium of the trade unions, created the Labour Party. Having once brought it to life, the trade unions then found themselves compelled to finance it. To do this, supplementary contributions from the organised workers were required.

The bourgeois parties protested unanimously against this "flagrant infringement of individual freedom". A worker is not just a worker but also a citizen and a human being, MacDonald teaches with profundity. Quite so, echo Baldwin, Asquith, and Lloyd George. As a citizen, a worker, whether he joins a trade union or not, has the right to vote for any party. To exact from him an obligatory levy in support of the Labour Party represents an act of force not only upon his purse but also upon his conscience. It is after all a direct violation of the democratic constitution that excludes any element of compulsion in the matter of supporting this or that party. Such arguments must in themselves make a powerful impact on the Labour Party leaders who would gladly reject the obligatory anti-Liberal, almost Bolshevik methods of the trade unions were it not for this accursed need of £sd[1] without which one cannot, even in a democratic Arcady, gain a seat in parliament. Such then is the sad fate of democratic principles that £sd gives them bruised heads and black eyes. Here lies the imperfection of the best of worlds.

The history of the question of the trade unions' political levies has by now become fairly rich in turns and dramatic episodes. We shall not recount it here. It was only the other day that Baldwin rejected (for the time being!) a fresh attempt by his Conservative friends to ban the collection of the political levy. The Trade Union (Amendment) Act of 1913,[2] currently in force, while permitting unions to collect the political levy entitles every trade union member to refuse to pay this levy, and at the same time forbids the trade unions to persecute members, expel them from the union, and so forth. If we believe the estimates of *The Times* (6 March 1925), about 10 per cent of organised workers avail themselves of their right to withhold payment of the political levy. In this way the principle of individual freedom is saved at least in part. The complete triumph of 'freedom' would be achieved only where the contributions could be collected solely from those members who had themselves declared their voluntary agreement.

But at present, where there is a union resolution to that effect, all members are obliged to pay the levy. Only those are exempted who give notice of this on the appropriate form in good time. In other words, the liberal principle is turned from a triumphant rule into a tolerated exception. But even this partial implementation of the principle of personal freedom was achieved – alas! – not by the will of the workers but the force of bourgeois legislation upon the organisations of the proletariat.

This circumstance gives rise to the question: how does it come about that the workers who constitute the vast bulk of the British population, and consequently of British democracy too, are driven along the path of violating

---

1   £sd – Spoken as "Pounds, shillings and pence".

2   Trade Union (Amendment) Act of 1913 – Allowed unions to collect political contributions from members who did not object. It was one of the few measures secured by the Labour Party in Parliament before the 1920s.

principles of 'personal freedom' in the whole course of its struggle, while the legislating bourgeoisie and the House of Lords in particular come forward as the bulwark of freedom, now categorically forbidding 'force' against the person of a trade unionist (the House of Lords judgement on the Osborne case of 1909)[3] and now substantially restricting such force (the 1913 act)? The crux of the matter is, of course, that the workers' organisations, by asserting their anti-Liberal, 'despotic', Bolshevik right of enforced collection of the political levy, are in effect fighting for the real and concrete, and not a metaphysical possibility of parliamentary representation for the workers; while the Conservatives and the Liberals, in upholding the principles of 'personal freedom', are in fact striving to disarm the workers materially, and thereby shackle them to the bourgeois parties.

It is sufficient merely to take a look at the division of roles: the trade unions are for the unconditional right to the enforced collection of the political levy; the House of Exhumed Lords is for the unconditional banning of such extortion in the name of sacred personal freedom; finally the House of Commons forces a concession from the trade unions which amounts in practice to a 10 per cent refund to the principles of Liberalism. Even a blind man can sense here the purely class nature of the principle of personal freedom which in the given concrete conditions signifies nothing but the possessing classes attempt politically to expropriate the proletariat by reducing its party to nil.

The Conservatives defend from the trade unions the 'right' of a worker to vote for any party – those same Tories who for centuries denied the workers the franchise altogether! For even today, in spite of all that we have seen and experienced, we cannot read the history of the struggle for a reform bill in Britain at the beginning of the 1830s without emotion. With what astonishing obstinacy, what tenacity, and what insolence did the slave-owning class of landlords, bankers, and bishops, in short, a privileged minority, beat back the assaults upon the stronghold of parliament by the bourgeoisie with the workers at their tail! The reform of 1832 was passed when it could no longer not be passed. The extension of the franchise was carried out with the

---

3 Osborne case – Osborne was a Liberal Party agent and member of the Amalgamated Society of Railway Servants who proceeded successfully against his union taking political contributions from him. This aroused a depth of feeling against the courts in the working-class movement comparable to the effect of the Taff Vale decision of 1901. Though it caused considerable financial difficulties, it was effectively reversed by the 1913 Act.

specific intention of separating the bourgeoisie from the workers. The Liberals were in essentials in no way distinguishable from the Conservatives, for once they had won the electoral reform of 1832 they left the workers in the lurch. When the Chartists demanded from the Tories and the Whigs that workers be granted the franchise, the opposition of the parliamentary monopolists took on a frantic character. Yet now that the workers have finally won the franchise, the Conservatives come out in defence of 'individual freedom' against the tyranny of the trade unions.

This vile, revolting hypocrisy does not meet its true appraisal in parliament. On the contrary, the Labour MPs thank the Prime Minister for magnanimously refraining from tightening a financial noose around the neck of the Labour Party today, while wholly and completely reserving the right to do so at a more suitable moment. The drivellers who amuse themselves with the terms 'democracy', 'equality' and 'individual freedom' should be sat down on a school bench and be forced to study the history of Britain as a whole and the history of the struggle to widen the franchise in particular.

The Liberal Cobden stated on one occasion that he would more willingly live under the rule of the Bey of Algiers than under the rule of a trade union. Cobden was here expressing his Liberal's indignation at the Bolshevik tyranny implanted in the very nature of the trade unions. In speaking for himself, Cobden was right. A capitalist who falls under the rule of a trade union will find it very tough: the Russian bourgeoisie will be able to tell a thing or two about that. But the whole point is that the worker has a perpetual Bey of Algiers over him in the form of the employer, and he cannot weaken the latter's tyrannical regime otherwise than by means of a trade union. Of course the worker has to make some sacrifices for this, not only financially, but also personally. However, his 'individual freedom', through the medium of the trade union will in the final count gain incomparably more than it loses. This is the class standpoint. It cannot be leapt over. From it there grows the right to contribute to the political levy. The bourgeoisie in its mass nowadays considers it essential to *reconcile itself* to the existence of trade unions. But it wants to restrict their activity to the point past which the struggle against individual capitalists passes over into a struggle against the capitalist state.

The Conservative MP Macquisten pointed out in parliament that a refusal by trade unions to make political levies is observable mainly in small-scale and scattered branches of industry; as for the concentrated branches of industry then there, he complains, "moral pressure and mass intimidation" is observable. This observation is in the highest degree interesting! And how typical of the British parliament that it was made by an extreme Tory, the sponsor of a prohibitive bill, and not a socialist. It signifies that the refusal of political contributions is observable in the most backward branches of industry where petty bourgeois traditions are strong and where, consequently, a petty bourgeois conception of individual freedom generally tied up with voting for the Liberal if not for the Conservative party is strong too. In the new, more modern branches of production the class solidarity and proletarian discipline reign supreme, and that is what appears as terror to the capitalists and their servants from the Labour renegades.

A certain Conservative MP related, as if delivering a thunderbolt, that in one trade union the secretary publicly threatened to display a list of members who refused to pay contributions to the party. The Labour MPs began indignantly to demand the name of this impious secretary. Yet such a course of action ought to have been recommended to every trade union. It is obvious that this will not be done by those bureaucrats who amid the howls of both bourgeois parties seek to chuck the communists out of workers' organisations. As soon as it is a question of the latter there is no more talk of individual freedom: at this point arguments about state security come on to the scene. One cannot, they say, let communists who reject the sanctity of democracy into the Labour Party.

Yet in the course of the debate on the political levy, the sponsor of the prohibitive bill, Macquisten, whom we are already acquainted with, let fall a phrase regarding this same democracy which the Opposition greeted with frivolous laughter, but which they really ought not only to have engraved on the walls of parliament but to have repeated and explained at every workers' meeting. In using figures to illustrate the importance of the trade unions' political contributions, Macquisten pointed out that prior to the Liberals' 1913 Act, the trade unions spent only about £10,000 for political purposes, but now, thanks to legalisation of political extortion, they had a fund of £250,000 in hand. It is natural, says Macquisten, that the Labour Party has grown strong. *"When you have an income of £250,000 a year you can form a party for any end you like."*

The furious Tory said a little more than he had intended. He openly admitted that a party *is made*, and that it is made with the aid of *money* and that funds play a *deciding role* in the mechanics of 'democracy'. Need it be said that bourgeois funds are immeasurably more abundant than proletarian ones? This alone completely shatters the phoney mystique of democracy. Any awakened British worker must tell MacDonald: it is a lie that the principles of democracy form the highest criterion for our movement. The principles themselves fall under the control of financial resources by which they are distorted and falsified.

Yet, nonetheless, it must be admitted: if we stand by a formally democratic point of view and if we operate with a concept of an ideal citizen and not a proletarian, a capitalist, or a landlord, then the most reactionary gorillas of the Upper House will prove to tie the most consistent. Every citizen has, damn it, the right freely to support with his purse and his vote the party that his free conscience dictates! The only trouble is that this ideal British citizen does not exist in nature. He represents a legalistic fiction. Nor has he ever existed previously. But the petty and middle bourgeois does come fairly close to this ideal concept. Today it is the Fabian who considers himself to be the yardstick of the ideal middle citizen, for whom the capitalist and the proletarian are nothing but a 'deviation' from the ideal type of citizen. But there are not really that many Fabian philistines on earth, though there are still rather more than there need be. But in general voters can be divided into property-owners and the exploiters on the one hand, and proletarians and exploited on the other.

The trade unions – and here no amount of Liberal casuistry is of avail – represent the class association of wage labourers for the struggle against the greedy and avaricious capitalists. One of the principal instruments of the trade union is the strike. Members' dues go to support the strike. During a strike the workers wage a ruthless struggle against strike-breakers who are exercising another Liberal principle – the 'freedom to work'. During any major strike the union requires political support and is compelled to turn to the press, the parties, and parliament. The hostile attitude of the Liberal Party towards the struggle of the trade unions was indeed one of the causes that forced them to form the Labour Party.

If you go into the history of the origin of the Labour Party it becomes clear that from a trade union standpoint the party in a sense forms its political section. It needs a strike fund, a network of officials, a newspaper, and a trusted member of parliament. The expense of voting a member into parliament is just as legitimate, necessary, and obligatory as that of a secretarial apparatus. A Liberal or Conservative trade union member may say: I punctually pay my usual member's dues to the trade union, but I refuse the extortions for the Labour Party as by my political convictions I vote for the Liberal (or for the Conservative). To this a trade union representative can reply: in the course of the struggle for improving working conditions – and that after all is the aim of our organisation – we require the support of the Labour Party, its press, and its MPs; but the party for which you vote (the Liberals or the Conservatives) in such circumstances always cracks down upon us, tries to compromise us, sows dissension in our midst or directly organises strike-breakers; we have no need of those members who would organise as strike-breakers! Thus what appears from the standpoint of capitalist democracy to be freedom of the individual is shown from the standpoint of proletarian democracy to be freedom of political strike-breaking.

The 10 per cent rebate which the bourgeoisie have gained is by no means an innocuous item. It means that one out of every ten members of a trade union is a political, in other words a class, opponent. Of course, some of these may be won over, but the rest can prove an invaluable weapon in the hands of the bourgeoisie against the proletariat at a time of serious struggle. A further struggle against the breaches made in the walls of the unions by the 1913 Act is therefore inevitable.

Speaking generally, we Marxists hold that every honest, uncorrupted worker may be a member of his trade union, irrespective of political, religious, or other convictions. We regard the trade unions on the one hand as militant economic organisations, and on the other hand as a school of political education. While we stand for permitting backward and non-class-conscious workers to join trade unions, we do so not from an abstract principle of freedom of opinion or freedom of conscience, but from considerations of revolutionary expediency. And these same considerations tell us that in Britain, where 90 per cent of industrially organised workers pay political levies – some consciously, others because they do not wish to violate the spirit of solidarity – and only 10 per cent decide to throw down an open challenge to the Labour Party, a systematic struggle must be carried on against this 10 per cent, to make them feel like renegades, and to secure the *right* of the trade unions to exclude them as strike-breakers. After all, if the citizen, taken in abstract, has the right to vote for any party, then workers' organisations have the right not to allow into their midst citizens whose political behaviour is hostile to the interests of the working class. The struggle of the trade unions to debar unorganised workers from the factory has long been known as a manifestation of 'terrorism' by the workers – or in more modern terms, Bolshevism. In Britain these methods can and must be carried over into the Labour Party, which has grown up as a direct extension of the trade unions.

The debate on the question of the political levies quoted above, which took place in the British parliament on 7 March this year (1925), holds quite exceptional interest as a typical example of parliamentary democracy. Only in Baldwin's speech could tentative hints be heard as to the real dangers rooted in Britain's class structure. The old relations have disappeared, and today there are no longer any good old British enterprises with patriarchal customs – such as Mr. Baldwin himself ran in the days of his youth. Industry is concentrating and combining. Workers are uniting in trade unions and these organisations can present a danger to the state itself.

Baldwin was speaking about the employers' federations as well as the trade unions. It is quite self-evident that he sees the real danger to the democratic state only in the shape of the trade unions. What the so-called struggle against trusts amounts to, we know sufficiently well from the example of America. Roosevelt's noisy agitation against trusts proved to be a soap bubble. Trusts both in his time and afterwards have become even stronger and the American government forms their executive organ to a far greater degree than the Labour Party forms the political organ of the trade unions. Although in Britain trusts as a form of association do not play such a great role as in America, the capitalists do play no less a role. The danger of the trade unions is that they do put forward – for the moment, gropingly, indecisively, and half-heartedly – the principle of a workers' government, *which is impossible without a workers' state*, as opposed to a capitalist government which can today exist only under the cover of a democracy. Baldwin is wholly in agreement with the principle of 'individual freedom' which lies at the basis of the prohibitive bill introduced by his parliamentary friends. He also considers the political levies to be a "moral evil". But he does not want to upset the peace.

The struggle, once started, can have dire consequences: "we do not in any event wish to fire the first shot". And Baldwin finishes: "Oh Lord, grant us peace in our time!" Virtually the entire House welcomed this speech including many Labour MPs: the Prime Minister had, on his own admission, made a "gesture of peace". Thomas, the Labour MP who is always on the scene when a gesture of toadying requires to be made, rose to hail Baldwin's speech and to remark on its truly human note; he declared that both sides would gain from a close intercourse between employers and workers; he quoted with pride the fact that quite a few left-wing workers in his own union refuse to pay the political levy in view of the fact that they had such a reactionary secretary as himself, Mr. Thomas. The whole debate on the question in which the vital interests of the two conflicting classes intersect was conducted in this tone of conventions, reservations, official lies, and purely British parliamentary cant.

The reservations of the Conservatives had a Machiavellian character; the reservations of the Labour Party stemmed from a contemptible cowardice. The front bench of the bourgeoisie resembles a tiger that retracts its claws and half closes its eyes with affection; the Labour leaders, like Thomas, resemble a beaten dog which droops its tail between its legs.

The insolvency of Britain's economic situation is reflected most directly in the trade unions. On the day following the end of the war, when in the heat of the moment it seemed that Great Britain was the unbounded sovereign of the world's destinies, the working masses, aroused by the war, poured in their hundreds of thousands and millions into the trade unions. The high point was reached in 1919: after that an ebb began. At the present time the number of members of trade union organisations has sharply dropped and continues to drop.

John Wheatley, a 'left' member of MacDonald's ministry, expressed himself at one of the March meetings in Glasgow to the effect that nowadays the trade unions are but a shadow of themselves and that they were equally unfit to fight or to conduct negotiations. Fred Bramley, the General Secretary of the Trades Union Congress, spoke out in clear opposition to this estimation. The polemic between these two, theoretically perhaps equally helpless adversaries, does present an eminent symptomatic interest. Fred Bramley referred to the fact that the political movement, by being more "rewarding" that is to say, by opening up wider career possibilities, draws the most valuable officials away from the trade unions. "On the other hand", Bramley asks, "what would the party be without the political levies from the trade unions?" Bramley does not in the end deny the decline in the economic power of the trade unions and explains it by reference to Britain's economic position.

But we would seek in vain from the General Secretary of the Trades Union Congress any indication of a way out of this impasse. His thinking does not go beyond the bounds of a hidden rivalry between the trade union apparatus and the party apparatus. Yet the problem does not lie here at all. At the root of the radicalisation of the working class, and consequently of the growth of the Labour Party too, there lie those same causes that have dealt cruel blows to the economic might of the trade unions. The one is doubtless developing at the expense of the other. But it would be extremely shallow thinking to draw from this the conclusion that the role of the trade unions is played out. On the contrary, these industrial alliances of the British working class still have a great future before them. It is just because there are no further prospects for the trade unions within the framework of capitalist society in Great Britain's present situation that the industrial workers' unions are compelled to take the path of the socialist reorganisation of the economy. The trade unions themselves, when reconstructed accordingly, become the main lever for the country's economic transformation.

But the necessary prerequisite for this is the taking of power by the proletariat – not in the sense of the wretched vulgar farce of a MacDonald ministry but in a real, material, revolutionary class sense. The whole apparatus of the state has to become an apparatus subordinated to the proletariat. The working class, as the only class with an interest in a socialist overturn, has to win the opportunity to dictate its will to society. The whole administration and all the judges and public servants must be as deeply instilled with the socialist spirit of the proletariat as today's public servants are instilled with the spirit of the bourgeoisie. Only the trade unions can provide this vital human personnel. It will be in the end the trade unions that will throw up the management organs of the nationalised industry.

The trade unions will in the future become schools for educating the proletariat in the spirit of socialist industry. Their future role will therefore be immense. But at present they are in an undoubted impasse. There is no solution to it through palliatives and half-measures. The decay of British capitalism inevitably gives rise to the impotence of the trade unions. Only a revolution can save the British working class and with it its organisations. In order to take power it is essential for the proletariat to have a revolutionary party at its head. To make trade unions equal to their future role they must be freed from their conservative functionaries, from superstitious dimwits who are waiting for 'peaceful' miracles from god knows where, and, finally, simply from the agents of big capital and renegades after the Thomas style. The reformist, opportunist, liberal Labour Party can only weaken the trade unions by paralysing the initiative of the masses. A revolutionary Labour party resting upon the trade unions will become in turn a powerful instrument for their recovery and resurgence.

In the compulsory, anti-Liberal, 'despotic' collection of the political levies there is contained, like the future stem and ear in a grain of wheat, all those methods of Bolshevism against which MacDonald never tires of sprinkling the holy water of his own indignant narrow-mindedness. The working class has the right and the duty to set its own considered class will above all the fictions and sophisms of bourgeois democracy. It must act in the spirit of the revolutionary self-confidence that Cromwell fostered in the young English bourgeoisie. The raw Puritan recruits were, as we have said, inspired thus by Cromwell:

> I will not cozen you with perplexed expressions in my commission about fighting for King and Parliament. If the King chanced to be in the body of the enemy, I would as soon discharge my pistol upon him as upon any private man; and if your consciences will not let you do the like, I advise you not to enlist yourselves under me.

It is not bloodthirstiness nor despotism that sounds in these words, but the awareness of a great historical mission which affords the right to annihilate all obstacles in its path. The young progressive class, sensing its vocation for the first time, speaks through the lips of Cromwell. If one is seeking national traditions then the British proletariat should borrow this spirit of self-confidence and aggressive courage from the old Independents. The MacDonalds, Webbs, Snowdens, and others have taken over from Cromwell's comrades-in-arms only their religious prejudices and combine them with a purely Fabian cowardice.

The proletarian vanguard has to combine the Independents' revolutionary courage with a materialist clarity of world-outlook.

—

The British bourgeoisie takes unerring stock of the fact that the chief danger threatens it from the quarter of the trade unions, and that only under the pressure from these organisations can the Labour Party, having replaced its leadership, turn itself into a revolutionary force.

One of the latest methods of struggle against the trade unions is the independent organisation of administrative and technical staff (technicians, engineers, managers, supervisors, and so forth) as a 'third party in industry'. *The Times* is conducting a very clever and a very ingenious struggle against the theory of "the unity of interests between mental and manual workers". In this as in other cases, the bourgeois politicians make very skilful use of the ideas of Fabianism which had been suggested by themselves. The opposition of labour to capital would be disastrous to national development, says *The Times*, in concert with all the Labour Party leaders, and from this draws the conclusion: engineers, managers, administrators, and technicians who stand between capital and labour are best of all capable of assessing the interests of industry "as a whole" and of introducing peace into the relations between the hirers and the hired. For just this reason administrative and technical staff must be set apart as a third party of industry.

In essence, *The Times* here goes wholly to meet the Fabians. The position in principle of these latter is directed in a reactionary and Utopian fashion against the class struggle and above all coincides with the social position of the petty-bourgeois or middle bourgeois intellectual, the engineer, or the administrator who stands between capital and labour, being to all effects a tool in the capitalists' hands, but wants to imagine himself to be independent. The more he emphasises his independence from proletarian organisations, the more completely he falls into the bondage of capitalist organisations. We can predict without difficulty that Fabianism, as it is displaced from the trade unions and the Labour Party, will increasingly merge its destiny with the destiny of the intermediate elements of the industrial, commercial, and state bureaucratic apparatus. The Independent Labour Party will, after its current momentary upturn, be inevitably cast down and, as the "third party in industry", will end up entangled between the feet of capital and labour.

8. Prospects

Arising out of the fact that Mrs. Lloyd George, the ex-Prime Minister's wife, had lost an expensive necklace, the *Daily Herald*, the organ of the Labour Party, meditated on the Liberal leaders who go over to the side of the enemy and give their wives valuable necklaces. The newspaper's leading article came to the following instructive conclusion on this matter: "The existence of the Labour Party depends on its success in restraining the workers' leaders from following this same disastrous road." Arthur Ponsonby, a hopeless Liberal, who even in the ranks of the Labour Party has not ceased to be a Liberal, in the same issue of the paper gives himself over to reflections on how the Liberal leaders, Asquith and Lloyd George, ruined the great Liberal Party. "Yes", the leader-writer repeats after him, "the Liberal leaders have changed their simple habits and manners for the manner of life of the wealthy with whom they continually associate; they have assimilated arrogance in reference to the lower orders", and so on.

One would have thought that there was nothing astonishing in the fact that Liberal leaders, in other words, of one of the two bourgeois parties, lead a bourgeois style of life. But for the Liberals in the Labour Party, Liberalism is represented as an abstract system of high ideas, and Liberal Ministers who buy their wives necklaces are represented as traitors to the ideas of Liberalism.

The reflection on how to save the workers' leaders from following this disastrous road is, however, more instructive. It is absolutely clear that these considerations are timid and stammering warnings to the semi-Liberal Labour leaders on the part of the semi-Liberal Labour journalists who have to reckon with the mood of its working-class readers. One can without difficulty imagine the careerist depravity which rules among the ministerial upper ten of the Labour Party! It is enough to mention that Mrs. Lloyd George herself, in a letter of protest to the editor of the *Daily Herald*, herself alluded to one or two facts like the "regal" present received by MacDonald from his capitalist friend. After these recollections the editors immediately bit their tongues. It is wretchedly puerile to imagine that the conduct of the Labour Party leaders can be regulated by cautionary tales of Lloyd George's wife's necklace and that politics can in general be guided by abstract moral prescriptions. On the contrary, the morals of a class, its party, and its leaders derive from politics taken in the broadest historical sense of the word. This is nowhere more clearly seen than in the organisations of the British working class.

The *Daily Herald* has hit upon the idea of the harmful effect that hobnobbing with the bourgeoisie has upon the worldly morals of 'leaders'. But this of course is wholly dependent upon the *political* attitude towards the bourgeoisie. If they stand on the position of an implacable class struggle there will be no place for any kind of hail-fellow-well-met relations: Labour leaders will not yearn to be in bourgeois circles nor will the bourgeoisie let them in. But the leaders of the Labour Party defend the idea of the collaboration of classes and the rapprochement of their leaders. "Cooperation and mutual trust between employers and workers is the essential condition for the well-being of the country" – so, for example, Mr. Snowden taught at one of the parliamentary sittings this year. We hear similar speeches from Clynes, the Webbs, and all the other leading lights. The trade union leaders adopt the same standpoint: all we hear from them is the necessity of frequent meetings between employers and workers' representatives around a common table.

Yet at the same time, the policy of a perpetual 'amicable' dialogue of the workers' leaders with bourgeois businessmen in the quest for common ground, that is to say, the setting aside of what distinguishes the one from the other, presents, as we have heard from the *Daily Herald*, a danger not only to the morals of the leaders but also for the development of the party. What should be done then? When John Burns[1] betrayed the proletariat he began to say: "I do not want a special workers' point of view any more than I want workers' boots or workers' margarine." The fact that John Burns, who became a bourgeois minister, considerably improved his butter and his boots along this path is beyond question. But Burns' evolution hardly improved the boots of the dockers who had raised Bums up on their shoulders. Morality flows from politics. For Snowden's budget to please the City it is necessary

---

1 John Burns (1858-1943) – Trade union leader and Liberal politician.

for Snowden himself, both in his way of life and his morality, to stand closer to the bigwigs of the banks than the miners of Wales.

And what is the case with Thomas? We told above of the banquet of railway owners at which Thomas, the secretary of the National Union of Railwaymen, swore that his soul belonged not to the working class but to "truth" and that he, Thomas, had come to the banquet in search of this truth. It is, however, noteworthy that while the whole of this foul affair is related in *The Times*, there is not a word on it in the *Daily Herald*. This woeful little paper occupies itself with moralising in thin air. Just try reining in Thomas with the parable of Mrs. Lloyd George's necklace. Nothing would come of it. The Thomases have to be driven out. To do this it is necessary not to hush up Thomas' banqueting and other embraces with the enemies, but to cry out about them, expose them, and summon workers to a ruthless purging of their ranks. In order to change the morality it is necessary to change the politics.

At the time that these lines are being written (April 1925), in spite of the Conservative government, Britain's official politics stand under the sign of compromise: there must be 'collaboration' of both sides of industry, mutual concessions are essential, workers must somehow or other be made the 'participants' in the revenue of industry, and so forth. This frame of mind of the Conservatives reflects both the strength and the weakness of the British proletariat. By creating its own party it has forced the Conservatives to orientate themselves towards 'conciliation'. But it still allows the Conservatives to place their hopes in 'conciliation' because it leaves MacDonald, Thomas, and Co. at the head of the Labour Party.

Baldwin delivers speech after speech on the need for mutual tolerance so that the country can get out of the difficulties of its present situation *without a catastrophe*. The workers' 'leader' Robert Smillie expresses his complete satisfaction with these speeches. "What a wonderful call for tolerance on both sides!" Smillie promises to follow this call to the full. He hopes that the captains of industry will likewise take a more humane approach to the workers' demands. "This is a wholly legitimate and reasonable desire", the leading newspaper, *The Times*, assures us with the most solemn air. All these unctuous speeches are made under the conditions of commercial and industrial difficulties, chronic unemployment, the loss of British shipbuilding orders to Germany, and threatening conflicts in a whole series of industries. And this in Britain with all its experience of class battles. The memory of the labouring masses is truly short and the hypocrisy of the rulers immeasurable! The historical memory of the bourgeoisie lies in its traditions of rule, in institutions, the law of the land, and in accumulated skills of statesmanship. The memory of the working class is in its party. The reformist party is a party with a short memory.

The conciliationism of the Conservatives may be hypocrisy, but it is compelled by solid causes. At the centre of the efforts of Europe's governing parties today there lies a concern to maintain external and internal peace. The so-called 'reaction' against war and the methods of the first post-war period can in no way be explained merely by psychological causes. During the war the capitalist regime showed itself to be so powerful and elastic that it gave birth to the special *illusions of war capitalism*. Boldly centralised guidance of economic life, military seizure of the economic values that it lacked, the piling up of debts, unrestricted issues of paper money, the elimination of social danger by means of bloody force on the one hand and sops of all kinds on the other – it seemed in the heat of the moment that these methods would solve all problems and overcome all difficulties.

But economic reality was soon to clip the wings of war capitalism's illusions. Germany approached the very edge of the abyss. The rich state of France failed to emerge from thinly disguised bankruptcy. The British state was compelled to support an army of unemployed twice the size of the army of French militarism. The riches of Europe have proved to be in no way limitless. A continuation of wars and upheavals would signify the inevitable doom of European capitalism. Hence the concern about 'regularising' the relations between states and classes.

During the last elections the British Conservatives played skilfully upon fear of upheavals. Now in power, they come forward as the party of conciliation, compromise and social benevolence. "Security – that is the key to the position" – these words of the Liberal Lord Grey are repeated by the Conservative Austen Chamberlain. The British press of both bourgeois camps lives on rehashing them. The striving for pacification, the creation of 'normal' conditions, the maintenance of a firm currency, and the resumption of trade agreements do not of themselves solve a single one of the contradictions that led to the imperialist war and were yet more aggravated by it. But only by starting from this aspiration and from the political groupings that have been formed out of it can the current trend of home and foreign policy of Europe's governing parties be understood.

Needless to say, pacifist tendencies run into the opposition of post-war economics at every step. The British Conservatives have already started to undermine the Unemployed Insurance Act. Making British industry *as it is now* better able to compete cannot be done otherwise than by a reduction of wages. But this is incompatible with the maintenance of the present unemployment benefit, which raises the power of resistance of the working class. The first forward skirmishes on this ground have already started. They can lead to serious battles. In this sphere the Conservatives will in any case be quickly forced to speak up with their natural voice. The chiefs of the Labour Party will thereupon fall into an increasingly awkward situation.

Here it is quite apposite to recall the relations that were established in the House of Commons after the 1906 General Election when a strong Labour group appeared on the parliamentary scene for the first time. In the first two years, the Labour MPs were surrounded with special courtesies. In the third year, relations were upset considerably. By 1910 parliament was 'ignoring' the Labour group. This was brought about not by intransigence on the part of the latter, but because outside parliament the working masses were becoming more and more demanding. Having elected a significant number of MPs they were expecting substantial changes in their lot. These expectations were one of the factors that prepared the way for the mighty strike wave of 1911 to 1913.

One or two conclusions for today arise from this case. The flirting of Baldwin's majority with the Labour group must all the more inevitably turn into its converse the more determined the pressure of the workers upon their group, upon capital, and upon parliament. We have already spoken about this in connection with the question of the role of democracy and revolutionary force in the reciprocal relations between classes. Here we wish to approach the same question from the standpoint of the *inner development of the Labour Party itself.*

—

The leading role in the British Labour Party is, as is well known, played by the leaders of the Independent Labour Party headed by MacDonald. The Independent Labour Party not only before but also during the war took a pacifist position, 'condemned' social-imperialism, and belonged in general to the centrist trend. The programme of the Independent Labour Party was aimed "against militarism in whatever form". Upon the termination of war, the Independent party left the Second International, and in 1920 upon a conference resolution the Independents even entered into dealings with the Third International and set it twelve questions, each one more profound than the previous. The seventh question read: "can communism and the dictatorship of the proletariat only be established by armed force or are parties which leave this question open allowed to participate in the Third international?" The picture is highly instructive: the butcher is armed with a jagged knife but the calf leaves the question open. Yet at that critical point the Independent party did raise the question of entering the Communist International while now it expels communists from the Labour Party.

The contrast between yesterday's policy of the Independent party and today's policy of the Labour Party, especially in the months where it was in power, hits one in the eye. Today the policy of the Fabians in the Independent Labour Party are distinct from the policy of the same Fabians in the Labour Party. In these contradictions there sounds a weak echo of the struggle between tendencies of centrism and social-imperialism. These tendencies intersect and combine in MacDonald himself – and as a result the Christian pacifist builds light cruisers in anticipation of the day when he will have to build heavy ones.

The main feature of socialist centrism is its reticence, its mediocre, half-and-half nature. It keeps going so long as it does not draw the ultimate conclusions and is not compelled to answer the basic questions set before it point-blank. In peaceful, 'organic' periods centrism can keep going as the official doctrine even of a large and active workers' party, as was the case with German Social-Democracy before the war, for in that period the solution of major problems of the life of the state did not depend on the party of the proletariat. But as a rule centrism is mostly typical of small organisations which precisely through their lack of influence absolve themselves from the need to provide a clear answer to all questions of politics and to bear practical responsibility for this answer. Just such is the centrism of the Independent Labour Party.

The imperialist war revealed only too clearly that the labour bureaucracy and the labour aristocracy had been able over the preceding period of capitalist boom to undergo a deep petty-bourgeois degeneration, in terms of its way of life and overall mental outlook. But the petty bourgeois preserves the *appearance* of independence until the first shock.

At one stroke the war disclosed and strengthened the political dependence of the petty bourgeois upon the great and greater bourgeoisie. Social-imperialism was the form of such a dependence within the workers' movement. But centrism insofar as it was preserved or reborn during the war and after it, expressed in itself the terror of the petty bourgeois among the Labour bureaucrats in the face of their complete and, what is more, open enslavement to imperialism.

German Social-Democracy, which for many years, even as early as Bebel's time, had followed an essentially centrist policy, could not as a result of its very strength maintain this position during the war: it had then to be either against the war, that is to take an essentially revolutionary path, or for the war, that is to cross openly over to the camp of the bourgeoisie. In Britain the Independent Labour Party as a propaganda organisation within the working class was able not only to preserve but even to strengthen its centrist features during the war by "absolving itself of the responsibility", busying itself with platonic protests and a pacifist sermon without carrying through their ideas to their conclusion or causing the belligerent state any embarrassments. The opposition of the Independents in Germany[2] was also of a centrist character, when they "absolved themselves of responsibility", though without preventing the Scheidemanns and Eberts from placing the whole might of the workers' organisations at the service of warring capital.

In Britain, after the war we had an entirely unique 'combination' of social-imperialist and centrist tendencies in the workers' movement. The Independent Labour Party, as has already been said, could not have been better adapted to the role of an irresponsible centrist opposition which criticises but does not cause the rulers great damage. However, the Independents were destined in a short time to become a political force, and this at the same time changed their role and their physiognomy.

The Independents became a force as a result of the intersection of two causes: in the first place because history has confronted the working class with the need to create its own party; secondly because the war and the post-war period which stirred millions-strong masses created in the beginning favourable repercussions for the ideas of labour pacifism and reformism. There were of course plenty of democratic pacifist ideas in the heads of British workers before the war too. The difference is nevertheless colossal: in the past the British proletariat, insofar as it took part in political life, and especially during the first half of the nineteenth century, tied its democratic pacifist illusions to the activity of the Liberal Party. The latter did 'not justify' these hopes and had forfeited the workers' confidence. A special Labour Party arose as an invaluable historical conquest which nothing can now take away. But it must be clearly realised

---

2 This refers to the Independent Social Democratic Party of Germany (USPD) which was formed under the leadership of Kautsky and Haase and in 1917 broke away from the SPD, mainly over its opposition to the war. In the 1920 congress the majority of delegates voted to leave the party and join the KPD, affiliating to the Comintern. The rump rejoined the SPD in 1922.

that the masses of workers became disillusioned more in Liberalism's goodwill than in democratic pacifist methods of solving the social question, and the more so now that new generations and new millions are being drawn into politics for the first time. They transferred their hopes and illusions to the Labour Party. For this very reason and only for this reason the Independents gained the opportunity to head it.

Behind the democratic pacifist illusions of the working masses stand *their awakened class will, a deep discontent with their position and a readiness to back up their demands with all the means that the circumstances require*. But the working class can build a party out of those ideological and personal leading elements which have been prepared by the entire preceding development of the country and all its theoretical and political culture.

Here, generally speaking, is the source of the great influence of the petty-bourgeois intellectuals, and including here of course both the Labour aristocrats and the bureaucrats. The formation of the British Labour Party became an inevitability precisely because a deep shift to the left took place in the masses of the proletariat. But the political staging of this shift to the left fell to the lot of those representatives of impotent conservative protestant pacifism who were at hand. Yet in transferring their headquarters on to the foundation of several million organised workers, the Independents could not remain themselves, that is to say, they could not simply impose their centrist stamp onto the party of the proletariat. Finding themselves suddenly the leaders of a party of millions of workers they could no longer confine themselves to centrist reservations and pacifist passivity. They had, first as a responsible opposition and then as the government, to answer either "yes" or "no" to the sharpest questions of political life. From the very moment that centrism became a political force it had to pass beyond the bounds of centrism, that is either draw revolutionary conclusions from its opposition to the imperialist state or openly enter its service.

The latter, of course, is what happened. MacDonald, the pacifist, started to build cruisers, to put Indians and Egyptians in jail, and to operate diplomatically with forged documents. Once having become a political force, centrism as centrism became a cipher. The deep swing *to the left* of the British working class that brought MacDonald's party to power unexpectedly rapidly, facilitated the latter's manifest swing *to the right*. Such is the link between yesterday and today, and such is the reason why the little Independent Labour Party looks at its successes with a bitter perplexity and attempts to pretend to be centrist.

The practical programme of the British Labour Party led by the Independents has an essentially Liberal character and forms, especially in foreign policy, a belated echo of Gladstonian impotence. Gladstone was 'compelled' to seize Egypt rather as MacDonald was 'compelled' to build cruisers. Beaconsfield rather than Gladstone reflected capital's imperialist requirements. Free Trade no longer solves a single problem. The refusal to fortify Singapore is absurd from the standpoint of the whole system of British imperialism. Singapore is the key to two oceans. Whoever wishes to preserve colonies, that is, to continue a policy of imperialist plunder, must have this key in his hands.

MacDonald remains on the ground of capitalism but he introduces cowardly amendments to it that solve nothing, save it from nothing, yet increase all the difficulties and dangers. On the question of the fate of British industry there is no serious difference between the policies of the three parties. The basic feature of this policy is a confusion born out of a fear of upheaval. All three parties are conservative and fear above all industrial conflicts. A conservative parliament refuses to establish a minimum wage for the miners. The MPs elected by the miners say that the behaviour of parliament is "a direct summons to revolutionary actions" although not one of them is seriously thinking in terms of revolutionary actions. The capitalists propose to the workers that the slate of the coal industry should be jointly investigated, hoping to prove what has no need of proof, namely that with the coal industry as it stands disorganised by private ownership, coal comes expensive even with a low wage. The Conservative and Liberal press sees salvation. The Labour leaders are following the same path. They all fear strikes that might strengthen the preponderance of foreign competitors. Yet if any sort of rationalisation at all can be realised under the conditions of capitalism it cannot be achieved save under the greatest pressure of strikes on the part of the workers. By paralysing the working masses through the trade unions, the leaders are supporting the process of economic stagnation and decay.

One of the pretty clear reactionaries inside the British Labour Party, Dr. Haden Guest, a chauvinist, a militarist, and a protectionist in parliament, mercilessly poured scorn on his own party's line on the question of free trade and protectionism: MacDonald's position, in Guest's words, has a purely negative character and does not indicate any way out of the economic impasse. That the days of Free Trade are over really is absolutely obvious: the break-up of Liberalism has also been conditioned by the break-up of Free Trade.

But Britain can just as little seek a way out in protectionism. For a young capitalist country just developing, protectionism may be an unavoidable and progressive stage of development. But for the oldest industrial country whose industry was geared to the world market and had an offensive and conquering character, the transition to protectionism is historical testimony to the beginning of a process of mortification, and signifies in practice the maintaining of certain branches of industry that are less viable in the given world situation, at the expense of other branches of the same British industry that are better adapted to the conditions of the world and the home market. The programme of senile protectionism of Baldwin's party can be countered not by an equally senile and moribund Free Trade policy, but only by the practical programme of a socialist overturn. But in order to tackle this programme it is necessary as a preliminary to purge the party both of the reactionary protectionists like Guest and reactionary free traders like MacDonald.

—

From what side and in what way can there come the change in the policy of the Labour Party that is inconceivable without a radical change in its leadership?

As the overall majority on the Executive Committee and other leading bodies of the British Labour Party belongs to the Independent Labour Party, the latter forms a ruling faction in the Labour Party. This system of inter-relations within the British Labour movement incidentally provides extremely valuable material on the question of 'the dictatorship of a minority', for it is just so that the leaders of the British party define the role of the Communist Party in the Soviet Republic – as the dictatorship of a minority. It can, however, be seen that the Independent Labour Party, which numbers some 30,000, has obtained a leading position in an organisation that rests through the trade unions upon millions of members. But this organisation, the Labour Party, comes to office thanks to the numerical strength and role of the British proletariat. Thus a most trifling minority of 30,000 people takes power in its hands in a country with a population of 40 million and ruling over hundreds of millions. A most real 'democracy' consequently leads to the dictatorship of a party minority.

Admittedly the dictatorship of the Independent Labour Party is in a class sense not worth a rotten egg, but this is a question on an entirely different plane. If, however, a party of 30,000 members without a revolutionary programme, without being tempered in struggle, and without solid traditions can come to power by the methods of bourgeois democracy and through the medium of an amorphous Labour Party resting upon the trade unions, why are these gentlemen so indignant and surprised when a theoretically and practically steeled communist party, with decades of heroic battles at the head of the popular masses behind it, a party that numbers hundreds of thousands of members, comes to power resting upon the mass organisations of the workers and peasants? In any case, the coming to power of the Independent Labour Party is incomparably less radical and deep-going than the coming to power of the Communist Party in Russia.

But the Independent Labour Party's dizzy career presents interest not only from the standpoint of a polemic against arguments about the dictatorship of a communist minority. It is immeasurably more important to assess the rapid upsurge of the Independents from the standpoint of the future destiny of the British Communist Party. Several conclusions suggest themselves here.

The Independent Labour Party was born in a petty-bourgeois environment and being close in its sentiments and moods to the milieu of the trade union bureaucracy, together with it quite naturally headed the Labour Party when the masses forced their secretaries to create the latter under pressure. However, the Independent Labour Party is, by its fabulous advance, its political methods and its role, preparing and clearing the path for the Communist Party. In the course of decades the Independent Labour Party has gathered some 30,000 members in all. But when deep changes in the international situation and in the inner structure of British society gave birth to the Labour Party there at once arose an unexpected demand for the leadership of the Independents. The same course of political development is preparing at the next stage an even heavier 'demand' for communism.

At the present time the Communist Party is numerically very small. At the last elections it collected only 53,000 votes – a figure which by comparison to the 5.5 million Labour votes may create a dispiriting impression if the logic of Britain's political development is not fully understood. To think that the communists will grow over the decades step by step, acquiring at each new parliamentary election a few tens or hundreds of thousands of new votes, would be to have a fundamentally false concept of the future. Of course, for a certain relatively prolonged period communism will develop comparatively slowly but then an unavoidable and sudden change will occur:

the Communist Party will occupy the place in the Labour Party that is at present occupied by the Independents.

What is necessary for this? A general answer is quite plain. The Independent Labour Party has accomplished its unprecedented rise because it assisted the working class to create a third, that is, its own, party. The last election shows what enthusiasm the British workers have for the instrument that they have created. But the party is not an end in itself. From it workers expect action and results. The British Labour Party grew up almost immediately as a party directly claiming government power and having already joined in it. In spite of the deeply compromising character of the first 'Labour' government, the party acquired more than a million fresh votes at the new elections. Within the party, however, there took shape the so-called left wing, formless, spineless, and devoid of any independent future. But the very fact of the emergence of an opposition bears witness to the growth of the demands of the masses and a parallel growth of anxiety at the top of the Party. A brief reflection on the nature of the MacDonalds, Thomases, Clyneses, Snowdens, and all the others is sufficient to appreciate how catastrophically the contradictions between the demands of the masses and the numbskulled conservatism of leading top dogs of the Labour Party will mount, especially in event of its return to power.

In outlining this perspective we are starting out from the proposition that the current international and domestic situation of British capital is not only not improving, but on the contrary continuing to worsen. Were this prognosis incorrect and had Britain been able to strengthen the empire and regain its former position on the world market, raise the level of industry, give work to the unemployed, and increase wages, then political development would move in reverse: the aristocratic conservatism of the trade unions would be again reinforced, the Labour Party would enter a decline, within it the right wing would grow stronger and draw closer to Liberalism, which would in turn feel a certain surge in its vital forces. But there are not the least grounds for such a prognosis. On the contrary, whatever the partial fluctuations in the economic and political conjuncture, everything points to a further aggravation and deepening of those difficulties which Britain is currently undergoing and thereby to a further acceleration of the tempo of revolutionary development. But in these conditions it seems highly likely that the Labour Party will come to power at one of the subsequent stages, and then a conflict between the working class and the Fabian top layer now standing at its head will be wholly unavoidable.

The Independents' current role is brought about by the fact that their path has crossed the path of the proletariat. But this in no way means that these paths have merged for good. The rapid growth in the Independents' influence is but a reflection of the exceptional power of working-class pressure; but it is just this pressure, generated by the whole situation, that will throw the British workers into collision with the Independent leaders. In proportion as this occurs, the revolutionary *qualities* of the British Communist Party will, given, of course, a correct policy, pass over into a *quantity* of several millions.

A certain analogy would appear to arise between the fate of the Communist and Independent parties. Both the former and the latter for a long time existed as propaganda societies rather than parties of the working class. Then at a profound turning-point in Britain's historical development the Independent party headed the proletariat. After a short interval the Communist Party will, we submit, undergo the same upsurge.[3] The course of its development will at a certain point merge with the historical highroad of the British proletariat. This merging of ways will, however, occur quite differently than it did with the Independent party. In the case of the latter the bureaucracy of the trade unions formed the connecting link. The Independents can head the Labour Party only in so far as the trade union bureaucracy can weaken, neutralise, and distort the independent class pressure of the proletariat. But the Communist Party will on the contrary be able to take the lead of the working class only in so far as it enters into an implacable conflict with the conservative bureaucracy in the trade unions and the Labour Party. The Communist Party can prepare itself for the leading role only by a ruthless criticism of all the leading staff of the British labour movement, and only by a day-to-day exposure of its conservative, anti-proletarian, imperialist, monarchist, and lackeyish role in all spheres of social life and the class movement.

The left wing of the Labour Party represents an attempt to regenerate centrism within MacDonald's social-imperialist party. It thus reflects the disquiet of a part of the labour bureaucracy over the link with the leftward moving masses. It would be a monstrous illusion to think that these left elements of the old school are capable of heading the revolutionary movement of the British proletariat and its struggle for power. They represent a historical stage which is over. Their elasticity is extremely limited and their leftness is

---

3 A prognosis of this kind has of course a relative and approximate character and should in no event be equated with astronomical predictions of lunar or solar eclipses. The real course of development is always more complex than a necessarily schematic forecast. – *Trotsky*

opportunist through and through. They do not lead nor are capable of leading the masses into struggle. Within the bounds of their reformist narrowness they revive the old irresponsible centrism without hindering, but rather, helping, MacDonald to bear the responsibility for the party's leadership and in certain cases for the destiny of the British Empire too.

This picture is nowhere more sharply revealed than at the Gloucester Conference of the Independent Labour Party (Easter 1925). While grumping about MacDonald, the Independents approved the so-called 'activity' of the Labour government by 398 votes to 139. But even the opposition could permit itself the luxury of disapproval only because a majority for MacDonald was guaranteed. The lefts' discontent with MacDonald is a discontent with themselves. MacDonald's policy cannot be improved by inbuilt changes. Centrism will, once in power, conduct MacDonald's, that is to say, a capitalist policy. MacDonald's line can be seriously opposed only by the line of a socialist dictatorship of the proletariat. It would be the greatest illusion to think that the Independents' party is capable of evolving into a revolutionary party of the proletariat. The Fabians have to be squeezed out, 'removed from their posts'. This can only be achieved by an implacable struggle against the centrism of the Independents.

The more clearly and acutely the question of conquering power comes to the fore, the more the Independent Labour Party will strive to evade an answer and substitute for the fundamental problem of revolution every kind of bureaucratic construction regarding the best parliamentary and financial methods of nationalising industry. One of the commissions of the Independent Labour Party came to the conclusion that purchasing of the land, plants, and factories should be preferred to confiscation, as in Britain, according to the presentiments of the commission, nationalisation will take place gradually, *à la* Baldwin, step by step; and it would be "unjust" to deprive one group of capitalists of its income while another group is still obtaining a return on its capital. "It would be another matter", the commission's report states (we are quoting from the report in *The Times*), "if socialism came to us not gradually but all at once as the result of a catastrophic revolution: then the arguments against confiscation would lose the greater part of their force. But we", says the report, "do not think that this combination is likely *and we do not feel called upon* to discuss this in the present report."

Speaking in general, there are no grounds to reject in principle the purchase of the land, factories, and plants. Unfortunately however, the political and financial opportunities to do this will never coincide. The financial state of the United States would make a purchasing operation wholly possible. But in America the question itself is not a practical one and there is not yet a party there that can pose it seriously. But by the time that such a party appears the economic position of the United States will have undergone extremely abrupt changes. In Britain, on the contrary, the question of nationalisation stands at point-blank range as a question of the salvation of the British economy. But the position of state funds is such that the feasibility of purchasing appears more than dubious.

However, the financial aspect of the question is only a secondary one. The main task consists in creating the political prerequisites for nationalisation regardless of whether by purchase or not. After all it is a matter of life and death for the bourgeoisie. A revolution is inevitable precisely because the bourgeoisie will never let itself be strangled by a Fabian banking transaction. Bourgeois society in its present state cannot accept even partial nationalisation except by besetting it with conditions which must impede the success of the measure in the extreme, while compromising the idea of nationalisation and with it the Labour Party. For to every really bold, even if partial, attempt at nationalisation, the bourgeoisie will respond as a class. Other industries will resort to lock-outs, sabotage, and the boycott of nationalised industries, that is to say, they will wage a life and death struggle. However cautious the original approach might be, the task will in the end be reduced to the need to crack the resistance of the exploiters. When the Fabians declare to us that they do not feel themselves "called upon" to consider "this contingency" it has to be said that these gentlemen are basically mistaken as to their calling. It is very possible that the most businesslike of them will be useful in this or that department of a future workers' state where they can occupy themselves with the accounting of individual items on a socialist balance-sheet. But they are of absolutely no use as long as it is still a question of creating the workers' state, that is to say, the basic prerequisite of a socialist economy.

In one of his weekly reviews in the *Daily Herald* (4 April 1925), MacDonald let slip a few realistic words: "The position of the parties", he said, "is these days such that the struggle will become increasingly hot and fierce. The Conservative Party will fight to the death and the more menacing that the power of the Labour Party becomes, the more monstrous the pressure of the reactionary MPs [the Conservative Party] will become".

This is absolutely true. The more immediate the danger of the Labour Party coming to power the stronger the influence of such people as Curzon (it is not by chance that MacDonald called him a "model" for future public figures) will grow in the Conservative Party. For once it might appear that MacDonald's appraisal of perspectives was correct. But in point of fact the Labour Party leader himself does not understand the meaning and weight of his own words. The observation that the Conservatives will fight to the death and the more frenziedly as time goes on, was required by him only to demonstrate the inexpediency of inter-party parliamentary committees. But in its essentials the prognosis given by MacDonald not only tells against inter-parliamentary committees, but cries out against the possibility of solving the whole of the present-day social crisis by parliamentary methods. "The Conservative Party will fight to the death". Correct! But that means that the Labour Party will only be able to defeat it in event of it exceeding their determination to struggle. It is not a matter of the competition between two parties, but of the fate of two classes. But when two classes fight each other to the death, the question is never solved by counting votes. This has never been so in history. And as long as classes exist it never will be so.

It is not, however, a question of MacDonald's general philosophy, nor of particular happy slips of his tongue, that is to say, not of how he justifies his activity, nor of what he wishes for, but of what he does and where his actions lead. If the question is approached from this angle then it turns out that MacDonald's party is by all its work preparing the gigantic sweep and extreme severity of the proletarian revolution in Britain. It is none other than MacDonald's party that strengthens the bourgeoisie's self-confidence and at the same time stretches the patience of the proletariat to the limit. And by the time that this patience cracks, the proletariat rising to its feet will collide headlong with the bourgeoisie whose consciousness of omnipotence has been only strengthened by the policy of MacDonald's party. The longer that the Fabians restrain Britain's revolutionary development the more terrible and furious will be the explosion.

The British bourgeoisie has been brought up on ruthlessness. Leading it along this path were the circumstances of an island existence, the moral philosophy of Calvinism, the practice of colonialism, and national arrogance. Britain is being forced increasingly into the background. This irreversible process also creates a revolutionary situation. The British bourgeoisie, compelled as it is to make its peace with America, to retreat, to tack, and to wait, is filling itself with the greatest bitterness which will reveal itself in terrible forms in a civil war. Thus the bourgeois scum of France, defeated in the war with the Prussians, took their revenge on the Communards; thus the officerdom of the routed Hohenzollern army took their revenge on the German workers.

All the cold cruelty that ruling-class Britain displayed towards the Indians, Egyptians and Irish, and which has the appearance of racial arrogance, in the event of a civil war will reveal its class nature and prove to be directed against the proletariat. On the other hand, the revolution will inevitably awaken in the British working class the deepest passions which have been so skilfully restrained and suppressed by social conventions, the church, and the press, and diverted along artificial channels with the aid of boxing, football, racing, and other forms of sport.

The concrete course of the struggle, its duration, and its outcome will depend wholly upon the domestic and especially the international conditions of the moment in which it develops. In the decisive struggle against the proletariat the British bourgeoisie will enjoy the most powerful support of the bourgeoisie of the United States, while the proletariat will rest for support primarily upon the working class of Europe and the oppressed popular masses of the colonies. The nature of the British Empire will inevitably give this gigantic struggle an international scale. This will be one of the greatest dramas in world history. The destiny of the British proletariat in this struggle will be linked with the destiny of all mankind. The whole world situation and the role of the British proletariat in production and in society will guarantee its victory – on condition there is a correct and resolute revolutionary leadership. The Communist Party must develop and come to power as the party of proletarian dictatorship. There are no ways round this. Whoever believes there are and propounds them can only deceive British workers. That is the main conclusion of our analysis.

V

Problems of the British Labour Movement

Notes on the Situation in Britain, 1925-1926

The article printed below consists of fragments written at various times since the end of last year. These fragments were originally intended to form the material for a more complete work. The General Strike, like any momentous event, at once shifted our perspectives, brought forward some problems and removed others. From the point of view of understanding and evaluating the General Strike and its outcome, it would now appear more appropriate to print these fragments in the form they were written, that is, chronologically following the facts and events to which they refer.

L. Trotsky,
19 May 1926

* * *

22 December 1925

We have already mentioned that we have in our possession two letters from a British 'left' socialist separated by an interval of several weeks. The first letter was written before the Liverpool Conference of the Labour Party (September 1925)[1] and the second after it.

---

1 The Liverpool Conference of the Labour Party was held from 29 September to 2 October 1925. The National Executive recommended that: (a) no member of the Communist Party should be eligible to become or remain a member of a local Labour Party, and that (b) no affiliated trade union ought to appoint delegates who are communists to national or local Labour Party conferences. Pollitt of the Communist

The most fateful question in the world of politics (writes our correspondent in the first letter) is without doubt the question of what will take place at Liverpool at the Annual Labour Party Conference… The Liverpool Conference will in all probability not only reverse last year's resolution banning communists from membership but it will possibly give rise to a decisive split in the ranks of the Labour Party.

As we now know exactly the opposite happened. The right wing were wholly victorious. The lefts presented the most wretched picture of impotence and confusion. The ban on communists was endorsed and strengthened.

In the second letter written just after the conference our correspondent makes the following admission:

With regard to the Liverpool Conference at which I was not present, I can make only one comment. The rights gained the upper hand while the lefts once again revealed insufficient cohesion. The communists also gained a victory. *The rights played directly into the hands of the communists…*

Our correspondent himself scarcely understands what this signifies. But nonetheless the logic of the facts is simple: if you wish for victory over MacDonaldism, over organised betrayal and over treachery elevated into a system, then you must operate not in the spirit of the 'lefts' but in the spirit of the Bolsheviks. It is in this sense and only in this sense that the rights play into the hands of the communists.

The working class is, in the words of the same critic, "burdened by both the extreme wings". How remarkably put! What our 'left' calls the right wing is the official leadership of the Labour Party. The political will of the British proletariat must pass willy-nilly through the customs house of Thomas and MacDonald. The opposite wing, that is the communists, represent a tiny persecuted minority inside the labour movement. In what way can the working class be "burdened" by them? It is at liberty to listen to them or not for they do not have in their hands any means of imposing themselves. Standing behind Thomas and MacDonald is the whole machine of the capitalist state. MacDonald expels the communists while Baldwin puts them

---

Party moved the reference back of (a), which was lost by 321,000 votes to 2,871,000. Shinwell moved the reference back of (b), which was lost by 480,000 to 1,692,000. In the period leading up to the conference, the Communist Party had mounted a campaign for the lifting of the ban on communists and motions to this effect were passed by seventy-five local Labour Parties and trades councils and three trade unions.

in jail. The one complements the other. The working class will be able to throw off MacDonald only when it genuinely wishes to throw off Baldwin. It is absolutely true that the working class is burdened by its dependence on the conservative Fabian bourgeois. But how it can rid itself of them and what path it should choose it still does not know. The lefts reflect the lethargy of the British working class. They convert its as yet vaguely defined but profound and stubborn aspiration to free itself from Baldwin and MacDonald into left phrases of opposition which do not place any obligations upon them. They convert the political feebleness of the awakening masses into an ideological mish-mash. They represent the expression of a shift but also its, brake.

We have already heard a prophecy to the effect that the Liverpool Conference would give rise to a decisive split in the ranks of the Labour Party, and we have seen what a cruel mockery life has made of this prophecy. The essential thing about centrists is that they do not make a decision to decide. It required the imperialist war to force the centrists to split away temporarily from the social-imperialists. As soon as the impact of events was relaxed, the centrists turned back. Centrism is incapable of an independent policy. Centrism cannot be the leading party in the working class. The essential thing about centrism is that it does not make a decision to decide, except where events seize it firmly by the throat. But it has not yet reached this stage in Britain: that is why there was no split at Liverpool.

But what would have happened if a split had nevertheless taken place? Our correspondent leaves us unclear on this question:

> As a result of such a split in the existing Labour Party two parties would in the end be formed, the one left-liberal and the other genuinely socialist. Even if you allow that development will lead to economic crises and revolutions, the socialist party which would emerge from the split would be able to place itself at the head of the revolution, yet Trotsky does not take this point into account.

In this argument grains of truth become lost in a welter of confusion. Of course a split by centrists like our critic away from the Fabian bourgeoisie would not be irrelevant to the labour movement. But to bring about such a split at present would require insight and determination, which are the very qualities of which the British 'opposition' has not the slightest trace. If the centrists do split away then it will be at the last minute when there is no other way out. But a party which hatches out at the 'last moment' cannot lead the revolution. This does not mean that the centrists who have split away could not find themselves temporarily "at the head" of the masses similar to the

German Independents and even Social-Democracy at the end of 1918, and to our Mensheviks and Socialist-Revolutionaries after February 1917. Such a stage in the development of the British revolution cannot be excluded. It may even prove to be inevitable if the sharpening of social contradictions proceeds more rapidly than the formation of the Communist Party. Under the pressure of a General Strike and a victorious uprising, a certain section of the 'left' leaders could even come to power – with approximately the same sensations and moods with which a calf goes to the slaughter. Such a state of affairs would not however last long. The independents despite all their policy might come to power. But they could not retain that power. From the centrists power must pass either to the communists or return to the bourgeoisie.

The German Independents who had against their will been elevated to the summit of power by the revolution immediately shared it with Ebert and Scheidemann. Ebert immediately entered into negotiations with General Groener to suppress the workers. The Independents criticised the Spartacists, the Social-Democrats slandered them, and the army officer-caste shot Liebknecht and Luxemburg. Events from then on followed their logical sequence. The coalition of the Social-Democrats and Independents gave way to a coalition of capitalists and Social-Democrats. And then the Social-Democrats proved unnecessary. Ebert died at the right moment. The revolution which had started out against Hindenburg ended up by electing Hindenburg President of the Republic. And by that time the Independents had already returned to Ebert's ranks.

In Russia, the Menshevik and Socialist-Revolutionary patriots who, in the name of defence, had opposed the revolution by every means, were raised to power by the revolution. The Bolshevik Party, despite a decade and a half of uncompromising educational, organisational, and militant work found itself in the early stages in an insignificant minority. While prepared at any moment to come forward on the left flank against every attempt at counter-revolution, it all the same set course for a ruthless ideological struggle against those parties which had found themselves against their will "at the head of the revolution". Only thanks to this did October become possible.

A split by the British independents from MacDonald and Thomas five minutes before the bell is not excluded. Nor, in the case of a precipitate development of events, is the centrists' coming to power excluded. One cannot doubt that in this event they will implore MacDonald and Webb to share their burden with them. Nor can one doubt that MacDonald, either personally or through Thomas, will conduct negotiations with Joynson-

Hicks. A powerful mechanism for liquidating the proletarian half-victory will be set in motion. It is quite possible that a new split will take place within the lefts. But the development will follow the 'Russian' rather than the 'German' path only where there is present a mass communist party armed with a clear understanding of the whole course of development.

* * *

28 December 1925

Our 'left' critic accuses us of the very fact that we place our stakes on the British Communist Party. This does not mean that he himself rejects it out of hand. No, the position of a 'left', drifting like a boat without rudder or sails, consists in neither acknowledging anything out of hand nor totally rejecting anything. Here we once again feel obliged to make a quotation:

> Instead of seeking to regenerate the masses they [the communists] attempted to drive them along with a bludgeon and the masses do not take to this at all. A striking testimony in support of the correctness of the principles they defend lies in the fact that in spite of their crude tricks at the expense of their friends and their enemies, and in spite of their very deep ignorance of the very masses that they wish to lead, they nevertheless do have a great influence. If workers join them then they do so *out of desperation* and because they can see no other answer – not because they approve of the party as it is now but because they are forced to accept its conclusions.

This statement is truly remarkable as an involuntary testimony by an opponent in support of those ideas and methods against which he is waging a struggle. The inner strength of communism proves to be so great that an increasing number come to support it in spite of the 'crude' character of the communists. "But the workers do so *out of desperation!*" – exclaims our critic, himself too apparently not without desperation. It is completely correct that workers come – and increasingly so as time goes on – to a state of real 'desperation' because of worthless, treacherous, cowardly, or dissolute leadership. Nor can one think that the British workers with their age-old traditions of liberal politics, parliamentarism, compromises, national self-esteem, and so on will take to the revolutionary path other than in a state of utter desperation with those very politics which had previously given them something but which all along the line deceived them. Here the critic has come to the crux of the matter. It is just herein that the strength of the communist party lies, in that despite its numerical weakness, its inexperience, and its mistakes, the whole situation increasingly compels the working masses to pay heed to it.

Bruce,[2] the Australian Prime Minister, in defending his policy of banishing revolutionary labour leaders, said on the eve of the last elections: "The Communist Party in Australia has a membership of less than a thousand. But it is able to direct 400,000 workers in the Commonwealth."

The Times quoted these words with great approval (see the leading article of 12 November 1925). While speaking about Australia, *The Times* of London has Britain in mind of course. In order to emphasise this the newspaper states with a blunt frankness:

> The truth is that the great majority of those Labour leaders in Australia who are moderate in their views are equally moderate in their ability. The control of the party is passing more and more into the hands of its 'wild men'.

This is what in Russian is called "beating the cat but slanging the sister-in-law". We are quite prepared to agree with the paper that the ability of the official leaders of the British Labour Party (this is what *The Times* implies) is just as moderate as their views. But in the last resort, independent abilities are not required of them for they transmit the will and the ideas of the British bourgeoisie into the milieu of the working class. They were 'skilful' for just as long as the bourgeoisie was all-powerful. We should say that even the sage *Times* seems to us somewhat inane when it mumbles away about the mutual relations between the United States and Britain. This stems from an inner consciousness of weakness together with an effort to preserve the appearance of strength and a restrained gnashing of teeth. In the final count, the cause of the decline of *The Times* as well as the disclosure of MacDonald's modest capabilities lies in the poor balance of trade and payments of Great Britain. And inasmuch as the most powerful historical factors are at work in the disruption of the British balance of payments there can be no doubt that the working masses will increasingly fall into desperation with their old leaders, and fall under the influence of the "wild men".

* * *

5 January 1926

In an American publication with pretensions to Marxism and even communism (*Freiheit*) it has been pointed out in condemnation that while criticising the British centrists I had failed to take into account that "revolution" which had already taken place in the British trade unions.

---

2 Stanley Melbourne Bruce (1883-1967) – Australian Prime Minister 1923-29. In 1925 his government took repressive measures against a wave of labour unrest.

There is no need at this point to mention the fact that the causes and prospects of the evolution of the trade unions have been noted in the chapter 'Trade Unions and Bolshevism'.[3] Nor is there any need to repeat the rudimentary concept that without a turn by the working class, and consequently by its trade unions too, towards a revolutionary road, there can be no talk of a conquest of power by the proletariat. But it would be the utmost disgrace to brush aside the struggle against opportunism in the top leadership by alluding to the profound revolutionary processes taking place in the working class. Such a supposedly 'profound' approach stems entirely from a failure to understand the role and the significance of the party in the movement of the working class and especially in the revolution. For it has always been centrism which has cloaked and continues to cloak the sins of opportunism with solemn references to the objective tendencies of development. Is it worth wasting time and energy in fighting the muddleheads of the type of Wheatley, Brailsford, Purcell, Kirkwood, and others, now that revolutionary aspirations are on the increase in the proletariat, now that the trade unions are turning towards cooperation with the Soviet trade unions and so on and so forth? But in actual fact, expressed in this alleged revolutionary objectivism is merely an effort to shirk revolutionary tasks by shifting them on to the shoulders of the so-called historical process.

And it is in Britain that the danger of this sort of tendency is particularly great. Yesterday we had to prove that objective conditions there are working in a revolutionary direction. To keep repeating this today is to knock at an open door. The growing preponderance of America; the burden of debts and military expenditure; the industrialisation of the colonies, dominions, and the backward countries in general; the economic strengthening of the Soviet Union and the growth of its attractive revolutionary force; the liberation movement of the oppressed nations – all these are factors which are growing. Through an inevitable series of fluctuations in the conjuncture of events, British capitalism is going to meet a catastrophe. It is clear what shifts in the correlations and consciousness of classes this implies. But the objective pre-conditions of the proletarian revolution are being prepared and are maturing far more rapidly than are the subjective. And this is what above all must be remembered *today*.

The danger is not that the bourgeoisie will again pacify the proletariat, nor that an era of liberal labour politics is again opening up before the trade unions: the United States has monopolised for itself the ability to give a

---

3   *Where is Britain Going?*, Chapter 7, from page 311 of the present edition.

privileged position to broad circles of the proletariat. The danger comes from another direction: *the formation of a proletarian vanguard can lag behind the development of a revolutionary situation.* While faced with the necessity for decisive actions, the proletariat might not find at its head the necessary political leadership. This is the question *of the party*. And this is the central question. The most mature revolutionary situation without a revolutionary party of due stature and without correct leadership is the same as a knife without a blade. This is what we saw in Germany in the autumn of 1923. A Bolshevik Party will take shape in Britain only in a perpetual and irreconcilable struggle against centrism which is becoming the substitute for the Liberal policy of Labour.

* * *

6 January 1926

The struggle for a united front has such importance in Britain precisely because it answers the elementary requirements of the working class in the new orientation and grouping of forces. The struggle for a united front will thereby pose the problem of leadership, that is, of programme and tactics, and this means the party. Yet the struggle for a united front will not in itself solve this task but will merely create the conditions for its solution. The ideological and organisational formation of a genuinely revolutionary, that is of a communist, party on the basis of the movement of the masses is conceivable only under the condition of a perpetual, systematic, inflexible, untiring, and irreconcilable unmasking of the quasi-left leaders of every hue, of their confusion, of their compromises, and of their reticence. It would be the crudest blunder to think – and this can be seen to happen – that the task of the struggle for a united front consists in obtaining a victory for Purcell, Lansbury, Wheatley, and Kirkwood over Snowden, Webb and MacDonald. Such an objective would contain within itself a contradiction. The left muddleheads are incapable of power; but if through the turn of events it fell into their hands they would hasten to pass it over to their elder brothers on the right. They would do the same with the state as they are now doing in the party.

The history of the German Independents, let us again recall, provides us with instructive lessons on this account. In Germany the process took place at a more rapid tempo owing to the directly revolutionary character of the recent years of German history. But the general tendencies of the development are the same whether you call MacDonald Ebert or you christen Wheatley and Cook, Crispien and Hilferding. The fact that Hilferding, the most vulgar Philistine, still makes references to Marx while Wheatley displays a preference for the Holy Father in Rome flows from the peculiarities of Britain's past as compared with that of Germany, but for the present day it is of tenth-rate importance.

* * *

7 January 1926

The left faction at the top of the trade unions leads the General Council on a number of questions. This expresses itself most clearly in the attitude towards the Soviet trade unions and to Amsterdam.[4] But it would be a mistake to overestimate the influence of these lefts upon the unions as the organisations of class struggle. This is not so much because the masses in the trade unions are not radical enough, on the contrary the masses are immeasurably more left than the most left of the leaders. In the British labour movement, international questions have always been a path of least resistance for the 'leaders'. In regarding international issues as a sort of safety valve for the radical mood of the masses, Messrs. leaders are prepared to bow to a certain degree to revolution (elsewhere), only the more surely to take revenge on the questions of the domestic class struggle. The left faction on the General Council is distinguished by a total *ideological* formlessness and for this very reason it is incapable of consolidating around itself *organisationally* the leadership of the trade union movement.

This too explains the impotence of the lefts within the Labour Party. The latter rests of course upon the same trade unions. It might appear that the left faction which 'leads' the General Council would have taken control of the Labour Party. But we see something quite different in reality. The extreme rights continue to control the party. This can be explained by the fact that a party cannot confine itself to isolated left campaigns but is compelled to have an overall system policy. The lefts have no such system nor by their very essence can they. But the rights do: with them stands tradition, experience and routine and, most important, with them stands bourgeois society as a whole which slips them ready-made solutions. For MacDonald has only to

---

4   This refers to the reformist or 'yellow' International Federation of Trade Unions re-established in 1919 at Amsterdam. It comprised trade union federations of European countries for the most part dominated by reformist and centrist socialist parties, and also the British Trades Union Congress. Trade unions controlled by or sympathetic to parties affiliated to the Communist International formed the Red International of Unions.

translate Baldwin's and Lloyd George's suggestions into Fabian language. The rights win despite the fact that the lefts are more numerous. The weakness of the lefts arises from their disorder and their disorder from their ideological formlessness. In order to marshal their ranks, the lefts have first of all to rally their ideas. The best of them will only be capable of doing so under the fire of the most ruthless criticism based upon the everyday experience of the masses.

* * *

12 January 1926

More influential leaders of the 'lefts' like Purcell, Cook, and Bromley, besides our 'left' critic in his letter, were as late as 17 September predicting that the Labour Party Conference would be distinguished by a great swing to the left. The opposite came about: the Liverpool Conference which was separated by a few weeks from the Scarborough Trades Union Congress[5] gave a complete victory to MacDonald. To ignore this fact, to gloss over it, to minimise it or to explain it by accidental secondary causes would be crass stupidity and courting defeats.

The party has fundamentally the same base as have the trade union leaders. But the General Council whose authority is extremely limited does not have any power over individual trade unions nor less over the country. But the Labour Party has already stood in power and is about to do so again. This is the gist of the question.

In connection with the Scarborough Congress, the liberal *Manchester Guardian* wrote that Moscow's influence made itself felt only in the left phraseology while in practice the trade unions remained under the leadership of wise and experienced leaders. The liberal newspaper has need of consolation. But there is in its assertions an element of truth and a large one at that. The resolutions of the congress were the more to the left the further removed they were from immediate practical tasks. Of course the leftness of

---

5   The Scarborough Congress of September 1925 marked the high point of a 'left wing interlude' at the TUC. Its President was left-winger Alonzo Swales of the Engineers and its policies included general support for socialism and a call for more power for the General Council. However, there was no discussion of how the former policy could be achieved or how the latter could be made to support the interests of the workers or resolve the inevitable confrontation in the coal industry that came in the following May. With extreme right wingers like Jimmie Thomas back on the General Council and Arthur Pugh in the Presidency, there was no serious prospect that the Congress could lead a struggle against the employers or the state.

the resolutions is symptomatic, marking a turn in the consciousness of the masses. But to think that the leading figures at Scarborough might become the leaders of a revolutionary overthrow of power would be to lull oneself with illusions. It is sufficient to recall that 3,802,000 votes were cast in favour of the right of oppressed nations to self-determination and even to secession, and only 79,000 against. What an enormous revolutionary swing this might appear to be! Yet on the question of forming shop committees – not for an armed uprising nor for a General Strike, but for nothing more than forming shop committees and only "in principle" at that – the voting was 2,183,000 in favour and 1,787,000 against; in other words congress was split almost in half. On the question of extending the powers of the General Council the lefts suffered a complete defeat. It is small wonder if after all the left resolutions the new General Council has proven to be more right than the old one. It must be clearly understood: this sort of leftism remains only as long as it does not impose any practical obligations. As soon as a question of action arises the lefts respectfully surrender the leadership to the rights.

* * *

13 January 1926

A spontaneous radicalisation of the trade unions expressing a deep shift in the masses is in itself totally inadequate to liberate the working class from the leadership of Thomas and MacDonald. National bourgeois ideology in Britain presents a formidable force – not only in public opinion but also in established institutions. 'Radical' trade unionism will break itself again and again against this force as long as it is led by centrists who cannot draw the necessary conclusions.

At the same time as the British unions fraternise with the Soviet trade unions which are under the leadership of communists, at Liverpool the British Labour Party which rests upon these same unions expels British communists from its ranks, thus preparing a government-fascist operation to smash their organisations. It would be criminal to forget for one day that lefts such as Brailsford and even Lansbury in effect approved of the Liverpool Conference resolution and blamed the communists for it all. It is true that when indignation with the reactionary police-state spirit of the Liverpool conference revealed itself from the lower ranks, the 'left' leaders readily changed their line. But to evaluate them one must take both sides of the matter into account. Revolutionaries need a good memory. Messrs. 'lefts' do not have a line of their own. They will go on swinging to the right under the pressure of bourgeois-Fabian reaction and to the left under the pressure of the masses. In difficult moments these, pious Christians are always ready to play the part if not of Herod then of Pontius Pilate, and facing the British working class there are many difficult moments ahead.

There is inside the Independent Labour Party a movement favouring unification of the Second and the Third Internationals. But try asking these people whether they would agree not to unification, but to a militant agreement with British communists, and they recoil there and then. In all matters relating to revolution there reigns supreme among the British 'lefts' a 'love for the distant'. They are for the October revolution, for Soviet power, for the Soviet trade unions, and even for a rapprochement with the Comintern, but under the immutable condition that the British Constitution, the system of parliamentarism, and the system of the Labour Party suffer no harm. It is necessary to direct the main blow against this repulsive two-faced policy of the lefts.

To this one should add in the sympathies of many lefts for the Soviet Union (alongside hostility towards their own communists) there is contained a good deal of the deference of the petty bourgeois towards a strong state power. This should not be forgotten. Of course the petty bourgeois who has turned his face towards the Soviet Union is more progressive than the petty bourgeois who goes on his knees before the United States. This is a step forward. But one cannot build revolutionary perspectives on such a deference.

* * *

25 December 1925

A foreign communist who knows Britain well and has only recently left there wrote to me the other day as follows:

> During my stay in England I had numerous conversations with certain prominent left leaders on the subject of the British revolution. I brought away approximately this picture: they are sure that in the near future they will win a majority in parliament and will commence a cautious but decisive implementation of the maximum demands of the working class such as the nationalisation of the mines, certain other branches of industry, the banks and so on. If the industrialists and bankers dare to resist then they will be straight away arrested and their enterprises will be nationalised too. To my question: what in this case will the fascist bourgeoisie who have the army and the Navy in their hands do? – they replied: in event of armed resistance on the part of the fascists they will be declared outlaws and the overwhelming majority of the British people will back the Labour Party in defence of the legal government. When I pointed out: since they will inevitably

resort to arms wouldn't it be better to prepare the working class now for such an outcome so that the armed forces of the bourgeoisie cannot catch it off guard? – they replied: such a preparatory move would be a premature signal for civil war and would prevent the Labour Party from winning a majority in parliament. To the question: on which side of the barricades will MacDonald, Snowden, Thomas and their friends be, they replied: on the side of the bourgeoisie most probably. Why then do you work together with them against the communists in order to strengthen a party leadership which will betray the working class at the critical moment? To this came the reply: we think that we will nevertheless retain a majority in parliament behind us and that a split by MacDonald and his liberal friends will not threaten in the slightest a favourable outcome to a peaceful revolution.

This sheaf of personal impressions and conversations is truly precious. These people have decided in advance to come to power in no other way than through the asses' gate which the enemy, armed to the teeth and standing guard, has shown them to. If they, the lefts, take power (through the indicated gate) and if the bourgeoisie rise up against this legal power, then the good British people will not tolerate this. And if MacDonald and Thomas whom the wise lefts are carrying on their backs are found by chance to be in a plot with the armed bourgeoisie against the unarmed workers, then this should not cause alarm to anyone for the lefts have provided for victory in this event. In a word, the brave spirits and wise men have firmly decided to conquer the bourgeoisie whatever the political combinations and at the same time maintaining the best relations with parliament, the law, the courts, and the police. The only trouble is that the bourgeoisie does not intend to surrender the privilege of the legal expropriation of power to the lefts. By advancing the fascist wing more energetically, as the threat of civil war becomes more immediate, the bourgeoisie will find sufficient means of provocation, of a legal coup d'état and so on. In the final count, the question is not who can best interpret laws and traditions, but who is master in the house.

The discussion which has recently flared up in the British Labour Press on the question of self-defence is in the highest degree significant. The question itself arose not as a question of armed uprising for the seizure of power but as a question of strikers repulsing blacklegs and fascists.

We have already shown elsewhere how trade unionism, by the logic of development – and especially in the period of capitalist decline – inevitably bursts the framework of democracy. It is not possible to postpone arbitrarily class conflicts until the conquest of a parliamentary majority. Cramped by its own decline, the bourgeoisie puts pressure on the proletariat. The latter defends itself. Hence the inevitable strike clashes. The government prepares strike-breaking organisations on a scale previously unheard of. The fascists link up with the police. The workers pose the question of self-defence. At this point the foundation of civil war has already been laid.

A worker writes in *Lansbury's Labour Weekly*:[6] "Fascism is purely and simply a military organisation and is not amenable to argument. It can only be successfully countered by a similar organisation on the other side." The author recommends taking the military organisation of fascism as a model. That is correct: the proletariat can and must learn military knowledge from the enemy.

And it is from the same source – the objective sharpening of class contradictions – that the aspiration of workers to draw soldiers over to their side flows. Agitation in the army and the navy is a second powerful element in the civil war, the development of which does not stand in a direct connection with the winning of a parliamentary majority. The defection of a considerable part of the armed forces to the side of the workers can guarantee the conquest of power by the proletariat without any parliamentary majority. The workers' majority in parliament can be destroyed if armed force is in the hands of the bourgeoisie. Whoever does not understand this is not a socialist but a numbskull.

In opposition to the slogan of arming the workers, the wise men of the left have scraped together all the prejudices and platitudes of centuries past: the superiority of the moral factor over force, the advantages of gradual reforms, the anarcho-pacifist idea of the peaceful General Strike, which they require not as a means of struggle but as an argument against insurrection, and a heroic readiness… to permit violence in the so-called "extreme case when it is forced on us". Obviously this means when the enemy has caught you off guard and is crushing you unarmed against the wall.

* * *

5 March 1926 (from a letter)

In Britain, more than in all the rest of Europe, the consciousness of the working masses, and particularly that of their leading layers, lags behind the

---

6 *Lansbury's Labour Weekly* – Newspaper run by George Lansbury as an alternative to the *Daily Herald* which was now entirely under the control of the right wing. It appeared in 1925-6 and reflected generally the policies of the 'left' union leaders in the TUC and an incoherent but largely undirected disillusionment following the failure of the 1924 Labour Government.

objective economic situation. And it is precisely in this direction that the main difficulties and dangers lie today. All shades of bosses of the British labour movement fear action because the historical impasse of British capitalism places every problem of the labour movement, however major, at point-blank range. This applies especially to the coal industry. The present miners' wages are maintained by a subsidy from the state, burdening an already crippling budget. To continue the subsidy means to accumulate and deepen the economic crisis. To withdraw the subsidy means to produce a social crisis.

The necessity of a technical and economic reconstruction of the coal industry represents a profoundly revolutionary problem and requires a political 'reconstruction' of the working class. The destruction of the conservatism of the British coal industry, this foundation of British capitalism, can only be through the destruction of the conservative organisations, traditions, and customs of the British labour movement. Britain is entering an entire historical phase of major upheavals. An 'economic' solution of the problem can be expected only by the conservative British trade union leaders. But it is just because the British trade union leaders direct their efforts towards an 'economic' (i.e., peaceful, conciliatory, conservative) solution of the problem, that is they run in defiance of the historical process, that the revolutionary development of the working class in Britain in the period to come will have higher overhead costs than in any other country. Both the rights and the lefts, including of course both Purcell and Cook, fear to the utmost the beginning of the *denouément*. Even when in words they admit the inevitability of struggle and revolution, they are hoping in their hearts for some miracle which will release them from these perspectives. And in any event they themselves will stall, evade, temporise, shift responsibility, and effectively assist Thomas over any really major question of the *British* labour movement (with regard to *international* questions they are a bit bolder!).

Hence the general situation can be characterised in this way. The economic blind alley of the country, which is most sharply expressed in the coal industry, thrusts the working class on to the path of seeking a solution, that is on to the path of an even sharper struggle. Its very first stage will as a result reveal the inadequacy of the 'usual' methods of struggle. The whole of the present-day 'superstructure' of the British working class – in all its shades and groupings without exception – represents a braking mechanism on the revolution. This portends over a prolonged period the heavy pressure of a spontaneous and semi-spontaneous movement against the framework of the old organisations and the formation of new revolutionary organisations on the basis of this pressure.

One of our principal tasks is to assist the British Communist Party to understand and think out this perspective fully. Inside the trade union apparatus and amongst its left wing the active elements, that is, the elements which are capable of understanding the inevitability of major mass battles, and who are not afraid of them but go to meet them, must be sifted out far more energetically and decisively than has been done up to now. The tactic of the united front must be increasingly and more firmly placed within the context of this perspective.

With regard to the miners' strike, it is not of course a question of an isolated strike, however big it may be, but the commencement of a whole series of social conflicts and crises. In this situation one cannot of course orientate oneself with the conceptions of Purcell and others. They fear the struggle more than anyone. Their thoughts and words can at best have in our eyes the importance of a symptom.

The British trade unions fear (in the form of their bureaucracy and even of its left) our 'intervention' in their internal affairs no less than Chamberlain does.

There are any number of inhibiting elements in the apparatus of the British working class. The whole situation can be summarised in the fact that the alarm, discontent, and pressure of the British working masses is all along the line running up against the organisational and ideological barriers of the conservatism of the apparatus. Under these conditions, to worry about how best to assist the impatient leaders is really to pour water into the ocean.

Everything goes to suggest that in Britain in the next period (I have in mind two or three years), a struggle will break out against the will of the old organisations, yet with the complete unpreparedness of the young ones. Of course, even with the firm revolutionary (i.e., active) footing of the Communist Party and of the best 'left' elements it cannot be assumed that the proletariat will come to power as the result of the first big wave by itself. But the question is this: Will this left wing pass through the first stage of the revolution at the head of the working masses as we passed through 1905; or will it miss a revolutionary situation as the German party did in 1923? This latter danger is in the highest degree a real one. It can only be reduced by helping the left wing (the really left wing and not Lansbury or Purcell), to an effective orientation. And to accomplish this task (that of assisting the revolutionary elements in Britain to a correct orientation), it must be clearly understood that all the traditions, organisational habits, and the ideas of all the already existing groupings in the labour movement in different forms and with different slogans predispose them either towards direct treachery or towards compromise, or else towards temporising and passivity in relation to the compromisers, and complaints about the traitors.

* * *

6 May 1926

A year ago, the Conservative government was still on its honeymoon. Baldwin was preaching social peace. With nothing to oppose to Conservatism, MacDonald rivalled it in hatred of revolution, civil war, and class struggle. The leaders of all three parties pronounced the institutions of Britain entirely adequate to ensuring peaceful collaboration between the classes. Naturally, the revolutionary prognosis for the future of the British Empire made in this book[7] was declared by the whole of the British press – from the *Morning Post* to *Lansbury's Labour Weekly* – to be hopeless drivel and Moscow phantasmagoria.

Today the situation looks somewhat different. Britain is convulsed by a huge mass strike. The Conservative government is carrying on a policy of frantic onslaught. From the top, everything is being done to provoke open civil war. The contradiction between basic social facts and the fraud of an outlived parliamentarism has been revealed in Britain as never before.

The mass strike arose from the imbalance between the current position of the British economy on the world market and the traditional industrial and class relations within the country. Formally the question at issue was one of reducing miners' wages, lengthening their working day, and throwing part of the sacrifices necessary for a serious reorganisation of the coal industry onto the workers' shoulders. Put in this way, the question is insoluble. It is perfectly true that the coal industry, and indeed the British economy as a whole, cannot be reorganised without sacrifices on the part of the British proletariat, and substantial ones at that. But only a wretched fool can imagine that the British proletariat will agree to shoulder these sacrifices on the old foundations of private property.

Capitalism has been portrayed as a system of continual progress and consistent improvement in the lot of the labouring masses. This used to be the case to a certain extent, at least in some countries during the

---

7   *Where is Britain Going?*, from page 251 of the present edition.

nineteenth century. In Britain the religion of capitalist progress was more potent than anywhere else. And it was just this that formed the foundation of the conservative tendencies in the labour movement itself and especially in the trade unions. Britain's wartime illusions (1914-1918), were, more than anywhere else, the illusions of capitalist might and social 'progress'. In the victory over Germany these hopes were supposed to find their highest fulfilment. Yet now bourgeois society says to the miners: "If you want to secure for yourselves at least the kind of existence you had before the war, you must reconcile yourselves to a worsening of all your conditions of life over an indefinite period." Instead of the perspective of uninterrupted social progress recently held out to them, the miners are invited to move down one step today so as to avoid tumbling down three or more steps tomorrow. This is a declaration of bankruptcy on the part of British capitalism. The General Strike is the answer of the proletariat, which will not and cannot allow the bankruptcy of British capitalism to signify the bankruptcy of the British nation and of British culture.

This answer, however, has been dictated by the logic of the situation far more than by the logic of consciousness. The British working class had no other choice. The struggle, whatever its backstage mechanics, was thrust upon it by the mechanical pressure of the whole set of circumstances. The world position of the British economy did not leave the material basis for a voluntary compromise. The Thomases, MacDonalds and the rest have ended up like windmills whose sails turn in a strong wind but fail to produce a single pound of flour because there is no corn for them to grind. The hopeless emptiness of present-day British reformism has found itself so convincingly unmasked that the reformists were left with no other recourse than to take part in the mass strike of the proletariat. This revealed the strength of the strike – but also its weakness.

A general strike is the sharpest form of class struggle. It is only one step from the general strike to armed insurrection. This is precisely why the general strike, more than any other form of class struggle, requires clear, distinct, resolute and therefore revolutionary leadership. In the current strike of the British proletariat there is not a ghost of such a leadership, and it is not to be expected that it can be conjured up out of the ground. The General Council of the Trades Union Congress set out with the ridiculous statement that the present General Strike did not represent a political struggle and did not in any event constitute an assault upon the state power of the bankers, industrialists, and landowners, or upon the sanctity of British parliamentarism. This most loyal and submissive declaration of war does not, however, appear the least bit convincing to the government, which feels the real instruments of rule slipping out of its hands under the effect of the strike. State power is not an 'idea' but a material apparatus. When the apparatus of government and suppression is paralysed, the state power itself is thereby paralysed. In modern society no-one can hold power without controlling the railways, shipping, posts, telegraphs, power stations, coal, and so on. The fact that MacDonald and Thomas have sworn to renounce any political objectives may typify them personally, but it in no way typifies the nature of the General Strike which if carried through to the end sets the revolutionary class the task of organising a new state power. Fighting against this with all their might, however, are those very people who by the course of events have been placed 'at the head' of the General Strike. And in this the main danger lies. Men who did not want the General Strike, who deny the political nature of the General Strike, and fear above all the consequences of a victorious strike, must inevitably direct all their efforts towards keeping it within the bounds of a semi-political semi-strike, that is to say, towards emasculating it.

We must look facts in the face: the principal efforts of the official Labour Party leaders and of a considerable number of official trade union leaders will be directed not towards paralysing the bourgeois state by means of the strike, but towards paralysing the General Strike by means of the bourgeois state. The government in the shape of its most die-hard Conservatives will without doubt want to provoke a small-scale civil war, so as to gain the opportunity of applying measures of terror before the struggle has fully unfolded and so throw the movement back. By depriving the strike of a political programme, dissipating the revolutionary will of the proletariat, and driving the movement up a blind alley, the reformists are thereby pushing individual groups of workers on to the path of uncoordinated revolts. In this sense the reformists go towards meeting the most fascist elements in the Conservative Party. There lies the principal danger of the struggle now opening up.

Now is not the time to predict the duration, the course, and still less the outcome of the struggle. Everything must be done on an international scale to aid the fighters and improve their chances of success. But it must be clearly recognised that such success is possible only to the extent that the British working class, in the process of the development and sharpening of the General Strike, realises the need to change its leadership, and measures up to that task. There is an American proverb which says that you cannot change horses in midstream. But this practical wisdom is true only within certain limits. The stream of revolution has never been crossed on the horse of reformism, and the class which has entered the struggle under opportunist leadership will be compelled to change it under enemy fire. The conduct of the really revolutionary elements in the British proletariat, and above all the communists, is pre-determined by this. They will uphold the unity of mass action by every means; but they will not permit even the semblance of unity with the opportunist leaders of the Labour Party and the trade unions. An implacable struggle against every act of treachery or attempted treachery and the ruthless exposure of the reformists' illusions are the main elements in the work of the genuinely revolutionary participants in the General Strike. In this they will not only aid the fundamental and protracted task of developing new cadres, without which the victory of the British proletariat is wholly impossible, but they will directly assist the success of this strike by deepening it, uncovering its revolutionary tendencies, thrusting the opportunists aside, and strengthening the position of the revolutionaries. The results of the strike, both the immediate and the more remote, will be the more significant the more resolutely the revolutionary force of the masses sweeps away the barriers erected by the counter-revolutionary leadership.

The strike cannot of itself alter the position of British capitalism, and the coal industry in particular, on the world market. This requires the reorganisation of the whole British economy. The strike is only a sharp expression of this necessity. The programme for reorganising the British economy is the programme of a new power, a new state, and a new class. The fundamental importance of the General Strike is that it poses the question of power point-blank. A real victory for the General Strike lies only in the winning of power by the proletariat and the establishment of the dictatorship of the proletariat. In view of the insolvency of British capitalism, the General Strike is less able than at any other time to be made a vehicle of reforms or partial gains. To be more precise, even if the mine-owners or the government were to make this or that economic concession under pressure of the strike, such concession could not, by virtue of the whole situation, be of a profound, still less of a lasting significance.

This in no way means, however, that the present strike faces the alternative: all or nothing. If the British proletariat had a leadership that came near to corresponding to its class strength and the ripeness of the conditions, power would pass out of the hands of the Conservatives and into the hands of the proletariat within a few weeks. But such an outcome cannot be relied upon. This again does not mean that the strike is futile. The more broadly it develops, the more powerfully it shakes the foundations of capitalism, and the further back it thrusts the treacherous and opportunist leaders, the harder it will be for bourgeois reaction to go over to the counter-offensive, the less proletarian organisations will suffer, and the sooner will follow the next, more decisive stage of the fight.

The present collision of the classes will be a tremendous lesson and have immeasurable consequences, quite apart from its immediate results. It will become plain to every proletarian in Britain that parliament is powerless to solve the basic and most vital tasks of the country. The question of the economic salvation of Britain will henceforth confront the proletariat as a question of the conquest of power. All the intervening, mediating, compromising, pseudo-pacifist elements will be dealt a mortal blow. The Liberal Party, however much its leaders may twist and turn, will emerge from such an ordeal even more insignificant than it entered it. Within the Conservative Party the most die-hard elements will obtain a preponderance. Within the Labour Party the revolutionary wing will gain in organisation and influence. The Communists will advance decisively. The revolutionary development of Britain will take a gigantic stride towards its *denouément*.

In the light of the mighty strike wave now under way, the questions of evolution and revolution, of peaceful development and the use of force, of reforms and class dictatorship, will grip the consciousness of British workers in their hundreds of thousands and millions, with all their acuteness. Of this there can be no doubt. The British proletariat, kept by the bourgeoisie and its Fabian agents in a state of horrifying ideological backwardness, will now spring forward like a lion. Material conditions in Britain have long been ripe for socialism. The strike has placed on the agenda the replacement of the bourgeois state by the proletarian state. If the strike itself does not produce this change, it will bring it far closer. The exact date we cannot say. But we should be prepared for it to be early.

* * *

From a speech to the 6th Congress of Textile Workers, 29 January 1926.

Take just a cursory glance at the situation in the chief European states today, and you are bound to conclude that history, in approaching its day of reckoning, is in no mood to play around with Europe. The strongest country in Europe is Britain. Leaning on Europe, Britain has grown accustomed to a position where ruling over the world comes as easily to her as breathing. The Englishman (I have in mind of course the *ruling* Englishman, a bourgeois or a lord), has thought of himself for centuries as nothing less than the ruler of the world. Yet today the former sovereign of the oceans and continents is staggering under irreversible blows: the rise of the colonies, their economic development and drive for independence; the national upsurge and the growth of industry in the Dominions; the growth of competition, first from Germany – who had to be strangled – and then from the United States – who will not be strangled, and will in fact do any strangling there is to be done. And finally, the growth of the might of the Soviet Union, reflecting the rise of the oppressed peoples and oppressed classes of the whole world. Britain is sliding further and further downhill before our eyes.

Today, I believe you sent greetings to the Anglo-Russian Trade Union Unity Committee. How did that come about? It grew out of the economic decline of Britain. Comrades of the older generation, those who were learning their Marxism twenty and twenty-five years ago, will remember how the British trade unions used to be regarded as a bulwark of conservatism. Where did our hopes lie? With the German workers first of all, and then the French workers, but we said that the British worker would be the third, fourth, or fifth to launch into struggle. And this because the upper layers were accustomed to an aristocratic position made possible only by the privileged position of British industry. Twenty-five years ago – and that's not such a long time – the Russian revolutionaries of the day had offered to fraternise with the British workers' leaders, and if twenty years ago Tomsky had been sent to London to join with British trade unionists they would have told him where to go. [*Laughter.*] But now the trade unions receive Tomsky as a brother. What is the reason for this change? It is that the last decades have undermined British industry, leaving not a trace of the privileged position of the working class, with the result that the British worker has become proletarianised politically. He is in search of a new source of support and it is no chance matter that he finds it first and foremost in our Soviet trade unions. The Anglo-Russian Trade Union Unity Committee is the highest expression of the shift in the situation of all Europe and especially Britain, which is taking place before our very eyes and will lead to the proletarian revolution. There can be no other solution.

Not so long ago, a Conservative government came to power in Britain promising to rectify the economic ills of the country with protectionist policies. We predicted failure for Mr. Baldwin along this road: Britain lives on imported agricultural produce, raw materials, and semi-finished goods, and therefore cannot become a protectionist country. If one branch of industry prospers from protective tariffs, another will perish. Baldwin nonetheless even lured along a considerable section of workers by promising to save British industry by means of a protectionist system of high customs duties. But what were the results? Protectionism was brought in for ladies' gloves, carpet tacks, and I believe for toilet paper [*laughter*], and for two or three other items equally necessary to life, but without this resurrecting the British economy. The last-mentioned commodity is possibly the most fitting symbol of the Conservative government's protectionist programme in action. [*Applause, laughter.*]

To be sure, back in his Leeds speech Baldwin instructed us all (especially transgressors like me) that the first requirement is gradualness. Don't hurry, don't overstep the mark, gradualness above all! But if Baldwin wishes to take protective measures for British industry with this gradualness then some 300 years will pass while he is carrying out his programme. Life, of course, does not wait: the working class is shifting to the left and the formation of the Anglo-Russian Trade Union Unity Committee was no accident. And we have yet to see how with God's help – for in Baldwin's realm nothing can happen without God's help – the British bourgeois regime will be 'gradually' overthrown.

* * *

13 May 1926, from *Pravda*, 25 and 26 May 1926.

The defeat of the General Strike is 'logical' at the present stage in that it flows from all the conditions of its origin and development. This defeat could have been foreseen. There is nothing demoralising about it. But we will deal with the lessons of the defeat and of the General Strike itself later.

Replies to Critics

From *Pravda* and *Izvestia*, 11 February 1926.

On the Tempo and Timescale of the Revolution

Events over the year which has passed since my book *Where is Britain Going?*[1] was written have in no way developed according to the scheme of either Baldwin or MacDonald. The starry-eyed idealism of the Conservative minister has faded away very rapidly. The communists who had been expelled from the Labour Party by MacDonald have been put in jail by King George's judges, thus putting the party on an illegal basis. These same judges pat young fascist thugs encouragingly on the back and recommend the violators of the law to join the police who are charged with safeguarding the law. The judges thereby bear witness to the fact that the difference between violation of the law by fascists and safeguarding the law by the police merely relates to the form and in no way to the essence. The fascists are good citizens but too impatient: their methods are premature. The class struggle has not yet reached civil war. MacDonald and Lansbury are still performing their functions restraining the proletariat with the fictions of democracy and the myths of religion. Fascism remains in reserve. But the capitalist politicians understand that matters do not end with the methods of democracy and in private Mr. Joynson-Hicks is trying on Mussolini's mask.

The tough repressiveness of the Baldwin government complements, out of necessity, its wretched confusion on economic problems. Faced with the new economic facts, the protectionism of the Conservative Party is just as feeble as

---

1 From page 213 of the present edition.

the free trade of the Liberals was. It was clear from the very start that the vain attempts at protectionism would run into the conflicts of interests of the basic branches of the British economy. But a year ago we still did not think that a protectionist programme would degenerate into such a farce. In the period since then, duties have been imposed on lace, gloves, musical instruments, gas mantles, penknives, and toilet paper. No more than 10,000 workers are employed in these branches of industry. Yet there are 1,231,900 miners. And the registered unemployed number 1,215,900. Isn't Mr. Baldwin abusing 'gradualness' just too much?

The Liberal Party, whose downfall continues to remain one of the sharpest political expressions of the decline of Britain, has for the most part abandoned any hopes of independent power, and while the right wing dreams of a role as a left brake on the Conservatives its left wing would like to support MacDonald from the right who, in turn, will have increasing need of such support as time goes on. When old Asquith commented ironically upon the speech of Snowden and Churchill, of whom the former urged the Liberals to enter the Labour Party and the latter to enter the Conservative Party, then Mr. Asquith was right in his way: between dying in the capacity of yes-men of old political adversaries and dying on the principles of independence, the difference is not so great.

The role of the MacDonald clique over this period can be adequately characterised by a simple juxtaposition of facts. In 1924 the MacDonald government convicted communists under the Incitement to Mutiny Act of 1797 (of the era of the French revolution!). At the end of 1925 MacDonald carried out the expulsion of communists from the Labour Party. The ultra-reactionary Home Secretary in the Conservative government, the already mentioned Benito Hicks, has convicted communists under the same Act of 1797 and has placed the leaders of the party in jail. The working masses protest. The MacDonald clique too is compelled to issue inarticulate sounds of protest. Against what? It is quite evident that it is against the rival Hicks taking the bread out of its mouth.

Neither the economics nor the politics of Britain over the last year provide any reason whatsoever to make alterations to the conclusions drawn in our book. There is no cause to react to the gnashing of teeth in the bourgeois press, of Britain and especially of America. "Behind the mask of a new book", howls one of the New York papers, "the author teaches Americans and Englishmen how to conduct an uprising". The paper then demands tough measures against the book on account of the geographical distance of the author. All this is in the order of things. There is no occasion to reply. Events will reply. The only thing that I have learnt from the criticisms in the British bourgeois press is that Mr. Winston Churchill is not yet a lord as I had mistakenly or at least prematurely supposed.

The official Menshevik Press says essentially the same thing; only the appeal to the bourgeois police against the "sermon of violence" has a somewhat more masked form. But here, neither, is there any place for polemics. For us at the present stage of development the British opposition on the left is far more interesting. From its literary representatives we will however hear little. "If the crazy Moscow tendencies are able to find roots here then it will be simply thanks to the greed of our bourgeoisie and the compliance of the leaders of the Labour Party" and so on and so forth. This is the gist of the articles of Lansbury, Brailsford, and others. The complete centrist stamp of thoughts and arguments could be predicted in advance. To hope for a positive attempt at an analysis of facts and reasoning on the part of these gentlemen is about equivalent to expecting milk from a billy-goat.

Fortunately we do have in our hands a document which is distinguished by a considerably greater spontaneity and, as it were, naturalness. A Russian comrade who maintains a correspondence with figures in the British labour movement has sent me two letters from a 'left' member of the Independent Labour Party directed against my book *Where is Britain Going?* These letters seemed to me more interesting than the articles by British and other 'leaders', some of whom have lost the ability to think and others of whom had never acquired it. I do not at all mean to say by this that the writer of the letters argues correctly. On the contrary, it would be hard to conceive of a greater chaos than that which reigns in his thoughts, which, by the way, he himself regards to be his principal advantage over the finished compromisers of the MacDonald variety and over the "dogmatists of revolution", that is ourselves. Through our Russian and international experience we are pretty well familiar with confusionists of this type. If we nevertheless consider the critical letters of the 'left', which had not been intended for publication, more instructive than the glossy articles of the specialists of centrism then it is just because, in the honest-to-goodness eclectic mish-mash of the letters, the political shifts in the masses are more directly reflected. It goes without saying that we are using the letters with the kind permission of both the English and the Russian correspondents.

The ideological groupings in the British labour movement and particularly in its leading layer can be divided along three basic lines. The leading position in the Labour Party is occupied by the rights, as the Liverpool Conference once again showed. The official ideology of these gentlemen, who will stop at nothing in the defence of the foundations of bourgeois society, consists of the left-overs of bourgeois theories of the nineteenth century and primarily of its first half. At the other pole stands the small minority of communists. The British working class will achieve victory only under the leadership of the Bolshevik party. Today it is still walking in toddler's shoes. But it is growing and can grow up rapidly.

Between these two extreme groupings there stretches, as between two shores, an innumerable quantity of shades and tendencies which, though having no future in themselves, do prepare it. The 'theoreticians' and 'politicians' of this broad middle tendency are recruited from eclectics, sentimentalists, hysterical philanthropists, and, generally, muddlers of every type. For some, eclecticism is a complete life's vocation, while for others, a stage of development. The opposition movement headed by the lefts, semi-lefts and the extreme lefts reflects a profound social shift in the masses. The woolliness of the British 'lefts' together with their theoretical formlessness, and their political indecision, not to say cowardice, makes the clique of MacDonald, Webb, and Snowden master of the situation, which in turn is impossible without Thomas. If the bosses of the British Labour Party form a bridle placed upon the working class then Thomas is the buckle into which the bourgeoisie inserts the reins.

The present stage in the development of the British proletariat, where its overwhelming majority responds sympathetically to the speeches of the 'lefts' and supports MacDonald and Thomas in power is not of course accidental. And it is impossible to leap over this stage. The path of the Communist Party, as the future great party of the masses, lies not only through an irreconcilable struggle against capital's special agency in the shape of the Thomas-MacDonald clique but also through the systematic unmasking of the left muddleheads by means of whom alone MacDonald and Thomas can maintain their positions. This is our justification for paying attention to the 'left' critic.

It goes without saying that our critic accuses our pamphlet of rectilinearity, a mechanical posing of the question, a simplification of reality, and so on and so forth. "Running through his [i.e., my] book is the conviction that the decline of Britain will proceed for another four to five years [?!] before it will bring on serious internal complications." While in the opinion of the critic the next twelve months will form the peak of the crisis after which "subsequent development over the coming decade [?!] will take place without major difficulties". In this way, our critic first ascribes to me a firm prediction with regard to the sharpening of the crisis over four to five years, and then counterposes to this an even more firm prediction which divides the coming period of British history into two periods: twelve months of sharpening crisis and ten years of peaceful prosperity.

In the letter there are not, unfortunately, any economic arguments. In order to give the prophecy concerning a year of crisis and a secure decade any economic weight, it has to be allowed that the writer is linking his prognosis with the present acute financial difficulties which flow from the return to the gold standard and the regulation of the debt question. The economic crisis is apparently reduced by the writer to a deflationary crisis, and for this reason he assigns to it such a brief period. It is quite probable that after the most grave financial and credit difficulties have been overcome a certain relaxation of the money market will in fact ensue, and consequently likewise in commercial and industrial activity. But a general prognosis cannot be based upon fluctuations of this sort which have essentially a secondary nature. And in any case the prediction of a prosperous decade is derived from absolutely nothing. Britain's fundamental difficulties are rooted in, on the one hand, the regrouping and relative movement of world economic and political forces, and on the other in the inner conservatism of British industry.

The immeasurable industrial and financial preponderance of the United States of America over Britain is a fact whose importance in the future can only grow. There are not nor cannot be any circumstances which can mitigate the mortal consequences which arise for Britain from the unparalleled superiority of America.

The development of modern technology, and in particular the growing importance of electrification, is aimed directly against the coal industry and obliquely against all of the generally extremely conservative British industry which is based largely upon coal.

The growth of the industrial and political self-sufficiency of Canada, Australia, and South America, which revealed its full proportions after the war, is inflicting continually fresh blows upon the metropolis. The dominions are, for Britain, turning from sources of enrichment into sources of economic deficit.

The national movement in India, Egypt, and in all the East is directed first and foremost against British imperialism. There are hardly any grounds to expect that this movement will begin to weaken "in twelve months".

The existence of the Soviet Union – and in this one can agree with British Conservative and Liberal politicians – contains within itself considerable economic and political difficulties for Great Britain. There are here once again no grounds for thinking that these difficulties will diminish in twelve months.

If the so-called pacification of Europe continues it will entail the rebirth and strengthening of German competition. And if pacification is succeeded by a military or a revolutionary crisis this too will strike at the economy of Great Britain.

The coming period will therefore create even more severe conditions for British capital and thereby the question of power will stand out before the proletariat with still greater sharpness. I did not set any time scale. The only remark in my book in this regard stated that the revolutionary development of the British working class will be measured in quinquennia rather than decades. It is clear that by this I did not mean that a social overturn would take place "in four years" (although I do not consider even this excluded). My point was that the prospects of revolutionary development should be reckoned not over a number of decades, not on sons and grandsons, but on the generation living now.

At this point I am obliged to include an extensive quotation from the 'left' critic's letter:

Trotsky speaks nearly all the time about decades. But can you speak of decades when applied to the economic or even to the political situation? I think not in any instance. It is impossible, as Trotsky himself has previously pointed out, to assign and fix an exact date when the explosion of the revolution will begin, and although he had in mind more the impossibility of indicating the day [?] I consider it to be impossible to predict even the year [?]. A revolution depends above all upon economic factors and *at the present time there are an endless number of economic factors which may prove to favour or oppose a revolution in Britain.* A revolution could have flared up on 1 August 1925 as a result of the crisis in the coal industry. A revolution may break out with the renewal of the crisis next May. A revolution may be accelerated by the Far Eastern crisis, war, the economic collapse of other countries, the short-sightedness of a few industrialists at home, the inability of the government to solve the unemployment problem, a crisis in other branches of industry besides coal, and also by socialist propaganda among workers which elevates their demands and hopes. *Each of these possibilities is highly probable in the conditions of the present day and not a single one of them can be predicted even to the month.* The present day is characterised by extreme economic and consequently political instability; one move can ruin the whole game but on the other hand the existing system can be artificially maintained for many years more. Thus the British revolution, if you understand a political revolution by that, is marked by uncertainty...

The confusion in these lines is absolutely unimaginable, and yet it is not a personal confusion, but on the contrary it is deeply typical. It is the confusion of the people who 'speaking generally' recognise the revolution, but who fear it to the marrow of their bones and who are ready to adopt any theoretical justification for their political fear.

Indeed, let us take a closer look at the writer's line of argument. He is knocking at an open door when he proves that the tempo of development of the revolution and consequently its date depend on the interaction of numerous factors and circumstances of both an accelerating and a retarding effect. Hence he draws the conclusion indisputable in itself of the impossibility of predicting the timing of the revolution. But he contrives to formulate this most elementary thought thus:

Trotsky considers it impossible to predict the day of the revolution but he, the sage critic, considers it impossible to predict even the year. This contraposition appears to be completely implausible by its childishness. It may even seem that it does not deserve an answer at all. But as a matter of fact how many 'extreme lefts' are there who have not thought over, even in the rough, the most elementary problems of the revolution and for whom the very fact of reflections about its day and year represent a huge step forward, similar for example to the transition from total illiteracy to the muddled reading of individual syllables?

If indeed I had considered it impossible to determine in advance the day (?!) of the revolution then I would have probably attempted to determine the week, month, or the year. But you see I did not make such an attempt. I merely indicated that the social development of Britain had entered a revolutionary phase. At the end of the last century one could speak of a revolution in Britain only within the context of the most general foresight. In the years immediately preceding the imperialist war one could already point with certainty to a number of symptoms which evidenced the approach of a turning point. After the war this turn, and in the event a sharp one, set in. *In the past the British bourgeoisie had, by oppressing the toilers and plundering the colonies, led the nation on the path of material growth and thus guaranteed its rule. Today the bourgeois regime is not only incapable of leading the British nation forward but neither can it maintain for it the level already achieved.* The British working class is beating against the contradictions of capitalist decline. There is not a single question of economic life: the nationalisation of the mines, and the railways, the fight against unemployment, free trade or protectionism, housing, and so on which does not lead directly to the question of power. Here is the social-historical foundation of a revolutionary situation. Of course, it is a question of the struggle of living historical forces and not of an automatic accumulation of arithmetical quantities. And this alone makes impossible a passive prediction of the stages of the process and timing of the denouement. A finger must be kept on the pulse of the British economy and politics, and, while not omitting overall perspectives for a moment, one must attentively follow all the partial fluctuations, the flows and the ebbs, and determine their place in the process of the capitalist decline. Only upon the basis of such a general orientation can the revolutionary party conduct its policy, the flexibility of which is expressed by the fact that it *does* take partial fluctuations into account but in no way loses sight of the basic line of development.

My 'left' critic has evidently heard something – in quite another connection – about the determination of the "day" of the revolution, and has not grasped that then we were referring to the moment of armed insurrection placed on the order of the day by the revolution. Here are two questions which, although interlinked, are quite distinct.

In the one case it is a question of a historically based prognosis and the general strategic line flowing from this; in the other, of a tactical plan which presupposes a more or less exact determination of a place and time. It would not enter anyone's head – except perhaps that of the British Attorney-General – to say that in Britain at the present moment armed uprising is on the order of the day, and that fixing its plan and thus its date is a practical task. And yet only in this connection could we speak of the day or of days. In Germany in the autumn of 1923 matters stood in just this way. Today in Britain the question is not one of assigning a 'day' for the revolution – we are a long way from this! – but in clearly understanding that the whole objective situation is bringing this 'day' closer and into the ambit of the educational and preparatory work of the party of the proletariat, and at the same time creating conditions for its rapid revolutionary formation.

In his second letter, the same critic brings to the aid of his scepticism about dates (in fact scepticism about revolution) still more unexpected arguments. "The domain of economics", he argues, "is, practically sneaking, limitless [...] new inventions, regrouping of capitalist forces [...] the other side also recognises the danger. [...] America too may take measures against an impending collapse of Britain. In a word", the critic concludes, "the possibilities are very many and Trotsky has by no means exhausted them all." Our 'left' has need of all possibilities except one: that of revolution. While playing hide-and-seek with reality he is ready to seize hold of any fantasy. In what sense for example can "new inventions" alter the social conditions of the development of Great Britain? Since the time of Marx there have been plenty of inventions through which the effect of Marx's law of the concentration of capital and the sharpening of class contradictions has not weakened, but on the contrary has become stronger. New inventions will in the future also provide advantages to the more powerful, i.e., not to Great Britain but to the United States. That the "other side", that is the bourgeoisie, is aware of the danger and will fight against it by all means is beyond question. But just this is the most important prerequisite for revolution. To hope for a saving hand from America is in the end completely preposterous. It is more than probable that, in the event of a civil war in Britain, America will attempt to assist the bourgeoisie, but this merely signifies that the British proletariat will have to seek allies beyond its frontiers too. We think that it will find them. Hence it follows that a British revolution will inevitably acquire an international scale. We least of all intend to dispute this. But our critic means something else. He expresses the hope that America will so relieve the existence of the British bourgeoisie that it can assist it to avoid revolution altogether. It is hard to think of a better one than that! Each new day testifies that American capital forms a historical battering ram which intentionally or unintentionally is dealing the most crushing blows to Britain's world position and internal stability. This however does not in the least prevent our 'left' from hoping that American capital will kindly squeeze up to help British capital. For a start he must evidently expect that America will relinquish the discharge of the British debt; that she will hand over to the British Treasury the $300 million which form her reserve of British currency without compensation; that she will support Great Britain's policy in China; that perhaps she will also hand over to the British Navy a few new cruisers and sell back her Canadian shares to British firms at a discount of 50 per cent. He must, in a word, expect that the Washington government will put the management of the affairs of state into the hands of the ARA[2] having picked for this the most philanthropic Quakers.

---

2 The American Relief Administration, which as an official body ostensibly provided medical aid and civilian supplies for areas under famine and epidemic primarily in central and eastern Europe at the end of the First World War. It also sent aid to White-held areas of Russia if not to the White armies themselves.

People who are capable of consoling themselves with nonsense of this sort must not lay claim to the leadership of the British proletariat!

* * *

From *Pravda*, No. 60, 14 March 1926.

Brailsford and Marxism[3]

The London edition of *Where is Britain Going?* has appeared with an unexpected foreword by Brailsford, the former bourgeois radical who after the war joined the Independent Labour Party and now edits its organ. Mr. Brailsford despite his socialist sympathies has not ceased to be a radical. And as moderate liberals stand at the head of the Independent Labour Party, Brailsford has ended up on the left wing.

The fact that it is not in backward China, nor even in Japan, where radical bourgeois publishers consider it still useful to issue books by Russian communists, but in Britain, with her crying social contradictions, that the appearance of a book by a communist with a patronising foreword by a member of MacDonald's party is possible, serves in the eyes of any Marxist as evidence of the inconceivable backwardness of British political ideology as compared with her material relations. In this judgement which needs no proof there is at once a condemnation of this sort of unexpected literary bloc. We do need a unity of front with the working masses. But the unity or a semi-unity of a literary front with Brailsford signifies but an aggravation of that ideological chaos in which the British labour movement is rich enough as it is.

There is however no mistake here on Brailsford's part. His historical mission consists in 'correcting' Thomas and MacDonald, in creating a safety valve for the discontent of the masses, in blurring the edges, and in dissolving cogent thought into a formless 'leftism'. It is of political advantage to Brailsford, whose intentions we do not in the least suspect (though we do bear firmly in mind that it is from reformist intentions that highways to hell are built), to appear within the same covers as us. The working masses of Britain are immeasurably more to the left than Brailsford. By 'fraternising' with Moscow communists, Brailsford camouflages his adherence to a party which expels British communists.

But we have different tasks. We do not want masks. Our first obligation is that of destroying ideological masks. The British working masses are

---

3 See p. 475 for Brailsford's introduction.

immeasurably more to the left than Brailsford but they have not yet found the appropriate language for their own inclinations. The rubbish of the past still separates the leftward moving masses from the programme of communism with a thick layer. So much more impermissible is it then to add even a shred to this garbage. In fighting for the interests of the miners, the communists are prepared to take several steps alongside Mr. Brailsford in this struggle. But with no ideological blocs, and no united front in the field of theory and programme! And this very Brailsford himself puts it thus with regard to the American edition of our book: "We are separated from these people by a gulf." Correct, correct, and three times correct! But from the standpoint of Marxism there is nothing more criminal than to throw literary olive branches across this political gulf: the worker who is deceived by the camouflage will set his foot down and fall through.

For Mr. Brailsford camouflage is necessary. He makes use of a revolutionary book in order to fight against revolution. Brailsford, a defender of democratic illusions and parliamentary fetishes, is saying in his foreword: "Just look, in our British democracy we can publish a Bolshevik book without fear, thereby demonstrating the breadth and power of democracy." Moreover, by his little demonstration Brailsford would like to gloss over the, for him, inconvenient outcome of the recent trial of the communists. Brailsford himself openly admits this. The sentencing of the British communists now, when the revolution is taking shape only at a remote distance, is an immeasurably sharper and more convincing refutation of democratic illusions than all our books and pamphlets. Brailsford understands this. In fighting for the preservation of democratic illusions he "greets" the appearance of our book in these words: "If it may come freely from the Press in public, if it may be discussed [...] then the nightmare of this trial is dissipated." By sparing democratic illusions at such a cheap price Brailsford wants to give the British proletariat the idea that once a revolutionary book accompanied by an appropriate dose of antidote in the shape of a pacifist foreword appears on the British book market, it is thereby proven that the British bourgeoisie will tamely bow its head when the banks, land, mines, factories, and shipyards start to be taken 'democratically' away from them. In other words, Brailsford unceremoniously admonishes our book with concepts directly contrary to its aim, sense, spirit, and letter.

It is not surprising if Brailsford reproachfully describes the "Russian methods" of polemic as ruthless and hopes that they will produce in the

British reader quite a different impression from that intended. Let us wait for the "impressions". Readers vary. Methods of polemic flow from the essence of the politics. "Ruthlessness" is caused by the necessity to reveal the reality behind a deliberate falsehood. Nowhere in Europe does canonised hypocrisy – 'cant' – play such a role as in Great Britain. Different political groupings, and even the most 'extreme' of them, are, when fighting against each other, accustomed not to touch upon certain questions or to call certain things by their proper names. The reason is that from time immemorial the political struggle has been waged inside the ranks of the possessing classes who have never forgotten that a third party is listening in. The system of conventions, implications, and reservations has over the ages worked itself downwards and today finds its most reactionary expression in the liberal Labour Party, including its radical opposition wing. Here it is not a question of literary style but of politics. Our polemic repels Brailsford because it lays the class contradictions absolutely bare. It is quite true that in those enlightened readers who have been brought up in the parliamentary tradition of political cant this polemic will produce not sympathy but annoyance. But Brailsford notwithstanding this is just the effect that the author, rightly, intends. It is also quite true that politicians with such an education still form a dense stratum between the working class and the programme of communism. Nevertheless, in Britain too, class realities are more powerful than traditional hypocrisy. Once aroused, British workers, blazing themselves a trail through the thicket of inherited prejudices – both those of Baldwin and Brailsford – will find in our polemic a particle of their own struggle. And this again will be the effect that we intend.

Brailsford's foreword represents an intermixture of immoderate praise and moderate censure. The praise relates to what is secondary, the form of the book. The censure is directed against the essence. The immoderate nature on the praise is to lend extra weight to the careful attacks on Bolshevism. Brailsford operates expediently. He fulfils his assignment. He is interested in camouflage. But we need complete clarity. That is why we reject equally both Brailsford's praises and his censure.

Brailsford operates expediently but is utterly impotent all the same. But then this is not his fault. He cannot leap out of the historical task of centrism: blurring realities in order to sustain illusions. We have seen how ridiculously Brailsford dealt with the lessons of the trial of the communists. This same impotence lies at the root of the whole of his appraisal of our book. On the one hand, for him it emerges that the book is based on the knowledge of facts and an understanding of the logic of their development. On the other, it turns out that the author of the book is "a man of another world" who is incapable of comprehending either the nature of British Protestantism or the force of parliamentary traditions. It is not only in parliament, but also in the Church, trade unions, and even clubs, Brailsford tries to convince us, that respect for the majority has been instilled into generations of British people. "What does a Russian know about this and how can he assess the force of traditions in our ancient civilisation?" Brailsford's arrogant helplessness lies in his method: he does not understand the material basis of social development as the decisive factor. He halts before traditions, before the ideological residue of old struggles and thinks that this crust is an eternal one. He does not know the simplest laws of the dependence of ideology upon class foundations. Arguing with him on these matters is as good as trying to convince the inventor of *perpetuum mobile* who denies the law of the conservation of energy. It is plain to any literate Marxist that the more firmly the conservative forms of British society have ossified, the more catastrophically new eruptions of the social volcano will explode the crust of the old traditions and institutions.

The ideas and prejudices which have been handed down from generation to generation become a factor of great historical force. This 'independent' force of prejudices condensed by history is only too evident in Brailsford himself. But material facts are nevertheless stronger than their reflection in ideas and traditions. And of this it is not hard to be convinced at the present day, faced with the most instructive picture that we have of British liberalism in its death throes. Can one find another tradition more powerful than this? At its source, liberalism was connected with the first Protestant movements and consequently with the revolution of the seventeenth century, which opened the history of the new England. And yet this mighty liberalism is before our eyes warping and crumbling like a sheet of parchment tossed on to a hot hearth. Living facts are more powerful than dead ideas. The decline of the middle classes in Britain and the decline of British capitalism in the world are material facts which are mercilessly settling the fate of British liberalism. The figure of the agrarian reformer Gracchus Lloyd George who in the evening denies what he said in the morning in itself forms a marvellous mockery of liberal traditions.

We heard from Brailsford that for "a man of another world" an understanding of "how deeply the *instinct of submission to the will of the majority* is stamped in the consciousness of the British people" is unattainable. But it is a remarkable thing that when Brailsford descends from the heights of doctrinairism into

the sphere of living political facts he himself unexpectedly reveals at times
the mystery of "submission to the will of the majority". Thus in tracing the
course of the last Liberal conference which against all its "traditions", and
more important, against its own wishes, adopted (in half-measure) Lloyd
George's charlatan programme of land nationalisation, Brailsford wrote in the
New Leader of 26 February: "The payment of expenses from a central fund (in
Lloyd George's hands) and the provision of a gratuitous luncheon apparently
created the right sort of majority." Luncheons *created* a majority! From these
realistic words it is evident that the democratic instinct of submission to the
majority instilled by a number of British generations and unattainable to men
"of another world" every so often requires in addition free roast beef and other
auxiliary resources to display its omnipotence. Brailsford could scarcely write
better words than these. Our idealist has here collided with the thing that
usually spoils metaphysical schema: a slice of reality. It has been long known
that German Kantian professors in the course of devising an eternal morality
stumbled on such obstacles as inadequate wages, intrigues of their colleagues,
or a cantankerous aunt. The democratic socialist Brailsford has slipped up,
far more dangerously than he might imagine, on roast beef. Of course, we
people of another world are incapable of appreciating the noble worship
by all British people of parliamentary methods. But then why embarrass us
with the report that inside the Liberal Party, the creator of parliamentarism,
a majority is achieved by means of hand outs and a series of lunches, free,
but we must suppose, quite copious. A majority achieved in this way is very
like a fraudulent or falsified majority. But here of course at the moment,
only the struggle for parliamentary seats and portfolios is at stake. What will
happen when the issue is posed point blank: who should have state power:
the bourgeoisie or the proletariat? And who shall have the property: the
capitalist or the people? If through considerations of parliamentary careerism
the leaders of the Liberal Party successfully set bribery and falsification into
motion, then at what violent means and at what crimes would the ruling
classes stop when the whole of their historical fate is on the order of the day?
I very much fear that if, out of the two of us, one is a man of another world
who does not understand the most important thing about British politics,
then it is Mr. Brailsford. He is a man of another era. The new era is ours.

———

In his foreword Brailsford does not miss the opportunity to take up a defence
of religion. It is curious that in doing so he calls himself an agnostic. In Britain

this word tends to be used as a polite, drawing-room, emasculated name for an atheist. More often it characterises a semi-atheism which is unsure of itself, i.e., the variety of idealism which on the question of God abstains from voting, to put it in parliamentary language. And so we see here once again the force of cant, convention, the half-truth, the half-lie, and philosophical hypocrisy. Implying his atheism and calling himself an agnostic, Brailsford here takes on the defence of religion. These are the ambiguous customs which British revolutionaries will have to expel from the ranks of the labour movement. Enough of hide-and-seek, call things by their names!

Brailsford defends religion by denying its class character. Not a single Russian is able, don't you see, to understand what British religion is, with its "traditions of free discussion, its democratic form, and its relative freedom from any other-worldliness", and so on and so forth. There is not a single democratic priest who could pronounce a more apologetic speech in defence of religious dope than does our "agnostic". His evidence in support of the Church must acquire the greater weight since he declares himself to be an unbeliever. Here is duplicity and falsehood at every step. While attempting to refute the bourgeois character of Protestantism, Brailsford accusingly asks whether Trotsky has ever been to a Non-Conformist chapel in a mining area, whether he has read Bunyan, and whether he has ever taken a look at the revolutionary history of the Anabaptists and the men of the Fifth Monarchy. I must admit that I have not been in a miners' Non-Conformist chapel and that I am very insufficiently familiar with the historical facts of which Brailsford speaks. I promise to visit a mining area and its chapel as soon as Brailsford's party takes power and permits me, in accordance with the principles of democracy, unimpeded passage through the possessions of His Majesty. I will attempt to acquaint myself with Bunyan and the history of the Anabaptists in the Fifth Monarchy before that date. But Brailsford is cruelly mistaken if he thinks that the facts and circumstances he has enumerated can alter a general evaluation of religion, and in particular of Protestantism. I once visited, together with Lenin and Krupskaya a 'free church' in London where we heard socialist speeches interspersed with psalms. The preacher was a printer who had just returned from Australia. He spoke about the social revolution. The congregation begged God in the psalms that he establish such an order where there would be neither poor nor rich. Such was my first practical acquaintance with the British labour movement nearly a quarter of a century ago (1902). What role, I asked myself at the time, does a psalm play in connection with a revolutionary speech? That of a safety-valve. Concentrated vapours of discontent issued forth beneath the dome of the Church and rose into the sky. This is the basic function of the Church in class society.

To be sure, different Churches fulfil this task in different ways. The Orthodox Church, while not having overcome primitive peasant mythology as time went on, turned into an external bureaucratic apparatus existing alongside the apparatus of tsarism. The priest walked hand in hand with the constable and any development of dissent was met with repression. It was for this reason that the roots of the Orthodox Church proved to be so weak in the popular consciousness, and especially in the industrial centres. In shaking off the bureaucratic ecclesiastical apparatus, the Russian worker in his overwhelming mass and the peasant milkmaid together with him, shook off religious thinking altogether. Protestantism is quite another matter: it came to its feet as the banner of the bourgeoisie and the small people of the towns and the countryside against the crowns of the privileged and courtly, and against the cavaliers and the bishops. The genesis and development of Protestantism is so closely bound up with the development of urban culture and the struggle of the bourgeoisie for a firmer and more stable position in society that there is really no need to prove it. The bourgeoisie could not of course fight successfully for, and then retain power if it had not made its banner to some degree or other the banner of lower social layers, that is, the artisans, peasants, and workers. In its struggle against the nobility the bourgeoisie tied the lower layers very firmly to itself using the Protestant religion. Of course, the Scottish woodcutter would not put into his psalms the same subjective content as the respectable Mr. Dombey, or his honourable grandson sitting in the House of Commons either to the right or to the left of Mr. MacDonald. And just the same applies to liberalism too. The liberal workers, not the trade union bureaucrats but the proletariat, understood the liberal programme completely differently from Gladstone. They introduced a class instinct into their liberalism, but a helpless one. But will Brailsford dispute on these grounds that liberalism was the programme of the middle and small merchant, the industrial bourgeoisie, and the bourgeois intelligentsia socially rising upwards?

It is true, and this is what Brailsford wants to adduce, that many petty-bourgeois radicals and opponents of the class struggle were inclined towards atheism while the pioneers of trade unionism stood in equal measure for Christianity and for the class struggle. But there is no contradiction here with what has been said above. Marxism in no way teaches that every man receives his share of religious and philosophical convictions depending upon the scale of his income or his wages. The question is more complex. Religious, as indeed any other, ideas being born out of the soil of the material conditions of life and above all the soil of class contradictions, only gradually clear themselves a way and then live on by force of conservatism longer than the needs which gave birth to them, and disappear completely only under the effect of serious social shocks and crises. The petty-bourgeois British radicals from the utilitarian and Owenite schools could be militant atheists only as long as they seriously believed that they possessed the painless means of solving all social problems. But in proportion as class contradictions sharpened, militant radicalism disappeared or moved over into the Labour Party bringing into it its threadbare idealistic arrogance and its political impotence. The organisers of the trade unions who had been thrown up by workers' strikes could not renounce the basis of their activity and the source of their influence, that is the class struggle. But they at the same time remained within the narrow limits of trade unionism, not leading the struggle to the necessary revolutionary conclusions, and this allowed and still does allow them to reconcile trade unionism with Christianity, i.e., with a discipline which imposes upon the proletariat the faith and morality of another class.

It is completely indisputable that the revolution will find a good share of the Welsh miners still in the grip of religious prejudices. It cannot be doubted that despite this the miners will do their job. From some prejudices they will free themselves in the heat of the struggle while from others only after victory. But we categorically deny that the Welsh miners and the British proletariat in general can be shown the correct path by people who have not separated themselves from infantile nonsense, do not understand the structure of human society, do not grasp its dynamics, do not understand the role of religion in it, and to one degree or another are ready to subordinate their actions to the precepts of ecclesiastical morality which unites oppressors with oppressed. Such leaders are unreliable. For their part the working class can expect capitulation or direct treachery – justified by the Sermon on the Mount – at the most crucial hour.

The traditional force of British Protestantism is clear to us. Brailsford depicts the matter in vain, as if he were judging Protestantism by orthodoxy. Nonsense. We Marxists are accustomed to taking historical phenomena in their social context, in their concrete aspect, and to judge them not by their names but by that content which living, that is class-divided, society imparts to them. The traditional power of Protestantism is great but not limitless. In its very essence, that is as a religious and not political teaching, Protestantism is more elastic than liberalism, which represents its younger brother. But the elasticity of Protestantism has its limits. The profound turn in the fate of Britain predetermines them. All her national traditions will undergo a test. What was shaped by centuries will be destroyed in the course of years. The revolution will bring a process of verification based on inexorable facts which will reach into those last refuges of consciousness where the inherited religious prejudices are concealed. Our task is to assist this cleansing operation and not to block its way, as the ambiguous agnostics do by implying their atheism only to defend religion.

We can see in this way that on the most important questions on which the historical life and death of the proletariat depend, we and Brailsford stand on different sides of the ideological barricade. That is why our appearance before the British reader within the same covers forms the crudest misunderstanding. With the present article I am correcting this misunderstanding as well as I can.

* * *

From *Derites Kak Cherti*, May 1926, Crimea, *en route*
(A reply to *The New Leader*, 26 February 1926,
'Trotsky on Our Sins' by Bertrand Russell).

Once More on Pacifism and Revolution –
A Reply to Bertrand Russell[4]

The majority of British critics of my book see its chief failing in that the author is not British and that consequently he is incapable of understanding British psychology, British traditions, and so on. It must however be said that the more the British Fabians clutch at this argument the less they appear to be British: in the final analysis they add very little to the arguments which we have heard more than enough of from the Russian Mensheviks and before that, from the populists.

Today, when we are victorious, British and European socialists in general are inclined to permit us to be left alone in view of the peculiarities of our country and its national culture. They want in this way to erect an essentially ideological barrier along the same frontiers where Lloyd George, Churchill, Clemenceau, and others attempted to set up a material barbed wire blockade. "It may be all right for Russians" – so the 'lefts' say to all intents, "but just let the Russians dare to cross the Russian frontiers with their experience and

---

4   See p. 479 for Russell's article.

their conclusions." The peculiarities of the British character are introduced as a philosophical justification for the theory of Bolshevik 'non-intervention'.

Fabian and other critics do not know that we have been well tempered by all our past against arguments of this brand. But the irony in it is that while the Fabians are agreed nowadays, that is after our victory, to recognise Bolshevism, that is Marxism in action, as corresponding to the national peculiarities of Russia, the old traditional Russian ideology, and not just that of the government but that of the opposition, invariably regarded Marxism as a creature of western culture and would proclaim its total incompatibility with the peculiarities of Russian national development.

My generation can still remember how the overwhelming majority of the Russian press declared the Russian Marxists to be ideological aliens who were trying in vain to transplant Britain's historical experience on to Russian soil. On every pretext we were reminded that Marx created his theory of economic development in the British Museum and through observing British capitalism and its contradictions. How could the lessons of British capitalism have any relevance to Russia with its enormous 'peculiarities', its predominantly peasant population, its patriarchal traditions, its village commune, and its Orthodox Church? Thus spoke the Russian reactionaries and the Russian populists with the appropriate right and left variations. And it was not only before and during the war but even after the February revolution of 1917, when Mr. Henderson came over to Russia to try to persuade the Russian workers to continue the war against Germany, that there was scarcely a single 'socialist' in the world, right or left, who considered that Bolshevism suited the national peculiarities of Russia. No, at that time we were regarded at best as maniacs. Our own Fabians, the Russian Mensheviks and the so-called Social-Revolutionaries, brought against us all the same arguments which today we hear from Lansbury, Brailsford, Russell, and their more right-wing colleagues, presented as the conquests of a pure British philosophy. In the final count, resorting to the question of national peculiarities forms the last tool of any ideological reaction in shielding itself from the revolutionary demands of the time. By this we do not at all mean that there do not exist national peculiarities or that they are of no substance. The residue of the past represents in institutions and customs a great conservative force. But in the final analysis the living forces of the present decide. The position of the British coal industry on the world market cannot be rectified by any recourse to national traditions. At the same time, the role of the coal industry in the fate of Great Britain is immeasurably more important than all the devices and ceremonies of parliamentarism. The House of Commons rests upon coal and not the converse. The conservatism of British forms of property and the means of production comprise just that national 'peculiarity' which is capable only of deepening the social crisis together with all the revolutionary contradictions which flow from it.

Mr. Bertrand Russell, a philosopher of mathematicians, a mathematician of philosophers, an aristocrat of democracy, and a dilettante of socialism, has considered it his duty to set his hand also, and not for the first time, to the destruction of those pernicious ideas *which emanate* from Moscow and are inimical to the Anglo-Saxon spirit.

On the question of religion, Russell takes a step forward from Brailsford. He admits that in present conditions any organised religion must become a reactionary force (this does not stop Russell from leaving a loop-hole on this point: personal religion, well that's another matter). Russell approves of our arguments concerning the fact that even the most economic king cannot become a component part of a socialist society. Russell refuses to regard the parliamentary road as a guaranteed road to socialism. But all these admissions as well as certain others are made by Russell only in order to reveal more sharply the anti-revolutionary character of his thinking on the question of the future road of the British working class. Russell declares the proletarian revolution in Britain not only to be dangerous but also disastrous. Britain is too dependent upon overseas countries and above all upon the United States of America. If cut off by a blockade from the outside world, the British Isles would not be able to feed a population of more than 20 million. "While [such a reduction of] the population was being effected by starvation", Russell taunts us, "Trotsky's sympathy would be a great comfort. But until Soviet Russia can place a fleet in the Atlantic stronger than that of America it is not clear what we should gain by sympathy, however enthusiastic." These strategic considerations are most interesting from the lips of a pacifist. We find that in the first place the fate of British pacifism, as far as it attempts to link itself to the working class, depends upon the strength of the American Navy. We find in the second place that it would not be at all a bad thing if British pacifism could be protected from its enemies by a Soviet navy of the necessary strength. Our worthy idealist disdainfully tosses aside an ideological sympathy which is not reinforced by sufficient quantities of shells and mines. But for us, however, it evidently more than suffices.

Russell's own sympathies for the October Revolution (which are however very much like antipathies) have not over the last few years provided us with any "comfort". But the sympathies of the British and European workers in general saved us. Of course Churchill caused us as much trouble as he could. Chamberlain is doing everything he can. But we would have been crushed long ago if the ruling classes of Great Britain and Europe had not been afraid to send their armed forces against us. Of course this safeguard is not an absolute one. But along with the antagonisms between the capitalist states it proved sufficient to protect us from intervention on a major scale during the most critical first years. And yet both before October and after October, our own Russells would assure us that we would be crushed by either the armies of Hohenzollern or the armies of the Entente.

They told us that the Russian proletariat, as the most backward and numerically small one, could take power into its hands only in the event of a victory of the world revolution. To make reference to the international revolution as a preliminary condition for the overthrow of the bourgeois state in one's own country represents a masked denial of revolution. For what is the international revolution? It is a chain – and not an even one either – of national revolutions within which each one feeds the others with its successes and, in turn, loses from the failures of the others. In 1923 when the revolutionary situation reached its sharpest point in Germany, the left Social-Democrats in their struggle against the communists argued the danger of military intervention by France and Poland. The German left Mensheviks were totally prepared, at least in words, to seize power in Germany under the condition of a preliminary victory of the proletariat in France. This Menshevik agitation was one of the factors *which paralysed* the revolutionary initiative of the German working class. In the event of a decisive sharpening of the political situation in France – and this is the way things are going – the French socialists will doubtless intimidate the French workers with the danger of a German *revanche* on the one hand and with that of a British blockade on the other. But who would have the slightest doubt that Leon Blum, Jean Longuet, and other heroes would agree to the conquest of power under the condition of a preliminary, and what is more, a complete victory of the working class of Great Britain and Germany? And the socialists of small states consider it to be doubly impossible to start a revolution at home as long as the bourgeoisie maintains power in the large states. The Mensheviks of the different countries toss the right to revolutionary initiative back and forth with about as much skill as performing seals at the circus toss burning torches from one to another.

Russell the pacifist considers it impossible to embark upon a revolution in Britain as long as the United States retains its powerful navy. It would of course be pretty good if the American proletariat seized power in its hands in the near future and with it the navy. But then wouldn't the American Russells tell us that proletarian power in the United States would inevitably be threatened by the combined navies of Great Britain and Japan? True, this argument could be ignored if the proletarian revolution really was on the immediate agenda in the United States. Unfortunately it is not yet. Great Britain from every point of view is immeasurably closer to revolution than North America. Consequently, we have to reckon with the fact that the struggle of the proletariat for power in Britain will take place in the face of the still unshaken rule of the American bourgeoisie. So what can we do? Russell indicates, more in irony it is true, a solution to the problem: he proposes to the Soviet Union that it creates a navy capable of guaranteeing free access to proletarian Britain. Unfortunately, the poverty and technological backwardness of our country do not permit us at the moment to fulfil such a programme. Of course, it would be more advantageous, economical, and simpler if the proletarian revolution commenced in the United States and extended through Britain, and from the West eastwards across Europe and Asia. But the actual course of development is not like this: the chain of capitalist rule like any other chain breaks at its weakest link. After tsarist Russia, Austro-Hungary, Germany and Italy came closest of all to the proletarian revolution. For France and Britain the day of reckoning for the war is merely still to come. Europe as a whole is immeasurably closer to the revolutionary overthrow than the United States. And this has to be taken into account.

Of course, the situation of a blockaded Britain would, in view of its vital dependence upon imports and exports, be more grave than the situation of any other European country. However the resources of a revolutionary Britain in its struggle against hardships would also be extremely great.

While referring to the American Navy, Russell for some reason forgets about the British Navy. In whose hands would it be? If it remained in the hands of the bourgeoisie then the closer and more acute danger to threaten the proletarian revolution would be not from the American Navy but from the British Navy. But if the latter ended up in the hands of the proletariat then the position would at once become immeasurably more favourable than Russell depicts it. From our critic there is not a word on this question of no little importance. But we must dwell on it in somewhat more detail.

The major peculiarities of British development have been determined by its island position. The role of the British Navy in the fate of the country has formed the sharpest expression of these peculiarities. At the same time, the British socialists who reproach us for ignorance or incomprehension of the hidden and imponderable peculiarities of the British spirit forget without exception when discussing the question of the proletarian revolution such an extremely ponderable quantity as the British Navy. Russell, while ironically appealing for assistance from the Soviet navy, says nothing about the navy which continued to be reinforced with light cruisers when the party of MacDonald, Brailsford, and Lansbury was in power.

Here we have a question of conquering power in a country where the proletariat constitutes the preponderant majority of the population. The political prerequisite for success must only be the aspiration of the proletariat itself to master power at any cost, that is, at the price of any sacrifice. Only a revolutionary party is capable of uniting the working masses in this aspiration. The second prerequisite of success is a clear understanding of the paths and methods of struggle. Only a workers' party freed from pacifist cataracts in its eyes can see itself and explain to the proletariat that the real transfer of power from the hands of one class into the hands of another depends in immeasurably greater degree upon the British army and the British Navy than upon parliament. The struggle of the proletariat for power must therefore be its struggle for the navy. Sailors, not of course the admirals but the stokers, electricians and ratings, must be schooled to understand the tasks and aims of the working class. A road to them must be found across all obstacles. Only systematic, stubborn, and insistent preparatory work can create a situation where the bourgeoisie cannot rely upon the navy in the struggle against the proletariat. And without this condition it is senseless to talk about victory.

It is of course impossible to conceive the question as though in the first period of the revolution the navy will *en bloc* and in full combat order go over to the side of the proletariat. Matters will not proceed without deep internal unrest inside the navy itself. The history of all revolutions bears witness to this. Unrest in the navy connected with an overall renewal of the officer corps inevitably signifies a general weakening of a navy over a fairly long period. Once again, one cannot close one's eyes to this. But a period of crisis and an internal weakening of the navy will proceed more rapidly the more decisive the leading party of the proletariat, the more contacts it has in the navy during the preparatory period, the bolder it is during the period of the struggle, and the more clearly it shows to all oppressed people that it is capable of seizing power and retaining it. Pacifism only to a very insignificant extent affects the military machine of the ruling class. The best evidence of this is provided by Russell's own courageous but generally futile experience during the war. It resulted merely in a few thousand young people being put in prison on account of their 'conscience'. In the old tsarist army, members of sects and especially followers of Tolstoy frequently suffered persecution for this kind of passive anti-militarism. But they did not solve the problem of the overthrow of tsarism. And in Britain they did not and could not prevent the war being carried on until the end. Pacifism turns its face not so much towards the military organisation of the bourgeois state, as towards the working masses. Here its influence is absolutely pernicious. It paralyses the will of those who as it is suffer no shortage of it. It preaches the harmfulness of armaments to those who are, as it is, disarmed and represent the victims of class violence. Under the present conditions of British life when the problem is posed point-blank, Russell's pacifism is reactionary through and through.

Not so long ago, Lansbury, according to the newspapers, invoked British soldiers not to fire on strikers. Thousands of those present at the meeting of working men and women raised their hands to show their solidarity with this appeal which, it is true, hardly reconciles itself with MacDonald's policy and yet represents a certain step forward on the road to revolution. One must be very naive to think that Lansbury's appeal opens up the possibility of a peaceful, bloodless, pacifist solution to the problem of power. On the contrary, this appeal, inasmuch as it makes any headway, in practice will inevitably bring on the sharpest military conflicts. It cannot be imagined that all soldiers and all sailors will simultaneously refuse to fire on workers. In actual fact the revolution will drive a wedge into the army and navy; a rift will pass through every company and through the crew of every warship. One soldier will have firmly made his mind up not to fire even though it may cost him his life. A second will waver. A third will be prepared to fire on the one who refuses to fire. And in the early stage most numerous are those who waver. How was it with us in 1905 and 1917? The soldier or sailor who showed in practice his solidarity with the workers fell under the fire of an officer. In the next stage an officer would fall under the fire of soldiers inspired by the heroic example of their more advanced comrades. Such conflicts spread. A regiment in which revolutionary elements hold control stands against a regiment where the command of the old officer corps is maintained. At the same time the workers, finding support in the revolutionary regiments, arm themselves. In the navy it was no different. We would very much advise Russell and his sympathisers to see the Soviet film *The Battleship Potemkin* which shows quite graphically the mechanism of the revolution inside an armed mass of people. Even more important it would be to show this film to British workers and sailors. Let us hope that the Labour Party will do so when it comes to power.

The congenital bourgeois bigots and the civilised cannibals will of course speak with the greatest vexation of how we are striving to set brother against brother, soldier against officer, and so forth. The pacifists will echo them. They will once again not fail to remind us that we see everything in a bloody light because we do not know the peculiarities of Great Britain, and because we underestimate the beneficial influence of Christian morality upon the naval officers, the policemen, and Joynson-Hicks. But this cannot stop us. A revolutionary policy requires above all that we look facts openly in the face so as to foretell the course of their subsequent development. A revolutionary policy appears fantastic to philistines only because it is able to predict the day after next, while they do not dare to give a thought to the next day.

In conditions where the national organism as a whole can be saved not by conservative therapy but only by surgical intervention and amputating the malignant organ – that is, the class which has outlived itself – the pacifist sermons flow in essence from an attitude of complacent indifference. The highest degree of 'mercy' in such conditions demands the greatest firmness so as to reduce the time-span and minimise the pain. The more decisively the British proletariat sets its hand upon all means and implements of the British bourgeoisie, the less temptation the American bourgeoisie will have to intervene in the struggle. The more speedily and fully the proletarian power dominates the British Navy, the less opportunity the American Navy will have to destroy that power in Britain. We do not mean by this that military intervention by the transatlantic republic is excluded. On the contrary, it is very probable and within certain limits entirely inevitable. But the results of such an intervention will depend in enormous measure upon our own policy before and during the revolution.

To impose a total blockade of the British Isles, and above all their isolation from the European continent, the behaviour of the French navy will be of no little significance. Will the French bourgeoisie send its warships against the proletarian revolution in Britain? On this score we have had certain experiences. In 1918 Millerand sent French warships to the Black Sea against Soviet ports. The result is well known. The cruiser *Waldeck-Rousseau* raised the banner of mutiny. Neither did everything go well with the British in the Russian North. Revolution is highly infectious. And sailors are, more than anyone else, susceptible to revolutionary infection. At the time when the French sailors Marty[5] and Badin[6] mounted the uprising because they did not wish to go into action against the proletarian revolution in Russia, France seemed to be at the summit of her power. But today the period of reckoning for the war has begun for her too, no less than for Britain. To think that even in the event where in Britain the monarchy, landlords, bankers and industrialists have been thrown overboard the French bourgeoisie will retain the possibility of playing the part of the gendarme in the Atlantic Ocean or even just in the English Channel is to display a monstrous optimism on behalf of the bourgeoisie, and a shameful pessimism as regards the proletariat. Britain, that is her bourgeoisie, was not for nothing the ruler of the waves. The British revolution will set ripples in motion throughout the oceans. Its first result will be to upset the discipline of all navies. Who knows whether in these conditions the American naval commanders will have to abandon the idea of a tight naval blockade and to withdraw their vessels away from the European infection?

But in the end, even in America itself the navy is not the final decisive factor. The capitalist regime is more powerful in America than anywhere else. We know as well as Russell does the counter-revolutionary character of the American Federation of Labour[7] of which he reminds us. Just as the bourgeoisie of the United States has raised the power of capital to an unprecedented height, so the American Federation of Labour has brought the methods of conciliation to the lowest limit. But this does not at all mean that the American bourgeoisie is all-powerful. It is immeasurably more powerful against the European bourgeoisie than against the European proletariat. Under the lid of the American labour aristocracy, the most privileged of all the world's labour aristocracies, there slumber and ferment the revolutionary instincts and moods of the multi-racial working masses of North America. A revolution in the Anglo-Saxon country on the other side

---

5 André Marty (1886-1956) – French sailor who led the mutiny in the Black Sea fleet on 16 April 1919 when French units were operating in support of the Whites in Russia. Became a leading member of the French Communist Party.

6 A lesser-known associate of Marty in the leadership of the French sailors' uprising.

7 Founded in 1881 as the Federation of Organised Trades and Labour Unions, in 1886 it became the American Federation of Labour. Led by Samuel Gompers, the federation linked craft unions which preserved a wide degree of independence. The leaders were extremely patriotic and anti-revolutionary, basing themselves on the most skilled and conservative sections of American workers.

of the Atlantic will affect the proletariat of the United States more strongly than any other revolution previously. This still does not mean that the rule of the American bourgeoisie will be toppled the day after the conquest of power by the British proletariat. A series of serious economic, military, and political crises will be required before the kingdom of the dollar is toppled. The American bourgeoisie is itself today preparing these crises by investing its capital throughout the world and thereby tying its rule to the European chaos and to the powder magazines of the East. But the revolution in Britain will inevitably evoke a powerful reaction on the other side of the 'great water', both on the New York Stock Exchange and in the workers' ghettoes of Chicago. A change will immediately take place in the self-awareness of the bourgeoisie and the proletariat of the United States: the bourgeoisie will feel weaker and the working class stronger. And the self-awareness of classes is a major component element of the so-called balance of forces. Again, this does not mean that the American bankers and tycoons will be unable to make attempts with their navy to choke economically the revolution of the British proletariat. But such an attempt will in itself mean a further crisis in the internal regime of the United States. In the final count, in the very heart of every American warship, in the engine room, not only the revolutionary events in Great Britain but also the new moods produced by them in the proletariat of the United States will take their effect. Taken together all this does not signify that the proletarian revolution in Britain is not fraught with hardships and dangers. On the contrary, both the former and the latter are colossal. But they exist on both sides. And this is in fact what the essence of revolution consists of. The greater the place occupied by a given nation in the world, the more sweeping will be the forces of action and counteraction that the revolution awakens and releases. Our "sympathies" can in these conditions prove to be of some use.

Revolutions are not made in the order of the most advantageous sequence. Revolutions are not generally made at will. If one could rationally map out a revolutionary itinerary then it would probably avoid revolution altogether. But this is just the point, for revolution forms the expression of the impossibility of reconstructing class society by rational methods. Logical arguments, even if elevated by Russell to the status of mathematical formulae, are impotent against material interests. The ruling classes will sooner condemn all civilisation, including mathematics, to ruin rather than renounce their privileges. In the struggle between the miners and the coal owners of Great Britain, the coming revolution already wholly exists in embryo just as in the grain of corn the future stalk and ear exists in embryo. The irrational factors of human history operate most brutally of all through class contradictions. Over these irrational factors one cannot leap. Just as mathematics by working with irrational quantities arrives at completely realistic conclusions, so in politics one can rationalise, that is bring a social system into a reasonable order, only by clearly taking into account the irrational contradictions of society so as to overcome them finally – not by avoiding revolution, but through its agency.

We could essentially finish at this point. Russell's objections have given us an opportunity to examine additionally those sides of the question which our pamphlet left in the shade. But perhaps it would not be superfluous to touch upon the last and most powerful argument of the pacifist critic. Russell declares that our attitude towards the British revolution is dictated by... our Russian patriotism. He says:

> I am afraid that like the rest of us Trotsky is a patriot when it comes to the pinch: a communist revolution in England would be advantageous to Russia; and therefore he advises it without considering impartially whether it would be advantageous to us.

This argument has everything in its favour except novelty. Chamberlain's and Joynson-Hicks' Press – the *Morning Post*[8] takes this up with the greatest fervour – long ago proved that the international communist movement serves the aims of Soviet imperialism which in turn continues the traditions of tsarist policy. This sort of accusation started at the time when the bourgeoisie became convinced that our party had taken power in earnest and was not about to give up. In the period preceding the seizure of power and directly following it the accusations had, as is well known, a directly converse nature. The Bolsheviks were accused of being alien to national feelings and patriotic considerations and of carrying out Hohenzollern policy in relation to Russia. And this was not at all so long ago. Arthur Henderson, Emil Vandervelde, Albert Thomas, and others made visits to Russia to convince the Russian workers that the Bolsheviks were prepared to betray the basic interests of Russia in favour of their international chimera (or according to another version for the German Kaiser's gold). Again it was the *Morning Post* which developed this theme with the most sharpness and vigour. In exactly the same way as Russell now accuses us of being ready to reduce the population of Great Britain to 20 million for the benefit of Soviet imperialism, nine

---

8   The *Morning Post* was a conservative daily paper published in London from 1772 to 1937 when it was purchased by the *Daily Telegraph*.

years ago we were accused of a heartless readiness to reduce the population of Russia two- and three-fold in the name of our international aims. Our party, as is well known, took the point of view that the defeat of tsarist Russia in the war would be advantageous as much for the Russian as for the international working class. The socialist lackeys of the Entente could not shift us from this position. In the period of the Brest-Litovsk peace, accusations of an anti-national policy (in the other version – of collaboration with Hohenzollern) reached fever pitch. Nevertheless, our party did not allow itself to be drawn into the war in the interests of American capital. The Hohenzollern regime fell and in its downfall the October revolution played no less a role than did the arms of the Entente. The antagonism between the Soviet Republic and the governments of the victorious Entente moved into the foreground. The most reactionary world role is played by the ruling class of Great Britain: in Europe, in Egypt, in Turkey, in Persia, in India, and in China. Any changes in the world situation, either economically or politically, are directed against the ruling class of Great Britain. Hence the obsolete British bourgeoisie in its struggle for its dwindling power furiously fights against changes. The American bourgeoisie is more powerful. Its struggle against the revolution will be on a larger scale. But America stands for the moment in the second line. The most active and vicious enemy of the revolutionary movement in Europe, in Asia, and in Africa is the dominant class of Great Britain. It would appear that for a socialist this fact is more than sufficient to explain the antagonism between the Soviet Union and the British Empire. Are we "patriots"? To the same degree as we were "anti-patriots" during the imperialist war. By the methods of state power we are defending the same interests for which we fought by the methods of insurrection: the interests of the world proletariat.

When Russell says that we are prepared in the interests of the Soviet state to make a sacrifice of the interests of the British working class then this is not only false but absurd. Any weakening of the British proletariat and even more so its defeat in open struggle must inevitably inflict a heavy blow both to the international and to the internal position of the Soviet Union. When in March 1921 the German communists made an attempt artificially to force the proletarian revolution they were subjected to sharp criticism at the Third World Congress of the Communist International. They justified themselves by referring to the difficult position of the Soviet Republic and to the necessity of assisting it. Lenin and ourselves said to them: neither heroic outbursts nor even less revolutionary adventures can help the Soviet Republic; we need the same thing that the German proletariat needs: that is a victorious revolution; it would be fundamentally wrong to think that the proletariat of any country must, in the interests of the Soviet state, undertake any steps which do not flow from its own interests as a class fighting for its complete liberation. This standpoint which has entered our flesh and blood is alien to socialists who, if not always then at least at the decisive moment, invariably end up on the side of their own bourgeoisie. And Russell does not form an exception. To be sure, during the war he displayed brave, *though politically* quite hopeless, resistance to his government: this was an individual demonstration, the tribute of conscience – the fate of the regime was not in slightest degree placed in jeopardy. But when it comes to the revolution of the proletariat, Russell cannot find in his intellectual arsenal any other arguments beyond those which make him kindred to the *Morning Post* and all the Churchills of his country.

The principal peculiarity of British politics, and its past history, is summed up in the blatant disparity between the revolutionary maturity of the objective economic factors and the extreme backwardness of ideological forms, particularly in the ranks of the working class. Least of all is this basic peculiarity understood by the very people who most sharply demonstrate it: the bourgeois humanists and the latter-day enlighteners and pacifists. Along with the reactionary petty-bourgeois reformists they consider themselves to be the anointed leaders of the proletariat. Bertrand Russell is not the worst among them. But his writings on social and political topics, his outcry against war, his polemic with Scott Nearing regarding the Soviet regime, characterise his unmistakable superficial dilettantism, his political blindness, and his complete lack of comprehension of the basic mechanism of historical development; that is, the struggle of living classes which grow out of the basis of production. To history he counterposes the propaganda of a few pacifist slogans which he formulates quite wretchedly. And in the process he forgets to explain to us why pacifist enlightenment has not saved us from wars and revolutions despite the fact that such eminent people as Robert Owen in the first half of the nineteenth century, the French enlighteners of the eighteenth century, the Quakers beginning in the seventeenth century and many, many, others concerned themselves with this question. Russell is a latter-day enlightener who has inherited from the old enlightenment not so much its enthusiasm as its idealistic prejudices. Russell is a sceptic through and through. He counterposes the peaceful and gradual methods of science and technology to the violent methods of revolution. But he believes just as little in the salutary force of scientific thought as he does in the force of revolutionary action. In his polemic with Nearing, he attempts under the cover of pseudo-socialist phrases to belittle, discredit, and compromise the revolutionary initiative of the Russian proletariat. In his polemic against the biologist Holden he makes a mockery of scientific-technical optimism. In his pamphlet *Icarus*, he openly expresses his conviction that the best outcome would be the destruction of all our civilisation. And this man, worm-eaten through and through with scepticism, egoistic, reclusive and aristocratic, considers himself called upon to give advice to the British proletariat and to warn it against our communist intrigues! The British working class is entering a period when it requires the greatest belief in its mission and its strength. To gain this there is no need for any stimulants like religion or idealist morality. It is necessary and sufficient that the British proletariat understands the position of its country in relation to the position of the whole world, that it has become clear about the rottenness of the ruling classes, and that it has thrown out of its way the careerists, quacks, and those bourgeois sceptics who imagine themselves to be socialists only because they from time-to-time vomit in the atmosphere of rotting bourgeois society.

—

P. S. – These lines were being written during the days when the question of the miners' strike and the General Strike hung on a thin thread. Today a final solution has still not come about or at least news of it has not reached us. But whatever direction events in Britain take in the coming days and weeks the questions to which the present article in particular is devoted can no longer be taken off the agenda of British political life.

The General Strike

From a speech to the All-Russian
Conference of Agricultural Workers, 28 June 1926
(*For Quality, Against Bureaucratism, For Socialism!*)

Comrades, as I speak to you the miners are on strike in Britain. The General Strike has been strangled but the miners' strike goes on. It is not out of the question that this miners' strike holds within itself new revolutionary possibilities. But whatever the outcome, the miners' struggle is a struggle of the world working class and therefore our struggle too. There is no going back from the General Strike. It is not out of place at this meeting to note a seemingly minor, but highly indicative fact: the importance of the strike was expressed in the production of such phenomena as wall newspapers and worker-journalists among the British working class. Wall newspapers in Britain! No one had dreamt of such a thing before the strike, but two or three weeks later wall newspapers were appearing there. There is a general strike, no newspapers, they need communications and so out comes the wall newspaper.

The General Strike was strangled not so much by the capitalists as by the perfidious leaders. The miners' strike goes on and if the signs are not deceptive, it will be sharp and bitter. Britain has entered a period of prolonged revolutionary shocks. There will of course be pauses and lulls, but *The Times* will not be able to relapse into the peaceful and prosperous existence it would like.

The gigantic upsurge experienced in this country during the days of the British General Strike was a truly great demonstration of the intimate ties linking the labouring masses of our Union with the life and struggle of the British proletariat, and the world working class as a whole.

When our workers collected money and the trade unions sent it to the strikers, the British bourgeois press wrote that the Russians were supporting the strike out of patriotism, in order to wreck the British economy. It is curious that a few weeks before the strike the British quasi-socialist Bertrand Russell wrote that the Bolsheviks' positions and advice regarding the revolutionary development of Britain were dictated by patriotism. The Russians, it is said, want to drag Britain into an armed uprising, and bring about her downfall in order to strengthen their own position.

These gentlemen forget that in 1917 there came to us in Petrograd a British quasi-socialist, Arthur Henderson, one of the purported leaders, but actual betrayers, of the recent General Strike. What he said to us was more or less this:

> The Bolsheviks are traitors to Russia, they are serving German imperialism, they have not a drop of healthy national feeling or patriotism in their hearts. The Mensheviks and Socialist-Revolutionaries are patriots who support the struggle for political independence and democracy.

Thus spoke the voice of official British socialism in 1917 at the most crucial moment when the Bolsheviks were fighting against imperialist war. But now when the Comintern transplants the very same principles and methods to British soil, reflecting the objective course of events, the position of the British economy, the growth of its contradictions, and the desperate situation of the British proletariat under declining capitalism – when all these circumstances likewise transplant the methods of Bolshevism in British soil: then the selfsame Henderson, along with the *Daily Mail* on the one hand, and Russell on the other, no longer says that the Bolsheviks are turncoats and traitors to their country. No, he says: "The Bolsheviks are very crafty patriots, they are serving the national, Great Russian idea, they wish to continue the policy of tsarism and undermine the power of old Britain." These gentlemen hedge, lie, and turn themselves inside out. But we remain the same as we were. Whether Messrs. Hendersons call us traitors to Russia or the most bloodthirsty Russian patriots is neither here nor there to us. We have been, are and shall remain the same as we were. If we are patriots then we are patriots to the entire working class, including the British workers, and patriots to the international proletarian revolution! [*Applause.*]

VI

The Lessons of the General Strike

The Opposition's Fight for Clarity

A Speech to the Politburo, 3 June 1926.

In our party life legends are playing an ever-increasing part. One such legend is the absurd rumour, which is being spread systematically, concerning my 'fear' of the harvest. On the same ideological and political level is based a new legend to the effect that I regard the British Communist Party as a reactionary organisation, an obstacle in the path of the working class. Anyone who has merely glanced at my little book *Where Is Britain Going?*[1] will easily understand how foolish, how absurd are these assertions, the object of which is not to elucidate the essence of the question, but to put me at odds with the British Communist Party.

On the eve of great events in Britain, in a letter to the Politburo, I expressed the fear that the British Communist Party, like the Bulgarian, in a critical moment of mass activity, might adopt too passive or temporising an attitude – the more so because against it would be ranged the immense pressure of a bourgeois state, of bourgeois social opinion, and of all the officialism of the working class. What conclusion did I draw from this? Well, here it is. "One of our principal tasks is to assist the British Communist Party to understand and think out this prospect fully." We must help it to select and group around itself those elements "which are capable of understanding the inevitability of major mass battles and are not afraid of them but go

---

1 From page 251 of the present edition.

out to meet them."[2] This is the conclusion which I drew from my own doubts and misgivings. Can this really be said to be directed against the British Communist Party? Since when has uttering a caution, before great struggles, against the dangers of passivity, recommending a choice of more active elements, implied speaking against the Communist Party? And this in Lenin's party.

At an extended plenary session of the Executive Committee, some British comrades warned against overestimating the critical state of British capitalism. By this they revealed they underestimate the depth of the crisis and the imminence of social clashes. An incomparably less significant fact, namely the publication of my book with a preface by Brailsford, was for me a further symptom of a willingness to compromise by an important section of the British Communists. They have not yet had experience of leadership by mass action. Taken together, all this aroused quite reasonable fears of excessive caution, lack of decision, and even passivity on the part of the powerful bureaucratic opposition in all the old administrative organisations of the working class.

Does not fundamental revolutionary teaching suggest that in these circumstances it was indeed necessary to stress, to repeat, to emphasise the danger that in all the old organisational superstructure, the imminent strike would meet counter-activity, resistance, sabotage, and from the side of the Communist Party, a lack of decision? I consider that the main task of our party in the International consists in warning before the action and not in punishing by bureaucratic means after the action. In a letter reporting on the British party, we read:

> Unfortunately, in some of our regional organisations, it could be noted that there still remained in the party sectarian survivals; these organisations have not taken root sufficiently deeply in the trade unions; by which is also explained the fact that, during the strike, they lagged behind the mass.[3]

Thus, from the words of the British Communists themselves it is apparent that shortcomings of this kind had emerged, shortcomings which could and must be feared. Fortunately, the revolutionary activity of the party was, on the whole, at a reasonably high level. This is our general achievement, which, however, does not minimise the necessity for issuing a warning. Without criticism of certain British comrades on the Executive Committee of the

---

2 See p. 358 of the present edition.

3 Letter from T. Stewart to the secretary of the Comintern of 21 May 1926.

Comintern, without friendly cautions and warnings, the elements of passivity and indecision might have proved more influential than, fortunately, they were found to be.

Yet it is criminal to portray the matter in this way, as if the British Communist Party had coped with all its problems. The discrepancy between its strength, its resources, its means, and these objective tasks which are becoming increasingly imminent, is gigantic; and about this we must speak openly, not replacing revolutionary policy by party legends and formulas.

But meanwhile, in view of the monstrous conservatism of British social life, the young British Communist Party needs to increase tenfold its implacability, its criticism, its counter-activity, to the pressure of bourgeois social opinion and its 'worker' organisation.

* * *

Resolution on the General Strike in Britain, submitted to the Central Committee and Central Control Commission joint plenum, July 1926, written by Trotsky and signed by Zinoviev, Trotsky, Kamenev, Pyatakov and Krupskaya.

In view of the completely indisputable fact that the General Council, having betrayed the miners on 12 May by viciously breaking the General Strike, is now preparing for the final betrayal of the miners' strike, already isolated by the Council's action;

In view of the fact that the General Council, in this work of betrayal, is trying to gain time and apparently wants to conceal its treacherous work from the eyes of the masses, at least for a certain time longer, by maintaining the formality of the Anglo-Russian Committee;

In view of the fact that it is for these and only these purposes that the traitors of the General Council have need of the Paris conference of the Anglo-Russian Committee;

The plenum instructs the Politburo:

To hasten the convening of the Anglo-Russian Committee in every way, not allowing the Paris conference to be put off for a single day;

To pose all questions at the Paris conference with full bluntness and sharpness, denying the traitors any opportunity to dodge or evade the question and once again deceive the workers;

And having exposed the traitors' intents in all respects, since we may not either directly or indirectly conceal or go along with the betrayers of the miners' continuing struggle, to immediately break off the Anglo-Russian Committee. At the same time, to intensify every effort to strengthen the *united front*, from below, relying above all on the ties that have been established with the mineworkers' union.

In addition, the plenum declares that the Politburo majority has pursued a profoundly incorrect policy on the question of the Anglo-Russian Committee. The point at which the working masses of Britain exerted the greatest opposing force to the General Council was when the General Strike was being broken. What was necessary was to keep step with the most active forces of the British proletariat and to break at that moment with the General Council as the betrayer of the General Strike. For many decades the bourgeois Labour politicians of Great Britain have periodically deceived the working masses, each time arousing the workers' indignation. But the absence of a genuinely revolutionary party has always allowed them to let some time pass for the anger of the masses to cool down and then to resume their treacherous work once again. Therefore, it was necessary to break with the General Council without hesitation over the question of the betrayal of the strike at the moment of the betrayal and before the eyes of the masses. The traitors should not have been allowed to appear as our 'allies' for a single hour after the breaking of the strike. Only the British workers can throw out the present General Council, but they should be supported in this work by our example, and not hindered, even by indirect support to the General Council through the maintenance of organisational ties.

It would be an impermissible error, bordering on the criminal, if we allowed the General Council in the future to move this question back, step by step, and to gradually and imperceptibly reduce the Anglo-Russian Committee to nothing or to break with it themselves over some second-rate question, as over the statutes of the Committee or the like. Every conscious British worker would then ask us why we did not break with the General Council when it betrayed the General Strike or later, when on top of that, it betrayed the miners' strike, but rather broke with it on this or that secondary question after the miners' strike had been liquidated. For all the efforts of the General Council are aimed in that direction. A passive, wait-and-see policy on our part would contribute to the success of this policy of the General Council chiefs, a policy that counts on the Anglo-Russian Committee being buried unobtrusively with the minimum of losses for the British traitors.

To defend the maintenance of the Anglo-Russian Committee with the argument that we cannot leap over the organisations of the proletariat that are 'historically given' is to engage in crude sophistry, which will invariably lead to opportunist conclusions. We cannot leap over the trade unions, since they are 'historically given' organisations of the proletariat. But the Anglo-Russian Committee is a temporary formation, brought into existence by a temporary situation.

We were absolutely correct to conclude this alliance when we did, but in order to turn it against the opportunists; in order to push vacillating leaders forward as far as possible; and in order to expose them and break with them in the event of their betrayal. But to break with the betrayers of the General Strike in the way that we have done by our example and our actions is to say to the British masses: "Curse your leaders as traitors but let them stay in their posts; that is, do as we have done in relation to the Anglo-Russian Committee."

All the arguments about the impermissibility of 'leaping over' the treacherous General Council can and should be applied with tenfold force to the question of entering the Amsterdam International. From this point of view the very existence of the Profintern could be declared an attempt to 'leap over' Amsterdam… The most consistent advocates of maintaining the Anglo-Russian Committee, no matter what, are in fact gradually sliding over to support for entry into the Amsterdam International.

The attempt to justify the existence of the present Anglo-Russian Committee is fundamentally wrong. True, Baldwin is fighting against the General Council – just as Hindenburg fought against the German Social Democrats. It does not follow from either of these facts that it is necessary or permissible for us to form a bloc with Purcell or Scheidemann.

The tactic of the united front still retains all its power as the most important method in the struggle for the masses. A basic principle of this tactic is: "With the masses – always; with the vacillating leaders – sometimes, but only so long as they stand at the head of the masses." It is necessary to make use of vacillating leaders while the masses are pushing them ahead, without for a moment abandoning criticism of these leaders. And it is necessary to break with them at the right time when they turn from vacillation to hostile action and betrayal. It is necessary to use the occasion of the break to expose the traitorous leaders and to contrast their position to that of the masses. It is precisely in this that the *revolutionary essence* of the united front policy consists. Without this, the struggle for the masses always threatens to turn into an opportunist kowtowing to spontaneity covered up by an in-no-way-binding criticism of opportunism in words alone. The line of the Politburo majority on the question of the Anglo-Russian Committee was clearly a transgression in terms of the revolutionary essence of the united front policy.

The trade unions are the main mass organisations in Britain. But the struggle for influence with the masses organised in these unions should in no case lead to bowing down before the conservative forms of trade unionism in the spirit of completely opportunistic tail-ending formations. The more rapid the revolutionary development in Britain and the more sharply new organisational forms (shop stewards, action committees) are counterposed to the old ones, not in circumvention of the trade unions but based on them – the more attention the British Communists should pay to the formation and development of new organisational forms based on the mass movement.

The plenum emphatically rejects the attempt to use Lenin's teaching on the need for constant, untiring, and stubborn struggle within every kind of workers' organisation as a justification for a passive, conciliatory, wait-and-see attitude toward the treacherous leaders on the pretext that they reflect the present stage of development of the working class, that "they are the best there is", that "there is no one yet ready to replace them", and so forth. Lenin allowed the possibility of a temporary bloc even with opportunist leaders under the condition that there would be a sharp and audacious turn and a break based on the actions of the masses when these leaders began to pull back, oppose, or betray. An attempt to abandon this truly intransigent aspect of Lenin's teaching on taking the offensive, which is in the sharpest contrast with Menshevik passivity and watchful waiting, would signify nothing less than the devitalisation of the revolutionary doctrine of Leninism.

The plenum expresses its unshakable conviction that the international interests of the USSR, as the first state in the world consisting of a proletarian dictatorship, coincide totally and completely with those of the workers of the world and with those of the oppressed peoples. The development of the revolutionary movement on the basis of fraternal solidarity remains as before the main guarantee of the USSR's inviolability and the possibility for us of world socialist development.

At the same time the plenum declares with all its energy that the crudely erroneous policy stands exposed, which aroused hopes that the present General Council headed by Thomas, MacDonald, and Purcell would be ready and able to conduct a struggle against imperialism, military intervention, etc. These compromising leaders who so basely betrayed their own workers during the strike will all the more inevitably and shamefully betray the British proletariat, and the Soviet Union, and the cause of peace along with them, at the moment of the danger of war. Only an unrelenting exposure of the traitors in the eyes of the masses, only their removal from their posts, will prevent the bourgeoisie from catching the workers unprepared when it decides to try to start a war. Linking up with the British working masses on the basis of an effective unmasking of their present treacherous general staff, the General Council, will be the firmest guarantee against a war. The Thomases, MacDonalds and Purcells are as little able to prevent an imperialist attack as the Tseretelis, Dans and Kerenskys were to stop the imperialist slaughter. It would be a great crime toward the peoples of the USSR and the world proletariat to sow any kind of illusions whatsoever on that score.

The Comintern's tactics, which were worked out in all essentials under Vladimir Ilyich's leadership, ought to remain hard and fast. The following elements of these tactics are of special importance: (1) the necessity for Communists to work in the most reactionary trade unions in order to fight to win over the masses under conditions of all kinds; (2) the necessity for British Communists to enter the Labour Party and to fight against being expelled from that organisation, since the experience of the past five years fully confirms what Lenin said on this question at the Second World Congress of the Comintern and in his *Left-wing Communism: An Infantile Disorder*; and (3) the necessity for a struggle against the right opportunist deviation as well as against the ultra-left.

"Anarchism", Lenin wrote, "has often enough served as a kind of punishment for the opportunist sins of the labour movement. The two types of deformity mutually reinforce one another."

The plenum regards as totally impermissible the ever more obvious course of the Politburo majority toward the replacement of Lenin's statement of the question by a struggle (sometimes an entirely principled one) against the ultra-left alone and by a glossing over of the right opportunist dangers (Poland,[4] Britain, Germany[5]). The situation is especially dangerous since the

---

4   In May 1926 József Piłsudski, retired marshal and Polish head of state, staged a coup and overthrew the Wito government which was attempting to reduce the power of parliament. The Communist Party supported this coup d'état on the grounds that it would remove the threat of fascism, and joined the social democrats in a general strike. With Piłsudski's troops they fought Wito's forces in the streets of Warsaw. On taking power, Piłsudski rejected the social democrats' proposals for a left coalition government and himself established a dictatorship.

5   On 12 October 1923 three German Communists, Heckert, Brandler and Bottcher entered as a minority into a coalition government in Saxony together

more people warn against the growing rightward danger, the more they are accused of being ultra-left.

The plenum calls attention to the changes introduced into the statutes of most of our trade unions by the leading clique in the All-Union Central Council of Trade Unions [AUCCTU] without the knowledge of the party or of the mass membership of these unions. Whereas before the end of last year the trade union statutes spoke of their adherence to the Red International of Labour Unions, through the AUCCTU, at the end of last year and early this year, the Red International of Labour Unions was replaced by the International Federation of Trade Unions. A change of such importance in principle cannot be understood as anything but the setting up of preconditions for entering the Amsterdam International.

The plenum categorically condemns these efforts and proposes that the faction in the AUCCTU take steps to see that all union statutes indicate clearly and precisely that our unions, in full agreement with the opinions and wishes of the working masses, belong to the Red International of Labour Unions.

The plenum regards as totally unjustified the action of a number of comrades in carrying disputes within the Politburo on the question of the Anglo-Russian Committee into the press and into meetings outside the Politburo, spreading the crudest distortions of the views of the members of the Politburo minority, making crude personal attacks, etc.

Politburo members who are in the minority on this question, which was by no means decided in advance (or even discussed) at the Fourteenth Party Congress, were not given the opportunity to state their actual views on this question. As a result a distorted and one-sided 'discussion', poisoning the atmosphere in the party, has developed.

---

with left social democrats headed by Zeigner. Participation in such governments (similar steps were taken in Thuringia) was advised by the Executive Committee of the Communist International under Zinoviev as a means of gaining access to stocks of arms in preparation for a hastily planned all-German uprising. Nine days later, the two state governments were overthrown by troops sent from Berlin. At the Fifth World Congress held the following year, the leadership of the Communist Party under Brandler, Thalheimer, Walcher, and others, was condemned not so much for its hesitancy and then lack of preparation for revolution but because of opportunist speeches made by Communist Party ministers in the state parliaments, and their failure to press for arming the workers at the last minute.

In the Moscow party organisation and in those of other cities, reports were given and theses introduced with the aim of exacerbating the differences in the Politburo and of carrying the one-sided 'discussion' into the Comintern.

This kind of activity brings very serious injury to the cause of party unity in the All-Union Communist Party and can substantially damage the Comintern.

The plenum rejects the motion for approval of the tactics of the Politburo, since that would mean the following:

a. To maintain the bloc with the strike-breakers and traitors of the General Council as long as possible;

b. To leave uncriticised and uncondemned the plainly erroneous shift to the right in the politics of the Politburo majority;

c. To leave uncriticised as well the corresponding changes in trade union statutes, pointing towards entry into the Amsterdam International;

d. To leave the trend towards entering the Amsterdam International itself uncriticised; and

e. To strike a blow at those members of the party who have criticised the errors listed above and have demanded their correction. To do this would inevitably result in a deepening of the opportunist deviation and would not only strengthen Purcell but would also give preponderance to the rightward tendencies in the British Communist Party, which are already significant enough without that.

/ * * *

Resolution of the Opposition on the Anglo-Russian Committee,
first published in the *Bulletin Communiste*, March 1927.

After the betrayal of the British General Strike by the right and 'left' trade union leaders, the Anglo-Russian Committee has not only lost all meaning, but has become simply the source of deception of the British and of the international working class.

All the more incomprehensible, then, is the official report on the last Berlin conference of this committee. Therein was announced, without even a single resolution being referred to, "complete unanimity" and "cordial understanding" between the Russian and the British delegates. Present among the British delegates was one of the most typical, most right-wing British social-imperialists, the notorious Citrine, so that even the former threadbare excuse for maintaining this committee, namely, that behind the left reformists stand workers who consider them revolutionary, is unmasked as a conscious lie.

The Conference of Party Workers condemns most resolutely:

- The methods of secret diplomacy which were employed at the conference of the Anglo-Russian Committee;
- The complete inactivity of this committee with regard to all questions of pressing importance at the present time (war transport to China,[6] imperialist war preparations, the fascist *putsch* in Latvia);
- The "cordial understanding" with right-reformist leaders, which by its very nature can only occur upon a reformist, never on a communist basis;

and demands the immediate break-up of this committee by putting forward feasible demands for action, which are clearly rejected by the reformists:

- Boycott of the murderously fascist country of Latvia;
- Prevention of all further troop transport to China;
- Revolutionary propaganda among the troops already sent there;
- International conferences of transport workers, seamen, arms, munitions and chemical workers for the preparation in a revolutionary manner of real resistance to every imperialist war.

---

6 The British government was shipping war material to Chiang Kai-Shek's government for his counter-revolutionary operations against the communists and the workers' movement in China.

The Anglo-Russian Committee
and Comintern Policy

Amendments to the ECCI resolution on the situation in Britain,
first published in *Documents de l'Opposition de Gauche
de l'Internationale Communiste*, October 1927.

1. The plenum states that for the whole direction of our work in the British labour movement, especially for the correct understanding and carrying out of the tactic of the united front, the question of the Anglo-Russian Committee at the present moment has a decisive significance. Without a clear principled attitude to this question, the Comintern, and above all the British Communist Party, will be condemned to ever newer mistakes and vacillations. In the struggle against the war danger, the resolution of the question of the Anglo-Russian Committee is the basic prerequisite for resolving all other questions, just as (by way of example), in the year 1914 no step forward could be made without first resolving the question whether Social-Democratic deputies could vote for the war budget.

2. In the British trade union movement, just as in the Labour Party, the leading role is played by reformists of different varieties, *the majority of whom are liberal Labour politicians.* In view of the profound leftward development of the working masses, it must be acknowledged that the most dangerous variety of the liberal Labour politicians are politicians of the type of Purcell, Hicks, Brailsford and Co. The tottering structure of British imperialism is being supported at present not so much on Thomas and MacDonald as on Purcell, Brailsford and the like, without whom

politicians such as Thomas and MacDonald, despite the fact that they are supported by the bourgeoisie, would no longer be able to maintain their leading position in the workers' movement. The irreconcilable and relentless struggle against the left lackeys of imperialism, both in the trade unions and in the Labour Party, is becoming especially urgent now, when the sharpening international and domestic situation will strike mercilessly at every indecision and hypocrisy.

3. The trade unions and the party have without doubt their special characteristics, their special methods of work, in particular their special methods of carrying out the united front. But it is precisely on the question of the political bloc with the reformist leaders that the distinction between the trade unions and the party is completely effaced. In all important and critical cases, the General Council proceeds hand in hand with the Executive Committee of the Labour Party and the parliamentary fraction. In calling off the great strike, the leading politicians and trade unionists went hand in hand. In such conditions, not a single honest worker will understand why Purcell is said to be politically *a left lackey of the bourgeoisie*, while on the other hand with respect to the trade unions we stand in "cordial relations", "mutual understanding", and "unanimity" with him.

4. In particular cases, the tactic of the united front can lead to temporary agreements with this or that left group of reformists against the right wing. But such agreements must not in any circumstance be transformed into a lasting political bloc. Whatever concessions of principle we make for the purpose of artificially preserving such a political bloc must be recognised to be contrary to the basic aim of the united front and to be extremely harmful for the revolutionary development of the proletariat. During the last year, the Anglo-Russian Committee has become just such an extremely harmful, thoroughly conservative factor.

5. The creation of the Anglo-Russian Committee was at a certain juncture an absolutely correct step. Under the leftward development of the working masses, the liberal Labour politicians, just like the bourgeois liberals at the start of a revolutionary movement, made a step to the left in order to maintain their influence among the masses. To reach out to them at that time was absolutely correct. However, it had to be clearly kept in mind that, just like all liberals, the British reformists would inevitably make a leap backwards to the side of opportunism, as the mass movement openly assumed revolutionary forms. This is just

what happened at the moment of the General Strike. From the time of this gigantic event, the temporary agreement with the leaders had to be broken, and the break with the compromising of the "left" leaders used to advantage among the broad proletarian masses. The attempt to cling to the bloc with the General Council after the open betrayal of the General Strike, and even after the betrayal of the miners' strike, was one of the greatest mistakes in the history of the workers' movement. The Berlin capitulation is a black mark in the history of the Comintern and represents the inevitable consequence of this false line.

6. One must be blind or a hypocrite to see the 'main defect' of the Berlin decisions in the fact that they narrowed the competence of the Anglo-Russian Committee instead of broadening it. The "competence" of the Anglo-Russian Committee during the last year consisted of this: that the All-Union Central Council of Trade Unions [AUCCTU] was trying to support the General Strike, while the General Council was breaking it. The AUCCTU was helping the miners' strike on a broad scale, while the General Council was betraying it. If one talks about the broadening of the activity of the Anglo-Russian Committee (see No. 29 of the Resolution of the Commission), one is hypocritically pretending that this activity served some real interest of the workers, while in reality the Anglo-Russian Committee merely shielded and covered over the base and treacherous work of the General Council. To broaden this "activity" contradicts the basic interests of the working class. Ridiculous and disgraceful is the attempt to get free from the Berlin decisions simply by appealing to the fact that the General Council bears responsibility for them (see again No. 29 of the draft Resolution). That strike-breakers who descend lower and lower, seek to protect their strike-breaking work from outside intervention; that strike-breakers take pains to cover over their strike-breaking with the capitulation of the All-Union Central Council of Trade Unions; all that is quite in the order of things. But all that does not justify our capitulation one iota.

7. The plenum indignantly rejects the vulgar, philistine, thoroughly Menshevik argument that Chamberlain "also" wants the break-up of the Anglo-Russian Committee. The very attempt to determine our revolutionary line according to the arbitrary guidance of the enigma of what at every given moment Chamberlain wants or doesn't want is nonsensical. His task consists in getting the left lackeys, as far as possible, into his hands. For this purpose he squeezes them, unmasks

them, blackmails them, and demands they break with the Bolsheviks. Under the influence of this pressure and this blackmail, the General Council blackmails the All-Union Council of Trade Unions and, for its part, threatens it with a split. Under the pressure of the General Council, the AUCCTU agrees to capitulate. In this devious way Chamberlain's task has been completed, for his blackmail has led to the capitulation of the AUCCTU.

8. If we were to break with the General Council in order to discontinue all intervention in the affairs of the British working class; if, after the break, we were to confine ourselves to our internal affairs, while the British Communist Party was not developing with redoubled energy its campaign against the General Council; then Chamberlain would have every cause to be satisfied with this state of affairs. But the break-up of the Anglo-Russian Committee ought to mean the very opposite. Since we flatly reject the Berlin principle of non-interference as the principle of chauvinism and not of internationalism, we must support with redoubled energy the British Communist Party and the Minority Movement[1] in their redoubled struggle against the left lackeys of Chamberlain. In the presence of such a policy, Chamberlain will very soon be convinced that the revolutionary wing of the movement grew stronger after it shed the reactionary connection with the General Council.

9. The plenum therefore considers it absolutely necessary to break up in the shortest space of time the political bloc, which carries a disastrous ambiguity into our whole policy towards British reformism. The plenum is of the opinion that the British Communist Party must at once openly pose the question of the mutual relationship between the AUCCTU and the General Council. The British Communist Party, as well as the left-wing trade union Minority Movement, must demand the immediate summoning of the Anglo-Russian Committee in order to develop, in the name of the AUCCTU, a clear revolutionary programme of struggle against war and the offensive of the bourgeoisie against the proletariat. The programme must be so formulated that it provides no scope to the charlatan trickery of Baldwin's pacifist

---

1   Minority Movement – Body of trade unionists was organised under the leadership of the Communist Party of Great Britain in 1924 from the militant rank and file in many industries. It built up support and its conferences secured increasing representation up to the 1926 General Strike. However, it never really broke from its syndicalist antecedents and eventually came under the control of the Stalinists.

party. Refusal of the General Council to summon the Anglo-Russian Committee, or refusal of its delegation to accept the programme of struggle, is to lead to immediate breaking up of the bloc from our side and to a broad campaign against the reformists, especially the left variety who, better and on a wider scale than all the rest at the present moment, are helping the British Conservatives drag the British working class into war, without themselves being aware of it.

10. While giving all-round support to the movement of the truly revolutionary minority and particularly while giving support to acceptable candidacies of representatives of this minority for this or that position in the trade union movement (always on the basis of a specific practical programme), the British Communist Party must not in any circumstances or under any conditions identify itself with the Minority Movement or merge the organisations. The British Communist Party must maintain full freedom of criticism with respect to the Minority Movement as a whole as well as with respect to its individual leaders, their mistakes and vacillations.

11. The sharpening class struggle in Britain and the approaching danger of war are creating conditions under which the policy of the particular 'labour' parties, organisations, groups and 'leaders' will quickly be put to the test by the course of events.

The inconsistency of word and deed should manifest itself in the shortest space of time. In such a period the Communist Party can rapidly enhance its revolutionary authority, its numbers, and especially its influence, provided that it conducts a clear, firm, bold, revolutionary policy, calls everything by its right name, makes no concessions of principle, keeps a sharp eye on its temporary alliance partners and fellow travellers and their vacillations, and mercilessly exposes trickery and above all direct treachery.

* * *

From *The Chinese Revolution and the Theses of Comrade Stalin* (dated 7 May 1927), first published in *Documents de l'Opposition de Gauche de l'Internationale Communiste*, October 1927.

In the direction of the Chinese revolution we are confronted not by tactical errors, but by a radically false line. This follows clearly from everything that has been presented above. It becomes still clearer when the policy in China is compared with our policy towards the Anglo-Russian Committee. In the latter case the inconsistency of the opportunistic line did not express itself so tragically as in China, but no less completely and convincingly.

In Britain, as in China, the line was directed towards a rapprochement with the 'solid' leaders, based on personal relations, on diplomatic combinations, while renouncing in practice the deepening of the abyss between the revolutionary or leftward-developing masses and the traitorous leaders. We ran after Chiang Kai-shek and thereby drove the Chinese Communists to accept the dictatorial conditions put by Chiang Kai-shek to the Communist Party. In so far as the representatives of the All-Russian Central Council of Trade Unions ran after Purcell, Hicks, Citrine and Co., and adopted in principle the position of neutrality in the trade union movement, they recognised the General Council as the only representative of the British proletariat and obligated themselves not to interfere in the affairs of the British labour movement.

The decisions of the Berlin Conference of the Anglo-Russian Committee mean our renunciation of support in the future to strikers against the will of avowed strike-breakers. They are tantamount to a condemnation and a flat betrayal of the trade union minority, all of whose activity is directed against the traitors whom we have recognised as the sole representatives of the British working class. Finally, the solemn proclamation of "non-interference" signifies our capitulation in principle to the national narrowness of the labour movement in its most backward and most conservative form.

Chiang Kai-shek accuses us of interfering in the internal affairs of China just as Citrine accuses us of interfering in the internal affairs of the trade unions. Both accusations are only transcriptions of the accusation of world imperialism against a workers' state which dares to interest itself in the fate of the oppressed masses of the whole world. In this case as in others, Chiang Kai-shek, like Citrine, under different conditions and at different posts, remain the agents of imperialism despite temporary conflicts with it. If we chase after collaboration with such 'leaders', we are forced ever more to restrict, to limit and to emasculate our methods of revolutionary mobilisation.

Through our false policy we not only helped the General Council to maintain its tottering positions after the strike betrayal, but, what is more, we furnished it with all the necessary weapons for putting impudent demands to us which we meekly accepted. Under the tinkling of phrases about "hegemony", we acted in the Chinese revolution and the British labour movement as if we were morally vanquished, and by that we prepared our material defeat. An opportunist deviation is always accompanied by a loss of faith in one's own line.

The businessmen of the General Council, having received a guarantee of non-interference from the All-Russian Central Council of Trade Unions, are undoubtedly persuading Chamberlain that their method of struggle against Bolshevik propaganda is far more effective than ultimatums and threats. Chamberlain, however, prefers the combined method and combines the diplomacy of the General Council with the violence of British imperialism.

If it is alleged against the Opposition that Baldwin or Chamberlain "also" wants the dissolution of the Anglo-Russian Committee, then one understands nothing at all of the political mechanics of the bourgeoisie. Baldwin justly feared and still fears the harmful influence of the Soviet trade unions upon the leftward-developing labour movement of Britain. The British bourgeoisie set its pressure upon the General Council against the pressure of the All-Russian Central Council of Trade Unions upon the treacherous leaders of the trade unions, and on this field the bourgeoisie triumphed all along the line. The General Council refused to accept money from the Soviet trade unions and to confer with them on the question of aid for the mineworkers. In exercising its pressure upon the General Council, the British bourgeoisie, through it, exerted pressure upon the All-Russian Central Council of Trade Unions and at the Berlin Conference obtained from the latter's representatives an unprecedented capitulation on the fundamental questions of the class struggle. An Anglo-Russian Committee *of this kind* only serves the British bourgeoisie (see the declaration of *The Times*). This will not hinder it from continuing its pressure in the future upon the General Council, and demanding of it a break with the All-Russian Central Council of Trade Unions, for by such a policy of pressure and blackmail the British bourgeoisie wins everything we lose by our senseless and unprincipled conduct.

The insinuations that Chiang Kai-shek is "in solidarity" with the Opposition, because he wants to drive the Communists out of the Kuomintang, have the same value. A remark by Chiang Kai-shek is being circulated in which he is supposed to have said to another general that he agrees with the Opposition in the All-Union Communist Party on this point. In the text of the document from which this "quotation" was picked out, the words of Chiang Kai-shek are not adduced as an expression of his views, but as a manifestation of his readiness and aptitude to deceit, to falsehood, and even to disguise himself for a few days as a "Left Communist" in order to be better able to stab us in the back. Still more, the document in question is one long indictment against the line and the work of the Comintern's representatives in China. Instead of picking quotations out of the document and giving them a sense contrary to that contained in the text, it would be better to make the document itself known to the Comintern. Leave aside, however, the misuse of alleged "quotations" and there remains the "coincidence" that Chiang Kai-shek has always been against a bloc with the Communists, while we are against a bloc with Chiang Kai-shek. The school of Martynov[2] draws from this the conclusion that the policy of the Opposition "generally" serves the reaction. This accusation is not new either. The whole development of Bolshevism in Russia proceeded under the accompaniment of Menshevik accusations that the Bolsheviks were playing the game of the reaction, that they were aiding the monarchy against the Cadets, the Cadets against the SR's and Mensheviks, and so on without end. Renaudel accuses the French Communists of rendering aid to Poincaré when they attack the bloc of the radicals and the socialists. The German social-democrats have more than once pretended that our refusal to enter the League of Nations plays the game of the extreme imperialists, etc., etc.

The fact that the big bourgeoisie, represented by Chiang Kai-shek, needs to break with the proletariat, and the revolutionary proletariat on the other hand needs to break with the bourgeoisie, is not an evidence of their solidarity, but of the irreconcilable class antagonism between them. The hopeless compromisers stand between the bourgeoisie and the proletariat and accuse both the 'extreme' wings of disrupting the national front and rendering assistance to the reaction. To accuse the Opposition of playing the game of Chamberlain, Thomas, or Chiang Kai-shek is to show a narrow-minded opportunism, and at the same time to recognise involuntarily the proletarian and revolutionary character of our political line.

The Berlin Conference of the Anglo-Russian Committee which coincided with the beginning of British intervention in China, did not even dare to allude to the question of effective measures to take against the hangman's work of British imperialism in the Far East. Could a more striking proof be found that the Anglo-Russian Committee is incapable of moving as much as a finger towards really preventing war? But it is not simply useless.

---

2 Alexander Martynov (1865-1935) – Right-wing Menshevik who opposed the
    October Revolution and joined the Soviet Communist Party only in 1923. He then
    became a leading opponent of 'Trotskyism', using all his old arguments in favour of
    the two stages' theory of revolutionary development. He was the main theorist of the
    'bloc of four classes', Stalin's justification for the betrayal of the Chinese Revolution
    of 1927.

It has brought immeasurable harm to the revolutionary movement, like every illusion and hypocrisy. By referring to its collaboration with the All-Russian Central Council of Trade Unions in the "struggle for peace", the General Council is able to soothe and lull the consciousness of the British proletariat, stirred by the danger of war. The All-Russian Central Council of Trade Unions now appears before the British working class and the working class of the whole world as a sort of guarantor for the international policy of the traitors of the General Council. The criticism directed by the revolutionary elements in Britain against the General Council thereby becomes weakened and blunted. Thanks to Purcell, Hicks, and Company, the MacDonalds and Thomases get the possibility of keeping the working masses in a stupor up to the threshold of war itself, in order to call upon them then for the defence of the democratic fatherland. When comrade Tomsky, in his last interview (*Pravda*, 8 May), criticised the Thomases, Havelock Wilsons and the other hirelings of the Stock Exchange, he did not mention by a single word the subversive, disintegrating, lulling, and therefore much more pernicious work of Purcell, Hicks and Company. These "allies" are not mentioned by name in the interviews as though they do not even exist. Then why a bloc with them? But they do exist. Without them Thomas does not exist politically. Without Thomas there exists no Baldwin, that is, the capitalist regime in Britain. Contrary to our best intentions, our support of the bloc with Purcell is actually support of the whole British regime and the facilitation of its work in China. After all that has happened, this is clear to every revolutionary who has gone through the school of Lenin. In a like manner, our collaboration with Chiang Kai-shek blunted the class vigilance of the Chinese proletariat, and thereby facilitated the April coup d'état.

* * *

Dated 16 May 1927, and first published in
*Documents de l'Opposition de Gauche de
l'Internationale Communiste*, October 1927.

The Struggle for Peace and the Anglo-Russian Committee

The whole international situation and all the tendencies of its development make the struggle against war and for the defence of the USSR as the first workers' state the central task of the international proletariat. But it is just the tension of the situation that demands clarity, a precise political line and firm correction of the errors made...

1. War is the continuation of politics by other means. The struggle against war is a continuation of revolutionary policy against the capitalist regime. To grasp this idea means to find the key to all opportunist errors in questions relating to war. Imperialism is no external factor existing by itself; it is the highest expression of the basic tendencies of capitalism. War is the highest method of imperialist policy. The struggle against imperialist war can and must be the highest expression of the international policy of the proletariat.

    Opportunist, or radicalism that is turning to opportunism, always inclines to estimate war as such an *exceptional* phenomenon that it requires the annulment of revolutionary policy and its basic principles. Centrism reconciles itself to revolutionary methods but does not believe in them. That is why it is always inclined, at critical moments, to refer to the *peculiarity* of the situation, to *exceptional* circumstances, and so on, in order to substitute opportunist methods for revolutionary ones. Such a shift in the policy of centrism or pseudo-radicalism is of course acutely provoked by the war danger. With all the greater intransigence must this touchstone be applied to the main tendencies of the Communist International.

2. It is already clear to everybody that the Anglo-Russian Committee must not be regarded as a trade union organisation into which the Communists enter to fight for influence over the masses, but as a 'peculiar' political bloc with well-defined aims, directing its activities primarily against the war danger. With tenfold attention to the experience and the example of the Anglo-Russian Committee, the methods of struggle against the war danger must be closely re-examined so as to be able to tell the revolutionary proletariat openly and precisely *what must not be done* if the Comintern is not to be destroyed and the bloody work of imperialism against the international proletariat and the USSR facilitated.

3. In the presidium of the ECCI [Executive Committee of the Comintern] on 11 May, Comrade Bukharin advanced a new interpretation of our capitulation to the General Council in Berlin. He declared that the capitulation must not be considered from the standpoint of the international revolutionary struggle of the proletariat, but from the standpoint of a "diplomatic" counteraction to the offensive of imperialism against the USSR.

    Various weapons of international action are at our disposal: the party (Comintern), the trade unions, diplomacy, the press, etc. Our activities in the trade union field are dictated to us by the tasks of the class struggle. But only "as a general rule". In certain cases, as exceptions, we must – according to Bukharin – use the organs of the trade union movement as instruments of diplomatic action. This is what happened with the Anglo-Russian Committee. We capitulated to the General Council not as the General Council, but as the agent of the British government. We obligated ourselves not to interfere not out of party reasons, but for reasons of state. That is the substance of the new interpretation of the Berlin capitulation which, as we will soon show, only makes it still more dangerous.

4. The Berlin agreement of the Trade Union Central Council of the Soviet Union with the General Council was discussed a short time ago at the April plenum of the Central Committee of our party. The decisions of the Berlin Conference were defended by Comrades Tomsky, Andreev and Melnichansky, that is, our outstanding trade unionists, but not our diplomats. All these comrades, in defending the Berlin capitulation, accused the Opposition of not understanding the role and methods of the trade union movement, and declared that the masses of trade unionists cannot be influenced by breaking with the apparatus, that the apparatus cannot be influenced by breaking with its upper sections, and that these were just the considerations that dictated the attitude of our trade unionists in Berlin.

Now Comrade Bukharin explains that the decisions of the Berlin Conference constitute, on the contrary, an exceptional case, an exception from the principled Bolshevik method of influencing the trade unions, an exception in the name of temporary, but acute, diplomatic tasks. Why did not Comrade Bukharin, and Comrade Tomsky with him, explain this to us at the last plenary session of our Central Committee?...

5. Where did such an appalling contradiction come from in the course of a few weeks? It grew out of the impossibility of standing, if even for a single month, on the April position. When our delegation left for Berlin, it did not have Bukharin's subsequent explanation of the position it was to take. Did Comrade Bukharin himself have this explanation at that time? At all events, it was nowhere expressed by anybody... It is quite clear that this explanation was thought up after the event.

6. It becomes still clearer when we go back further, that is, to the origin of the question. After the criminal calling off of the General Strike

by the General Council, the "left" vying with the right for the palm, the Opposition in the All-Union Communist Party demanded an immediate break with the General Council so as to make easier and accelerate the liberation of the proletarian vanguard from the influence of the traitors. The majority of the Central Committee opposed to this their viewpoint that the retention of the Anglo-Russian Committee was allegedly required in the interests of our revolutionary influence on the British proletariat, despite the counter-revolutionary policy of the General Council during the strike.

It was precisely at this moment that Comrade Stalin advanced his theory of stages that cannot be skipped over. By the word "stage", in this case, must not be understood the political level of the masses, which varies with different strata, but of the conservative leaders who reflect the pressure of the bourgeoisie on the proletariat and conduct an irreconcilable struggle against the advanced sections of the proletariat.

In contradiction to this, the Opposition contended that the maintenance of the Anglo-Russian Committee after its open and obvious betrayal, which closed the preceding period of "left development", would have as its inevitable conclusion an impermissible weakening of our criticism of the leaders of the General Council, at least of its "left" wing. We were answered, primarily by this same Bukharin, that this is a revolting slander; that the organisational alliance does not hinder our revolutionary criticism in the slightest degree; that we would not permit any kind of principled concessions; that the Anglo-Russian Committee would only be an organisational bridge to the masses for us. It occurred to nobody at that time to justify the maintenance of the Anglo-Russian Committee by referring to grounds of a diplomatic character which necessitate a temporary abandonment of the revolutionary line…

7. The Opposition foretold in its writings that the maintenance of the Anglo-Russian Committee would steadily strengthen the political position of the General Council, and that it would inevitably be converted from defendant to prosecutor. This prediction was explained as the fruit of our "ultra-leftism". Incidentally, an especially ridiculous theory was created, namely, that the demand for the dissolution of the Anglo-Russian Committee was equivalent to the demand for the workers to leave the trade unions. By that alone, the policy of maintaining the Anglo-Russian Committee was invested with the character of an exceptionally important question of principle.

8. Nevertheless, it was very quickly proved that the choice must be made between maintaining organisational connections with the General Council or calling the traitors by their name. The majority of the Politburo inclined more and more to maintain the organisational connections at any cost. To achieve this aim, no "skipping over stages" was required, it is true; but it did require sinking politically one degree after another. This can most distinctly be followed in the three conferences of the Anglo-Russian Committee: in Paris (July 1926), in Berlin (August 1926), and most recently in Berlin (April 1927). Each time our criticism of the General Council became more cautious, and completely avoided touching on the "left", that is, on the most dangerous betrayers of the working class.

9. The General Council felt all along, by its consistent pressure, that it held the representatives of the All-Union Central Council of Trade Unions in its hand. From the defendant it became the prosecutor. It understood that if the Bolsheviks did not break on the question of the General Strike, which had such a tremendous international importance, they would not break later on, no matter what demands were placed before them. We see how the General Council, under the pressure of the British bourgeoisie, conducted its offensive against the All-Union Central Council of Trade Unions with ever greater energy. The Central Council retreated and yielded. These retreats were explained on the grounds of revolutionary strategy in the trade union movement, but by no means for diplomatic motives...

   The line of the Politburo ended naturally and inevitably with the Berlin conference of the Anglo-Russian Committee at the beginning of April. The capitulation of the All-Union Central Council of Trade Unions on the basic questions of the international working-class movement was neither an unexpected side-leap nor an abrupt manoeuvre. No, it was the inevitable crowning, predicted by us long before, of the whole line followed in this question.

10. At the beginning of June of last year (1926), Comrade Bukharin, as we said, was the creator of a theory according to which the necessity of working in reactionary trade unions allegedly brought with it the maintenance of the Anglo-Russian Committee under all circumstances. In the face of all the evidence, Bukharin at that time flatly denied that the Anglo-Russian Committee was a political bloc and called it a "trade union organisation".

Now Bukharin creates a new theory, according to which our remaining in the Anglo-Russian Committee, bought at the price of an absolutely unprincipled capitulation, was not called forth by the needs of a "trade union organisation," but by the necessity of maintaining a *political bloc* with the General Council in the name of diplomatic aims.

Bukharin's theory of today is in direct contradiction to his theory of yesterday. They have only this in common, that they are both 100 per cent deceitful, that they were both dragged in by the hair in order to justify after the fact, at two different stages, the sliding down from a Bolshevik to a compromising line.

11. That the right will betray us in the event of war, is recognised as indisputable even by Bukharin. So far as the "left" is concerned, it will "probably" betray us. But if it betrays us, it will do it, according to Bukharin, "in its own way", by not supporting us but by playing the role of ballast for the British government. Pitiful as these considerations may be, they must nevertheless be demolished.

Let us assume for a moment that all of this is really so. But if the "left" betrays us "in its own way", that is, less actively, in a more veiled manner than the right, it will surely not be because of the lovely eyes of the delegation of the All-Union Central Council of Trade Unions, but because of the British workers. That is the general line of policy of the "left" in all questions, internal as well as external: to betray, but "in its own way". This policy is profitable for it. Then why are we obliged to pay the "left" with the abandonment of our policy, for a policy which they are forced in any case to carry out in their own interests?

12. But in what sense will the "left" be a ballast for the British government? Obviously, in the same sense that they were "ballast" during the imperialist war, or are now, during the war of Britain against revolutionary China, and during the campaign of the Conservatives against the trade unions. The "left" criticises the government within such limits as do not interfere with its role as exploiter and robber. The "left" gives expression to the dissatisfaction of the masses within these limits, so as to restrain them from revolutionary action.

In case the dissatisfaction of the masses breaks through to the outside, the "left" seeks to dominate the movement in order to strangle it. Were the "left" not to criticise it, not to expose, not to attack the bourgeoisie, it would be unable to serve it "in its own way."

If it is admitted that the "left" is a ballast, then it is admitted that it is the useful, appropriate, necessary, succouring ballast without which the ship of British imperialism would long ago have gone down.

To be sure, the [Tory] diehards are fulminating against the "left." But this is done to keep the fear of God in it, so that it will not overstep the bounds prescribed for it, so that no unnecessary expense be incurred for their "ballast". The diehards are just as necessary an ingredient in the imperialist mechanism as the "left".

13. But under the pressure of the masses cannot even the "left" overstep the bounds prescribed for it by the bourgeois regime? This unexpected argument is also launched.

That the revolutionary pressure of the masses can undo the game of Chamberlain-Thomas-Purcell is incontestable. But the dispute does not hinge on whether the international revolutionary movement of the proletariat is advantageous for a workers' state, but rather whether we are helping or obstructing it by our policy.

The pressure of the masses, all other conditions being equal, will be all the stronger the more the masses are alarmed by the perspective of war, the less they rely upon the General Council, and the less confidence they have in the "left" traitors (traitors "in their own way"). If we sign "unanimously" a pitiful, lying, hypocritical declaration on the war together with the General Council, we thereby pacify the masses, appease their restlessness, lull them to sleep, and consequently reduce their pressure on the "left".

14. The Berlin conference can be justified by the "international interests of the USSR"! Here the mistake of Bukharin becomes especially atrocious. Precisely the interests of the USSR will suffer chiefly and most directly as a result of the false policy of the political bureau towards the General Council. Nothing can cause us such harm as mistakes and hypocrisy in the revolutionary camp of the proletariat. We will not deceive our enemies, the experienced and shrewd imperialists. Hypocrisy will help the vacillating pacifists to vacillate in the future. And our real friends, the revolutionary workers, can only be deceived and weakened by the policy of illusions and hypocrisy.

15. Bukharin will reply to this: "The Berlin decisions would be inadmissible if we worked only in the trade union movement. However, everything we have done in Berlin can be extended and improved with the means

that the party has. Just look: we even criticise the General Council in *Pravda*, in speeches by British Communists, etc."

This argument amounts to poisoning of the revolutionary consciousness. Bukharin's words mean only that we support the General Council "in our fashion" while it in turn "in its fashion" supports the imperialist state. If we criticise the General Council, then under the present circumstances, that is only to cover our political support of it and our political alliance with it.

The articles in *Pravda* (which are extremely foolish in regard to Purcell and Co.) are not read by the British workers. But the decisions of the Berlin conference are distributed through the press over the whole world. For the moment only a small minority of the British proletariat knows anything of the articles by the British Communists. But all the British workers know one thing: that Purcell and Tomsky maintain "friendly relations" with each other, "understand each other", and "are in agreement with each other". The attitude of the Russian trade union delegation, which represents the victorious proletariat of the Soviet Republic, is much more decisive than the speeches of the British Communists and thus belies their criticism, *which –* by the way *– is inadequate, since their freedom is limited by the Anglo-Russian Committee.*

In short: the capitulation of the Russian trade union movement in the name of the alliance with Purcell is one of the most important facts in the international workers' movement at the present moment. The "critical" articles in *Pravda* and Bukharin's ever-new theories are only the sauce on it.

That is just why Lenin wrote in his instructions for our delegation to the pacifist congress at the Hague,[3] where we had to deal with the same trade unionists, cooperators, and so forth:

> I think that if we have several people at the Hague Conference who are capable of delivering speeches against war in various languages, the most important thing would be to refute the opinion that the delegates at the Conference are opponents of war, that they understand how war may and will come upon them at the most unexpected moment, that they to

---

3 The Hague International Peace Conference was convened by the Amsterdam International of trade unions and met from 10-15 December 1922. The reformist majority rejected the proposal of the Soviet delegation on the question of war.

any extent understand what methods should be adopted to combat war, that they are to any extent in a position to adopt reasonable and effective measures to combat war.[4]

What interests did Lenin have in mind in writing these words: the international interests of the USSR or the revolutionary interests of the international proletariat? In such a basic question Lenin did not and could not set the one against the other. Lenin was of the opinion that the slightest yielding to the pacifist illusions of the trade unionists would render more difficult the real struggle against the war danger and injure the international proletariat as much as the USSR.

Lenin had conscientious pacifists in mind here, and not branded strike-breakers who are condemned by their whole position after May 1926 to a further chain of betrayals...

16. In what manner can the thoroughly rotten, pseudo-pacifist agreement with traitors, whom we have already declared by common accord to be the "only representatives" of the British proletariat, strengthen our international position? How? The Berlin conference took place in the period of the opening of hostilities by the British government against China and the preparation of similar hostilities against us. The interests of our international position demanded above all that these facts be openly called by their proper name. Instead, we passed them over in silence.

Chamberlain knows these facts and is obliged to conceal them. The British masses do not correctly know these facts and are obliged to learn them from us. Honest pacifists among the workers can go over to a revolutionary line in the face of these facts. The base merchants of pacifism in the General Council cannot speak aloud about facts which would, at best and without doubt, expose their silent conspiracy with Chamberlain against the British workers, against China, against the USSR, and against the world proletariat.

Now what did we do in Berlin? With all the authority of a workers' state, we helped the "pacifist" lackeys of imperialism to preserve their thieves' secret. We proclaimed before the whole world that we are "in unanimous accord" with the agents of Chamberlain in the General Council in the cause of the struggle against war. We thereby weakened the resistance power of the British workers against the war. We thereby

---

4 V. I. Lenin, *Collected Works*, Vol. 33, Lawrence and Wishart, 1960, pp. 448-9.

increased Chamberlain's freedom of action. We thereby injured the international position of the USSR.

It must be said more concretely: the Berlin capitulation of the All-Union Central Council of Trade Unions to the General Council extraordinarily facilitated Chamberlain's attack on the Soviet institutions in London, with all the possible consequences of this act.

17. It must not be forgotten that thanks especially to the insular position of Britain and the absence of a direct threat to its borders, the British reformists, during the war, allowed themselves a somewhat greater 'freedom' of words than their brothers-in-treason on the Continent. But in general they played the same role. Now, with the experiences of the imperialist war, the reformists, especially of the "left," will endeavour in the event of a new war to throw even more sand in the eyes of the workers than in the years 1914-18.

It is entirely probable that as a result of the attack on the Soviet institutions in London, which was prepared by the whole policy of the "left", they will protest in a little louder tone than the Liberals. But if the Anglo-Russian Committee were in any way capable of helping, not Chamberlain, but us, then would not both sides have come to an agreement in the first twenty-four hours, sounded the alarm, and spoken to the masses in a language corresponding to the seriousness of the circumstances? But nothing of the sort occurred, and nothing will. The Anglo-Russian Committee did not exist during the General Strike when the General Council refused to accept the "damned gold" of the All-Union Central Council of Trade Unions: the Anglo-Russian Committee did not exist during the miners' strike; the Anglo-Russian Committee did not exist during the bombardment of Nanking; and the Anglo-Russian Committee will not exist in the event of the breaking of diplomatic relations between England and the USSR. These harsh truths must be told to the workers. They must be honestly warned. *That* will strengthen the USSR!

18. It may be replied: But concessions on our part to the bourgeoisie are permissible, and if the present General Council is considered an agent of the bourgeoisie within the working-class movement, why should we not make concessions to the General Council out of the same considerations that we make concessions to imperialism? Certain comrades are beginning to play with this formula which is a classic example of the falsification and overthrow of Leninism for opportunist political aims.

If we are forced to make concessions to our class enemy, we make them to the master himself, but not to his Menshevik clerk. We never mask and never embellish our concessions. When we resigned ourselves to Curzon's ultimatum, we explained to the British workers that at the present moment we, together with them, are not yet strong enough to take up the challenge of Curzon immediately. We bought ourselves off from the ultimatum to avert a diplomatic break, but we laid bare the real relations of classes by a clear presentation of the question; by that, we weakened the reformists and strengthened our international position as well as the position of the international proletariat.

In Berlin, however, we got absolutely nothing from Chamberlain. The concessions we made to the interests of British capitalism (new crowning of the General Council, principle of "non-interference", and so forth), were not exchanged for any concession at all on their part (no breaking-off of relations, no war). And at the same time we camouflaged everything by depicting our concessions to capitalism as a triumph of the unity of the working class. Chamberlain received a great deal *gratis*. The traitors of the General Council received a great deal. We received – a compromise. The international proletariat received – confusion and disorder. British imperialism came out of the Berlin conference stronger. We came out weaker.

19. But, it is said, to break with the General Council at such a critical moment would mean that we could not so much as live in peace with the organised workers of Britain; it would give the imperialists a trump card, and so on and so forth.

This argument is false to its very roots. Of course it would have been incomparably more advantageous had we broken with the General Council immediately after its betrayal of the General Strike, as the Opposition demanded. The year would then not have been frittered away with doleful gallantries towards the traitors, but would have been used for their merciless exposure. The past year was not lacking in occasions for this.

Such a policy would have forced the "left" capitulators of the General Council to fight for remnants of their reputation, to separate themselves from the right, to half-expose Chamberlain, in a word, to show the workers that they, the "left", are not half as bad as the Moscow people present them. This would have deepened the split in the General Council. And when the swindlers of reformism come to blows, many secrets come to light, and the workers can only gain by it. Such a struggle against the General Council would have been the sharpest form of struggle against the policy of Chamberlain in the labour movement. In this struggle, the revolutionary working-class cadres in Britain would have learned in a year more skilfully to catch the sharpers of the General Council at their swindles and to expose the policy of Chamberlain. British imperialism would have had to face much greater difficulties today. In other words: *Had the policy proposed by the Opposition been adopted in June of last year, the international position of the USSR would now be stronger.*

Even if belatedly, the break should have been made at least during the miners' strike, which would have been quite clear to the million miners, as well as the millions of workers betrayed in the General Strike. But our proposals in this respect were rejected as incompatible with the interests of the international trade union movement. The consequences are well known. They were registered in Berlin. Today it is declared that the radically false line that already caused so much harm must be maintained in the future as well because of the difficulties of the international situation, which means in essence that the international position of the USSR is being sacrificed in order to conceal the errors of the leadership. All the new theories of Bukharin have no other meaning.

20. A correction of the errors now, even after a year's delay, would only be of benefit and not detriment. Chamberlain will say, of course, that the Bolsheviks are not able to maintain peace with his trade unionists. But every honest and even partly conscious British worker will say: the far too patient Bolsheviks, who did not even break with the General Council during our strikes, could no longer maintain any friendship with it when it refused to struggle against the suppression of the Chinese revolution and the new war that is being hatched by Chamberlain. The putrid decorations of the Berlin Anglo-Russian Committee will be cast aside. The workers will see the real facts, the real relationships. Who will lose thereby? Imperialism, which needs putrid decorations! The USSR and the international proletariat will gain.

21. But let us return again to the latest theory of Bukharin. In contradiction to Tomsky, Bukharin says, as we know, that the Berlin decisions are

not the policy of the united front, but an exception to it, evoked by exceptional circumstances.

What are these circumstances? The war danger, that is, the most important question of imperialist policy and the policy of the world proletariat. This fact alone must forthwith compel the attention of every revolutionist. It would appear from this that revolutionary policy serves for more or less "normal" conditions; but when we stand before a question of life or death, the revolutionary policy must be substituted by a policy of compromise.

When Kautsky justified the iniquity of the Second International in 1914, he thought up the *ex post facto* theory that the International was an instrument of peace but not of war. In other words, Kautsky proclaimed that the struggle against the bourgeois state is normal, but that an exception must be made under the "exceptional conditions" of war, and a bloc made with the bourgeois government, while we continue to "criticise" it in the press.

For the international proletariat, it is now a question not only of the struggle against the bourgeois state, but of the direct defence of a workers' state. But it is precisely the interests of this defence that demand of the international proletariat not a weakening but a sharpening of the struggle against the bourgeois state. The war danger can only be averted or postponed for the proletariat by the real danger to the bourgeoisie that the imperialist war can be transformed into a civil war. In other words, the war danger does not demand a passing over from the revolutionary policy to a policy of compromise, but on the contrary, a firmer, more energetic, more irreconcilable execution of the revolutionary policy. War poses all questions forcefully. It admits of evasions and half-measures infinitely less than does a state of peace. If the bloc with the Purcells who betrayed the General Strike was a hindrance in peaceful times, in times of war danger it is a millstone around the neck of the working class.

If one admits that the turning back from Bolshevism to opportunism is justified by circumstances on which the life and death of the workers' state depend, then one capitulates in principle to opportunism: for what value has a revolutionary policy that must be abandoned under the most critical circumstances?

22. In general, can the trade unions be utilised at one time in the interests of international class policy, and at another time for any sort of alleged

diplomatic aims? Can such a situation be established where the same representatives of the AUCP(B), the Comintern, and the All-Union Central Council of Trade Unions say at one moment that the General Council is a traitor and strike-breaker, and at another time that it is a friend with whom we are in hearty accord? Is it sufficient to whisper secretly that the former must be understood in the revolutionary class sense and the latter in a diplomatic sense? Can such a policy be spoken of seriously? Can one speak seriously to people who propose and defend such a policy?

After the Berlin conference, the word "traitor", as used for a Menshevik agent of the bourgeoisie, became terribly cheap. But such expressions as "hearty accord", "mutual understanding", and "unanimity" (the words of Comrade Tomsky), became equally cheap. Who benefits by this unusually artful combination of methods? It does not deceive our enemy for a moment. It only confuses our friends and reduces the weight of our own words and deeds.

23. Bukharin's new theory is not an isolated one. On the one hand, we are told that the unprincipled agreement with the notoriously treasonable General Council allegedly facilitated the defence of the USSR. On the other hand, we hear ever more loudly that the building of workers' and peasants' soviets in China would be a threat to the defence of the USSR. Doesn't this mean turning the foundations of Bolshevik policy upside down? Workers' and peasants' soviets in China would signify a magnificent extension of the soviet front and the strengthening of our world position. The agreement with the General Council signifies on the contrary a weakening of the internal contradictions in Britain and the greatest facility to Chamberlain in his work of brigandage against China and against us.

Once it is avowed that soviets in China are harmful to our international position, but that the General Council is useful, then the recognition of the principle of "non-interference" is essentially correct; but then supplementary conclusions must be drawn, at least with regard to Amsterdam. One can be sure that these conclusions will be drawn today or tomorrow, if not by Bukharin himself then by someone else. The new principle of opportunist exceptions "in particularly important cases" can find a broad application. The orientation on the opportunist chiefs of the labour movement will be motivated everywhere by the necessity of avoiding intervention. The possibility of building socialism in one country will serve to justify the principle of "non-interference". That is how the various ends will be knotted together into a noose that will strangle to death the revolutionary principles of Bolshevism. And end must be made to this once and for all!

We must make up for lost time. A broad and politically clear international campaign against war and imperialism is necessary. Our bloc with the General Council is now the principal obstacle in the road of this campaign, just as our bloc with Chiang Kai-shek was the chief obstacle in the road of the development of the workers' and peasants' revolution in China and, because of that, was used by the bourgeois counter-revolution against us. The more acute the international situation becomes, the more the Anglo-Russian Committee will be transformed into an instrument of British and international imperialism against us. After all that has happened, only he can fail to understand who does not want to understand. We have already wasted far too much time. It would be a crime to lose even another day.

The Break-up of the Anglo-Russian Committee

From a speech to a session of the Central
Control Commission, June 1927.

We declare that we shall continue to criticise the Stalinist *régime* so long as
you do not physically seal our lips. Until you clamp a gag on our mouths we
shall continue to criticise this Stalinist *régime* which will otherwise undermine
all the conquests of the October Revolution. Back in the reign of the Tsar
there were patriots who used to confuse the fatherland with the ruling
administration. We have nothing in common with them. We will continue
to criticise the Stalinist *régime* as a worthless *régime*, a *régime* of back-sliding,
an ideologically emasculated, narrow-minded and short-sighted *régime*.

For one year we tried to hammer into your heads the meaning of the
Anglo-Russian Committee. We told you that it was ruining the developing
revolutionary movement of the British proletariat. In the meantime, all your
authority, the entire accumulated experience of Bolshevism, the authority of
Leninism – all this you threw on the scales in support of Purcell. You will say,
"But we criticise him!" This is nothing else than a new form of support to
opportunism by backsliding Bolsheviks. You "criticise" Purcell – ever more
mildly, ever more rarely – and you remain tied to him. But what is he enabled
to say in reply to revolutionists in his own country when they brand him as
the agent of Chamberlain? He is able to say, "Now look here! Tomsky himself,
a member of the Political Bureau and Chairman of the All-Russian Central
Council of the Trade Unions who sent money to the British strikers, has

made criticisms of me but nevertheless we are working hand in hand. How dare you call me the agent of imperialism?" Would he be right or wrong? He would be right. In a devious way you have placed the entire machinery of Bolshevism at the disposal of Purcell. That is what we accuse you of. This is a very grave accusation – far graver than bidding Smilga farewell at the Yaroslav station. What have you done to Bolshevism? What have you done in the space of a few years to all the authority of Bolshevism, all its experience, and the entire theory of Marx and Lenin? You have told the workers of the world, and above all our Moscow workers, that in the event of war the Anglo-Russian Committee would be the organising centre of the struggle against imperialism. But we have said and still say that in the event of war the Anglo-Russian Committee will be a ready-made trench for all the turn-coats of the breed of the false, half-way friends of the Soviet Union, and for all the deserters to the camp of the enemies of the Soviet Union. Thomas gives open support to Chamberlain. But Purcell supports Thomas, and that is the main thing. Thomas maintains himself upon the support of the capitalists. Purcell maintains himself by deceiving the masses and lends Thomas his support. And you are lending support to Purcell. You accuse us of giving support to Chamberlain. No! It is you yourselves who are linked up with Chamberlain through your Right wing. It is you who stand in a common front with Purcell who supports Thomas and, together with the latter, Chamberlain. That is the verdict of a political analysis and not a charge based on calumny.

The devil only knows what is already being said about the Opposition at meetings, particularly at meetings of workers' and peasants' nuclei. Questions are raised as to the "resources" used by the Opposition to carry on its "work". It may be that illiterate and unconscious workers, or your own plants, are sending up such questions as are worthy of the Black Hundred. And there are scoundrels acting as reporters who have the audacity to give evasive answers to such written questions. If you were really a Central Control Commission, you would be duty-bound to put an end to this dirty, abominable, contemptible and purely Stalinist campaign against the Opposition. We, on the other hand, are not preoccupied with spreading calumny. We present an open political declaration: Chamberlain and Thomas are in a common front; they are supported by Purcell, without whose support they are ciphers; but you are supporting Purcell and thereby weakening the USSR and strengthening imperialism. This is an honest political declaration! And you yourselves are feeling the weight of it at this very moment.

* * *

From a speech to the Central Committee and Central
Control Commission joint plenum, 1 August 1927.

Trotsky: Is it possible to pose seriously the question of a revolutionary struggle
against war and of the genuine defence of the USSR while at the same time
orienting toward the Anglo-Russian Committee? Is it possible to orient the
working-class masses toward a general strike and an armed insurrection
in the course of a war while simultaneously orienting towards a bloc with
Purcell, Hicks and other traitors? I ask: *Will our defencism be Bolshevik or trade
unionist?* That is the crux of the question!

Let me first of all remind you of what the present leadership has taught
the Moscow proletariat during the whole of the last year. Everything
centres round this point. I read you the verbatim directives of the Moscow
Committee: "The Anglo-Russian Committee can, must and undoubtedly
will play a tremendous role in the struggle against all types of intervention
directed at the USSR. It [the Anglo-Russian Committee!] will become the
organising centre for the international forces of the proletariat in the struggle
against all attempts of the international bourgeoisie to start a new war."

Molotov has made here the remark that "through the Anglo-Russian
Committee we disintegrated Amsterdam". It is as clear as noon-day that
even now he has grasped nothing. We disintegrated the Moscow workers
together with the workers of the entire world, deceiving them as to where
their enemies were, and where their friends.

Skrypnik: What a tone!

Trotsky: The tone is suited to the seriousness of the question. You consolidated
Amsterdam, and you weakened yourselves. The General Council is now more
unanimously against us than ever before.

It must be said, however, that the scandalous directive I just read expresses
much more fully, clearly and honestly the actual standpoint of those who
favoured the preservation of the Anglo-Russian Committee than does the
scholastic hocus-pocus of Bukharin. The Moscow Committee taught the
Moscow workers and the Political Bureau taught the workers of the entire
Soviet Union that in the event of a war danger our working class would be
able to seize hold of the rope of the Anglo-Russian Committee. That is how
the question stood politically. But this rope proved rotten. Saturday's issue
of *Pravda*, in a leading article, speaks of the "united front of traitors" in
the General Council. Even Arthur Cook, Tomsky's own beloved Benjamin,
keeps silent. "An utterly incomprehensible silence!" cries *Pravda*. That is your

eternal refrain: "This is utterly incomprehensible!" First you staked everything on the group of Chiang Kai-shek; I mean to say Purcell and Hicks, and then you pinned your hopes on 'loyal' Wang Ching-wei, that is, Arthur Cook. But Cook betrayed even as Wang Ching-wei betrayed two days after he had been enrolled by Bukharin among the loyal ones. You turned over the Minority Movement bound hand and foot to the gentlemen of the General Council. And in the Minority Movement itself you likewise refuse to counterpose and are incapable of counterposing genuine revolutionists to the oily reformists. You rejected a small but sturdier rope for a bigger and an utterly rotten one. In passing across a narrow and unreliable bridge, a small but reliable prop may prove one's salvation. But woe to him who clutches at a rotten prop that crumbles at a touch – for, in that case, a plunge into the abyss is inevitable. Your present policy is a policy of rotten props on an international scale. You successively clutched at Chiang Kai-shek, Feng Yu-hsiang, Tang Cheng-chih, Wang Ching-wei, Purcell, Hicks and Cook. Each of these ropes broke at the moment when it was most sorely needed. Thereupon, first you said, as does the leading article in *Pravda* in reference to Cook, "This is utterly incomprehensible!", in order to add on the very next day, "We always foresaw this."

* * *

Dated 23 September 1927, first published in
The New International, September-October 1934.

What We Gave and What We Got

In his report at the general membership meeting of the Moscow railwaymen, Comrade Andreev made the first – and still the only – attempt to put two and two together in the question of the Anglo-Russian Committee [ARC]. Comrade Andreev did not succeed in putting two and two together, but instead – despite his own intentions – he did make a serious contribution toward explaining just where lies the difference between opportunist and Bolshevik policies.

1. Comrade Andreev begins by very plaintively relating how the British busted up the ARC just at the time when it should have gone on living for many, many years. Imperialism has passed over to the offensive, strangling China, preparing a war against the USSR: "That is why the existence and activities of the ARC and similar organisations are most urgently needed right now." Again, further on: "It is precisely right

now, at the time of this offensive of capital against the working class, that the urgent need for the existence of the ARC becomes especially clear." And so on, in the same vein.

Concurrently, Comrade Andreev supplies a lot of direct information about the measures that were taken to preserve the ARC (in enumerating these measures, however, he religiously avoids the Berlin conference of the ARC in April of this year). But all these exertions availed nothing: the ARC broke up just at the moment when the need for it became most acute.

As a matter of fact, this presentation as it stands is of itself a merciless condemnation of the very policy that Andreev is defending. One may suffer defeat at the hands of an enemy despite the most correct policy… because the enemy is stronger. But when, in the course of many months, one forges a weapon against the enemy and then complains that this weapon went to pieces in one's hands on the eve of the battle – that is tantamount to self-condemnation: either the blacksmith is bad, or he forged out of worthless material.

2. After the General Council had broken the general strike in May 1926, the defenders of the official line said to us: "But didn't we know all along that the General Council is composed of reformist traitors?" Let us allow that we knew. But did we foresee that the General Council would collapse precisely when the need for it would be most urgent? Obviously this was not foreseen. Because not even the worst blacksmith would begin forging a weapon that he knew beforehand would fall apart on the eve of the battle.

Yet the controversy between the Opposition and the majority revolved precisely around this question. The Opposition said:

> The members of the General Council are liberal Labour politicians of diverse shades. As is always the case with liberals, they have been plunged to the left by the first and still formless revolutionary wave. The General Strike swept them to the right. They can have no independent policy; swept to the right, they become transformed into the active agency of the bourgeoisie. Their role will be counter-revolutionary. Since they have betrayed the general strike of their own workers, and the strike of their own miners, only a pathetic philistine can pin any hope on the possibility that these people would protect the Chinese revolution or the Soviet Union from the blows of British imperialism. Quite the contrary. In the critical moment they will come to the aid of imperialism against the revolution.

Such was our prognosis in this question. But after the British had broken the ARC, Comrade Andreev comes before the Soviet workers with his pathetic lamentations: the ARC left this world just at the time when its activity was "most urgently needed".

In politics, Comrade Andreev, this is called bankruptcy!

3. We said above: let us allow that the representatives of the official line did actually know whom they were dealing with – in which case their responsibility would be all the greater. As a matter of fact, they are vilifying themselves after the event. Their appraisal of the General Council was false, they did not understand the internal processes in the British working class, and they sowed illusions because they shared them themselves.

    a. There is no need of going into the period prior to the strike: during that period Purcell, Hicks, and the others were pictured as our most trustworthy friends, almost our adherents. A veritable cloud of proof can be produced. We shall confine ourselves to a single instance. In his pamphlet, *The Practical Questions of the Trade Union Movement*, published in 1925, Comrade Tomsky said:

        > Those [trade unionists] who have entered into the agreement with us are maintaining themselves staunchly both against bourgeois lies and slanders, and against the former [?] leaders of the British movement: Thomas, Clynes and MacDonald. The leaders of the British trade unions, the section that is farthest to the left – one can say with assurance, the majority – are working harmoniously with us. This gives us the assurance of and the occasion for hoping that the British who are averse to striking quick agreements, who take a long time to think, weigh, discuss, and hesitate prior to coming to this or another decision, *will strictly fulfil the agreement*; and that we shall not have to put to ourselves the question: What will the unity of the world trade union movement give the Russian worker? (p. 48.)

    b. In the nature of things, matters did not improve very much after the strike was broken, either. Even after the Opposition came out with utmost decisiveness for a break with the Anglo-Russian Committee as an institution which was false and rotten to the core and which served only to befuddle the workers by its existence, the Moscow Committee lectured the party as follows in the special theses issued against the Opposition:

The Anglo-Russian Committee can, must, and undoubtedly will play a tremendous role in the struggle against all types of intervention directed against the USSR. It will become the organising centre for the international forces of the proletariat in the struggle against all attempts of the international bourgeoisie to start up a new war.[1]

As a matter of fact, in the agitation among the rank and file, that is, in the really important agitation embracing the masses, the fundamental, chief and pertinent argument against the Opposition was the following: We are threatened by the war danger and the General Council will help us to ward it off, but the Opposition, pursuing its "factional Aims", demands that we break with the General Council. And from this sprang the stupid and base accusation of semi-defencism, defeatism, etc.

On the other hand, the Opposition maintained that the General Council would dilly-dally so long as no serious danger threatened its masters, the bourgeoisie, and then later on it would break with us at the moment when it best serves the bourgeoisie, i.e., when most dangerous to us.

Now Comrade Andreev comes forward and tearfully laments that the General Council broke with us, you see, just at a time when the activity of the ARC was "most urgently needed". Needed by whom – us or the British bourgeoisie? For the General Council is the agency of the British bourgeoisie in the workers' movement. It is clear that it broke the bloc with us when this break happened to be "most urgently needed" by Chamberlain.

In politics, Comrade Andreev, this is precisely what is meant by bankruptcy.

c. As for the famous argument of Comrade Rykov to the effect that since Baldwin was demanding the dissolution of the ARC, therefore the Opposition was aiding Baldwin – didn't this argument in its entirety flow from the false appraisal of the General Council, from the misunderstanding of its class nature and its social role?

The General Council is the agency of the British bourgeoisie. A good master must watch his agency like a hawk. Agents have their own personal interests. The agent in his operations may go

---

1 *Materials Toward the Summary of the July 1926 Plenum of the CC of the AUCP(B)*, Agitprop Department of the Moscow Committee.

further than is profitable to the master. Baldwin watches sharply after his agency, he exerts pressure on it, frightens it and presents it with demands for an accounting. Baldwin had to see to it that the General Council makes no extra promises, and that it will be able to make a timely break with us. The closer the approach of great problems the more inevitable the rupture. Among us, those who made a false appraisal of the General Council, painted it up, cherished illusions on this score and hoped that in a major and serious question the ARC would carry out a policy directed against Chamberlain – they failed to understand this. The Opposition took its point of departure from the fact that a break was inevitable and that this break must occur over *such questions as would be most clear and comprehensible to the British working masses.*

4. But even during the very last period, even after the Berlin conference, Comrade Tomsky continued to paint up the General Council. He rejected indignantly all references to the fact that the ARC had become a reactionary impediment in the way of the workers' movement. He asserted that the ARC is playing and can play a progressive role, even in the case of war. True, in April 1927 he expressed himself much more cautiously: 99 per cent in favour of the General Council's betraying us in case of war, as against one chance in a hundred that it might not betray. Can we – demanded Tomsky – reject even one chance against ninety-nine in so great a cause?

    To reason in such a manner is to turn politics into a lottery. But guaranteeing the defence of the USSR by lottery methods is a pitiful policy indeed, all the more so since the odds to lose are 100 per cent. And when the loss became patent, Comrade Andreev, with many sighs, told the assembled railwaymen how fine it would have been had the opportunists turned out to be not as they are in reality but as Comrade Andreev had imagined them to be.

    All this, Comrade Andreev, is precisely what is called the opportunistic policy of illusions.

5. Today, after the event, there is no lack of volunteers anxious to renounce the wretched crib of Comrade Uglanov upon the subject that the Anglo-Russian Committee "will become the organising centre of the international forces of the proletariat in the struggle against all attempts of the international bourgeoisie to start up a new war."

But precisely in this hope lay the crux of our entire official policy. It was precisely in this that the party was fooled. It was precisely by this that the Opposition was "beaten".

In the July 1926 joint plenum, Comrade Stalin lectured to us complacently:

> The aim of this bloc [the ARC] consists in organising a wide working-class movement against new imperialist wars in general, and against intervention into our country on the part [especially so!] of the most powerful of the imperialist powers of Europe – on the part of Britain in particular.[2]

Instructing us Oppositionists that it is necessary to "be concerned about the defence of the first workers' republic in the world from intervention", Stalin added for good measure:

> If the trade unions of our country in this cause, meet with the support on the part of the British, even if reformist, trade unions, then this should be hailed.
>
> *Voices:* Correct![3]

We may be quite sure that among those shouting "correct" was also the voice of Comrade Andreev. Yet these were the voices of blind men who were exposing the defence of the USSR to the danger of a sudden blow. It is not enough for one to "be concerned about the defence of the USSR", one must also be concerned about the Marxist line of the policies; one must know the basic forces of the world struggle, understand class relations and the mechanics of parties; and one must be a Marxist-Leninist and not a philistine.

Stalin keeps chewing his ideas with the smugness of a provincial wiseacre. Each vulgarity is numbered: first, second, third, and fourth. First, pinning hope on Chiang Kai-shek; second, pinning hope on Wang Ching-wei; third, on Purcell; fourth on Hicks. Today's hope is being pinned on the French Radicals,[4] who, if you please, will "repel the French imperialists", but this falls under fifth… It is not

---

2   *Minutes*, first issue, p. 71.

3   Ibid.

4   One of the main parties of the bourgeoisie during the Third Republic of 1871 to 1940. It was characterised by anti-clericalism and gained support from lower sections of the middle class. It participated in many governments of the period, including the Popular Front in 1936.

enough for one to "be concerned about the defence"; one must have some inkling as to what's what. In the same speech Stalin goes on to sermonise:

> If the reactionary British trade unions are willing to enter into a bloc with the revolutionary trade unions of our country against the counter-revolutionary imperialists of their own country – then why not hail this bloc?[5]

Stalin cannot understand that were the "reactionary trade unions" capable of waging a struggle against their own imperialists, they would not be reactionary trade unions. Falling into middle-class superficiality, Stalin loses all sight of the line of demarcation between the concepts reactionary and revolutionary. Out of sheer habit he refers to the British trade unions (i.e., obviously their leadership) as reactionary, but he really cherishes entirely Menshevik illusions about them.

Stalin sums up his philosophy as follows:

> And so, the ARC is the bloc between our trade unions and the reactionary trade unions of Britain [...] for the purpose of struggle against imperialist wars in general, and against intervention in particular.[6]

That's just it: both in general and in particular. In general, and in particular – middle class narrowness (suggested topic for the 'red' professors of the Stalinist school).

With the smugness of a provincial wiseacre, Stalin concludes his sermonising with an attempt at irony: "Comrades Trotsky and Zinoviev should remember this, and remember it well."[7]

That's just it! We have remembered everything very firmly indeed. We have remembered that our criticisms of the Stalinist hopes in Purcell as the guardian angel of the workers' state were called by Stalin a deviation from "Leninism to Trotskyism".

Voroshilov: Correct!

A Voice: Voroshilov has affixed the seal!

Trotsky: Fortunately all this will appear in the minutes.[8]

---

5   Ibid.
6   Ibid.
7   Ibid., p. 72.
8   Ibid., p. 71.

Yes, this is all to be found in the minutes of that very same July plenum which removed Zinoviev from the Politburo, which thundered against "Trotskyism", which assumed the defence of the Uglanov-Mandelstamm crib.

We now propose that the speeches of Stalin together with our speeches on the question of the ARC be published for the congress. This would provide an excellent examination as to whose views stand the test of events and of time: the views of Stalin or the views of the Opposition?

6. We shall pass over the scholastic constructions of Bukharin. Upon this question he observed seven theoretical Fridays a week. Here is the sophism that the ARC is a trade union organisation and not a political bloc. Here is also the sophism that the ARC is not the union of leaders but the union of the masses. Here, too, is the defence of the April capitulation in Berlin by an argumentation of a state and diplomatic character. And many, many other things besides.

We evaluated these theories in their own time for what they were worth. It would be a fruitless waste of time to unwind, after the event, Bukharin's talmudic knots. The course of events has swept away Bukharin's scholasticism, as so much rubbish, out of which only one fact emerges clearly: *the ideological and political bankruptcy*. And just to think that all this put together is being served up as the general line of the Comintern!

> From the moment the General Strike was broken [relates Andreev] there was begun the preparation of a plan how best to destroy the ARC, or to reduce the ARC completely to a cipher, to such a position as would keep it from being a hindrance to the General Council… This is what the plan of the present leaders of the General Council amounted to. And what happened at the last congress was the fulfilment of this plan.

All of which is entirely correct. The General Council did have its own plan, and it did execute this plan methodically. "The break is the fulfilment of a carefully thought-out plan which the General Council had prepared and which it executed during the last congress." This is absolutely correct. The General Council knew what it wanted. Or rather, the masters of the General Council knew where it had to be led. But did Comrade Andreev know where he was going? He did not. Because not only did he fail to hinder but he also assisted the

General Council to fulfil its perfidious plan to the greatest benefit of the General Council itself and its actual political principals i.e., the British bourgeoisie.

8. If the General Council did have a plan and if it was able to execute this plan methodically, then couldn't this plan have been understood, deciphered and foreseen? The Opposition did foresee. As early as 2 June 1926, two weeks after the General Strike was broken, we wrote to the Politburo:

> But may not the General Council itself take the initiative to break away? This is more than probable. It will issue a statement that the CEC [Central Executive Committee] of the Russian trade unions is striving not toward the unity of the world working class but to fan discord among trade unions, and that it, the General Council, cannot travel along the same road with the CEC of the Russian unions. Then once more we shall call after them: *Traitors!* – which will express all the realism there is in the policy that consists of supporting rotten fictions.[9]

Hasn't this been confirmed literally, almost letter for letter? We did not break with the General Council after it had betrayed the General Strike and had aroused against itself the extreme exasperation of millions of English workers. We did not break with it under conditions already less favourable to us, after it had broken the miners' strike, together with the priests of the bourgeoisie. Nor did we break with it under still less favourable conditions – on the question of British intervention in China. And now the British have broken with us over the question of our interfering in their internal affairs, our striving to "give orders" to the British working class, or to turn the English trade unions into instruments of our state policies. They broke on those questions which are most favourable to them, and which are most apt to fool the British workers. Which is precisely what we had been forecasting. Whose policy, then, turns out to be correct, sober and revolutionary? The one that penetrates the machinations of the enemy and foresees the morrow? – or the policy that blindly assists the enemy to carry its perfidious plan to completion?

9. During the July 1926 plenum, a cable was received from the General Council with its gracious consent to meet with the representatives of the CEC of the Russian unions. At that time, this cable was played up as

---

9 *Minutes of the Politburo*, 8 June 1926, p. 71.

a victory not over the General Council but over the Opposition. What an effect there was when Comrade Lozovsky brought up this telegram!

> What will you do [he demanded from the Opposition] if they [the General Council] do consent; more than that, what will you do if they have already consented? We have received such a cable today.

> *Trotsky:* They have consented that we shield them temporarily by our prestige, now when they are preparing a new betrayal. [*Disorder, laughter.*][10]

All this is recorded in the minutes. At that time our forecasts were the subject for taunts, disorder, and laughter. Comrade Tomsky did indeed crow over the receipt of the cable.

> *Tomsky:* Our little corpse is peering out of one eye... [*Loud laughter.*][11]

Yes, the laughter was loud. Whom were you laughing at then, Comrade Andreev? You were laughing at yourselves.

And how Comrade Lozovsky did taunt the Opposition with the fact that its expectations had not materialised.

> What makes you so certain [he inquired] that your second supposition will materialise? Wait...[12]

To which we answered.

> *Trotsky:* This means that for the moment the wiser and the more astute among them have gained the day, and that is why they have not broken as yet. [*Disorder.*][13]

Again "disorder". To Andreev, Lozovsky, and others it was absolutely clear that the Opposition was motivated by "gross factional considerations", and not by the concern for how we should distinguish correctly friends from enemies, and allies from traitors. Hence, the laughter and the disorder in the production of which Comrade Andreev by no means took the last place. "What makes you so certain that your second supposition will materialise?", inquired Comrade Lozovsky. "Wait..." The majority was with Andreev and Lozovsky.

---

10 Ibid., p. 53.
11 Ibid., p. 58.
12 Ibid., p. 53.
13 Ibid.

We had to wait. We waited more than a year. And it so happened that the Anglo-Russian Committee, which according to Rykov should have tumbled bourgeois strongholds – assisted instead its own bourgeoisie to deal us a blow, and then screened Chamberlain's blow by dealing its own supplementary blow.

When the test of great events comes, Comrade Andreev, one must always pay heavily for the policy of opportunistic illusions.

10. We have already recalled that Andreev in his report skipped completely over the Berlin conference of the ARC, April 1927, as if no such conference had ever been. Yet this conference marks the most important stage in the history of the ARC after the General Strike was broken. At the Berlin conference, the delegation of the CEC of the Russian unions renewed its mandate of faith in the General Council. The delegation behaved as if there had been neither the betrayal of the General Strike, nor the betrayal of the coal miners' strike, nor the betrayal of the Chinese revolution, nor the betrayal of the USSR. All the notes of credit were renewed and Comrade Tomsky boasted that this was done in the spirit of perfect "mutual understanding" and "heart-to-heart relations".

It is impossible to give traitors aid. What did we get for it? The disruption of the ARC within four months, at the time when our international position became worse. In the name of what did we capitulate in Berlin? Precisely upon this question, Comrade Andreev didn't have a word to say to the membership meeting of the railwaymen.

Yet in Berlin capitulation was no accident. It flowed in its entirety from the policy of "preserving" the ARC at all costs. From the end of May 1926, the Opposition hammered away that it was impermissible to maintain a bloc with people we call traitors. Or the converse: we cannot call traitors people with whom we maintain a bloc.

We must break with the traitors at the moment of their greatest betrayal, in the eyes of loyal and indignant masses, aiding the masses to invest their indignation with the clearest possible political and organisational expression. This is what the Opposition demanded. And it also forewarned that if the bloc was not broken, the criticism of the General Council would necessarily have to be adapted to the bloc, i.e., reduced to nothing. This forecast was likewise completely verified.

The manifesto of the CEC of the Red International of Labour Unions on 8 June 1926, contained a rather sharp, although inadequate, criticism of the General Council. Subsequent manifestos and resolutions became paler and more diffuse. And on 1 April 1927, the Russian delegation capitulated completely to the General Council.

At no time was the position of the British trade union leaders so difficult as in May, June and July 1926. The fissure between the leaders and the revolutionary vanguard of the proletariat stood revealed during that period as never before.

We had two courses open to us: to deepen this fissure or to assist the General Council to plug it up. Thanks to the assistance we gave the strikers, our prestige was very high. Our breaking relations with the General Council would have been a powerful supplementary blow to its authority and position. On the contrary, the preservation of the political and organisational bloc assisted the General Council to negotiate with least losses the frontier most dangerous to it. "Thank you", it said to those who helped keep it in the saddle. "I can go on from here myself." Incidentally, there was no gratitude expressed; the CEC of the Russian trade unions merely received a kick.

On one point Andreev is correct: this break is the fulfilment of a carefully thought-out plan.

11. But did Andreev have a plan himself? We have already stated that he had none whatsoever. Perhaps the most severe indictment of Andreev lies in his silence about the Berlin conference of April 1927. Yet at the April plenum of the CEC, Comrade Andreev spoke very decisively in defence of this conference. Here is what he said then:

> What did we set as our task? At this Anglo-Russian Committee [in Berlin] we set as our task to force the British to give us a direct and clear [!] answer to what their views were about continuing the existence of the Anglo-Russian Committee. And in my opinion, *we did force them to do this.* [?!] Jointly with us, they said that they were for continuing the existence of the Anglo-Russian Committee, for activising it, and so forth. At this Anglo-Russian Committee we were to force through a definite decision upon the question of unity and to a certain degree the condemnation of the Amsterdam International for its evasion of unity proposals… *We forced such a decision.* [?!] We forced through a resolution on this question. We had to force an answer from them on the question of the war danger, and imperialist mobilisation. In my opinion, *in this sphere also, we forced through,* of course not a 100 per cent Bolshevik decision [?!], but a

maximum possible decision that could have been forced through under the given conditions.[14]

Such were the victories gained by Comrade Andreev at the Berlin conference: the British expressed themselves "directly and clearly" in favour of continuing the existence of the ARC; more than that, in favour of "activising it". It is no laughing matter indeed! Andreev forced a clear answer from the British on the question of trade union unity, and finally – hear! hear! – on the question of war. Small wonder that in that very same speech of his, Comrade Andreev – poor fellow! – spoke of how the Opposition "has hopelessly sunk in the mire of its mistakes".

But what to do now? In April "we forced the General Council to give us clear and direct answers". The Opposition, sunk in the mire of its mistakes, alone failed to understand these successes. But in September, the Trades Union Congress arranged by the General Council broke with the Anglo-Russian Committee. Whence comes this contradiction between April and September? Right now, Andreev admits that the collapse of the ARC is the fulfilment of a plan conceived back at the time of the General Strike, that is, in May 1926. What then was the import of the "clear and direct" answers of the British in April 1927? Hence, it follows that these answers were neither clear nor direct, but swindles. The job of the General Council consisted in hoodwinking, gaining time, causing a delay, preparing the congress, and using it as a shield.

The Opposition issued timely warning on this score as well. Open the minutes of the April 1926 plenum to page 31. We said at that time:

> "A particular danger to world peace is lodged in the policy of the imperialists in China." This is what they have countersigned. How come their tongues didn't turn inside out, or why didn't we pull them by the tongue and compel them to speak out precisely who the imperialists were? It is no mere coincidence that all this was signed on the first day of April, this date is symbolic… [*Laughter.*]

> *Kaganovich:* You mean to say we fooled them!

As may be observed, Comrade Kaganovich hit the bull's eye. Now it has become quite clear as to who fooled whom. Andreev has some cause

---

14 Ibid., p. 32.

to be plaintive over the fact that after all his victories in April 1927 the British liquidated the ARC at that very moment when it was most urgently needed.

This, Comrade Andreev, is what one would call having hopelessly sunk in a mire.

12. But this wasn't enough; Comrade Andreev expressed himself even more harshly about the Opposition at the April plenum:

> Our Opposition comes out with the demand that we break with the British unions. Such a position is a position to isolate us at the most difficult moment, when imperialism is mobilising its forces against us. You maintain that your position is presumably revolutionary, but you are giving objective aid to the Chamberlains because the Chamberlains want no connections whatever between our trade union movement and the English trade union movement, and they want no Anglo-Russian Committees to hinder them.[15]

The Opposition proposed that we do not seize hold of a rotten twig while passing over a precipice. But the policies defended by Comrade Andreev did bring us into isolation "at the most difficult moment, when imperialism is mobilising its forces against us." That is the job which was literally fulfilled by the official policies. By supporting the General Council, we weakened the Minority Movement.

Within the minority itself, by our conciliationist line, we supported the right elements against the left. By this policy we put a brake on the revolutionary education of the proletarian vanguard, including the Communist Party among the number. We assisted the General Council to hold its position without losses, to prepare a reactionary congress of trade union bureaucrats in Edinburgh, and to break with us against the resistance only of a small minority. We assisted the General Council to isolate us in our most difficult moment and thus to realise the plan conceived by the General Council far back during the time of the General Strike.

This, Comrade Andreev, implies giving objective aid to the Chamberlains!

13. But now, defending the policies of bankruptcy before a non-party meeting, Comrade Andreev says:

---

15 Ibid., p. 33.

A few hotheads from the Opposition in our Communist Party proposed to us during the entire period the following tactic: "Break with the English traitors, break with the General Council."

This utterly cheap, philistine phrase about "hotheads" is taken from the dictionary of middle-class reformism and opportunism, which are incapable of a long-range policy, that is to say, the policy of Marxist prescience and Bolshevik resolution. In April 1927, Andreev reckoned that he had forced serious commitments from the British. To this we replied:

> Political swindlers in the staff of the Amsterdam agency of capitalism commonly sow pacifist bargains of this type in order to lull the workers and thus keep their own hands free *for betrayal at the critical moment.*[16]

Who proved to be correct? Policies are tested by facts. We saw above what Andreev expected in April of this year, and what he received in September. Wretched niggardliness, shameful near sightedness! That is the name for your policy, Comrade Andreev!

14. Andreev has one remaining solace:

> The responsibility [!] or the breaking up of this organisation falls entirely and squarely [!!] upon the leaders of the British trade union movement.

This statement proves that Andreev has learned nothing. The "responsibility" for the breaking of the ARC! One might think that this was the most frightful of crimes against the working class. The General Council broke the General Strike, assisted the coal barons to enslave the miners, screened the destruction of Nanking, supported the policies of Chamberlain against the workers' state, and will support Chamberlain in case of war. And Andreev seeks to scare these people by "responsibility" for breaking the ARC.

What did the British workers see of the ARC, particularly from the time of the General Strike: banquets, hollow resolutions, hypocritical and diplomatic speeches.

And on the other hand, since when have we become afraid of assuming the responsibility for breaking with traitors and betrayers? What sort of a pathetic, wishy-washy, rotten liberal way is this of putting the question, anyway! To prolong the life of the ARC for four

---

16 Ibid., p. 38.

months we paid by the most disgraceful capitulation it Berlin. But in return, don't you see, we have rid ourselves of the most horrendous "responsibility" – the responsibility of having broken with the betrayers of the working class. But the entire history of Bolshevism is impregnated with the determination to assume responsibility of this sort!

Comrade Andreev, you are also one of those who babble about Trotskyism but who have yet to grasp the main thing in Bolshevism.

15. The perplexed reporter says:

> Now every proletarian must give himself a clear accounting, weigh the documents, and compare our policy with theirs.[17]

This is, of course, a praiseworthy manner of putting the question. One shouldn't accept anyone's say so. On this score Lenin had the following to say: "He who accepts somebody's word is a hopeless idiot." This Leninist aphorism applies to all countries, the Soviet Union among them. It is essential that our workers gain a clear conception of the policies of Comrade Andreev, i.e., the entire official policy in the question of the Anglo-Russian Committee. To this end, all the documents must be published and made available to every worker.

We trust that Comrade Andreev will support this proposal of ours. Otherwise he'll be in the position of one who maintains that what is good for the British is death for Russians. But this is the viewpoint of chauvinists and not internationalist revolutionists.

16. But what to do now, after the rotten stage decoration has collapsed completely? Comrade Andreev replies:

> The leaders refuse to make agreements with us – we will carry on this policy of the united front over the heads of the leaders and against their wishes, we shall carry it on from below, by means of our ties with the masses, their rank-and-file organisation, and so forth.

Fine. But didn't Manuilsky say more than a year ago, at the July plenum:

> Comrade Zinoviev appears here to console us that after breaking with the Anglo-Russian Committee we shall have to build new bridges to the workers' movement. But I want to ask – *have you seen these bridges?* Did Comrade Zinoviev outline new ways for realising the idea of trade union

---

17 Andreev, *Report at the Meeting of Railwaymen.*

unity? What is worst in the entire Opposition of Comrades Zinoviev and Trotsky is *this state of helplessness* [!!!].[18]

Thus a year ago the proclamation read that the liquidation of the Anglo-Russian Committee must create a state of helplessness: there being no other bridges in sight. He was considered a true revolutionary optimist who believed in the Purcellian bridge. And now this bridge has collapsed. Cannot one draw the conclusion that precisely Manuilsky's position is the position of helplessness and occlusion? It may be objected that no one would take Manuilsky seriously. Agreed. But didn't all the other defenders of the official line declare that the ARC is the "incarnation" of the brotherhood between the Russian and British proletariat, the bridge to the masses, the instrument of the defence of the USSR, and so forth and so on…?!

To the Opposition – such was the objection of the representatives of the official line – the Anglo-Russian Committee is the bloc between leaders, but for us it is the bloc of toiling masses, the incarnation of their union. Now, permit us to ask: Is the breaking of the ARC the breaking of the union of the toiling masses? Comrade Andreev seems to say – no. But this very same answer goes to prove that the ARC did not represent the union of toiling masses, for it is impossible to make a union with strikers through the strike-breakers.

17. It is incontestable that we must find ways other than the General Council. Moreover, after this *reactionary partition* has been eliminated, only then do we obtain the possibility of seeking genuine connections with the genuine masses. The first condition for success on this road is the merciless condemnation of the official line toward the Anglo-Russian Committee for the entire recent period, i.e., from the beginning of the General Strike.

18. The tremendous movements of the English proletariat have naturally not passed without leaving a trace. The Communist Party has become stronger – both in numbers and in influence – as a result of its participation in the mass struggles. The processes of differentiation within the many-millioned masses continue to take place. As is always the case after major defeats, certain and rather wide circles of the working class suffer a temporary drop in activity. The reactionary bureaucracy entrenches itself, surmounting internal shadings. At the

---

18 Ibid., p. 24.

left pole a selection of revolutionary elements and the strengthening of the Communist Party takes place at a rate more rapid than prior to the strike.

All these phenomena flow with iron inevitability from the gigantic revolutionary wave which broke against the resistance not only of the bourgeoisie but also of its own official leadership. One can and must continue building on this foundation. However, the thoroughly false policy restricted to the extreme the sweep of the offensive and weakened its revolutionary consequences. With a correct policy, the Communist Party could have garnered immeasurably more abundant revolutionary fruits. By the continuation of the incorrect policies it risks losing what it has gained.

19. Comrade Andreev points to the workers' delegations as one of the ways toward establishing connections with the British masses. Naturally, workers' delegations, well-picked and well-instructed, can also bring benefit to the cause of workers' unity. But it would be a rock-bottom mistake to push this method to the foreground. The import of workers' delegations is purely auxiliary. Our fundamental connection with the British working class is through the Communist Party.

It is possible to find the road to the toiling masses organised into trade unions not through combinations, nor through false deals at the top but through the correct revolutionary policy of the British Communist Party, the Comintern, Profintern, and the Russian unions. The masses can be won over only by a sustained revolutionary line. Once again this stands revealed in all its certainty, after the collapse of the ARC. As a matter of fact, the point of departure for the erroneous line in the question of the ARC was the straining to *supplant* growth of the influence of the Communist Party by skilled diplomacy in relation to the leaders of the trade unions.

If anyone tried to leap over actual and necessary and inevitable stages, it was Stalin and Bukharin. It seemed to them that they would be able through cunning manoeuvres and combinations to promote the British working class to the highest class without the Communist Party, or rather with some cooperation from it. This was also the initial error of Comrade Tomsky. Again, however, there is nothing original in this mistake. That is how opportunism always begins. The development of the class appears to it to be much too slow and it seeks to reap what it has not sown, or what has not ripened as yet. Such, for example, was the source of the opportunistic mistakes of Ferdinand Lassalle.

But after the methods of diplomacy and combination have described a complete circle, opportunism then returns, like the fishwife in the fable, to its broken trough. Had we from the very beginning correctly understood that the ARC is a temporary bloc with reformists which can be maintained only up to their first shift to the right; had we generally understood that a united front with the 'leaders' can have only an ephemeral, episodic, and subordinate significance; had we, in correspondence with all this, broken with the Anglo-Russian Committee on that very day when it refused to accept the assistance of the Russian workers to the British strikers – this entire tactical experiment would have been justified. We would have given impetus to the movement of the left minority and the British Communist Party would have received a lesson in the correct application of the tactic of the united front.

Instead of this, we shifted the tactical axis over to the side of the bloc with the reformist leaders. We attempted to transform a temporary and an entirely legitimate agreement into a permanent institution. This institution was proclaimed by us to be the core of the struggle for the unity of the world proletariat, the centre of the revolutionary struggle against war, and so forth and so on. Thus we created political fictions, and we preached to the workers to have faith in these fictions, i.e., we were performing work which is profoundly harmful and inimical to the revolution.

To the extent that the treacherous character of our allies became revealed – to which we tried to shut our eyes as long as possible – we proclaimed that the crux of the matter lay not in them, not in the General Council: that the ARC is not a bloc between leaders but a union of masses, that the ARC is only the "incarnation", only a "symbol", and so forth and so on. This was already the direct policy of lies, falsehoods, and rotten masquerades. This web of falseness was crumpled by great events. Instead of lisping, "the responsibility for this does not fall on us", we must say, "to our shame – we deserve no credit for it".

Andreev says that the whole truth must be told to every British worker. Of course, everything possible must be done. But this is not at all easy. When Andreev says: "Now no one will believe the members of the General Council any longer", that is simply a cheap phrase. As the Edinburgh congress shows, our policy strengthened the General Council. The Berlin conference alone – disregarding all the rest – did not pass scot-free for us. We shall have not only to scrub but to scrape away the ideological confusion we have spread. This primarily refers to the British Communist Party, and in the second place to the left-wing Minority Movement.

As far back as the time of the General Strike, as well as the miners' strike, the leadership of the British Communist Party was far from always able to display initiative and resolution. One must not forget that the CEC of the British Communist Party long refused to print the 8 July manifesto of the Russian unions as too sharp toward the General Council.

For him who is able to judge symptoms, this episode must appear as extremely alarming. A young Communist Party, whose entire strength lies in criticism and irreconcilability, reveals at the decisive moment a surplus of qualities of the opposite order. At bottom of it is the false understanding and the false application of the policy of the united front.

Day in and day out the British Communist Party was taught that the union with Purcell and Hicks would aid the cause of the defence of the USSR and that the Russian Opposition, which does not believe this, was guilty of defeatism. Everything was stood on its head. This could not pass without leaving its traces upon the consciousness of the British Communist Party...

This could not and it did not pass scot-free. The right-wing tendencies have become extremely strengthened among the leading circles of the British Communist Party: enough to recall the dissatisfaction of a number of the members of the British Central Committee with the Comintern theses on war as being too far 'left'; enough to recall Pollitt's speech in Edinburgh, the speeches and articles of Murphy, and so on.

All these symptoms indicate one and the same thing: for a young Party, still lacking real Bolshevik tempering, the policies of the Anglo-Russian Committee inevitably implied the opportunistic dislocation of its entire line.

This applies even to a larger measure to the left-wing Minority Movement. The evil caused here is not so easily remedied. It is pregnant with party crises in the future. Of course these words will supply pathetic functionaries with the pretext to speak of our hostility toward the British Communist Party and so forth. We have witnessed this in the past more than once, particularly in the case of China. Up to the last moment the Chinese Communist Party was proclaimed as the exemplar of Bolshevik policies, and after the collapse – as the progeny of Menshevism. We have nothing in common with such repulsive political sliminess. It has already brought the greatest harm both to our party and to the Comintern. But this will not cause us to pause on the road of fulfilling our revolutionary duty.

Andreev's report aims to smear over one of the greatest tactical lessons of the recent period. In this lies the most serious harmfulness of the report and of similar speeches and documents. It is possible to move forward only on the basis of an all-sided examination of the experience with the Anglo-Russian Committee. To this end all the basic documents that shed light on this question must be made available to all Communists. In order to move forward it is necessary to tell the truth, the whole truth, and nothing but the truth, both to the Russian and British workers.

The Struggle in Retrospect

From *Strategy and Tactics in the Imperialist Epoch*
(dated 28 June 1928), first published in *Die Internationale
Revolution und die Kommunistische Internationale*, 1929.

In the hunt after an artificial acceleration of the periods, not only were Radic,[1] LaFollette,[2] the peasant millions of Dombal,[3] and even Pepper clutched at, but a basically false perspective was also built up for Britain. The weaknesses of the British Communist Party gave birth at that time to the necessity of replacing it as quickly as possible with a more imposing factor. Precisely then was born the false estimate of the tendencies in British trade unionism. Zinoviev gave us to understand that he counted upon the revolution finding an entrance, not through the narrow gateway of the British Communist Party, but through the broad portals of the trade unions. The struggle to win the masses organised in the trade unions through the Communist Party was replaced by the hope for the swiftest possible utilisation of the ready-made apparatus of the trade unions for the purposes of the revolution. Out of this false position sprang the later policy of the Anglo-Russian Committee which dealt a blow to the Soviet Union, as well as to the British working class; a blow surpassed only by the defeat in China.

---

1 Stjepan Radic (1871-1928) – Croatian politician; founder of the Croatian Peasant Party in 1905.

2 Robert LaFollette Sr. (1855-1925) – American Republican; presidential candidate of his own Progressive Party in 1924.

3 Tomasz Dombal (1890-1937) – Polish communist and peasant leader; leader of Polish Communist Party.

In the *Lessons of October*, written as early as the summer of 1924, the idea of an accelerated road – accelerated through friendship with Purcell and Cook, as the further development of this idea showed – is refuted as follows:

> Without the party, independently of the party, skipping over the party, through a substitute for the party, the proletarian revolution can never triumph. That is the principal lesson of the last decade. To be sure, the British trade unions can become a powerful lever of the proletarian revolution. They can, for example, under certain conditions and for a certain period, even replace the workers' Soviets. But they cannot play such a role without the Communist Party and certainly not against it, but only provided that communist influence in the trade unions becomes decisive. We have paid too dearly for this conclusion as to *the role and significance of the party for the proletarian revolution to renounce it so lightly or even to have it weakened.* [4]

The same problem is posed on a wider scale in my book *Where is Britain Going?*[5] This book, from beginning to end, is devoted to proving the idea that the British revolution, too, cannot avoid the portals of communism and that with a correct, courageous, and intransigent policy which steers clear of any illusions with regard to detours, the British Communist Party can grow by leaps and bounds and mature so as to be equal in the course of a few years to the tasks before it.

The Left illusions of 1924 rose thanks to the Right leaven. In order to conceal the significance of the mistakes and defeats of 1923 from others as well as from oneself, the process of the swing to the Right that was taking place in the proletariat had to be denied and revolutionary processes within the other classes optimistically exaggerated. That was the beginning of the downsliding from the proletarian line to the centrist, that is, to the petty bourgeois line which, in the course of the increasing stabilisation, was to liberate itself from its ultra-Left shell and reveal itself as a crude collaborationist line in the USSR, in China, in Britain, in Germany and everywhere else…

As to the Anglo-Russian Committee, the third most important question from the strategical experiences of the Comintern in recent years, there only remains for us, after all that has already been said by the Opposition in a series of articles, speeches, and theses, to make a brief summary.

The point of departure of the Anglo-Russian Committee, as we have already seen, was the impatient urge to leap over the young and too slowly

---

4   L. Trotsky, *Works*, Vol. 3, Part 1, p. 9.

5   From page 251 of the present edition.

developing communist party. This invested the entire experience with a false character even prior to the General Strike.

The Anglo-Russian Committee was looked upon not as an episodic bloc of the tops which would have to be broken and which would inevitably and demonstratively be broken at the very first serious test in order to compromise the General Council. No, not only Stalin, Bukharin, Tomsky and others, but also Zinoviev saw in it a long lasting "co-partnership" – an instrument for the systematic revolutionisation of the British working masses, and if not the gate, at least an approach to the gate through which would stride the revolution of the British proletariat. The further it went, the more the Anglo-Russian Committee became transformed from an episodic alliance into an inviolable principle standing above the real class struggle. This became revealed at the time of the General Strike.

The transition of the mass movement into the open revolutionary stage threw back into the camp of the bourgeois reaction those liberal labour politicians who had become somewhat Left. They betrayed the General Strike openly and deliberately; after which they undermined and betrayed the miners' strike. The possibility of betrayal is always contained in reformism. But this does not mean to say that reformism and betrayal are one and the same thing at every moment. Not quite. Temporary agreements may be made with the reformists whenever they take a step forward. But to maintain a bloc with them when, frightened by the development of a movement, they commit treason, is equivalent to criminal toleration of traitors and a veiling of betrayal.

The General Strike had the task of exerting a united pressure upon the employers and the state with the power of the 5 million workers, for the question of the coal mining industry had become the most important question of state policy. Thanks to the betrayal of the leadership, the strike was broken in its first stage. It was a great illusion to continue in the belief that an isolated economic strike of the miners would alone achieve what the General Strike did not achieve. *That is precisely where the power of the General Council lay.* It aimed with cold calculation at the defeat of the mineworkers, as a result of which considerable sections of the workers would be convinced of the "correctness" and the "reasonableness" of the Judas directives of the General Council.

The maintenance of the amicable bloc with the General Council, and the simultaneous support of the protracted and isolated economic strike of the mineworkers, which the General Council came out against, seemed, as it were, to be calculated beforehand to allow the heads of the trade unions to emerge from this heaviest test with the least possible losses.

The role of the Russian trade unions here, from the revolutionary standpoint, turned out to be very disadvantageous and positively pitiable. Certainly, support of an economic strike, even an isolated one, was absolutely necessary. There can be no two opinions on that among revolutionists. But this support should have borne not only a financial but also a revolutionary-political character. The All-Russian Central Council of Trade Unions should have declared openly to the British mineworkers' union and the whole British working class that the mineworkers' strike could seriously count upon success only if by its stubbornness, its tenacity, and its scope, it could prepare the way for a new outbreak of the General Strike. That could have been achieved only by an open and direct struggle against the General Council, the agency of the government and the: mine owners. The struggle to convert the economic strike into a political strike should have signified, therefore, a furious political and organisational war against the General Council. The first step to such a war had to be the break with the Anglo-Russian Committee, which had become a reactionary obstacle, a chain on the feet of the working class.

No revolutionist who weighs his words will contend that a victory *would have been guaranteed* by proceeding along this line. But a victory was *possible* only on this road. A defeat on this road was a defeat on a road that could lead *later* to victory. Such a defeat educates, that is, strengthens the revolutionary ideas in the working class. In the meantime, mere financial support of the lingering and hopeless trade union strike (trade union strike – in its methods; revolutionary-political – in its aims), only meant grist to the mill of the General Council, which was biding calmly until the strike collapsed from starvation and thereby proved its own 'correctness'. Of course, the General Council could not easily bide its time for several months in the role of an open strike-breaker. It was precisely during this very critical period that the General Council required the Anglo-Russian Committee as its political screen from the masses. Thus, the questions of the mortal class struggle between British capital and the proletariat, between the General Council and the mineworkers, were transformed, as it were, into questions of a friendly discussion between allies in the same bloc, the British General Council and the All-Russian Central Council of Trade Unions, on the subject of which of the two roads was better at that moment: the road of an agreement, or the road of an isolated economic struggle. The inevitable outcome of the strike led to the agreement, that is, tragically settled the friendly 'discussion' in favour of the General Council.

From beginning to end, the entire policy of the Anglo-Russian Committee, because of its false line, provided only aid to the General Council. Even the fact that the strike was long sustained financially by the great self-sacrifice on the part of the Russian working class, did not serve the mineworkers or the British Communist Party, but the self-same General Council. As the upshot of the greatest revolutionary movement in Britain since the days of Chartism, the British Communist Party has hardly grown while the General Council sits in the saddle even more firmly than before the general strike.

Such are the results of this unique 'strategical manoeuvre'.

The obstinacy evinced in retaining the bloc with the General Council, which led to downright servility at the disgraceful Berlin session in April 1927, was explained away by the ever recurring reference to the very same 'stabilisation'. If there is a setback in the development of the revolution, then, you see, one is forced to cling to Purcell. This argument, which appeared very profound to a Soviet functionary or to a trade unionist of the type of Melnichansky, is in reality a perfect example of blind empiricism – adulterated by scholasticism at that. What was the significance of 'stabilisation' in relation to the British economy and politics, especially in the years 1926-1927? Did it signify the development of the productive forces? The improvement of the economic situation? Better hopes for the future? Not at all. The whole so-called stabilisation of British capitalism is maintained only upon the conservative forces of the old labour organisations with all their currents and shadings in the face of the weakness and irresoluteness of the British Communist Party. On the field of the economic and social relations of Britain, the revolution has already fully matured. The question stands purely politically. The basic props of the stabilisation are the heads of the Labour Party and the trade unions which, in Britain, constitute a single unit but which operate through a division of labour.

Given such a condition of the working masses as was revealed by the General Strike, the highest post in the mechanism of capitalist stabilisation is no longer occupied by MacDonald and Thomas, but by Pugh, Purcell, Cook and Co. They do the work and Thomas adds the finishing touches. Without Purcell, Thomas would be left hanging in mid-air and along with Thomas also Baldwin. The chief brake upon the British revolution is the false, diplomatic masquerade 'Leftism' of Purcell which fraternises sometimes in rotation, sometimes simultaneously with churchmen and Bolsheviks, and which is always ready not only for retreats but also for betrayal. *Stabilisation is Purcellism.* From this we see what depths of theoretical absurdity and blind opportunism are expressed in the reference to the existence of 'stabilisation' in order to justify the political bloc with Purcell. Yet, precisely in order to shatter the 'stabilisation', Purcellism had first to be destroyed. In such a situation, even a shadow of solidarity with the General Council was the greatest crime and infamy against the working masses.

Even the most correct strategy cannot, by itself, always lead to victory. The correctness of a strategical plan is verified by whether it follows the line of the actual development of class forces and whether it estimates the elements of this development realistically. The gravest and most disgraceful defeat which has the most fatal consequences for the movement is the typically Menshevist defeat, due to a false estimate of the classes, an underestimation of the revolutionary factors, and an idealisation of the enemy forces. Such were our defeats in China and Britain.

What was expected from the Anglo-Russian Committee for the USSR?

In July 1926, Stalin lectured to us at the joint plenum of the Central Committee and the Central Control Commission as follows:

> The task of this bloc [the Anglo-Russian Committee] consists in organising a broad movement of the working class against new imperialist wars and generally against an intervention in our country (especially) on the part of the mightiest of the imperialist powers of Europe, on the part of Britain in particular.

While he was instructing us Oppositionists, to the effect that "care must be taken to defend the first workers' republic of the world against intervention" (we, naturally, are unaware of this), Stalin added:

> If the reactionary trade unions of Britain are ready to conclude a bloc with the revolutionary trade unions of our country against the counter-revolutionary imperialists of their own country, then why should we not hail such a bloc?

If the "reactionary trade unions" were capable of conducting a struggle against their own imperialists they would not be reactionary. Stalin is incapable of distinguishing any longer between the conceptions *reactionary* and *revolutionary*. He characterises the British trade unions as reactionary as a matter of routine but in reality he entertains miserable illusions with regard to their "revolutionary spirit".

After Stalin, the Moscow Committee of our party lectured to the workers of Moscow:

> The Anglo-Russian Committee can, must, and will undoubtedly play an enormous role in the struggle against all possible interventions directed against the USSR.

It will become the organising centre of the international forces of the proletariat for the struggle against every attempt of the international bourgeoisie to provoke a new war.[6]

What did the Opposition reply? We said:

> The more acute the international situation becomes, the more the Anglo-Russian Committee will be transformed into a weapon of British and international imperialism.

This criticism of the Stalinist hopes in Purcell as the guardian angel of the workers' state was characterised by Stalin at the very same plenum as a deviation "from Leninism to Trotskyism".

Voroshilov: Correct

A Voice: Voroshilov has affixed his seal to it.

Trotsky: Fortunately all this will be in the Minutes.

Yes, all this is to be found in the Minutes of the July plenum at which the blind, rude and disloyal opportunists dared to accuse the Opposition of "defeatism".

This dialogue which I am compelled to quote briefly from my earlier article, *What We Gave and What We Got*,[7] is far more useful as a strategical lesson than the entire sophomoric chapter on strategy in the draft programme. The question – *what we gave (and expected) and what we got?* – is in general the principal criterion in strategy. It must be applied at the Sixth Congress to all questions that have been on the agenda in recent years. It will then be revealed conclusively that the strategy of the ECCI, especially since the year 1926, was a strategy of imaginary sums, false calculations, illusions with regard to the enemy, and persecutions of the most reliable and unwavering militants. In a word, it was the rotten strategy of Right-Centrism.

* * *

From 'The Errors in Principle of Syndicalism',
Byulleten Oppozitsii, November-December 1929.

… In the capitalist states, the most monstrous forms of bureaucratism are to be observed precisely in the trade unions. It is enough to look at America, Britain and Germany. Amsterdam is a powerful international organisation of the trade

---

6 *Theses of the Moscow Committee.*

7 From page 440 of the present edition.

union bureaucracy. It is thanks to it that the whole structure of capitalism now stands upright, above all in Europe and especially in Britain. If there were not a bureaucracy of the trade unions, then the police, the army, the courts, the lords, the monarchy, would appear before the proletarian masses as nothing but pitiful ridiculous playthings. The bureaucracy of the trade unions is the backbone of British imperialism. It is by means of this bureaucracy that the bourgeoisie exists, not only in the metropolis, but in India, in Egypt and in the other colonies. One would have to be completely blind to say to the British workers: "Be on guard against the conquest of power and always remember that your trade unions are the antidote to the dangers of the state." The Marxist will say to the British workers: "The trade union bureaucracy is the chief instrument for your oppression by the bourgeois state. Power must be wrested from the hands of the bourgeoisie and for that its principal agent, the trade union bureaucracy, must be overthrown." Parenthetically, it is especially for this reason that the bloc of Stalin with the strike-breaker Purcell was so criminal.

From the example of Britain, one sees very clearly how absurd it is to counterpose in principle trade union organisation to state organisation. In Britain, more than anywhere else, the state rests upon the back of the working class which constitutes the overwhelming majority of the population of the country. The mechanism is such that the bureaucracy is based *directly* on the workers, and the state indirectly, *through the intermediary* of the trade union bureaucracy.

Up to now, we have not mentioned the Labour Party which, in Britain, the classic country of trade unions, is only a political transposition of the same trade union bureaucracy. The same leaders guide the trade unions, betray the General Strike, lead the electoral campaign and later on sit in the ministries. The Labour Party and the trade unions – these are not two principles, they are only a technical division of labour. Together they are the fundamental support of the domination of the British bourgeoisie. The latter cannot be overthrown without overthrowing the Labourite bureaucracy. And that cannot be attained by opposing the trade union as such to the state as such, but by the active opposition of the Communist Party to the Labourite bureaucracy in all fields of social life. In the trade unions, in strikes, in the electoral campaign, in parliament, and in power. The principal task of a real party of the proletariat consists of putting itself at the head of the working masses, organised in trade unions and unorganised, to wrest power from the bourgeoisie and to strike a death-blow to the "dangers of state-ism".

* * *

From Chapter 42 of *My Life* (1930).

Stalin, Bukharin and, in the first period, Zinoviev as well, considered as the crowning achievement of their policy, the policy of a diplomatic bloc between the top circles of the Soviet trade unions and the General Council of the British trade unions. In his provincial narrowness Stalin had imagined that Purcell and the other trade union leaders were ready or capable of giving support to the Soviet republic against the British bourgeoisie in a difficult moment. As for the trade union leaders they, not without grounds, considered that in view of the crisis of British capitalism and the growing discontent of the masses it would be advantageous for them to have a cover from the left in the shape of an official friendship with the leaders of the Soviet trade unions that committed them to nothing. Both parties beat carefully about the bush most of all fearing above all to call things by their real names. A rotten policy has more than once before foundered on great events. The General Strike of May 1926 was a great event not only in the life of Britain but also in the internal life of our party.

Britain's fate after the war presented exceptional interest. The abrupt change in her world position could not but produce an equally abrupt change in the internal balance of forces. It was absolutely clear that even if Europe, including Britain, was again to reach a certain social equilibrium for a more or less prolonged period, Britain could not arrive at such an equilibrium other than through a series of the gravest conflicts and upheavals. I considered it probable that the conflict in the coal industry in Britain especially could lead to a general strike. From this I deduced that in the near future the deep contradiction between the old organisations of the working class and its new historical tasks would be inevitably revealed. In the winter and spring of 1925 in the Caucasus I wrote a book on this topic (*Where is Britain Going?*)[8]. The book was in essence directed against the Politburo's official conception with its hopes for a leftward swing in the General Council and for a gradual and painless penetration of communism into the ranks of the Labour Party and the trade unions. Partly in order to avoid unnecessary complications and partly in order to test out my opponents I passed the manuscript of the book for scrutiny by the Politburo. As it was a question of a prognosis and not a criticism in retrospect none of the Politburo members decided to make observations. The book passed the censorship favourably and it was printed just as it was written without the slightest alternation. It quickly appeared in English too. The official leaders of British socialism treated it as

---

8   From page 251 of the present volume.

the fantasy of a foreigner who did not know British conditions and dreamt of transplanting a 'Russian' general strike onto the soil of the British Isles. Such reactions could be counted in dozens if not in hundreds beginning with MacDonald himself to whom in the political banalities competition first place must unquestionably belong. Meanwhile, hardly had several months passed when the miners' strike turned into a general strike. I had not at all reckoned on such a speedy confirmation of the prognosis. If the General Strike demonstrated the correctness of a Marxist prognosis as opposed to the homespun estimations made by British reformism then the behaviour of the General Council during the General Strike signified the dashing of Stalin's hopes in Purcell. In the clinic I gathered and brought together with great eagerness all the material characterising the course of the General Strike and the inter-relations of the masses and the leaders in particular. I was above all exasperated by the nature of the articles in the Moscow *Pravda*. Its main task lay in covering up bankruptcy and saving face. This could not be achieved in any other way than by a cynical distortion of the facts. There can be no greater ideological decline for a revolutionary politician than deceiving the masses!

Upon my arrival in Moscow I demanded the immediate break of the bloc with the General Council. Zinoviev after the inevitable wavering supported me. Radek was against. Stalin clung to the bloc and even to the semblance of one for all his worth. The British trade union leaders waited until the end of their sharp internal crisis and then shoved their generous if dull-witted ally out with an impolite movement of the foot.

* * *

From 'The mistakes of the Right Elements of
the French Communist League on the Trade Union Question'
(dated 4 January 1931), *Byulleten Oppozitsii*, March 1931.

The disastrous experience with the Anglo-Russian Committee was based entirely upon effacing the independence of the British Communist Party. In order that the Soviet trade unions might maintain the bloc with the strike-breakers of the General Council (allegedly in the state interests of the USSR!), the British Communist Party had to be deprived of all independence. This was obtained by the actual dissolution of the party into the so-called 'Minority Movement', that is, a 'left' opposition inside the trade unions.

The experience of the Anglo-Russian Committee was unfortunately the least understood and grasped even in the Left Opposition groups. The demands for a break with the strike-breakers appeared even to some within our ranks as... sectarianism. Especially with Monatte, the original sin which led him into the arms of Dumoulin was most clearly manifested in the question of the Anglo-Russian Committee. Yet, this question has a gigantic importance: without a clear understanding of what happened in Britain in 1925-1926, neither Communism as a whole nor the Left Opposition in particular will be able to find its way on the road.

Stalin, Bukharin, Zinoviev – in this question they were all in solidarity, at least in the first period – sought to replace the weak British Communist Party by a 'broader current' which had at its head, to be sure, not members of the party, but 'friends', almost Communists, at any rate, fine fellows and good acquaintances. The fine fellows, the solid 'leaders', did not, of course, want to submit themselves to the leadership of a small, weak Communist Party. That was their full right; the party cannot force anybody to submit himself to it. The agreements between the Communists and the 'Lefts' (Purcell, Hicks and Cook), on the basis of the partial tasks of the trade union movement were, of course, quite possible and in certain cases unavoidable. But on one condition: the Communist Party had to preserve its complete independence, even within the trade unions, act in its own name in all the questions of principle, criticise its 'Left' allies whenever necessary, and in this way, win the confidence of the masses step by step.

This only possible road, however, appeared too long and uncertain to the bureaucrats of the Communist International. They considered that by means of personal influence upon Purcell, Hicks, Cook and the others (conversations behind the scenes, correspondence, banquets, friendly back-slapping, gentle exhortations), they would gradually and imperceptibly draw the 'Left' opposition ('the broad current') into the stream of the Communist International. To guarantee such a success with greater security, the dear friends (Purcell, Hicks and Cook) were not to be vexed, or exasperated, or displeased by petty chicanery, by inopportune criticism, by sectarian intransigence, and so forth… But since one of the tasks of the Communist Party consists precisely of upsetting the peace of and alarming all centrists and semi-centrists, a radical measure had to be resorted to by actually subordinating the Communist Party to the 'Minority Movement'. On the trade union field there appeared only the leaders of this movement. The British Communist Party had practically ceased to exist for the masses.

What did the Russian Left Opposition demand in this question? In the first place, to re-establish the complete independence of the British Communist Party towards the trade unions. We affirmed that it is only under the influence of the independent slogans of the party and of its open criticism that the

Minority Movement could take form, appreciate its tasks more precisely, change its leaders, fortify itself in the trade unions while consolidating the position of communism.

What did Stalin, Bukharin, Lozovsky and company reply to our criticism? "You want to push the British Communist Party on to the road of sectarianism. You want to drive Purcell, Hicks and Cook into the enemy's camp. You want to break with the Minority Movement."

What did the Left Opposition rejoin? "If Purcell and Hicks break with us, not because we demand of them that they transform themselves immediately into Communists – nobody demands that! – but because we ourselves want to remain Communists, this means that Purcell and company are not friends but masked enemies. The quicker they show their nature, the better for the masses. We do not at all want to break with the Minority Movement. On the contrary, we must give the greatest attention to this movement. The smallest step forward with the masses or with a part of the masses is worth more than a dozen abstract programmes of circles of intellectuals, but the attention devoted to the masses has nothing in common with capitulation before their temporary leaders and semi-leaders. The masses need a correct orientation and correct slogans. This excludes all theoretical conciliation and the patronage of confusionists who exploit the backwardness of the masses."

What were the results of the Stalinists' British experiment? The Minority Movement, embracing almost a million workers, seemed very promising, but it bore the germs of destruction within itself. The masses knew as the leaders of the movement only Purcell, Hicks and Cook, whom, moreover, Moscow vouched for. These 'left' friends, in a serious test, shamefully betrayed the proletariat. The revolutionary workers were thrown into confusion, sank into apathy, and naturally extended their disappointment to the Communist Party itself which had only been the passive part of this whole mechanism of betrayal and perfidy. The Minority Movement was reduced to zero; the Communist Party returned to the existence of a negligible sect. In this way, thanks to a radically false conception of the party, the greatest movement of the English proletariat, which led to the General Strike, not only did not shake the apparatus of the reactionary bureaucracy, but, on the contrary, reinforced it and compromised Communism in Great Britain for a long time.

Appendices

Introduction to the English Edition of 'Where is Britain Going?'[1]

H. N. Brailsford

At the close of the Communist trial, the judge at the Old Bailey summoned seven of his prisoners to choose between a six months' sentence and the opinions expressed in this book. They are, if we must read this summons in its literal meaning, prohibited opinions on which the law has put its ban. If this were really our case, then the thesis which Trotsky maintains in these pages is established already. For we should have to admit that even before violence had been attempted, the mere appearance in our politics of a tiny revolutionary party has sufficed to frighten the ruling class out of its respect for the liberty of opinion on which democracy is founded. It needs no energetic exercise of the imagination to predict from this episode what would happen if the challenge grew to a formidable threat.

But the battle for freedom is not yet lost. It is precisely those of us who differ from Trotsky's reading of our inevitable destiny who are bound in duty to welcome the appearance of this book. If it may come freely from the press, if it may be discussed, as it deserves to be, with equal freedom for assent or dissent, then, for the moment at least, the nightmare of this trial is dissipated. Of all parties in Great Britain, the Labour Party has the chief interest in demanding for this ruthless attack upon itself both liberty and attention. We can hold our faith in the democratic approach to Socialism as a reasoned

---

1 See p. 376 for Trotsky's reply to this article.

conviction only if the opposite opinion may be argued in perfect liberty, and only then if it finds worthy and capable advocates. If the law forbids a man to draw from the study of history and the survey of contemporary politics the conclusion that force is the only adequate instrument for social change, in that moment our contrary opinion ceases to be a reasoned conviction and becomes an imposed dogma.

The opinion which Trotsky maintains has never been more brilliantly argued. Behind its wit and its logic there is the prestige of experience. The pamphleteer who tells us that if we mean to achieve Socialism we cannot escape civil war has himself conducted a civil war against terrific odds to a triumphant conclusion. It is obvious, moreover, that he has taken pains to equip himself for his task and has applied his versatile intellect to the study of our history and our contemporary life. He makes some mistakes, it is true, in his facts, but none of these really invalidate his argument.

His book is a slashing attack on our whole movement. We shall make a grave mistake if we allow its manner to blind us to the fact that he has a strong case to argue. He assails Left and Right with equal vehemence. Sometimes in his criticisms of persons he is arrogant and offensive; sometimes his wit is irresistible; sometimes (it seems to me) he assails things in our record and muddles in our thinking which deserve to be assailed. But the odds are that with these ruthless Russian methods he will produce in the minds of most English readers an effect which is far from his intention.

Trotsky is far too able a man not to realise that there are differences in the English and Russian national characters. He emphasises again and again the lesson that history has made each of us what we are. Yet the more he displays his acquaintance with the external facts of our history, the less does he seem to understand us. His attitude to the religious beliefs of most of our readers is for me the test of his failure to understand us – and this I may say calmly, since I am myself an agnostic. No Russian that I ever met, even when he had been long in England, ever grasped the fact that English religion with its long tradition of open discussion, the democratic form of its 'free' churches, its emphasis on conduct rather than ritual or belief, and its relative freedom from other worldliness, has literally nothing in common with the Eastern Church. I wonder, would Trotsky's conviction that Protestant religion is necessarily a "bourgeois" creed which no worker can honestly profess survive a visit to a Dissenting chapel in a mining district? Has he ever read Bunyan, or glanced at the revolutionary history of Anabaptists and Fifth Monarchy men? What would he make of the queer disputes between the middle-class

Freethinker Robert Owen (who hated class war) and the pioneers of English Trade Unionism, who clung with equal obstinacy to their Christianity and their belief in the class war?

One feels the same failure of a man from another world to understand us when Trotsky laughs at the idea that a Labour majority in Parliament will ever be allowed to do anything fundamental.

Assuredly it will be a tremendous adventure; certainly it will want will and courage. No sane man will deny the risks to which Trotsky points. But equally, I think, every man who realises how deeply the Parliamentary tradition and the instinct of obedience to the majority are graven on the English mind will admit that the adventure is worth attempting. Not only in Parliament, but in churches, Trade Unions, and even clubs, this respect for the majority has been inculcated on generations of Englishmen. What can a Russian know of that? What estimate can he make of the power of tradition in our older civilisation? We should answer, in the last resort, that if he is right, if the propertied class will in the end defend its privileges by force, then we prefer to fight, as Cromwell fought, with the Parliament behind us, and the rights of a majority on our side.

But it is not the business of an introducer to enter into controversy with the author. The book with all its vitality and assurance is doubly valuable – as a revelation of the Russian mind, and a criticism of our English ways. It is the work of a shrewd and realistic intellect. It will not convert many of us to the Russian standpoint. But we shall fail to use it to the full unless we take it as a challenge that forces us to think out our position anew. Trotsky sees, as some of us do not, the difficulty of our unparalleled enterprise. He realises that the tactics which will avail to transform an old society cannot be the tactics of an opportunist Liberalism. The book may confirm us in our resolve by all means to avoid civil war, but it is a formidable challenge to us to test our own sincerity, and to ask ourselves whether, with a will and a courage that equal the audacity of these Russian pioneers, we are moving with single minds towards the achievement of our goal.

Trotsky on Our Sins[1]

Bertrand Russell

From *The New Leader*, 26 February 1926.

Trotsky's new book is one of the most interesting that I have read for a long time, and up to a certain point, extraordinarily penetrating. There are certain errors of fact, but they are not important – e.g., that Joseph Chamberlain left Gladstone on the Protectionist issue, and that the present Parliamentary constituencies are gerrymandered so as to give a great advantage to the Conservatives.

On the politics of the British Labour Movement, Trotsky is remarkably well informed. A great deal of his criticism is to my mind, quite convincing. I leave on one side his personalities about leaders, which will be liked or disliked according as the reader dislikes or likes the leader in question. What is more important is his complaint that the Labour Party lacks a coherent theoretical outlook. Take, for example, the question of Republicanism. He quotes British Labour pronouncements to the effect that the royal authority does no harm, and that a king is cheaper than a president. He argues that in a time of critical conflict the bourgeoisie can make use of the royal authority with great success, as the concentration point for all the extra-parliamentary, that is to say, the real forces directed against the working class… To proclaim a socialist programme, and at the same time declare that the royal authority "does not hinder" and works out cheaper, is absolutely the same as, for example, acknowledging materialistic science and making use of the incantation of a sorcerer for toothache, on the ground that the sorcerer is cheaper.

---

1   See p. 384 for Trotsky's reply to this article.

To hope to achieve Socialism without Republicanism is the sort of thing that could only occur among English-speaking people; it would hardly be possible for men with any profound knowledge of history, or any understanding of the economic and psychological links between different institutions. In spite of Mr. Brailsford's remark to the contrary in the introduction, I should agree with Trotsky in saying the same of the Churches. Personal religion is a private matter; but organised religion, in the modern world, must be a reactionary force, even when its adherents ardently desire the opposite.

"But", I shall be told, "how many Labour members would you get into Parliament if you attacked the monarchy and antagonised the Churches?" Here we come up against a most disastrous fallacy. It is thought that the important thing is to get Socialists elected to Parliament by hook or by crook, even if, in order to get elected, they have had to let it be understood that they will refrain from carrying out large parts of the Socialist programme. To secure a Government composed of professing Socialists is not the same thing as to secure Socialism; this has been proved in many European countries since the war. Socialism will never be actually established until the leaders are in earnest in desiring it; by this I mean not merely that they should favour it in the abstract, but that they should be willing, for its sake, to forego the amenities of bourgeois success, which are enjoyed by successful Labour politicians so long as they refrain from abolishing bourgeois privileges.

Another important point is illustrated by the analogy of Cromwell, upon which Trotsky dwells at some length. Cromwell, unlike most of the Parliament men, expressed a preference for soldiers convinced of the justice of the cause rather than 'gentlemen', and only by this means succeeded in achieving victory in spite of the opposition of his superior officers. In our day, in England, there seems to be hardly anyone whose belief in anything is sufficient to make him indifferent to 'gentlemanliness'; certain Labour leaders are constantly led into weaknesses by the desire to have their opponents consider them 'gentlemen'. They do not seem to realise that the ideal of a 'gentleman' is one of the weapons of the propertied classes; it precludes dirty tricks against the rich and powerful, but not against the poor and oppressed. This weakness is peculiarly British. We shall achieve nothing until we desire Socialism more than the approval of our enemies, which is only to be won by treachery, conscious or unconscious.

Our British passion for inconsistency and lack of philosophy is leading the Labour Movement astray. Cromwell had a complete philosophy, however absurd it may seem to us; so had the Benthamites who created the Liberal Party and the whole democratic movement of the nineteenth century. The Russian Communists have achieved what could never have been achieved by men who were content with a hotch-potch of amiable sentiments. It is useless to pretend, for instance, that Socialism is merely Christianity consistently carried out. Christianity is an agricultural religion, Socialism is industrial; it is not so much an affair of sentiment as of economic organisation. And we British, like the young man who had great possessions, are prevented from thinking clearly by the vague realisation that, if we did, we should have to abandon our imperialism; it is only by a skilful muddle-headedness that the Labour Party can inveigh against imperialists while taking care to retain the Empire and to carry on the tradition of oppression, as the late Government did in practice.

Let us, at least for the sake of argument, admit the whole of Trotsky's indictment of our movement; what, then, shall we say of his programme for Britain? I say it is a programme which could only be advocated by an enemy or a fool; and Trotsky is not a fool. His view is that when we at last have a Labour Government with a clear parliamentary majority, the present leaders, both of the Right and the Left, will be as helpless as Kerensky, and will be swept away by resolute men of action.

> The police, the courts, the army, and the territorial forces will always be on the side of the disruptors, saboteurs, and fascists. The administrative machinery will have to be broken up and the reactionaries replaced by Labour Party members. [But such meagre measures] will sharpen the legal and illegal opposition of unified bourgeois reaction in the extreme. In other words: this will also be a path of civil war.

> [...] in the event of the victory of the proletariat [there will ensue] the shattering of the resistance of the exploiters by means of the revolutionary dictatorship.[2]

It is odd how Trotsky's realism fails him at this point. Much of his book is taken up in proving how our economic position has deteriorated, and how we have become dependent upon the United States. Yet when he speaks of a Communist revolution, he always argues as though we were economically self-subsistent. It is obvious that French (if not British) aeroplanes and American (if not British) warships would soon put an end to the Communist regime; or, at the lowest, an economic blockade would destroy our export trade and therefore deprive us of our food supply.

2　See p. 292 of the present edition.

There are some bombastic sentences about the sympathy to be expected from Soviet Russia. But until Soviet Russia can place a fleet in the Atlantic stronger than that of America, it is not clear what we should gain by sympathy, however enthusiastic. To secure economic independence without naval supremacy, we should have to reduce our population to about 20 millions. While this was being effected by starvation, no doubt Trotsky's sympathy would be a great comfort; but, on the whole, most of us would rather remain alive without it than die with it.

The fact is that Trotsky hates Britain and British imperialism, not without good reason, and is therefore not to be trusted when he gives advice. We have become, through our dependence upon foreign food, so hopelessly entangled in world politics that it is impossible for us to advance at a pace which America will not tolerate.

Trotsky himself says:

> In the decisive struggle against the proletariat the British bourgeoisie will enjoy the most powerful support of the bourgeoisie of the United States, while the proletariat will rest for support primarily upon the working class of Europe and the oppressed popular masses of the colonies.[3]

It is scarcely credible that he should suppose our food supply would continue under such circumstances. I am afraid that, like the rest of us, he is a patriot when it comes to the pinch: a Communist revolution in England would be advantageous to Russia, and therefore he advises it without considering impartially whether it would be advantageous to us. The arguments against it, so far from being sentimental or visionary, are strategical and economic. The Pacifism which he dislikes in the British Labour Movement is forced upon it by the dependence upon America which has resulted from our participation in the Great War. If he really desires the spread of Communism, and not merely the collapse of England, it is time for him to turn his attention to the American Federation of Labour.

---

3   See p. 339 of the present edition.

Trotsky and His English Critics

R. Palme Dutt

Labour Monthly, Vol. VIII, No. 4 April 1926.

No one would guess from reading the reviews of Trotsky's book[1] that it is a serious piece of work. However, it is. From the reviews the book might be considered to consist mainly of brilliant wit, revolutionary romance from a Russian who has never ventured beyond the borders of Russia, and malicious personalities. Actually the book is an objective estimate of the English situation, rapid, but carried out with a sure hand; and the polemic is strictly subordinate to the objective argument.

A word must be said at the outset on the common plea that Trotsky "knows nothing of England" (the threadbare escape of every single reformist reviewer to avoid having to meet Trotsky's merciless argument). It would be more true to say that his critics know nothing of England – a charge that could be substantiated by every single statement of the reformist school for the past fifty years. Trotsky himself points out that:

> The 'leaders' of the British working class imagined for decades that an independent workers' party was the gloomy privilege of continental Europe. Nowadays, nothing is left of that naive and ignorant conceit. The proletariat forced the trade unions to create an independent party. It will not stop at this however.

> The Liberal and semi-Liberal leaders of the Labour Party still think that a social revolution is the gloomy prerogative of continental Europe. But here again events will expose their backwardness.[2]

---

1 *Where is Britain Going?*, from page 213 of the present edition.

2 Ibid., p. 252.

In fact, Trotsky is able justly to claim and substantiate that:

> We Marxists can, thanks to this, understand far better the course of development of the British labour movement, and better foretell its future than can the present-day 'theoreticians' of the Labour Party. The old call of philosophy to "know thyself" has not sounded in their ears.[3]

This self-ignorance of the reformist idealist school, which is so naively exposed in their reviews of Trotsky and their 'British' repudiations of his 'Russian' standpoint, can be illustrated in a very simple form. A challenge may safely be issued to the critics to name a single book by a single English author or politician, bourgeois or labour leader, which is as close to the essentials of the English situation as Trotsky's book. It cannot be done. And yet Trotsky is admittedly a busy man, for whom the English situation is only one factor in a complex of problems; his sketch could obviously be improved and amplified by fuller study, knowledge, contact, etc.; these English authors have abundance of time (for their narrow horizon England is usually the world), copious information, contact on the spot and all the rest of it. Nevertheless there is none. And why not? The reason goes to the heart of the English situation. The expressions and books produced in England about English questions are all marked by the same subjective unscientific character, the same insular ignorance and unconsciousness (*My Ideals for Labour, Ethics of Empire, England's Awakening, The Future of Citizenship, Creative Socialism*, and all the rest of the dreary crew). In other words they are all 'idealist', that is, unable to deal with the facts of the social process in their actual movement, unable to think dialectically. There is no social scientific, i.e., Marxist, school in England yet; a fact which reflects the immaturity of the working class movement and the overpowering weight of the past bourgeois tradition. As Trotsky points out, the same conditions which gave England priority in the past make for backwardness in every sphere today. English Capitalism was the pioneer in the past, empirically finding out a way. This fact has stamped a deeply empirical character on English thought, and a contempt for all non-English thought and methods. Today this traditional outlook has been inherited by the English labour leaders from the bourgeoisie just at a time when its foundation in fact has completely disappeared, and when England most needs to learn from the development of world scientific thought.

The notion that Trotsky is unfit to write on England because he is not an Englishman is a piece of abysmal national ignorance and self-conceit. It

3 Ibid., 254.

would be as sensible to argue that Marx could not write on *Capital* because he was not a capitalist. In point of fact, the best view of cheesemites at the end of a microscope is not necessarily at the cheesemites' end. When the critics proudly put Trotsky right on some irrelevant point of detail (and in nine cases out of ten they are wrong even in their facts, and merely misunderstanding Trotsky's point),[4] they are only giving a measure of their own smallness. In short, the cheesemites are showing that they are cheesemites. Certainly the scientific handling needs, when we are concerned with the living problems

---

4   One or two examples may be given of these corrections of Trotsky's "ignorance."

1. Johnston takes as his principal proof of the falsity of Trotsky's facts the statement that MacDonald operated in the realm of diplomacy with the aid of false documents. This is a simple question of history. MacDonald was responsible head of the Foreign Office when it issued the Zinoviev forgery; he wrote and amended with his own hand the note utilising the forgery; he never repudiated the issue of the forgery; and he has never apologised for it since. In the light of these facts Johnston's ingenuous plea that "MacDonald did not operate the Zinoviev letter; it was operated against him" (which, even if it were true, would make of the Leader of the Labour Party an innocent baby unfit to be left in charge of a halfpennyworth of working class interests among the foxes of the bourgeoisie – and MacDonald is not entirely an innocent baby) makes no difference to the historical facts. The constitutional, legal and political responsibility for the Zinoviev forgery rests solely with MacDonald, and cannot be lifted by his lackeys on to any other shoulders.

2. Brailsford, Russell, and others complain that Trotsky dares to suggest that the English electoral districts are weighted in favour of the Conservatives. Yet this is notoriously so, although the extent may be a matter for discussion. The agricultural districts, which are the Conservative strongholds, are heavily over-represented by the apportionment of electoral districts; and, in addition, there are the University seats, bogus 'City' and 'Exchange' constituencies, etc. Compare Dalton in the March Socialist Review: "Broadly, the industrial vote predominates in more than 400 constituencies, the agricultural in less than 200… In the country as a whole, the agricultural areas are over-represented in relation to their electorates." This overweighting of agriculture – in industrial England – is a significant evidence of the reactionary character of the whole electoral system in England.

The same will be found to be the case with most of the other points raised, if subjected to closer analysis. The superficiality rests with the critics, who are startled at unsuspected angles of vision turned on to the conventional hypocritical bourgeois picture of events and conditions in England.

of the class struggle, to be carried beyond a treatment of principles, and to be realised, elaborated, and worked out in closest relation to the fullest living information, experience, and action. But to imagine that the important thing is the possession of details of local information (which 50 million Englishmen have had for a generation without being any the wiser), and not the scientific handling, is childishness.

With this prelude we may come to Trotsky's analysis of the English situation.

Trotsky argues that England has reached a turning point at which no further capitalist development is possible, and the only path forward is along the lines of Socialist reorganisation. This conception needs understanding correctly, as it is the basis of the whole argument. The decline of English Capitalism dates back for forty years, since the development of the more scientifically, organised German and later American industry, and was already diagnosed by Engels in its main lines in 1885. This decline was partially veiled by the Imperialist expansion of the past forty years, which was in reality accelerating the decline, although giving an artificial appearance of prosperity. It is only the war and the post-war period that has carried forward the whole process at a tremendous pace, and now laid bare to all the point of open decline reached and the emergence of new world forces. American industrial and financial preponderance, which grows more exacting and dominating each year; the centrifugal forces of the Empire and growth of the Dominions to an independent capitalist policy; the revolutionising and struggle to independence of the colonial and semi-colonial nations, which afforded the indispensable basis of English capitalist industry and exploitation; the loss of strategic immunity and sea power; the strangling weight of debt, inflated capital, and long continued accumulation; the historic disorganisation of industry and failure of development: all these are factors not affected by unbased hopes of a possible 'revival of trade' (as if it were only a question of the ups and downs of 'normal' capitalism); they are contradictions which no capitalist statesman can solve, because the economic reorganisation which alone can solve them, cannot be accomplished without cutting across the whole historic tangle of private property interests and legal rights which stand in the way. This is why only a revolution can solve the English situation: a legal transformation is not in practice possible, because the whole existing legal state framework and machine is in practice bound up with the maintenance of existing property rights.

What is the character of this revolution? It is here that comes the second essential point of Trotsky's argument. A political revolution is the necessary preliminary of carrying out the economic reorganisation. This point is the key to Trotsky's book: for the first point – the basic necessity of a unitary economic reorganisation on the lines of the social organisation of production – is beginning in varying degrees to be understood. But the economic reorganisation cannot take place so long as power is in the hands of the capitalist class; since the capitalist class will not carry out their own extinction. The economic reorganisation can only be carried out when power is in the hands of the working class, whose existence and future is bound up with the social organisation of production. The revolutionary conception is commonly treated in the vulgar bourgeois and reformist writers as the conception of a 'sudden' transition to a socialist economy. This of course is nonsense, as the transition to a full socialist economy is a heavy process, involving many stages. But the reorganisation cannot begin until class power is changed: this is the essence of the revolutionary conception. Trotsky shows how the bourgeois political revolution of the seventeenth century (itself the outcome of the gradual rise of the bourgeoisie within the preceding state) was the necessary preliminary of the industrial revolution of the eighteenth century and the consequent full flourishing of capitalism. In the same way the working class has to win power into its own hands now. This is not accomplished by the sham of a 'Socialist' ministry within the existing system, which in itself is no more than a cover for capitalist power. The actual transference means that the working class apparatus has to become the ruling apparatus throughout the country. This involves the certainty of struggle and civil war with the existing ruling capitalist class, which has already shown, by its action all over the world that it will use all its resources to maintain itself by every means without limit. In comparison with the certainty of this struggle, for which the working class must prepare, the question of parliamentary right in relation to it is absolutely secondary, and; if allowed to occupy the foreground, even to the extent of hoping to avoid the struggle, is a deluding and disarming of the workers and a guaranteeing of capitalist armed power.

This brings us to the third stage in Trotsky's argument – the working class movement in England, and its readiness for the future struggle. This is the central issue of the whole argument. A revolution that involves an actual transference of class power cannot be carried out by the working class without absolute clearness and determination of leadership, freedom from dependence on bourgeois ideology, and strong central organisation – in other words, a revolutionary mass party, leading the workers to the struggle for proletarian dictatorship. These conditions do not yet exist in the English working class, and this weakness in the subjective readiness of the workers is the retarding fact in the development of the English situation. What is the explanation of this, and what is the line of development? What are the traditions and forces that stand in the way? Here Trotsky brings to bear all his wealth of polemical power and analysis to shatter the existing confusion, cant, and humbug of the ruling leadership and ideology in the existing Labour Movement, and to show the workers the plain path forward.

The existing leadership in the Labour Movement is the inheritor of the Liberal, that is of the bourgeois tradition from the time of secure capitalist supremacy. All its outlook is bounded by the capitalist framework, by the permitted legal forms of parliamentary and trade union activity. All its beliefs are the echo of capitalism; of the bourgeois national tradition, of Protestant Christianity, of the sanctity of the Empire, of the sinfulness of revolution, of the necessity of very gradual change, of the unity of classes, and all the other cults which Capitalism has laboured to instil into the workers. The more conscious elements of this leadership, the Right Wing, work in direct cooperation with the capitalists. The more confused elements, the centre and so-called left, combine occasional verbal hankerings after socialism, with subordination in practice to the same policy and ideology. Repeated episodes show that the basic ideology of all is the same (Trotsky groups it collectively as Fabianism), and that the differences are still only differences of sentiment and phrase, of responsibility in the governmental sense and irresponsibility.

But this leadership is in complete conflict with the whole existing development of events, and with the development of the working class. Capitalism is no longer ascending, but descending; and there is therefore no longer any room for Liberalism. The capitalist class can no longer make concessions, but must cut the conditions of the workers; in consequence is no longer driven in a progressive direction by the fear of revolution, but in the opposite; develops increasingly to Conservatism, to police repression, to Fascism. On the other hand the workers are driven to more and more revolutionary struggle; first to maintain their conditions, and then, as this becomes more and more visibly impossible in the existing capitalist situation, to the political struggle for power. The revolutionary pressure of the workers throws up into existence the Labour Party against all the opposition of the old Liberal leaders. But the Labour Party is only a stage in the process. As certainly, the workers will throw off the old Liberal leadership, and find revolutionary leadership. And the form of this process will be the transition from the leadership of the Independent Labour Party to the leadership of the Communist Party.

This struggle for emancipation demands a break with the old traditions that still tie the workers to the leading strings of the bourgeoisie. Therefore Trotsky delivers the full force of his assault on these traditions; and this assault is an essential part of the attack on capitalism in England. These traditions or conceptions to which Trotsky returns again and again, may be summed up under four heads: (1) Religion; (2) Pacifism; (3) Parliamentary Democracy; and (4) Gradualism. All these, when analysed, reduce in the end to one thing: submission to the ruling class.

The attack on Religion has been widely misunderstood. Protestant religion has been the principal form in England for the transmission of bourgeois influence to the working class. Religion seeks to blur all class distinctions in a fictitious spiritual 'brotherhood' alongside actual material relations of inequality and exploitation, and has therefore been the invariable weapon of an exploiting class. Religion is the negation of science, and therefore enslaves the mind, destroying mental clearness and honesty, and replacing revolutionary realism by illusion, fables, and aspirations. For this reason the revolutionary working-class movement, fighting on a scientific basis, necessarily combats Religion, not only as an organised social force, but also as an individual ideology.

Nothing more completely exposes the mental stage of development of the Fabian Socialists than the universal disapproval and disagreement that Trotsky's attack on Religion in the Labour Movement has aroused. It is not merely that such an attack is repudiated by every reformist critic (even Russell the philosopher, while agreeing with the attack on "organised religion", comes out with the old vicious social democratic distinction that "personal religion is a private matter" – without seeing that this is precisely what Trotsky is attacking). It is that Trotsky's attack has actually to be 'explained away' by the solemn statement that he, Trotsky (with his abundant West European and American experience) can only be thinking of – the Old Russian Orthodox Eastern Church! This is a truly comic failure of Malvolio to recognise himself. Every page of Trotsky's book shows that he is thinking precisely of that ethical Protestant, Puritan, musty, dusty hymn-singing Christianity which was the basis of the old Liberal Party yesterday and of the upper sections of the Labour Movement today, and which, despite all its sham 'democratic' pretensions, has always been the sheet-anchor of the Lloyd Georges and MacDonalds and all that is canting and reactionary in politics for the degradation of the workers and their enslavement. Nevertheless Brailsford, who ought to know enough at least of the facts of Marxism to know better, comes out with this foolish, fable – which is solemnly repeated after him by all the scribes – and goes on to talk of Trotsky's failure to understand the "free" and "democratic" traditions of "English religion":

> I wonder, would Trotsky's conviction that Protestant religion is necessarily a "bourgeois" creed which no worker can honestly profess [what a pitiful and disingenuous parody of Trotsky's argument! Plenty of workers have 'honestly professed' Liberalism, which was none the less a bourgeois creed] survive a visit to a Dissenting chapel in a mining district?

To which the answer is that precisely in the mining districts the principal battle has notoriously been in case after case between Religious Revivalism with its ally Spiritualism on the one hand, and the Revolution and Communism on the other.[5]

What of Pacifism and Capitalist Democracy? Both are, on analysis, hypocritical forms of submission to the ruling class. Pacifism soon becomes entangled in an impossible network of distinctions between permissible and impermissible force, which in practice bases itself on one simple criterion – the bourgeois criminal code. In grosser forms (MacDonald, Ponsonby, etc.), Pacifism supports the armed forces of the Capitalist State and imperialist repression, the guns, tanks, and cruisers of the bloody capitalist order; and only preaches submission and non-resistance to the workers and subject peoples. In subtler, more refined forms, the ugly contrast is veiled beneath phrases of centrist irresponsibility ("against all force"), but the practical basis remains the police Capitalist State. The same is true of Capitalist Democracy. It is soon found that there is very little democracy in Capitalist Democracy; and that the preaching of submission to Capitalist Democracy means, not

---

5 The most complete and pathetic misunderstanding of the whole issue of religion and materialists is expressed by Lansbury:

> As I understand our comrade, he bases his whole philosophy of life on materialism. Well: he may be right, but my experience is that when men or women join our movement purely and simply because they think it is going to bring them individually a better life, they very soon find their way into the other camp.

It is a shame that his staff, who should know some scraps of Marxism, should have been so malicious as to let this pass.

submission to the ideal principle of democracy (in that case, the House of Commons, which legislates for 400 millions on a basis of one elector to eight colonial slaves, would have no claim to authority), but submission to the existing legal apparatus of the bourgeoisie, and the obedient attempt to pass through whatever "asses' gate" the bourgeoisie choose to set as the only permitted path to proletarian freedom. Pacificism and Capitalist Democracy are in fact fine phrases which mean in reality the slavery of the working class.

'Gradualism' is subjected to a no less severe analysis. It is not difficult to see that 'gradualism', as soon as it is examined, disappears into a phrase meaning nothing at all save that progress must be slow, i.e., a catchphrase for the maintenance of the existing order. Its bombastic pseudo-scientific pretensions have no foundation either in fact, experience or in real science. It is an arbitrary and illegitimate jump from the conception of Evolution, i.e., of development, which is the basis of scientific thinking, to the conception that Evolution contains no leaps or conflicts, which is contrary to all the facts of nature and experience. The whole opposition of 'Evolution' and 'Revolution' is childish and meaningless. 'Evolution' leads to 'Revolution', and 'Revolution' is a part of 'Evolution'. Trotsky has no difficulty in showing that even in the plant and animal world (from which the obsolete MacDonald type of preachers profess to draw their social wisdom!), the accumulation of gradual changes leads up to the necessity of sharp transformation or conflict: the butterfly bursts forth from the chrysalis; the chicken has to smash the prison of its egg. Much more so in the social world of human development, where the factors are so much more complex as to render biological metaphors worthless child's play, and where the consciousness of men enters in as direct agents of the social process, this conscious role being expressed in the conflict of classes. But in fact to argue with these preachers in scientific terms is waste of time. Their arguments are not seriously meant save as a hypocritical cover for conservatism. The Baldwins and MacDonalds never think of using 'gradual' and 'persuasive' means when it comes to the tasks of imperialist repression. Guns, tanks and air-bombing are then their forms of 'gradualism'. It is only to the working class that they preach 'gradualism', i.e., to put a brake on their advance.

Finally, what of the subtler arguments which profess to recognise the possibility of struggle and civil war with the bourgeoisie, but urge the necessity to exploit to the full the possibilities of parliamentary democracy, the desirability of fighting with the legal right of a parliamentary majority on the workers' side, and so forth? Here again the same double-dealing is visible.

Communism has always advocated the fullest exploitation of the possibilities of parliament, but not as a substitute for the inevitable real struggle; if it is once advocated as a substitute for the real struggle, it becomes only an instrument of enslavement. Is the 'recognition' of the possibility of civil war serious, or is it only a counter in an argument? If it is said that it is serious, then all the acts and daily propaganda of its spokesmen belie it.

> But heroic promises to put up lightning resistance in the event the Conservatives should 'dare' and so forth are not worth a rotten egg. One cannot lull the masses day in and day out with claptrap about a peaceful, painless transition to socialism and then at the first solid punch on the nose summon the masses to an armed response. This is the surest way of assisting reaction in the rout of the proletariat.[6]

In burning words Trotsky describes how a real revolutionary situation arises, with how little regard for the niceties and forms of parliamentary right (how would these heroes act, if the Fascist attack were to develop on the working class movement, as in Italy, *before* any Parliamentary majority or Labour Government?), and throwing the responsibilities of action and of facing armed force on the leaders of the working class movement. The 'passive' general strike inevitably gives rise to the necessity to protect it from guerilla attacks, saboteurs, and provocateurs. The smaller conflicts inevitably extend to larger ones. The Government, once threatened, inevitably brings the armed troops into play. The coming over of the wavering troops inevitably depends on the determination of the revolutionary leaders and the direct attack on the 'loyal' troops. The fate of the proletariat, the difference between victory and the scorpions of reaction let loose after defeat, depends on the political and organising preparations of the working class forces, and on the determination and strategy of the leaders, and not at all save in the most secondary degree on the legal and formal parliamentary and other 'rights' – which will be covered at once in a cloud of arguments and counter-arguments, as in wartime, so soon as the fight begins ("an assault upon the House of Commons by the Conservatives would form a most 'noble' motive for agitation, but such a circumstance has in the end but a third – or fifth – rate importance"[7] – and in addition the choice for this may not lie with the workers).

> The more procrastinatory, hesitant, and evasive the policy of the leaders of the general strike, the less will be the waverings in the soldiers' ranks, the more

---

6 Ibid., p. 295.
7 Ibid., p. 296.

resolutely they will support the existing power, and the more chances the latter will have of emerging the victor from the crisis so as then to loose all the scorpions of bloody repression on to the heads of the working class.

Only the highest resoluteness in the revolutionary struggle is capable of striking the arms out of the hands of reaction, shortening the duration of civil war, and minimising the number of its victims. Whoever does not take this road should not take to arms at all; and without taking to arms a general strike cannot be organised. And if the general strike is rejected there can be no thought of serious struggle. The only thing that then remains is to educate workers in the spirit of total prostration which is already the concern of official education, governing parties, the priests of every church, and… the socialist preachers of the impermissibility of force.[8]

These words deserve to be burnt into the consciousness of every centre of the working class movement. They represent the kernel of the situation for the future in England, as in every Capitalist State, whatever the momentary liberal forms and phrases.

The treatment of this question of revolutionary and bourgeois force by the reviewers is deeply significant. Every reviewer combines to oppose Trotsky's argument: that is, to advocate unchallenged submission to the supremacy of bourgeois force and acceptance of only such methods of agitation as are permitted by the bourgeoisie. But the arguments of every reviewer are different, contradictory, and in reality nothing but a catchword repetition of exactly the threadbare formulas Trotsky has been patiently pulling to pieces, without the slightest attempt to meet Trotsky's argument.

The arguments (if they can be so called) need only to be set out together to see their general character.

a. Force is useless. "In the long run force accomplishes nothing" (Hunter). "The final word about violence is that this has been the weapon all through the ages, and we are as we were" (Lansbury). These confused 'Tolstoyan' arguments bear no relation to the policy of the leadership of the Labour Party, who believe in and use imperialist force, and are therefore irrelevant. To use these arguments in defence of the policy of the existing leaders of the Labour Party against the policy of Trotsky is indefensible.

b. Force is nasty. This is the argument of the Editor of the *Daily Herald*. Under the title 'Two views of Life in Conflict' he quotes a phrase of Trotsky concerning Cromwell, about the right of a historic mission to

---

8 Ibid., p. 280.

cut through all obstacles and triumphantly affirms the "breakdown" of this argument because Mussolini and British Imperialism also believe in their "historic mission". Certainly they do, and this is precisely why their force can only be met by force, and the talk of arguing them out of their positions (let Fyfe try converting Mussolini) is transparent make-believe, and evading the issue of repressive force confronting the working class. Fyfe rejects this as a "gloomy view." He prefers to set against it the "hope of persuading people that Force is futile", etc. In other words, he puts his "hopes", wishes, personal feelings in front of the facts that he himself admits, because the latter are "gloomy". This is Illusionism. (In addition it is of course as indefensible as the first as a defence of official Labour policy, which accepts bourgeois force and only opposes working class force.)

c. Force is unnecessary. "The battle for freedom is not yet lost. [...] Not only in Parliament, but in churches, Trade Unions, and even clubs, this respect for the majority has been inculcated on generations of Englishmen" (Brailsford). "Our traditions and training in majority rule" (Johnston). Here the wish is father to the thought. This is nowhere more curiously illustrated than in Brailsford's own introduction, where he is so eager to reaffirm the existence of English "freedom" after the "nightmare" of the Communist trial, that he actually declares that, if Trotsky's book is successfully issued in England and permitted to be discussed, "then for the moment at least the nightmare of this trial is dissipated." Unfortunately the twelve remain in prison; Hicks remains Home Secretary; the O. M. S. and Special Police recruiting go on; the intentions of the Conservatives are open. But for Brailsford all these mere facts are "dissipated", because a book is issued and he has written an introduction. The "dissipation" is in Brailsford's own mind. Once again, in all this 'democratic' view, 'hopes' are put forward instead of facing facts.

d. We will fight if... etc. These are the 'heroic promises' dealt with by Trotsky in the quotation already given, as "not worth a rotten egg." These promises are actually trotted out again by Brailsford, Johnston and others in exactly the same form as before without the slightest attempt to meet Trotsky's destructive arguments: that such promises are practically valueless without previous preparation, that the bourgeoisie will not necessarily allow the proletariat free choice of a strategic ground before attacking, etc.

e. We can't fight because… etc. This is an alternative line of argument favoured by Johnston, Russell and others. The 'because' always brings up some purely technical reason for inability to face the ruling class. Before the war the favourite argument was modern artillery. After the Russian Revolution had disposed of that technical argument, the modern favourite argument follows the line of chemical warfare, the air force or – in England – the food supply.

It is worth noting the effect of this line of argument which places technical in front of political considerations. This means of course simple surrender to the bourgeoisie. It makes a present to the bourgeoisie of a public declaration that they are impregnable, and that the workers cannot face a struggle. If that were true, why enter on a struggle at all of which the end is thus foreseen? To imagine that in such circumstances the bourgeoisie would let themselves be circumvented by the paper formalities of parliament is excess of innocence. Nothing remains, as Trotsky says, but to "educate workers in the spirit of total prostration",[9] etc. In fact the calculation is false, and based on a completely formal unrealistic view of the actual factors and development. But its principal importance at the present moment is the light that it throws on the socialist determination of those who make it. As with all mensheviks in face of every practical difficulty, what should be a technical problem for the revolution to solve becomes at once (without even any attempt at serious consideration) a political reason *against* the revolution.

Johnston himself uses both the last two arguments together. On the one hand he argues, quoting Brailsford, that, if the bourgeoisie compel us we will fight. On the other hand he argues that if we fight, and are presumably certain to be blockaded, "we would perish". How he reconciles his two arguments he does not stop to consider; but in fact both his arguments serve the same purpose – to put off Trotsky's challenge.

Russell's argument is even more instructive. He "agrees" benignly with almost all the points of Trotsky that the rest deny: he finds that "on the politics of the British Labour Movement, Trotsky is remarkably well informed"; he agrees on the question of monarchy, on the question of religion, on the imperialism of the Labour Party, on the intellectual and social subservience of the leaders to the bourgeoisie, etc. Nor does he even dispute the inevitability of civil war with the bourgeoisie. But then comes his little 'practical' difficulty which enables him, as a British citizen, to avoid any revolutionary conclusion

---

9 Ibid., p. 280.

to the revolutionary principles, to which, as a philosopher, he has given his assent. Nothing can be done because – Britain is dependent on America. "[I]t is impossible for us to advance at a pace which America will not tolerate." Here is the true English version of Austro-Marxism. Enlarging and developing this liberating conception, Russell discovers that this is the true unguessed-at explanation of the "Pacifism" of the British Labour leaders. "The Pacifism which he dislikes in the British Labour Movement is forced upon it by the dependence upon America which has resulted from our participation in the Great War." Unfortunately for the truth of this statement, the "Pacifism" existed in the British Labour Movement long before there was any question of a "Great War" or dependence on America. The fact that Russell should be reduced to such a demonstrably false argument reveals the straits to which these theoreticians of the Labour Party have been reduced in their efforts to escape the issue raised by Trotsky.

Now these arguments, if placed together, are all mutually contradictory. We are told by these official spokesmen of the Labour Party in reply to Trotsky: (1) that force is useless, (2) that force is nasty, (3) that force is unnecessary, (4) that we will fight if necessary, (5) that we can't fight. The argument that all force is wrong is in complete contradiction to the practice of the official Labour leadership. The argument that all force is useless is in complete contradiction to the argument that we will use force if necessary. The argument that we will use force if necessary is in complete contradiction to the argument that we could not fight if we would. And so on endlessly (for the arguments here reproduced are only a selection of the maze offered). But all these contradictory arguments agree in one thing, and in one thing only, and that is the practical conclusion: that we need do nothing now to face the question of bourgeois force and the working class struggle. This common principle alone unites these motley ranks. This is a very striking fact. It means that the arguments themselves are indifferent, variable, taken up and thrown aside at random, individually reached, unthought out, contradictory – that is to say, on a central problem confronting the working class there is no attempt at a serious concerted answer: on one thing alone there is agreement; one thing alone, that is to say, is serious for these 'leaders'; and that is servility to the existing State apparatus and bourgeois legality and force. This is the inevitable conclusion reached from the aggregate of the replies issued to Trotsky on behalf of the official Labour Party leadership.

This conclusion – the complete frivolousness and emptiness of the existing leadership in relation to the actual problems of the working class struggle, and their seriousness only in the question of bourgeois state servility – is the most important outcome of the replies issued to Trotsky on behalf of the official leadership. It is for this very reason that the divorce between these leaders and the working class inevitably grows greater, as the workers are compelled in daily life to find an answer to their problems and to find a leadership which is ready and able to drive a way forward.

In the concluding section of his argument Trotsky shows how the workers in England are already developing as a revolutionary class force, in spite of all the obstacles to hold them in. This is shown most clearly in the development of the trade unions more and more into the political sphere. The history of the Labour Party is only a stage in this process. The real character of this process is shown unmistakeably in the trade union political levy, which is the very basis of the Labour Party, and which Trotsky seizes on with sure insight as the germ of the whole Bolshevist principle:

> In the compulsory, anti-Liberal, 'despotic' collection of the political levies there is contained, like the future stem and ear in a grain of wheat, all those methods of Bolshevism against which MacDonald never tires of sprinkling the holy water of his own indignant narrow-mindedness. The working class has the right and the duty to set its own considered class will above all the fictions and sophisms of bourgeois democracy.

What is the future of the Trade Unions? As the economic situation is increasingly bringing home, the Trade Unions have no longer any future in the capitalist framework of society. But this does not mean that they are played out, as the politicians of the Labour Party would like to suggest. On the contrary, the Trade Unions have a tremendous future as the main lever of the economic transformation of the country, as the apparatus and source of personnel of the working class regime, and the schools of education of the proletariat in the spirit of socialist production. But to accomplish this role they need to win power in the hands of the working class, and for this purpose they need to throw up and place at their head a revolutionary party, capable of carrying through the struggle for power.

> The reformist, opportunist, liberal Labour Party can only weaken the trade unions by paralysing the initiative of the masses. A revolutionary Labour party resting upon the trade unions will become in turn a powerful instrument for their recovery and resurgence.[10]

---

10 Ibid., p. 320.

This transformation is the immediate task. The workers have already driven past the old Liberal Party. They have thrown forward the Independent Labour Party leaders, and these in their turn are being exposed today. The so-called Left leaders will in their turn be put to the test.

> But those who will in all probability form the first substitutes, people of the ilk of Lansbury, Wheatley, and Kirkwood, will inevitably reveal that they are but a left variant of the same basic Fabian type. Their radicalism is constrained by democracy and religion, and poisoned by the national arrogance that ties them spiritually to the British bourgeoisie. The working class will in all probability have to renew its leadership several times before it creates a party really answering the historical situation and the tasks of the British proletariat.[11]

But the needs of the workers and the force of events will drive forward to the future which must be reached.

> The Communist Party must develop and come to power as the party of proletarian dictatorship. There are no ways round this. Whoever believes there are and propounds them can only deceive British workers. That is the main conclusion of our analysis.[12]

It will be seen even from the very incomplete survey here given that there is here an argument solidly built, based on a careful and exact estimate of the objective situation in England and the forces in the English working class movement, and requiring at least an equally exact and responsible treatment for an attempt at its refutation.

The bankruptcy of the answers published in the official Labour press is very striking. There is no attempt (with the single exception of the well-intentioned, but extremely innocent and uncomprehending, notice in the *Socialist Review*) to meet Trotsky's objective argument. There is no attempt to consider the objective situation in England, the line of development, the policy of the bourgeoisie, the line of development of the working class movement, the next problems of the working class struggle. These questions, which are of very serious importance for the working class, do not exist for the light and airy writers of the official Labour press. For them everything is turned into the personal. Trotsky is "brilliant", "witty", but "arrogant", "offensive", with "execrable taste". Trotsky has "attacked" the Labour leaders, and the natural desire is to attack him back: it is felt as a personal quarrel

---

11 Ibid., p. 256.
12 Ibid., p. 339.

(Lansbury, after admitting that the book is "theoretically sound" – as if this were an issue of only minor importance like a question of style – goes on to say: "If those of us whom he criticises were put into the mirror of truth, we should be in effect saying to him: 'Yes, and we do not like the look of you either'"). Trotsky is a "Russian"; his standpoint – familiar enough in every country since the Communist Manifesto of 1847 – is "the Russian standpoint" (Brailsford – perhaps Brailsford thinks the Communist Manifesto a "Russian" document?); he sees everything through "Russian spectacles" and imagines every country must imitate Russia (Hunter); his real aim in advocating revolution in England is because it would be "advantageous to Russia" (Russell – what a childish little piece of spite!). Occasionally some critic discovers some incidental point or other at random, without reference to the context or the line of argument (like Johnston's indignant discovery that Trotsky dares to advocate the abolition of the monarchy as one among a series of demands for a decisive attack on bourgeois class power), and at once sets up an excited clucking, without even waiting or troubling to understand the point first. When finally an attempt is made to touch on any of the central themes and issues raised by Trotsky, such as the issue of bourgeois and revolutionary force or bourgeois democracy, the critic at once falls back on personal feelings, emotions, opinions, hopes, aspirations, dismisses Trotsky's view as "a gloomy view", and expresses warmly, as if they were arguments, his private hopes and faiths, without even attempting to consider the alternative if his faiths should prove unfounded.

This bankruptcy is of course not accidental, but is simply the expression of the ideological bankruptcy of the whole school of Fabian Socialism and the Independent Labour Party. Today it is becoming more and more widely clear that the only coherent view of actual problems possible is the Communist view. Marxism is conquering in England also by the power of facts. Just as thirty years ago the Independent Labour Party was permeating and capturing the trade union bureaucracy, so today the younger trade union masses are advancing to Communism. The contrast and conflict between Trotsky's book, with its objective firmness and militant confidence, and his reviewers, with their vague confusion and shoddy sentiment in place of argument, is the contrast between two worlds and the conflict between two classes. Between these two worlds there can be no real contact. The older school of leaders who were bred up in the Liberal tradition (and their younger apprentices at the same trade) will never understand, but will go on repeating their catchphrases and empty sentiments until they pass away or are pushed aside. But the younger workers, who have been bred up in the conditions of the war and after, and whose eyes and ears are eager to take in the facts, the Labour students, the younger trade unionists, the workers' leaders of tomorrow, are learning very fast: and Trotsky's book will help them to learn. Among these Trotsky's book will be eagerly read, and will give stimulus and help; will help to break the chains of enslavement to old ideas and leadership, to give confidence and clearness and strength, and to show the plain path forward of the struggle. The English working class has cause to be grateful to Trotsky for his book; and to hope that he will not stay his hand at this short sketch, but will carry forward his work of interpretation, polemic and elucidation, and elaborate his analysis further, which is so much needed in England. For despite all the national philistines, the problems of England, more than of any country, will only be solved by the united force of the whole international movement.

Volume Three

VII

*From World Slump
to World War*

1929-40

British 'Democratic' Traditions

From Chapter 45 of *My Life* (1930).

On 5 June 1929, the Independent Labour Party, of which Ramsay MacDonald is a member, sent me an official invitation, on its own initiative, to come to England and deliver a lecture at the party school. The invitation, signed by the general secretary of the party, read: "With the formation of the Labour government here, we cannot believe that any difficulties are likely to arise in connection with your visit to England for this purpose." Nevertheless difficulties did arise. I was neither allowed to deliver a lecture before the supporters of MacDonald, nor was I allowed to avail myself of the aid of English physicians. My application for a visa was flatly refused. Clynes, the Labour Home Secretary, defended this refusal in the House of Commons. He explained the philosophical meaning of democracy with a directness that would have done credit to any minister of Charles II. According to Clynes, the right of asylum does not mean the right of an exile to demand asylum, but the right of the state to refuse it. Clynes' definition is remarkable in one respect: by a single blow it destroys the very foundations of so-called democracy. The right of asylum, in the style of Clynes, always existed in tsarist Russia. When the Shah of Persia failed to hang all the revolutionaries and was obliged to leave his beloved country, Nicholas II not only extended to him the right of asylum, but supplied him with sufficient comforts to live in Odessa.[1] But it never occurred to any of the Irish revolutionaries to

---

1 The Persian bourgeois revolution which began in 1905 eventually deposed the pro-Russian reactionary Shah Muzaffor Ud-Din in 1907, after he had made a number of attempts to hold back the tide of reform. He fled to Russia after being deposed, and

seek asylum in tsarist Russia, where the constitution consisted entirely of the principle expounded by Clynes, namely, that the citizens must be content with what the state authorities give them or take from them. Mussolini accorded the right of asylum to the King of Afghanistan in exact agreement with this very principle.[2]

The pious Mr. Clynes ought at least to have known that democracy, in a sense, inherited the right of asylum from the Christian church, which, in turn, inherited it, with much besides, from paganism. It was enough for a pursued criminal to make his way into a temple, sometimes enough even to touch only the ring of the door, to be safe from persecution. Thus the church understood the right of asylum as the right of the persecuted to an asylum, and not as an arbitrary exercise of will on the part of pagan or Christian priests. Until now, I had thought the pious Labourites, though little informed in matters of socialism, certainly well versed in the tradition of the church. Now I find that they are not even that.

But why does Clynes stop at the first lines of his theory of the state law? It is a pity. The right of asylum is only one component part of the system of democracy. Neither in its historical origin, nor in its legal nature, does it differ from the right of freedom of speech, of assembly, etc. Mr. Clynes, it is to be hoped, will soon arrive at the conclusion that the right of freedom of speech stands not for the right of citizens to express their thoughts, whatever they may be, but for the right of the state to forbid its subjects to entertain such thoughts. As to the freedom of strikes, the conclusion has already been drawn by British law.[3]

Clynes' misfortune is that he had to explain his actions aloud, for there were members of the Labour faction in Parliament who put respectful but inconvenient questions to him. The Norwegian premier found himself

---

was protected by Tsar Nicholas. In July 1911 the ex-Shah led an army of invasion which was defeated. Later in the same year Russian forces intervened, and they remained there until after the October 1917 revolution.

2   King Amanullah was forced to flee from Afghanistan in 1929 following the success of a palace coup backed by British imperialism. After a brief period in India, he arrived in Rome in July and, under the protection of the fascist regime, occupied the Afghan embassy.

3   The 1927 Trade Disputes and Trade Union Act, passed by the Tories in the wake of the General Strike, had, among other attacks on trade union rights, declared illegal all sympathetic strikes as well as those considered to be "calculated to coerce the government", or to inflict "hardship upon the community". It was repealed in 1945.

in the same unpleasant situation.[4] The German cabinet was spared this discomfiture because in the whole Reichstag there was not a single deputy who took any interest in the question of the right of asylum. This fact assumes special significance when one remembers that the president of the Reichstag, in a statement that was applauded by the majority of deputies, promised to accord me the right of asylum at a time when I had not even asked for it.[5]

The October revolution did not proclaim the abstract principles of democracy, nor that of the right of asylum. The Soviet state was founded openly on the right of revolutionary dictatorship. But this did not prevent Vandervelde or other social-democrats from coming to the Soviet republic and even appearing in Moscow as public defenders of persons guilty of terrorist attempts on the lives of the leaders of the October revolution.

The present British ministers were also among our visitors. I cannot remember all of those who came to us – I haven't the necessary data at hand – but I remember that among them were Mr. and Mrs. Snowden. This must have been as far back as 1920.[6] They were received not simply as tourists but

---

4 The Prime Minister of Norway at this time was Johan Mowinckel (1870-1943), leader of the so-called 'Left Party', who presided over a coalition of various bourgeois parties from 1928 to 1931. Trotsky was to fare little better with the subsequent social-democratic government, which in 1935 permitted him to enter Norway only then to subject him to detention and deportation.

5 Before his deportation from the Soviet Union, Stalin's Politburo informed Trotsky that his application to visit Germany had been refused by the Müller government. Soon afterwards Paul Loebe, Social Democratic Speaker of the Reichstag, made a speech asserting that Trotsky would be granted asylum in Germany. He therefore requested asylum, but the application was repeatedly blocked. Trotsky was told he could enter the country only if in need of medical treatment; when he replied that he was, the government decided that he was not ill enough for them to be obliged to grant entry. As Trotsky relates in *My Life*: "I could thus appreciate the full advantages of democracy only as a corpse." (Wellred Books, 2018, p. 505.)

6 During the visit of the British Labour Delegation of that year. The delegation was sent as a the result of a motion passed at a special meeting of the Trades Union Congress on 10 December 1919 deciding to initiate an independent and impartial inquiry into the industrial, political and economic conditions in Russia. Its members arrived there in May 1920, and remained for three to six weeks respectively. Those representing the Labour party included Ethel Snowden and Robert Williams, and the TUC delegates included A. A. Purcell. They issued a generally favourable report later in 1920, though

as guests, which was probably carrying it a little too far. A box in the Grand Theatre was placed at their disposal. I remember this in connection with a little episode that it may be worth recounting at this point. I had arrived in Moscow from the front, and my thoughts were far away from the British guests; in fact I did not even know who those guests were, because in my absorption in other things I had hardly read any newspapers. The commission that was receiving Snowden, Mrs. Snowden, and if I am not mistaken, Bertrand Russell and Williams, as well as a number of others, was headed by Lozovsky, who told me by telephone that the commission demanded my presence in the theatre where the English guests were. I tried to excuse myself, but Lozovsky insisted that his commission had been given full power by the Politburo and that it was my duty to set others an example of discipline. I went unwillingly. There were about a dozen British guests in the box. The theatre was crammed to overflowing. We were gaining victories at the front, and the theatre applauded them violently. The British guests surrounded me and applauded too. One of them was Snowden. Today of course he is a little ashamed of this adventure. But it is impossible to erase it. And yet I too should be glad to do so, for my "fraternising" with the Labourites was not only a mistake, but a political error as well. As soon as I could get away from the guests, I went to see Lenin. He was much disturbed. "Is it true that you appeared in the box with those people?" (Lenin used a different word for "people".) In excuse, I referred to Lozovsky, to the commission of the Central Committee, to discipline, and especially to the fact that I had not the remotest idea who the guests were. Lenin was furious with Lozovsky and the whole commission in general and for a long time I too couldn't forgive myself for my imprudence.

One of the present British ministers visited Moscow several times, I believe; at any rate, he rested in the Soviet republic, stayed in the Caucasus and called on me. It was Mr. Lansbury. The last time I met him was at Kislovodsk. I was urged to drop in, if only for a quarter of an hour, at the House of Rest where some members of our party and a few foreign visitors were staying. A goodly number of people were sitting around a large table. It was in the nature of a modest banquet. The place of honour was held by the guest, Lansbury. On my arrival, he offered a toast and then sang: *For he's a jolly good fellow.* Those

---

Mrs. Snowden published her own hostile account called *Through Bolshevik Russia*. Philip Snowden was not a member of the delegation, nor was Bertrand Russell, though he was one of many British visitors to the Soviet Union at about this time, and produced his own unfriendly picture in *The Practice and Theory of Bolshevism*.

were Lansbury's feelings toward me in the Caucasus. Today, he too would probably like to forget about it.

When I applied for the visa, I sent special telegrams to Snowden and Lansbury, reminding them of the hospitality that had been accorded them by the Soviets and in part by myself. My telegrams had little effect. In politics, recollections carry as little weight as democratic principles.

Mr. and Mrs. Sidney Webb most courteously paid me a visit quite recently, early in May of 1929, when I was already on Prinkipo.[7] We talked about the possible advent of the Labour party to power. I remarked in passing that immediately after the formation of MacDonald's government, I intended to demand a visa. Mr. Webb expressed the view that the government might find itself not strong enough, and because of their dependence on the Liberals, not free enough either. I replied that a party that isn't strong enough to be able to answer for its actions had no right to power. Our irreconcilable differences needed no new test. Webb came into power. I demanded a visa. MacDonald's government refused my application, but not because the Liberals prevented it from following its democratic convictions. Quite the contrary. The Labour government refused the visa, despite the protests of the Liberals. This was a variant that Mr. Webb did not foresee. It must be pointed out, however, that at that time he was not yet Lord Passfield.

Some of these men I know personally. Others I can judge only by analogy. I think that I measure them correctly. They have been raised up by the automatic growth of labour organisations, especially since the war, and by the sheer political exhaustion of liberalism. They have completely shed the naive idealism that some of them had twenty-five or thirty years ago. In its stead, they have acquired political routine and unscrupulousness in the choice of means. But in their general outlook they have remained what they were – timid petty bourgeois whose methods of thought are far more backward than the methods of production in the British coal industry. Today, their chief concern is that the court nobility and the big capitalists may refuse to take them seriously. And no wonder. Now that they are in power, they are only too sharply aware of their weakness. They have not and cannot have the qualities possessed by the old governing cliques in which traditions and habits of rulership have been handed down from generation to generation, and often take the place of talent and intellect. But neither do they have what might have constituted their real strength – faith in the masses and the ability

---

7   Trotsky was exiled in February 1929, arriving on the island of Prinkipo the following month. The Webbs arrived to visit him on 29 April 1929.

to stand on their own feet. They are afraid of the masses who put them there, just as they are afraid of the conservative clubs whose grandeur staggers their feeble imaginations. To justify their coming to power, they must show the old ruling classes that they are not simply revolutionary upstarts. God forbid! No, they really deserve every confidence because they are loyally devoted to the church, to the King, to the House of Lords, to the system of titles; that is to say, not simply to the sacrosanct principle of private property, but to all the rubbish of the Middle Ages. For them to refuse a visa to a revolutionary is really a happy opportunity to demonstrate their respectability once again. I am very glad that I gave them such an opportunity. In due time, this will be taken into account, since, in politics, as in nature, there is no waste.

One needs no great imagination to picture Mr. Clynes' interview with his subordinate, the chief of the political police. During the interview, Mr. Clynes feels as if he were undergoing an examination, and is afraid that he will not seem firm enough to the examiner, or statesmanlike or conservative enough. Thus it needs little ingenuity on the part of the chief of the political police to prompt Mr. Clynes to a decision that will be greeted with full approval in the conservative papers next day. But the conservative press does not merely praise – it kills with praise. It mocks. It does not take the trouble to conceal its disdain for the people who so humbly seek its approval. No one will say, for instance, that the *Daily Express* belongs to the most intelligent institutions in the world.[8] And yet this paper finds very caustic words to express its approval of the Labour government for so carefully protecting the "sensitive MacDonald" from the presence of a revolutionary observer behind his back.

* * *

From an interview given to the *Daily Express*, 18 March 1929.

Trotsky: Doesn't Britain realise that her industrial success is now so in the balance that it depends entirely on how soon she throws aside her quarrel with Russia? America does and if Great Britain is not careful she will find the ground cut away from under her feet; the second-comers will only get the crumbs.

Daily Express: What are your views on resuming relations?

---

8 This paper was of course known for its right-wing views even before a controlling interest was taken in it in 1916 by Sir Max Aitken (later Lord Beaverbrook). Thereafter, it was closely identified with various reactionary causes, notably with strong support for the maintenance of the British Empire.

Trotsky: My views? Well, Great Britain is apparently blind but she will get a serious knock very soon that will restore her sight when it is too late and this knock will come from America. Great Britain's fear of communism reminds me of a child which closes its eyes when it is frightened, yet she is big enough to act like a man and grapple with anything she considers menaces her. With Anglo-Russian relations resumed she will still be able to say who shall enter her territory. Every government has this prerogative: look at me, I am not wanted so out I have gone. Then again, the fact of Great Britain being on friendly terms with Soviet Russia would give her an advantage in getting friendly consideration of her desires. But to continue her stand for reparations for alleged damages will only result in Great Britain being outrun by America. Russia has a score of millions of millions marked up against Great Britain for blame for the bloody revolution attaches to her, or rather to her soldiers and her gold. To persist in making Russia only a debtor will never lead to any good, and the sooner this is realised so much the better for England.

Daily Express: Where are you going after leaving Turkey?

Trotsky: I have as yet had no reply from Germany. I suppose it is because of the cabinet crisis there but I have no doubt they will give me a visa. I only sent in my request after Herr Löebe's favourable speech. Reports that I have applied to France, Czechoslovakia, and Holland are lies. I wonder what would be the result if I asked to go to England. You know I spent a happy period in London visiting the British Museum in 1902 and I sometimes think I would like to see it again. Apparently the mere mention in the House of Commons of the possibility of my requesting a visa for England was sufficient to bring the House down in laughter. I have studied what appears to be the joke for some time but I fail to see the point of it.

* * *

Interview with the *Daily Express*, 19 June 1929.

My state of health has obliged me to decline all interviews during the past few weeks, but I now desire to receive a representative of an English newspaper, especially after false information concerning me has been spread throughout the world by a prominent London newspaper from its Constantinople correspondent,[9] and in view of its inconceivable refusal to publish the formal

---

9   *The Times*, 10 May 1929: "He [Trotsky] has just sent a request to Moscow for permission to return to Russia and support Stalin and the ruling clique." *The Times*, 30 May 1929: "Trotsky has been given permission to return in July to Russia." The

denial which I forwarded to it immediately this information came to my knowledge.

It is untrue that I have addressed a demand to return to Russia to the Stalinist faction, which for the moment governs Soviet Russia. Nothing is changed in my situation as an exile, and it ought not to have been necessary to make a denial to the fantasy of a poor imagination, which is without scruples concerning so-called plans in the Orient and the Extreme Orient. The Near East begins in Turkey, and my sojourn here has shown that I understand the right of refuge.

I have just addressed a request to the British government for permission to go to England. This is not because I have any reason to complain of the treatment which I have received at the hands of the Turkish authorities. On the contrary, they have shown themselves to be perfectly loyal and hospitable. I should not dream of leaving Turkey were I not compelled to do so for a number of important reasons.

My state of health and that of my wife demands treatment which it is impossible to obtain here. Furthermore, residence in London would allow me to pursue my scientific work and enable me to superintend the publication of my books in English. Here I am deprived of the necessary sources of information. The smallest verification entails a great loss of time.

I do not wish to conceal that there is besides, at this moment, a special interest for me to go to England, where a great political change has just taken place.

The party which for the second time assumes power in Great Britain believes that the difficulties created by private ownership can be surmounted through the medium of democracy.[10] I want to see how it will be done.

I do not think that democracy which believes it can solve the gravest problems by democratic methods can begin by refusing the right of asylum – a democratic institution – to an adversary who has no intention of interfering with or intervening in British political affairs, but who desires only to observe and to learn.

It is well known that the German Government refused to give me a visa for Germany. I was therefore unable to receive that lesson in democracy which Herr Löebe, the President of the Reichstag, had promised me. The

_____

Constantinople correspondent alleged that Trotsky had left Russia only to do secret work on Stalin's behalf.

10 The second minority Labour Government was returned to office in the General Election of May 1929.

right of asylum exists in Germany only for its political friends, which means that it does not exist at all, despite the fact that it is continually affirmed that Germany is the freest country in the world.

The Norwegian Government, which, by the way, I had not approached, declared itself unable to undertake responsibility for my personal security. Suffice it to say that I am the only private person whose security is dependent on oneself and one's friends. To put the question on a humane basis, I demand that less importance be attributed to my security and more to my health.

(Signed) Leon Trotsky

—

I asked Mssr. Trotsky then how he would reconcile the offer of refuge by Great Britain to a man exiled from Russia with a renewal of diplomatic relations between the two countries. He replied that he saw nothing in that connection whereby difficulties might arise.

> On the contrary [he said], for the British Government, clinging firmly to the principle of non-intervention, the right of refuge is entirely one of an internal order. Equally am I sure that with the re-establishment of diplomatic relations the British Government would not think of demanding that the Soviet Government should modify its internal regime.

He added laughingly that of course he would never have dreamed of asking for permission to enter England while Sir Austen Chamberlain was at the Foreign Office.

> Sir Austen [he said] for some reason has a personal objection to me which he has aired on not a few occasions.

> Yes [he continued, speaking of the question of resumed relations], I hope the new Government will repair the mistake committed by its predecessor. That British industry should be made to suffer merely because of discontent with the Communist International is a thing I cannot understand. I believe, moreover, that this is also the opinion of British industrialists, who found it necessary to send an important delegation to Russia to study the situation.

Mssr. Trotsky spoke of his works which are now in preparation, citing especially that which has for its subject the world situation since the war, notably the situation of the United States *vis-à-vis* Europe in general and in particular *vis-à-vis* Great Britain.

What is my opinion [he concluded] concerning the possibilities of the new Socialist Government and the perspectives open before it? It is precisely these questions which I shall treat in my new book on world politics.

The great experiment which begins with Mr. MacDonald's new Cabinet will furnish me with new elements for appreciation and discussion.

* * *

John O'London's Weekly, Saturday, 20 April 1929.

Mr. Churchill is Wrong

In 1918-1919 Mr. Churchill attempted to overthrow Lenin by force of arms. In 1929 he attempts a psychological and political portraiture of him in his book, *The Aftermath* (Thornton Butterworth). Perhaps he was hoping thereby to secure some sort of literary revenge for his unsuccessful appeal to the sword. But his methods are no less inadequate in the second mode of attack than they were in the first.

"His [Lenin's] sympathies cold and wide as the Arctic Ocean. His hatreds tight as the hangman's noose", writes Mr. Churchill. Verily, he juggles with antitheses as an athlete with dumbbells. But the observant eye soon notices that the dumbbells are painted cardboard, and the bulging biceps are eked out with padding.

The true Lenin was instinct with moral force – a force whose main characteristic was its absolute simplicity. To try to assess him in terms of stage athletics was bound to spell failure.

Mr. Churchill's facts are miserably inaccurate. Consider his dates, for instance. He repeats a sentence, which he has read somewhere or other, referring to the morbid influence exercised on Lenin's evolution by the execution of his elder brother. He refers the fact to the year 1894. But actually the attempt against Alexander III's life was organised by Alexander Ulyanov (Lenin's brother) on 1 March 1887. Mr. Churchill avers that in 1894 Lenin was sixteen years of age. In point of fact, he was then twenty-four, and in charge of the secret organisation at Petersburg. At the time of the October revolution he was not thirty-nine, as Mr. Churchill would have it, but forty-seven years old. Mr. Churchill's errors in chronology show how confusedly he visualises the period and people of which he writes.

But when from the point of view of chronology and fisticuffs we turn to that of the philosophy of history, what we see is even more lamentable.

Mr. Churchill tells us that discipline in the Russian army was destroyed, after the February revolution, by the order abolishing the salute to officers.

This was the point of view of discontented old generals and ambitious young subalterns; otherwise, it is merely absurd. The old army stood for the supremacy of the old classes, and was destroyed by the revolution. When peasants had taken away the landowners' property, the peasants' sons could hardly continue to serve under officers who were sons of landowners. The army is no mere technical organisation, associated only with marching and promotion, but a moral organisation, founded on a definite scheme of mutual relations between individuals and classes. When a scheme of this kind is upset by a revolution, the army unavoidably collapses. It was always thus...

Mr. Churchill grants that Lenin had a powerful mind and will. According to Lord Birkenhead, Lenin was purely and simply non-existent: what really exists is a Lenin myth (see his letter in *The Times*, 26 February 1929). The real Lenin was a nonentity upon which the colleagues of Arnold Bennett's Lord Raingo[11] could look down contemptuously. But despite this one difference in their appraisement of Lenin, both Tories are exactly alike in their utter incapacity to understand Lenin's writings on economy, on politics, and on philosophy – writings that fill over twenty volumes.

I suspect that Mr. Churchill did not even deign to take the trouble carefully to read the article on Lenin which I wrote for the *Encyclopaedia Britannica* in 1926. If he had, he would not have committed those crude, glaring errors of dates which throw everything out of perspective.

One thing Lenin could not tolerate was muddled thought. He had lived in all European countries, mastered many languages, had read and studied and listened and observed and compared and generalised. When he became the head of a revolutionary country, he did not fail to avail himself of this opportunity to learn, conscientiously and carefully. He did not cease to follow the life of all other countries. He could read and speak fluently English, German, and French. He could read Italian and a number of Slavonic languages. During the last years of his life, though overburdened with work, he devoted every spare minute to studying the grammar of the Czech language in order to have access, without intermediaries, to the inner life of Czechoslovakia.

What can Mr. Churchill and Lord Birkenhead know of the workings of this forceful, piercing, tireless mind of his, with its capacity to translate

---

11 *Lord Raingo* is a satirical novel published in 1926 by the English writer Arnold Bennett (1867-1931). Raingo, a self-made millionaire who became a Cabinet Minister, is supposed to represent the 'new men' who were beginning to replace the established leaders of the landed aristocracy and the industrial bourgeoisie.

everything that was superficial, accidental, external into terms of the general and fundamental? Lord Birkenhead, in blissful ignorance, imagines that Lenin never had thought of the password: "Power to the Soviets" before the revolution of February 1917. But the problem of the Soviets and of their possible functions was the very central theme of the work of Lenin and of his companions from 1905 onwards, and even earlier.

By way of completing and correcting Mr. Churchill, Lord Birkenhead avers that if Kerensky had been gifted with a single ounce of intelligence and courage, the Soviets would never have come into power. Here is, indeed, a philosophy of history that is conducive to comfort. The army falls to pieces in consequence of the soldiers having decided not to salute the officers whom they meet. The contents of the cranium of a Radical barrister happen to have been one ounce short, and this deficiency is enough to lead to the destruction of a pious and civilised community! But what indeed can a civilisation be worth which at the time of dire need is unable to supply the needful ounce of brain!

Besides, Kerensky did not stand alone. Around him was a whole circle of Entente officials. Why were they unable to instruct and inspire him, or if need was, replace him? To this query Mr. Churchill can find but this reply: "The Statesmen of the Allied nations affected to believe that all was for the best, and that the Revolution constituted a notable advantage for the common cause" – which means that the officials in question were utterly incapable of understanding the Russian revolution – or, in other words, did not substantially differ from Kerensky himself.

Today, Lord Birkenhead is incapable of seeing that Lenin, in signing the Brest-Litovsk peace,[12] had shown any particular foresight.[13] He considers, today, that the peace was then inevitable. In his own words, "only hysterical fools" could have imagined that the Bolsheviks were capable of fighting Germany: a very remarkable, though tardy, acknowledgement!

---

12 The Brest-Litovsk Peace Treaty was signed on 3 March 1918 after three months of negotiations in which the Soviet delegation was led by Trotsky. The policy was carried through by Lenin and Trotsky against the opposition of Bukharin and the 'Left Communists'. This faction wished to make it a principle to carry on a 'revolutionary war' in the face of threats that German imperialism would renew the offensive after talks were broken off at one point. Trotsky deals with the Stalinist distortion of this history in *The Stalin School of Falsification*.

13 I do not insist upon the fact that Lord Birkenhead represents me as in favour of war with Germany in 1918. The honourable Conservative, on this point, follows far too docilely the utterances of the historians of the Stalin school. – *Trotsky*

The British Government of 1918, and, indeed, all the Entente Governments of that time, categorically insisted on our fighting Germany, and when we refused to do so replied by blockade of, and intervention in, our country. He may well ask, in the energetic language of the Conservative politician himself: Where were, at that moment, the hysterical fools? Was it not they who decided the fate of Europe? Lord Birkenhead's view would have been very far-seeing in 1917: but I must confess that I, for one, have little use for far-sight which asserts itself twelve years after the time when it could have been of use.

Mr. Churchill brings up against Lenin – and it is the very keystone of his article – statistics of the casualties of the civil war. These statistics are quite fantastic. This, however, is not the main point. The victims were many on either side. Mr. Churchill expressly specifies that he includes neither the deaths from starvation nor the deaths from epidemics. In his would-be athletic language he declares that neither Tamerlane[14] nor Genghis Khan[15] were as reckless as Lenin in expenditure of human lives. Judging by the order he adopts, one would hold that Mr. Churchill considers Tamerlane more reckless than Genghis Khan. In this he is wrong… statistical and chronological figures are certainly not the strong point of this Finance Minister. But this is by the way.

In order to find examples of mass expenditure of human life, Mr. Churchill goes to the history of Asia in the thirteenth and fourteenth centuries. The great European war of 1914-1918, in which 10 million men were killed and 20 million crippled, appears to have entirely escaped his memory. The campaigns of Genghis Khan and Tamerlane were child's play in comparison with the doings of civilised nations from 1914 to 1918. But it is in a tone of lofty moral indignation that Mr. Churchill speaks of the victims of civil war in Russia – forgetting Ireland, and India, and other countries.

In short, the question is not so much the victims as it is the duties and the objects for which war was waged. Mr. Churchill wishes to make clear that all sacrifices, in all parts of the world, are permissible and right so long as the object is the power and sovereignty of the British Empire – that is, of its governing classes. But the incomparably lesser sacrifices are wrong which result from the struggle of peoples attempting to alter the conditions under

---

14 Timur (known as Tamerlane in Europe) (1336-1405) – Mongol ruler and conqueror who carried out some of the most ambitious military campaigns in history. Won historical notoriety for his massacres, in one instance of 100,000 Indian prisoners.

15 Genghis Khan (1167-1227) – Founder of the Mongol world empire, won through sweeping military campaigns against China and throughout Asia, in the course of which the Tartars were exterminated.

which they exist – as occurred in England in the seventeenth century, in France at the end of the eighteenth, in the United States twice (eighteenth and nineteenth centuries), in Russia in the twentieth century, and as will occur more than once in the future.

It is vainly that Mr. Churchill seeks assistance in the evocation of the two Asiatic warrior chiefs, who both fought in the interests of nomadic aristocracies, but yet aristocracies coveting new territories and more slaves – in which respect their dealings were in accordance with Mr. Churchill's principles, but certainly not with Lenin's. Indeed, we may recall that Anatole France,[16] the last of the great humanists, often expressed the idea that of all kinds of the bloodthirsty insanity called war, the least insane was civil war, because at least the people who waged it did so of their own accord and not by order.

Mr. Churchill has committed yet another mistake, a very important one and, indeed, from his own point of view, a fatal one. He forgot that in civil wars, as in all wars, there are two sides; and that in this particular case, if he had not come in on the side of a very small minority, the number of the victims would have been considerably less. In October, we conquered power almost without a fight. Kerensky's attempt to reconquer it evaporated as a dewdrop failing on a red-hot stone. So mighty was the driving power of the masses, that the older classes hardly dared attempt to resist.

When did the civil war, with its companion, the Red Terror, really start? Mr. Churchill being weak in the matter of chronology, let us help him. The turning point was the middle of 1918. Led by the Entente diplomatists and officers, the Czechoslovakians got hold of the railway line leading to the East.[17] The French ambassador, Noullens, organised the resistance at Yaroslavl.[18] Another foreign representative organised deeds of terror and an attempt to cut off the water supply of Petersburg. Mr. Churchill encourages

---

16 Pseudonym of Jacques Thibault (1844-1924), the French novelist. Trotsky had been re-reading his works on the journey into exile, in the weeks before the writing of this article (see *My Life*, Wellred Books, 2018, p. 499).

17 The Czechoslovaks were prisoners of war from the Austro-Hungarian Army who were formed into a legion to fight on the Allied side. The officers were bourgeois nationalists hostile to Austrian rule but also to Bolshevism. For a period during 1918 they held Kazan and other strategic points on the route from Moscow to the East. The recapture of Kazan in September was the first victory of the newly formed Red Army and marked a turning point in the fight to beat back the imperialist invasion.

18 A rising of White Guards in the summer of 1918. Noulens was aided by the British agent Bruce Lockhart in instigating it. Yaroslavl is only 160 miles North-East of Moscow.

and finances Savinkov, he is behind Yudenich. He determines the exact dates on which Petersburg and Moscow are to fall. He supports Denikin and Wrangel. The monitors of the British fleet bombard our coast. Mr. Churchill proclaims the coming of "fourteen nations". He is the inspirer, the organiser, the financial backer, the prophet of civil war: a generous backer, a mediocre organiser, and very bad prophet.

He had been better advised not to recall the memories of those times. The number of the victims would have been not ten times, but a hundred or a thousand times smaller but for British guineas, British monitors, British tanks, British officers, and British food supplies.

Mr. Churchill understands neither Lenin nor the duties that lay before him. His lack of comprehension is at its worst when he attempts to deal with the inception of the New Economic Policy. For him, Lenin thereby gave himself the lie. Lord Birkenhead adds that in ten years the very principles of the October revolution were bankrupt. Yes: he who in ten years failed to do away with the miners' unemployment, or to palliate it,[19] expects that in ten years we Russians can build up a new community without committing one mistake, without one flaw, without one setback; a wonderful expectation which gives us the measure of the primitive and purely theoretical quality of the honourable Conservative's outlook. We cannot foretell how many errors, how many set-backs, will mark the course of history; but to see, amid the obstacles and deviations and set-backs of all kinds, the straight line of historical evolution was the achievement of Lenin's genius. And had the Restoration been successful at the time, the need for radical changes in the organisation of the community would have remained as great.

When the Stuarts came back to power, they had far better reasons to think of a bankruptcy of Cromwell's principles. Yet, despite the triumphant Restoration, despite the many ebbs and flows of the following periods, the contest between Whigs and Tories, Freetraders and Protectionists, it was the Cromwellian leaven that gave rise to the new England.[20] And it is only in the last quarter of the nineteenth century that this ferment began to lose its potency, whence the unavoidable decrease of the part played by England in the world's affairs.

---

19 In his years as a minister of the successive Tory governments of the 1920s.

20 Though Cromwell's death was followed by the restoration of Charles II in 1660 and Cromwell's body was dug up to be hung, drawn and quartered, the bourgeois revolution of the seventeenth century was by then accomplished. Capital ruled while permitting the aristocracy to govern. The revolution of 1640 was what laid the basis for Britain's industrial supremacy in the nineteenth century.

The Labour Party and Britain's Decline

From *Disarmament and the United States of Europe,*
(dated 4 October 1929) *Byulleten Oppozitsii,* October 1929.

Briand senses the need to improve the fate of 350 million Europeans who are the bearers of the highest civilisation yet find it impossible to live through a single century without a dozen wars and revolutions. MacDonald has in the interests of pacifying our planet made the crossing of the Atlantic Ocean. The United States of Europe, disarmament, freedom of trade, and peace are on the agenda. Capitalist diplomacy is everywhere preparing a pacifist broth. Peoples of Europe, peoples of the world – get out your soup spoons and gulp it down!

Why? Surely the socialists are in power in the most important countries of Europe or else are preparing to take power? Yes, that is just why! It is already apparent that Briand's plan and MacDonald's plan pursue the pacification of mankind from diametrically opposed directions. Briand wants to unify Europe as a defensive measure against America. MacDonald wants to earn the gratitude of America by helping her oppress Europe. The two trains are rushing headlong at each other in the effort to save the passengers from the crash.

The Anglo-French Naval Agreement of July 1928[1] was liquidated on a wink and a nod from the United States. This fact forms sufficient proof of the

---

1   Drawn up according to the full quota of ships requested by Britain at the talks of the previous year with the United States and Japan, which had broken down over Britain's refusal to lower this quota. The Anglo-French agreement also permitted unrestricted

current world balance of power. "Don't you think", hinted America, "that I can accommodate myself to the negotiations which you are holding around the English Channel? – But to hold a *serious* conversation you must take the trouble to cross over the Atlantic Ocean." So MacDonald booked his passage. That proved to be the most practicable part of the pacifist programme.

At Geneva[2] the future unifiers of the European continent felt not much better than the bootleggers on the other side of the ocean: they were glancing over their shoulders in fear at the American police. Briand began and finished his speech with an avowal that the unification of Europe would in no case and under no circumstances be directed against North America. God forbid! On reading those lines American politicians must have experienced a double feeling of satisfaction: "Briand is pretty scared of us... but he doesn't fool us..."

While repeating Briand's words about America, Stresemann at the same time engages in a veiled polemic against him. Henderson polemicises with them both but especially with the French Prime Minister. The Geneva talks must have developed along roughly the following lines:

Briand: In no case against the United States.

Stresemann: Absolutely right, but someone has ulterior motives – America can count only on Germany.

MacDonald: I swear upon the Bible that fidelity in friendship is a quality belonging only to the British, and more especially to the Scots.

The weakness of present-day Europe is caused first and foremost by its economic fragmentation. The strength of the United States in turn lies in its economic unity. They are asking: how can matters be arranged so that the unification of Europe is not directed against America, i.e., without changing the balance of power to America's disadvantage?

The Daily Herald, MacDonald's semi-official organ, in its issue of 10 September, called the idea of a United States of Europe "grotesque" and even

---

re-equipment in small vessels including submarines, which were the speciality of the French. The US Embassy in London issued a strong public protest in September 1928 when these terms became known. MacDonald, once in office, hastened to make a deal with the Americans and the agreement with the French was pushed aside in favour of the London Conference settlement of 1930, which fixed a ratio of 5:5:3 vessels between the US, Britain and Japan, and placed a five-year moratorium on naval shipbuilding. For all the long negotiations it involved this 'agreement' was no more than a cover for the ongoing preparations for the next imperialist war.

2 The meeting-place of the League of Nations.

provocative. Should, however, such a fantasy be realised, then the United States of Europe would erect a monstrous tariff barrier against the United States – so argued MacDonald's semi-official organ – and as a result Britain would be caught in a vice between two continents. And the *Daily Herald* then went on to add: How could one expect aid from America if the course was set for the unification of Europe? "To act in this way would be insanity or worse." It could not be put more plainly.

* * *

From *Disarmament and the United States of Europe*,
(dated 4 October 1929) *Byulleten Oppozitsii*, October 1929.

Alongside the problem of unifying Europe, that of the reduction of armaments has just been put on the order of the day. MacDonald has declared that the road of gradual disarmament is the surest way of guaranteeing eternal peace. That is how a pacifist confutes us. If all the countries disarmed, it would obviously be a serious guarantee for peace. But such disarmament is excluded in the same way as the voluntary destruction of the customs walls. At the present time, there is only one great power in Europe that is really disarmed. But its disarmament was accomplished only as a result of a war by which Germany also tried to 'unify Europe' under its domination.

The question of 'gradual disarmament', if it is examined closely, assumes the aspect of a tragic farce. In place of disarmament, the cessation of armaments is first substituted, in order to end finally in parity of the fleets of the United States and England. At present, this 'aim' seems bound to be the great guarantee of peace. That amounts to saying that the regulating of revolvers is the surest way to suppress duelling. To decide the matter, it would rather be necessary to view it in the opposite sense. The fact that the two greatest naval powers haggle so furiously for a few thousand tons, clearly shows that each of them is trying to assure itself in advance, by diplomatic means, the most advantageous position in the coming military conflict.

What, however, does the creation of 'equality' between the American and British fleets represent from the point of view of the international situation? It means the establishment of a great 'inequality' between them – in America's favour. And that is understood perfectly by all the serious participants in this game, above all by the Admiralties of London and Washington. If they preserve silence on these matters, it is only out of diplomatic timidity. But we have no reason to imitate them.

After the experience of the last war, there is no one who does not understand that the next war to set the titans of the world by the ears, will be both long in preparation and in duration and not lightning-like. The issue will be determined by the respective powers of production of the two camps. This means that the war fleets of the powers will not only be supplemented and renewed, but in great measure created in the very course of the war.

We have seen the extraordinary place occupied by the German submarines in the military operations during the third year of the war. We have seen how Britain and America, in the very course of the war, created gigantic new armies and armaments, infinitely superior to the old armies of the European continent. It follows that the soldiers, sailors, cruisers, cannons, tanks, and aeroplanes existing at the outbreak of hostilities only constitute a point of departure. The decisive problem will depend upon the measure in which the given country will be able to create, under the enemy's fire, cruisers, cannons, soldiers, and sailors. Even the tsarist government was able to prepare a certain reserve at the beginning of the war. But what was above its power was to create a new one in the battle.

For Britain, in case of war with America, there is but one theoretical condition of success: that it be capable of assuring, before the outbreak of war, a technico-military preponderance in order to balance off to a certain extent the incomparable technical and economic preponderance of the United States. The equalisation of the two fleets before the war means that from the very first months of the war America will have an incontestable advantage. Not for nothing did America threaten a few years ago to turn out cruisers in an emergency like so many pancakes.

In the negotiations of Hoover and MacDonald, it is not a question of disarmament or even the limitation of naval armaments: it is solely a question of rationalising the preparation of war. The type of ships is becoming obsolete. At present, when the great experience of the war and the flood of inventions it let loose are improved only for military needs and usage, the delay in eliminating various kinds of arms of military technique will be infinitely briefer than before 1914. Consequently the main part of the fleet can be revealed to be obsolete even before it has been put into action. Under such conditions, is there any sense in accumulating ships in advance? Rationalisation in this matter requires having such a fleet as is necessary in the first period of the war and which, up to that point can serve as a laboratory for testing and experimenting with new inventions and discoveries, in view of the fact that in the period of war it would be necessary to pass over to standardised construction and production in series. All the great powers feel more or less interested in the 'regulation' of armaments, especially the very costly naval armaments. But destiny has transformed this 'regulation' into the greatest prerogative of the economically strongest country.

During these last years, the war and navy departments of the United States have applied themselves to adapting the entire American industry to the needs of the coming war. Schwab, one of the magnates of maritime war industry, concluded his speech to the War College a short time ago with the following words: "It must be made clear to you that war in the present period must be compared with a great big industrial enterprise."

The French imperialist press, naturally, is doing all it can to incite America against Britain. In an article devoted to the naval accord, *Le Temps* writes that parity of the fleets by no means signifies the equalisation of sea power, since America cannot even dream of securing naval leases comparable to those which Britain has held for centuries. The British naval bases give it an incontestable advantage. But the accord on the parity of the two fleets, in case it is concluded, will not be the last word of the United States. Its first demand is "freedom of the seas", that is, a regime that will appreciably limit Great Britain's use of its naval bases. The second: "the open door", is of no less importance; under this slogan, America will raise not only China but also India and Egypt against British domination. America will conduct its expedition against the British bases not on sea but on land, that is, across the colonies and dominions of Great Britain. America will put its war fleet into action when the situation is ripe enough for it. Of course all this is music of the future. But this future is not separated from us by centuries, nor even by decades. *Le Temps* need not be uneasy. The United States will take over piece-meal all that can be taken in morsels, changing the relation of forces in all fields – technical, commercial, financial, military – to the disadvantage of its principal rival, and it will not lose sight of the latter's exceptional naval bases for a single instant.

The American press has spoken scornfully of the British acclaim for Snowden when he wrested $20 million at the Hague Conference[3] to Britain's profit, that is, a sum that the American tourists spend for their cigars. Is

---

3   This took place in August 1929 to revise the post-war settlement between the European powers, particularly in the matter of German reparations. Snowden, representing the British government as Chancellor of the Exchequer, nearly wrecked it by refusing to accept a reduction of £2 million per year in Britain's share. In return for this gesture of defiance on behalf of declining British imperialism he was awarded the Freedom of the City of London. It was left to Henderson as Foreign Secretary to restore good feeling with the other imperialist powers.

Snowden the victor? – asked the *New York Times*. "No! The real victor is the Young Plan",[4] that is, American finance capital. Thanks to the Bank of International Settlements, the Young Plan gives America the possibility of holding its hand firmly on the golden pulse of Europe. From the financial irons forged on Germany's feet there extend strong chains which fetter the hands of France, the feet of Italy and the neck of Britain. MacDonald, who is now fulfilling the duties of keeper to the British lion, points with pride to the collar, and calls it the best instrument of peace. Just think: to attain this aim, it was enough for America to give its 'magnanimous aid' to Europe so that it might liquidate the war and to consent to equalise its fleet with that of the weaker Britain.

Since 1923, I had to conduct a struggle to have the leadership of the Communist International consent, finally, to take notice of the existence of the United States and to understand that Anglo-American antagonism constitutes the fundamental line of the groupings and conflicts in the world. This was considered a heresy even at the time of the Fifth Congress of the CI (middle of 1924). I was accused of exaggerating, of enlarging the role of America. A legend was conceived according to which I had prophesied the disappearance of European antagonisms in the face of the American peril. Ossinsky, Larin and others smeared up not a little paper in order to 'dethrone' powerful America. Radek, following the bourgeois journalists, affirmed that an epoch of Anglo-American collaboration is ahead of us, confusing temporary and episodic relations with the essence of world developments.

Little by little, however, America was 'recognised' by the official leadership of the Communist International which began to repeat my formulae of yesterday, not failing, of course, to add each time that the Opposition exaggerates the role of America. The correct estimation of America was at that time, as is known, the exclusive prerogative of Pepper and Lovestone.

From the moment when the orientation to the Left was established, the reservations disappeared. Now it is obligatory upon the official theoreticians to predict that Britain and America are moving inevitably towards war. On this subject I wrote, some time in February of last year, to the deported comrades:

---

4 The agreement reached at the Hague Conference, relieving Germany of allied control in return for a final settlement, at a reduced rate, of reparations payments. A new Bank for International Settlements was set up through which Germany was to pay at the re-negotiated rates over a period of fifty-nine years.

The Anglo-American antagonism is at last seriously recognised. It seems that Stalin and Bukharin are beginning to understand what it is all about. Nevertheless, our papers are simplifying the problem too much when they picture the situation as if Anglo-American antagonisms were becoming continuously aggravated and must lead to war right away. There is no doubt that there will still be a few crises in the course of its development. War would be a too dangerous business now for the two rivals. They will still make many efforts to come to an understanding and make peace. But at the end of all this there is a bloody denouement towards which they are proceeding with great strides.

The present stage assumes anew the aspect of military 'collaboration' between America and Britain and even some French journals fear to see the rise of an Anglo-Saxon dictatorship. It is evident the United States can use, and will use, their 'collaboration' with Britain to hold Japan and France in check with the same bridle. But all this will be a stage not towards an Anglo-Saxon domination but towards an American dictatorship weighing down on the world, including Great Britain.

* * *

From an interview with *The Manchester Guardian*,
28 March 1931.

Mr. MacDonald esteems the results achieved on his American journey[5] as the loftiest triumph of peace politics. As I am speaking here in an interview, wherein one does not so much explain one's opinion as proclaim it, I shall allow myself to turn to a speech that I made in 1924 about the relations between America and Europe. At that time, if I remember aright, Curzon was foreign minister and was engaging in sabre-rattling against Soviet Russia. In a polemic against Lord Curzon (which now, of course, has lost all political interest) I observed that he was only treading on Russia's heels in consequence of the unsatisfactory power of the United States and by the world situation generally. His protests against Soviet Russia were to be interpreted as the result of his dissatisfaction at having to negotiate accords with the United States that were not of equal advantage to both parties. "When it comes to the point", I said, "it will not be Lord Curzon who will execute this unpleasant task; he is too spirited. No, it will be entrusted to MacDonald. All the pious eloquence of MacDonald, Henderson and the Fabians will be needed to make that capitulation acceptable."

* * *

---

5   In October 1929, shortly after the formation of the second Labour government.

From *Ou va la France?*, *La Verité*, 9 November 1934.

The most recent electoral victories[6] of the British Labour Party do not at all invalidate what is said above. Even if we were to allow that the next parliamentary elections will give the Labour Party an absolute majority, which is not assured in any case; if we were further to allow that the party would actually take the road of socialist transformations – which is scarcely probable – it would immediately meet with such fierce resistance from the House of Lords, the king, the banks, the stock-market, the bureaucracy, the press, that a split in its ranks would become inevitable, and the Left, more radical wing would become a parliamentary minority. Simultaneously the Fascist movement would acquire an unprecedented sweep. Alarmed by the municipal elections, the British bourgeoisie is no doubt already actively preparing for an extra-parliamentary struggle actively while the tops of the Labour Party lull the proletariat with the successes and are compelled, unfortunately, to see the British events through the rosy spectacles of Jean Longuet. In point of fact, the less the leaders of the Labour Party prepare for it, the more cruel will be the civil war forced upon the proletariat by the British bourgeoisie.

* * *

From the Introduction to the second English edition of
Terrorism and Communism, 10 January 1935.

In the period before the war Karl Kautsky and the leaders of the British Labour Party seemed to be standing at opposite poles of the Second International. Our generation, which then was young, in the fight against the opportunism of MacDonald, Henderson, and their brethren, not seldom made use of weapons taken from Kautsky's arsenal. But in truth even in those days we went a great deal further than that wavering and ambiguous teacher was willing to go. Even before the war, Rosa Luxemburg, who had a closer

---

6   Following on MacDonald's treacherous turn to coalition with the Tories and the disastrous losses for Labour in the 1931 General Election, the determination of the working class to fight back against the slump was reflected in a series of by-election victories, eight in all, between April 1932 and October 1934. On 25 October 1933 the Conservative candidate for Fulham East, who had campaigned for a strengthening of the armed forces, was defeated by the Labour candidate, who accused him of preparing war. A conservative majority of 14,521 was replaced by a Labour majority of 4,840. On 1 November, Labour won control of 200 boroughs in municipal elections, and in March 1934 captured the London County Council.

knowledge of Kautsky than others, had ruthlessly exposed the pinchbeck in his radicalism. These last years, anyhow, have thrown a full light on the facts: politically Kautsky belongs to the same camp as Henderson. If the former still goes on quoting from Marx, while the latter chooses rather the psalms of King David, this difference in habits does no harm whatever to their solidarity. All that is essentially uttered in this book against Kautsky can likewise almost unreservedly be applied to the leaders of the British trade union movement and of the Labour Party.

One of the chapters in the book is given to the so-called Austrian school of Marxism (Otto Bauer, Karl Renner, and others).[7] Essentially this school fulfilled the same function: with the help of sterilised formulae from Marxism it gave shelter to a policy of cowering opportunism and, coward-like, it refused to make those bold decisions which were inevitably called for by the course of the class struggle. Events put both Kautskianism and Austrian Marxism to a ruthless test. The once powerful social-democratic parties of Germany and Austria, raised (against their own will) by the revolutionary movement in 1918 to the heights of power, freely yielded up bit by bit their positions to the bourgeoisie, until they were seen to have been ruthlessly crushed by it. The history of these two parties will be found to be a priceless illustration in the question of the part played by revolutionary and counter-revolutionary violence in history.

For the sake of continuity I have kept the title for the book under which the first English edition came out: *The Defence of Terrorism*. But it must at once be said here that this title, which is that of the original publishers and not the author's, is too wide and may even give grounds for misunderstanding. What we are concerned with is not at all the defence of 'terrorism' as such. Methods of compulsion and terrorisation down to the physical extirpation of its opponents have up to now advantaged, and continue to advantage in an infinitely higher degree the cause of reaction, as represented by the outworn exploiting classes, than they do the cause of historical progress, as represented by the proletariat. The jury of moralists who condemn 'terrorism'

---

7 First put forward by some of the leaders of Austrian Social Democracy in the period before 1914, including Otto Bauer, Max Adler, and Karl Renner (who was later Chancellor in 1918 and President in 1946). They were proponents of theories about cultural autonomy within the Austrian Empire. Took a pacifist position during the war, and afterwards associated themselves with centrist international currents, providing the home of the 'Vienna Union' or Two-and-a-Half International, returning to the fold of the Second International in 1923.

of whatever kind have their gaze fixed really on the revolutionary deeds of the persecuted who are seeking to set themselves free. The best example of this is Mr. Ramsay MacDonald. In the name of the eternal principles of morality and religion he was unwearied in condemning violence. But when the collapse of the capitalist system and the sharpening of the class struggle made the revolutionary fight of the proletariat for power an actual and living question for Britain also, MacDonald left the Labour camp for that of the Conservative bourgeoisie with just as little bother as when a passenger changes from a smoking compartment to a non-smoking. Today the pious enemy of terrorism is keeping up by the help of organised violence a 'peaceful' system of unemployment, colonial oppression, armed forces, and preparation for fresh wars.

The present work, therefore, is far away from any thought of defending terrorism in general. It champions the historical justification of the proletarian revolution. The root idea of the book is this: that history down to now has not thought out any other way of carrying mankind forward than that of setting up always the revolutionary violence of the progressive class against the conservative violence of the outworn classes.

The incurable Fabians, it is true, keep on saying that, if the arguments of this book are true for backward Russia, they are utterly without application to advanced lands, especially to old democracies like Great Britain. This consoling illusion may have worn a cloak of persuasiveness up to fifteen or ten years ago. But since then a wave of Fascist or militarised police dictatorships has overwhelmed a great part of the European states. The day after I was exiled from the Soviet Union, on 25 February 1929, I wrote – not for the first time, indeed – with reference to the situation in Europe:

> Democratic institutions have shown that they cannot withstand the pressure of present-day antagonisms both international and national – more often, both together... On the analogy with electrical science democracy may be defined as a system of safety switches and fuses to guard against too strong currents of national or social hostility. There has never been one period in the history of mankind even within the slightest degree so filled with antagonisms as our own. The overloading of the current shows itself more and more at various points in the European system. Under the too high tension of class and international oppositions the safety switches of democracy fuse or burst. This is the essence of the short-circuit of dictatorship. The first to give way, of course, are the weakest switches. Internal and world oppositions, however, are not losing strength, but growing. It is hardly a ground for consolation that the process has taken hold only

of the edge of the capitalistic world; gout begins with the big toe, but, once it has begun, it reaches the heart.

In the six years that have gone by since these lines were written the "short-circuits" of dictatorship have arisen in Germany, Austria, and Spain – in this last after a short-lived revolutionary flowering of democracy. All those democratic illusionary dreamers who tried to explain Italian Fascism as a passing phenomenon that had arisen in a relatively backward land as the result of an after-war psychosis, met with the sternest refutation from the facts themselves. Among the great European countries the parliamentary regime is now left only in France and in Britain. But after what has happened in Europe anyone would have to be extraordinarily blind if he believes France and Britain to be safe from civil war and dictatorship. On 6 February 1934, French parliamentarianism was given its first warning.[8]

Extraordinarily superficial is the idea that the comparatively strong resisting power of the British political system arises out of the great age of its parliamentary traditions, and that as the years go on it automatically draws fresh strength from these for resistance. It has nowhere been found that old things, other circumstances being the same, are set firmer than new things. The fact is that British parliamentarianism holds together better than the others amid the crisis of the capitalist system only because their former world domination allowed the ruling classes of Great Britain to heap up an immense wealth, which now goes on lighting up the gloom of their days. In other words: the British parliamentary democracy holds together not through a mystic power of tradition, but from the plump savings which have been handed down from thriving times.

The future lot of British democracy depends not on its inner characteristics, but on the lot of British and world capitalism. If the jugglers and wonder-workers in power were really to find out the secret of giving youth to capitalism there is no doubt that along with it bourgeois democracy would find its own youth again. But we see no grounds for believing in the jugglers and wonder-workers. The last imperialistic war, indeed, came as an expression, and at the same time a proof, of the historical truth that world capitalism has drunk its progressive mission to the last drop. The development of the productive powers comes to rest against two reactionary barriers: private ownership of

---

8   On 6 February 1934 the Radical government led by Daladier was brought down amid riots by armed fascist bands in the pay of big capital, and the right-wing Bonapartist regime headed by Doumergue was installed. See Trotsky's *Whither France?*

the means of production and the frontiers of the national state. Unless these two barriers are swept away, that is to say, unless the means of production are concentrated in the hands of the community, and unless there is an organised planned economy which can gradually enfold the whole world, the economic and cultural collapse of mankind is foredoomed. Further short-circuitings by reactionary dictatorships would in such a case inevitably spread to Great Britain also; the successes won by Fascism are seen to be no more than the political expression of the decay of the capitalist system. In other words: even in Britain a political state of things is not impossible wherein some coxcomb such as Mosley will be able to play an historical part like that played by his teachers Mussolini and Hitler. From the Fabians we may hear it objected that the British proletariat have it quite in their own hands to come to power by way of Parliament, to carry through peacefully, within the law and step by step, all the changes called for in the capitalist system, and by so doing not only to make revolutionary terrorism needless, but also to dig the ground away under the feet of counter-revolutionary adventurers. An outlook such as this has at first sight a particular persuasiveness in the light of the Labour Party's very important successes in the elections – but only at first sight, and that a very superficial one. The Fabian hope must, I fear, be held from the very beginning to be out of the question. I say "I fear", since a peaceful, parliamentary change over to a new social structure would undoubtedly offer highly important advantages from the standpoint of the interests of culture, and therefore those of socialism. But in politics nothing is more dangerous than to mistake what we wish for what is possible. On the one hand, a victory for the Labour Party at the elections would by no means bring with it the immediate concentration of real power in its hands. On the other hand, the Labour Party does not, indeed, aim at full power, for, as represented by its leaders, it has no wish to expropriate the bourgeoisie. Henderson, Lansbury and the others have nothing about them of the great social reformers; they are nothing else than small bourgeois conservatives. We have seen social democracy in power in Austria and Germany. In Britain we have twice beheld a so-called Labour Government. Today there are social democratic governments at the head of Denmark and of Sweden. In all these cases not one hair has fallen from the head of capitalism. A Henderson-Lansbury Government would not differ in the slightest from a Hermann Müller Government in Germany. It would not dare to lay a finger on the property of the bourgeoisie, and would be doomed to try paltry reforms, which, while disappointing the workers, would irritate the bourgeoisie. Far-reaching social reforms cannot be carried out amid the conditions of crumbling capitalism. The workers would be more and more insistent in demanding more determined measures from the Government. In the parliamentary section of the Labour Party the revolutionary wing would split off, the right wing would be drawn more and more openly to a capitulation on the MacDonald pattern. As a counter-weight to the Labour Government and a safeguard against revolutionary action by the masses, big capital would set about energetically supporting (this it has already begun to do) the Fascist movement. The Crown, the House of Lords, the bourgeois minority in the House of Commons, the bureaucracy, the military and naval commands, the banks, the trusts, the main body of the press, would merge into a counter-revolutionary bloc, ever ready to bring up the bands of Mosley or of some other more efficient adventurer to help the regular armed forces. In other words the "parliamentary outlook" would inevitably and fatally lead along the road to civil war, a civil war which, the less the leaders of the Labour Party were ready for it, would threaten the more to take on a long drawn, embittered, and for the proletariat, unfavourable character.

The conclusion to be drawn from all this is that the British proletariat must not reckon on any historic privileges. It will have to struggle for power by the road of revolution and keep it in its hands by crushing the fierce resistance of the exploiters. There is no other way leading to socialism. The problems of revolutionary violence, or 'terrorism', therefore have their practical interest for England also. That is why I agreed to a new English edition of this book... If in Britain in spite of the highly favourable conditions, the Communist Party is still an organisation without importance, without influence, without authority, and without a future, then the responsibility for this lies above all with the Soviet bureaucracy.

Everything in Britain is heading for a revolutionary explosion. A happy issue from the economic crisis – and this is quite a possibility in itself and even inevitable – could never have more than a transitory character, and would quickly yield once more to a fresh and devastating crisis. There is no way to salvation through capitalism. The coming into power of the Labour Party will have only this meaning for progress, that once more it will show – infinitely clearer even than before – the bankruptcy of the methods and illusions of parliamentarianism amidst the crumbling ruins of the capitalist system. And so the absolute need for a new, a truly revolutionary party will stand forth clear-cut before our eyes. The British proletariat will enter upon a period of political crisis and theoretical criticism. The problems of revolutionary violence will stand in their full height before it. The teachings of Marx and Lenin for the first time will find the masses as their audience. Such being the case, it may also be that the present book will turn out to be not without its use.

*   *   *

From *Diary in Exile* (1935), first published in 1958.

11 April

Baldwin thinks that Europe is a lunatic asylum; England is the only country that has kept her reason: she still has the King, the Commons, the Lords: England has avoided revolution, tyranny, and persecution (see his speech in Llandrindod).[9]

As a matter of fact, Baldwin understands exactly nothing about what is taking place before his very eyes. There is a much greater distance between Baldwin and Lenin, as intellectual types, than between the Celtic druids and Baldwin. England is nothing but the last ward of the European madhouse, and quite possibly it will prove to be the ward for particularly violent cases.

Before the last Labourite government, just at the time of the election, the Webbs, Sydney and Beatrice, came to visit us at Prinkipo. These 'socialists' were quite willing to accept Stalin's socialism in one country for Russia. They expected, not without gloating, a cruel civil war in the US. But for England (and Scandinavia) they reserved the privilege of peaceful evolutionary socialism. In order to account for unpleasant facts – such as the October Revolution, outbursts of the class struggle, and fascism – and at the same time preserve their Fabian prejudices and predilections, the Webbs – to suit their Anglo-Saxon empiricism – had created a theory of 'types' of social development and made a bargain with history to obtain a peaceful type for England. In fact, at that time Sydney Webb was about to receive from his King the title of Lord Passfield, so that he might peacefully reconstruct society as His Majesty's minister.[10]

---

9   Llandrindod Wells is a spa in Radnorshire, Wales. Baldwin spoke there on 8 April 1935 to the National Council of Evangelical Free Churches. He defended the government's White Paper on defence, and urged an increase in the size of the Air Force.

10 An amusing touch: Sydney Webb informed me, with particular emphasis, that he was able to leave England for a few weeks only because he was not standing for Parliament. He obviously expected me to ask, "Why?" – in order to inform me about his pending elevation to the peerage. I saw in his eyes that he was expecting a question, but refrained from asking anything in order to avoid causing any embarrassment. The question of the peerage never even occurred to me; rather I thought that Webb, in

Of course, the Webbs are closer to Baldwin than to Lenin. I listened to the Webbs as if they were emanations from the next world, although they are very educated people. It's true that they boasted of not belonging to any church.

—

14 April

In Stresa,[11] three socialist turncoats, Mussolini, Laval, and MacDonald, represent the 'national' interests of their countries. The most contemptible and incompetent is MacDonald. There is something of the flunkey running all through him, even in his posture when talking to Mussolini (see the newspaper picture). It is so characteristic of this man that during his first ministry he hastened to grant a position to Mosley, the aristocratic coxcomb who had only recently joined the Labour Party as a short cut to a career. And now that same Mosley is trying to change sane old England into merely another ward of the European lunatic asylum. And if he does not succeed in this, somebody else certainly will – the minute Fascism is victorious in France. This time the possible advent to power of the Labourites will give a great stimulus to the development of British fascism and in general will open up a stormy chapter in the history of England, contrary to all the historical and philosophic conceptions of the Baldwins and the Webbs.

In September 1930, about two or three months after the Webbs, Cynthia Mosley, the wife of the adventurer and daughter of the notorious Lord Curzon, visited me at Prinkipo. At that stage her husband was still attacking MacDonald 'from the left'. After some hesitation I agreed to a meeting which, however, proved banal in the extreme. The 'Lady' arrived with a female travelling companion, referred contemptuously to MacDonald, and spoke of her sympathies toward Soviet Russia. But the enclosed letter from

---

his old age, had renounced active political life, and naturally I did not want to pursue that subject. Only later, when the new ministry was formed, I understood what had been going on: the author of research reports on industrial democracy was proudly looking forward to bearing the title of Lord! – *Trotsky*

11 This conference in April 1935 between the British, French, and Italian governments, represented the last attempt to keep together the anti-German alliance of imperialist powers which had won victory in 1918 and enforced the Treaty of Versailles in the following year. Nothing concrete could be agreed, and by October relations had been disrupted by the Italian invasion of Ethiopia. Mussolini was now in open alliance with Hitler; Laval went on later to become a leader of the Vichy regime of Nazi collaborators.

her is an adequate specimen of her attitude at that time.[12] About three years later the young woman suddenly died. I don't know if she lived long enough to cross over to the fascist camp.

About that time or a little later I received a letter from Beatrice Webb in which – on her own initiative – she tried to justify or explain the refusal of the Labour Government to grant me a visa. (This letter ought to be looked up, but I am without a secretary now. I did not answer her: there was no point…)

* * *

From Appendix to *The Revolution Betrayed*, 1936.

For the first time a powerful government provides a stimulus abroad not to the respectable right, but to the left and extreme left press. The sympathies of the popular masses for the great revolution are being very skilfully canalised and sluiced into the mill of the Soviet bureaucracy. The 'sympathising' Western press is imperceptibly losing the right to publish anything which might aggrieve the ruling stratum of the Soviet Union. Books undesirable to

---

12 The copy of Cynthia Mosley's letter which was pasted into Trotsky's diary reads as follows:

Istanbul, 4 September 1930

Dear Comrade Trotsky,

I would like above all things to see you for a few moments. There is no good reason why you should see me as (1) I belong to the Labour Party in England who were so ridiculous and refused to allow you in, but also I belong to the ILP and we did our very best to make them change their minds, and (2) I am daughter of Lord Curzon who was Minister for Foreign Affairs in London when you were in Russia! On the other hand I am an ardent socialist. I am a member of the House of Commons. I think less than nothing of the present Government. I have just finished reading your *Life* which inspired me as no other book has done for ages. I am a great admirer of yours. These days when great men seem so very few and far between it would be a great privilege to meet one of the enduring figures of our age and I do hope with all my heart you will grant me that privilege. I need hardly say I come as a private person, not a journalist or anything but myself – I am on my way to Russia, I leave for Batum-Tiflis-Rostov-Kharkov and Moscow by boat Monday. I have come to Prinkipo this afternoon especially to try to see you, but if it were not convenient I could come out again any day till Monday. I do hope however you could allow me a few moments this afternoon.

Yours fraternally,

Cynthia Mosley

the Kremlin are maliciously unmentioned. Noisy and mediocre apologists are published in many languages. We have avoided quoting throughout this work the specific productions of the official 'friends', preferring the crude originals to the stylised foreign paraphrases. However, the literature of the 'friends', including that of the Communist International, the most crass and vulgar part of it, presents in cubic metres an impressive magnitude, and plays not the last role in politics. We must devote a few concluding pages to it.

At present the chief contribution to the treasury of thought is declared to be the Webbs' book, *Soviet Communism*.[13] Instead of relating what has been achieved and in what direction the achieved is developing, the authors expound for 1,200 pages what is contemplated, indicated in the bureaux, or expounded in the laws. Their conclusion is: When the projects, plans and laws are carried out, then communism will be realised in the Soviet Union. Such is the content of this depressing book, which rehashes the reports of Moscow bureaux and the anniversary articles of the Moscow press.

Friendship for the Soviet bureaucracy is not friendship for the proletarian revolution, but, on the contrary, insurance against it. The Webbs are, to be sure, ready to acknowledge that the communist system will sometime or other spread to the rest of the world. "But how, when, where, with what modifications, and whether through violent revolution, or by peaceful penetration, or even by conscious imitation, are questions we cannot answer." This diplomatic refusal to answer – or, in reality, this unequivocal answer – is in the highest degree characteristic of the 'friends', and tells the actual price of their friendship. If everybody had thus answered the question of revolution before 1917, when it was infinitely harder to answer, there would have been no Soviet state in the world, and the British 'friends' would have had to expend their fund of friendly emotion upon other objects.

The Webbs speak as of something which goes without saying about the vanity of hoping for a European revolution in the near future, and they gather

---

13 Published in 1935 when the Webbs were in their 70s. Previously they had been anti-Soviet but now they made Russia respectable. They praised the Russian system of planning and policy of "peace and non-interference"; they discovered that "force of example is the most promising way of spreading Soviet ideas" and that "Stalin is universally considered to have justified his leadership by success". The Moscow Trials are glossed over as a necessary part of the birth pangs of the "New Civilisation". The book was part of the brief vogue for Russia among some British intellectuals in the 1930s. The full title of the first edition was *Soviet Communism – A New Civilisation?* By the time of the second edition in 1937, the question mark had disappeared.

from that a comforting proof of the correctness of the theory of socialism in one country. With the authority of people for whom the October revolution was a complete, and moreover an unpleasant, surprise, they give us lessons in the necessity of building a socialist society within the limits of the Soviet Union in the absence of other perspectives. It is difficult to refrain from an impolite movement of the shoulders! In reality, our dispute with the Webbs is not as to the necessity of building factories in the Soviet Union and employing mineral fertilisers on the collective farms, but as to whether it is necessary to prepare a revolution in Great Britain and how it shall be done. Upon that question the learned sociologues answer: "We do not know." They consider the very question, of course, in conflict with "science".

Lenin was passionately hostile to the conservative bourgeois who imagines himself a socialist, and, in particular, to the British Fabians. By the biographical glossary attached to his *Works*, it is not difficult to find out that his attitude to the Webbs throughout his whole active life remained one of unaltered fierce hostility. In 1907 he first wrote of the Webbs as "obtuse eulogists of English philistinism," who "try to represent Chartism, the revolutionary epoch of the English labour movement, as mere childishness." Without Chartism, however, there would have been no Paris Commune. Without both, there would have been no October revolution. The Webbs found in the Soviet Union only an administrative mechanism and a bureaucratic plan. They found neither Chartism nor Communism nor the October revolution. A revolution remains for them today, as before, an alien and hostile matter, if not indeed "mere childishness."

In his polemics against opportunists Lenin did not trouble himself, as is well known, with the manners of the salon. But his abusive epithets ("lackeys of the bourgeoisie", "traitors", "boot-lick souls") expressed during many years a carefully weighed appraisal of the Webbs as the evangels of Fabianism – that is, of traditional respectability and worship for what exists. There can be no talk of any sudden change in the views of the Webbs during recent years. These same people who during the war supported their bourgeoisie, and who accepted later at the hands of the King the title of Lord Passfield, have renounced nothing, and changed not at all, in adhering to Communism in a single, and moreover a foreign, country. Sidney Webb was Colonial Minister – that is, chief jail-keeper of British imperialism – in the very period of his life when he was drawing near to the Soviet bureaucracy, receiving material from its bureaux, and on that basis working upon this two-volume compilation.

As late as 1923, the Webbs saw no great difference between Bolshevism and tsarism (see, for example, *The Decay of Capitalist Civilisation*, 1923). Now, however, they have fully recognised the 'democracy' of the Stalin regime. It is needless to seek any contradiction here. The Fabians were indignant when the revolutionary proletariat withdrew freedom of activity from 'educated' society, but they think it quite in the order of things when a bureaucracy withdraws freedom of activity from the proletariat. Has not this always been the function of the Labourites' workers' bureaucracy? The Webbs swear, for example, that criticism in the Soviet Union is completely free. A sense of humour is not to be expected of these people. They refer with complete seriousness to that notorious "self-criticism' which is enacted as a part of one's official duties, and the direction of which, as well as its limits, can always be accurately foretold.

Naïveté? Neither Engels nor Lenin considered Sidney Webb naïve. Respectability rather. After all, it is a question of an established regime and of hospitable hosts. The Webbs are extremely disapproving in their attitude to a Marxian criticism of what exists. They consider themselves called to preserve the heritage of the October revolution from the Left Opposition. For the sake of completeness we observe that in its day the Labour Government in which Lord Passfield (Sidney Webb) held a portfolio refused the author of this work a visa to enter Great Britain. Thus Sidney Webb, who in those very days was working on his book upon the Soviet Union, is theoretically defending the Soviet Union from being undermined, but practically he is defending the Empire of His Majesty. In justice be it said that in both cases he remains true to himself.

The Outbreak of War

From *Mysteries of Imperialism* (dated 4 March 1939),
Byulleten Oppozitsii 75-76, March-April 1939.

The Socialist Léon Blum and the Conservative Chamberlain, in equal measure friends of 'peace', were for non-intervention in the Spanish affair.[1] Hand in hand with them went Stalin, the ex-Bolshevik, through his ambassador Maisky, the ex-Menshevik. Nuances of programmes did not hinder them from friendly collaboration in the name of one and the same high aim.

Now, however, Chamberlain declares that if, after recognition of Franco, Italy and Germany do not withdraw the so-called volunteers from Spain, Britain is prepared to take the most serious measures, not short of war. The Radical Socialist Daladier, another well-known supporter of the policy of "non-intervention", completely supports Chamberlain in this question. From love of peace, these gentlemen refused to defend democracy with arms. But there is a limit to everything, even to the love of peace of these experienced friends of humanity. Chamberlain openly says: the arrival of Italian and German soldiers on the Iberian Peninsula would break the 'balance' in the Mediterranean. This cannot be endured! England and France were not at all inclined to support Spanish democracy; but now, when they have helped Franco to stifle it, they are fully prepared to support with arms the 'balance' in the Mediterranean – a mysterious technical term which is to be understood as meaning the defence by the enslavers of their colonial possessions and the seaways leading to them.

---

1 "Non-intervention" meant leaving the field open to Germany and Italy to give Franco every form of aid in crushing the Spanish working class. It was the policy laid down by the Chamberlain government in Britain and Blum's Popular Front in France.

We humbly ask the gentlemen of the Second and Third Internationals exactly what historical, political, and other conditions are required to establish the promised grand alliance in defence of democracy in the whole world? The government of France relied on the Popular Front.[2] The struggle of the Popular Front in Spain was waged in the name of democracy. What other example can be invented in which the duty to defend democracy would appear in a more imperative form? If a 'Socialist' government supported by a 'National Front' refused to defend a democracy also headed by 'Socialists', then the question arises just where and when will what kind of government occupy itself with the task of defending democracy? Perhaps the augurs of Social Democracy and the Comintern can, nevertheless, manage to explain that?

In fact, the two imperialist democracies, in the person of their ruling classes, were from the very beginning completely on the side of Franco; they merely did not at first believe in the possibility of his victory, and were afraid of compromising themselves by premature disclosure of their sympathies. As Franco's chances improved, however, the real faces of the possessing classes of the 'great democracies' were revealed ever more clearly, ever more openly, ever more shamelessly. Both Great Britain and France know perfectly well that it is considerably easier to control colonies, semi-colonies, and simply weak nations through a military dictatorship than through a democratic or even semi-democratic regime.

Alliance with the Conservative [Chamberlain] government is just as immutable a commandment for the 'Socialist' petty-bourgeois Blum as for the most extreme reactionaries of the French Chamber of Deputies. This commandment emanates from the French stock exchange. England's plan in relation to Spain was fixed from the very start: let them fight; whoever wins will need money to revive the economy of the country. Neither Germany nor Italy will be able to give this money; consequently, the victor will have to turn to London, and partly to Paris. Thus it will be possible to dictate terms.

Blum was initiated into the English plan perfectly well from the beginning. He could have no plan of his own because his semi-socialist government was completely dependent on the French bourgeoisie, and the French

---

2 After the rise to power of Hitler, the Comintern in 1934-5 enunciated a new policy of support for all those forces on the side of 'democracy', including bourgeois parties, Liberals and Conservatives, against fascism. This policy denied the duty of Marxists to fight for the leading position of the working class, or indeed for its revolutionary role at all. The counter-revolutionary consequences of this policy, the other side of the coin of the previous ultra-leftism, are outlined in Trotsky's writings of this period.

bourgeoisie on Great Britain. Blum shouted about the preservation of peace as an even more sacred task than the salvation of democracy. But in fact he was concealing the plan of British capital. After he had carried out this piece of dirty work, he was thrown into the opposition camp by the French bourgeoisie, and again obtained the possibility of shouting about the sacred duty of helping the Spanish republicans. Without a cheap left phrase, he would not have preserved the possibilities of again rendering other just as treacherous services to the French bourgeoisie at a critical moment.

The Moscow diplomats also, of course, speak somewhat through gritted teeth in favour of Spanish democracy, the very thing they have destroyed by their policy. But in Moscow they now express themselves very carefully, because they are groping for a way to Berlin.[3] The Moscow Bonapartists[4] are ready to betray all the democracies in the world, not to speak of the international proletariat, just to prolong their rule for an additional week. It is possible that both Stalin and Hitler have started with bluff; each wants to frighten Chamberlain, Daladier, and even Roosevelt. But if the 'democratic' imperialists are not frightened, the bluff may go considerably further than was at first supposed in Moscow and Berlin. To cover up their manoeuvres, the Kremlin clique needs the assistance of the leaders of the Second and Third Internationals, the more so as that does not cost too much…

In the veins of the Spanish people, there still remains unshed blood. Who will dispose of it, Hitler and Mussolini or Chamberlain with his French accomplices, is a question that will be decided by the relations of the imperialist forces in the near future. The struggle for peace, for democracy, for race, for authority, for order, for balance, and for dozens of other high and imponderable things means the struggle for a new division of the world. The Spanish tragedy will go down in history as an episode on the path of preparation of a new world war. The ruling classes of all shades are afraid of it and at the same time are preparing for it with all their might. The charlatanism of Popular Fronts serves one part of the imperialists to conceal their plans from the popular masses, as the other gang uses phrases about blood, honour, and race for the same purpose. The petty-bourgeois windbags

---

3　I.e., towards the Nazi-Soviet Pact, which was ultimately signed in August 1939.

4　Trotsky began to use this term about the Stalinist bureaucracy in 1935 when he spoke of the Stalinists as having made a decisive break with the revolutionary gains of October, though without yet having destroyed the workers' state. (See his article *The 'Workers' State and the Question of Thermidor and Bonapartism'*, reprinted in *The Class Nature of the Soviet State*.)

and phrasemongers only make it easier for the imperialists to prepare war, by preventing the workers from seeing the naked truth.

* * *

Letter to Emrys Hughes[5] (dated 22 April 1939),
first published in *Forward*, 31 August 1940.

Dear Comrade Hughes,

Thank you sincerely for your letter of 3 April. Undoubtedly there are thousands upon thousands of British workers and honest and revolutionary intellectuals who think as you do. They are simply stifled, but not so much by the state machine as by the machine of the official workers' organisations. The war they are preparing will break both these machines.

In the catastrophe of war, the most disoriented, confused, and cowardly will be the present magnificent leaders of the workers' organisations, of the Second and Third Internationals. The masses will look for a new orientation, a new direction, and will find them.

You are right that the first chapter of the war will be a chapter of nationalistic madness. But the more terrible the war and the war hysteria, the more crushing will be the mass reaction. Not to lose one's head and to look toward the future – the near future – with open eyes, is the highest revolutionary duty.

With fraternal greetings,
Leon Trotsky,
Coyoacán, D. F.

* * *

From a stenographic record of an interview with
Hubert Herring, 23 July 1939.

Q – How do you interpret the underlying purposes of the Chamberlain government?

A – I believe the underlying factors are panic and headlessness. It is not an individual characteristic of Mr. Chamberlain. I do not believe he has any worse head than any other person, but the situation of Great Britain is very difficult, the same as that of France. England was a leading world power in the

---

5 Emrys Hughes (1894-1969) – Labour politician, editor of *Forward*, the Scottish ILP paper, from 1931-46. MP for South Ayrshire from 1946 until his death, during which time he wrote a number of books of a mildly reformist character.

past – in the nineteenth century – but no more. But she has the greatest world empire. France, with her stagnating population and more or less backward economic structure, has a second colonial empire. This is the situation. It is very difficult to be inventive as a British Prime Minister in this situation. Only the old formula of 'wait and see'. This was good when Great Britain was the strongest power in the world and they had enough power to reach their aims. No more now. The war can only crush and disrupt the British empire and the French empire. They can gain nothing by the war – only lose. That is why Mr. Chamberlain was so friendly to Hitler during the Munich period.[6] He believed that the question was about central Europe and the Danube, but now he understands that it is the question of world domination. Great Britain and France cannot avoid a war, and now they do everything they can in a feverish tempo to avoid the war threatened by the situation created by the rearmament of Germany. That war is inevitable.

* * *

Exchange of telegram messages between *The Daily Herald* and Trotsky. First published in *Socialist Appeal*, 3 November 1939.

Leon Trotsky
Cable prepaid
Mexico

600 word article by return cable giving your reasons for opposing negotiations allies with Russia.[7] Bernard Shaw article supporting Stalin will appear same page. Prepared order £15 if published.

Editor, *Daily Herald*,
London, 20 October

---

6   An agreement was signed at Munich on 30 September 1938 by Hitler, Chamberlain, and Daladier allowing the Germans to annex parts of Czechoslovakia, and soon to occupy the entire country. Virtually all of the British press supported this agreement and no Conservative MP voted against it. As a method of providing 'peace in our time' between British and German imperialism it proved singularly ineffective, with the Second World War breaking out less than a year later.

7   The British Tories and their French equivalents had not been prepared to negotiate an anti-German pact with Stalin, since they would not agree to any of the Western movement of Soviet troops necessary to enforce it. As a result, as Trotsky had always predicted, a Nazi-Soviet pact was agreed on 23 August. This caused demoralisation

—

Leon Trotsky
Cable prepaid
Mexico

Would welcome immediate reply if prepared cable article requested last
Friday or not. If agreeable please cable article today at latest.

Editor, *Daily Herald*,
London, 23 October

—

Editor, *Daily Herald*
Cable collect
London

You did not publish my letter protesting imperialist London policy against
Mexico. You did not publish my statement on coming war granted to your
own correspondent Vincent. Now you want to adapt me to your anti-socialist
policy.[8] That will not succeed.

Leon Trotsky,
Coyoacán, 23 October

* * *

From the *Manifesto of the Fourth International on Imperialist War
and Proletarian Revolution* adopted by the Emergency Conference
of the Fourth International 26 May 1940.

The immediate cause of the present war is the rivalry between the old wealthy
colonial empires, Great Britain and France, and the belated imperialist
plunderers, Germany and Italy.

The nineteenth century was the era of the incontestable hegemony of the
oldest capitalist power, Great Britain. From 1815 to 1914 – true enough,
not without isolated military explosions – 'British peace' reigned. The British

---

among many who had followed the Popular Front policies of the Stalinists in the
previous period. The call by the *Herald* for the resumption of negotiations with Stalin
was part of an effort in radical and social-democratic circles to return to that situation.

8 The social-democrats of the *Daily Herald* were trying to use Trotsky as an ally in
opposition to communism itself and the Soviet workers' state.

fleet, mightiest in the world, played the role of policeman of the seas. This era, however, has receded into the past. As early as the end of the last century, Germany, armed with modern technology, began to move toward first place in Europe. On the other side of the ocean an even more powerful country arose, a former British colony. The most important economic contradiction which led to the war of 1914-1918 was the rivalry between Britain and Germany. As for the United States, its participation in the war was of a preventive character – Germany could not be permitted to subjugate the European continent.

The defeat hurled Germany back into complete impotence. Dismembered, encircled by enemies, bankrupted by indemnities, weakened by the convulsions of civil war, she appeared to be out of the running for a long time to come, if not forever. On the European continent, first violin turned up temporarily in the hands of France. For victorious Britain, the balance sheet of the war left in the last analysis liabilities: increasing independence of the dominions; colonial movements for independence; loss of naval hegemony; lessening of the importance of her Navy through the development of aviation.

Through inertia Britain still attempted to play the leading role on the world arena in the first few years after victory. Her conflicts with the United States began to assume an obviously threatening character. It seemed as though the next war would flare up between the two Anglo-Saxon aspirants to world domination. Britain, however, soon had to convince herself that her specific economic weight was inadequate for combat with the colossus across the ocean. Her agreement with the United States on naval equality signified formal renunciation of naval hegemony, already lost in actuality. Her replacement of free trade by tariff walls signified open admission of the defeat of British industry on the world market. Her renunciation of the policy of "splendid isolation" drew in its wake the introduction of compulsory military service. Thus all the sacred traditions were dusted away.

A similar lack of correspondence between her economic weight and her world position is characteristic of France too, but on a smaller scale. Her hegemony in Europe rested on a temporary conjuncture of circumstances created by the annihilation of Germany and the artificial combinations of the Versailles Treaty.[9] The size of her population and the economic foundation supporting this hegemony were far too inadequate. When the hypnosis of

---

9   The agreement between the main combatants that ended the First World War. Concluded at Versailles near Paris in 1919, the treaty imposed crushing military and economic sanctions against Germany.

victory wore off, the real relationship of forces surged to the surface. France proved to be much weaker than she had appeared not only to her friends but to her enemies. Seeking cover, she became in essence Britain's latest dominion.

Germany's regeneration on the basis of her first-rate technology and organisational abilities was inevitable. It came sooner than was thought possible, in large measure thanks to Britain's support of Germany against the USSR, against the excessive pretensions of France and, more remotely, against the United States. Such international combinations proved successful for capitalist Britain more than once in the past, so long as she remained the strongest power. In her senility she proved incapable of dealing with those spirits she had herself evoked.

Armed with a technology, more modern, of greater flexibility, and of higher productive capacity, Germany once again began to squeeze Britain out of very important markets, particularly south-eastern Europe and Latin America. In contrast to the nineteenth century, when the competition between capitalist countries developed on an expanding world market, the economic arena of struggle today is narrowing down so that nothing remains open to the imperialists except tearing pieces of the world market away from each other.

The initiative for the new redivision of the world this time as in 1914 belonged naturally to German imperialism. Caught off guard, the British government first attempted to buy its way out of war by concessions at the expense of others (Austria, Czechoslovakia). But this policy was short-lived. 'Friendship' with Britain was only a brief tactical phase for Hitler. London had already conceded Hitler more than he had calculated on getting. The Munich agreement, through which Chamberlain hoped to seal a long-time friendship with Germany, led, on the contrary, to a hastening of the break. Hitler could expect nothing more from London – further expansion of Germany would strike at the life lines of Britain herself. Thus the 'new era of peace' proclaimed by Chamberlain in October 1938 led within a few months to the most terrible of all wars.

While Great Britain has exerted every effort since the first months of the war to seize blockaded Germany's vacated positions in the world market, the United States has almost automatically been driving Britain out. Two-thirds of the world's gold is concentrated in the American vaults. The remaining third is flowing to the same place. Britain's role as banker for the world is a thing of the past. Nor are matters in other spheres much better. While Britain's Navy and merchant marine are suffering great losses, the American shipyards are building ships on a colossal scale which will secure the predominance of the American fleet over the British and the Japanese. The United States is obviously preparing to adopt the *two-power standard* (a navy stronger than the combined fleets of the next two strongest powers). The new programme for the air fleet envisages securing the superiority of the United States over all the rest of the world.

However, the industrial, financial and military strength of the United States, the foremost capitalist power in the world, does not at all insure the blossoming of American economic life, but on the contrary, invests the crisis of her social system with an especially malignant and convulsive character. Gold in the billions cannot be made use of nor can the millions of unemployed! In the theses of the Fourth International, *War and the Fourth International*, published six years ago, it was predicted:

> Capitalism in the United States is running head on into those problems which impelled Germany in 1914 upon the road of war… For Germany it was a question of 'organising' Europe. For the United States it is a question of 'organising' the world. History is taking mankind directly into the volcanic eruption of American imperialism.

The 'New Deal' and the 'Good Neighbour' policy[10] were the final attempts to postpone the climax by ameliorating the social crisis through concessions and agreements. After the bankruptcy of this policy, which swallowed up tens of billions, nothing else remained for American imperialism but to resort to the method of the mailed fist. Under one or another pretext and slogan the United States will intervene in the tremendous clash in order to maintain its world dominion. The order and the time of the struggle between American capitalism and its enemies is not yet known – perhaps even by Washington. War with Japan would be a struggle for 'living room' in the Pacific Ocean. War in the Atlantic, even if directed immediately against Germany, would be a struggle for the heritage of Britain…

---

10 The term 'New Deal' was coined by F. D. Roosevelt in his acceptance speech for nomination as Democratic Party candidate for President in 1932. What was intended at first simply as an electoral catch-phrase later came to represent a whole series of capitalist policies for dealing with depression, from the granting of certain rights to trade unions to state intervention in the economy, and ultimately to methods of government deficit financing and other measures proposed by the British economist Keynes. The 'Good Neighbour' policy was the name given to Roosevelt's efforts to impose United States control throughout the Americas less by direct political sanctions and armed intervention and more by the economic penetration of her capitalists.

The weakness of France and Britain was not unexpected. The theses of the Fourth International (1934) state: "The collapse of the League of Nations is indissolubly bound up with the beginning of the collapse of French hegemony on the European continent." This programmatic document declares further that "Britain's rulers are increasingly less capable of carrying out their plans", that the British bourgeoisie is "alarmed by the disintegration of its empire, the revolutionary movement in India, the instability of its positions in China." The power of the Fourth International lies in this, that its programme is capable of withstanding the test of great events.

The industry of Britain and France, thanks to the assured flow of colonial super-profits, has long lagged both in technology and organisation. In addition, the so-called 'defence of democracy' by the socialist parties and trade unions created an extremely privileged political situation for the British and French bourgeoisie. Privileges always foster sluggishness and stagnation. If Germany today reveals so colossal a preponderance over France and Britain, then the lion's share of the responsibility rests with the social-patriotic defenders of democracy who prevented the proletariat from tearing Britain and France out of atrophy through a timely socialist revolution.

VIII

Trotsky Versus Centrism in Britain

Questions of Perspective

From *Germany: The Key to the International Situation*
(dated 26 November 1931), *Byulleten Oppozitsii*,
November-December 1931.

The situation in Britain can likewise be termed, with a certain degree of justification, pre-revolutionary, provided it is strictly agreed that a period covering several years of partial ebbs and flows can elapse between the pre-revolutionary and the immediately revolutionary situation. The economic situation in Britain has reached extreme in the economic acuteness. Still, the political superstructure this arch-conservative country extraordinarily lags behind the changes in its economic basis. Before having recourse to new political forms and methods, all the classes of the British nation are attempting time and again to ransack the old storerooms, to turn the old clothes of their grandfathers and grandmothers inside out. The fact remains, that despite the dreadful national decline, there does not exist in Britain as yet either a revolutionary party of any significance or its antipode – the Fascist party. Thanks to these circumstances, the bourgeoisie has had the opportunity of mobilising the majority of the people under the 'national' banner, that is, under the most hollow of all possible slogans. In the pre-revolutionary situation, the most dull-witted of conservatisms has acquired tremendous political predominance. It will in all probability take more than one month, perhaps more than one year, for the political superstructure to become adapted to the real economic and international situation of the country.

There is no ground for assuming that the collapse of the 'national' bloc – and such a collapse is inevitable in the relatively near future – will lead directly to the proletarian revolution (it is a matter of course, that there can be no other revolution in Britain) or to the triumph of 'Fascism'. On the contrary, it may be assumed with much greater probability that on her path to the revolutionary solution Britain will go through a lengthy period of the radical-democratic and social-pacifist demagogy *à la* Lloyd George and of Labourism. There can therefore be no doubt that Britain's historical development will grant British Communism ample time to transform itself into the genuine party of the proletariat by the time it is confronted with the solution. From this, however, it does not at all follow that we can afford to continue losing time with disastrous experiments and centrist zigzags. In the present world situation, time is the most precious of raw materials.

* * *

From *The Third Period of the Mistakes of the Comintern*
(dated 26 January 1930), *Byulleten Oppozitsii*, January 1930.

But there is yet another important tactical conclusion drawn from the "third period" which is expressed by Molotov in the following words: "Now, more than ever before, the tactic of coalitions between revolutionary organisations and organisations of reformists are unacceptable and harmful."[1]

Agreements with reformists are impermissible now "*more than ever before*". Does this mean they were impermissible before? How then can the whole policy of 1926-1928 be explained? And why exactly have agreements with reformists which are impermissible in general become *especially* impermissible now? – Because, as they explain to us, we have entered a phase of revolutionary upsurge. But we cannot help recalling that the formation of the bloc with the General Council of the British trade unions was in its time justified precisely by the fact that Britain was entering a period of revolutionary upsurge and that the radicalisation of the British working masses was driving the reformists leftwards. Upon what occasion was yesterday's tactical wisdom of Stalinism turned upon its head? We would seek a solution in vain. All that can be said is that the empiricists of centrism burned their fingers in the experience of the Anglo-Russian Committee and wish by making a solemn oath to protect themselves from such a scandal in the future. But oaths will not help. Our strategists have to this day not understood the lessons of the Anglo-Russian Committee.

The mistake lay not in concluding an episodic agreement with the General Council which in actual fact did 'turn left' in that period (1926) under the

---

1   *Pravda*, 4 August 1929.

pressure of the masses. The first and initial error lay in that the bloc was founded not upon concrete practical tasks but upon general pacifist phrases and false diplomatic formulas. But the chief error, which grew into a gigantic historic crime, lay in the fact that our strategists proved unable to break immediately and publicly from the General Council when the latter turned its weaponry against the General Strike, that is, when it turned from unsteady half-ally into an open enemy.

* * *

From *The Tasks of the Left Opposition in Britain and India*
(dated 7 November 1931), *The Militant*, 12 December 1931.

Two comrades, Ridley and Chandu Ram, have worked out theses dedicated to the situation in Britain, the Left Opposition and its relations to the Comintern. The authors consider themselves supporters of the Left Opposition despite their having serious differences with it. In their document they defend several times the necessity of an open and free inner criticism. This is absolutely correct. This free and open criticism we will employ therefore in relation to their own theses.

1. "Great Britain is at the present time in a transitional phase between democracy and fascism". Democracy and fascism are here considered as two abstractions without any social determinants. Evidently the authors wish to say: British imperialism prepares itself to free her dictatorship from the decomposing parliamentary covering, and to enter upon the path of open and naked violence. In general this is true, but only in general. The present government[2] is not an 'anti-parliamentary' government: on the contrary, it has received unheard of support from 'the nation'. Only the growth of the revolutionary movement in Britain can force the government to tread the path of

---

2 In August 1931, at a time of enormous international economic crisis, a section of the minority Labour government led by MacDonald and Snowden joined the Tories and Liberals to form a so-called 'National' government. On 27 October MacDonald called an election, and in an atmosphere of red-baiting and the demoralisation of the working-class leadership, the coalition secured a majority of 497 seats, dramatically reducing the number of Labour MPs to forty-six. The National Government then set about cutting the dole and making various other attacks on the working class which its predecessor had found it impossible to carry out. The coalition survived a further General Election in 1935, though it had long since given up the pretence of being anything other than a creature of the Tories who dominated it.

naked, ultra-parliamentary violence. This will without doubt take place. But at the present time this is not so. To place today the question of fascism on the first plane is not here motivated. Even from the standpoint of a distant perspective one can doubt in what measure it is in place to speak of 'fascism' for Britain. Marxists must, in our opinion, proceed from the idea that fascism represents a different and specific form of the dictatorship of finance capital, but it is absolutely not identical with the imperialist dictatorship as such. When the 'Party' of Mosley[3] and the 'Guild of St. Michael'[4] represent the beginnings of fascism, as the thesis declares, it is precisely the total futility of both named groups that shows how unwise it is to reduce already today the whole perspective to the imminent coming of fascism.

In the analysis of the present situation in Britain, we should not preclude the variants through which the rule of conservatism will pass, not directly to the dictatorship of open violence, but will put forward, as a result of a swift parliamentary dislocation to the Left, through any block of Henderson and Lloyd George, a transitory government of the British Kerenskiade. Lloyd George counts, manifestly, on the inevitable Left turn of open opinion and precisely, therefore, does not fear to remain today in a futile minority.[5] In what degree the British Kerenskiade is probable, how durable it will be, etc., depends on the further development of the economic crisis, on the tempo of the bankruptcy of the 'national' government, and, mainly, upon the speed of the radicalisation of the masses.

Obviously, the Kerenskiade, when it appears, must for its own part uncover its insufficiency and consequently push the bourgeoisie along the road of open and naked violence. In this case, the British workers must convince themselves that their monarchy is not just an innocent and decorative institution: the King's power will inevitably become the centre of the united imperialist counter-revolution.

2. A profound error is to be found in the second paragraph, directed against activity in the trade unions with the object of their capture,

---

3 The New Party – Formed in 1931 by Oswald Mosley. Renamed the British Union of Fascists in 1932.

4 The 'Guild of St. Michael' – A short-lived right-wing group that soon disappeared after the formation of British Union of Fascists.

5 I have just received the *Resignation Letter* of Lloyd George to his parliamentary party, which totally confirms this supposition. – *Trotsky*

which for a Marxist and Bolshevik is obligatory. According to the thought of the thesis, the trade unions from their origin represent "imperialist organisations". They can live so long as they benefit by the super-profits of British capitalism; now, when her privileged position is forever lost, the trade unions can only disappear. To struggle to capture the present trade unions is nonsense. The revolutionary dictatorship will, in the proper time, build new "economic organisations".

In this judgement there is nothing new. It renews long ago clarified and rejected propositions. The trade unions are not considered by the authors as the *historic organisation* of the British proletariat, which reflects its destiny, but as a creation which from its inception is penetrated with the sin of imperialism. But the trade unions have had their rich and instructive history. They had previously carried on a heroic struggle for the right to organisation. They gloriously participated in the Chartist movement. They led the struggle for the shorter working day, and these struggles were recognised by Marx and Engels as having great historical importance. A number of trade unions entered the First International. Alas, history does not exist for our authors. In all their opinions, there is not a drop of dialectics. They limit themselves under metaphysical principles: 'fascism', 'democracy', 'imperialist organisations'. To the living and real processes they oppose their own inventions.

We hear from them that the leaders of the trade unions did not betray the General Strike of 1926. To acknowledge them as 'betrayers' would indicate acknowledgement that they were previously 'revolutionary'. See what kind of a Derby metaphysics runs! The reformists have not always betrayed the workers. In certain periods and under certain conditions, the reformists carried through some progressive work, insufficient though it be. The epoch of imperialist decline snatches the rug from under the reformists. That is why the reformists, insofar as they are forced to attach themselves to the movement of the masses, betray it at a certain stage. Even so, the masses accept the conduct of the reformists. To this living conception of the masses, the authors oppose the theory of the original sin of the trade unions. This theory is remarkable in that it does not allow a betrayer to be called a betrayer.

Since 1920, the trade unions have lost more than 40 per cent of their membership. The authors, therefore, say that in the course of the next two years they will lose another 40 per cent. When these 80 per cent of workers come to communism, comrades Ridley and Ram have not a dozen workers behind them. The trade unions still embrace millions of workers who in 1926 demonstrated that they are capable of carrying on a revolutionary struggle. We must look for the workers where they are to be found today, and not where they may be tomorrow – the organised as well as the unorganised. The question does not go so far as the economic organisations which the future revolutionary dictatorship will create, but rather to the present British worker, without whom to speak of the dictatorship of the proletariat signifies playing with phrases. Can in reality the workers enter the path of insurrection in one leap, without in the preceding period deepening its struggle against capitalism, without radicalising themselves, their methods of struggle and their organisations? How can the revolutionisation of the working class take place outside of the trade unions, without reflecting itself inside of the trade unions, without changing its physiognomy, and failing to call forth a selection of new leaders? If it is true that the trade unions originated on the fundamentals of the capitalist super-profits of Great Britain – and this is so *to a limited degree* – so must the destruction of the super-profits radicalise the trade unions, understood, of course, from below and not from above, understood in the struggle against the leaders and traditions. This struggle will be all the more successful if the Communists participate in it.

The authors of the thesis go so far as to identify the struggle for the trade unions with the Anglo-Russian Committee. An overwhelming argument! The Left Opposition accused Stalin, Tomsky, and Co. that through the political friendship with Citrine, Purcell, Cook *et al.* the communists in the trade unions were hindered from unmasking these traitors. Comrades Ridley and Ram bring forth a new discovery: To unite with the betrayers and to unmask them before the masses – are one and the same thing. Can we take such arguments seriously?

The American comrade, Glotzer, in speaking of the necessity of working in the trade union organisations for their conquest, appeals in absolute correctness to the pamphlet of Lenin's *Left Wing Communism: An Infantile Disorder*. To this, comrades Ridley and Ram answer with four objections:

a.   They ask for arguments and not appeals to authorities. This is right. But the pamphlet of Lenin's contains many arguments which their thesis entirely fails to answer.

    b. The authors deny Roman Catholic dogmas of infallibility. We agree with that. But we counsel them to begin with a criticism of the infallibility of their own gospel.

    c. "Lenin was neither God nor an infallible Pope!" This is a repetition of the preceding argument. Without a Pope, Lenin successfully struggled against metaphysics and sectarianism.

    d. Lenin wrote in the year 1920. The situation since then has changed considerably. But the authors abstain from explaining in what these changes really consist, aside from considering their allusion to the diminishing membership of the trade unions, which does not have a decisive significance.

We see that the arguments of the authors have an extremely abstract even a purely formal character. The allusion to the year 1920 is in direct opposition to the fundamental thoughts of the thesis. If the trade unions from their origin were and remain to this day pure imperialist organisations incapable of revolutionary deeds, the allusion to the year 1920 loses all significance. We would have to say simply that the attitude of Marx, Engels, and Lenin was false to the roots.

3. The third paragraph is dedicated to the Comintern. The authors stand for the creation of a Fourth International,[6] and, here too, manifest the fundamental quality of their thoughts: absolute metaphysics. We reply that Engels, after Hegel, understood metaphysics as considering phenomenon, fact, power, tendencies, etc., as unchangeable substances, and not as developing processes and, therefore, developing in constant contradictions. If the trade union is a vicious imperialist substance from below to above, in all epochs and periods, so likewise the Comintern is for our innovators a vicious bureaucratic substance. The inner processes of the Comintern, the inevitable contradiction between the masses of members and the bureaucratic apparatus, are entirely left out of

---

6 Trotsky opposed early calls for such an organisation made by some of those who considered themselves to be his supporters. It was only when Stalin's policies in Germany split the working class and allowed Hitler to come to power that the Third International showed it had without qualification gone over to the side of counter-revolution. It was at this point that he began to oppose those, like the ILP and their supporters in the 'London Bureau', who would not break decisively from Stalinism as well as from social democracy. From 1933 until his death Trotsky considered the establishment of the Fourth International, which ultimately took place in 1938, to be the most important task he had to perform.

consideration in their calculations. The authors ask us: Do we believe
that the bureaucracy under the influence of our thesis will surrender
their interests? And is such a supposition to be described as idealism
or materialism? – inquire further Ridley and Ram with inimitable
irony, not observing that their own posing of the question must be
characterised as lifeless metaphysics.

The bureaucracy is very strong, but it is certainly not as omnipotent as
Ridley and Ram believe. In the USSR, the sharpening contradictions of
economic development pose ever more before the millions of members
of the party and youth, the fundamental questions of programme
and tactics. Insofar as the bureaucrats will not be able to solve these
contradictions, the millions of communists and young communists will
be forced to think independently of their solution. To these masses we say
today, and we will say tomorrow: "The centrist bureaucracy conquered
the apparatus of the party, thanks to certain historic conditions. But
you, worker-communists, hold to the party, not in the name of the
bureaucrats but in the name of its great revolutionary past and its possible
revolutionary future. We understand you fully. The revolutionary
workers do not leap from organisation to organisation with lightness,
like individual students. We Bolshevik-Leninists are fully ready to help
you worker-communists regenerate the party."

Supporting the German Communist Party are millions of workers.
The catastrophic crisis in Germany places before it revolutionary
problems as problems of life or death. On this ground without doubt
will develop a deeper and deeper ideological struggle in the party. If
the few hundred Left Oppositionists remain on the side, they will
become transformed into a powerless lamentable sect. If, however, they
participate in the inner ideological struggles of the party, of which
they remain an integral part despite all expulsions, they will win an
enormous influence among the proletarian kernel of the party.

No; the Left Opposition has no reason to tread the path which
Ridley and Ram call for. Within the Comintern – even when one
does not consider the USSR – are to be found tens of thousands
of workers who have lived through serious experiences, through a
whole stream of disillusionments, and are forced to search for correct
answers to all fundamental questions of politics. We must approach
these workers and not turn our backs to them. It would be very sad if
the critical members of the official British Communist Party would

imagine that the opinions of Ridley and Ram represent the opinions of the Left Opposition.

4. The authors of the thesis accuse the Left Opposition, especially the American League,[7] of "absurdly over-rating" the importance of the British Communist Party. In no way do we over-rate its importance. The last elections sufficiently, clearly, and openly exhibited the weakness of the British Communist Party. But the Left Opposition in Great Britain is today many hundred times weaker than this weak party. Ram and Ridley have as yet nothing. Supporting them are nobody but individuals who are not bound up with the struggle of the proletariat. Have they really attempted to draw an honest criticism of the Party? Where is their activity? Where are their programme theses? Have they held discussions with the rank and file of the party? Have they tried to convert them and win them to their support? Have Ram and Ridley, out of the 70,000 voters for the official party, 700 or even seventy supporters? But in spite of this they are ready to organise the Fourth International. The proletariat must believe in them implicitly – on credit, that they are really capable of building an International and leading it.

The entire posing of the question is absolutely wrong. To this we must add that if the Left Opposition entertained this pernicious error and decided to create a Fourth International comrades Ridley and Ram, who differ with us on fundamental questions, must openly and immediately build a Fourth International.

5. The paragraph which concerns itself with India, also suffers an extraordinary abstraction. It is absolutely indisputable that India can accomplish its full national independence only through a really great revolution which will put in power the Indian proletariat. Another path of development is imaginable only, in this case, if the proletarian revolution in Britain comes to victory prior to the revolution in India. In such an event, the national liberation of India would come before – one must suppose for a short time only – the dictatorship of the proletariat uniting with it the poor peasantry. But from these

---

7 Communist League – The title adopted by sections supporting the International Left Opposition in the period before the call to establish a new International in 1933. It was adopted by Trotsky's followers in the United States under the leadership of James P. Cannon, Martin Abern, and Max Shachtman after their expulsion from the CPUSA in 1928. In 1933 the American Communist League changed its name to the Workers' Party when it fused with A. J. Muste's Conference for Progressive Labour Action.

perspectives, which are absolutely correct, it is still a long way to say that India is already ripe for the dictatorship of the proletariat, that the proletariat have outlived their transitory illusions, etc. No: before Indian Communism stands a task not yet begun. The Bolshevik-Leninists[8] of India must accomplish an immense, audacious, daily, and difficult work. They must penetrate into all organisations of the working class. The first cadres of worker-communists must be trained. There must be participation in the 'prosaic' life of the workers and their organisations. There must be study of the relations existing between the cities and the rural districts.

To fulfil such a work, naturally programmatical and tactical theses are necessary. But it would be incorrect to begin to work with the convention of an international conference over the question of India, as our authors propose. A conference without sufficient preparation will produce nothing. If the Indian Left Oppositionists will occupy themselves with the selection of recent material and working it up, or at least translate it into one of the European languages (strikes, demonstrations, matters of the peasant movement, the parties and the political groups of the different classes, the activity of the Comintern, its appeals and slogans), they will do such an important work, greatly facilitate the possibility of a collective elaboration of the programme and tactics of the proletarian vanguard in India.

One must begin with the building of a serious nucleus of the Left Opposition of Indian comrades, who must stand upon the point of view of the Bolshevik-Leninists.

* * *

Notes from a discussion with Albert Glotzer of the
Communist League of America, (17 November 1931),
The Militant, 19 December 1931.

1. For an analysis of a situation from a revolutionary point of view, it is necessary to distinguish between the economic and social premises of a revolutionary situation and the revolutionary situation itself.

2. The economic and social premises for a revolutionary situation begin, generally speaking, at that moment when the productive forces of the country are going not up but down, that is diminishing; when

---

8 Bolshevik-Leninists – The name used by Left Oppositionists in the early period to draw the line against the Stalinists' break from Leninist theory and practice.

the specific weight of a capitalist country on the world markets is systematically reduced and when the incomes of the classes are likewise systematically reduced; when unemployment becomes not a conjunctural event of fluctuation but a permanent social evil with a tendency to growth. All the foregoing characterise the situation in Britain completely and we can affirm that the economic and social premises for a revolutionary situation exist there in this form and are always becoming more and more acute. But we must not forget that the expression, revolutionary situation, is a political term, not alone sociological. This explanation includes the subjective factor, and the subjective factor is not only the question of the party of the proletariat. It is a question of the consciousness of the whole class, foremost, of course, of the proletariat and the party.

3. The revolutionary situation, however, begins only from the moment that the economic and social premises of a revolution produce a break in the consciousness of society and its different classes. What must be produced in this way for creating a revolutionary situation?

    a. In every situation which we must analyse, it is necessary to distinguish three classes of society; the capitalists, the middle class (or petty bourgeoisie) and the proletariat. Those changes in the consciousness of these classes in order to characterise a revolutionary situation are very different for every one of these classes.

    b. That the economic situation is very acute, the British proletariat know very well, far better than all theoreticians. But the revolutionary situation begins only at the moment when the proletariat begins to search for a way out, not on the basis of the old society but along the path of a revolutionary insurrection against the existing order. This is the most important subjective condition for a revolutionary situation. The acuteness of the revolutionary feelings of the masses is one of the most important measures for the ripeness of the revolutionary situation.

    c. But a revolutionary situation is one which must, in the next period permit the proletariat to become the ruling power of society, that depends in Britain, less than in any other country, but also there to a degree, on the political thoughts and feelings of the middle class; the revolutionary situation would be characterised by the loss of confidence of the middle class in all the traditional parties (including the Labour Party, which is reformist), and its turn of hope to a radical, revolutionary change in the society (and not a counter-revolutionary change, viz., a fascist change).

d. Both the changes in the consciousness of the proletariat and the middle class correspond to the change in the consciousness of the ruling class which sees that it has not the means to save its system, loses confidence in itself, decomposes and splits into factions and cliques.

4. It cannot be foreseen or indicated mathematically at what point in these processes the revolutionary situation is totally ripe. The revolutionary party can only establish that fact by its struggles, by the growth of its forces, through its influence on the masses, on the peasants and the petty-bourgeoisie of the towns, etc., and by the weakening of the resistance of the ruling class.

5. If we adapt these criteria to the British situation we can see:
   a. That the economic and social premises, as we stated, are existing and becoming more effective and acute.
   b. The bridge, however, from these economic premises to the psychological results has not been crossed. For the revolutionary situation in Britain it is not necessary for great changes in the economic conditions, which are already unbearable, to come about. What is necessary is a new adjustment of the consciousness of the different classes to this unbearable catastrophic situation in Britain.

6. The economic change of society is very slow and is measured by centuries and decades. But when the economic conditions are radically changed a transformation of the retarded psychological factors can be produced very quickly. However, quickly or slowly, such changes must inevitably be effected in the consciousness of the classes. Only then can we have a revolutionary situation.

7. In political terms it signifies:
   a. That the proletariat must have lost its confidence not only in the conservatives and liberals, but also in the Labour Party. It must concentrate its will and its courage for revolutionary aims and methods.
   b. That the middle class must lose its confidence in the big bourgeoisie, in the lords and turn their eyes to the revolutionary proletariat.
   c. That the rich classes, the ruling cliques, rejected by the masses lose confidence in themselves.

8. These phenomena will inevitably come. However, they do not exist today. They can come in a short period of time through the acute crisis. They can arrive in two or three years, or perhaps only a year. But this

is a perspective and not a fact today. We must base our policy on the facts of today and not of tomorrow.

9. The political conditions of a revolutionary situation are developing more or less parallel and simultaneously, but this does not signify that they all become ripe at the same moment – there is the danger of the British situation of tomorrow. In the ripening political conditions, the most retarded is the revolutionary party of the proletariat. It is not excluded that the general revolutionary change of the proletariat and the middle class, and the political decomposition of the ruling class, will develop more quickly than the ripening of the Communist Party. It signifies that it does not exclude after tomorrow a genuinely revolutionary situation without an adequate revolutionary party. It would be to a certain degree a reproduction of the situation in Germany of 1923.[9] But to affirm that Britain is in such a situation today is absolutely false.

10. We say that it is not excluded that the development of the Party can remain retarded in relation to the other elements of the revolutionary situation, but that is not in any case inevitable. On this question we cannot make any prognosis, but the question is not merely a question of prognoses. It is a question of our own action.

11. How much time will the British proletariat need in the present state of capitalist society to break up its connections with the three bourgeois parties? By a correct policy of the Communist Party, it is entirely possible that its growth will take place in proportion to the bankruptcy and decomposition of the other parties. It is our aim, it is our duty to realise this possibility.

Conclusions. That explains sufficiently why it is totally false to affirm that Britain is now between democracy and fascism. The era of fascism begins seriously after an important and, for a certain time, decisive victory of the bourgeoisie over the working class. But the great struggles in Britain are not behind us, rather ahead of us. As we discussed in another connection, most probably the next political chapter in Britain, after the decomposition of the National Government and the Conservative government which will probably succeed it, will be a Liberal-Labour reformist era which can, namely in Britain, become in the near future more dangerous than the spectre of fascism. We called this period, conditionally, the British Kerensky phase.

---

9   See footnote on page 143.

But it is necessary to add that the Kerensky phase is not obliged to be in every situation, in every country, as weak as the Russian Kerensky phase. The weakness of the Kerensky phase there was a result of the great power of the Bolshevik Party. We see now, for example, in Spain[10] that the Kerenskiade – the coalition of the liberals and the 'socialists' – is by no means as weak as it was in Russia, and this is the result of the weakness of the Communist Party, which is thereby becoming a great danger to the Spanish Revolution. The Kerensky phase signifies for us the employment of reformist, 'revolutionary', 'democratic', 'socialist' phrases, certain secondary democratic and social reforms, while at the same time carrying on repression against the left wing of the working class.

This method is contrary to the method of fascism, but it serves the same aim. To condemn the future Lloyd George era to a weakness, is only possible when we are not hypnotising ourselves with the spectre of fascism which is further away than Lloyd George and his instrument of tomorrow – the Labour Party. The danger of tomorrow can become the reformist party, the bloc of the liberals and the socialists; the fascist danger is still in the third or fourth stage away. The struggle to eliminate the fascists and to eliminate or reduce the new reformist period signifies for the Communist Party the struggle for the winning of the working class.

---

10 The 1929 economic crisis was reflected in Spain in the following year with the collapse of the military dictatorship of Primo de Rivera. During the course of 1931 the constitution was restored, the King followed Rivera into exile, and a government was established which consisted of a coalition of liberal bourgeois parties and the Spanish Socialist Party of Francisco Caballero and Indalecio Prieto.

The First British Trotskyists

Letter to Reg Groves (dated 10 November 1931),
The Militant, 5 December 1931.

Dear Comrade Groves,

I have your letter of four weeks ago. Excuse me for not answering sooner. I am at present busy with extremely important work. Aside from this, it is very difficult for me to write in English and it would take me a great deal of time to do so. In addition I did not know whether you could read German or French. At the present time there is an American comrade here who will translate this letter into English. Because of all these reasons you can understand the exceptional delay in answering you.

The same necessary work, which will take at least one and a half months, prevents me from paying close attention to the British question, which is of immeasurable importance to us. Even with regard to reading the British papers, I find little time for it. I trust that the second volume of my *History of the Russian Revolution* which I am now completing will serve in good stead the communists over the entire world, and especially Britain, in the current era which will bring great tremors in Europe and the rest of the world.

The above will explain why it is difficult for me to give a precise opinion at the present time on the question of the next practical steps for the British Communists and the Left Opposition. In one or two months I shall turn my attention to this. For the present I am forced to confine myself to considerations of a most general character.

One of my English friends wrote to me on 9 October, prior to the parliamentary elections, about the fast growth of the Communist Party, and of a certain approach of the rank-and-file members in the ILP towards communism. My correspondent speaks also of a regrowth of the Minority Movement in the trade unions and the growing leadership of the same minority in the sporadic strike movements. These isolated instances in the background of the world crisis and the *national crisis* which Britain is going through allows us to accept the idea that in the last two years there has been a strengthening of the Communist Party. The elections brought an absolute disillusionment in this respect. Of the many hundreds of thousands of votes which the Labourites lost, the Party at best swung to its support 20,000 which is, in consideration of the increased total number of voters, an invalid conjunctural fluctuation, and not by any means a serious political conquest. Where is the influence of the Party among the unemployed? Among the coal miners? Among the young generation of workers who, for the first time, voted? Actually, the election results are a horrible condemnation of the policies of the Party and the Comintern.

I have observed very little the tactics of the British party during the last year and I do not want to give judgement about what it learned, or whether it really learned anything. However, it is clear to me that independent from its recent and latest errors, the Communist Party is paying by its impotence of the past year, for the shameful and criminal politics of the Comintern, bound up with the Anglo-Russian Committee and later with the 'Third Period' These errors were ruinous especially for Britain.

It surprises one anew what a terrible load of humiliation, conservatism, bigotry, conciliation, respect to the summits, to titles, to riches, to the Crown, drags in its thoughts the British working class which is at the same time capable of grand revolutionary insurrections Chartism, pre-war movements of 1911, movements following the war, the strike movements of 1926.

The British proletariat, the oldest with the most traditions, is, in its thinking methods, most empirical, carries in its chest two souls, and turns, as it were, with two faces to historical events. The contemptible mercenary and servile bureaucrats of the Trade Unions and the Labour party give expression to all that is rotten, humiliating, serf-like, and feudal in the British working class. Against this, the tasks of the Communist Party consist in giving expression to the potential revolutionary qualities of the British working class, which is very great and capable of developing immense explosive powers. But in the very critical period of British history, 1925-1927, all the policies of the

British Communist Party and the Comintern consisted in the slave-like assimilation of the trade union leadership, its idealisation, blotting out its treason, and fastening the confidence of the working class to it. The young British Communist Party was because of this deeply demoralised. The whole authority of the October Revolution, USSR and Bolshevism, was in this year attached to the support and solidification of the conservative and servile tendencies of the British working class.

After the Labourites had used the Stalinites to the end and kicked them aside, the chapter of Trade Unionism was mechanically substituted under the caption of the ultra-Left jump to the glory of the 'Third Period'. The slogan of 'Class against Class' was now issued, interpreted as a slogan of the struggle of a handful of Communists against the 'social fascist' proletariat. When yesterday Purcell and Cook were friends and trustworthy allies of the Soviet Union, today the workers who voted for Purcell and Cook transformed themselves into class enemies. This is the political orbit of the British Communist Party, or, rather, of the Communist International. Can we expect another surer way to trample the prestige of Communism and to undermine the confidence of the Party by the awakening workers?

The Moscow bureaucracy of the Communist International at every step runs against a blind alley with its nose, commands a turn either to the Left or to the Right. That is not difficult. All these Kuusinens, Manuilskys, Lozovskys, etc., are apparatus men, free not only of serious Marxist training and revolutionary horizon, but also – and this is the important thing – from every control of the masses. Its politics has a pure chancery character. A tactical turn is for them only a new circular. The CC of the British Communist Party, according to its strength, carries out the orders. But all of these circulars, through the corresponding politics, transport themselves into the consciousness of the workers. The bureaucratic bankrupts believe that one can mechanically fasten our leadership, onto the working class: on the one side with the aid of cash and repression, on the other side with the help of abrupt leaps, the blotting out of traces, with lies and calumnies. But this is totally untrue.

The British workers think slowly, since their consciousness is filled with the rubbish of centuries. But they think. Single articles, appeals, slogans, generally pass them by unnoticed. However, whole periods of politics (Anglo-Russian Committee, 'Third Period') in no respect pass without a trace, at least, with the most progressive, militant, critical, and revolutionary section of the working class. When one imagines the education of the revolutionary consciousness as the cutting of threads on a screw, one must say that the leadership of the Comintern, at each time, does not employ the proper tool nor proper calibre, and not in the direction necessary, thereby breaking the grooves, crumbling, and demolishing. Without the smallest exaggeration one can confirm that from 1923 (for Britain especially from 1925) had the Comintern not existed, we would have today in Britain an incomparably more important revolutionary party. The last elections illustrate with power that frightful conviction.

Here begins the task of the Left Opposition. The English communists, among whom are naturally many devoted, honest, self-sacrificing revolutionaries, cannot but be discouraged with the results of a decade of activity, and that in exclusively opportune conditions. Pessimism and indifference can also take hold of very good revolutionaries when they do not understand the causes of their own weaknesses, nor find the way out. Criticism, i.e., in the light of Marxism that openly illuminates the path of the party, its zig-zags, its errors, the theoretical roots of these errors – that is the foremost and necessary condition for the regeneration of the party. It is especially necessary, when this has not been done, to begin the publication of the most important documents of the International Left Opposition concerning the question of the Anglo-Russian Committee. This is the point of departure for the British left wing

The Left Opposition in Britain, just as communism generally, has the right to count upon a promising future: British capitalism falls from great historical heights to an abyss that is clear to all. One can, with assuredness, say that the recent elections represent the last gigantic rise of the natural 'grandeur' of the British bourgeoisie. However, it is the rise of a dying lamp. For these elections, official British politics will in the coming period pay heavily.

The bankruptcy of the great national heroes of the three parties, just as the bankruptcy of British capitalism, are absolutely inevitable. Despite all obstacles from the Communist International, the mole of the British revolution burrows much too well its earthy path. One has every right to hope that these elections are the last rise of reliance of the millions of workers on the capitalists, lords, intellectuals, educated and rich persons, those united with MacDonald and the Sunday Pudding. These gentlemen will find no secret. The real secret is this: the proletarian revolution. Just as the actual elections prepare to smash the conservative and servile soul of the British proletariat, it will be followed by the powerful blossom of their revolutionary soul.

Yet, immediately the victory of the conservatives brings heavy trials for the British proletariat and the deepening of international dangers. Especially does this endanger the USSR. Here we can see what little aid was brought to the USSR through the uninterrupted cry for her 'defence'. For a period of two or three years, one expected this defence from Purcell, Hicks, Citrine, and later this defence was taken up by the Communist Party against the 'social-fascist' proletariat. And, now, it has in the defence of the USSR all in all received 70,000 votes. All that the Left Opposition demanded, the rupture of the shameful bloc with Purcell, was charged by Stalin as a refusal to defend the USSR from British imperialism. Now we can draw the balance: Nobody has given such service to the expiring British imperialism as the Stalin school. Of course, the chief of this school earned two orders of the Garter.

The British Left Opposition must begin systematic work. You must establish our staff-centre though a small one. You must build your own publication, even on a modest scale... It is necessary to have a steady, uninterrupted activity, to educate our cadres, although in the first stages few. The fundamental power of history is in our favour. When, in Britain, more so than elsewhere, communism in a short time can conquer the consciousness of the wide masses, so can conquer, in the same short time, within the communist movement, the supremacy of the ideas of the Left Opposition, that is, the ideas of Marx and Lenin. I sincerely wish our British friends success on this path.

With best Communist greetings,
Yours, L. Trotsky

* * *

Letter of greetings to *Red Flag* (dated 19 May 1933),
The Militant, 22 July 1933.

Dear Comrades,

You have begun publication of a little monthly, *The Red Flag*. This is a modest step forward. We must hope that other steps will follow.

The advance of communism in Great Britain in no way corresponds to the rate of decay of British capitalism. The conservative traditions of British politics, including the politics of the working class, are in themselves obviously insufficient to explain this. We only declare what is true and cannot be refuted when we say that above all, and, alas, with greater effect than any other factor, the progress of communism during the last years has been hindered by the leadership of the British Communist Party. It of course has not acted independently, but has only blindly followed the orders given by the leaders of the Comintern. But this does not free the British Communist bureaucracy from its responsibility or lessen the damage it has done.

A critical examination of the policy of the British Communist Party during the last eight or ten years constitutes a most important task in the education of the Left Opposition itself. You should study the official publications of the Party throughout this period carefully, digest them, and reveal the party line on the main strategical problems: its attitude towards the Labour Party, the trade unions, the Minority Movement, the colonial revolution, the united-front policy, the ILP, etc. The mere selection of the most striking quotations and the presentation of them in chronological order would expose not only the glaring contradictions of the 'general line', but also the inner logic of these contradictions, that is, the violent oscillation of the centrist bureaucracy between opportunism and adventurism. Each one of these tactical zigzags pushed Communists, sympathisers, and potential friends to the right, to the left, and finally into the swamp of indifference. We can say without the least exaggeration that the British Communist Party has become a political thoroughfare and retains its influence only in that section of the working class which has been forcibly driven to its side by the decomposition of both capitalism and reformism.

Along with the new printed publication, you have at your disposal a hectographed (excellently hectographed!) bulletin, *The Communist*. It would be extremely desirable to devote the greatest possible space in this publication to an examination of the policy of the British Communist Party along the lines indicated above, and also to a discussion of controversial questions within the Left Opposition itself. While persistently striving to widen our influence among the workers, we must at the same time concentrate on the theoretical and political education of our own ranks. We have a long and labourious road ahead of us. For this we need first-class cadres.

With all my heart I wish you success,
Leon Trotsky

The ILP After Disaffiliation

Letter to the Independent Labour Party (dated 8 August 1933),
New Leader, 25 August 1933.

To the Comrades of the Independent Labour Party,

You have published my Copenhagen speech on the Russian Revolution in pamphlet form.[1] I can of course, only be glad that you made my speech accessible to British workers. The foreword by James Maxton recommends this booklet warmly to the Socialist readers. I can only be thankful for this recommendation.

The foreword, however, contains an idea to which I feel obliged to take exception. Maxton refuses in advance to enter into the merits of those disagreements which separate me and my co-thinkers from the now ruling fraction in the USSR. "This is a matter", he says, "on which only Russian socialists are competent to decide."

By these few words the international character of socialism as a scientific doctrine and as a revolutionary movement is completely refuted. If socialists (communists) of one country are incapable, incompetent, and consequently have no right to decide the vital questions of the struggle of socialists (communists) in other countries, the proletarian International loses all rights and possibilities of existence.

I will allow myself, moreover, to affirm that, while refraining formally from judging the struggle which split the Russian Bolsheviks, Maxton, possibly

---

1 *In Defence of October* – A lecture to an audience of Social-Democratic students in Copenhagen, 27 November 1932.

without wishing it, has nevertheless expressed himself in hidden form on the essence of the dispute and, in effect, in favour of the Stalinist fraction, since our struggle with it concerns precisely the question as to whether socialism is a national or international matter. Admitting the possibility of the theoretical and practical solution of the problems of socialism within national limits, Maxton admits the correctness of the Stalinist fraction which bases itself on the theory of "socialism in one country."[2]

In reality, the disputes between the Russian Bolsheviks are not only Russian disputes, just as the conflicts between the Labour Party, the Independent Labour Party, and the Communist Party of Great Britain are not only British conflicts. The matter concerns not only the fate of the present Communist International but of a proletarian International in general.

The grouping of forces, not only in the USSR, but also far beyond its limits, goes along the dividing line between "socialism in one country" and International Socialism. Sections of true Internationalists, taking as the point of departure the theory of permanent revolution, are to be found now in almost all the countries of the world. Their number and influence grows. I consider that on the basic questions of the struggle between us and the Stalinists, every member of the ILP not only can, but is by duty bound to arrive at his independent opinion.

On my part I am ready to help as much as I can, in print, writing or orally, every British socialist, every British worker, in the study of the disputed questions of the International.

I will be very grateful to you if you will publish this letter in your organ.

Comradely yours,
L. Trotsky

* * *

2 The theory of 'socialism in one country' was developed by Bukharin and taken up in 1924 by Stalin as the platform of the rising bureaucracy in the Soviet Union. It represented a complete break from Marxism. In the next period, it became the programme of betrayal of revolutionary opportunities in Germany and China, and also led to the failure of the General Strike in Britain, further consolidating the position of the bureaucracy within the Soviet Union. This same theory was used to impose the needs of the Soviet bureaucracy on the Communist International as a whole, in the form of the draft programme for the Sixth Congress in 1928. Trotsky's reply to this document, which analyses the class roots of 'socialism in one country', is contained in *The Third International After Lenin*.

Written on 24 August 1933 and published in
Red Flag, October-November 1933

Whither the ILP?

The latest political decisions[3] of the National Council of the British Independent Labour Party show clearly that after its break with the reformists the party continues to move leftward. Similar processes are to be observed in other countries: a left wing forms within the social-democratic parties which splits off at the following stage from the party and tries with its own forces to pave for itself a revolutionary path. These processes reflect on one side the deep crisis of capitalism and of reformism which is inseparably bound up therewith, and on the other – the inability of the Comintern to group around itself revolutionary currents within the proletariat.

In Britain, however, the situation is complicated more by an unheard-of combination. Whereas, in other countries, the Comintern continues to treat the left socialist organisations as "left social fascists" and as "the most dangerous counter-revolutionists", a permanent collaboration has been established between the ILP and the Communist Party of Great Britain. How these leaders of the Comintern combine this collaboration with the theory of social-fascism, remains a mystery. In the July issue of the theoretical organ of the Comintern, Fenner Brockway, the newly appointed secretary of the ILP, is called a "counter-revolutionist" as heretofore. Why the British Communist Party made a united front this time not from below but from above, moreover, with leaders who prove to be "counter-revolutionists", and a united front made not for one single practical action but for collaboration in general – no mortal can solve these contradictions. But if the principles be left aside, the matter can be explained very simply: under the exceptionally favourable conditions of Great Britain the Comintern managed completely to isolate and weaken its British section by the ruinous policy of the Anglo-Russian Committee, the 'Third Period', 'social-fascism', and the rest; on the other hand, the deep social crisis of

---

3   A year after breaking from the Labour Party, the ILP's NAC meeting in July 1933 attempted to hammer out a programme in which the parliamentary struggle would be secondary to a campaign of agitation industrially. The ILP was to intervene more forcibly in trade unions, trades councils, the NUWM, and to set up 'Workers' Councils' to agitate against wage cuts etc., and "to act for the working class in a revolutionary crisis".

British capitalism pushed the ILP sharply towards the left; not heeding consistency or logic the totally discouraged Comintern grabbed this time with both hands the alliance proposed to it.

We could have and should have welcomed and heartily supported the collaboration of the ILP with the Communist Party had it not been based on evasiveness, suppressions, and ambiguities on both sides.

Of the Communist Party the National Council says that it is "revolutionary in outlook as ourselves." That is all we learn with regard to the appraisal of the Communist Party and of its policy. Every serious and thinking worker will inevitably ask: why are two parties necessary if they have both an equally revolutionary outlook. This worker will be even more astonished upon learning that the leaders of one of the equally revolutionary parties consider the leaders of the other Party as "counter-revolutionaries" and "left social-fascists". Possibly the National Council refrains from a critical estimation of its ally so as not to undermine the alliance itself. But an alliance of revolutionary organisations which is based not on open mutual criticism but on diplomacy will be thrown over by the first gust of the political storm, like a house of cards.

The theses of the National Council explain the bloc with the Communist Party, first as a step towards the united front, secondly as a stage in the creation of a mass revolutionary party. Each of these two arguments has its weight; but mechanically placed side by side they contradict each other. The theses repeat that the united front should embrace any and all organisations of the proletariat insofar as they wish to participate in the struggle: the Labour Party, the trade unions, even the Co-operative Party. But we know well, and not from literature but from the tragic experience of the German catastrophe,[4] that the Comintern rejects the united front with reformist ('social-fascist') organisations. How does the ILP intend to build a united front with reformist organisations in alliance with the Communist Party: only from below and under the leadership of the communist bureaucracy guaranteed in advance? To this question there is no answer.

Mentioning in passing that the bloc with the Communist Party has pushed certain sections of the "official movement" to the right, the National

---

4 When Hitler came to power in 1933 the German working class was not only disarmed by the refusal of the Social Democratic leaders to fight (they went so far as to offer to participate in the Nazi Labour Front), but by the ultra-left policy of the Stalinists, who branded the Social-Democrats as 'social fascists' and wrecked the possibility of uniting social-democratic and communist workers in defence of rights.

Council expresses the hope that these prejudices can be conquered by an active participation in daily struggles. The fact that the reactionary prejudices of the leaders of the Labour Party and of the General Council of trade unions do not frighten the leaders of the ILP only does the ILP credit. Unfortunately, however, it is not only a question of prejudices. When the communist bureaucracy declares that reformism and fascism are twins, it not only criticises the reformist leaders incorrectly, but it provokes the rightful indignation of the reformist workers. The theses, it is true, say that the criticism of reformism should correspond to actual facts and push the reformist workers forward and not back; but the Communist Party is not mentioned in this connection by one word. What can be made of the theory of 'social-fascism'? And how can the policy of the united front be built on this theory? To pass such questions in silence in the resolution does not mean to remove them from life. An open discussion could possibly force the Communist Party to adopt a correct position; diplomatic evasiveness can only pile up contradictions and prepare a new catastrophe for the next mass movement.

Without defining in principle their attitude to official communism (Stalinism) the theses of the National Council stop midway in their relation to reformism. The reformists must be criticised as conservative democrats and not as fascists, but the struggle with them must be no less irreconcilable because of it, since British reformism is the main hindrance now to the liberation not only of the British but also of the European proletariat. The policy of a united front with reformists is obligatory but it is of necessity limited to partial tasks, especially to defensive struggles. There can be no thought of making the socialist revolution in a united front with reformist organisations. The principal task of a revolutionary party consists in freeing the working class from the influence of reformism. The error of the Comintern bureaucracy consists, not in the fact that they see the most important condition for the victory of the proletariat in the leadership of a revolutionary party – that is entirely correct – but in that being incapable of gaining the confidence of the working masses in daily struggle, starting as a minority in modest roles, it demands this confidence in advance, presents ultimatums to the working class and disrupts attempts at a united front because other organisations are not willing to hand it over voluntarily the marshal's baton. This is not Marxist Policy but bureaucratic sabotage. A secure and firm victory of the proletarian revolution – we repeat it again – is possible only under the condition that a revolutionary, that is a truly communist, party will succeed in gaining the firm confidence of the majority of the working class before the overthrow. This central question is not touched in the theses. Why? Out of 'tact' with regard to the ally? Not only that. There are deeper causes. Insufficient clarity of the theses with regard to the united front flows from the incomplete realisations of the methods of the proletarian revolution. The theses speak of the necessity "to wrest the control of the economic system and the state from the capitalist class and to transfer it to the working class." But how solve this gigantic problem? To this pivotal question of our epoch the theses reply with a naked phrase: "this can only be achieved through united action by the working class." The struggle for power and the dictatorship of the proletariat remain abstractions which can be easily dissolved in the amorphous perspectives of the united front.

In the realm of ready-made revolutionary formulae the bureaucracy of the British Communist Party is immeasurably better equipped. Precisely in this lies now its advantage over the leadership of the ILP. And it must be said openly: this superficial, purely formal advantage may under the present circumstances lead to the liquidation of the ILP without any gain accruing to the Communist Party and to the revolution. The objective conditions have more than once pushed tens and even hundreds of thousands of workers towards the British section of the Comintern, but the leadership of the Comintern was capable only of disillusioning them and of throwing them back. If the ILP as a whole should enter today the ranks of the Communist Party, within the next couple of months one third of the new members would return to the Labour Party, another third would be expelled for "conciliatory attitude towards Trotskyism" and for similar crimes, finally, the remaining third, disillusioned in all its expectations would fall into indifferentism. As a result of this experiment the Communist Party would find itself weaker and more isolated than now.

The ILP can save the workers' movement of Britain from this new danger only by freeing itself from all unclarity and haziness with regard to the ways and methods of the socialist revolution and by becoming a truly revolutionary party of the proletariat. There is no necessity of inventing anything new in this field, all has been said well by the first four congresses of the Comintern. Instead of feeding on bureaucratic substitutes of the epigones it is better to put all the members of the ILP to the study of the resolutions of the first four congresses of the Comintern. But this alone does not suffice. It is necessary to open a discussion in the party on the lessons of the last decade which was marked by the struggle between the Stalinist bureaucracy and the Left Opposition. The content of this struggle was made up of the most important stage of the world revolutionary movement; economic and political tasks of the USSR; problems of the Chinese revolution; the policy of the Anglo-Russian committee; methods of the united front; problems of party democracy; the causes of the German catastrophe. This enormous cycle of problems cannot be passed by. These are not Russian but international problems.

In our epoch a revolutionary party cannot but be *international*. What is the position of the ILP on this? Having entered into an alliance with the Communist Party the ILP has not determined its international position. It broke with the Second International and made an alliance with the Third, but it also enters into a labour alliance with left socialist parties. This alliance, in its turn, is not homogeneous. There are elements in it which gravitate towards Bolshevism, but there are also elements which pull towards the Norwegian Workers' Party. That is, in reality towards the social-democracy. What position does the ILP take on all these questions? Is it willing to share the fate of the historically already doomed Comintern, does it want to try to remain in an intermediary position (which means to return by round about ways to reformism), or is it ready to participate in the building of a new International on the foundations laid by Marx and Lenin?

To the serious reader it is clear that our criticism is least of all inspired by animosity towards the ILP. On the contrary, we see too clearly that if this party should ingloriously disappear from the scene socialism would suffer a new hard blow. And this danger exists and it is not far removed. In our epoch it is impossible to remain long in intermediary Positions. Only political clarity can save the ILP for the proletarian revolution. The aim of these lines is to help revolutionary clarity to pave its way.

* * *

Written on 4 September 1933 and published in
The Militant, 30 September 1933.

The ILP and the New International

After a brief interval I am returning again to the policy of the Independent Labour Party. This is occasioned by the declaration of the ILP delegation at the Paris Conference,[5] which permits a clear idea of the general direction the ILP is heading as well as of the stage at which it now finds itself.

---

5   This was the meeting in August 1933 of the group of centrist organisations then known as the International Labour Community, but more usually as the 'London

The delegation considers it necessary to call a world congress of "all" revolutionary parties beginning with those adhering to the Third International. "If the Third International proves unprepared to change its tactics and organisation, the time will have come to consider the formation of a new International." This sentence contains the very essence of the present policy of the ILP. Having shifted decisively to the left, to communism, the members of this Party refuse to believe that the Communist International, which has numerous cadres and material and technical means at its disposal, is lost for the revolutionary movement. It is necessary, they say, to make one more test of the ability or inability of the Comintern to change its policy.

It is incorrect, even naive, to pose the question in this manner. The ability or inability of a party is not determined at a congress but in daily struggle, and particularly in times of great dangers, momentous decisions, and mass action. After the victory of Hitler, for which the Comintern bears a direct responsibility, the leadership of the Comintern not only has left its policy unchanged but also has intensified its disastrous methods. This historic test has a thousand times more weight than all the declarations that the representatives of the Comintern might make at any one congress. It must not be forgotten that congresses represent elements of 'parliamentarism' in the workers' movement itself. While parliamentarism is inevitable and necessary, it cannot add anything fundamentally new above what has been actually attained in mass struggle. This refers not only to the parliamentarism of the bourgeois state but also to the 'parliamentary' institutions of the proletariat itself. We must orient ourselves by the real activity of working-class organisations and not expect any miracles from the proposed world congress.

During a period of ten years (1923-33), the Left Opposition acted as a *faction* of the Comintern, hoping to attain an improvement in its policy and regime by systematic criticism and an active participation in the life of the Comintern and its sections. The Left Opposition, therefore, has a colossal experience of an international character. There was not a single, important, historic event that did not force the Left Opposition to counterpose its slogans and methods to the slogans and methods of the bureaucracy of the Comintern. The struggle around the questions of the Soviet economy and the regime of the Communist Party of the Soviet Union, the Chinese Revolution, Anglo-Russian Committee, etc., etc., remained comparatively little known

---

Bureau'. These organisations in some cases rallied to the Fourth International, but mostly disintegrated or liquidated themselves into Stalinism or social democracy.

to the workers' parties of the West.[6] But two chapters of this struggle passed before the eyes of the advanced workers of all the world: they deal with the theory and practice of the 'third period' and with the strategy of the Comintern in Germany.

If the Left Opposition can be blamed for anything, it is certainly not for an impatient break with the Comintern. Only after the German Communist Party, which had been gathering millions of votes, proved incapable of offering even the least resistance to Hitler, and after the Comintern refused to recognise not only the erroneousness of its policy but even the very fact of the defeat of the proletariat (in reality the victory of Hitler is the greatest defeat of the proletariat in the history of the world!), and replaced the analysis of its mistakes and crimes by a new campaign of persecution and slander against real Marxists – only after this did we say: nothing can save these people any more. The German catastrophe, and the role of the Comintern in it, is infinitely more important for the world proletariat than any organisational manoeuvres, congresses, evasive declarations, diplomatic agreements, etc. The historical judgement on the Comintern has been pronounced. There is no appeal from this verdict.

The history of the Comintern is almost unknown to the members of the ILP, which has just recently taken the revolutionary path. Besides, no organisation learns *only* by books and files. The ILP wants independently to undergo an experience that others have already undergone on a much larger scale. Had this involved only the loss of a few months, one could have reconciled oneself to it despite the fact that each month of our time is much more precious than years of another period. The danger, however, is that, aspiring to 'test' the Comintern by drawing closer to it, the ILP may, without realising it, follow the ways of the Comintern – and ruin itself.

The trade union question remains the most important question of proletarian policy in Great Britain, as well as in the majority of old capitalist countries. The mistakes of the Comintern in this field are innumerable. No wonder: a party's inability to establish correct relations with the working class reveals itself most glaringly in the area of the trade union movement. That is why I consider it necessary to dwell on this question.

6　This material is in print, however, in a series of studies and documents published partly also in foreign languages. For the British comrades, the publications of the American League (Pioneer Publishers) are of great importance. Whoever wishes to study seriously the ten-year struggle of the Left Opposition for the reform and improvement of the Comintern must study all these documents. – *Trotsky*

The trade unions were formed during the period of the growth and rise of capitalism. They had as their task the raising of the material and cultural level of the proletariat and the extension of its political rights. This work, which in Britain lasted over a century, gave the trade unions tremendous authority among the workers. The decay of British capitalism, under the conditions of decline of the world capitalist system, undermined the basis for the reformist work of the trade unions. Capitalism can continue to maintain itself only by lowering the standard of living of the working class. Under these conditions trade unions can either transform themselves into revolutionary organisations or become lieutenants of capital in the intensified exploitation of the workers. The trade union bureaucracy, which has satisfactorily solved its own social problem, took the second path. It turned all the accumulated authority of the trade unions against the socialist revolution and even against any attempts of the workers to resist the attacks of capital and reaction.

From that point on, the most important task of the revolutionary Party became the liberation of the workers from the reactionary influence of the trade union bureaucracy. In this decisive field, the Comintern revealed its complete inadequacy. In 1926-27, especially in the period of the miners' strike and the General Strike, that is, at the time of the greatest crimes and betrayals of the General Council of the Trades Union Congress, the Comintern obsequiously toadied to the highly placed strike-breakers, cloaked them with its authority in the eyes of the masses and helped them remain in the saddle. That is how the Minority Movement was struck a mortal blow. Frightened by the results of its own work, the Comintern bureaucracy went to the extreme of ultra-radicalism. The fatal excesses of the "third period" were due to the desire of the small Communist minority to act as though it had a majority behind it. Isolating itself more and more from the working class, the Communist Party counterposed to the trade unions, which embraced millions of workers, its own trade union organisations, which were highly obedient to the leadership of the Comintern but separated by an abyss from the working class. No better favour could be done for the trade union bureaucracy. Had it been within its power to award the Order of the Garter, it should have so decorated all the leaders of the Comintern and Profintern.

As was said, the trade unions now play not a progressive but a reactionary role. Nevertheless, they still embrace millions of workers. One must not think that the workers are blind and do not see the change in the historic role of the trade unions. But what is to be done? The revolutionary road is seriously compromised in the eyes of the left wing of the workers by the zigzags and adventures of official communism. The workers say to themselves: the trade unions are bad, but without them it might be even worse. This is the psychology of one who is in a blind alley. Meanwhile, the trade union bureaucracy persecutes the revolutionary workers ever more boldly, ever more impudently replacing internal democracy by the arbitrary action of a clique, in essence, transforming the trade unions into some sort of concentration camp for the workers during the decline of capitalism.

Under these conditions, the thought easily arises: is it not possible to by-pass the trade unions? Is it not possible to replace them by some sort of fresh, uncorrupted organisation, such as revolutionary trade unions, shop committees, Soviets and the like? The fundamental mistake of such attempts is that they reduce to organisational experiments the great political problem of how to free the masses from the influence of the trade union bureaucracy. It is not enough to offer the masses a new address. It is necessary to seek out the masses where they are and to lead them.

Impatient leftists sometimes say that it is absolutely impossible to win over the trade unions because the bureaucracy uses the organisations' internal regimes for preserving its own interests, resorting to the basest machinations, repressions and plain crookedness, in the spirit of the parliamentary oligarchy of the era of 'rotten boroughs'.[7] Why then waste time and energy? This argument reduces itself in reality to giving up the actual struggle to win the masses, using the corrupt character of the trade union bureaucracy as a pretext. This argument can be developed further: why not abandon revolutionary work altogether, considering the repressions and provocations on the part of the government bureaucracy? There exists no principled difference here, since the trade union bureaucracy has definitely become a part of the capitalist apparatus, economic and governmental. It is absurd to think that it would be possible to work against the trade union bureaucracy with its own help, or only with its consent. Insofar as it defends itself by persecutions, violence, expulsions, frequently resorting to the assistance of government authorities, we must learn to work in the trade unions *discreetly*, finding a common language with the masses but not revealing ourselves prematurely to the bureaucracy. It is precisely in the present epoch, when the reformist bureaucracy of the proletariat has transformed itself into the

---

7 These were parliamentary seats before the Reform Act of 1832 where very small electorates were controlled by rich patrons who could decide on the MP and his policies.

economic police of capital, that revolutionary work in the trade unions, performed intelligently and systematically, may yield decisive results in a comparatively short time.

We do not at all mean by this that the revolutionary party has any guarantee that the trade unions will be completely won over to the socialist revolution. The problem is not so simple. The trade union apparatus has attained for itself great independence from the masses. The bureaucracy is capable of retaining its positions a long time after the masses have turned against it. But it is precisely such a situation, where the masses are already hostile to the trade union bureaucracy but where the bureaucracy is still capable of misrepresenting the opinion of the organisation and of sabotaging new elections, that is most favourable for the creation of shop committees, workers' councils and other organisations for the immediate needs of any given moment. Even in Russia, where the trade unions did not have anything like the powerful traditions of the British trade unions, the October Revolution occurred with Mensheviks predominant in the administration of the trade unions. Having lost the masses, these administrations were still capable of sabotaging elections in the apparatus, although already powerless to sabotage the proletarian revolution.

It is absolutely necessary right now to prepare the minds of the advanced workers for the idea of creating shop committees and workers councils at the moment of a sharp change. But it would be the greatest mistake to 'play around' in practice with the slogan of shop councils, consoling oneself with this 'idea' for the lack of real work and real influence in the trade unions. To counterpose to the existing trade unions the abstract idea of workers' councils would mean setting against oneself not only the bureaucracy but also the masses, thus depriving oneself of the possibility of preparing the ground for the creation of workers' councils.

In this the Comintern has gained not a little experience: having created obedient, that is, purely Communist, trade unions, it counterposed its sections to the working masses in a hostile manner and thereby doomed itself to complete impotence. This is one of the most important causes of the collapse of the German Communist Party. It is true that the British Communist Party, insofar as I am informed, opposes the slogan of workers' councils under the present conditions. Superficially, this may seem like a realistic appraisal of the situation. In reality, the British Communist Party only rejects *one form* of political adventurism for *another*, more hysterical form. The theory and practice of social fascism and the rejection of the policy of the united front creates insurmountable obstacles to working in the trade unions, since each trade union is, by its very nature, the arena of an ongoing united front of revolutionary parties with reformist and non-party masses. To the extent that the British Communist Party proved incapable, even after the German tragedy, of learning anything and arming itself anew, to that extent can an alliance with it pull to the bottom even the ILP, which only recently has entered a period of revolutionary apprenticeship.

Pseudo-Communists will, no doubt, refer to the last congress of trade unions, which declared that there could be no united front with Communists against fascism. It would be the greatest folly to accept this piece of wisdom as the final verdict of history. The trade union bureaucrats can permit themselves such boastful formulas only because they are not immediately threatened by fascism or by communism. When the hammer of fascism is raised over the head of the trade unions, then, with a correct policy of the revolutionary party, the trade union masses will show an irresistible urge for an alliance with the revolutionary wing and will carry with them onto this path even a certain portion of the apparatus. Contrariwise, if communism should become a decisive force, threatening the General Council with the loss of positions, honours and income, Messrs. Citrine and Co. would undoubtedly enter into a bloc with Mosley and Co. against the Communists. Thus, in August 1917, the Russian Mensheviks and Social Revolutionaries together with the Bolsheviks repulsed General Kornilov. Two months later in October, they were fighting hand in hand with the Kornilovists against the Bolsheviks. And in the first months of 1917, when the reformists were still strong, they spouted, just like Citrine and Co., about the impossibility of their making an alliance with the dictatorship either of the right or left.

The revolutionary proletarian Party must be welded together by a clear understanding of its historic tasks. This presupposes a scientifically based programme. At the same time, the revolutionary party must know how to establish correct relations with the class. This presupposes a policy of revolutionary realism, equally removed from opportunistic vagueness and sectarian aloofness.

From the point of view of both these closely connected criteria, the ILP should review its relation to the Comintern as well as to all other organisations and tendencies within the working class. This concerns first of all the fate of the ILP itself.

* * *

From a letter to *New Leader* (dated 2 October 1933),
published 13 October 1933.

In the *Daily Worker* of 14 September I found the letter of Comrade C. A.
Smith, who defends the ILP from the accusation that its delegates have
participated in Paris in the building of a Two-and-a-Half International. I
have no basis whatsoever to interfere in the essence of this polemic. I must
point out, however, that from the letter of Comrade Smith the conclusion
might be drawn that in Paris there was actually laid the foundation for a Two-
and-a-Half International, although without the participation of the ILP. I
consider it necessary to dispel any misunderstandings that the readers of the
New Leader might have on this score.

It is true that certain organisations which occupy an intermediate position
between the Second and the Third International, such as the Norwegian
Workers' Party, the French Party of the Proletarian Unity (PUP),[8] the
Italian Maximalists[9] and others, have participated in the Paris Conference.
But precisely *all these organisations expressed themselves against the new
International.*

For the creation of the new International, not a Two-and-a-Half, but a
Fourth International, were the following organisations: The International
Left Opposition, the Socialist Workers' Party (SAP) of Germany and two
Dutch Socialist Parties, the Independent Socialist Party and the Revolutionary
Socialist Party of Holland.

I urge the readers of the *New Leader*, as, however, also the readers of the
Daily Worker, to acquaint themselves with the declaration of the named
organisations *On the Necessity and Principles of a New International.* Here I
shall quote only one paragraph (eight) out of eleven.

> While ready to cooperate with all the organisations, groups and fractions which
> are actually developing from reformism or bureaucratic centrism (Stalinism)
> towards revolutionary Marxist policy, the undersigned at the same time declare
> that the new International cannot tolerate any conciliation towards reformism,
> or centrism. The necessary unity of the workers' movement cannot be attained
> by the blurring of reformist and revolutionary conceptions, or the adaptation

---

8   French Party of the Proletarian Unity (PUP) – Trotsky characterised them as a
    rightward-moving group comparable to the followers of Brandler and Lovestone.
9   A centrist tendency within the Italian Socialist Party which continued to exist in
    exile after Mussolini's suppression of the working-class movement. Affiliated to the
    London Bureau.

to the Stalinist *policy*, but only by combating the policies of both bankrupt Internationals. To remain equal to its task the new International must not permit any deviation from revolutionary principles in the questions of insurrection, proletarian dictatorship, Soviet form of the State, etc.

In conclusion, I allow myself to say that the International Left Opposition (Bolshevik-Leninists) is much further removed from centrism (two-and-a-half) than the present Barbussised[10] Comintern.

With revolutionary greetings,
L. Trotsky

* * *

Interview with C. A. Smith (29 August 1933),
New Leader, 13 October 1933.

It was all rather breathtaking. Driven at midnight to a station in Paris; put on a train but kept ignorant of destination; leaving the train according to instructions at a certain time; recognised by a comrade, armed with a telegraphed description of us; whirled off for a further journey; admitted past various obstacles; and finally greeted with tempestuous heartiness by Leon Trotsky himself.

We settled down to business immediately, and for over ten hours, with breaks only for meals, plied one of the world's most distinguished revolutionaries with questions. No one could fail to be impressed by the man's enormous vitality, or charmed by his frank and eager courtesy. Clear analytical exposition, supplemented by a wealth of vivid imagery and forceful metaphor, made his conversation both an intellectual and an aesthetic delight.

"You are aware", I said, "that at the Paris Conference of Revolutionary Socialist Parties the ILP voted against the main resolution (because we considered the condemnation of the Comintern unbalanced or exaggerated), and also against the proposal to form a Fourth International. We are consequently particularly desirous of hearing: (a) Your chief criticism of the Comintern; (b) Why you despair of its reform; (c) What action you propose taking?"

Trotsky's criticisms, delivered with great verve and clarity, related both to the Communist International's policy and to its organisation. The latter he declared to be bureaucratic, and corruptly bureaucratic at that. Discussion is

---

10 Henri Barbusse (1873-1935) – French novelist; joined the Communist Party in 1923 and became a notorious Stalin-worshipper. He was associated with the earliest steps in Popular Front policy such as the 1932 Amsterdam Conference.

stifled, criticism regarded as disloyalty, and all who oppose the bureaucratic tops expelled as heretics.

Bolshevik self-criticism, said Trotsky, is a departed glory. In the early days, even during the Civil War, perfect freedom of discussion was the rule. In the Red Army there was strict military discipline with severe punishment, yet even there in policy discussions private soldiers, as party members, frequently attacked Lenin (as well as Trotsky himself), or the Central Committee as a whole, and criticised them unsparingly. During the Civil War a Congress was held every year, with an additional Congress in a case of emergency; now five years pass and there is no Comintern Congress.

Functionaries of the Comintern Praesidium are changed by the decree of the Political Bureau of the CPSU (Communist Party of the Soviet Union). Brandler, the German CP leader, criticised the Comintern policy in Germany. He was summoned to Moscow and detained there several *years*, finally getting away by extraordinary methods. If a man refuses to go to Moscow when ordered thither he is immediately expelled from the party.

This suppression of internal criticism, insisted Trotsky, arises from the determination of the Stalinist faction to retain control in the teeth of a wrong policy. But the results of bureaucratic rule themselves influence policy. The bureaucratic mind has an essential distrust of the masses, and in consequence develops the usual characteristics of bureaucracies, whatever their time or place. Specifically, the present Russian bureaucracy differs from the bourgeois bureaucracies of the capitalist countries, in that the former desires to preserve the Soviet Union and the latter desire to overthrow it. Generically, however, they are identical in outlook and methods.

Decisions are taken without consulting the rank and file, and every art of lying, concealment and repression is used to compel acceptance of the line laid down by the executive, often out of touch with the situation it is attempting to control. Further, the bureaucracy never dares to admit its mistakes, which are the more grave the more the bureaucracy considers itself infallible. The most glaring instance of this refusal to admit mistakes is afforded by the German debacle.

The CI line there was tragically wrong, declared Trotsky, and many of the ablest communist leaders recognise this. It led the German workers to certain and frequently predicted disaster. Yet immediately after the disaster, the CI solemnly declared that its line had been correct!

This same distrust of the masses was revealed through the history of the Anglo-Russian Committee, when the CI recognised as the representatives of the British workers the trade union bureaucracy – even during the actual days of their betrayal of the General Strike of 1926! – and worse still, after it. Bureaucratic distrust was shown in the CI's terrible mishandling of the Chinese Revolution,[11] when they placed it under the direction of the bourgeois Kuomintang, which, as Trotsky had foretold, soon after betrayed it with massacre and torture.

Bureaucratic distrust is shown repeatedly, continued Trotsky, in the CI's attitude to other organisations, where, despite the slogan of United Front from Below, the aim has been not so much to mobilise the revolutionary workers as to capture the organisational apparatus. All of this, reinforced by the financial control of the CI bureaucracy over its national sections, breeds a mentality of dependence, of unquestioning obedience, which is the very antithesis of the critical and independent mind required for a revolutionary.

"What were the Comintern errors in Germany?", I interpolated.

The mistakes have continued for ten years: missing the revolutionary situation in 1923 (the Occupation of the Ruhr); steering a course to armed uprising after the relationship of forces had radically changed against the proletariat; a turn towards 'courting' the Social-Democracy (1926-1927); a new turn towards adventurism ('Third Period', conquest of the streets, etc.); a radically false policy with regard to the trade unions; the replacement of educational work by 'ultimatism'; the creation of tiny parallel trade unions – that is, the isolation of the party from the class; the theory of social-fascism and the renunciation of the policy of the united front; nationalistic agitation and the adaptation to fascism ('national liberation' of Germany, the participation in the Prussian plebiscite together with the Nazis);[12] systematic destruction of all defence organisations established by local workers' organisations.

---

11 In this period the Comintern leadership under Stalin forced the young Communist Party to work under the control of the bourgeois nationalist Kuomintang, then coming under the leadership of the reactionary Chiang Kai-shek. CP members pushed the revolution forward in the cities and were murdered in their thousands by Chiang. All efforts to come to terms with the Kuomintang, including its left section under Wang Ching-wei, came to nothing. Wang became a Japanese puppet and died in 1934 and Chiang ultimately accepted the patronage of the American imperialists to be dictator of a regime set up in the island of Taiwan. The full story of the Comintern's role in the events of 1926-7 can be found in Trotsky's *Problems of the Chinese Revolution*.

12 In 1931 the Nazis and their right-wing allies managed to get a plebiscite in Prussia in an effort to force out of office the regional government, then run by the Social Democrats. Although the German Communist Party leaders at first wanted to oppose

Social-democracy and fascism are *not* twins, as the CI declared [insisted Trotsky]. True, Social-Democracy supports the bourgeoisie; but it does not (despite treacherous leaders) support fascism, whose victory signifies the extermination of Social-Democracy as a party.

"What are your chief criticisms of the *present* policy of the CI?", I asked.

"Chiefly, the theory of 'Socialism in one country' and its resultant policy of 'centrism'." Trotsky defined centrism as the sum total of all the tendencies between Marxism and reformism which move from one to the other. The CI bureaucracy is predisposed to become reformist, but cannot do so because it is tied to the Soviet state. Yet it cannot be revolutionary because it has abandoned the theory of world revolution. So it swings between the two poles and remains centrist.

> Secondly, the theory of socialism in one country is not an abstract principle, but a matter of life and death. The present crisis in capitalism arises not only from the contradiction between productive forces and private property, but also from that between productive forces and national states. The task of socialism is not to push back the productive forces within the boundaries of a single state, but, on the contrary, to organise them on a world scale. And this presupposes the world revolution, which ought to be the basis of the Comintern.

This is not incompatible with the rapid industrialisation of Russia. It was Trotsky who in 1923 was pleading in speech and writing for a Five-Year Plan, when Stalin was deriding him as an optimist. When the bureaucracy was at length converted to this optimism, they swung into the opposite extreme and fell into the error of 'Socialism in one country'.

"Do you support the proposal for an industrial and transport boycott of fascist Germany at the earliest possible moment?"

"Yes, at the earliest *suitable* moment; it is only a question of capacity."

"At the Paris Conference", I said, "The ILP urged an amendment calling for a protest or demonstration strike of definite and limited duration with regard to some special Nazi outrage, but this was rejected."

"This time the ILP line was the perfectly correct revolutionary policy", replied Trotsky.

Next I asked: "Why do you despair of the Comintern's correcting its policy?"

---

this, under the direct orders of the Comintern they decided to vote with the Nazis against the Social Democrats. This incident represented for Trotsky one of the most criminal results of the 'Third Period' policies of Stalin.

First, because there is no democracy within the party and critics who attempt to correct its line are expelled. Secondly, this fight is not of recent origin: it started ten years ago. The crucial instance is Germany. If *that* cannot convince the bureaucracy of its errors, then *nothing* can. And if the ILP is still to wait hopefully a little longer, how much longer will you wait, and what evidence will finally satisfy you? The destruction of the now endangered Soviets would surely be too high a price for the enlightenment of the ILP!

"Then what do you think must be done?"

Form the Fourth International [said Trotsky] to include all revolutionaries who accept the principles of Marx and Lenin, and know that the Second and Third Internationals are both bankrupt – the one through reactionary reformism and the other through bureaucratic centrism. We of the International Left Opposition are ready, however, to make a united front with the Comintern bureaucracy for the specific purpose of defending the Soviet Union.

"And what is your advice to the ILP?"

To remain independent at all costs, until it has completed its movement from reformism to revolution, from an empirical to a theoretical basis. You require a firm grasp of the revolutionary theory of the capitalist state, a correct evaluation of social and economic forces, adequate information of the movement of revolution and reaction outside Great Britain and a definite plan of the revolutionary course within Britain – a plan flexible in detail but rigid in principle.

Regretfully we took our leave to catch the night train to Paris. More than once we turned back to salute the erect figure of the former Red Army leader, who stood waving repeated farewells. While not prepared to accept all his conclusions, we were glad to have heard his own statement of his case. So, too, we believe, will be the majority of revolutionary socialists in Britain.

The 'Marxist Group' in the ILP

From a letter on *The International Left Opposition and the ILP* (dated 3 September 1933), *Internal Bulletin*, British Section of the Left Opposition, 24 October 1933.

On the question of the ILP, the Secretariat has altered so much of my proposition that it suggests to our British section[1] – if my information is correct – that some comrades should not enter the ILP, so that they can continue publishing the paper. This plan, after a long conversation with Smith[2] (who makes the best impression personally), seems to me of no use. The ILP, and this is to its credit, has expelled two members because they were also members of the Communist Party. The ILP will also distrust us for the same reason. This distrust can only be overcome if our people get into the ILP with the desire to influence the party as a whole and to become powerful there but not to work toward breaking away a small part from the whole party.

The publication of a small, monthly paper under the circumstances is senseless, because the same articles are published at the same time or earlier in *The Militant*. We can make good use of *The Militant* as a 'central organ' for our internal work within the ILP.

---

1 After their expulsion from the CPGB in August-September 1932, mainly for their opposition to the Amsterdam Conference's policies, the so-called 'Balham Group' formed themselves into the 'Communist League' and in May 1933 began to produce the *Red Flag*. At this point the group began to discuss Trotsky's suggestion that they should enter the ILP, though by the end of the year only a minority agreed they nevertheless proceeded to do so.

2 See p. 587 of the present edition for Smith's interview with Trotsky.

Comrade Witte is travelling to Britain, and it would be very good if he would discuss and examine the whole question from this point of view with the British comrades.

I am of the opinion, under the given circumstances, that the British section in relation to the ILP must use the tactic applied by the Brandlerite minority toward the SAP. If we only send a part of our membership into the ILP and keep a publication going outside of it, then we are in danger of getting our members expelled from the ILP in a very short time. Our mutual relations would be poisoned by this, and we would lose, because of our outside action, the possibility of gaining considerable influence.

* * *

Letter to the British Section, Bolshevik-Leninists
(dated 16 September 1933), *Internal Bulletin*, British Section
of the Left Opposition, 24 October 1933.

Dear Comrades,

I have not yet received your letter in which you motivate your negative attitude to the entry into the ILP. But, so as not to delay this matter, I shall try to examine the principled considerations for and against the entry. If it should happen that your letter contains additional arguments I shall write you again.

In its present state, the ILP is a left-centrist party. It consists of a number of factions and shadings that are indicative of the different stages of evolution from reformism to communism. Should the Bolshevik-Leninists enter into the Official Communist Parties, which they had long designated, and with full reason, as centrist organisations? For a number of years, we have considered ourselves Marxist factions of centrist Parties. A categorical answer – yes, yes; no, no – is insufficient also in this case. A Marxist party should, of course, strive to full independence and to the highest homogeneity. But in the process of its formation, a Marxist Party often has to act as a faction of a centrist and even a reformist party. Thus the Bolsheviks adhered for a number of years to the same party with the Mensheviks. Thus, the Third International only gradually formed itself out of the Second.

Centrism, as we have said more than once, is a general name for most varied tendencies and groupings spread out between reformism and Marxism. In front of each centrist grouping it is necessary to place an arrow indicating the direction of its development: from right to left or from left to right. Bureaucratic centrism, for all its zigzags, has an extremely conservative character corresponding to its social base: the Soviet bureaucracy. After a ten-year experience, we came to the conclusion that bureaucratic centrism does not draw nearer and is incapable of drawing nearer to Marxism, from the ranks of which it emerged. It is precisely because of this that we broke with the Comintern.

While the official Communist Parties have been growing weaker and decomposing, left flanks have separated from the reformist camp, which has grown considerably in numbers. These flanks also have a centrist character, but they move towards the left and, as demonstrated by experience, are capable of development and yield to Marxist influence. Let us recall once more that the Third International originated from organisations of this sort.

A clear example of the above is furnished by the history of the German SAP. A few hundred communists who split off from the Brandlerite opposition and entered the SAP have succeeded in a comparatively short time in placing themselves at the head of this organisation, which, for the most part, consists of former Social-Democratic members. At that time we criticised the group of Walcher, Frölich, Thomas[3] and others not because they resolved to enter a left-centrist party, but because they entered it without a complete programme and without an organ of their own. Our criticism was and remains correct. The SAP bears even now traces of shapelessness. Some of its leaders even now consider irreconcilable Marxist criticism as 'sectarianism'. In reality, however, if the Left Opposition with its principled criticism had not been standing at the side of the SAP, the position of the Marxists within the SAP would have been incomparably more difficult; no revolutionary group can live without a constantly creative ideological laboratory. Nevertheless, the fact remains that the movement of the centrist party (SAP) to the left was so decisive that the communist group, even without a complete programme and without an organ of its own, found itself very soon at the head of the party.

The history of the SAP is neither a chance one nor an exceptional one. For a number of years the Comintern prevented by its policy the going-over of the socialist workers to the revolutionary road. A mass of explosive material accumulated, therefore, in the camp of reformism. The frightful crisis of capitalism and the triumphal march of fascism, accompanied by the absolute impotence of both Internationals, gave the left-centrist organisations an impulsion towards communism; this is one of the most important prerequisites for the creation of new parties and of a new International.

---

3 These were all Brandlerites who assumed the leadership of the SAP in 1933.

In the area of theory, the ILP is completely helpless. This gives an advantage to the official Communist Party – herein lies the danger. This opens up the field for the intervention of our British section. It is not sufficient to have correct ideas. In a decisive moment one must know how to show one's strength to the advanced workers. As far as I call judge from here, the possibility for influencing the further development of the ILP as a whole is not yet missed. But in another couple of months, the ILP will have completely fallen between the gear wheels of the Stalinist bureaucracy and will be lost, leaving thousands of disappointed workers. It is necessary to act and to act immediately.

It is worth entering the ILP only if we make it our purpose to help this party, that is its *revolutionary majority* to transform it into a truly Marxist party. Of course, such an entry would be inadmissible if the Central Committee of the ILP should demand from our friends that they renounce their ideas, or the open struggle for those ideas in party. But it is absolutely admissible to take upon oneself the obligation to fight for one's views on the basis of the party statutes and within the limits of party discipline. The great advantage of the Left Opposition lies in the fact that it has a theoretically elaborated programme, international experience, and international control. Under these conditions, there is not the slightest basis for the fear that the British Bolshevik-Leninists will dissolve without a trace in the ILP.

Some comrades point out that the ILP has greatly weakened, that behind the old front a ramshackle structure hides itself. This is very possible. But this is not an argument against entry. In its present composition, it is clear, the ILP is not viable. It is getting weaker and is losing members not only on the right but also on the left, because its leadership has no clear policy and is not capable of imbuing the party with confidence in its strength. It is possible to stop this further disintegration of the ILP only by imparting to it Marxist views on the problems of our epoch, and in particular a Marxist analysis of the Stalinist bureaucracy. Only the Bolshevik-Leninists can do this work. But to do this they must courageously destroy the wall that divides them today from the revolutionary workers of the ILP. If the apparatus of the ILP should not admit our section into the ranks of its Party, this would be the best proof that the leadership has completely submitted to the Stalinist bureaucracy behind the back of the party. In this worst case we would acquire a strong weapon against the leaders and would gain the sympathy of the rank-and-file members of the ILP.

It may be objected that the small size of our British section would not permit it to play the same role with regard to the ILP that the group of Walcher-Frölich played with regard to the SAP. Possibly.

But even if the ILP is doomed to disintegrate, the Bolshevik-Leninists can save for the revolution an important kernel of this party. It must also not be forgotten that the group of Walcher-Frölich was completely isolated, while our British friends can count on international help in their work.

I am very much afraid that our British friends, at least some of them, are restrained from entering the ILP by the fear of malicious criticism of the Stalinists. There is nothing worse in revolutionary policy than to be actuated by purely external, superficial criteria or by the fear of public opinion of the bureaucracy only because we were connected with it in the past. It is necessary to determine one's road in accordance with the deep currents within the proletarian vanguard, to trust more in the power of one's ideas without looking back at the Stalinist bureaucracy.

G. Gourov [Leon Trotsky]

* * *

Letter to the British Section, Bolshevik-Leninists
(dated 16 September 1933), *Internal Bulletin*,
British Section of the Left Opposition, 24 October 1933.

Dear Comrades,

Comrade Paton of the ILP offered to place my articles on the ILP in the magazine *Adelphi*. My reply will be clear from the copy of my letter attached hereto.

No doubt you have received the extract from the minutes of the plenum of the International Secretariat from which it is clear that the suggestion to enter the ILP was adopted by the plenum unanimously. I cannot understand who could have supplied you with such false information. At any rate, it was not Comrade Witte, who participated actively in the meetings of the plenum and voted for the general resolution. It is clear, of course, that I am far from the thought that the unanimous opinion of the plenum obligates you to submit to it silently. The plenum adopted not a *decision* but a *proposal*. The proposal, however, was considered and discussed very seriously and adopted unanimously.

Comrade Fenner Brockway asked my permission to print in *The New Leader* an article by Comrade Smith relating my conversation with him. Of course, I gave my approval. Thus you will get an idea of the general nature of my conversation which coincides almost to the dot with the contents of my article sent to you.

I continue to believe that the fate of our British section for the next couple of years depends on a correct attitude toward the ILP. It was Shakespeare who counselled taking advantage of the time of the tides so as not to remain on the strand all life long.[4] With great impatience and concern I am awaiting your final decision in this matter.

Comradely Yours,
L. Trotsky

* * *

Letter to the British Section (dated 2 October 1933),
Internal Bulletin, British Section of the
Left Opposition, 24 October 1933.

Dear Comrades,

I received a copy of your letter of 5 September and allow myself to express a few additional considerations on the question of entry into the ILP.

1. We do not exaggerate the significance of the ILP. In politics as in the physical world, everything is relative. In comparison with your small group, the ILP is a big organisation. Your small lever is insufficient to move the Labour Party but can have a big effect on the ILP.

2. It seems to me that you are inclined to look at the ILP through the eyes of the Stalinist party, that is, to exaggerate the number of petty-bourgeois elements and minimise the proletarian elements of the Party. But if we should estimate that the workers make up only 10 per cent (an obvious underestimation since you ignore the [illegible words]), even then you will get 1000 revolutionary-minded workers, and in reality many more.

3. The jump from 1,000 to 10,000 is much easier than the jump from forty to 1,000.

---

4   "There is a tide in the affairs of men,

Which taken at the flood, leads onto fortune;

Omitted, all the voyage of their life

Is bound in shallows or in miseries."

– Brutus' speech, *Julius Caesar*, IV, iii, 217.

4. You speak of the advantages of influencing the ILP from the outside. Taken on a wide historical scale, your arguments are irrefutable, but there are unique, exceptional circumstances that we must know how to make use of by exceptional means. Today the revolutionary workers of the ILP still hold on to their Party. The perspective of joining a group of forty, the principles of which are little known to them, can by no means appeal to them. If within the next year they should grow disappointed with the ILP, they will go not to you but to the Stalinists, who will break these workers' necks.

    If you enter the ILP to work for the Bolshevik transformation of the party (that is, of its revolutionary kernel), the workers will look upon you as upon fellow workers, comrades, and not as upon adversaries who want to split the party from outside.

5. Had it been a question of a formed, homogeneous party with a stable apparatus, entry in it would not only be useless but fatal. But the ILP is altogether in a different state. Its apparatus is not homogeneous and, therefore, permits great freedom to different currents. The revolutionary rank and file of the party eagerly seek solutions. Remaining as an independent group, you represent, in the eyes of the workers, only small competitors to the Stalinists. Inside the party you can much more successfully insulate the workers against Stalinism.

6. I believe (and this is my personal opinion) that even if you should give up your special organ you will be able to use to advantage the press of the ILP, *The New Leader* and the discussion organ. The American *Militant* as well as the *International Bulletin* could well supplement your work.

7. Should all the members of your group enter the ILP? This is a purely practical question (if your members who work inside the Communist Party of Great Britain have a wide field for their activity, they can remain there longer, although I personally believe that the useful effect of their work would be, under the present conditions, a few times greater in the ILP).

8. Whether you will enter the ILP as a faction or as individuals is a purely formal question. In essence, you will, of course, be a faction that submits to common discipline. Before entering the ILP you make a public declaration: "Our views are known. We base ourselves on the principles of Bolshevism-Leninism and have formed ourselves as a part of the International Left Opposition. Its ideas we consider as the only

basis on which the new International can be built. We are entering the
ILP to convince the members of that party in daily practical work of
the correctness of our ideas and of the necessity of the ILP joining the
initiators of the new International."

In what sense could such a declaration lower the prestige of your group? This
is not clear to me.

Of course, the International Secretariat did not intend to and could not
intend to force you by a bare order to enter the ILP. If you yourselves will
not be convinced of the usefulness of such a step, your entry will be to no
purpose. The step is an exceptionably responsible one; it is necessary to weigh
and consider it well. The aim of the present letter, as well as of the foregoing
ones, is to help in your discussion.

With best comradely greetings,
L. Trotsky

Cardinal Questions Facing the ILP

Letter to a member of the ILP (dated 5 January 1934),
The Militant, 27 January 1934.

For the Fourth International

I am informed that the ILP has weakened considerably in the last period. Its membership, it is claimed, has fallen to 4,000. It is possible, even very probable, that this report is exaggerated. But the general tendency does not seem to me improbable. I will say more: the leadership of the ILP bears a considerable share of responsibility for the weakening of the organisation before which all the conditions opened up and – I want to hope – still open up a wide perspective.

If a worker barely awakened to political life seeks a *mass* organisation, without distinguishing as yet either programmes or tactics, he will naturally join the Labour Party. A worker disillusioned with reformism and exasperated by the betrayals of the political and trade union leaders has attempted more than once – and to some extent is attempting even now – to join the Communist Party, behind which he sees the image of the Soviet Union. But where is the worker who will join the ILP? And exactly what political motives will impel him to take this step?

It seems to me that the leaders of the ILP have as yet not given themselves a clear answer to this cardinal question. Working masses are not interested in shadings and details but in great events, clear slogans, far-seen banners. What is the situation with the ILP's banner? Not well. I say this with great regret. But it must be said. To suppress or embellish the facts would be rendering a poor service to your party.

The ILP broke away from the Labour Party. That was correct. If the ILP wanted to become the revolutionary lever, it was impossible for the handle of this lever to be left in the hands of the thoroughly opportunist and bourgeois careerists. *Complete and unconditional political and organisational independence of a revolutionary party is the first prerequisite for its success.*

But while breaking away from the Labour Party, it was necessary immediately to turn toward it. Of course, this was not to court its leaders, or to pay them bittersweet compliments, or even to suppress their criminal acts – no, only characterless centrists who imagine themselves revolutionaries seek a road to the masses by *accommodating* themselves to the leaders, by humouring them and reassuring them at every step of their friendship and loyalty. A policy of this sort is a road that leads down to the swamp of opportunism. One must seek a way to the reformist masses not through the favour of their leaders, but against the leaders, because opportunist leaders represent not the masses but merely their backwardness, their servile instincts and, finally, their confusion. But the masses have other, progressive, revolutionary traits that strive to find political expression. The future of the masses is most clearly counterposed to their past in the struggle of programmes, parties, slogans, and leaders. *Instinctively* working masses are always 'for unity'. But besides class instinct there is also political wisdom. Harsh experience teaches the workers that a break with reformism is the prerequisite for real unity, which is possible only in *revolutionary action*. Political experience teaches all the better and faster, the more firmly, logically, convincingly, and clearly the revolutionary party interprets the experience to the masses.

The Leninist method of the united front and political fraternisation with reformists exclude each other. *Temporary practical fighting* agreements with mass organisations even headed by the worst reformists are inevitable and obligatory for a revolutionary party. Lasting political alliances with reformist leaders without a definite programme, without concrete duties, without the participation of the masses themselves in militant actions, are the worst type of opportunism. The Anglo-Russian Committee remains forever the classic example of such a demoralising alliance.

One of the most important bridges to the masses is the trade unions, where one can and must work without accommodating to the leaders in the least, on the contrary, struggling irreconcilably against them openly or under cover, depending on the circumstances. But besides the trade unions, there are numerous ways of participating in the daily life of the masses – in the factory, on the street, in sport organisations, even in church and saloon, under the condition that the greatest heed to be paid to what the masses feel and think, how they react to events, what they expect and what they hope for, how and why they let themselves be deceived by reformist leaders. Observing the masses constantly and most thoughtfully, the revolutionary party must not, however, adapt itself passively to them (*chvost*-ism [tail-ending]); on the contrary, it must counterpose their judgement to their prejudices.

It would be particularly wrong to ignore or minimise the importance of parliamentary work. Of course, parliament cannot transform capitalism into socialism or improve the conditions of the proletariat in rotting capitalist society. But revolutionary work in parliament and in connection with parliament, especially in Britain, can be of great help in training and educating the masses. One courageous exclamation of McGovern refreshed and stirred the workers, who had been deceived or stupefied by the Pious, hypocritical, flag-waving speeches of Lansbury, Henderson and other gentlemen of 'His Majesty's Opposition' of flunkeys.

Unfortunately, having become an independent party, the ILP turned not toward the trade unions and the Labour Party, not toward the masses altogether, but toward the Communist Party, which had during a number of years conclusively proven its bureaucratic dullness and absolute inability to approach the class. If even the German catastrophe taught these people nothing, then the doors of the Comintern should bear the same inscription as the entrance to hell: *Lasciate ogni speranza* [Abandon all hope].[1]

The ILP had not freed itself by far of all the defects of the Left wing of the Labour Party (theoretical vagueness, lack of a clear programme, of revolutionary methods, of a strong organisation) when it hastened to take upon itself the responsibility for the incurable failings of the Comintern. It is clear that in this situation new revolutionary workers will not join the ILP; rather, many of its old members will leave it, having lost patience. If semi-reformists, petty-bourgeois radicals and pacifists leave the ILP, we can only wish them a happy journey. But it is a different matter when discontented workers quit the party.

The causes for the enfeeblement of the ILP are seen with special clarity and precision when the problem is approached from the international point of

---

1 From Dante Alighieri's *Inferno*: "*Lasciate ogne speranza, voi ch'intrate*" – "Abandon all hope, ye who enter here".

view, which is of decisive importance in our epoch. Having broken with the Second International, the ILP approached the Third, but did not join it. The ILP is simply hanging in mid-air. Meanwhile, every thinking worker wants to belong to the kind of party that occupies a definite international position: in the unbreakable union with co-thinkers of other countries he sees the confirmation of the correctness of his own position. True, the ILP enters the so-called London Bureau. But the chief characteristic of this Bureau consists, unfortunately, in the absence of all position. It would suffice to say that the Norwegian Labour Party, which under the leadership of the treacherous opportunist Tranmael goes ever more openly along the Social-Democratic road, belongs to this Bureau. Tranmael and Co. need the temporary alliance with the ILP and with other left organisations to pacify their own left-wing and gradually to prepare for themselves the way to the Second International. Now Tranmael is approaching the harbour.

On the other side, the Socialist Workers Party of Germany (SAP) and the Independent Socialist Party of Holland (OSP) also belong to the London Bureau. Both these organisations stand on the point of view of the Fourth International. Their adherence to the Bureau merely reflects their past. We, the International Communist League (Left Opposition), have considered and now consider it a great mistake of our allies, the SAP and the OSP, that they have not yet broken openly and decisively with Tranmael and with the London Bureau in general. We do not doubt, however, that the hour of such a rupture is near.

What is the position of the ILP? Entering the London Bureau, it becomes by this very fact an ally of Tranmael, that is, essentially of the Second International. Through the SAP and the OSP, it becomes a sort of ally, or semi-ally, of the Fourth International. This is not all – outside the London Bureau, the ILP finds itself in a temporary alliance with the British Communist Party, that is, with the Third International. Are there not somewhat too many Internationals for one party? Can the British worker make head or tail out of this confusion?

At the Paris Conference, the ILP delegates said that they did not lose hope of attracting the Comintern to participate in the building of a broad revolutionary International. Nearly a half year has elapsed since then. Is it possible that no answer has come yet? How much time do the leading comrades of the ILP need to understand the *Comintern is incapable of making one step forward*, that it is completely ossified, that as a revolutionary party it is dead? If the ILP wants to continue waiting for miracles, that is, to live in hopes on the Comintern, or to remain outside of the main historic currents, its own members will inevitably lose confidence in it.

The same fate awaits the Swedish Independent Communist party. For fear of making an error, it abstains from all decision, not realising that precisely this is the greatest error. In general, there are not a few politicians who consider evasiveness and waiting for problems to solve themselves as the highest wisdom. "Do not hurry with the Fourth International", they say, "now is not the time". *It is a matter not of bureaucratically 'proclaiming' the new International but of uninterrupted struggle for its preparation and building.* "Not to hurry" means in practice to lose time. "Perhaps the new International will not be needed", perhaps "a miracle will happen, perhaps…" This policy, which seems to some people very realistic, is the *worst type of utopianism*, spun out of passivity, ignorance and belief in miracles. If the Swedish Independent Communist Party will not shake off its pseudo-realistic superstitions, it will weaken, waste away and finally be torn between three Internationals.

"But the masses", object some pseudo-realists, "are as afraid of a new International as of a new split". This is absolutely natural. The masses' fear of a new party and of a new International is a reflection (*one* of the reflections) of the great catastrophe, the terrible defeat, the disillusionment of the masses, their bewilderment, their disbelief in themselves. How long these moods will last depends mainly on the course of events but to a certain extent also on us. We do not bear any responsibility for the course of events, but we answer fully for our own attitude. The advantage of the vanguard over the masses is that we illuminate theoretically the march of events and foresee its future stages. The formless passive longing for 'unity' will receive blow after blow. The rottenness of the Second and Third Internationals will be revealed at each step. Events will confirm *our* prognosis and *our* slogans. But it is necessary that we ourselves not be afraid to unfurl our banner right now.

Lassalle used to say that a revolutionary needs the "physical power of thought". Lenin liked to repeat these words, although, in general, he did not like Lassalle much. The physical power of thought consists in analysing the situation and perspectives to the very end and, having come to the necessary practical conclusions, defending them with conviction, courage, intransigence, not fearing someone else's fears, not bowing before prejudices of the masses but basing oneself on the objective course of development.

The ILP of Great Britain must place itself right now under the banner of the Fourth International, or it will disappear from the scene without leaving a trace.

* * *

From a summary of discussion at a meeting of the
Communist League of America (6 August 1934), *Internal Bulletin*
No. 17 of the Communist League of America, October 1934.

The lack of a real ideological position on the part of Comrades Bauer[2] and
P. N.[3] appears most plainly on the question of the ILP. Bauer was in favour
of the entry of the British section into the ILP from its beginning. P. N.
was against this, but after his trip to Britain, having become aware of the
actual situation at first hand, he recognised the incorrectness of his original
position. To set up an ideological difference between the ILP and the SFIO,[4]
especially the latter's Parisian organisation and the Young Socialists, is simply
ridiculous. Neither P. N. nor Bauer has made any attempt to explain the
difference in their ideological stand with regard to Britain and France.

However the experience of the British section, on a small scale, is highly
instructive. The 'majority' maintaining its 'organisational autonomy' actually
finds itself in a state of constant internal strife and division. Certain leaders
have left the organisation altogether. On the other hand, the 'minority' that
entered the ILP has maintained its internal solidarity and its connection with
the international Bolshevik-Leninists, has made large use of the publications
of the League in America and has had a series of successes inside the ILP. We
must learn from the example.

---

2 Eugene Bauer, pseudonym of Erwin Ackerknecht (1906-1988) – Though a member
   of the International Secretariat, broke from the movement on this question, and in
   October joined the SAP.

3 Pierre Naville (1904-1993) – One of Trotsky's earliest supporters in France and
   eventually followed the rest of the section into the Socialist Party. After further
   disagreements, he left the Trotskyist movement during the Second World War, and
   after it was a member of various centrist organisations.

4 After the chief organisations of French social democracy (the Socialist Party of France
   led by Jules Guesde and the French Socialist Party of Jean Jaurès) were united in 1905,
   they adopted the title French Section of the (Second) Workers' International, partly
   to symbolise the role of the International in the fusion. The majority of this party
   seceded at the Tours Congress of 1920 to form the French Communist Party and
   those reformists who remained kept this title.

The ILP and the Fourth International

ILP and the Fourth International, Written on 18 September 1935 (postscript dated 20 October), *New International*, December 1935.

The Middle of the Road

If we were to leave aside the Revolutionary Socialist Party of Holland which stands under the banner of the Fourth International, we could assuredly say that the ILP of Britain stands on the left wing of the parties that adhere to the London-Amsterdam Bureau. In contrast to the SAP which has shifted recently to the right to the side of crassest petty bourgeois pacifism, the ILP has indubitably undergone a serious evolution to the left. This became definitely revealed by Mussolini's predatory assault upon Ethiopia.[1] On the question of the League of Nations, on the role played in it by British imperialism, and on the 'peaceful' policy of the Labour Party,[2] the *New Leader* has perhaps carried

---

1 The invasion of this feudal kingdom on 3 October 1935 by the Italian fascists precipitated a crisis in the so-called 'collective security' Policy of the League of Nations. The Stalinists and social democrats called for 'sanctions' by the League. The Trotskyist movement on other hand tried to develop working class opposition to the war and fought for this perspective, for example within the ILP.

2 The attitude of the executive of the Labour Party was that full support should be given to League of Nations sanctions against Italy, including military ones. This view, though not shared by Lansbury, the party leader, nor by Cripps, won majority support at the 1935 Party Conference.

the best articles in the entire Labour press. But a single swallow does not make a spring, nor do a few excellent articles determine as yet the policy of a party. It is comparatively easy to take a 'revolutionary' position on the question of war; but it is extremely difficult to draw from this position *all the necessary theoretical and practical conclusions*. Yet, this is precisely the task.

Compromised by the experience of 1914-18, social-patriotism has found today a new source to feed from, namely, Stalinism. Thanks to this, bourgeois chauvinism obtains the opportunity to unleash a rabid attack against the revolutionary internationalists. The vacillating elements, the so-called centrists, will capitulate inevitably to the onset of chauvinism on the eve of the war, or the moment it breaks out. To be sure, they will take cover behind the argument from 'unity', the need not to break away from mass organisations, and so on. The formulas of hypocrisy are quite diversified, which supply the centrists with a screen for their cowardice in the face of bourgeois public opinion, but they all serve the self-same purpose: to cover up the capitulation. 'Unity' with the social-patriots – not a temporary coexistence with them in a common organisation with a view to waging a struggle against them, but unity as a principle – is unity with one's own imperialism, and consequently, an open split with the proletariat of other nations. The centrist principle of *unity at any price* prepares for the most malignant split possible, along the lines of imperialist contradictions. Even today, we can observe in France the Spartacus group[3] which translates into the French language the ideas of the SAP, advocating, in the name of 'unity' with the masses, the political capitulation to Blum who was and who remains the chief agent of French imperialism within the working class.

After its split with the Labour Party, the ILP came into close contact with the British Communist Party, and through it, with the Communist International. The acute financial difficulties under which the *New Leader* labours right now indicate that the ILP was able to preserve complete financial independence from the Soviet bureaucracy, and its methods of corruption. This can only be a source of gratification. Nevertheless, the connection with the Communist Party did not pass without leaving a trace: despite its name, the ILP did not become really *independent* but turned into a sort of appendage to the Communist International. It did not pay the necessary attention to mass work, which cannot be carried on outside of the trade unions and the Labour Party; instead it became seduced by the Amsterdam-

---

3 A group of French supporters of Brandler Right Oppositionists, though they were very small and insignificant.

Pleyel masquerade, the Anti-Imperialist League, and other surrogates for revolutionary activity. As a result, it appeared to the workers to be a *second grade Communist Party*. So disadvantageous a position for the ILP did not arise accidentally: it was conditioned by its lack of a firm principled basis. It is a secret to nobody that Stalinism long over-awed the leaders of the ILP with those rubber-stamp formulas which comprise the miserable bureaucratic falsification of Leninism.

More than two years ago the writer of this article sought to arrive at an understanding with the leaders of the ILP by means of several articles, and in letters; the attempt was barren of results: during that period, our criticism of the Communist International seemed to the leaders of the ILP to be 'preconceived', and 'factionally', perhaps even 'personally' motivated. Nothing remained except to yield the floor to time. For the ILP, the last two years have been scanty in successes, but bountiful in experience. The social-patriotic degeneration of the Communist International, the direct consequence of the theory and practice of 'socialism in one country', was turned from a *forecast* into a living, incontestable *fact*. Have the leaders of the ILP fully plumbed the meaning of this fact? Are they ready and able to draw all the necessary conclusions from it? The future of the ILP depends upon the answer to these questions.

From pacifism towards proletarian revolution – such has indubitably been the general tendency of the evolution of the ILP. But this development has far from reached a rounded-out programme as yet. Worse yet: not uninfluenced by the hoary and expert opportunistic combinations of the German SAP, the leaders of the ILP have apparently halted in the middle, and keep marking time.

In the following critical lines, we intend to dwell primarily upon two questions: the attitude of the ILP toward the *general strike* in connection with the struggle against war, and the position of the ILP on the question of the *International*. In the latter as well as the former question there are to be found elements of a half-way attitude: on the question of the general strike this hesitancy assumes the guise of irresponsible *radical phraseology*; on the question of the International hesitancy pulls up short of the *radical decision*. And yet Marxism, and Leninism as the direct continuation of its doctrine, is absolutely irreconcilable both with an inclination to radical phraseology, and with the dread of radical decisions.

The question of the general strike has a long and rich history, in theory as well as practice. Yet the leaders of the ILP behave as if they were the first to run across the idea of general strike, as a method to stop war. In this is their greatest error. Improvisation is impermissible precisely on the question of the general strike. The world experience of the struggle during the last forty years has been *fundamentally* a confirmation of what Engels had to say[4] about the general strike towards the close of the last century, primarily on the basis of the experience of the Chartists, and in part of the Belgians.[5] Cautioning the Austrian Social Democrats against much too flighty an attitude towards the general strike, Engels wrote to Kautsky, on 3 November 1893, as follows:

> You yourself remark that the barricades have become antiquated (they may, however, prove useful again should the army turn one-third or two-fifths socialist and the question arises of providing it with the opportunity to turn its bayonets), but the political strike must either prove victorious immediately by the threat alone (as in Belgium, where the army was very shaky), or it must end in a colossal fiasco, or, finally *lead directly to the barricades*.

These terse lines provide, incidentally, a remarkable exposition of Engels' views on a number of questions. Innumerable controversies raged over Engels' famous introduction to Marx's *The Class Struggles in France* (1895), an introduction which was in its time modified and cut in Germany with a view to censorship. Philistines of every stripe have asserted hundreds and thousands of times during the last forty years that "Engels himself" had apparently rejected once and for all the ancient "romantic" methods of street fighting. But there is no need of referring to the past: one need only read the contemporary and inordinately ignorant and mawkish discourses of Paul Faure, Lebas and others[6] on this subject, who are of the opinion that the very question of armed insurrection is 'Blanquism'.[7] Concurrently, if

---

4 The statements by Engels quoted in this paragraph were only beginning to see the light of day at the time this paragraph was written. The Introduction to *The Civil War in France*, for example, was only published in full in English in 1933.

5 This was called by the Belgian Labour Party on the demand for manhood suffrage at twenty-five. About 300,000 workers came out in April 1893 and major changes in the electoral law were introduced.

6 The leaders of French social democracy in this period.

7 After Louis Auguste Blanqui (1805–1881) – French revolutionary of the nineteenth century, who stood at the extreme left of the turbulent Parisian movement of his time. In contrast to Marxism, Blanquism favoured an insurrectionary movement organised conspiratorially and conducted by a small, active minority which, without basing itself on a broad working-class movement, would seize power by a single, sudden

Engels rejected anything, it was first of all, *putsches*, i.e., *untimely* flurries of a *small minority*; and secondly, antiquated methods, that is to say, forms and methods of street fighting which did not correspond to the new technological conditions. In the above quoted letter, Engels corrects Kautsky, in passing, as if he were referring to something self-evident: barricades have become "antiquated" only in the sense that the bourgeois revolution has receded into the past, and the time for the socialist barricades has not come as yet. It is necessary for the army, one-third, or better still, two-fifths of it (these ratios, of course, are given only for the sake of illustration), to become imbued with sympathy for socialism; then the insurrection would not be a 'putsch', then the barricades would once again come into their own – not the barricades of the year 1848, to be sure, but the new 'barricades', serving, however, the self-same goal: to check the offensive of the army against the workers, give the soldiers the opportunity and the time to sense the power of the uprising, and by this to create the most advantageous conditions for the army's passing over to the side of the insurrectionists. How far removed are these lines of Engels – not the youth, but the man seventy-three years of age! – from the asinine and reactionary attitude to the barricade, as a piece of 'romanticism'! Kautsky has found the leisure to publish this remarkable letter just recently, in 1935! Without engaging in a direct polemic with Engels, whom he never understood *fully*, Kautsky tells us smugly, in a special note, that toward the end of 1893, he had himself published an article in which he "developed the advantages of the democratic-proletarian method of struggle in democratic countries as against the policy of violence." These remarks about "advantages" (as if the proletariat has the freedom of choice!) have a particularly choice ring in our day, after the policies of the Weimar democracy, not without Kautsky's cooperation, have fully revealed all their... disadvantages. To leave no room for doubt as to his own attitude on Engels' views, Kautsky goes on to add, "I defended then the self-same policy I defend today." In order to defend "the self-same policy" Kautsky needed only to become a citizen of Czechoslovakia: outside of the passport, nothing has changed.

---

stroke, establish a proletarian party dictatorship and inaugurate the new social order by the decrees of the revolutionary government. Lenin, accused in 1917 of Blanquism, even by many of his own party friends, dealt in his writings at great length with the distinctions between Blanquism and the Marxist conception of "insurrection as an art" based upon the preparation, guidance and active participation of a broad mass movement.

But let us return to Engels. He differentiates, as we have seen, between three cases in relation to the political strike:

1. The government *takes fright* at the general strike, and at the very outset, without carrying matters to an open clash, takes to concessions. Engels points to the "shaky" condition of the army in Belgium as the basic condition for the success of the Belgian general strike (1893). A somewhat similar situation, but on a much more colossal scale, occurred in Russia, October 1905. After the miserable outcome of the Russo-Japanese War, the tsarist army was, or, at any rate, seemed extremely unreliable. The Petersburg government, thrown into a mortal panic by the strike, made the first constitutional concessions.

    It is all too evident, however, that without resorting to decisive battles, the ruling class will make only such concessions as will not touch the basis of its rule. That is precisely how matters stood in Belgium and Russia. Are such cases possible in the future? They are inevitable in the countries of the Orient. They are, generally speaking, less probable in the countries of the West, although, here too, they are quite possible as partial episodes of the unfolding revolution.

2. If the army is sufficiently reliable, and the government feels sure of itself; if a political strike is promulgated from above, and if, at the same time, it is calculated not for decisive battles, but to 'frighten' the enemy, then it can easily turn out a mere adventure, and reveal its utter impotence. To this we ought to add that after the initial experiences of the general strike, the novelty of which reacted upon the imagination of the popular masses as well as governments, several decades have elapsed – discounting the half-forgotten Chartists – in the course of which the strategists of capital have accumulated an enormous experience. That is why a general strike, particularly in the old capitalist countries, requires a painstaking Marxist accounting of all the concrete circumstances.

3. Finally, there remains a general strike which, as Engels put it, "leads directly to the barricades". A strike of this sort can result either in complete victory or defeat. But to shy away from battle, when the battle is forced by the objective situation, is to lead inevitably to the most fatal and demoralising of all possible defeats. The outcome of a revolutionary, insurrectionary general strike depends, of course, upon the relationship of forces, covering a great number of factors: the class differentiation of society, the specific weight of the proletariat, the mood

of the lower layers of the petty-bourgeoisie, the social composition and the political mood of the army, etc. However, among the conditions for victory, far from the last place is occupied by *the correct revolutionary leadership, a clear understanding of conditions and methods of the general strike and its transition to open revolutionary struggle.*

Engels' classification must not, of course, be taken dogmatically. In present day France not partial concessions but power is indubitably in question: the revolutionary proletariat or Fascism – which? The working-class masses want to struggle. But the leadership applies the brakes, hoodwinks and demoralises the workers. A general strike can flare up just as the movements flared in Toulon and Brest.[8] Under these conditions, independently of its immediate results, a general strike will not of course be a 'putsch' but a necessary stage in the mass struggle, the necessary means for casting off the treachery of the leadership and for creating within the working class itself the preliminary conditions for a victorious uprising. In this sense the policy of the French Bolshevik-Leninists is entirely correct, who have advanced the slogan of general strike, and who explain the conditions for its victory. The French cousins of the SAP come out against this slogan, the Spartacists who at the beginning of the struggle are already assuming the role of strikebreakers.

We should also add that Engels did not point out another 'category' of general strike, exemplars of which have been provided in Britain, Belgium, France and some other countries: we refer here to cases in which the leadership of the strike previously, i.e., without a struggle, arrives at an agreement with the class enemy as to the course and outcome of the strike. The parliamentarians and the trade unionists perceive at a given moment the need to provide an outlet for the accumulated ire of the masses, or they are simply compelled to jump in step with a movement that has flared over their heads. In such cases they come scurrying through the backstairs to the Government and obtain the permission to head the general strike, this with the obligation to conclude it as soon as possible, without any damage being done to the state crockery. Sometimes, far from always, they manage to haggle beforehand some petty concessions, to serve them as fig leaves. Thus did the General Council of British Trade Unions (TUC) in 1926. Thus did

---

8   The scene of massive local strike action and demonstrations in the period before the election of the 1936 Popular Front government. At Brest, where the town was taken over for a time, the Trotskyists played an active part.

Jouhaux in 1934. Thus will they act in the future also. The exposure of these contemptible machinations behind the backs of the struggling proletariat enters as a necessary part into the preparation of a general strike.

To which type does a general strike belong which is specially intended by the ILP in the event of mobilisation, as a means to stop war at the very outset?[9] We want to say beforehand: it pertains to the most inconsidered and unfortunate of all types possible. This does not mean to say that the revolution can never coincide with mobilisation or with the outbreak of war. If a widescale revolutionary movement is developing in a country, if at its head is a revolutionary party possessing the confidence of the masses and capable of going through to the end; if the government, losing its head, despite the revolutionary crisis, or just because of such a crisis, plunges headlong into a war adventure – then the mobilisation can act as a mighty impetus for the masses, lead to a general strike of railwaymen, fraternisation between the mobilised and the workers, seizure of important key centres, clashes between insurrectionists and the police and the reactionary sections of the army, the establishment of local, workers' and soldiers' councils, and, finally, to the complete overthrow of the government, and consequently, to stopping the war. Such a case is theoretically possible. If, in the words of Clausewitz, "war is the continuation of politics by other means", then the struggle against war is also the continuation of the entire preceding policy of a revolutionary class and its party. Hence follows that a general strike can be put on the order of the day as a method of struggle against mobilisation and war only in the event that the entire preceding developments in the country have placed revolution and armed insurrection on the order of the day. Taken, however, as a 'special' method of struggle against mobilisation, a general strike would be a sheer adventure. Excluding a possible but nevertheless an exceptional case of a government plunging into war in order to escape from a revolution that directly threatens it, it must remain, as a general rule, that precisely prior to, during, and after mobilisation the government feels itself strongest, and, consequently, least inclined to allow itself to be scared by a general strike. The patriotic moods that accompany mobilisation, together with the war terror make hopeless the very execution of a general strike, as a rule. The most intrepid elements who, without taking the circumstances into account, plunge into the struggle, would be crushed. The defeat, and the partial annihilation of the vanguard would make revolutionary work difficult for a long time in the atmosphere of dissatisfaction that war breeds. A strike

---

9   See *What the ILP Stands For*, a compendium of the basic party documents. – *Trotsky*

called artificially must turn inevitably into a *putsch*, and into an obstacle in the path of the revolution.

In its theses accepted in April 1935 the ILP writes as follows: "The policy of the party aims at the use of a *general strike* to stop war and at *social revolution* should war occur." An astonishingly precise, but – sad to say – absolutely fictitious obligation! The general strike is not only separated here from the social revolution but also counterposed to it as a specific method to "stop war". This is an ancient conception of the anarchists which life itself smashed long ago. A general strike without a victorious insurrection cannot "stop war". If, under the conditions of mobilisation, the insurrection is impossible, then so is a general strike impossible.

In an ensuing paragraph we read: "The ILP will urge a General Strike against the British Government, if this country is in any way involved in an attack on the Soviet Union…" If it is possible to forestall *any* war by a general strike, then of course it is all the more necessary to stop *war against the USSR*. But here we enter into the realm of illusions: to inscribe in the theses a general strike as *punishment* for a given *capital crime* of the government is to commit the sin of revolutionary phrasemongering. If it were possible to call a general strike at will, then it would be best called today to prevent the British government from strangling India and from collaborating with Japan to strangle China. The leaders of the ILP will of course tell us that they have not the power to do so. But nothing gives them the right to promise that they will apparently have the power to call a general strike on the day of mobilisation. And if they be able, why confine it to a strike? As a matter of fact, the conduct of a party during mobilisation will flow from its preceding successes and from the situation in the country as a whole. But the aim of revolutionary policy should not be an isolated general strike, as a special means to "stop war", but the proletarian revolution into which a general strike will enter as an inevitable or a very probable integral part.

The ILP split from the Labour Party chiefly for the sake of keeping the independence of its parliamentary fraction. We do not intend here to discuss whether the split was correct at the *given moment*, and whether the ILP gleaned from it the expected advantages. We don't think so. But it remains a fact that for every revolutionary organisation in England its attitude to the masses and to the class is almost coincident with its attitude toward the Labour Party, which bases itself upon the trade unions. At *this time* the question whether to function inside the Labour Party or outside it is not a principled question, but a question of actual possibilities. In any case, without a strong faction in the trade unions, and, consequently, in the Labour Party itself, the ILP is doomed to impotence even today. Yet, for a long period, the ILP attached much greater importance to the 'united front' with the insignificant Communist Party than to work in mass organisations. The leaders of the ILP consider the policy of the opposition wing in the Labour Party incorrect out of considerations which are absolutely unexpected: although "they (the Opposition) criticise the leadership and policy of the party but, owing to the block vote and the form of organisation of the Party, they cannot change the personnel and policy of the Executive and Parliamentary Party within the period necessary to resist capitalist reaction, fascism and war". The policy of the opposition in the Labour Party is unspeakably bad. But this only means that it is necessary to counterpose to it inside the Labour Party another, a correct Marxist policy. That isn't so easy? Of course not! But one must know how to hide one's activities from the police vigilance of Sir Walter Citrine and his agents, until the proper time. But isn't it a fact that a Marxist faction would not succeed in changing the structure and policy of the Labour Party? With this we are entirely in accord: the bureaucracy will not surrender. But the revolutionists, functioning outside and inside, can and must succeed in winning over tens and hundreds of thousands of workers. The criticism directed by the ILP against the left-wing faction in the Labour Party is of an obviously artificial character. One would have much more reason for saying that the tiny ILP by involving itself with the compromised Communist Party and thus drawing away from the mass organisations, hasn't a chance to become a mass party "within the period necessary to resist capitalist reaction, fascism and war".

Thus, the ILP considers it necessary for a revolutionary organisation to exist independently within the *national* framework even at the present time. Marxist logic, it would seem, demands that this consideration be applied to the international arena as well. A struggle against war and for the revolution is unthinkable without the International. The ILP deems it necessary for it to exist *side by side* with the Communist Party, and consequently, *against* the Communist Party, and by this very fact it recognises the need of creating against the Communist International – a New International. Yet the ILP dares not draw this conclusion. Why?

If in the opinion of the ILP the Comintern could be reformed, it would be its duty to join its ranks, and work for this reform. If, however, the ILP has become convinced that the Comintern is incorrigible, it is its duty to join with us in the struggle for the Fourth International. The ILP does neither. It halts midway. It is bent on maintaining a 'friendly collaboration' with the Communist International. *If it is invited to the next Congress of the Communist International* – such is the literal wording of its April theses of this year! – it will there fight for its position and in the interests of the "unity of revolutionary socialism". Evidently, the ILP expected to be "invited" to the International. This means that its psychology in relation to the International, is that of a *guest*, and not of a *host*. But the Comintern did not invite the ILP. What to do, now?

It is necessary to understand first of all that really *independent* workers' parties – independent not only of the bourgeoisie, but also of both bankrupt Internationals – cannot be built unless there is a close international bond between them, on the basis of self-same principles, and provided there is a living interchange of experience, and vigilant mutual control. The notion that national parties (which ones? on what basis?) must be established first, and coalesced only later into a new International (how will a common principled basis then be guaranteed?) is a caricature echo of the history of the Second International: the First and Third Internationals were both built differently. But, today, under the conditions of the imperialist epoch, after the proletarian vanguard of all countries in the world has passed through many decades of a colossal and common experience, including the experience of the collapse of the two Internationals, it is absolutely unthinkable to build new Marxist, revolutionary parties, without direct contact with the self-same work in other countries. And this means the building of the Fourth International.

To be sure, the ILP has in reserve a certain international association, namely, the London Bureau (IAG). Is this the beginning of a new International? Emphatically, no! The ILP comes out against 'split' more decisively than any other participant: not for nothing has the Bureau of those organisations who themselves *split away* inscribed on its banner… 'unity'. Unity with whom? The ILP itself yearns exceedingly to see all revolutionary-socialist organisations and all sections of the Communist International united in a single International, and that this International have a good programme. The road to hell is paved with good intentions. The position of the ILP is all the more helpless since nobody else shares it inside of the London association itself. On the other hand, the Communist International, having drawn social-patriotic conclusions from the theory of socialism in one country, seeks today an alliance with powerful reformist organisations, and not at all with weak revolutionary groups. The April theses of the ILP console us: "… but they [i.e., the other organisations in the London association] agree that the question of a new International is now theoretical [!], and that the form [!] which the reconstructed International will take will depend upon historical events [!] and the development of the actual working class struggle." (p. 20.) Remarkable reasoning! The ILP urges the unity of the "revolutionary-socialist organisations" with the sections of the Communist International; but there is not and there cannot be any desire on the part of either for this unification. "But", the ILP consoles itself, the revolutionary-socialist organisations are agreed upon... what? Upon the fact that it is still impossible to foresee today what "form" the reconstructed International will take. For this reason, the very question of the International ("Workers of the World Unite!") is declared to be "theoretical". With equal justification one might proclaim the question of socialism to be theoretical, since it is unknown what form it will take; besides, it is impossible to achieve the socialist revolution by means of a "theoretical" International.

For the ILP, the question of a *national* party and the question of the *International* rest on two different planes. The danger of war and fascism demands, as we were told, *immediate* work for the building of a national party. As regards the International, this question is... "theoretical". Opportunism reveals itself so clearly and incontestably in nothing else as in this principled counterposing of a national party to the International. The banner of "revolutionary socialist unity" serves only as a cover for the yawning gap in the policy of the ILP. Are we not justified in saying that the London association is a temporary haven for vacillators, waifs, and those who hope to be "invited" to one of the existing Internationals?

While acknowledging that the Communist Party has a "revolutionary and theoretical basis", the ILP discerns "sectarianism" in its conduct. This characterisation is superficial, one-sided, and fundamentally false. Which "theoretical basis" has the ILP in mind? Is it Marx's *Das Kapital*, Lenin's *Works*, the resolutions of the first Congresses of the Comintern? – or the eclectic programme of the Communist International accepted in 1928, the wretched theory of the 'Third Period', 'social-fascism', and, finally, the latest social patriotic avowals.

The leaders of the ILP make believe (at any rate, such was the case up to yesterday) that the Communist International has preserved the theoretical basis that was lodged by Lenin. In other words, they identify Leninism with Stalinism. To be sure, they are unable to make up their minds to say it in so many words. But, in their passing silently over the enormous critical struggle that took place first inside the Communist International and then outside it; in their refusal to study the struggle waged by the 'Left Opposition' (the Bolshevik-Leninists) and to determine upon their attitude towards it, *the leaders of the ILP turn out to be backward provincials in the sphere of the questions of the world movement.* In this they pay tribute to the worst traditions of the insular working class movement. As a matter of fact the Communist International has no theoretical basis. Indeed, what sort of theoretical basis can there be, when yesterday's leaders, like Bukharin, are pronounced to be "bourgeois liberals", when the leaders of the day before yesterday, like Zinoviev, are incarcerated in jail as "counter-revolutionists", while the Manuilskys, Lozovskys, Dimitrovs together with Stalin himself never generally bothered much with questions of theory.[10]

The remark in relation to "sectarianism" is no less erroneous. *Bureaucratic Centrism* which seeks to dominate the working class is not sectarianism but a specific refraction of the autocratic rule of the Soviet bureaucracy. Having burnt their fingers, these gentlemen are abjectly crawling today before reformism and patriotism. The leaders of the ILP took for gospel the assertion of the leaders of the SAP (poor counsellors!) that the Comintern would rest on the pinnacle, if not for its "ultra-left sectarianism". In the meantime, the Seventh Congress has spurned the last remnants of "ultra-leftism"; but, as a result, the Communist International did not rise higher but fell still lower, losing all right to an independent political existence. Because the parties of the Second International are, in any case, more suitable for the policy of blocs with the bourgeoisie and for the patriotic corruption of workers: they have behind them an imposing opportunist record, and they arouse less suspicion on the part of the bourgeois allies.

Aren't the leaders of the ILP of the opinion that after the Seventh Congress they ought to reconsider radically their attitude toward the Communist International? If it is impossible to reform the Labour Party, then there are immeasurably less chances for reforming the Communist International. Nothing remains except to build the new International. True, in the ranks of the Communist parties quite a few honest revolutionary workers are still to be found. But they must be led out from the quagmire of the Comintern onto the revolutionary road.

Both the revolutionary conquest of power and the dictatorship of the proletariat are included in the programme of the ILP. After the events in

---

10 In August 1935 the Comintern held its seventh (and last) Congress, declaring its support for the policies of the Popular Front.

Germany, Austria and Spain,[11] these slogans have become compulsory. But this does not at all mean that in every case they are invested with a genuine revolutionary content. The Zyromskis of all countries find no embarrassment in combining the "dictatorship of the proletariat" with the most debased patriotism, and besides, such fakery is becoming more and more fashionable. The leaders of the ILP are not social-patriots. But until they blow up their bridges to Stalinism, their internationalism will remain semi-platonic in character.

The April theses of the ILP enable us to approach the same question from a new standpoint. In the theses two special paragraphs (27 and 28) are devoted to the future British Councils of Workers' Deputies. They contain nothing wrong. But it is necessary to point out that the Councils (Soviets) as such are only an *organisational form* and not at all a sort of immutable principle. Marx and Engels provided us with the theory of the proletarian revolution, partly in their analysis of the Paris Commune, but they did not have a single word to say about the Councils. In Russia there were Social-Revolutionary and Menshevik Soviets (Councils), i.e., anti-revolutionary Soviets. In Germany and Austria the Councils in 1918 were under the leadership of reformists and patriots and they played a counter-revolutionary role. In autumn 1923, in Germany, the role of the Councils was fulfilled actually by the shop committees that could have guaranteed fully the victory of the revolution were it not for the craven policy of the Communist Party under the leadership of Brandler and Co. Thus, the slogan of Councils, as an organisational form, is not in itself of a principled character. We have no objection, of course, to the inclusion of Councils as "all-inclusive organisations" in the programme of the ILP. Only, the slogan must not be turned into a fetish, or worse yet – into a hollow phrase, as in the hands of the French Stalinists ("Power to Daladier!" – "Soviets Everywhere!").[12]

---

11 This refers to the coming to power of reactionary groups in all three countries. Hitler had come to power in Germany in 1933. In Austria in February 1934 the labour movement had been subjected to violent attack and most of its leaders imprisoned or exiled by the clerical-fascist Chancellor Dolfuss. Though Dolfuss was murdered in an unsuccessful Nazi coup in July 1934, a similar regime under Schusnigg remained in power until the Nazis eventually did take over in 1938. In Spain, the right-wing government of Leroux from 1933 began to dismantle the democratic reforms won from previous administrations and to smash strike and insurrectionary movements of workers and peasants.

12 This slogan of 1934 expressed an attempt to cover over the new right-wing policies of the Popular Front era with a verbal leftism inherited from the 'Third Period'. They

But we are interested in another aspect of the question. Paragraph 28 of the theses reads, "The Workers' Councils will arise in their final form in the actual revolutionary crisis, but the Party must *consistently prepare for* their organisation" (our italics). Keeping this in mind, let us compare the attitude of the ILP toward the future Councils with its own attitude toward the future International: the erroneousness of the ILP's position will then stand before us in sharpest clarity. In relation to the International we are given generalities after the spirit of the SAP: "the form which the reconstructed International will take will depend upon historic events and the actual development of the working-class struggle." On this ground the ILP draws the conclusion that the question of the International is purely "theoretical", i.e., in the language of empiricists, *unreal*. At the same time we are told that: "the Workers' Councils will arise in their final form in the actual revolutionary crisis, but the Party must *consistently prepare for their organisation*". It is hard to become more hopelessly muddled. On the question of the Councils and on the question of the International, the ILP resorts to methods of reasoning that are directly contradictory. In which case is it mistaken? In both. The theses turn topsy-turvy the actual tasks of the party. The Councils represent an *organisational form*, and only a *form*. There is no way of "preparing for" Councils except by means of a correct revolutionary policy applied in all spheres of the working-class movement: there is no special, specific "preparation for" Councils. It is entirely otherwise with the International. While the Councils can arise only under the condition that there is a revolutionary ferment among the many-millioned masses, the International is always necessary: both on holidays and weekdays, during periods of offensive as well as in retreat, in peace as well as in war. The International is not at all a "form" as flows from the utterly false formulation of the ILP. The International is first of all a *programme*, and a system of *strategic, tactical and organisational* methods that flow from it. By dint of historic circumstances the question of the British Councils is deferred for an indeterminate period of time. But the question of the International, as well as the question of national parties, cannot be deferred for a single hour: we have here in essence two sides of one and the same question. Without a Marxist International, national organisations, even the most advanced, are doomed to narrowness, vacillation and helplessness; the advanced workers are forced to feed upon surrogates for internationalism. To proclaim as

---

were calling for the formation of organs of dual power – to install a government of the main bourgeois party. The position of the CP was soon clarified by a sharp shift to the right.

"purely theoretical", i.e., needless, the building of the Fourth International, is cravenly to renounce the basic task of our epoch. In such a case, slogans of revolution, of the dictatorship of the proletariat, Councils, etc., lose nine-tenths of their meaning.

The 30 August issue of the *New Leader* carries an excellent article: *Don't Trust the Government!* The article points out that the danger of "national unity" draws closer with the approaching danger of war. At the time when the ill-fated leaders of the SAP call for the *emulation* – literally so! – of British pacifists, the *New Leader* writes: "It [the government] is actually using the enthusiasm for peace to prepare the British people for imperialist war." These lines, which are printed in italics, express with utmost precision the political function of petty-bourgeois pacifism: by providing a platonic outlet for the horror of the masses to war, pacifism enables imperialism all the easier to transform these masses into cannon fodder. The *New Leader* lashes the patriotic position of Citrine and other social-imperialists who (with quotations from Stalin) mount upon the backs of Lansbury and other pacifists.[13] But this same article goes on to express its "astonishment" at the fact that the British Communists are supporting Citrine's policy on the question of the League of Nations and the "sanctions" against Italy ("astonishing support of Labour line"). The "astonishment" in the article is the Achilles heel of the entire policy of the ILP. When an individual "astonishes" us by his unexpected behaviour, it only means that we are poorly acquainted with this individual's real character. It is immeasurably worse when a politician is compelled to confess his "astonishment" at the acts of a political party, and what is more, of an entire International. For the British Communists are only carrying out the decisions of the Seventh Congress of the Communist International. The leaders of the ILP are "astonished" only because they have failed up to now to grasp the real character of the Communist International, and its sections. Yet, there is a twelve years' history behind the Marxist criticism of the Communist International. From the time the Soviet bureaucracy made as its symbol of faith the theory of 'socialism in one country' (1924), the *Bolshevik-Leninists forecast the inevitability of the nationalist and patriotic degeneration of the sections of the Communist International*, and from then on they followed this process critically through all its stages. The leaders of the ILP were caught off

---

13 The policy of Citrine and the TUC at this stage was for full support for the League of Nations sanctions against Italy over the threatened invasion of Ethiopia. Such policies won the support of Stalinism internationally, and had nothing in common with Lenin's denunciation of the League as a "thieves' kitchen" of imperialism.

guard by events only because they had ignored the criticism of our tendency. The privilege of becoming "astonished" by major events is the prerogative of a pacifist and reformist petty-bourgeois. The Marxists, especially those claiming the right to leadership, must be capable not of astonishment but of foresight. And, we may remark in passing, it is not the first time in history that Marxist misdoubt turned out more penetrating than centrist credulity.

The ILP broke with the mighty Labour Party because of the latter's reformism and patriotism. And today, retorting to Wilkinson,[14] the *New Leader* writes that the independence of the ILP is fully justified by the patriotic position of the Labour Party. Then what are we to say about the ILP's interminable flirtation with the British Communist Party that now tails behind the Labour Party? What are we to say about the ILP's urge to fuse with the Third International that is now the first violinist in the social patriotic orchestra? Are you "astonished", comrades Maxton, Fenner Brockway, and others? That does not suffice for a party leadership. In order to put an end to becoming astonished, one must critically evaluate the road that has been travelled, and draw the conclusion for the future.

Back in August 1933, the Bolshevik-Leninist delegation issued a special declaration officially proposing to all the participants in the London Bureau, among them the ILP, that they review jointly with us the basic strategic problems of our epoch, and in particular, that they determine their attitude to our programmatic documents. But the leaders of the ILP deemed it below their dignity to occupy themselves with such matters. Besides, they were afraid they might compromise themselves by consorting with an organisation which is the target of a particularly rabid and vile persecution at the hands of the Moscow bureaucracy: we should not overlook the fact that the leaders of the ILP awaited all the while an "invitation" from the Communist International. They waited, but the awaited did not materialise…

Is it conceivable that even after the Seventh Congress the leaders of the ILP will be so hardy as to present the matter as if the British Stalinists turned out to be the squires of the little honoured Sir Walter Citrine only through a misunderstanding, and only for a split-second? Such a dodge would be unworthy of a revolutionary party. We should like to entertain the hope that the leaders of the ILP will come at last to an understanding of how lawful is the complete and irremediable collapse of the Communist International, as a revolutionary organisation, and that they will draw from this all the necessary conclusions. These are quite simple:

---

14 Ellen Wilkinson (1891-1947) – Labour politician.

- Work out a Marxist programme.
- Turn away from the leaders of the Communist Party and face towards…
  the mass organisations.
- Stand under the banner of the Fourth International.

On this road we are ready to march shoulder to shoulder with the ILP.

—

A Necessary Addition: In my article I approved the attitude of this party on the question of sanctions. Later, friends sent me a copy of an important letter of Comrade Robertson to the members of the ILP. Comrade Robertson accuses the leadership of the party of maintaining pacifist illusions, particularly in the matter of "refusal" of military service. I can only associate myself wholly with what is said in Comrade Robertson's letter. The ILP's misfortune is that it doesn't have a truly Marxist programme. That too is why its best activities, such as sanctions against British imperialism, are always influenced by pacifist and centrist mixtures.

* * *

From *The Treachery of the Spanish POUM* (dated 23 January 1936),
New Militant, 15 February 1936.

The POUM is a member of the celebrated London Bureau of 'Revolutionary Socialist Parties' (the former IAG). The leadership of this bureau is now in the hands of Fenner Brockway, secretary of the Independent Labour Party (ILP). We have already written that, despite the antiquated and apparently incurable pacifist prejudices of Maxton and others, the ILP has taken an honest revolutionary position on the question of the League of Nations and its sanctions. Each of us has read with pleasure a number of excellent articles in the *New Leader*. During the last parliamentary elections, the Independent Labour Party refused to give even electoral support to the Labourites, precisely because the latter supported the League of Nations. In itself this refusal was a tactical error. Wherever the ILP was unable to run its own candidates, it should have supported a Labour candidate against a Tory. But this is incidental. In any case, even talk of any 'common programmes' with the Labourites was excluded. Internationalists would have combined support in elections with an exposure of the crawling of the British social patriots before the League of Nations and its 'sanctions'.

We take the liberty of putting a question to Fenner Brockway: just what is the purpose of this 'International' of which he is the secretary?

The British section of this 'International' rejects giving even mere electoral support to Labour candidates if they support the League of Nations. The Spanish section concludes a bloc with *bourgeois* parties on a common programme of support to the League of Nations. Is not this the extreme in the domain of contradictions, confusion, and bankruptcy? There is no war as yet, but the sections of the London 'International' are already pulling in completely opposite directions. What will happen to them when the ominous events break?

* * *

Interview with Robertson (November 1935),
New International, February 1936.

Once Again the ILP

Question: What do you mean specifically when you say, at the conclusion of your article,[15] that the ILP must still "work out a Marxian programme"?

Answer: My whole article was a documentation of the instances in which ILP policy still fails to be Marxist, to be revolutionary: its failure to break sharply with pacifism and with Stalinism, and to turn its face fully to the British masses and to reach a clear position on international organisation. These defects are one and the same. Take, for example, pacifism. Despite the revolutionary phraseology of *What the ILP Stands For*, it is still possible in the ILP that Maxton, McGovern, and Campbell Stephen can issue an authoritative statement urging the workers not to bear arms when war comes. This is a bankrupt policy; this is only defeatism against the workers, not revolutionary defeatism against capitalism. Moreover, war is an *international* product of capitalism and can be fought only internationally. Which are the workers' organisations in other countries that the revolutionists in the ILP must unite with? Not the CI as your pacifist leaders had fondly imagined, for the CI is committed to social-patriotism. Not with the International Bureau of Revolutionary Socialist Unity (IAG, i.e., London Bureau) for of the ten groups forming this Bureau some have expired, others are pacifist or even social-patriotic, and only the Dutch party (RSAP) is in agreement with the ILP on the fight against sanctions and for independent workers' action only. This party has long since declared for the Fourth International and this week (about 21 November 1935) declared also for a break with the Bureau. It is, then, the Dutch party and the other parties openly fighting for the Fourth

---

15 See p. 607 of the present edition for Trotsky's article.

International with whom the ILP must of necessity solidarise itself if it is to join in the international revolutionary fight against war.

In the *New Leader* I read that the Lancashire and London and Scottish divisions of the ILP have already declared themselves to be in opposition to the pacifist statements of the Inner Executive, and the similar utterances of McGovern in the House of Commons. But this is not enough. Their fight can succeed only if it is *positive* – not simply "against pacifism", but *for* revolutionary defeatism. This can only mean that the main fight will be *for the Fourth International.*

Q: Was the ILP correct in running as many candidates as possible in the recent General Elections, even at the risk of splitting the vote?[16]

A: Yes. It would have been foolish for the ILP to have sacrificed its political programme in the interests of so-called unity, to allow the Labour Party to monopolise the platform, as the Communist Party did. We do not know our strength unless we test it. There is always a risk of splitting, and of losing deposits but such risks must be taken. Otherwise we boycott *ourselves.*

Q: Was the ILP correct in refusing critical support to Labour Party candidates who advocated military sanctions?

A: No. Economic sanctions, if real, lead to military sanctions, to war. The ILP itself has been saying this. It should have given critical support to *all* Labour Party candidates, i.e., where the ILP itself was not contesting. In the *New Leader* I read that your London Division agreed to support only *anti*-sanctionist Labour Party candidates. This too is incorrect. The Labour Party should have been critically supported not because it was for or against sanctions but because it represented the working-class masses.

The basic error which was made by some ILPers who withdrew critical support was to assume that the war danger necessitated a change in our appreciation of reformism. But as Clausewitz said, and Lenin often repeated, *war is the continuation of politics by other means.* If this is true, it applies not only to capitalist parties but to social democratic parties. The war crisis does not alter the fact that the Labour Party is a workers' party, which the governmental party is not. Nor does it alter the fact that the Labour Party

---

16 In the 1935 General Election the ILP stood seventeen candidates of whom four were elected, all in Glasgow. In Bradford East the Conservatives were elected on a minority vote as the result of the ILP intervention, but in most cases the ILP received very few votes.

leadership cannot fulfil their promises, that they will betray the confidence which the masses place in them. In peace-time the workers will die of hunger if they trust in social democracy; in war, for the same reason, they will die from bullets. Revolutionists never give critical support to reformism on the assumption that reformism, in power, could satisfy the fundamental needs of the workers. It is possible, of course, that a Labour government could introduce a few mild temporary reforms. It is also possible that the League could postpone a military conflict about secondary issues – just as a cartel can eliminate secondary economic crises only to reproduce them on a larger scale. So the League can eliminate small episodic conflicts only to generalise them into world war.

Thus, both economic and military crises will only return with an added explosive force so long as capitalism remains. And we know that social democracy cannot abolish capitalism.

No, in war as in peace, the ILP must say to the workers: "The Labour Party will deceive you and betray you, but you do not believe us. Very well, we will go through your experiences with you but in no case do we identify ourselves with the Labour Party programme."

Morrison, Clynes, etc., represent certain prejudices of the workers. When the ILP seeks to boycott Clynes it helps not only Baldwin but Clynes himself. If successful in its tactic, the ILP prevents the election of Clynes, of the Labour government, and so prevents their exposure before the masses. The workers will say: "If only we had Clynes and Morrison in power, things would have been better."

It is true, of course, that the mental content of Clynes and Baldwin is much the same except, perhaps, that Baldwin is a little more 'progressive' and more courageous. But the class content of the support for Clynes is very different.

It is argued that the Labour Party already stands exposed by its past deeds in power and its present reactionary platform. For example, by its decision at Brighton.[17] For us – yes! But not for the masses, the 8 million who voted

---

17 The Labour Party conference of 1935, held in Brighton, approved a National Executive Committee (NEC) resolution supporting the League of Nations measures against Italy's attack on Abyssinia. This was the main discussion, and the lengthiest in the party's history. The resolution was opposed by Lansbury from a pacifist position and by Cripps on the principle that the League was an "International Burglars' Union", and that Labour ought not to "join without power in the responsibility for capitalist and imperialist war that sanctions may entail". Cripps was opposed to demanding that a Tory government exercise sanctions. Ernest Bevin attacked Cripps and the resolution

Labour. It is a great danger for revolutionists to attach too much importance to conference decisions. We use such evidence in our propaganda – but it cannot be presented beyond the power of our own press. One cannot shout louder than the strength of his own throat.

Let us suppose that the ILP had been successful in a boycott tactic, had won a million workers to follow it, and that it was the absence of this million votes which lost the election for the Labour Party. What would happen when the war came? The masses would in their disillusionment turn to the Labour Party, not to us. If Soviets were formed during the war the soldiers would elect Labour Party people to them, not us. Workers would still say that *we* handicapped Labour. But if we gave critical support and by that means helped the Labour Party to power, at the same time telling the workers that the Labour Party would function as a capitalist government, and would direct a capitalist war – then, when war came, workers would see that we predicted rightly, at the same time that we marched with them. *We* would be elected to the Soviets and the Soviets would not betray.

As a general principle, a revolutionary party has the right to boycott parliament only when it has the capacity to overthrow it, that is, when it can replace parliamentary action by general strike and insurrection, by direct struggle for power. In Britain the masses have yet no confidence in the ILP. The ILP is therefore too weak to break the parliamentary machine and must continue to use it. As for a *partial* boycott, such as the ILP sought to operate, it was unreal. At this stage of British politics it would be interpreted by the working class as a certain contempt for them; this is particularly true in Britain where parliamentary traditions are still so strong.

Moreover, the London Division's policy of giving critical support only to anti-sanctionists would imply a fundamental distinction between the social-patriots like Morrison and Ponsoriby or – with your permission – even Cripps. Actually, their differences are merely propagandistic. Cripps is actually only a second-class supporter of the bourgeoisie. He has said, in effect: "Pay no attention to my ideas; our differences are only small." This is the attitude of a dilettante, not a revolutionist. A thousand times better an open enemy like Morrison. Lansbury himself is a sincere but extravagant and irresponsible old man; he should be in a museum not Parliament. The other pacifists are more duplicitous – more shifty: like Norman Angell, who demands more sanctions now, they will easily turn into social-patriots as

---

to support sanctions was carried by 2,168,000 votes to 102,000. Lansbury resigned as leader of the parliamentary party, to be followed by Attlee.

war develops. Then they could say to the workers: "You know us. We were anti-sanctionists. Even the ILP supported our struggle. Therefore you can have confidence in us now when we say that this war is a just war." No, the ILP should have applied the same policy of critical support to the whole of the Labour Party, only varying our arguments to meet the slightly varied propaganda of pacifists and social-patriots. Otherwise illusions are provoked that pacifism has more power to resist than has social-patriotism.

This is not true; their differences are not fundamental. Even among the Tories there are differences on sanctions and war policies. The distinction between Amery[18] and Lansbury is simply that Amery is more of a realist. Both are anti-sanctionists; but for the working class, Lansbury with his illusions and sincerity is more dangerous.

Most dangerous of all, however, is the Stalinist policy. The parties of the Communist International try to appeal especially to the more *revolutionary* workers by denouncing the League (a denunciation that is an apology) by asking for "workers' sanctions" and then nevertheless saying: "We must use the League when it is for sanctions." They seek to hitch the revolutionary workers to the shafts so that they can draw the cart of the League. Just as the General Council in 1926 accepted the General Strike but behind the curtains concluded a deal with the clergy and pacifist radicals and in this way used bourgeois opinion and influence to 'discipline' the workers and sabotage their strike, so the Stalinists seek to discipline the workers by confining the boycott within the limits of the League of Nations.

The truth is that if the workers begin their own sanctions against Italy, their action inevitably strikes at their own capitalists, and the League would be compelled to drop all sanctions. It proposes them now just because the workers' voices are muted in every country. Workers' action can begin only by absolute opposition to the national bourgeoisie and its international combinations. Support of the League and support of workers' actions are fire and water; they cannot be united.

Because of this, the ILP should have more sharply differentiated itself from the CP at the elections than it did. It should have critically supported the Labour Party against Pollitt and Gallacher.[19] It should have been declared openly that the CP has all the deficiencies of the Labour Party without any of its advantages. It should have, above all, shown in practice what *true* critical support means. By accompanying support with the sharpest and widest

18 Leo Amery (1873-1955) – Tory politician, protectionist, and pro-Imperialist.
19 William Gallacher (1881-1965) – Leader of British Stalinism.

criticism, by patiently explaining that such support, only for the purpose of exposing the treachery of the Labour Party leadership, the ILP would have completely exposed, also, the spurious 'critical' support of the Stalinists themselves, a support which was actually whole-hearted and *uncritical*, and *based on an agreement in principle with the Labour Party leadership.*

Q: Should the ILP seek entry into the Labour Party?

A: At the moment the question is not posed this way. What the ILP must do, if it is to become a revolutionary party, is to turn its back on the CP and face the mass organisations. It must put 99 per cent of its energies into building of fractions in the trade union movement. At the moment I understand that much of the fractional work can be done openly by ILPers in their capacity of trade union and cooperative members. But the ILP should never rest content; it must build its influence in the mass organisations with the utmost speed and energy. For the time may come when, in order to reach the masses, it must enter the Labour Party, and it must have tracks laid for the occasion. Only the experience that comes from such fractional work can inform the ILP if and when it must enter the Labour Party. But for all its activity an absolutely clear programme is the first condition. A small axe can fell a large tree only if it is sharp enough.

Q: Will the Labour Party split?

A: The ILP should not assume that it will automatically grow at the expense of the Labour Party, that the Labour Party left wingers will be split off by the bureaucracy and come to the ILP. These are possibilities. But it is equally possible that the left wing, which will develop as the crisis deepens, and particularly now within the trade unions after the failure of the Labour Party to win the elections, will be successful in its fight to stay within the Labour Party. Even the departure of the Socialist League to join the ILP would not end these possibilities, for the Socialist League is very petty bourgeois in character and is not likely to organise the militancy within the Labour Party. In any case, the history of the British General Strike of 1926 teaches us that a strong militant movement can develop in a strongly bureaucratised trade union organisation, creating a very important minority movement without being forced out of the trade unions.

Instead, what happens is that the labour fakers swing left in order to retain control. If the ILP is not there at the critical moment with a revolutionary leadership the workers will need to find their leadership elsewhere. They might still turn to Citrine, for Citrine might even be willing to shout for Soviets, for the moment, rather than lose his hold. As Scheidemann and Ebert[20] shouted for Soviets, and betrayed them, so will Citrine. Leon Blum, rather by the revolutionary pressure of the French masses, runs headlines in his *Populaire*, '*Sanctions – but the workers must control*', etc. It is this treacherous 'heading in order to behead' which the ILP must prevent in Britain.

Q: Is Stalinism the chief danger?

A: Of all the radical phrasemongers, the ones who offer the greatest danger in this respect are the Stalinists. The members of the CPGB are now on their bellies before the Labour Party – *but this makes it all the easier for them to crawl inside.* They will make every concession demanded of them, but once within – they will still be able to pose as the left-wing because the workers still retain some illusions about the revolutionary nature of the Comintern – *illusions which the ILP in the past has helped to retain.* They will use this illusion to corrupt the militants with their own social-patriotic policy. They will sow seed from which only weeds can sprout. Only a clear and courageous policy on the part of the ILP can prevent this disaster.

Q: Would you recommend the same perspective for the ILP Guild of Youth[21] as the adult party?

A: Even more. Since the ILP youth seem to be few and scattered, while the Labour Youth[22] is the mass youth organisation. I would say: "Do not only build fractions – seek to enter." For here the danger of Stalinist devastation is extreme. The youth are *all-important.* Unlike the older generation they have little actual experience of war; it will be easier for the Stalinists and the other pseudo-revolutionary patriots to confuse the youth on the war issues than to confuse those who survived the last war. On the other hand, the willingness of the Stalinists to drive these same youths into another actual war will make

20 Leaders of the German Social Democratic Party responsible for the bloody suppression of the revolutionary movements of the German working class in 1918-19.

21 Formed in 1924, the ILP Guild of Youth had 171 branches by 1925. Catered for young people between fourteen and twenty-one, it organised football leagues, swimming and hiking, as well as meetings. Penetrated by the CP. When in May 1934 the English section decided to "seek sympathetic affiliation to the YCL", the ILP EC took measures to dissolve it.

22 This was established by the Youth sections of the Labour Party in 1926, largely in response to the initial successes of the ILP Guild of Youth.

the young workers properly suspicious. They will listen more easily to us – *if we are there to speak to them*. No time must be lost. Out of the new generation comes the new International, the only hope for the world revolution. The British section will recruit its first cadres from the 30,000 young workers in the Labour League of Youth. Their more advanced comrades in the ILP youth must not allow themselves to be isolated from them, especially now at the very moment when war is a real danger.

Q: Should the ILP terminate its united front with the CP?

A: Absolutely and categorically – yes! The ILP must learn to turn its back on the CP and towards the working masses. The permanent 'unity committees' in which the ILP has sat with the CP were nonsense in any case. The ILP and the CPGB were propaganda organisations not mass organisations; united fronts between them were meaningless if each of them had the right to advance its own programme. These programmes must have been different or there would have been no justification for separate parties, and with different programmes there is nothing to unite around. United fronts for certain specific actions could have been of some use, of course, *but the only important united front for the ILP is with the Labour Party, the trade unions, the cooperatives.* At the moment, the ILP is too weak to secure these; it must first conquer the right for a united front by winning the support of the masses. At this stage, united fronts with the CP will only compromise the ILP. Rupture with the CP is the first step towards a mass basis for the ILP and the achievement of a mass basis is the first step towards a proper united front, that is, a united front with the mass organisations.

Q: Should the ILP forbid groups?

A: It can scarcely do that without forbidding its leadership, which is also a group, a centrist group, protected by the party machinery, or without denying the very fractional principle by which it must build its influence in the mass organisations.

Factions existed in the Bolshevik party as temporary groupings of opinion during its whole life – except for a brief period in 1921 when they were forbidden by unanimous vote of the leadership as an extreme measure during an acute crisis.

Q: How far can factions develop with safety to the party?

A: That depends on the social composition of the party, upon the political situation and upon the quality of the leadership. Generally it is best to let petty-bourgeois tendencies express themselves fully so that they may expose themselves. If there are no such tendencies, if the membership is fairly homogeneous, there will be only temporary groupings – unless the leadership is incorrect. And this will be shown best in practice. So, when a difference occurs, a discussion should take place, a vote be taken, and a majority line adopted. There must be no discrimination against the minority; any personal animosity will compromise not them but the leadership. Real leadership will be loyal and friendly to the disciplined minority.

It is true, of course, that discussion always provokes feelings which remain for some time. Political life is full of difficulties – personalities clash – they widen their dissensions – they get in each other's hair. These differences must be overcome by common experience, by *education of the rank and file*, by the leadership *proving* it is right. Organisational measures should be resorted to only in extreme cases. Discipline is built by education, not only by statutes. It was the elastic life within it which allowed the Bolshevik party to build its discipline. Even after the conquest of power, Bukharin and other members of the party voted against the government in the Central Executive on important questions, such as the German peace, and in so doing lined themselves with those Socialist-Revolutionaries who soon attempted armed insurrection against the Soviet state. But Bukharin was not expelled. Lenin said, in effect: "We will tolerate a certain lack of discipline. We will demonstrate to them that we are right. Tomorrow they will learn that our policy is correct, and they will not break discipline so quickly." By this I do not advise the dissenting comrades to imitate the arrogance of Bukharin. Rather do I recommend that the leadership learns from the patience and tact of Lenin. Though when it was necessary, he could wield the razor as well as the brush.

The authority of the national leadership is the necessary condition of revolutionary discipline. It can be immensely increased when it represents an international agreement of principles, of common action. Therein lies one of the sources of strength of the new International.

Q: What do you think of the ILP colonial policy?

A: So far, it seems to be mainly on paper. Fenner Brockway has written some very good articles on the Mohmand struggles[23] and upon Ethiopia. But there

---

23 The Mohmands are a tribe on the North-West frontier of India who engaged in spasmodic battles with British imperialism from the middle of the nineteenth century onwards. They are based primarily in the Mohmand territory, which is located in Nangarhar, Afghanistan and Mohmand Agency, Pakistan.

should be many more – and beyond words, there should be action. The ILP should long ago have created some kind of colonial bureau to coordinate those organisations of colonial workers who are striving to overthrow British imperialism. Of course, only the real revolutionists in the ILP will bother to work for such policies. It is the test of their revolutionary understanding.

Q: What should be the basic concept of illegal work?

A: Illegal work is work in the mass organisations – for the ILP it is systematic entry and work in the trade unions, cooperatives, etc. In peace-time and in war, it is the same. You will perhaps say: "They will not let us in. They will expel us." You do not shout: "I am a revolutionist", when working in a trade union with reactionary leadership. You educate your cadres who carry on the fight under your direction. You keep educating new forces to replace those expelled, and so you build up a mass opposition. Illegal work must keep you in the working masses. You do not retire into a cellar as some comrades imagine. The trade unions are the schools for illegal work. The trade union leadership is the unofficial police of the state. The protective covering for the revolutionist is the trade union. Transition into war conditions is almost imperceptible.

Q: What specifically do you think the ILP should do in order to build a new International?

A: The ILP, if it intends to become a genuine revolutionary party must face honestly the question of the new International.

The Second International is bankrupt, the ILP has already said. It now recognises the betrayal of the Third International. It should also realise that the International Bureau for Revolutionary Socialist Unity [IBRSU] is a myth. It should draw the only possible conclusion and add its name to the *Open Letter for the Fourth International.*

Q: You mention that the IBRSU offers no basis for the struggle against war. What is the policy of this Bureau? What is its future?

A: The Bureau has no common policy; its parties are going in all directions. The SAP of Germany now marches steadily rightwards toward social democracy and Stalinism. Today I have news that the congress of the RSAP, one of the largest parties in the Bureau has voted by an overwhelming majority to sever its old close cooperation with the SAP and also to break off completely with the Bureau and to associate with parties which work to build the Fourth International. It even passed a vote of censure on the

Central Committee for having maintained a connection with the SAP as long as it did.

The Spanish POB[24] is, in a certain sense, similar to the ILP. Its leadership is not internationalist in perspective but its membership includes an important section who are for the Fourth International. The USP of Romania is also developing towards a revolutionary internationalist position. Recently it expelled the tiny Stalinist faction within it, and it is already being accused of 'Trotskyism'. I hope that in the near future they will recognise the necessity of joining in the great work of building the Fourth International.

As for the other members of the Bureau, they are either nonentities or they have no real relation to the Bureau. The Italian SP (Maximalist)[25] is not a party, only a microscopic group living for the most part in exile. The Austrian Red Front[26] only two years ago had 1,000 members in illegality. Today it is non-existent, dissolved. Why? Because it had no programme – no banner! The Polish ILPZ[27] is only a topic for humour, a caricature organisation of no political importance, while the Bulgarian LSG[28] is never heard of. Like the Norwegian 'Mot-Dag' – another 'member' of the Bureau – it is only a small left-wing group of intellectuals which is in process of decomposition. Here in Norway, the only workers' party is the NAP.[29] It belonged to the Bureau

---

24 The Workers' and Peasants' Bloc established by Joaquin Maurin (1896-1973) in 1931 after his expulsion from the Spanish Communist Party. It joined with the Left Opposition group of Andres Nin (1892-1937) in 1935 to form the POUM. It is known as the BOC from its Spanish initials, and POB more usually refers to the Belgian Social Democratic party.

25 The Italian SP (Maximalist) was a faction within the exile Italian Social Democracy that aligned itself with the London Bureau.

26 The Austrian Red Front was a faction within the underground Austrian Social Democracy that aligned itself with the London Bureau.

27 A small group adhering to the London Bureau. It consistently supported the British ILP within the Bureau.

28 An organisation of no significance in the history of Bulgarian socialism. A small Trotskyist movement did however have some influence in the period 1931-33, under the leadership of Stefan Manov and Sider Todorov, when it published a paper called *Osvobozhdenie* (*Liberation*).

29 *Mot Dag* (*Towards Day*) is the name of a left-wing magazine which existed from 1921 to 1936, and of the group of intellectuals which formed round it under the leadership of Erling Falk. In the early period, from within the Labour Party (NAP) Falk was a

for two years, but does so no more and is in no way desirous of building a new International. Just now, I have received word that the NAP decided (on the very same day that the Dutch party withdrew from the Bureau) to sever even formal connections – for opposite political reasons. Only two parties of consequence remain to be considered – the ILP and the Swedish SP.[30] Already the latter grows cold to the Bureau as the SP turns to the right like the NAP. It is altogether likely that it will follow.

The Bureau suffers the fate of all centrist organisations in times of acute class struggle; it is destroyed by the release of the centrifugal forces within itself. We predicted that the IAG would lose both to the right and to the left. It is happening before our eyes, and even more quickly than we had expected. History could not arrange a better demonstration of the correctness of our analysis of centrism. If the ILP does not soon make up its mind it will find itself sitting in lonely possession of the Bureau.

Q: Was not Doriot also a member of the "Seven Lefts"?[31]

A: Certainly. He may never, for his own reasons, have adhered formally, but he was chosen with Schwab[32] and Gorkin[33] to form the Bureau's World Committee for Peace Work. The committee, of course, never functioned. Later, when Doriot came to terms with Laval he slipped out of the Committee as quickly as possible. Before, the IAG had met in St. Denis, under his protection. Later, when they called him on the phone it was always busy – connected with the government. Doriot is quite openly a traitor. It is interesting that at the last IAG conference Doriot was the loudest in condemning the Trotskyists for their slogan of the new International, and the SAP quoted him with enthusiastic approval.

Q: May not the Bureau recoup its losses from other forces?

particularly virulent opponent of its affiliation to the Communist International. The group was expelled from the NAP in 1925, but eventually rejoined it in 1936.

30 Formerly known as the Swedish Independent Communist Party.

31 Jacques Doriot (1898-1945) – a leader in turn of the Communist Party and of fascism in France. For a short period between 1934 and 1936 he took a centrist position, supporting the London Bureau (the 'Seven Lefts'), but winning no approval from Trotsky. He set up a fascist party in 1936.

32 Schwab, the real name of J. Walcher (1887-1970), a leader of the German SAP.

33 Gorkin, whose real name was Julian Gomez (1901-1987) – a leading member of the Spanish CP during the 1920s. Supported the Spanish Left Opposition for a time, later becoming a leader of the POUM.

A: The course of events is not that way. Zyromski, in France, has been the great hope of the IAG. He was, together with Pivert, a year in the Bataille Socialiste. Since that time, the Bataille Socialiste has ceased to exist. The reason? Like the Austrian Red Front, it had no clear programme, no banner. Pivert has moved further left and Zyromski has had to solidarise himself with the right, with Blum himself. Zyromski now plays the perfidious role of Stalinist social-patriot within the SFIO.

Pivert has now built up another left group, but this too will not last six months. It is composed of one element afraid of the patriots and another afraid of the Bolshevik-Leninists. The group calls itself 'Revolutionary Left'. It is a little left, but it is not yet revolutionary.

Q: What do you think of the Lovestoneite argument, which we hear in the ILP, that the CPSU must still be a good party because it exists in a workers' state.

A: That is not a Marxian argument, that is metaphysics. If a workers' state automatically produced a good government there would be no need for a communist party within it. The fact is that the CP as the government of the workers' state is not a 'thing-in-itself', but is subjected to the play of different historical forces. It can deviate, degenerate, become a danger to the existence of the workers' state. That is precisely what has happened in Russia.

* * *

Written 3 April 1936 and published in *Unser Wort*, May 1936.

Open Letter to an English Comrade

Dear Comrade,

The article written against me in the *New Leader* of 20 March of this year is sharp but incorrect. The sharpness is good. One must always welcome it when a revolutionary defends his ideas with sharpness and precision. Unfortunately, in spite of all the sharpness I fail to notice the necessary precision.

The polemical article sets itself the task of protecting the 'International Bureau for Revolutionary Socialist Unity' against my attacks. My criticism of the parties affiliated to the Bureau is said to be totally wrong. These parties are said to be by no means disintegrating, but on the contrary to be showing themselves more and more unified in the international struggle.

Let us try to verify these assertions. As far as I am concerned I know of only one single common international action of the London Bureau. That is the creation of the 'World Committee for Peace'. I carefully criticised at the time the programme of this committee proposed by the SAP on the basis of their document, and branded it with perfect justification, I think, as an expression of the shallowest petty-bourgeois pacifism. No one, not even the leaders of the SAP, has ever given to this criticism a material and pertinent answer. My point of view, consequently, remains valid. The parties which on the question of war adopt a pacifist attitude cannot be looked upon by a Marxist as revolutionary proletarian parties. Maxton, for instance, is a pacifist and not a Marxist. His war policy can perhaps contribute much to the saving of his soul but scarcely to the liberation of the working class.

The above-mentioned Committee was formed of three people: the German Schwab, the Frenchman Doriot (!), and the Spaniard Gorkin. Since then Doriot, the host of the last conference of the so-called Socialist Revolutionary Parties, has gone over with his clique to the reaction. Gorkin fought his election in Spain with a miserable democratic-pacifist programme of the People's Front. And, the third member, Schwab, has up to now not yet explained that the Committee for Peace was an anti-revolutionary undertaking and that the programme laid down by him, Schwab, of the 'Fight for Peace' mocks the whole teaching of Marx and Lenin in every word. (Incidentally there are still a few lamb-like people who think that they can still convince the minority of the SAP by endless, totally abstract discussion. We certainly believe that Schwab and some other leaders with their reactionary ideas are in the minority – but that this minority is to be won by good words, no, we are really not so naïve as to believe that.)

This, then, is at present the growing capacity of the London Bureau for 'united international action'.

I have never put a low value on small organisations merely because they are small. Even here the *New Leader* twists the Marxist criterion. The mass organisations have value precisely because they are mass organisations. Even when they are under patriotic reformist leadership one cannot discount them. One must win the masses who are in their clutches: whether from outside or from inside depends on the circumstance.

Small organisations which regard themselves as selective, as pioneers, can only have value on the strength of their programme and of the schooling and steeling of their cadres. A *small* organisation which has no unified programme and no really revolutionary will is less than nothing, is a negative quantity. In this sense I have spoken very contemptuously of the small groups in Bulgaria, Romania and Poland. Their confusion is really too big for their small compass. The revolutionary movement is only injured by them. On the other hand, the smallest of our groups are valuable because they know what they want and because they look back on the great tradition of Bolshevism with which they are internationally closely bound. Sooner or later every one of these groups will show its value.

The Austrian 'Red Front', which had united in itself the really militant worker elements, has united itself ostensibly with the Revolutionary Socialist Party of Austria, i.e., with the old Austro-Marxist Party.[34] Fenner Brockway's bulletin affirms: "The united party, although it is affiliated to the Second International, supports the anti-war policy of the IBRSU". This representation of Austro-Marxism is utterly wrong and confusing. Anyone who has read the theses of Messrs. Otto Bauer, Dan and Zyromski knows that Austro-Marxism represents even now nothing else than a cowardly, wretched falsification of Marxism, i.e., has remained completely true to its tradition. The 'Red Front' could accomplish revolutionary work in the Austro-Marxist Party under two closely related conditions: firstly, it must itself have clear principles; secondly, it must see clearly the rottenness of Austro-Marxism. Both conditions are completely missing (incidentally, one might mention that the *Neue Front*, the organ of the SAP, makes propaganda for *Der Kampf*, the Austro-Marxist organ). Actually the point is that the 'Red Front' is being absorbed in the Austro-Marxist slough.

The Norwegian group 'Mot-Dag' adopts the point of view of the Locarno Powers[35] and is now preparing to be absorbed in the Labour Party. This group too has been for years nothing else but confusion worse confounded.

It is really hardly worthwhile losing any more words about the Italian section (the Maximalists). It is enough to say that this 'revolutionary' organisation, together with the Italian Socialist Party (Second International) and the Italian Communist Party (Third International), has signed a common appeal in which it calls on the League of Nations to widen sanctions, and tries to instil into the Italian people that imperialist sanctions are a means of peace! Perhaps Fenner Brockway does not know of this appeal? Let him become acquainted with it. And if he does know why

---

34 This was the name adopted by the Austrian Social Democrats when they were made illegal by the clerical-fascist regimes of Dollfuss and Schuschnigg from 1933 onwards, and after they had broken from some of the older and more discredited right-wing leaders like Renner and Bauer.

35 Locarno was the venue for the conference held in 1925 of the main European powers except for the Soviet Union, i.e., France, Germany, Belgium, Britain, and Italy. It resulted in the non-aggression pact known as the Locarno Treaty.

does he treat these people as revolutionary friends and not as *traitors to proletarian internationalism?*

The policy article of the *New Leader* maintains that the Swedish Socialist Party feels itself more closely connected with the London Bureau than I have maintained. It is quite possible that this connection has recently become somewhat closer. But that the Swedish Socialist Party has an international attitude – that is either a naïve or consciously false legend. It is of course anti-war and it declares itself to be anti-League of Nations. But its 'fight' against war leads it hand-in-hand with the peace companies in the form of petitions. One could with the same success hold divine services for peace. But this method of action which manifests a shrieking contradiction between goal and method is enough to make us understand that the leaders of the Swedish Socialist Party with all their phraseology, which by the way changes very easily, are pacifistic philistines and certainly not proletarian revolutionaries, The peace policy of Kilboom, like that of a Schwab, is in the final analysis a small edition of the policy of Lord Cecil.[36] Every important event *in Sweden* will confirm this explanation.

The ILP cannot and will not admit that the Swedish Party is an anti-Marxist organisation, because its own leadership shows that it itself is through and through a pacifist-centrist party. We have heartily welcomed the series of truly revolutionary *New Leader* articles about sanctions[37] without any of those mental reservations with which the critic has reproached us. But one swallow does not make a summer. But even these articles bestow no Marxist halo upon the ILP. Maxton and the others remain what they were: petty-bourgeois pacifists, and *they* decide the party's course today as yesterday.

May I be permitted to point out that I publicly warned the ILP more than two years ago against the sterile alliance with the CPGB, as this alliance only multiplies the defects of both parties and diverts the attention of the ILP from the workers' mass organisations. Were these warnings right or not? The CPGB is ending in the slough of opportunism. But the ILP is now politically weaker than ever, and its own ideas remain as indefinite and hazy as they were two years ago.

Lastly a few more words about what the *New Leader* says concerning the organisations of the Fourth International: it calls them "merest cliques". In this

---

36 Lord Robert Cecil (1864-1958) – Tory MP from 1906-1923, President of the League of Nations Union from 1923-1945, and of the ad hoc 'National Declaration Committee' which conducted the 'Peace Ballot' of 1935.

37 See *Unser Wort*, Nos. 67 and 68.

characterisation ignorance surpasses dishonesty. Clique is the word used by us Marxists for a group of individuals who have neither programme nor high aim but who cluster round a leader in order to satisfy personal and certainly not praiseworthy desires. ('Sect', on the other hand, is the designation of a group with definite ideas and methods.) 'Clique' also implies lack of honour. Does the *New Leader* believe that our party, organisations and groups possess no principles, no programme, and no revolutionary consciousness? It would be really interesting to hear this sometime from Maxton or Fenner Brockway. On our side we maintain: we are the only international organisation which has developed in a struggle of many years an absolutely definite programme, which the greatest events confirm and strengthen every day. The passion with which all our organisations enter into discussion in order to clarify all the questions of the international workers' movement, the independence with which they develop their opinion, proves how seriously they understand Marxism and how many miles distant they are from an unprincipled clique spirit.

According to figures, too, they do not stand in any way inferior to the organisations around the London Bureau. A short time ago I proved, using the official Soviet press, that in the last few months of the year 1935 about 20,000 Bolshevik-Leninists had been expelled from the official Communist Party. I believe that in the Soviet Union alone we have more followers than the London Bureau has in the whole world. According to figures the Dutch party stands hardly inferior to the ILP. We have a courageous and militant section in France,[38] the focal point of European politics. Although the French comrades of the Fourth International have no representative in Parliament

---

38 Trotsky was well known to many of the leaders of French Communism and he secured the support of some of their number as early as 1923 when he warned in *The New Course* of the bureaucratic degeneration of the Russian Revolution. Various of them were expelled from the CP and began to produce the documents of the Soviet Left Opposition in different magazines. Eventually they came together to produce *La Verité* from August 1929, and in April 1930 established the 'Ligue Communiste'. Trotsky took a close interest in the development of his French supporters after that, and considered that the issues raised there had a significance that went well beyond France itself. In August 1934, with strong encouragement from Trotsky, the group entered the SFIO. Twenty-six prominent Bolshevik-Leninists were expelled from the SFIO in September 1935 as the party leadership lined up with the Popular Front. This led to further debate among the Trotskyists about how to proceed, and Trotsky gave firm support to those in favour of establishing an independent organisation, which was achieved with the founding of the Parti Communiste Internationaliste in March 1936.

they play a much more important part today in French political life. The fascist and capitalist press of France is an irrefutable proof of this. And this is not to be wondered at: the Bolshevik-Leninists put forward in a revolutionary situation a really revolutionary programme. It is true that our earlier Spanish section has declined into the worst opportunism. But why? Because it has fused with the section of the London Bureau in order to pursue 'big politics' in the wake of Señor Azaña.[39] Our friends in Belgium have fought their way to a significant influence.[40] Even in South America we have important and growing sections. Our American section, which has now joined the Socialist Party,[41] has gained within it considerable sympathy for its ideas. Incidentally, it seems to me that the flag of the Fourth International has some supporters even inside the ILP. And the number of these is systematically increasing.

The difference between the London Bureau and the association of the Fourth International is as follows: in the first case it is a question of different hybrid organisations with quite a different past, with different ideas and a different future which, being without a roof, have *temporarily* associated themselves with the International London Bureau; in contrast to this the sections of the Fourth International are selective bodies which came into existence on the basis of quite definite ideas and methods worked out in the struggle with the Second and Third Internationals and the London Bureau. That is the reason why we increase systematically in spite of enormous difficulties, why the influence of the Fourth International grows stronger and stronger, why the two old Internationals have entered into a holy alliance against it, and why, when all is said and done, the sections of the London Bureau associate themselves everywhere with this holy alliance. The article in the *New Leader* is only one of the many proofs of these circumstances.

With the same certitude with which we some years ago warned the ILP against the alliance with the CPGB, we affirm today that the ILP under its present leadership and on its present course is marching directly towards the abyss. We are at the same time no less certain that the best elements of the English workers' movement will group themselves around the standard of the Fourth International, for it is now the only flag of the proletarian revolution.

---

39 Manuel Azaña (1880-1940) – Leading bourgeois politician in Spain. Prime Minister in the republican government in June 1931 and again in 1936, and President of the Republic from May 1936 until his resignation in 1939.

40 The Belgian Workers Party (POB) which entered the Social Democratic party in 1935.

41 In June 1936 the American Trotskyists dissolved their organisation and joined the Socialist Party, at Trotsky's prompting.

The Decline of the ILP

A letter to a British comrade (dated 22 April 1936),
published in *Unser Wort*, May 1936.

On Dictators and the Heights of Oslo

Dear Comrade,

It is with great astonishment that I read the report of the conference of the Independent Labour Party in the [London] *New Leader* of 17 April 1936. I really never entertained any illusions about the pacifist parliamentarians who run the ILP. But their political position and their whole conduct at the conference exceeds even those bounds that can usually be expected of them. I am sure that you and your friends have drawn approximately the same conclusions as we have here. Nevertheless I cannot refrain from making several observations.

1. Maxton and the others opine that an Italo-Ethiopian war is conflict between two rival dictators. To these politicians it appears that this fact relieves the proletariat of the duty of making a choice between two dictators. They thus define the character of the war by the political *form* of the state, in the course of which they themselves regard this political form in a quite superficial and purely descriptive manner, without taking into consideration the social foundations of both 'dictatorships'. A dictator can also play a very progressive role in history. For example: Oliver Cromwell, Robespierre, etc. On the other hand, right in the midst of the English democracy Lloyd George exercised a

highly reactionary dictatorship during the war. Should a dictator place himself at the head of the next uprising of the Indian people in order to smash the British yoke – would Maxton then refuse this dictator his support? Yes or no? If no, why does he refuse his support to the Ethiopian 'dictator' who is attempting to ward off the Italian yoke?

If Mussolini triumphs, it means the re-enforcement of fascism, the strengthening of imperialism and the discouragement of the colonial peoples in Africa and elsewhere. The victory of the Negus,[1] however, would mean a mighty blow not only at Italian imperialism but at imperialism as a whole and would lend a powerful impulsion to the rebellious forces of the oppressed peoples. One must really be completely blind not to see this.

2. McGovern puts the 'poor little Abyssinia [Ethiopia]' of 1935 on the same level with the 'poor little Belgium' of 1914; in both cases it means support of war. Well, 'poor little Belgium' has 10,000,000 slaves in Africa, whereas the Abyssinian people are fighting in order not to become the slave of Italy. Belgium was and remains a link of the European imperialist chain. Abyssinia is only a victim of imperialist appetites. Putting the two cases on the same plane is sheerest nonsense.

On the other hand, to take up the defence of Abyssinia against Italy in no way means to encourage British imperialism to war. At one time this is just what was very well demonstrated in several articles of the *New Leader*. McGovern's conclusion that it should have been the ILP's task "to stand aside from quarrels between dictators", is an exemplary model of the spiritual and moral impotence of pacifism.

3. The most shameful thing of all, however, only comes after the voting. After the conference had rejected the scandalous pacifist quackery by a vote of seventy to fifty-seven, the tender pacifist Maxton put the revolver of an ultimatum at the breast of the conference and forced a new decision by a vote of ninety-three to thirty-nine. So we see that there are dictators not only in Rome and in Addis Ababa, but also in London. And of the three dictators, I consider most harmful him who grabs his own party by the throat in the name of his parliamentary prestige and his pacifist confusion. A party that tolerates such conduct is no revolutionary party; for if it surrenders (or 'postpones') its principled position in a highly important and topical question because of threats

---

1 Haile Selassie (1892-1975) – Emperor of Ethiopia 1930-1974. "Negus" is Amharic for "King".

of resignation made by Maxton, then at the grave moment it will never withstand the immeasurably mightier pressure of the bourgeoisie.

4. By an overwhelming majority, the conference forbade the existence of groups inside the party. Good! But in whose name did Maxton put an ultimatum to the conference? In the name of the parliamentary group which regards the party machine as its private property and which actually represents the only faction that should have been sharply drubbed into respect for the democratic decisions of the party. A party which dissolves the oppositional groups but lets the ruling clique do as it jolly well pleases, is no revolutionary party. It will not be able to lead the proletariat to victory.

5. Fenner Brockway's position on this question is a highly instructive example of the political and moral insufficiency of centrism. Fenner Brockway was lucky enough to adopt a correct point of view in an important question, a view that coincides with ours. The difference lies in this, however, that we Marxists really mean the thing seriously. To Fenner Brockway, on the contrary, it is a matter of something 'incidental'. He believes it is better for the British workers to have Maxton as chairman with a false point of view than to have a correct point of view without Maxton. That is the fate of centrism – to consider the incidental serious and the serious thing incidental. That's why centrism should never be taken seriously.

6. In the question of the International, the old confusion was once more sealed, despite the obvious bankruptcy of the previous perspective. In any case, nothing more is said about the 'invitation' from the Third International. But the centrist doesn't take anything seriously. Even when he now admits that there is no longer a proletarian international, he nevertheless hesitates to build one up. Why? Because he has no principles. Because he can't have any. For if he but once makes the sober attempt to adopt a principled position in only one important question, he promptly receives an ultimatum from the right and starts to climb down. How can he think of a rounded-out revolutionary programme under such circumstances? He then expresses his spiritual and moral helplessness in the form of profound aphorisms, that the new International must come 'from the development of socialist movements', that is, from the historical process which really ought to produce something some day. This dubious ally has various ways, however: he even got to the point of reducing the Leninist International

to the level of the Second. Proletarian revolutionists should therefore strike out on their own path, that is, work out the programme of the new International and, basing themselves on the *favourable* tendencies of the historical process, help this programme gain prevalence.

7. Fenner Brockway, after his lamentable capitulation to Maxton, found his courage again in struggle against the undersigned. He, Brockway, cannot allow a new International to be constructed from "the heights of Oslo". I leave aside the fact that I do not live in Oslo and that, besides, Oslo is not situated on heights. The principles which I defend in common with many thousand comrades, bear absolutely no local or geographical character. They are Marxian and international. They are formulated, expounded and defended in theses, brochures and books. If Fenner Brockway finds these principles to be false, let him put up against them his own. We are always ready to be taught better. But unfortunately Fenner Brockway cannot venture into this field, for he has just turned over to Maxton that oh-so-paltry parcel of principles. That is why there is nothing left for him to do save to make merry about the "heights of Oslo", wherein he promptly commits a threefold mistake: with respect to my address, to the topography of the Norwegian capital and, last but not least, to the fundamental principles of international action.

My conclusions? The cause of the ILP seems to me to be hopeless. The thirty-nine delegates who, despite the failure of the Fenner Brockway faction, did not surrender to Maxton's ultimatum, must seek ways of preparing a truly revolutionary party for the British proletariat. It can only stand under the banner of the Fourth International.

Leon Trotsky

*   *   *

Interview with Collins,[2] *Internal Bulletin* of the
Marxist Group, Summer 1936.

Collins: Should the Marxist Group[3] oppose or favour Communist Party affiliation to the Labour Party?

---

2 Sam Collins – British Trotskyist and a member of the Marxist Group in the ILP. This interview with Trotsky was the last direct contact the British movement had with him.

3 This was the name adopted by the main group of Trotsky's supporters in Britain in this period. At this point, in mid-1936, their period of entry in the ILP was just coming

Trotsky: The question becomes sheer pedantry and completely meaningless in view of the smallness, the weakness and lack of clear perspective in the group itself. However, whatever the position of the group, it is essential to support critically the affiliation of the Communist Party – for two reasons. 1) If we refuse to support, we shall be riding against the mass desire for unity. 2) That the mistakes of the Communist Party in the Labour Party and their inevitable alliance with the bureaucracy will give us the opportunity of winning their best elements. *But only if we are inside the Labour Party ourselves.* The whole question revolves around the italicised sentence. If that is ignored, all speculation is metaphysical and has nothing in common with Marxism.

Collins: Whom do you think is correct – Cooper[4] or Matlow[5] – on the question of the group perspective?

Trotsky: In my opinion, Matlow is 100 per cent correct. In view of the international situation England must inevitably develop in common with the rest of Europe. That must give rise to a strike wave in the near future, which will drive the last nail into the coffin of the ILP. The ILP is not a mass but a propaganda organisation, and since their propaganda is centrist and not revolutionary, this dying corpse must be completely swept away during a working class resurgence. I consider that the rigid, formalistic position of the Cooper paper has no relationship to Marxism at all. It shows a complete lack of comprehension of the class struggle. The idea of remaining inside the ILP for a further period in order to win a few more wavering elements, whilst the Communist Party is rapidly penetrating into the mass organisations, is ridiculous. We can only win these wavering elements in the ILP by our entry into the Labour Party and the effective work we will do in there. The

---

to an end. The same name was then taken over by one of the main groups to emerge, under the leadership of C. L. R. James.

4 Arthur Cooper – British Trotskyist. Expelled from the CPGB in 1933 then joining the ILP, and afterwards the Marxist Group within it. In 1936 he proposed that the Trotskyists should remain within the ILP but was nevertheless expelled himself in the September of that year. Opposed the subsequent entry into the Labour Party, but remained active in the Trotskyist movement.

5 Albert Matlow (1898-1987) – British Trotskyist. Played a leading part in founding the Marxist Group. In the summer of 1936 he advocated that all British Trotskyists should join the Labour Party and took the chair at the founding conference of the Militant Labour League at the end of 1937. He remained active in the Labour Party from some time after, though as a left social democrat.

waverers remaining in the ILP will inevitably leave in disgust as the ILP disintegrates further, and in their attempt to find a new orientation must inevitably come to us in the Labour Party, if we adopt a correct line at once. The argument that it is still possible to win a few more of the waverers in the ILP is sheer formalism, as for every one that we might win in the ILP there are hundreds in the Labour Party. The argument that we may be able to capture the apparatus of the ILP is at best hypothetical, and even if successful must mean a struggle of years in view of the strength of the bureaucracy. We have not eternity before us. We are too generous with our time, which is very precious; and we are not rich enough to spend it at such a rate. The experience of the Belgian and French sections[6] demonstrates conclusively the tremendous possibilities that unfold themselves inside the mass reformist organisations. Unless we accept that perspective we can play no significant revolutionary role in the history of Great Britain.

---

6   In July 1934 Trotsky proposed that the members of the French Communist League join the SFIO – the tactical change known as the 'French turn'. At that time the SFIO was about five times larger than the CP, with much greater trade union influence. In November 1933 the right-wing 'Neos' had split away. The left-wing groupings expelled by them were invited to return, factions were permitted to operate and to produce their own papers. Centrist and leftward-moving currents were rapidly developing, especially among the youth. Trotsky saw, not only the possibilities for the building of a revolutionary tendency, but also the danger of not intervening, as the Stalinists dropped their ultra-left 'social-fascist' line and began moving towards making a pact with the social-democratic leaders. Later in 1934, Trotsky made similar proposals in relation to the Spanish Socialist Party and the Socialist Party of Belgium. He also supported the merger of the Communist League of America with A. J. Muste's American Workers' Party. In 1936, the fused organisation entered the American Socialist Party.

The tactic of 'entry' into social-democratic parties aimed at enabling the groups adhering to the International Communist League (ICL) (formally the International Left Opposition) to make important experiences within the developing struggles of the working class in the fight for the Fourth International. It was fiercely opposed within the ICL, especially by the followers of Oehler in the American group. Some of these opponents later found their way into the centrist parties of the London Bureau. But when the opportunities arose in each case of 'entry' to break from the social democracy and form open revolutionary parties as sections of the Fourth International, there was opposition to the break, in some cases from those who had opposed 'entry'.

Collins: Since we have already missed the opportunity of the plebiscite issue, what issue can we raise in order to split from the ILP?

Trotsky: It is essential to choose a political issue comprehensible to the broad mass of workers. To raise a fight on the existence of legal groups within the ILP would be completely useless. I can only offer some suggestions from this distance. A struggle raised to commit the ILP on our theses at our recent conference is one possibility, particularly the thesis on the revolutionary upsurge already printed in the French paper. Possibly, however, a better example would be the question of the ILP affiliation to the Labour Party. That question we must pose immediately and as strongly as possible.

Collins: Should the group place any conditions upon the entry of the ILP into the Labour Party?

Trotsky: That kind of knightly courtesy has no place in politics. Since the ILP bureaucracy have made our group illegal and have suppressed our paper,[7] it would be ridiculous for us to fight for privileges on behalf of the ILP. Our duty is to get into the Labour Party, with or without the ILP, as rapidly as possible. It is not possible for me from this distance to choose either the precise issue or the time to be taken in the struggle for the split. If we remember that time is precious and the matter is extremely urgent, we will not go far wrong. In any event, the suggestion of a time limit such as the next annual conference of the ILP in April is incomprehensible to me. The European situation is developing so rapidly that history will not wait for the ILP conference.

Collins: How shall we enter the Labour Party and how shall we work within it?

Trotsky: In view of the weakness of the Marxist Group, it may be necessary to cater as individuals first and spend one, two, or three months in exploring the avenues of work. The important thing is to get in. Once in, opportunities will rapidly unfold. It is understood that regardless of how we enter, we will have a secret faction from the very beginning. Our subsequent actions will depend on our progress within the Labour Party. It is very important that we do not lay ourselves open at the beginning to attacks from the Labour Party bureaucracy, which will result in our expulsion without having gained any appreciable strength. Our first attacks must be directed against the

---

7   At the ILP National Conference in Keighley, Easter 1936, the bloc of Brockway and Maxton secured a majority for prohibiting the existence of organised factions in the party. Its purpose was to prevent the Marxist Group in the ILP from circulating Trotskyist material through their journal, *The Marxist Bulletin*.

inconsistency of the centrists and not the bureaucracy. That again must be determined by what we find once we are inside. Obviously, we will not be able to raise the issue of the Fourth International immediately. History will provide the opportunity for raising that issue. The question of the Fourth International is not a burning issue to the masses of Great Britain today. If we take a revolutionary position on the popular issues that concern the masses today, then inevitably we will be able to develop towards the question of the Fourth International. At all costs we must be very careful to avoid either sectarianism or opportunism – we must continually have our fingers on the pulse of the masses. It is well to remember that as the political situation develops, revolutionary work will be increasingly dangerous and we will be better protected within the broad masses of the Labour Party than in the isolated and rotting corpse of the ILP, if even a corpse remains by then. It will undoubtedly be correct to leave a few capable comrades within the ILP to do fraction work. As regards the Marxist Group when we enter the Labour Party, a situation may rapidly arise requiring one or two of our best speakers to bring forth our complete revolutionary position thus deliberately inviting expulsion for themselves, as martyrs are useful to every movement. Such expelled comrades will find useful avenues of work, e.g., in the Lenin Club.

Collins: Do you think that the idea of the Lenin Club, as developed by the ILP group, will be useful in our future work within the Labour Party?

Trotsky: That will also depend on the concrete conditions that we find in the Labour Party, but from this distance it would appear that it could serve a useful function. But if it is to be of any use, it must be democratically controlled with representatives from all the Bolshevik-Leninists and not merely the ILP group. Anything else would be pure sectarianism.

Collins: Should the paper proposed by [C. L. R.] James be run as an independent organ of the acknowledged Trotskyists within the political organisations such as the Labour Party or as the organ of the Lenin Club without party affiliation?

Trotsky: That is difficult to say, as it must obviously depend on objective conditions. In any case, we must first make every effort to merge with the Groves-Dewar group.[8]

---

8 Reg Groves and Hugo Dewar were ex-members of the CPGB expelled in August 1932 as supporters of Trotsky, who formed the majority of the Communist League, opposing the entry into the ILP advised by the International Secretariat in 1934. They

I understand from Comrade Collins that previous approaches to Groves-Dewar have met with rebuffs. Even if that remains true once we are inside the Labour Party, the supporters of Groves-Dewar must realise that we are 100 per cent with them and further rebuffs from their two leaders should result in their coming over to us. In the event of our failure to secure the *Red Flag* as the organ of our tendency, then we will have to decide which is better for our work – an independent Lenin Club organ, or a group paper within the Labour Party. To me this question is not of first-rate importance, as in any case the Stalinists would expose our connection with a Lenin Club paper. This development on the part of the Stalinists we can anticipate without any question. Just as the Labour bureaucracy serves as the police of capitalism within the ranks of the working class, so the Stalinist leaders will act as the police of the Labour Party bureaucracy. This identification of the Labour Party and Communist Party bureaucracies will afford us an excellent opportunity to win over the rank and file of the Communist Party. The entire question of a paper and of a Lenin Club becomes formalistic and unreal while we remain outside the Labour Party and isolated from the masses.

Collins: What should our attitude be towards Peace Councils?[9]

Trotsky: The question of the Peace Council bears a certain resemblance to that of the People's Front. For example, in France, we tell the workers that we know that the People's Front is all wrong. While the workers support it, we say to them that we are perfectly willing to collaborate loyally with the working-class organisations, the Communist Party, and the Socialist Party, but we refuse under any circumstances to have anything to do with the bourgeois participants in the People's Front. We do not shout: "Down with the People's Front!" at present because we have nothing to replace it as yet. In the same manner, we cannot turn our backs on the Peace Councils and say: "Down with the Peace Councils!" because as yet there is no revolutionary party to give a clear lead on the question of war and peace. In the analogy, however, there is this fundamental difference. One is a question of state

---

remained as an 'open party', continuing to produce *Red Flag*. During the course of 1935 they rejoined the Labour Party and in 1936 declined to accept the advice of the Geneva pre-conference of the Fourth International that they should unite with others in the Labour Party claiming allegiance to Trotskyism. They were considered to be acting in an opportunist manner.

9 Peace Councils – CP front organisations, which appear never to have achieved mass support.

power in a revolutionary situation. The other is a question of using existing committees as long as they are supported by mass workers' organisations. Therefore, it is necessary to get representatives wherever possible on the Peace Councils and to direct our attacks in the beginning against certain of the bourgeois participants (who these will be depends on the reaction of the workers to our propaganda). It is understood, of course, that the very first task of revolutionaries in any mass organisation is to demand that it be democratically controlled by the workers. That agitation will give us our first opportunity of attacking the private invitations given out by the Communist Party bureaucrats to so-called progressive bourgeois figures. By attacking the leading bourgeois pacifists and subsequently the participation of all bourgeois elements, we will inevitably run counter to the class-collaborationist policies of the LP-CP bureaucrats. We can then say to the workers: "We have our differences with Comrades Morrison, Pollitt, and Lansbury, but we are perfectly willing to work loyally with them. They, however, wish to expel us because we refuse to work with open class enemies." This will have the effect of making the LP-CP bureaucrats bear the responsibility of open class collaboration before the workers. This situation correctly used will discredit not only the bureaucrats but also the entire idea of Peace Councils. *But it is first necessary to get on to them.*

Collins: How can we best deal with the very important colonial question, a fundamental question which we have so far almost entirely ignored?

Trotsky: A study of the First Four Congresses of the Comintern is essential. In addition, the general theses of the Fourth International of the colonial question will serve to indicate the general line, but the concrete application will be determined by the special situation.

Collins: Is it even possible to consider at this stage an independent existence outside the mass organisations?

Trotsky: The fact that Lenin was not afraid to split from Plekhanov in 1905 and to remain as a small isolated group bears no weight because the same Lenin remained inside the Social Democracy until 1912 and in 1920 urged the affiliation of the British Communist Party to the Labour Party. While it is necessary for the revolutionary party to maintain its independence at all times, a revolutionary group of a few hundred comrades is not a revolutionary party and can work most effectively at present by opposition to the social patriots within the mass parties. In view of the increasing acuteness of the international situation, it is absolutely essential to be within the mass organisations while there is the possibility of doing revolutionary work within them. Any such sectarian, sterile, and formalistic interpretation of Marxism in the present situation would disgrace an intelligent child of ten.

* * *

From a letter to the Central Committee of the RSAP (Holland) (dated 15 July 1936), *Informatie en Discussie Bulletin*, 1 July 1937.

Let us take the ILP question. I really cannot reproach myself with any precipitateness on this question. For years I followed the evolution of this party, quite calmly and objectively. After Schmidt's[10] and Paton's visit to me,[11] from which I learned a great deal, I wrote a series of articles and letters of an entirely friendly kind to the ILP people, sought to enter into personal contact with them, and counselled our English friends to join the ILP in order, from within, to go through the experience systematically and to the very end. Since the last visit of Comrades R. and A., I formulated my observations in this sense, that there isn't much to be done with the ILP. The three of us worked out a definite proposal for our British comrades (a manifesto to the party, collection of signatures, etc.). Comrade Schmidt went to England and judged the plan to be incorrect. Naturally, this was not without its influence on the comrades, as well as on me. I immediately said to myself: Schmidt knows the situation in the ILP better than I do; perhaps he sees in the ILP such aspects as escape me; therefore the decision should perhaps be postponed in order to see the effect of the latest big events (the war in Abyssinia, etc.) at the coming party conference of the ILP. To lose two to three months in a critical period is always a great loss. But it seemed to me, after comrade Schmidt's intervention, that it is necessary to go through this new experience. Well, it is now already behind us. To continue now with an effort to revive the illusion which has been shattered to bits, would be nothing less than to inflict a bad service on the cause. In times of calm, one can live on illusions for a long

---

10 Peter J. Schmidt (1896-1962) – Leader of the Dutch social democrats and associated with the Stalinists in the 1920s. In 1932 he split away and formed the Dutch Independent Socialist Party. Chairman of the Paris conference of the 'London Bureau' in August 1933.

11 They visited Trotsky, who was in France at the time, while the Paris conference was taking place, discussing with him the building of a new International. For Trotsky the role of the Comintern in Hitler's rise to power earlier that year had proved the necessity for this.

period; in a period of crisis, if one does not take into account the hard facts, that is, the actual policy of centrism and pacifism, and consequently their deeds, but considers one's own wishes and sentiments, one courts the danger of becoming the shadow of the centrists and pacifists and of compromising and destroying one's own organisation. That is why I deem it absolutely necessary for our comrades to break openly with the ILP and to transfer to the Labour Party where, as is shown especially by the experience in the Youth, much more can be accomplished.

* * *

From the transcript of a discussion with C. L. R. James, held in April 1939, published in the *Internal Bulletin* (Socialist Workers Party), 20 December 1939.

Trotsky: Great Britain and the ILP? It is also a special task. I followed it a bit more closely when I was in Norway. It seems to me that our comrades who entered the ILP had the same experience with the ILP that our American comrades made with the Socialist Party. But not all our comrades entered the ILP and they developed an opportunistic policy so far as I could observe, and that is why their experience in the ILP was not so good. The ILP remained almost as it was before while the Socialist Party is now empty. I do not know how to approach it now. It is now a Glasgow organisation. It is a local machine and they have influence in the municipal machine, and I have heard that it is very corrupt. It is a separate job of Maxton. Rebellions of the rank and file are a familiar thing in the ILP. In preparing for a new convention, Fenner Brockway becomes a patron of the rebellious section and secures a majority. Then Maxton says he will resign. Then Fenner Brockway says: "No, we will abandon our victory. We can give up our principles, but not our Maxton." I believe that the most important thing is to compromise them – to put them in the mud – the Maxtons and the Brockways. We must identify them with class enemies. We must compromise the ILP with tremendous and pitiless attacks on Maxton. He is the sacrificial goat for all the sins of the British movement and the especially the ILP. By such concentrated attacks on Maxton, systematic attacks in our press, we can expedite the split in the ILP. At the same time we must point out that if Maxton is the lackey of Chamberlain, then Fenner Brockway is the lackey of Maxton.

James: What do you think of an independent paper for the work of slashing at Maxton, etc?

Trotsky: It is a practical question. In France, if our section enters the PSOP I believe that the International Secretariat should publish the *Quatriéme Internationale* for all French-speaking countries twice-monthly. It is simply a question of the juridical possibility. I believe that even if we work inside the Labour Party we must have an independent paper, not as opposed to our comrades within, but rather to be outside the control of the ILP.

* * *

From a letter to Daniel Guerin (dated 10 March 1939),
Byulleten Oppozitsii March-April 1939.

Of the ILP it is not worth while speaking at length. I will only recall a very recent fact. The leader of this party, Maxton, thanked Chamberlain in Parliament after the Munich pact and declared to astonished humanity that by his policy Chamberlain had saved the peace – yes, yes, had saved the peace! – that he, Maxton, knew Chamberlain well and he assured that Chamberlain had "sincerely" fought the war and "sincerely" saved the peace, etc., etc. This single example gives a conclusive and what is more a pretty crushing characterisation of Maxton and of his party. The revolutionary proletariat rejects Chamberlain's "peace" just as it does his war. The "peace" of Chamberlain is the continuation of the violence against India and other colonies and the preparation of the war in conditions more favourable for the British slaveholders. To take upon himself the slightest shadow of responsibility for the policy of "peace" of Chamberlain, is not possible for a socialist, for a revolutionist, but only for a pacifist lackey of imperialism. The party that tolerates a leader like Maxton and actions like his public solidarisation with the slaveholder Chamberlain is not a socialist party but a miserable pacifist clique.

* * *

From the transcript of a discussion with C. L. R. James held
in April 1939, published in the *Internal Bulletin* (SWP), January 1940.

Trotsky: What is… dangerous is the sectarian approach to the Labour Party. You say that I put forward the slogan of Blum-Cachin[12] without reservations. Then you remember "All power to the soviet!", and you say that the united front has no soviet. It is the same sectarian approach.

James: We have had difficulty in Britain with advocating a Labour government with the necessary reservations.

12 The call for a government of the main working-class parties, at that time the SFIO led by Léon Blum, and the PCF, whose leaders included Marcel Cachin (1869-1958).

Trotsky: In France in all our press, in our archives and propaganda, we regularly made all the necessary reservations. Your failure in Britain is due to lack of ability; also lack of flexibility, due to the long domination of bourgeois thought in Britain. I would say to British workers, "You refuse to accept my point of view. Well, perhaps I did not explain well enough. Perhaps you are stupid. Anyway I have failed. But now, you believe in your party. Why allow Chamberlain to hold the power? Put your party in power. I will help you all I can. I know that they will not do what you think, but as you don't agree with me and we are small, I will help you put them in." But it is very important to bring up the questions periodically. I would suggest that you write an article discussing these points and publish it in our press.

Letters to Sumner[1]

Avenida Londres 127
Coyoacán, D. F.
Mexico

21 May 1937

Dear Comrade Sumner,

I am sincerely grateful to you for your friendly and very informative letter. I can very well understand the obstacles you have to overcome, but it is beyond doubt that every new month will see the situation change in your favour. The only difficulty was to begin the investigation; now the truth will reveal itself almost as automatically as a natural force. All these ladies and gentlemen,

---

1 The following three letters were written by Trotsky to Hilary Sumner-Boyd, the then secretary of the Revolutionary Socialist League. The third of these letters (29 June 1938) was thought to be missing until it was rediscovered in May 2018. In this letter, Trotsky mentions receiving an English edition of his pamphlet on Spain and praises the accompanying introduction. This introduction was written by Ralph Lee and Ted Grant, leading members of the Workers' International League, a predecessor organisation to the International Marxist Tendency. Whilst the first two letters were published in Trotsky's *Works*, the third one never appeared. It was clearly suppressed by the leaders of the US Socialist Workers Party, especially James Cannon, for factional reasons. For a full explanation and for Grant's introduction see *Lessons of Spain*, International Marxist Tendency, 2019.

including such political old wives as Brailsford and Fenner Brockway, will soon notice that the ground is becoming hot under them, and they will try to join the camp of the truth to avoid being definitely compromised. We can, openly and with full assurance, predict our victory over the masters of frame-up and their agents of the first and second degrees. The shift which is now occurring in the United States will undoubtedly influence your situation in England favourably.

Please transmit my respectful greetings to your mother and my best wishes to all our friends in England.

Fraternally yours,
Leon Trotsky

* * *

15 April 1938

Dear Comrade Sumner,

I haven't written you for a long time but you understand the reasons. We received your cable and your letter and both Natalia and I warmly appreciate your friendly feelings…

I don't know whether you have been informed about the trip of Comrade Cannon to Europe and in the first line to London. It is possible that Comrade Shachtman will also go with Cannon. I ascribe great importance to this trip especially for things in England. Cannon and Shachtman are our best comrades in the States, with a wide outlook and with serious organisational experience. One of their tasks is to meet all the English groups who belong or wish to belong to the Fourth International and to try to normalise the situation among these groups in order to help the crystallisation of a genuine British section of the Fourth International. I hope that you and your group will give Cannon and Shachtman your full cooperation in their task.

I doubt that they can remain in London for more than a week, possibly less. It is absolutely necessary to use this time as well as possible. The best procedure it seems to me would be to enter now into connection with the other groups and even to establish a technical committee with the purpose of arranging the meeting of the American friends with each of the British groups separately, and then with all of them together. You will surely receive in time a communication specifying the precise day of arrival of the American friends in London. I should be very glad to have a note from you about the preparation for the discussions with C and S and also later about the results of these discussions.

I receive your publications. Thanks. But I write today only on the 'C-S' trip. Best greetings from Natalia and me to you and all friends.

Yours fraternally,
Trotsky

Coyoacán, D. F.
LT: joe 61-18

———

P. S. – I have received a letter from Frank Maitland in the name of the 'Revolutionary Socialist Party'. He wished to publish my article upon Spain as a pamphlet and is ready to do it in cooperation with one of our British groups. The evolution of his party, he writes me, is totally in the direction of the Fourth International. Are you in connection with them? I am writing to Maitland today.

* * *

29 June 1938

Dear Comrade Sumner,

I received your edition of my Spain pamphlet with your excellent introduction. It was really a good revolutionary idea to create one's own printing shop.

We received Leon's letter to you which turned out to be his last letter. I don't remember whether I answered you at that time. Natalia was very touched by your attention.

I wrote you about Cannon's and Shachtman's trip to Europe and especially to England and the plans connected with this trip. Did you receive this letter? You never answered me on this matter.

My warmest greetings to you and to your friends.

Yours,
Leon Trotsky

Coyoacán, D. F.

LT: joe 71.2

Stalinism and Centrism

Written on 6 March 1937 and published in the
Information Bulletin of the British Committee for the
Defence of Leon Trotsky, July 1937.

Fenner Brockway – Pritt Number Two

The Secretary of the Independent Labour Party of Great Britain, Fenner
Brockway, runs to the aid of Pritt,[1] the King's Counsellor, with a plan to
save the Moscow falsifiers. Pritt Number One tried to resolve the task
juridically. Pritt Number Two considers the task politically. An international
inquiry into the Moscow trials, according to Fenner Brockway's way of
thinking, is impermissible because it might arouse "prejudice in Russia
and in Communist circles". Fenner Brockway thus recognises beforehand
that an impartial verification could not confirm the Moscow accusations
and justify the executions. On the contrary, Brockway is convinced that
an honest and open inquiry can only "prejudice" Stalin's clique and
"Communist circles". That is precisely why Pritt Number Two proposes
to organise an "inquiry into the role of Trotskyism in the Working-Class
Movement". In other words: instead of establishing the objective truth
regarding the monstrous, criminal accusations, Brockway proposes a
partisan political trial against his ideological adversary. Furthermore,
Brockway considers – and who can know Brockway better than himself –
that he is marked in advance by the finger of fate to assume an initiative

---

1   Denis Nowell Pritt (1887-1973) – Stalinist fellow-traveller of upper class background
    and Labour Party membership.

of this nature. He even points magnanimously to a future jury of "four or five persons" who have "objective analytical minds". As candidates Brockway names: the Austrian social-democrat Otto Bauer, the "Danish" (Swedish?) lawyer Branting, the head of the Socialist Party of the United States, Norman Thomas, and... a "good Frenchman". This commission, to which he hopes, according to his own words, to assure the indispensable finances, will pass a judgement on the "role of Trotskyism in the Working Class Movement". It is difficult to imagine a more ridiculous and, at the same time, a more cunning project! My "attitude in respect to the Working Class Movement", leaving aside my forty years of revolutionary activity, is expressed at present in the following formula:

The guiding apparatuses of the Second and Third Internationals have become obstacles on the road of the emancipation of the proletariat. If a new war is bearing down on humanity with implacable force, the responsibility for that circumstance falls on the leadership of the Second and Third Internationals. I believe that the creation of a new International is inevitable and necessary, on the basis of the programme which is explained and developed in my books and articles as well as in the works of my ideological friends. At the same time the so-called Trotskyites are always and everywhere ready to sustain every practical step of the Second and Third Internationals against fascism and reaction in general, when it is a question of real acts of struggle and not of cheap parades, deceitful shows of unification, or in general, of all those things which throw dust in one's eyes.

With bureaucratic charlatanism and 'democratic' verbiage *we have nothing* in common! For these ideas I fight entirely openly. My adversaries have the full right and the full possibility to submit me to the most severe criticism. Up to now they have made great use of this right. I have never complained on that score. The struggle goes on for the supreme ends of humanity. Only the ultimate advance of the historical process can resolve these implacable discords. I patiently await its verdict. If, however, Brockway, together with Otto Bauer and the anonymous "good Frenchman", wishes to anticipate the verdict of history, I can only wish them great successes. It is not the first time that such attempts have been made.

Messrs. Fenner Brockway and Otto Bauer have more than once judged Lenin, especially from 1914 to 1917, and also later, together with the Russian Mensheviks, as a sectarian, a splitter, a disorganiser and an auxiliary of counter-revolution. Such men, in alliance with "good Frenchmen" and also "good" Germans, in the middle of the nineteenth century, more than once judged and annihilated Marx and Engels. I am ready to submit to the same fate to which my great masters were very often subjected.

However, Brockway's plan takes on a manifestly *dishonest* character at the point where he tries to replace a juridical inquiry into the criminal accusations and the trials, more exactly, into the greatest frame-ups in the world,[2] with a factional political intrigue to avoid the "prejudice" of Stalin and his agents. Here the advanced workers will say: Stop! Brockway's fears, whatever may be their source, will not hinder the truth from triumphing over the lie!

As to the candidates indicated by Brockway for his political intrigue, I can say the following: in the last years I wrote a dozen articles in which I attempted to explain in a friendly manner to Fenner Brockway himself and to his friends that their unprincipled politics, zig-zagging from right to left under the whip of the Stalintern, would inevitably destroy the Independent Labour Party. Now this prognosis, alas, is completely confirmed. I have known Otto Bauer for thirty years as a political invertebrate, who has always adapted himself to the class enemy: to the defunct Habsburg monarchy, to the Austrian bourgeoisie, to Wilson, to the Entente, and who, precisely because of the fact, has become chiefly responsible for the crushing of the Austrian proletariat. Again, in 1922 Bauer thought that the Soviet dictatorship arrested 'progress', which, in his opinion, then demanded the return of Russia to the road of capitalism. Now Bauer bows low before the Soviet bureaucracy, which is arresting progress toward socialism. The analysis of Otto Bauer's rotten politics is given in dozens of my writings. Bauer himself has never tried to reply to them. I cannot say anything about Branting, who is recommended as a 'lawyer', although it is not a question of

---

2   The assassination in December 1934 of Sergei Kirov (1886-1934), boss of the Leningrad party machine, which was believed to have been engineered by the GPU itself, was the signal for a succession of murderous attacks on former leaders of the Russian Bolshevik Party, including Lenin's closest collaborators. This culminated in a series of show trials held in Moscow at which the leaders of all sections of the Russian Bolsheviks, including those who had at one time been the strongest supporters of Stalin himself, were forced to confess to crimes both fantastic and inconceivable. The first of these was held in August 1936 and the chief defendants were Zinoviev, Kamenev, and Smirnov. A second trial took place in January 1937, where the defendants included Radek and Pyatakov, and a third began at the end of February 1938, when Bukharin, Rykov, Rakovsky, and Yagoda appeared in the dock. In nearly all cases the main defendants were executed, though it seems that Radek may have survived in prison for a number of years.

juridical, but of theoretical and political, problems. As for Norman Thomas he has never hidden his disagreements with me, and on my part I have no reason to attenuate their profundity. But Norman Thomas thinks that however profound these differences may be, and however acute the struggle of tendencies and fractions, certain methods are inadmissible, criminal, corrupt, menacing equally all parts of the proletariat. Without purging the workers' ranks of terror, sabotage, espionage, etc. – if they exist – or of frame-ups, falsifications, despicable juridical assassinations – and they certainly exist! – the working-class movement as a whole is menaced by gangrene. Here there is common ground between myself and Norman Thomas and all those who seriously concern themselves with the internal morale of the working-class movement. With Brockway such a common ground does not and cannot exist. As a political man, Brockway can judge Trotskyism as he likes; that is his right. But as Pritt Number Two he must be met with a merciless counter-thrust.

* * *

Written on 5 September 1937 and published in
Socialist Appeal, 18 September 1937.

London Bureau Aids Stalin Frame-ups – Once More on Fenner Brockway

'The London Bureau of Revolutionary Socialist Parties' was invited, together with the Second and Third Internationals, to participate in the International Commission of Inquiry on the Moscow trials.[3] On 21 May Fenner Brockway, in the name of the London Bureau, rejected the invitation. The pertinent section of his reply reads verbatim as follows:

---

3   In order to counter the lies of the Moscow Trials, Trotsky decided after his arrival in Mexico in February 1936 and the beginning of the second trial to run a 'counter-trial' at which publicity could be given to the unstated case for the defence. In March 1937 a Joint Commission of Enquiry was set up by American, British, French, and Czech bodies for the defence of Trotsky. Its chairman was John Dewey, the American pragmatist philosopher and educationalist, and other members included American writers and academics and former Communist Party members of the German Reichstag. After a meticulous consideration of the evidence, the Commission decided that the first two Moscow Trials were frame-ups and that Trotsky and his son were not guilty of all the numerous charges against them which had been mentioned there. (For Trotsky's speech to the Commission, see the *Moscow Trials Anthology*, 1967.)

> The International Bureau is not able to endorse the American Commission of Inquiry or to be represented on it because it takes the view that a disastrous mistake has been made in initiating the inquiry through a Committee which describes itself as a 'Committee for the Defence of Trotsky'.

The London Bureau, it would seem, is vitally concerned in the success of the inquiry and if it refuses to give any assistance it is solely due to the fact that the investigation was initiated by the 'Defence' Committee. However, Mr. Brockway fails to specify just who should have initiated the inquiry. The new head of the GPU Yezhov? Or the secretary of the Comintern, Dimitrov? Or the King's Counsellor, Pritt? Or the secretary of the London Bureau, Fenner Brockway? Or, finally, the Archbishop of Canterbury? The most 'impartial' of the above-listed candidates, one should imagine, is Brockway himself. But, as is obvious from his letter of last February to the American Socialist, Devere Allen, none other than Brockway himself not only refused to initiate the inquiry but did everything in his power to prevent others from taking the initiative, and, furthermore, adduced arguments involving not the interests of impartiality but those of the Moscow bureaucracy. Here is what Brockway wrote to Allen: The inquiry "will merely arouse prejudice in Russia and in Communist circles". Isn't it astonishing? In a letter not intended for publication Brockway incautiously spoke up as a member of the 'Committee for the Defence of – Stalin, Dimitrov, Vyshinsky and Yagoda'. I pointed this out in the press at the time. Not a word came in reply from Brockway. Several months elapsed. In his letter of 28 May, Brockway again came out against the inquiry, but this time with a completely different set of arguments. But in essence he still remains a member of the undercover 'Committee for the Defence' of the falsifiers against their victims.

There is no juridical or moral ground whatever for the suspicion which Brockway, in the name of the London Bureau, seeks to cast over the inquiry. All that the American Committee did was to take the initiative. Furthermore, the sum and substance of its initiative consisted precisely in this: to assure, in collaboration with other organisations, an objective and a conscientious investigation through a special International Commission, entirely independent of the initiators.

The composition of the American Committee is not a homogeneous one. There are individuals in it who understood from the very outset the absurdity and vileness of the Moscow accusations. Other members had no settled opinions on this score but they were either alarmed by or indignant over the 'totalitarian' character of Moscow justice and over the fact that the Norwegian

'Socialist' flunkeys of the GPU had placed me behind lock and key at the very moment when I needed freedom most to defend not only myself but hundreds of others. It goes without saying that had the American Committee been composed of hypocrites it might have called itself 'The Committee for the Defence of Eternal Precepts of Morality'. But it chose to act openly. By 'Defence of Trotsky' the Committee had and has in mind not to provide the alliance between Trotsky and Hitler with a cover but to provide Trotsky with an opportunity to publicly refute the accusation made against him. Nothing more! It is quite sufficient.

The members of the Committee understood from the first just as well as Brockway did that the verdict of the International Commission would carry weight only if the inquiry were conducted with all the requisite guarantees for thoroughness and objectivity, in particular, with the participation in the Commission of representatives of the different trends in political thought. The Committee began by inviting publicly the representatives of the Moscow government, the Comintern, 'Friends of the Soviet Union', the Second International, the London Bureau, etc. It was, naturally, not a question of the *political* or *moral* evaluation of Stalinism, Trotskyism, Bolshevism, or Marxism. No political tendency would agree to serve as the object of appraisal by an inter-party commission; no rational commission would undertake such an insuperable task. The appraisal of political tendencies is made by the masses in the course of the political struggle. The final verdict is brought in by history.

The task of the inquiry of the International Commission did and does consist only of verifying certain specific charges made against certain individuals. The *political* conclusions from the verdict of the Commission will be drawn by each tendency in its own way. This made it all the more essential for every organisation interested in bringing out the truth to participate in the investigation. But the direct and indirect agents and 'friends' of the GPU and the friends of friends flatly refused to participate. Some of them, in the spirit of Fenner Brockway's first letter, argued that it was impermissible to arouse any prejudice against Stalin and his Comintern; others, in the style of Fenner Brockway's second letter, adjudged the commission not 'impartial' enough. Both the former and the latter had ample justification for fearing an investigation. The London Bureau protected their rear.

To reveal more vividly the unworthy role played by this Bureau we shall dwell on another, and more recent case. The gangsters of the GPU in Spain murdered Andres Nin, the leader of the POUM. Nin was an opponent of mine. Fenner Brockway, on the contrary, considered Nin a co-thinker. If the London Bureau and other 'impartial' Pontius Pilates had joined in an investigation of the Moscow frame-ups immediately after the Zinoviev-Kamenev trial, the GPU might not have dared to put in circulation the palpably false charge that the leaders of the POUM are collaborating with General Franco. But this was not done. The 'impartial' ones shielded the GPU. As a result, Nin has been murdered, together with scores and hundreds of others. The POUM has been crushed. What has been let slip cannot be retrieved. Does Mssr. Brockway think that the time has now come for an international investigation of the crimes of the GPU in Spain – of the frame-ups, pillages, and murders? Or are they waiting for the sterilised priests of impartiality to initiate the investigation? Let Brockway supply me with their addresses and telephone numbers. I will immediately get in touch with them. But if, as I suspect, they do not exist in nature, let the London Bureau take upon itself the initiative of calling the inquiry. Let the Bureau, emulating the example of the American Committee, turn to all the existing labour Internationals and to outstanding individuals in science, literature, and art who are known for their honesty and integrity. If someone were to say that Fenner Brockway would make a "disastrous mistake" by initiating the inquiry instead of allowing matters to rest with Stalin or Negrin, every rational and honest person would call such an "accuser" a brazen hypocrite.

In conclusion, I consider it necessary to recall here another not unimportant circumstance. In the very same February letter in which he expressed his touching concern for the interests of Stalin, Yagoda and Dimitrov, Fenner Brockway proposed to create an international commission of inquiry… into my *political* activity and, furthermore, with rather strange 'precipitancy' proposed to include in this commission Norman Thomas, Otto Bauer, Branting, and other bitter political enemies of mine. The very idea of an 'official' appraisal of the political activity of an individual or a party through the medium of a commission of inquiry is so absurd that it properly belongs only on the pages of a provincial humorous magazine. Of course, Fenner Brockway himself could not have failed to understand this. But he attempted to make use of the gory Moscow amalgams in order to deal a blow at Bolshevism ("Trotskyism") which he hates so much; in addition he tried to cover up his factional struggle with the cloak of an impartial "investigation". Specialists in morals are notoriously fond of fishing in troubled waters.

We, the 'amoral' Bolsheviks, proceed differently. We openly criticised Nin's policies when he was alive. We did not alter our evaluation of him after he died. But inasmuch as we never for a moment doubted the integrity of this proletarian fighter, we stand ready to do everything in our power to rehabilitate his name and mercilessly brand his executioners. We declare in advance to Fenner Brockway and all other specialists in morals that not a single one of our friends and co-thinkers will attempt to use the investigation of Nin's murder as a pretext to settle scores with Nin's policies. To wage a struggle against opportunism and centrism we have no need to hide behind a 'commission', created for a totally different purpose. We leave such methods to the Tartuffes[4] of idealistic morality. We, gross materialists, prefer to call a "nettle but a nettle and the faults of fools but folly". We deal blows to our adversaries openly and in our own names.

* * *

From *Hitler and Stalin* (dated 6 March 1939), *Byulleten Oppozitsii*, March-April 1939.

In Great Britain the Comintern is nowadays conducting agitation in favour of creating a 'People's Front' with the participation of the liberals. At first glance such a policy appears to be absolutely incomprehensible. The Labour Party represents a mighty organisation. One could easily understand an urge on the part of the social-patriotic Comintern to draw closer to it. But the liberals represent an utterly compromised and politically second-rate force. Moreover, they are split into several groups. In the struggle to maintain their influence the Labourites naturally reject any idea of a bloc with the liberals, so as not to infect themselves with a gangrenous poison. They are defending themselves rather energetically – by means of expulsions – against the idea of a 'People's Front'.

Why then doesn't the Comintern confine itself to fighting for a collaboration with the Labourites? Why does it instead invariably demand the inclusion of the liberal shadows of the past into the united front? The crux of the matter lies in this, that the policy of the Labour Party is far too radical for the Kremlin. An alliance between the Communists and the Labourites might assume some shade of anti-imperialism and would thereby render more difficult a rapprochement between Moscow and London. The presence of liberals in the 'People's Front' signifies a direct and an immediate

---

4 Tartuffe is the main character in the comedy of the same name by the seventeenth century French playwright Molière. He is a pious crook, outwardly ascetic but actually a sensual glutton, who tricks his way into a respectable household for the purpose of seducing the daughter.

censorship exercised by imperialism over the actions of the Labour Party. Under the cover of such a censorship Stalin would be able to render all the necessary services to British imperialism.

* * *

From the *Manifesto of the Fourth International on the Imperialist War and the World Proletarian Revolution*, adopted by the Emergency Conference of the Fourth International, 26 May 1940.

At first sight the conduct of the French and English sections of the Communist International appeared to be diametrically opposite.[5] In contradistinction to the Germans, they were compelled to attack their own government. But this sudden defeatism was not internationalism, but a distorted variety of patriotism – these gentlemen consider their fatherland to be the Kremlin, on which their welfare depends. Many of the French Stalinists behaved with unquestionable courage under persecution. But the political content of this courage was besmirched by their embellishment of the rapacious policy of the enemy camp. What must the French workers think of it?

Revolutionary internationalists have always been portrayed by reaction as agents of a foreign enemy. The Comintern created a situation for its French and English sections that made them provide the very grounds for such an accusation, and thereby forcibly drove the workers into the patriotic camp or condemned them to confusion and passivity.

---

5   This was written during the period of the Nazi-Soviet pact when Stalinists in every country were opposing the Allies' war plans. In Britain the *Daily Worker* was suppressed for a time, while in France, especially after surrender and occupation, the CP had to face even greater difficulties.

IX

*British Imperialism and
National Liberation Struggles*

The Principles Involved

From the *Manifesto of the Communist International to the Workers of the World*, adopted by the First World Congress on 6 March 1919.

The last war, which was by and large a war for colonies, was at the same time a war conducted with the help of colonies. The colonial populations were drawn into the European war on an unprecedented scale. Indians, Negroes, Arabs, and Madagascans fought on the territories of Europe – for the sake of what? For the sake of their right to continue to remain the slaves of Britain and France. Never before has the infamy of capitalist rule in the colonies been delineated so clearly; never before has the problem of colonial slavery been posed so sharply as it is today.

A number of open insurrections and the revolutionary ferment in all the colonies have hence arisen. In Europe itself, Ireland keeps signalling through sanguinary street battles that she still remains and still feels herself to be an enslaved country. In Madagascar,[1] Annam,[2] and elsewhere the troops of the bourgeois republic have more than once quelled the uprisings of colonial slaves during the war. In India the revolutionary movement has not subsided for a single day and has recently led to the greatest labour strikes in Asia, which the British government has met by ordering its armoured cars into action in Bombay.

---

1 A secret anti-French society set up in Madagascar in 1916, mostly by native government officials opposed to colonial rule established in 1896.

2 Annam, which covers the central area of modern Vietnam, saw many revolts against French authority, established there in 1884. These were led by local royalists, native troops, and others.

The colonial question has been thus posed in its fullest measure not only on the maps at the diplomatic congress in Paris but also within the colonies themselves. At best, Wilson's programme has as its task: to effect a change of labels with regard to colonial slavery. The emancipation of the colonies is conceivable only in conjunction with the emancipation of the working class in the metropolises. The workers and peasants not only of Annam, Algiers and Bengal, but also of Persia and Armenia,[3] will gain their opportunity of independent existence only in that hour when the workers of Britain and France, having overthrown Lloyd George and Clemenceau, will have taken state power into their own hands. Even now the struggle in the more developed colonies, while taking place only under the banner of national liberation, immediately assumes a more or less clearly defined social character. If capitalist Europe has violently dragged the most backward sections of the world into the whirlpool of capitalist relations, then socialist Europe will come to the aid of liberated colonies with her technology, her organisation and her ideological influence in order to facilitate their transition to a planned and organised socialist economy.

* * *

From the *Manifesto of the Second Congress of the
Communist International*, adopted 7 August 1920.

The toilers of the colonial and semi-colonial countries have awakened. In the boundless areas of India, Egypt, Persia, over which the gigantic octopus of British imperialism sprawls – in this uncharted human ocean vast internal forces are constantly at work, upheaving huge waves that cause tremors in the City's stocks and hearts.

In the movements of colonial peoples, the social element blends in diverse forms with the national element, but both of them are directed against imperialism. The road from the first stumbling baby steps to the mature forms of struggle is being traversed by the colonies and backward countries in general through a forced march, under the pressure of modern imperialism and under the leadership of the revolutionary proletariat.

---

3 Algiers was even at this point a centre of resistance to French colonial rule in North
   Africa. The events in Bengal referred to are perhaps those of 1907-9, though such
   manifestations of revolt continued in India in the following year. The weak Persian
   and Armenian regimes of this period were being bolstered up by the British in efforts
   to prevent the strengthening of local popular movements or the expansion of Soviet
   power. A Soviet government was later set up in Armenia in 1921.

The fruitful rapprochement of the Mohammedan and non-Mohammedan peoples who are kept shackled under British and foreign domination, the purging of the movement internally by doing away with the influence of the clergy and of chauvinist reaction, the simultaneous struggle against foreign oppressors and their native confederates – the feudal lords, the priests, and the usurers – all this is transforming the growing army of the colonial insurrection into a great historical force, into a mighty reserve for the world proletariat.

The pariahs are rising. Their awakened minds avidly gravitate to Soviet Russia, to the barricade battles in the streets of German cities, to the growing strike struggles in Great Britain, to the Communist International.

The socialist who aids directly or indirectly in perpetuating the privileged position of one nation at the expense of another, who accommodates himself to colonial slavery, who draws a line of distinction between races and colours in the matter of human rights, who helps the bourgeoisie of the metropolis to maintain its rule over the colonies instead of aiding the armed uprising of the colonies; the British Socialist who fails to support by all possible means the uprisings in Ireland, Egypt, and India against the London plutocracy – such a socialist deserves to be branded with infamy, if not with a bullet, but in no case merits either a mandate or the confidence of the proletariat.

* * *

From Chapter 9 of *Between Red and White* (1922).

The Allied powers do not intend to recede from the great principle of the self-determination of small nations. They will only repudiate this principle when they are faced with the fact that some of the temporarily independent nations prove themselves to be a peril to universal peace by their incapacity to maintain order, by their bellicose and aggressive acts, and even by constant, childish and unnecessary insistence on their own dignity. The Great Powers will not tolerate such nations, as they are determined to preserve universal peace.

With these energetic words the British General Walker impressed on the Georgian Mensheviks' minds the conception of the *relativity* of the national right to self-determination. Politically, Henderson stood, and still stands, behind his general. But "on principle", he is willing to turn national self-determination into an absolute principle, and to direct it against the Soviet Republic.

National self-determination is the fundamental democratic formula for oppressed nations. Wherever class oppression is complicated by national subjection, democratic demands take first of all the form of demands for national equality of rights – for autonomy or for independence.

The programme of bourgeois democracy included the right of national self-determination, but this democratic principle came into violent and open conflict with the interests of the bourgeoisie of the most powerful nations. The republican form of government seemed to be quite compatible with the domination of the Stock Exchange. Capitalism with the greatest ease established a dictatorship over the machinery of universal suffrage. However, the right of national self-determination has assumed and is still assuming in many instances the character of an acute and immediate peril of the dismemberment of the bourgeois states, or of the secession of their colonies.

The most powerful democracies have been transferred into imperialist autocracies. The financial oligarchy, the City, reigns supreme over the disfranchised human ocean of Asia and Africa through the medium of the 'democratically' enslaved people of the home country.

* * *

From Chapter 10 of *Between Red and White* (1922).

One more question must be cleared up: on what does the Second International base its demand that we, the Soviet Federation, the Communist Party, should evacuate Georgia! Even if we were to admit that Georgia has been forcibly occupied, and that this fact is the expression of our Soviet imperialism, what right has Henderson, a member of the Second International, a former British Cabinet Minister, to demand that the proletariat organised in a State, that the Third International, that revolutionary Communism, should disarm Soviet Georgia "merely for the sake of his pious eyes"? When Mr. Churchill makes these demands, he makes as well a significant gesture in the direction of the long barrels of the naval guns and the barbed wire of the blockade. Upon what does Henderson rely? Is it the Holy Scriptures, or a party programme, or his own record? But the Holy Scriptures are nothing but a naïve myth, Mr. Henderson's programme is a myth, if not a naïve one, and as to his record, it is a severe indictment against him.

Not so long ago Henderson was a Minister in one of the democracies, viz., of his own – the British democracy. Why then has he not insisted that his own democracy, for the defence of which he was ready to make all sacrifices, including the acceptance of a Ministerial portfolio from the Liberal-Conservative Lloyd George, should begin to put into practice not our principles (heaven forbid) but his own – Mr. Henderson's? Why has he not demanded the evacuation of India and Egypt? Why did he not, at the right time, support the demands of the Irish for their complete liberation from the yoke of Great Britain?

We are aware that Henderson, as well as MacDonald, does protest, on certain appointed days, by means of mournful resolutions against the excesses of British imperialism. But these feeble and irresolute protests have never imperilled, and do not now imperil, the interests of British capitalism, and have never led, nor are they leading, to courageous and decisive action. They are only intended to salve the conscience of the 'socialist' citizens of the ruling nation, and to serve as an outlet for the dissatisfaction of the British workers. They will not help to break the chains of the colonial slaves. The Hendersons regard British domination over the colonies not as political questions, but as a fact in natural history. They have never declared that Hindus, Egyptians, and other enslaved peoples have the right (nay, that it is their duty) to rise in armed revolt against British domination. Neither have they undertaken as 'socialists' to render armed assistance to the colonies in their struggle for liberation. On this point there can certainly be no doubt whatever, that this is a question of the most elementary, ultra-democratic duty, and that for two reasons: *firstly*, because the colonial slaves certainly constitute an overwhelming majority, as compared with the infinitesimal ruling British minority; *secondly*, because this same minority, and especially its official socialist section, recognises the principles of democracy as the guiding principle of its existence. There is India. Why does not Henderson organise a rising in favour of the evacuation of British troops from India? For there can be no more evident, monstrous, and shameless violation of the laws of democracy than the domination of all the consolidated forces of British capitalism over the prostrate body of this unhappy and enslaved country! It seems to us that Henderson, MacDonald, and the rest of them ought unceasingly to beat the tocsin, demand, appeal, denounce, and preach revolution to the Indians and to all British workers against this inhuman trampling upon all the principles of democracy. But they remain silent, or worse still, they from time to time, with obvious boredom, sign a reasonable resolution, which is as stale and meaningless as an English sermon, and has for its aim to prove that, while supporting colonial domination, they would like its roses without the thorns, and that, in any case, they are not willing to allow these thorns to prick the fingers of loyal British socialists. For 'democratic and patriotic' considerations, Henderson ensconced himself with the greatest equanimity in a Ministerial armchair, and it did not appear to strike him that his armchair was resting on the most anti-democratic pedestal in the world

– the domination of a numerically insignificant capitalistic clique, through the medium of some tens of millions of Britishers, over several hundred millions of coloured Asiatic and African slaves. And, what is worse still, on the plea of defending this monstrous domination concealed under the cloak of democratic forms, Henderson allied himself with the unashamed military and police dictatorship of Russian tsarism. In so far as you were a member of the British War Cabinet, Mr. Henderson, you were a Minister of Russian tsarism. Do not forget that.

Henderson, of course, would not even dream of asking the Tsar, his patron and ally, to remove the Russian forces from Georgia, or from the other territories which he had enslaved. At that time he would have described such a demand as rendering a service to German militarism. He looked upon every revolutionary movement in Georgia directed against the Tsar in the same light as upon a rising in Ireland, viz., as the result of German intrigue and German gold.

In the end one's brain reels from all these monstrous crying contradictions and inconsistencies! Nevertheless, they are in the order of things, for British domination, or rather the domination of its ruling upper 10 thousand over one quarter of the human race, is looked upon by the Hendersons not as a question of politics, but as a fact in natural history. These democrats, with all their Fabian, emasculated, and feeble socialism have always been and always will be the slaves of public opinion. They are thoroughly imbued with the anti-democratic exploiter, planter, and parasite views on races which are distinguished by the colour of their skins, by the fact that they do not read Shakespeare, or wear stiff collars.

Thus, although having tsarist Georgia, Ireland, Egypt, and India on their consciences, they dare to demand from us their opponents, and not their allies, the evacuation of Soviet Georgia. But, strange as it may seem, this ridiculous and thoroughly inconsistent demand is an unconscious expression of the respect of petty-bourgeois democracy for the proletarian dictatorship. Unconsciously, or half consciously, Henderson and Co. are saying: "Of course one cannot expect bourgeois democracy (whose Ministers we become when invited), to take the democratic principle of self-determination seriously. One cannot expect the socialists of this democracy, or the respectable citizens of the ruling nation who conceal our slave ownership with democratic fictions, to aid the colonial slaves against their slave owners. But you, the revolution, personified in the proletarian state, are obliged to do what we, owing to our cowardice, mendacity and hypocrisy, are unable to do."

In other words, while formally placing democracy above all else, they recognise, willingly or unwillingly, that one can put demands to the proletarian state which would seem ridiculous and even silly, if they were put to bourgeois democracy, whose ministers or loyal representatives they are.

However, they express this unwilling respect for the proletarian dictatorship, which they reject, in a way which is in keeping with their political vagaries. They demand that the dictatorship should maintain and defend its power, not by its own methods, but by the methods which (in words, but not in deeds) they consider obligatory for democracy, but which they never apply themselves. We have already dealt with this in the first manifesto of the Communist International. Our enemies demand that we defend our lives in no other way than according to the rules of French duelling – that is to say, by the rules laid down by our enemies – but they do not consider such rules binding for themselves in their struggle against us.

* * *

From a speech to the 7th Plenum of the Executive Committee of the Communist International, 9 December 1926.

Comrades, the premise of this theory [of socialism in one country] is the *unevenness of imperialist development*. Stalin accuses me of not recognising or insufficiently recognising this law. Nonsense! The law of the unevenness of development is not a law of imperialism but it is a law of all human history. In its first phase capitalist development abruptly heightened the disparity between the economic and cultural level of development of different nations; imperialist development, i.e., the highest phase of capitalism, has not increased this disparity of levels but on the contrary has considerably facilitated their levelling out. This levelling out can never in any way be complete. The difference in tempos of development will disrupt this levelling out over and over again, thereby rendering impossible the stabilisation of imperialism at any given level. Lenin attributed this unevenness by and large to two factors: first to the *tempo*; and secondly to the *level* of economic and cultural development of the different countries. As far as the tempo is concerned imperialism has brought unevenness to an extremely high point; as regards the level of different capitalist countries the very difference in tempo has brought about certain levelling tendencies. Whoever does not understand this does not understand the very root of the question. Take Britain and India. Capitalist development is in certain parts of India proceeding faster than did the capitalist development of Britain at its very start. Yet the difference, the economic gap between Britain and India – is this today greater or less than fifty years ago? It is less. Take Canada, South America, South Africa on the one hand and Britain on the other. The development of Canada and South America has gone ahead at a furious rate over the recent period. The 'development' of Britain consists of a slump or even a decline. Thus the tempo is more uneven than ever before in history. But the levels of development of these countries have today drawn closer together than thirty or fifty years ago. What conclusions flow from this? Very important ones. Just the very fact that the tempo of development in some backward countries has of late become feverish while on the other hand in some old capitalist countries development has slowed down and even gone into reverse, and this very fact totally excludes the possibility of realising Kautsky's hypothesis of systematically organised super-imperialism...[4]

* * *

From *Remarks on the Theses of the Communist League of
South Africa, Byulleten Oppozitsii*, July 1935.

The South African possessions of Great Britain form a dominion only from the point of view of the white minority. From the point of the black majority, South Africa is a slave colony.

No social upheaval (in the first instance, an agrarian revolution) is thinkable with the retention of British imperialism in the South African dominion. The overthrow of British imperialism in South Africa is just as indispensable for the triumph of socialism in South Africa as it is for Great Britain itself.

If, as it is possible to assume, the revolution will start first in Great Britain, the less support the British bourgeoisie will find in the colonies and dominions, including so important a possession as South Africa, the quicker will be their defeat at home. The struggle for the expulsion of British imperialism, its tools and agents thus enters as an indispensable part of the programme of the South African proletarian party.

The overthrow of the hegemony of British imperialism in South Africa can come about as the result of a military defeat of Great Britain and the disintegration of the empire. In this case, the South African whites could still,

---

4 Kautsky saw imperialism not as a product of advanced capitalism, but as a result of the activities of pre-industrial, aristocratic elements, and envisaged the possible disappearance of capitalist wars through the establishment of a system he called 'super-imperialism', by which international finance capital would exploit the world. This theory ignored the dynamic of imperialism and the conflicts it must inevitably provoke.

for a certain period – hardly a considerable one – retain their domination over the blacks.

Another possibility, which in practice could be connected with the first, is a revolution in Great Britain and her possessions. Three quarters of the population of South Africa (almost 6 million of the almost 8 million total) is composed of non-Europeans. A victorious revolution is unthinkable without the awakening of the native masses. In its turn, that will give them what they are so lacking today – confidence in their strength, a heightened personal consciousness, a cultural growth.

Under these conditions, the South African republic will emerge first of all as a 'black' republic; this does not exclude, of course, either full equality for the whites or brotherly relations between the two races – depending mainly on the conduct of the whites.

The revolutionary party must put before every white worker the following alternative: either with British imperialism and with the white bourgeoisie of South Africa or with the black workers and peasants against the white feudalists and slave owners and their agents in the ranks of the working class.

The overthrow of the British domination over the black population of South Africa will not, of course, mean an economic and cultural break with the previous mother country, if the latter will liberate itself from the oppression of its imperialist plunderers. A Soviet Britain will be able to exercise a powerful economic and cultural influence on South Africa through the medium of those whites who in deeds, in actual struggle, have bound up their fate with that of the present colonial slaves. This influence will be based not on domination but on proletarian mutual cooperation.

But more important in all probability will be the influence that a Soviet South Africa will exercise over the whole of the black continent. To help the Negroes catch up with the white race in order to ascend hand in hand with them to new cultural heights, this will be one of the grand and noble tasks of a victorious socialism.

Ireland, 1916

Nashe Slovo, 4 July 1916.

Results of the Dublin Events

The former prominent colonial bureaucrat of Great Britain, Sir Roger Casement, by conviction a revolutionary Irish nationalist, the go-between for Germany and the Irish uprising, on being sentenced to death declared, "I prefer to sit on the bench of the accused than in the seat of the accuser", before the reading of the sentence, which ran according to the old formula that Casement should be "hung by the neck until dead", at which God was invited to have mercy on his soul.

Should the sentence be carried out? This question must have given Asquith and Lloyd George many troubled hours. To execute Casement would make it even more difficult for the opportunist, nationalist, and purely parliamentary Irish party, led by Redmond, to ratify a new compromise with the government of the UK on the blood of the insurrectionaries. To pardon Casement, after having carried out so many executions, would mean an open "display of indulgence to a high-ranking traitor". This is the demagogic tune of the British social-imperialists of the Hyndman type – downright blood-thirsty hooligans. But however the personal fate of Casement is resolved the sentence on him will bring to a conclusion the dramatic episode of the Irish uprising.[1]

---

1 On Easter week, April 1916, the joint forces of the petty-bourgeois nationalist Irish Volunteers, under the leadership of Patrick Pearce, and of the proletarian Irish Citizen Army, led by James Connolly, declared a Provisional Government and seized a number of prominent buildings in Dublin, including the General Post Office which dominates

In so far as the affair concerned the purely military operations of the insurrectionaries, the government, as we know, turned out comparatively easily to be master of the situation. The general national movement, however it was expressed in the heads of the nationalist dreamers, did not materialise at all. The Irish countryside did not rise up. The Irish bourgeoisie, as also the upper, more influential layer of the Irish intelligentsia, remained on the sidelines. The urban workers fought and died, together with revolutionary enthusiasts from the petty-bourgeois intelligentsia. The historical basis for the national revolution had disappeared even in backward Ireland. Inasmuch as the Irish movements in the last century had assumed a popular character, they had invariably fed on the social hostility of the deprived and exhausted pauper-farmer towards the omnipotent English landlord.

But if for the latter Ireland was only an object of agrarian plunder and exploitation, for British imperialism it was a necessary guarantee of their dominion over the seas. In a pamphlet written on the eve of the war,[2] Casement, speculating about Germany, proves that the independence of Ireland means the "freedom of the seas" and the death blow to the naval domination of Britain. This is true in so far as an "independent" Ireland could exist only as an outpost of an imperialist state hostile to Britain and as its military naval base against British supremacy over the sea routes. It was Gladstone who first expounded with full clarity the military imperialist consideration of Great Britain over the interests of the Anglo-Irish landlords and laid the basis for the wide agrarian legislation by which the state transferred to the Irish farmers the landlords' land, very generously compensating the latter, of course. Anyway, after the agrarian reforms of 1881-1903, the farmers turned into conservative small property owners, whose gaze the green banner of national independence is no longer able to tear away from their plots of land.

The redundant Irish intelligentsia flowed in their thousands into the towns of Great Britain as lawyers, journalists, commercial employees, etc. In this way,

---

O'Connell Street. After resisting for six days, under siege and bombardment by the British army, the rebels were forced to surrender, and sixteen of their leaders were shot. Despite its defeat, the Rising was a turning point in Irish history, creating an unerasable revolutionary example and tradition, and galvanising a mood of anger against British imperialism.

2 *Ireland, Germany and the Freedom of the Seas*, written in 1911, published in 1914 in New York. Republished as *Crime Against Europe – Causes of War and Foundation of Peace* in Berlin, 1915.

for the majority of them, the 'national question' got lost. On the other hand, the independent Irish commercial and industrial bourgeoisie, in so far as it has formed over the past decades, immediately adopted an antagonistic position towards the young Irish proletariat, giving up the national revolutionary struggle and entering the camp of imperialism. The young Irish working class, taking shape in an atmosphere saturated with the heroic recollections of national rebellions, and clashing with the egoistic, narrow-minded, imperial arrogance of British trade unionism, naturally swing between nationalism and syndicalism, ever ready to unite these two concepts in their revolutionary consciousness. It attracts the young intelligentsia and individual nationalist enthusiasts, who, in their turn, supply the movement with a preponderance of the green flag over the red. In this way, the 'national revolution', even in Ireland, in practice has become an uprising of workers, and the obviously isolated position of Casement in the movement only serves to emphasise this fact still deeper.

In a pathetic and shameful article, Plekhanov recently pointed to the 'harmful' character of the Irish uprising for the cause of freedom, rejoicing that the Irish nation "to their credit" had realised this and not supported the revolutionary madmen. Only complete patriotic softening of all the joints could lead anyone to interpret the situation as if the Irish peasants had declined to participate in the revolution from the standpoint of the international situation, thus saving the 'honour' of Ireland. In actual fact they were led only by the obtuse egoism of the farmer and complete indifference to everything beyond the bounds of their plots of land. It was precisely because of this and only this that they supplied the London government with such a quick victory over the heroic defenders of the Dublin barricades. The undoubted personal courage, representing the hopes and methods of the past, is over. But the historical role of the Irish proletariat is only beginning. Already into this uprising – under an archaic banner – it has injected its class resentment against militarism and imperialism. That resentment from now on will not subside. On the contrary, it will find an echo throughout Great Britain. Scottish soldiers smashed the Dublin barricades. But in Scotland itself coal-miners are rallying round the red flag, raised by Maclean and his friends. Those very workers, who at the moment the Hendersons are trying to chain to the bloody chariot of imperialism, will revenge themselves against the hangman Lloyd George.

* * *

Nashe Slovo, 11 May 1916.

Clemency!

The Irish rising has been crushed. Those whom it was thought necessary to shoot first have been shot. The rest wait for their personal fate to be decided after that of the rising itself. The triumph of British rule is so complete that Prime Minister Asquith considered it possible to declare from his parliamentary platform the government's intention to show "reasonable clemency" towards the imprisoned Irish revolutionaries. In so doing Asquith referred to the good fruits of the clemency shown by General Botha to those who took part in the South African rising. Asquith refrained from mentioning General Botha himself. Twelve years before the present war he stood at the head of the Boers who shed their blood in a struggle against British imperialism; but at the beginning of the war he successfully put down a rising of his own fellow-countrymen. Thus Asquith remains wholly within the traditions of British imperialism when he crowns the work of the "law and order" specialists in Dublin and other places with a proclamation of the principles of "expedient" humanity – humanity, that is, within the limits of what is… expedient. So far, then, everything is clear, and there can be no doubt in the minds of our readers about Asquith's statement, which goes beyond what it is permissible to express in the French Republic in 1916.

But the matter does not end there. We have an uprising crushed, buildings razed, human corpses, men and women in chains. We have triumphant authority making a gesture of 'philanthropy'. But in this picture which history has set in the frame of the world war, on this 'stage within a stage', one other figure is missing: the French social-patriot, the standard bearer of 'liberating' war and the principles of national 'freedom', commenting on the official 'humanity' of the Dublin government.

To fill in this gap, and add the finishing touch to our picture of the official governmental, patriotic aspect of our epoch, Mssr. Renaudel published an article on *Clemency* in the pages of his paper *Humanité*, which until now has not carried a single word about the Irish rising.

Now of course he, Renaudel, knows that there were facts in the past which clouded relations between Ireland and Britain. He allows that these facts could not but leave bitterness to this day in the most irreconcilable Irish hearts. But the Irish chose the most fatal hour for their action. He, Renaudel, had not doubted for a moment that the British government would do everything necessary to remain master of the situation, and he was not mistaken. But, therefore, "Britain who is fighting with her allies for the rights of nations, can and must show magnanimity." And that is why being simultaneously a friend of Britain and of Ireland, of Britain which crushed down and of Ireland which was crushed, he, Renaudel, could only welcome Asquith's magnanimous gesture.

One might think that this was quite enough. One might think it physically impossible for social-patriotic cynicism to go any further than masquerading like this as the advocate of clemency to a set of frenzied butchers. But no, Renaudel has also to introduce a national French factor in order to explain and rationalise his sage statesmanlike pleading on behalf of the vanquished and justify it to official France. "Of course", he writes, "in a land which weeps over Corneille's verses and the noble farewell to Cinna by Auguste[3] – in such a land it causes no surprise if we counsel that clemency be shown."

Thus the spiritual heirs and political descendants of Thiers and General Gallifet[4] are reassured. For didn't they, who wept on reading Racine[5] show clemency to the fighters of the Paris Commune? Here is the real crowning of the spiritual reconciliation between Gallifet's descendants and the offspring of the movement in whose history the Commune is indelibly inscribed.

3　In Corneille's play *Cinna* (1641), the character in the title is a reluctant party to a conspiracy led by his uncle against the emperor, Augustus. He receives a political pardon.

4　Louis Adolph Thiers (1797-1877) and Gaston Gallifet (1830-1909) were respectively leaders of the political and military forces that suppressed the Paris Commune of 1871. Thiers led the bourgeois government of the day and was the first President of the Third Republic. Gallifet became a general in 1870, and distinguished himself by ordering summary executions of the Communards. He thus became a symbol of counter-revolutionary repression.

5　Jean Racine (1639-99) – French dramatist, mostly writing tragedies.

Afghanistan

From *May Day in the West and the East*
(speech at the commemorative plenum of the
Moscow Soviet, 25 April 1924).

There is yet another nation in the East which deserves special mention today in connection with the holiday of international brotherhood. This is Afghanistan.[1] Dramatic events are taking place there and the hand of British imperialism is embroiled in these events. Afghanistan is a backward country. Afghanistan is making its first step to Europeanise itself and guarantee its independence on a more cultured basis. The progressive nationalist elements of Afghanistan are in power and so British diplomacy mobilises and arms everything which is in any way reactionary both in that country and along its borders with India, and throws all this against the progressive elements in Kabul. Starting from the decrees by which not only the bourgeois but also the social-democratic authorities in Germany banned May Day demonstrations, passing through events in China and Afghanistan, we can see everywhere the parties of the Second International behind the work of suppression and oppression. For, you know, the onslaught against Kabul organised with British resources, takes place under the government of the pacifist MacDonald.

* * *

---

1 The movement for 'modernisation' under King Amanullah led to sharp social conflicts. The reforms included the abolition of feudal land tenure, and in April 1923 a 'democratic' constitution was promulgated. Pro-feudal elements exploited the discontent of the peasantry at these measures with the covert support of British imperialism, and Amanullah was overthrown in 1929.

From *Perspectives and Tasks in the East*
(Speech on the third anniversary of the Communist
University for the Toilers of the East, 21 April 1924).

That is why, comrades, I think that the danger of a national-democratic degeneration which of course exists and which will seize and carry off some people for it cannot be otherwise, that this danger is greatly reduced by the very fact of the existence of the Soviet Union and of the Third International. There is every ground for hoping that the basic nucleus which will emerge from the Communist University for Toilers of the East will occupy its due place as a class leaven, a Marxist leaven, and a Leninist leaven to the proletarian movement in the lands of the East. The demand for you, comrades, appears gigantic and it manifests itself, as I have already said, not gradually but all at once, also in its own way 'catastrophically'. Read over one of Lenin's last articles, 'Better Fewer, But Better': seemingly it is devoted to a specific organisational question, but it at the same time embraces the perspectives for the development of the countries of the East in connection with the development of Europe. What is the main idea behind the article? The fundamental idea is that the development of the revolution in the West may be held up. How can it be held up? By MacDonaldism, for the most conservative force in Europe is in fact MacDonaldism. We can see how Turkey abolished the Caliphate and MacDonald resurrects it. Is this not a striking example which sharply contrasts in deed the counter-revolutionary Menshevism of the West to the progressive national-bourgeois democracy of the East?

Taking place at present in Afghanistan are truly dramatic events: MacDonald's Britain is toppling the left national-bourgeois wing which is striving to Europeanise independent Afghanistan and is attempting there to restore to power the darkest and most reactionary elements imbued with the worst prejudices of pan-Islamism, the Caliphate and so forth. If you weigh up these two forces in their living conflict, it will at once become clear why the East will more and more gravitate towards us, the Soviet Union and the Third International.

We can see how Europe, which through its past development preserved the monstrous conservatism of the bosses of the working class, is more and more undergoing economic disintegration. There is no way out for her. And this finds an expression in particular in the fact that America does not give her loans, rightly not trusting her economic viability. On the other hand, we can see too that the same America and the same Britain are compelled to finance the economic development of the colonial countries, thereby driving them along the path of revolution at a frantic rate. And if Europe is to be kept back amid the present state of putrefaction of the numbskulled, parochial, aristocratic, privileged MacDonaldism of the labour bosses then the centre of gravity of the revolutionary movement is being transferred wholly and entirely to the East. And then it will emerge that although a number of decades of Britain's capitalist development was necessary to act as a revolutionising factor to raise up our old Russia and our old East on to their feet, then it will now be necessary for the revolution in the East to come back to Britain to smash through or, if necessary smash up some thick skulls and give an impulse to the revolution of the European proletariat. [*Applause.*] This is *one* of the historical possibilities. It must be kept in one's mind's eye.

India

From *The Crisis of Terrorism and its Party*,
Pravda (Vienna) No. 3, 27 March 1909.

Revolutionary terror has shifted far to the east – to the regions of the Punjab and Bengal.[1] There the slow political awakening of the 300 million strong nation creates a favourable atmosphere for it. There too the state regime seems even more absolute in its despotism over society, even more 'accidental' and alien; for the military and police apparatus of East India was imported from Britain together with printed cotton and office ledgers. And so the Indian intelligentsia, becoming acquainted with the ideas of Locke, Bentham, and Mill at the school bench, and in its ideological evolution overtaking the political development of its country, is predisposed to seek the forces it still lacks in the bottom of alchemic retorts.

* * *

From *On the Policy of the KAPD*, speech to the Executive Committee of the
Communist International, 24 November 1920.

Thus his assertion[2] that the proletariat remains isolated in Britain whereas in Russia it is leading the peasant masses behind it, is a generalisation naked

---

1 The partition of Bengal in 1905 by the British colonial administration resulted in the intensification of nationalist activity in a number of forms. There was a considerable growth in the organisation of the Congress which itself split in 1907 as a result of demands for more militant policies. In April 1908 a terrorist bomb at Muzatarpur killed two English women.

2 Herman Gorter (1864-1927) – Poet and a member of the Dutch Socialist Party. Rallied to the Communist International in 1919 but became a convinced ultra-left,

in point of form, one-sided, and therefore false. The British proletariat is far from being isolated, for after all Britain is a world state. British industry and the position of British capitalism depend wholly upon the colonies and, in consequence, the struggle of the British proletariat likewise depends on the struggle of the colonial popular masses. The tasks which the British proletariat sets itself in its struggle against British capitalism must likewise take their orientation in harmony with the interests and moods of the Indian peasantry. British proletarians cannot attain their final victory until the peoples of India rise and until the British proletariat provides this uprising with a goal and a programme; and in India victory is out of the question without the aid and the leadership of the British proletariat. Here you have the revolutionary collaboration between the proletariat and the peasantry within the confines of the British Empire.

* * *

Written on 30 May 1930 and published in *Byulleten Oppozitsii*, June-July 1930.

The Revolution in India – Its Tasks and Dangers

India is the classic colonial country as Britain is the classic metropolis. All the viciousness of the ruling classes, every form of oppression that capitalism has applied against the backward peoples of the East is most completely and frightfully summed up in the history of the gigantic colony on which the British imperialists have settled themselves like leeches to drink its blood for the past century and a half. The British bourgeoisie has diligently fostered every remnant of barbarism, every institution of the Middle Ages which could be of service in the oppression of man by man. It forced its feudal agents to adapt themselves to colonial capitalist exploitation to become its links, its organs, its convoys to the masses. The British imperialists boast of their railroads, their canals and industrial enterprises in India in which they have invested close to 4 billion gold dollars. Apologists for imperialism triumphantly compare present day India with what it was prior to colonial occupation. But who can doubt for a moment that a gifted nation of 320,000,000 people would develop immeasurably quicker and more successfully were it freed from the burden of systematic and organised plunder? It is enough to recall the 4 billion gold dollars which represent the British investment in India to imagine what Britain extracts from India in the course of only some five or six years.

---

attacking Lenin's *Left-Wing Communism* in his *Open Letter to Comrade Lenin*. This extract forms part of Trotsky's reply.

Allowing India carefully weighed doses of technique and culture, exactly enough to facilitate the exploitation of the riches of the country, the Shylock of the Thames could not however prevent the ideas of economic and national independence and freedom from penetrating more and more widely into the masses.

Just as in the older bourgeois countries, the various racial stocks that exist in India can only be fused into a nation by means of a binding political revolution. But in contradistinction to the older countries, this revolution in India is a colonial revolution directed against foreign oppressors. Besides this, it is the revolution of a historically belated nation in which the relations of feudal serfdom, caste divisions, and even slavery exist alongside of the class antagonisms of the bourgeoisie and proletariat which have grown greatly in the last period.

The colonial character of the Indian revolution against one of the most powerful oppressors masks to a certain extent the internal social antagonisms of the country, particularly to the eyes of those to whom such masking is advantageous. In reality the necessity of throwing off the system of imperialist oppression, with all its roots intertwined with the old Indian exploitation, demands the greatest revolutionary effort on the part of the Indian masses and by that itself assures a gigantic swing of the class struggle. British imperialism will not abandon its positions voluntarily; while dropping its tail before America, it will direct the remains of its energy and its resources against insurgent India.

What an instructive historical lesson it is that the Indian revolution, even in its present stage, when it has not yet broken loose from the treacherous leadership of the national bourgeoisie, is being crushed by the 'socialist' government of MacDonald. The bloody repressions of these scoundrels of the Second International who promise to introduce socialism peacefully in their own home countries represent so far that small deposit which British imperialism brings in today on its future accounting in India. The sweet social democratic deliberations about reconciling the interests of bourgeois Britain with democratic India are a necessary supplement to the bloody repressions of MacDonald, who is of course ready, between executions, for the thousand-and-first commission of reconciliation.

The British bourgeoisie understands too well that the loss of India would not only mean the crash of its sufficiently rotted world power but also a social collapse in its own metropolis. It is a struggle of life and death. All forces will be set in motion. This means that the revolution will have to mobilise irresistible energy. The many-millioned mass has already begun to stir. They showed their half-blind force to such an extent that the national bourgeoisie was compelled to come out of its passivity and master the movement in order to break the edge of the revolutionary sword. Gandhi's passive resistance is the tactical knot that combines the naivete and self-denying blindness of the disunited and petty bourgeois masses with the treacherous manoeuvres of the liberal bourgeoisie. The fact that the chairman of the Indian Legislative Assembly, that is, the official organ of the machinations with imperialism, gave up his post to head the movement for the boycott of British goods, is of a deeply symbolic character. "We will prove to you", say the national bourgeoisie to the gentlemen on the Thames, "that we are indispensable for you, that without us you will not calm the masses; but for this we will present you with our own bill."

By way of reply, MacDonald puts Gandhi in jail. It is possible that the lackey goes further than the master intends, being conscientious beyond reason in order to justify his faith. It is possible that the Conservatives, serious and experienced imperialists, would not at the present stage go so far with repressions. But on the other hand the national leaders of the passive opposition are themselves in need of repression as support for their considerably shaken reputations. MacDonald does them this service. While shooting down workers and peasants, he arrests Gandhi with an abundance of forewarning such as the Russian provisional government used to arrest the Kornilovs and Denikins.

If India is a component element in the internal rule of the British bourgeoisie, then on the other hand, the imperialist rule of British capital over India is a component element of the internal order of India. The question cannot at all be reduced to one of the mere expulsion of some tens of thousands of foreign exploiters. They cannot be separated from the internal oppressors, and the harder the internal oppressors and the harder the pressure of the masses will become the less will the latter want to separate. Just as in Russia the liquidation of tsarism together with its indebtedness to world finance capital became possible only because to the peasantry the abolition of the monarchy grew out of the abolition of the landowning magnates, to the same degree also in India the struggle with imperialist oppressions grows out of the countless masses of the oppressed and semi-pauperised peasantry, out of the necessity of liquidating the feudal landlords, their agents and intermediaries, the *chinovniks*[3] and sharks.

---

3 The lower-level civil servants of tsarist Russia. The word has much the same connotation as the English phrase "petty officialdom".

The Indian peasant wants a 'just' distribution of land. That is the basis of democratism. And this is at the same time the social basis of the democratic revolution as a whole.

At the first stages of their struggle the ignorant, inexperienced, and disunited peasantry which, in single villages, opposes the individual representatives of the hated regime, always resorts to passive resistance. It does not pay rent, does not pay taxes, it escapes to the woods, or deserts from military service, etc. The Tolstoyan formulae of passive resistance were in a sense the first stages of the revolutionary awakening of the peasant masses. Gandhi does the same in regard to the masses of the Indian people. The more 'sincere' he is personally, the more useful he is for the owners as an instrument for the disciplining of the masses. The support of the bourgeoisie for peaceful resistance to imperialism is only a preliminary condition for its bloody resistance to the revolutionary masses.

From passive forms of struggle, the peasantry has more than once in history passed over to the severest and bloodiest wars against their direct enemies: the land owners, the authorities, and the loan sharks. The Middle Ages were full of such peasant wars in Europe; but they are also full of merciless suppression of peasant wars. Passive resistance of the peasantry as well as its bloody uprisings can be turned into a revolution only under the leadership of the urban class which thus becomes the leader of the revolutionary nation and after the victory – the bearers of the revolutionary power. In the present epoch such a class can be only the proletariat, even in the Orient.

It is true that the Indian proletariat occupy a smaller numerical place in the composition of the population than even the Russian proletariat on the eve of 1905 and 1917. This comparatively small size of the proletariat was the main argument of all the philistines, all the Martinovs, all the Mensheviks against the perspective of the permanent revolution. They considered fantastic the very thought that the Russian proletariat, thrusting the bourgeois aside, would take hold of the agrarian revolution of the peasantry, would give it a bold swing, and rise on its wave to the revolutionary dictatorship. Therefore they considered realistic the hope that the liberal bourgeoisie, leaning on the masses of the city and village, would complete the democratic revolution. But it turned out that their social statistics of the population are far from measuring the economic or the political role of single classes. The October revolution, by experience has proved this once and for all and very convincingly.

If today the Indian proletariat is numerically weaker than the Russian this in itself does not at all pre-determine the smaller swing of its revolutionary possibilities, just as the numerical weakness of the Russian proletariat compared to the American and British was no hindrance to the dictatorship of the proletariat in Russia. On the contrary, all those social peculiarities which made possible and unavoidable the October revolution are present in India in a still sharper form. In this country of poor peasants, the hegemony of the city has no less clear a character than in tsarist Russia. The concentration of industrial, commercial, and banking power in the hands of the big bourgeoisie, primarily the foreign bourgeoisie, on the one hand; a swift growth of a sharply-defined proletariat, on the other, excludes the possibility of an independent role of the petty bourgeoisie of the city, and to an extent the intellectuals, and transforms by this the political mechanics of the revolution into a struggle of the proletariat with the bourgeoisie for the leadership of the peasant masses. So far there is 'only' one condition missing: a Bolshevik Party. And that is where the problem lies now.

We were witnesses to the way the leadership of Stalin and Bukharin carried out the Menshevik conception of the democratic revolution in China. Armed with a powerful apparatus this leadership had the opportunity of applying the Menshevik formulae in deeds and by that alone was compelled to carry them to a conclusion. In order best to secure the leading role of the bourgeoisie in the bourgeois revolution (this is the basic idea of Russian Menshevism) the Stalinist bureaucracy transformed the young Communist Party of China into a subordinate section of the national bourgeois party. In connection with that, according to the terms officially arrived at between Stalin and Chiang Kai-shek (through the intermediary of the present People's Commissar of Education, Bubnov), the Communists had no right to occupy more than one third of the posts within the Kuomintang. The Party of the proletariat this way entered the revolution as an official captive of the bourgeoisie with the blessings of the CI. The result is known: the Stalinist bureaucracy slew the Chinese revolution. History has never known a political crime equal in extent to this one. For India, just as for all countries of the Orient in general, Stalin advanced in 1924 simultaneously with the reactionary idea of socialism in one country, the no less reactionary idea of 'dual composition worker and peasant parties'. This was another formula for the same rejection of independent policy and of an independent party of the proletariat. The unfortunate Roy has ever since that time become the apostle of the super-class and supra-class 'people's' or 'democratic' party. The history of Marxism, the development of the nineteenth century, the experience of the three Russian revolutions, everything passed for these gentlemen without leaving a trace.

They have not yet understood that the 'worker-peasant party' is conceivable only in the form of a Kuomintang, that is, in the form of a bourgeois party leading behind itself the workers and peasants in order later on to betray and crush them. History has not yet invented another type of a supra-class, or intra-class party. After all, not in vain was Roy the agent of Stalin in China, the prophet of the struggle against 'Trotskyism', the executor of the Martinovist 'bloc of four classes', in order to become the ritualistic scapegoat for the crimes of the Stalinist bureaucracy, after the inevitable defeat of the Chinese revolution. Six years passed in India in weakening and demoralising experiments with the realisation of the Stalinist prescription for the two-class worker-peasant parties. The results are at hand: impotent, provincial 'worker-peasant parties', which waver, limp along, or simply melt away and are reduced to nothing precisely at a moment when they are supposed to act, that is, at a moment of revolutionary tide. But there is no proletarian party. It must still be created in the fire of events and at that it will be first necessary to remove the garbage piled up by the leading bureaucracy. Such is the situation! Beginning with 1924, the leadership of the Comintern has done everything that could be done to render impotent the Indian proletariat, to weaken the will of the vanguard, and to clip its wings.

While Roy and the other Stalinist pupils were wasting precious years in order to elaborate a democratic programme for a supra-class party, the national bourgeoisie used this dawdling to the maximum in order to seize the trade unions. If not politically, then in the trade unions, the Kuomintang has been accomplished in India, true, with the difference that the creators have in the meantime become frightened by their own handiwork, and have jumped aside heaping slander on the 'executors'.

This time the centrists jumped, as is known, to the 'Left', but matters did not improve by this. The official position of the Comintern on the questions of the Indian revolution is such a tangled ball of yarn which is apparently intended especially to derail the proletarian vanguard and bring it to despair. At any rate, half of it goes on because the leadership strives constantly and wilfully to conceal its mistakes of yesterday. The second half of the tangle must be credited to the hapless nature of centrism.

We have in mind at present not the programme of the Comintern which ascribes to the colonial bourgeoisie a revolutionary role, completely approving the constructions of Brandler and Roy who still continue to wear the Martinov-Stalin cloak. We also do not speak of the innumerable editions of the Stalinist *Questions of Leninism* where, in all the languages of the world, the discourse on the dual composition worker and peasant parties continues. No. We limit ourselves to the present, to today's latest posing of the question which is in conformity with the Third Period mistakes of the Comintern in the Orient.

The central slogan of the Stalinists for India, as well as for China, still remains the democratic dictatorship of the workers and peasants. Nobody knows, nobody explains, because nobody understands what this formula signifies at present, in the year 1930, after the experience of the past fifteen years. In what way is the democratic dictatorship of the workers and peasants supposed to be distinguished from the dictatorship of the Kuomintang which massacred the workers and peasants? The Manuilskys and Kuusinens will perhaps answer that they now talk about the dictatorship of three classes (workers, peasants, and the city petty bourgeoisie) and not four as it was in China where Stalin had so happily attracted to the bloc his ally, Chiang Kai-shek.

If so, we reply, then make an effort to explain to us why you reject the national bourgeoisie in India, that is, that ally for the rejection of whom in China you expelled Bolsheviks from the Communist Party and then imprisoned them? China is a semi-colonial country. In China, there is no powerful caste of feudal lords and feudal agents. But India is a classic colonial country with a mighty heritage of the feudal caste regime. If the revolutionary role of the Chinese bourgeoisie was deduced by Stalin and Martinov from the presence in China of foreign oppression and feudal remnants, then for India each of these reasons should hold with doubled force. This means that the Indian bourgeoisie, according to the exact basis of the programme of the Comintern, has immeasurably more rights to demand its inclusion in the Stalinist bloc than the Chinese bourgeoisie with its unforgettable Chiang Kai-shek and the 'true' Wang Ching-wei. And if this is not so, if in spite of the oppression of British imperialism and the whole heritage of the Middle Ages, the Indian bourgeoisie is capable only of a counter-revolutionary and not a revolutionary role – then condemn mercilessly your treacherous policy in China and correct immediately your programme in which this policy has left cowardly but sinister traces!

But this does not exhaust the question. If in India you construct a bloc without the bourgeoisie and against the bourgeoisie, then who will lead it? The Manuilskys and Kuusinens will perhaps answer with their characteristically gentle ardour: "The proletariat, of course!" Good, we answer, it is quite complimentary. But if the Indian revolution will develop on a basis of a union of workers, peasants and the petty bourgeoisie; if this union will be directed not only against imperialism, feudalism, but also against the national bourgeoisie which is bound up with them in all basic questions; if at the head of this union will stand the proletariat, if this union comes to victory only by sweeping away the enemies through armed uprising and in this way raises the proletariat to the role of the real all-national leader – then the question arises: in whose hands will the power be after the victory if not in the hands of the proletariat? What is the significance in such a case of the democratic dictatorship of the workers and peasants in distinction to the dictatorship of the proletariat leading the peasantry? In other words: in what way will the hypothetical dictatorship of the workers and peasants be distinguished in its type from the actual dictatorship which the October revolution established?

There is no reply to this question. There can be no reply to it. By this course of historical development the 'democratic dictatorship' has become not only an empty fiction but a treacherous trap for the proletariat.

That slogan is correct which admits the possibility of two diametrically opposed explanations: in the sense of the dictatorship of the Kuomintang and in the sense of the October dictatorship! There can be nothing in between these two. In China, the Stalinists explained the democratic dictatorship twice, at first as a dictatorship of the Kuomintang of the Right, and afterwards of the Left. But how do they explain it in India? They are silent. They are compelled to keep silent for fear of opening the eyes of their supporters to their crimes. This conspiracy of silence is actually a conspiracy against the Indian revolution. And all the present extremely Left or ultra-Left noise does not improve the situation one iota, for the victories of the revolution are not secured by noise and clatter but by political clarity.

But what has been said does not yet unwind the tangled yarn. No. Here is precisely where new threads are twisted into it. Giving the revolution an abstract democratic character and permitting it to pass to the dictatorship of the proletariat only after some sort of a mystical or mystifying 'democratic dictatorship' is established, our strategists at the same time reject the central political slogan of every revolutionary democratic movement, which is precisely the slogan of the Constituent Assembly. Why? On what basis? It is absolutely incomprehensible. The democratic revolution signifies equality to the peasant – above all equality in the distribution of land. On this is based the equality of rights. The Constituent Assembly, where the representatives of the whole people formally draw the balance with the past and the classes actually draw the balance with each other, is the natural and inevitable combination of the democratic tasks of the revolution not only in the consciousness of the awakening masses of the peasantry but also in the consciousness of the working class itself. We have spoken of this more fully with regard to China and we do not see here the necessity of repetition. Let us only add that the provincial multiformity of India, the variegated governmental forms, and their no less variegated bond with the feudal caste relations, saturates the slogan of the Constituent Assembly in India with a particularly deep revolutionary democratic content.

The theoretician of the Indian revolution in the Communist Party of the Soviet Union at present is Safarov, who with the price of a happy capitulation transferred his injurious activities to the camp of centrism. In a programmatic article in the *Bolshevik* about the forces and tasks of the revolution in India, Safarov carefully circles around the question of the Constituent Assembly just like an experienced rat circles around a piece of cheese on a hook – this sociologist does not by any means want to fall into the Trotskyist trap a second time. Disposing of the problem without much ceremony, he counterposes to the Constituent Assembly such a perspective:

> The development of a new revolutionary ascent on the basis [!] of struggle for the proletarian hegemony leads to the conclusion [whom? how? why? – *LT*] that the dictatorship of the proletariat and peasantry in India can be achieved only in the Soviet form.[4]

Amazing lines! Martinov multiplied by Safarov. Martinov we know and about Safarov Lenin said not without tenderness: "Safarchik will go Leftist, Safarchik will pull boners." The above-mentioned Safarovist perspective does not invalidate this characterisation. Safarov has gone considerably Leftist and it must be admitted that he did not upset the second half of Lenin's formula. To begin with, the question of the revolutionary ascent of the masses of the people develops "on the basis" of the struggle of the Communists for proletarian hegemony. The whole process is turned on its head. We think that the proletarian vanguard enters or is preparing to enter or should enter a struggle for hegemony on the basis of a new revolutionary ascent. The perspective of struggle, according to Safarov, is the dictatorship of the proletariat and peasantry. Here, for the sake of Leftism, the word 'democratic' is shaken off. But it is not said frankly what kind of a dual composition dictatorship this is: a Kuomintang or an October type. But for that we are assured on his word of honour that this dictatorship can

---

4 *Bolshevik*, 1930, No. 5, p. 100.

be accomplished "only in the Soviet form". It sounds very noble. Why the slogan of the Constituent Assembly? Safarov is ready to agree only with the Soviet 'form'.

The essence of epigonism – its contemptible and sinister essence – lies in the fact that from the actual processes of the past and its lessons it abstracts only the bare form and converts it into a fetish. This is what has happened to the Soviets. Without saying anything about the class character of the dictatorship – a dictatorship of the bourgeoisie over the proletariat, like the Kuomintang, or a dictatorship of the proletariat over the bourgeoisie, like the October? – Safarov lulls somebody, and primarily himself, by the Soviet form of the dictatorship. As if the Soviets cannot be a weapon for deceiving the workers and peasants! What else were the Menshevik-Socialist Revolutionary Soviets of 1917? Nothing but a weapon for the support of the power of the bourgeoisie and the preparation of its dictatorship. What were the social democratic Soviets in Germany and Austria in 1918-1919? Organs for saving the bourgeoisie and for deceiving the workers. With the further development of the revolutionary movement in India, with the greater swing of mass struggles and with the weakness of the Communist Party – and the latter is inevitable with a Safarovist muddle prevailing in its mind – the Indian national bourgeoisie itself may create workers' and peasants' Soviets in order to direct them just as it now directs the trade unions, in order thus to slaughter the revolution as the German social democracy, by getting at the head of the Soviets, slaughtered it. The treacherous character of the slogan of the democratic dictatorship lies in the fact that it does not close tightly to the enemies, once and for all, such a possibility.

The Indian Communist Party, the creation of which was held back for six years – and what years! – is now deprived, in the circumstances of revolutionary democratic ascent, of one of the most important weapons for mobilising the masses, precisely the slogan of the democratic Constituent Assembly. Instead of that, the young Party which has not yet taken its first steps is inflicted with the abstract slogan of Soviets as a form of abstract dictatorship, that is, a dictatorship of nobody knows what class. It is truly an apotheosis of confusion! And all this is accompanied as usual with disgusting colouring and sugaring of an as yet difficult and not in the least sweet situation.

The official press, particularly this same Safarov, depicts the situation as if bourgeois nationalism in India is already a corpse, as if communism either has got or is getting at the head of the proletariat, which, in its turn, is already almost leading the peasantry behind it. The leaders and their sociologists, in the most conscienceless manner, proclaim the desired as the existing. To put it more correctly, they proclaim that which might have been with a correct policy for the past six years, for what has actually developed as a result of the false policy. But when the inconsistency of the inventions and realities are revealed, the ones to be blamed will be the Indian Communists, as bad executors of the general inconsistency which is advanced as a general line.

The vanguard of the Indian proletariat is as yet at the threshold of its great tasks and there is a long road ahead. A series of defeats will be the reckoning not only for the general backwardness of the proletariat and the peasantry but also for the sins of the leadership. The chief task at present is a clear Marxist conception of the moving forces of the revolution, and a correct perspective, a far-sighted policy which rejects stereotyped, bureaucratic prescriptions, but which, in the accomplishment of great revolutionary tasks, carefully adjusts itself to the actual stages of the political awakening and the revolutionary growth of the working class.

* * *

Letter to an Indian comrade (dated 24 November 1939),
Internal Bulletin of the Socialist Workers Party, December 1939.

Dear Comrade Perera,

The question about the possible military intervention of the Red Army in India (not to speak about Ceylon) has been launched absolutely artificially by some of the American comrades. The possibility is not excluded, but it is not this question that is now on the order of the day. From the principled point of view I don't see here any new question in comparison with the Chinese or Spanish experience. The Red Army is not an independent political factor but a military instrument of the Bonapartist bureaucracy of the USSR. The military intervention would be only the continuation of the political intervention and the political intervention of Stalin's Comintern is developing in India as elsewhere every day. But our task is not to speculate about the possibilities of a future military intervention – rather it is to learn how to fight against the present political intervention. Every fight demands a correct appreciation of all the factors involved.

The first thing is not to forget that the direct enemy of the Indian workers and peasants is not the Red Army but British imperialism. Some comrades, who in the last period have replaced Marxist policy by anti-Stalinist policy, forget the political realities in India and imitate the Stalinists of yesterday who proclaimed – before the Stalin-Hitler pact of course – that the main enemy in India is... Japan.

The Stalinists in India directly support the bourgeois and petty-bourgeois national parties and do all they can to subjugate the workers and peasants through these parties. What we must do is create an absolutely independent proletarian party with a clear class programme.

The general historic role of the Stalinist bureaucracy and their Comintern is counter-revolutionary. But through their military and other interests they can be forced to support progressive movements. (Even Ludendorff felt himself forced to give Lenin a train – a very progressive action – and Lenin accepted it.) We must keep our eyes open to discern the progressive acts of the Stalinists, support them independently, foresee in time the danger, the betrayals, warn the masses and gain their confidence. If our policy is firm and intransigent and realistic at the same time, we would succeed in compromising the Stalinists on the basis of the revolutionary experience. If the Red Army intervenes we will continue the same policy, adapting it to military conditions. We will teach the Indian workers to fraternise with the rank-and-file soldiers and denounce the repressive measures of their commanders, and so on.

The main task in India is the overthrow of the British domination. This task imposes upon the proletariat the support of every oppositional and revolutionary action directed against imperialism.

This support must be inspired by a firm distrust of the national bourgeoisie and their petty-bourgeois agencies.

We must not confound our organisation, our programme, our banner with theirs for a moment.

We must observe strictly the old rule: march separately, strike together.

We must keep a suspicious eye on the temporary ally as well as on the foe.

We must use the dissensions of the bourgeois and petty-bourgeois tendencies in order to reinforce the self-confidence of the proletarian vanguard.

If we follow seriously these good old rules, the intervention of the Red Army would not take us unawares.

With warmest greetings to yourself and to the Ceylon comrades, and with best wishes for your trip,

Yours comradely,
L. Trotsky

* * *

Byulleten oppozitsii, August-October 1939.

India Faced with Imperialist War –
An Open Letter to the Workers of India

Dear Friends,

Titanic and terrible events are approaching with implacable force. Mankind lives in expectation of war which will, of course, also draw into its maelstrom the colonial countries and which is of vital significance for their destiny. Agents of the British government depict the matter as though the war will be waged for principles of 'democracy' which must be saved from fascism. All classes and peoples must rally around the 'peaceful', 'democratic' governments so as to repel the fascist aggressors. Then 'democracy' will be saved and peace stabilised forever. This gospel rests on a deliberate lie. If the British government were really concerned with the flowering of democracy then a very simple opportunity to demonstrate this exists: let the government give complete freedom to India. The right of national independence is one of the elementary democratic rights. But actually, the London government is ready to hand over all the democracies in the world in return for one tenth of its colonies.

If the Indian people do not wish to remain as slaves for all eternity, then they must expose and reject those false preachers who assert that the sole enemy of the people is fascism. Hitler and Mussolini are, beyond doubt, the bitterest enemies of the toilers and oppressed. They are gory executioners, deserving of the greatest hatred from the toilers and oppressed of the world. But they are, before everything, the enemies of the German and Italian peoples on whose backs they sit. The oppressed classes and peoples – as Marx, Engels, Lenin and Liebknecht have taught us – must always seek out their main enemy at home, cast in the role of their own immediate oppressors, exploiters. In India that enemy above all is the British bourgeoisie. The overthrow of British imperialism would deliver a terrible blow at all the oppressors, including the fascist dictators. In the long run the imperialists are distinguished from one another in form – not in essence. German imperialism, deprived of colonies, puts on the fearful mask of fascism with its sabre-teeth protruding. British imperialism, gorged, because it possesses immense colonies, hides its sabre-teeth behind a mask of democracy. But this democracy exists only for the metropolitan centre, for the 45,000,000 souls – or more correctly, for the ruling bourgeoisie – in the metropolitan centre. India is deprived not only of democracy but of the most elementary right of national independence. Imperialist democracy is thus the democracy of slave owners fed by the lifeblood of the colonies. But India seeks her own democracy, and not to serve as fertiliser for the slave owners.

Those who desire to end fascism, reaction and all forms of oppression must overthrow imperialism. There is no other road. This task cannot, however, be accomplished by peaceful methods, by negotiations and pledges. Never before in history have slave owners voluntarily freed their slaves. Only a bold, resolute struggle of the Indian people for their economic and national emancipation can free India.

The Indian bourgeoisie is incapable of leading a revolutionary struggle. They are closely bound up with and dependent upon British capitalism. They tremble for their own property. They stand in fear of the masses. They seek compromises with British imperialism no matter what the price and lull the Indian masses with hopes of reforms from above. The leader and prophet of this bourgeoisie is Gandhi. A fake leader and a false prophet! Gandhi and his compeers have developed a theory that India's position will constantly improve, that her liberties will continually be enlarged, and that India will gradually become a Dominion on the road of peaceful reforms. Later on, perhaps even achieve full independence. This entire perspective is false to the core. The imperialist classes were able to make concessions to colonial peoples as well as to their own workers, only so long as capitalism marched uphill, so long as the exploiters could firmly bank on the further growth of profits. Nowadays there cannot even be talk of this. World imperialism is in decline. The condition of all imperialist nations daily becomes more difficult while the contradictions between them become more and more aggravated. Monstrous armaments devour an ever-greater share of national incomes. The imperialists can no longer make serious concessions either to their own toiling masses or to the colonies. On the contrary, they are compelled to resort to an ever more bestial exploitation. It is precisely in this that capitalism's death agony is expressed. To retain their colonies, markets and concessions, from Germany, Italy and Japan, the London government stands ready to mow down millions of people. Is it possible, without losing one's senses, to pin any hopes that this greedy and savage financial oligarchy will voluntarily free India?

True enough, a government of the so-called Labour Party may replace the Tory government. But this will alter nothing. The Labour Party – as witness its entire past and present programme – is in no way distinguished from the Tories on the colonial question. The Labour Party in reality expresses not the interests of the working class, but only the interests of the British labour bureaucracy and labour aristocracy. It is to this stratum that the bourgeoisie can toss juicy morsels, due to the fact that they themselves ruthlessly exploit the colonies, above all India. The British labour bureaucracy – in the Labour Party as well as in the trade unions – is directly interested in the exploitation of colonies. It has not the slightest desire to think of the emancipation of India. All these gentlemen – Major Attlee, Sir Walter Citrine, and Co. – are ready at any moment to brand the revolutionary movement of the Indian people as 'betrayal', as aid to Hitler and Mussolini, and to resort to military measures for its suppression.

In no way superior is the policy of the present day Communist International. To be sure, twenty years ago the Third, or Communist, International was founded as a genuine revolutionary organisation. One of its most important tasks was the liberation of the colonial peoples. Only recollections today remain of this programme, however. The leaders of the Communist International have long since become the mere tools of the Moscow bureaucracy which has stifled the Soviet working masses and which has become transformed into a new aristocracy. In the ranks of the Communist Parties of various countries – including India – there are no doubt many honest workers, students, etc.: but they do not fix the politics of the Comintern. The deciding word belongs to the Kremlin which is guided not by the interests of the oppressed, but by those of the USSR's new aristocracy.

Stalin and his clique, for the sake of an alliance with the imperialist governments, have completely renounced the revolutionary programme for the emancipation of the colonies. This was openly avowed at the last Congress of Stalin's party in Moscow in March of the current year by Manuilsky, one of the leaders of the Comintern, who declared:

> The Communists advance to the forefront the struggle for the realisation of the right of self-determination of nationalities enslaved by *fascist* governments. They demand free self-determination for Austria [...] the Sudeten regions [...] Korea, Formosa, Abyssinia [...]

And what about India, Indo-China, Algeria, and other colonies of England and France? The Comintern representative answers this question as follows:

The Communists [...] demand of the imperialist governments of the so-called bourgeois democratic states the immediate [*sic*] drastic [!] improvement in the living standards of the toiling masses in the colonies and the granting of broad democratic rights and liberties to the colonies.[5]

In other words, as regards the colonies of England and France the Comintern has completely gone over to Gandhi's position, and the position of the conciliationist colonial bourgeoisie in general. The Comintern has completely renounced revolutionary struggle for India's independence. It "demands" (on its hands and knees) the "granting" of "democratic liberties" to India by British imperialism. The words "immediate drastic improvement in the living standards of the toiling masses in the colonies", have an especially false and cynical ring. Modern capitalism – declining, gangrenous, disintegrating – is more and more compelled to worsen the position of workers in the metropolitan centre itself. How then can it improve the position of the toilers in the colonies from whom it is compelled to squeeze out all the juices of life so as to maintain its own state of equilibrium? The improvement of the conditions of the toiling masses in the colonies is possible only on the road to the complete overthrow of imperialism.

But the Communist International has travelled even further on this road of betrayal. Communists, according to Manuilsky, "subordinate the realisation of this right of secession... in the interests of defeating fascism." In other words, in the event of war between England and France over colonies, the Indian people must support their present slave-owners, the British imperialists. That is to say, must shed their blood not for their own emancipation, but for the preservation of the rule of 'the City' over India. And these cheaply-to-be-bought scoundrels dare to quote Marx and Lenin! As a matter of fact, their teacher and leader is none other than Stalin, the head of a new bureaucratic aristocracy, the butcher of the Bolshevik Party, the strangler of workers and peasants.

The Stalinists cover up their policy of servitude to British, French, and USA imperialism with the formula of 'People's Front'. What a mockery of the people. 'People's Front' is only a new name for that old policy, the gist of which lies in class collaboration, in a coalition between the proletariat and the bourgeoisie. In every such coalition, the leadership invariably turns out to be in the hands of the right wing, that is, in the hands of the propertied class. The Indian bourgeoisie, as has already been stated, wants a peaceful horse trade and not a struggle. Coalition with the bourgeoisie leads to the

---

5　*Pravda*, Issue No. 70, 12 March 1939.

proletariat's abnegating the revolutionary struggle against imperialism. The policy of coalition implies marking time on one spot, temporising, cherishing false hopes, engaging in hollow manoeuvres and intrigues. As a result of this policy disillusionment inevitably sets in among the working masses, while the peasants turn their backs on the proletariat, and fall into apathy. The German revolution, the Austrian revolution, the Chinese revolution, and the Spanish revolution have all perished as a result of the policy of coalition.[6] The self-same danger also menaces the Indian revolution where the Stalinists, under the guise of 'People's Front', are putting across a policy of subordinating the proletariat to the bourgeoisie. This signifies, in action, a rejection of the revolutionary agrarian programme, a rejection of arming the workers, a rejection of the struggle for power, a rejection of revolution.

In the event that the Indian bourgeoisie finds itself compelled to take even the tiniest step on the road of struggle against the arbitrary rule of Great Britain, the proletariat will naturally support such a step. But they will support it with *their own* methods: mass meetings, bold slogans, strikes, demonstrations and more decisive combat actions, depending on the relationship of forces and the circumstances. Precisely to do this must the proletariat have its hands free. Complete independence from the bourgeoisie is indispensable to the proletariat, above all in order to exert influence on the peasantry, the predominant mass of India's population. Only the proletariat is capable of advancing a bold, revolutionary agrarian programme, of rousing and rallying tens of millions of peasants and leading them in struggle against the native oppressors and British imperialism. The alliance of workers and poor peasants is the only honest, reliable alliance that can assure the final victory of the Indian revolution.

All peacetime questions will preserve their full force in time of war, except that they will be invested with a far sharper expression. First of all, exploitation of the colonies will become greatly intensified. The metropolitan centres will not only pump from the colonies foodstuffs and raw materials, but they will also mobilise vast numbers of colonial slaves who are to die on the battlefields for their master. Meanwhile, the colonial bourgeoisie will have its snout deep in the trough of war orders and will naturally renounce opposition in the name of patriotism and profits. Gandhi is already preparing the ground for such a policy. These gentlemen will keep drumming: "We must wait patiently

---

6 The experience of the Chinese Revolution of 1925-1927 is of the most direct significance for India. I heartily recommend to the Indian revolutionists Harold Isaacs' excellent book, *The Tragedy of the Chinese Revolution.* – *Trotsky*

till the war ends – and then London will reward us for the assistance we have given." As a matter of fact, the imperialists will redouble and treble their exploitation of the toilers both at home and especially in the colonies so as to rehabilitate the country after the havoc and devastation of the war. In these circumstances there cannot even be talk of new social reforms in the metropolitan centres or of grants of liberties to the colonies. Double chains of slavery – that will be the inevitable consequence of the war if the masses of India follow the politics of Gandhi, the Stalinists, and their friends.

The war, however, may bring to India as well as to the other colonies not a redoubled slavery but, on the contrary, complete liberty: the proviso for this is a correct revolutionary policy. The Indian people must divorce their fate from the very outset from that of British imperialism. The oppressors and the oppressed stand on opposite sides of the trenches. No aid whatsoever to the slave-owners! On the contrary, those immense difficulties which the war will bring in its wake must be used so as to deal a mortal blow to all the ruling classes. That is how the oppressed classes and peoples in all countries should act, irrespective of whether Messrs. Imperialists don democratic or fascist masks.

To realise such a policy a *revolutionary party*, basing itself on the vanguard of the proletariat, is necessary. Such a party does not yet exist in India. The Fourth International offers this party its programme, its experience, its collaboration. The basic conditions for this party are: complete independence from imperialist democracy, complete independence from the Second and Third Internationals and complete independence from the national Indian bourgeoisie.

In a number of colonial and semi-colonial countries, sections of the Fourth International already exist and are making successful progress. First place among them is unquestionably held by our section in French Indo-China[7] which is conducting an irreconcilable struggle against French imperialism and 'People's Front' mystifications. "The Stalinist leaders", it is stated in the newspaper of the Saigon workers (*The Struggle – La Lutte*) of 7 April 1939:

> ... have taken yet another step on the road of betrayal. Throwing off their masks as revolutionists, they have become champions of imperialism and openly speak

---

7 The Vietnamese Trotskyist movement was established in 1933 and its leaders included Ta Thu Thau and Tran Van Trach. During the 1930s they held seats on the Saigon municipal council and in 1939 won a majority of votes on the Cochin Chinese Colonial Council. In 1945 Ta, Tran, and other leaders of the movement were murdered by the Stalinists when they led mass strikes and demonstrations against the return of French imperialist rule which the Stalinists were advocating.

out against emancipation of the oppressed colonial peoples. Owing to their bold revolutionary politics, the Saigon proletarians, members of the Fourth International, scored a brilliant victory over the bloc of the ruling party and the Stalinists at the elections to the colonial council held in April of this year.

The very same policy ought to be pursued by the advanced workers of British India. We must cast away false hopes and repel false friends. We must pin hope only upon ourselves, our own revolutionary forces. The struggle for national independence, for an independent Indian republic is indissolubly linked up with the agrarian revolution, with the nationalisation of banks and trusts, with a number of other economic measures aiming to raise the living standard of the country and to make the toiling masses the masters of their own destiny. Only the proletariat in an alliance with the peasantry is capable of executing these tasks.

In its initial stage the revolutionary party will no doubt comprise a tiny minority. In contrast to other parties, however, it will render a clear accounting of the situation and fearlessly march towards its great goal. It is indispensable in all the industrial centres and cities to establish workers' groups, standing under the banner of the Fourth International. Only those intellectuals who have completely come over to the side of the proletariat must be allowed into these groups. Alien to sectarian self-immersion, the revolutionary worker-Marxists must actively participate in the work of the trade unions, educational societies, the Congress Socialist Party[8] and, in general all mass organisations. Everywhere they remain as the extreme left-wing, everywhere they set the example of courage in action, everywhere, in a patient and comradely manner, they explain their programme to the workers, peasants, and revolutionary intellectuals. Impending events will come to the aid of the Indian Bolshevik-Leninists, revealing to the masses the correctness of their path. The party will grow swiftly and become tempered in the fire. Allow me to express my firm hope that the revolutionary struggle for the emancipation of India will unfold under the banner of the Fourth International.

With warmest comradely greetings,
Leon Trotsky

8   Established in 1933 by various participants in the Indian nationalist movement including the pro-Stalinist J. Narayan (1902-1979) and the former British Labour Party member, M. R. Masani (1905-1998). It worked in the so-called United Front with the Indian CP from 1937 to 1940, but eventually expelled all its CP members and moved to the right as the main bourgeois party in India.

* * *

From *Petty Bourgeois Moralists and the Proletarian Party, Socialist Appeal,* 4 May
1940, re-published in *In Defence of Marxism,* 1942.

India is participating in the imperialist war on the side of Great Britain.
Does this mean that our attitude towards *India* – not the Indian Bolsheviks
but India – is the same as toward Great Britain? If there exist in this world,
in addition to Shachtman and Burnham,[9] only two imperialist camps, then
where, permit me to ask, shall we put India? A Marxist will say that despite
India's being an integral part of the British Empire and India's participating
in the imperialist war; despite the perfidious policy of Gandhi and other
nationalist leaders, our attitude toward India is altogether different from our
attitude toward Britain. We defend India against Britain. Why then cannot
our attitude toward the Soviet Union be different from our attitude toward
Germany despite the fact that Stalin is allied with Hitler? Why can't we
defend the more progressive social forms which are capable of development
against reactionary forms which are capable only of decomposition? We
not only can but we must! The theoreticians of the stolen magazine replace
class analysis with a mechanistic construction very captivating to petty-
bourgeois intellectuals because of its pseudo-symmetry. Just as the Stalinists
camouflage their subservience to national socialism (the Nazis) with harsh
epithets addressed to the imperialist democracies, so Shachtman and Co.
cover up their capitulation to American petty-bourgeois public opinion with
the pompous phraseology of the 'third camp'. As if this 'third camp' (what is
it? a party? a club? a League of Abandoned Hopes? a 'People's Front'?) is free
from the obligation of having a correct policy toward the petty bourgeoisie,
the trade unions, India, and the USSR!

* * *

From the *Manifesto of the Fourth International on the Imperialist War and the World
Proletarian Revolution,* adopted by the Emergency Conference of the Fourth
International, 26 May 1940.

In the very first weeks of war the Indian masses exerted their growing pressure,
compelling the opportunist 'national' leaders to speak in an unaccustomed
tongue. But woe to the Indian people if they place trust in high-sounding
words! Under the mask of the slogan of national independence, Gandhi has

---

9   Leaders of the petty-bourgeois revisionist tendency in the Socialist Workers Party
    at this time, who denied the need to defend the Soviet Union against imperialism.
    Trotsky's struggle against them is documented in *In Defence of Marxism.* Shachtman
    later became a social democrat and Burnham a Cold War reactionary.

already hastened to proclaim his refusal to create difficulties for Great Britain during the present severe crisis. As if the oppressed anywhere or at any time have ever been able to free themselves except by exploiting the difficulties of their oppressors!

Gandhi's 'moral' revulsion from violence merely reflects the fear of the Indian bourgeoisie before their own masses. They have very good grounds for their foreboding that British imperialism will drag them down too in the collapse. London, for its part, warns that at the first display of disobedience it will apply "all necessary measures" – including, of course, the air force in which it is deficient at the Western Front. There is a clear-cut division of labour between the colonial bourgeoisie and the British government: Gandhi needs the threats of Chamberlain and Churchill in order more successfully to paralyse the revolutionary movement.

In the near future the antagonism between the Indian masses and the bourgeoisie promises to become sharper as the imperialist war more and more becomes a gigantic commercial enterprise for the Indian bourgeoisie. By opening up an exceptionally favourable market for raw materials it may rapidly promote Indian industry. If the complete destruction of the British empire slashes the umbilical cord linking Indian capital with the City of London, the national bourgeoisie would quickly seek a new patron in New York's Wall Street. The material interests of the bourgeoisie determine their politics with the force of the laws of gravitation.

So long as the liberating movement is controlled by the exploiting class it is incapable of getting out of a blind alley. The only thing that can weld India together is the agrarian revolution under the banner of national independence. A revolution led by the proletariat will be directed not only against British rule but also against the Indian princes, foreign concessions, the top layer of the national bourgeoisie, and the leaders of the National Congress as well as against the leaders of the Muslim League.[10] It is the pressing task of the Fourth International to create a stable and powerful section in India.

---

10 These were the leading parties of bourgeois nationalism in the Indian sub-continent in this period. The Indian National Congress was founded in 1885 to demand reforms, only gradually taking up the aim of national independence. The Muslim League was set up at Dacca in 1906 on the grounds that the Congress catered exclusively for the interests of Hindus. It also eventually came round to supporting national independence, which it thought could only be safeguarded by establishing a separate state for Muslims. The two organisations thus became the basis for the ruling parties of the states of India and Pakistan.

Britain and Mexico, 1938

Letter to the editor of the *Daily Herald* (dated 22 April 1938),
published in *Forward*, 7 May 1938.

Fair Play for Mexico

Dear Sir,

In the vocabulary of all civilised nations there exists the word, *cynicism*. As a classic example of brazen cynicism, the British government's defence of the interests of a clique of capitalist exploiters should be introduced into all encyclopaedias. I am therefore not mistaken if I say that world public opinion awaits the voice of the British Labour Party regarding the scandalous role of British diplomacy in the question of the expropriation of the Eagle joint-stock oil company by the Mexican government.[1]

The juridical side of the question is clear to a child. With the aim of exploiting the natural wealth of Mexico, the British capitalists placed

---

1 One of the measures of the bourgeois nationalist President of Mexico from 1934, Lazaro Cardenas. After land reforms, railway nationalisation, and various measures restricting the oil companies, in March 1938 the Cardenas government took over control of the property of all British and American oil companies. In retaliation the United States discontinued silver payments and the British broke off diplomatic relations. The measures, essential to the protectionist policies by which the Mexican bourgeoisie was attempting to survive the slump, had widespread support among the mass of workers and peasants.

themselves under the protection and at the same time under the control of Mexican laws and the Mexican authorities. No one compelled Messrs. Capitalists to do this either by military force or through diplomatic notes. They acted entirely voluntarily and consciously. Now Mr. Chamberlain and Lord Halifax wish to force mankind into believing that the British capitalists have pledged themselves to recognise Mexican laws only within those limits where they find it necessary. Moreover, it accidentally occurs that the completely 'impartial' interpretation of the Mexican laws by Chamberlain-Halifax coincides exactly with the interpretation of the interested capitalists.

The British government cannot, however, deny that only the *Mexican* government and the Supreme Court of the country are competent to interpret the laws of Mexico. To Lord Halifax, who nourishes warm sympathies for the laws and courts of Hitler, the Mexican laws and courts may seem unjust. But who gave the British government the right to control the inner politics and legal procedure of an independent state? This question already contains part of the answer: the British government, accustomed to command hundreds of millions of colonial slaves and semi-slaves, is trying to fit those same methods also to Mexico. Having encountered courageous resistance, it instructs its lawyers hurriedly to invent arguments in which juridical logic is replaced by imperialist cynicism.

The economic and social side of the problem is as clear as its juridical side. The executive committee of your party would, in my opinion, act correctly if it created a special commission for studying what British, and in general foreign, capital has contributed to Mexico and what it has extracted. Such a commission could within a short period present to the British public the stunning balance of imperialist exploitation!

A small clique of foreign magnates, in the full sense of the word, pumps out the living sap of Mexico as well as of a series of other backward or weak countries. The solemn speeches about foreign capital contributing 'civilisation', about it assisting in the development of the national economy and so forth, are the sheer Phariseeism. The question, in actuality, concerns plundering the natural wealth of the country. Nature required many millions of years in order to deposit gold, silver, and oil in the sub-soil of Mexico. The foreign imperialists wish to plunder these riches in the shortest possible time, making use of cheap labour power and the protection of their diplomacy and their fleet.

Visit any centre of the mining industry: hundreds of millions of dollars, extracted by foreign capital from the earth, have given nothing, nothing whatever to the culture of the country; neither highways nor buildings nor good development of the cities. Even the premises of the companies themselves often resemble barracks. Why, indeed, should one spend Mexican oil, Mexican gold, Mexican silver on the needs of far-away and alien Mexico when with the profits obtained it is possible to build palaces, museums, theatres in London or in Monaco? Such are the civilisers! In the place of historical riches they leave shafts in the Mexican soil and ill health among the Mexican workers.

The notes of the British government refer to 'international law'. Even irony powerlessly drops its hands in face of this argument. About what kind of international law are we talking? Evidently about the law which triumphed in Ethiopia and to which the British government is now preparing to give its sanction. Evidently about that same law which the aeroplanes and tanks of Mussolini and Hitler are already announcing in Spain for the second year with the British government's invariable support. The latter held endless conversations about the evacuation of foreign 'volunteers' from Spain.

Naive public opinion long thought this meant the halting of intervention by the foreign fascist bandits. Actually the British government demanded of Mussolini only one thing: that he remove his armies from Spain *only after* he guaranteed the victory of Franco. In this case, as in all others, the problem consisted not in defending 'international law' or 'democracy' but in safeguarding the interests of British capitalists in the Spanish mining industry from possible attempts on the part of Italy.

In Mexico, the British government carries on basically the same politics as in Spain – passively in relation to Spain, actively in Mexico. We are now witnessing the first steps of this activity. What will be its further development? No one can yet foretell. Chamberlain himself does not yet know. One thing we can affirm with assurance: the *further development* of the attempts of British imperialism against the independence of Mexico will to a great degree depend upon the conduct of the British working class. Here it is impossible to evade the issue by resort to indefinite formulas. Firm resoluteness is necessary to paralyse the criminal hand of imperialist violence. I therefore finish as I began: world public opinion awaits the firm voice of the British Labour Party!

—

P. S. – Several imperialist newspapers have attempted to represent me… as the initiator of the expropriation. Such nonsense does not even deserve refutation. I, a private person, enjoying the hospitality of this country, have learned only from the papers all the stages of the struggle of the foreign capitalists against the Mexican laws. But this was completely sufficient to form an opinion. To state this opinion aloud is the elementary duty of every participant in the liberating struggle of the proletariat.

* * *

Socialist Appeal (New York), 25 June 1938.

Mexico and British Imperialism

The international campaign which imperialist circles are waging over the expropriation of Mexican oil enterprises by the Mexican government has been distinguished by all the features of imperialism's propagandistic Bacchanalias – combining impudence, deceitfulness, speculation in ignorance with cocksureness in its own impunity.

The signal for this campaign was given by the British government when it declared a boycott upon Mexican oil. Boycott, as is known, always involves self-boycott, and is therefore accompanied by great sacrifices on the part of the boycotter. Great Britain was until recently the largest consumer of Mexican oil; naturally not out of sympathy for the Mexican people, but out of consideration for her own advantage.

Heaviest consumer of oil in Great Britain itself is the state with its gigantic fleet and rapidly-growing air force. A boycott of Mexican oil by the British government signifies, therefore, a simultaneous boycott not only of British industry but also of national defence. Mr. Chamberlain's government has shown with unusual frankness that the profits of Britain's capitalist robbers loom above state interests themselves. Oppressed classes and oppressed peoples must thoroughly learn this fundamental conclusion.

Both chronologically and logically the uprising of General Cedillo[2] grew out of Chamberlain's policy. The Monroe Doctrine[3] prevents the British admiralty from applying a military-naval blockade of the Mexican coast. They must act through internal agents, who, it is true, do not openly fly the

---

2 General Cedillo (1890-1938) – Right-wing Mexican general, provincial governor and minister in the Cardenas government, against which he led an abortive coup in 1938, losing his life in the course of it.

3 In 1823 President James Monroe of the United States announced in the wake of the South American Wars of Independence that his government would not allow any future outside interference in the affairs of any American state. This prohibition, which was frequently cited in justification of US policies during the nineteenth century, was never of course deemed to apply to the US themselves.

British flag, yet serve the same interests as Chamberlain – the interests of a clique of oil magnates. In the *White Book* issued by British diplomacy just a few days ago we may be sure that the negotiations of its agents with General Cedillo are not included. Imperialist diplomacy carries on its major business under cover of secrecy. In order to compromise the expropriation in the eyes of bourgeois public opinion, they represent it as a 'communist' measure. Historical ignorance combines here with conscious deceit. Semi-colonial Mexico is fighting for her national independence, political and economic. This is the basic meaning of the Mexican revolution at this stage. The oil magnates are not rank-and-file capitalists, not ordinary bourgeoisie. Having seized the richest natural resources of a foreign country, standing on their billions and supported by the military-diplomatic forces of their metropolis, they strive to establish in the subjugated country a regime of imperialistic feudalism, subordinating to themselves legislation, jurisprudence, and administration. Under these conditions expropriation is the only effective means of safeguarding national independence and the elementary conditions of democracy.

What direction the further economic development of Mexico may take depends decisively upon factors of an international character. But this is a question of the future. The Mexican revolution is now carrying out the same work as, for instance, the United States of America accomplished in three quarters of a century, beginning with the Revolutionary War for independence and finishing with the Civil War for the abolition of slavery and for national unification. The British government not only did everything at the end of the eighteenth century to retain the United States under the status of a colony, but later, in the years of the Civil War, supported the slaveholders of the South against the abolitionists of the North, striving for the sake of its imperialist interests to thrust the young republic into a state of economic backwardness and national disunity.

To the Chamberlains of that time, too, the expropriation of the slaveholders seemed a diabolical 'Bolshevik' measure. In reality the historic task of the Northerners consisted in clearing the arena for the independent democratic development of bourgeois society. Precisely this task is being solved at this stage by the government of Mexico. General Cardenas[4] stands in the series of those statesmen of his country who have been fulfilling work comparable to that of Washington, Jefferson, Abraham Lincoln, and General Grant. And,

---

4   Lazaro Cardenas (1895-1970) – Mexican general and politician, President of Mexico 1934-40. He granted Trotsky asylum in 1938.

of course, it is not accidental that the British government in this case, too, finds itself on the other side of the historic trench.

The world press, in particular the French, preposterous as it may seem, continues to drag my name into the question of the expropriation of the oil industry. If I have once already refuted this nonsense, it is not at all because I fear 'responsibility' as was insinuated by one talkative agent of the GPU. On the contrary, I would consider it an honour to carry even a part of the responsibility for this courageous and progressive measure of the Mexican government. But I do not have the least basis for it. I first learned of the decree of expropriation from the newspapers. But, naturally, this is not the question.

Two aims are pursued in interjecting my name – first, the organisers of the campaign wish to impart to the expropriation a 'Bolshevik' colouration; secondly, they are attempting to strike a blow at the national self-respect of Mexico. The imperialists are endeavouring to represent the affair as if Mexico's statesmen were incapable of determining their own road. A wretched and ignoble hereditary slaveholders' psychology! Precisely because Mexico today still belongs to those backward nations which are only now impelled to fight for their independence, greater audacity of thought is engendered among her statesmen than is granted to the conservative dregs of a great past. We have witnessed similar phenomena in history more than once!

The French weekly, *Marianne*, a notorious organ of the French People's Front, even asserts that on the oil question the government of General Cardenas acted not only as one with Trotsky but also… in the interests of Hitler. It is a question, you see, of depriving the great-hearted 'democracies' of oil in case of war and, contrariwise, of supplying Germany and other fascist nations. This is not one whit more clever than the Moscow trials. Humanity learns, not without amazement, that Great Britain is being deprived of Mexican oil because of the ill-will of General Cardenas and not because of Chamberlain's self-boycott. But then the 'democracies' possess a simple way of paralysing this 'fascist' plot: let them buy Mexican oil, once more Mexican oil, and again Mexican oil! To every honest and sensible person it is now beyond all doubt that if Mexico should find herself forced to sell her liquid gold to fascist countries the responsibility for this act would fall fully and completely upon the governments of the imperialist 'democracies'.

Behind the back of *Marianne* and her ilk stand the Moscow prompters. At first glance this seems preposterous, since other prompters of the same school use diametrically opposed librettos. But the whole secret consists in the fact that the friends of the GPU adapt their views to geographical gradations of latitude and longitude. If some of them promise support to Mexico, others picture General Cardenas as an ally of Hitler. From the latter point of view, Cedillo's oil rebellion should be viewed, it would seem, as a struggle in the interests of world democracy.

Let us, however, leave the clowns and intriguers to their own fate. We do not have them in mind, but the class-conscious workers of the entire world. Without succumbing to illusions and without fear of slander, the advanced workers will completely support the Mexican people in their struggle against the imperialists. The expropriation of oil is neither socialism nor communism. But it is a highly progressive measure of national self-defence. Marx did not, of course, consider Abraham Lincoln a communist; this did not, however, prevent Marx from entertaining the deepest sympathy for the struggle which Lincoln headed. The First International sent the Civil War president a message of greeting, and Lincoln in his answer highly appreciated this moral support.[5]

The international proletariat has no reason to identify its programme with the programme of the Mexican government. Revolutionists have no need of changing colour, adapting, themselves, and rendering flattery in the manner of the GPU school of courtiers, who in a moment of danger will sell out and betray the weaker side. Without giving up its own identity, every honest working-class organisation of the entire world, and first of all in Great Britain, is duty bound to take an irreconcilable position against the imperialist robbers, their diplomacy, their press, and their fascist hirelings. The cause of Mexico, like the cause of Spain, like the cause of China,[6] is the

---

5   This address, drafted by Marx, was sent to Lincoln in November 1864, on the occasion of his re-election as President and shortly before the end of the Civil War and his assassination. It denounced "the Confederate gentry" and described their "slaveholders' rebellion" as "a general holy crusade of property against labour". The reply, which was received in January 1865 through the American embassy in London, said that Lincoln hoped he would be worthy of "the confidence which has recently been extended to him by the friends of humanity and progress throughout the world." See *Marx and Engels Collected Works*, Vol. 20, Lawrence and Wishart, 1975, pp. 19-21.

6   The defence of China against the predatory assaults of Japanese imperialism. The Japanese invaded the province of Manchuria in 1931 and established a puppet state there. In 1935 further areas were taken over, and by 1938, when this was written, Japan exercised effective control over much of Northern China and was in a position to enforce the penetration of all sections of the Chinese economy under the Kuomintang regime of Chiang Kai-shek.

cause of the international working class. The struggle over Mexican oil is only one of the advance-line skirmishes of future battles between the oppressors and the oppressed.

Name Glossary

ADLER, Friedrich (1879-1960) – Austrian Social Democratic politician. From the mid-1920s he was Secretary General of the reconstituted Socialist International.

ADLER, Victor (1852-1918) – Founder of Austrian Social Democracy; supported Austria's involvement in the war; Foreign Minister in the interim government of Karl Renner after November 1918.

ASQUITH, Herbert Henry (1858-1928) – British Liberal politician and lawyer; Home Secretary 1892-95, Chancellor of the Exchequer 1905-8 and Prime Minister 1908-16.

BALDWIN, Stanley (1867-1947) – British Conservative politician; Prime Minister three times 1923-1924, 1924-1929 and 1935-1937; Prime Minister during the General Strike.

BENTHAM, Jeremy (1748-1832) – English jurist and philosopher, founder of utilitarianism.

BIRKENHEAD, Lord (Smith, Frederick Edwin) (1874-1930) – Right-wing Tory and lawyer. Solicitor-General in 1915, Attorney-General from 1915-18, Lord Chancellor from 1919-22, and Secretary of State for India from 1924-28. Resisted Irish Home Rule and led the prosecution at the trial of Sir Roger Casement.

BRAILSFORD, Henry Noel (1873-1958) – Socialist writer; joined the ILP in 1907 and took a pacifist position in the First World War; an opponent of MacDonald within the ILP. He was active in efforts to reunite the Second and Third Internationals and in the ILP campaign of 1926 entitled 'Socialism in Our Time'.

BRIAND, Aristide (1862-1932) – French politician and renegade socialist. Served as Prime Minister eleven times from 1909-29 and Foreign Minister from 1926-32.

BROCKWAY, Archibald Fenner (1888-1988) – Born in Calcutta, the son of a Christian missionary. Came to Britain and in 1907 joined the ILP. Pacifist during the First World War. Organising Secretary of the ILP in 1922, General Secretary in 1928 and 1933-39, Chairman from 1931-33. Editor of *New Leader* from 1926-29 and 1931-46. He acted as leader of the 'left' of the ILP following its disaffiliation from the Labour Party, and was the moving spirit behind the 'London Bureau' of centrist parties established in 1932. In this capacity he played an active role in such capitulations to the Stalinist 'Popular Front' as those perpetrated by the POUM in Spain, and was strongly opposed to Trotsky's call for a Fourth International. He took a centrist position during the Second World War and quietly rejoined the Labour Party in 1946.

BUCHANAN, George William (1854-1924) – British ambassador to Russia 1910-18. Encouraged British intervention against the Bolsheviks.

BUKHARIN, Nikolai (1888-1938) – Russian Bolshevik; after the introduction of the New Economic Policy (NEP) he adopted more right-wing positions, encouraging the peasantry to enrich itself; after Lenin's death he developed the theoretical basis for the theory of 'socialism in one country'; despite allying with Stalin against the Left Opposition he was executed during the Moscow Trials.

BUNYAN, John (1628-1688) – Former soldier in the revolutionary parliamentary army who became a radical preacher. While in prison for preaching without a licence he started *The Pilgrim's Progress*, one of the most widely read and translated works of seventeenth century English literature.

BURNHAM, James (1905-1957) – American political theorist. During the 1930s he was a leading member of the American Trotskyist movement. After the Soviet invasion of Finland in 1939 he was involved in the faction fight about the class nature of the Soviet Union that led him and Max Shachtman to split from the Socialist Workers Party and set up the Workers Party in 1940. Shortly afterwards he resigned from the Workers Party and moved to the right, eventually ending up as a leading supporter of the Cold War and theoretician of conservatism.

CALVIN, John (1509-1564) – French Protestant theologian during the Protestant Reformation. His ideas on civic and religious governance greatly influenced Scottish Presbyterianism, English (and later American) Puritanism, and the Dutch Reformed Church.

CASEMENT, Sir Roger David (1864-1916) – Irish nationalist, a leader of the Irish Volunteers. After the outbreak of war, he became convinced that the German imperialists could serve the cause of Irish freedom, and went to negotiate with them on this basis. Having failed to achieve his aim he nevertheless persuaded the Germans to send some arms to the Irish Volunteers on a ship called the *Aud* and to send him on a submarine so he could try to prevent the planned rising. Together with the arms, he was captured by the British in April 1916, tried for treason and executed the following August. Before the trial, the British government circulated excerpts said to be from his private journals, which detailed homosexual activities. Given prevailing views and existing laws on homosexuality, this material undermined support for clemency for Casement.

CHAMBERLAIN, Arthur Neville (1869-1940) – Tory leader. Chancellor of the Exchequer in 1923-24 and Prime Minister from 1937-40. Although his father, Joseph, had been something of a political outsider, Neville's policies were those of the mainstream of ruling class opinion, notably in his desire to fight communism at all costs on an international scale, and to arrive at an accommodation with the German fascists.

CHAMBERLAIN, Austen (1863-1937) – Tory politician. Chancellor of the Exchequer 1903-6. Secretary for India in Asquith's 1915 coalition and a member of Lloyd George's War Cabinet. Chancellor once again 1919-21. Helped to draft the plans for de-controlling the coal industry in 1921 which led to the 'Black Friday' defeat for the miners. Foreign Secretary in Baldwin government. Played an important part in framing the 1925 Locarno pact, an attempt to stabilise the capitalist powers in Europe. Known to enjoy family holidays with Mussolini.

CHAMBERLAIN, Joseph (1836-1914) – Imperialist politician and capitalist. After a period as Mayor of Birmingham he entered parliament as a Radical, joining the Liberal government in 1880. Although an advocate of social reforms, he was a strong supporter of all forms of imperialism and resigned from Gladstone's government in 1886 in opposition to Irish Home Rule. Subsequently led the 'Unionist' section of the Liberal Party which joined the Conservatives in 1895. Colonial Secretary until his resignation in 1903. Father of Austen and Neville Chamberlain.

CHARLES I of Great Britain and Ireland (1600-1649) – Came to the throne in 1625 and attempted to rule without calling parliament after 1629. Failing to arrive at agreement with his 1640 parliament he led the royalist forces against the parliamentary army in the Civil War from 1642 until his surrender in 1646. He was finally executed in 1649.

CHARLES II of Great Britain and Ireland (1630-1685) – Assumed the title of king in exile on his father's execution; crowned in Scotland in 1651. Tried unsuccessfully to regain rule over England. Re-installed with the fall of the Commonwealth in 1660. Formed an alliance with France to fight Holland in 1670. Built up British naval power. His reign was marked by a measure of economic development resulting from the bourgeois revolution.

CHIANG Kai-shek (1887-1975) – Generalissimo of the Chinese nationalist army that finally, with Communist support, overthrew the warlords in 1925 and then turned against the Communists and the working class, massacring the workers of Shanghai, Canton, and other cities. Defeated in the civil war by Mao Tse-tung and retreated to Formosa in 1949, where until his death he ruled over a statelet of his own under the patronage of US imperialism.

CHICHERIN, Georgi (1872-1936) – Russian Social Democrat, later Soviet diplomat; Menshevik before the First World War, adopted an anti-war position and drew closer to the Bolsheviks; jailed in Britain in 1917, Trotsky secured his release in exchange for hostages including Buchanan, British ambassador to Russia; formally joined the Bolsheviks early in 1918 and was appointed Trotsky's deputy at the Commissariat for Foreign Affairs; succeeded Trotsky on his resignation and remained Commissar for Foreign Affairs until 1930, when he was replaced due to bad health.

CHURCHILL, Winston Spencer (1874-1965) – Leading imperialist politician of twentieth century. Entered parliament as a Conservative in 1900 but joined the Liberal Party in 1906. As President of the Board of Trade from 1908 he was responsible for the introduction of Labour Exchanges. Home Secretary 1910. He called out troops against striking miners and dockers in 1911 and personally directed the burning to death of a group of armed anarchists in Sidney Street, London. Secretary for War and Air 1919-21 and the leading supporter of armed intervention against Soviet Russia. After the 1924 election he returned to the Conservative Party. Chancellor of the Exchequer in Baldwin's Cabinet 1924-29. Responsible for the disastrous return to the Gold Standard in 1925 which increased export prices and led to substantial wage cuts for miners and other workers. During the 1926 General Strike he organised the anti-labour blackleg government newspaper, the *British Gazette*. Observed with favour the rise of Mussolini and Hitler in this period, but later became the spokesman for the anti-German section of British imperialism. As a result, he was again in the Cabinet in 1939 and was appointed Prime Minister of the War Coalition Cabinet in May 1940 with Attlee as Lord Privy Seal. Defeated overwhelmingly in the 1945 General Election. Tory Prime Minister again 1951-55.

CITRINE, Walter McLennan (1887- 1983) – TUC General Secretary 1926-46.

CLEMENCEAU, Georges (1841-1929) – Leading French bourgeois politician. As Prime Minister from 1917-20 he was hailed as the 'architect of victory' and was the leading figure at the Versailles peace conference in 1919, as well as the inspirer of intervention against Soviet Russia.

CLYNES, Joseph Robert (1869-1949) – British trade unionist and Labour politician; supporter of British involvement in the First World War; became leader of the Labour Party after the war; served as Home Secretary in the second Labour government (1929-31), but split with Ramsay MacDonald in 1931 over the proposed austerity measures.

COOK, Arthur James (1883-1931) – Miners' leader. After the defeat of the miners in 1926 he denounced the General Council for its role. In 1927 he joined the General Council itself and attacked the collaborationist policies of the Mond-Turner talks. Though always a militant and never losing the confidence of the miners, Cook nevertheless remained a prisoner to his syndicalist prejudices and lacked any overall perspective to deal with the crushing attacks on his members.

CRIPPS, Sir Richard Stafford (1889-1952) – Labour MP for Bristol 1929-1950. Leading member of the Socialist League, founded in 1932, and affiliated to the Labour Party.

CROMWELL, Oliver (1599-1658) – Leader of the English Revolution. Born into a family of minor gentry in Cambridgeshire. MP in 1628 and again in 1640. One of the most uncompromising of the Puritans, he achieved prominence as a military commander in the Civil War, raising a New Model Army of those with strong religious convictions and military skill. This army not only defeated the Royalists, but also rebellions in Scotland and Ireland. After the Civil War Cromwell not only pushed hard for the execution of the King, he also opposed and defeated movements inside and outside the army such as the Levellers and Diggers who demanded greater democracy and social equality. After this he became virtual dictator, though refusing the title of King. He did much to extend the basis of capitalism not only in domestic affairs but through the pursuit of colonial wars. Tried many forms of government such as military rule and a nominated Parliament, but died as Lord Protector without having discovered a satisfactory political alternative to the monarchy. Though the Stuarts were restored less than two years after his death, the movement he led had irrevocably altered the relations between the classes and the balance of political power.

CURZON, George Nathaniel (Lord Curzon) (1859-1925) – Aristocrat educated at Eton and Oxford. Viceroy of India 1898-1905. Strengthened the apparatus of colonial rule, partitioning Bengal and fortifying the North-West Frontier against a threat from tsarist Russian imperialism. Became an earl in 1911 and joined Lloyd George's War Cabinet in 1916. Foreign Secretary first under Lloyd George in 1919 and then under Bonar Law and Baldwin, 1922-24. A leader of the right wing of the Conservative Party in this period, he combined traditional hostility to tsarist Russia with his class loyalty to act as an arch-enemy of Soviet Russia, against which he carried out endless diplomatic manoeuvres.

DENIKIN, Anton Ivanovich (1872-1947) – Tsarist general, organiser and commander of counter-revolutionary Volunteer Army in South Russia, 1918-1920.

DERBY, Earl of (Edward Stanley) (1865-1948) – Conservative politician. Actively opposed the social reforms of the pre-war Liberal administration. During the war he served at the War Office in both Asquith's and Lloyd George's administrations, perpetrating the notorious 'Derby scheme', which placed enormous pressure on young men to join the army.

DEWEY, John (1859-1952) – American philosopher, psychologist and educational reformer, one of the founders of Pragmatism. In 1937 he chaired the commission of enquiry that cleared Trotsky of the charges made against him by Stalin.

FOCH, Ferdinand (1851-1929) – French general; as supreme commander of the Allied armies in 1918 he accepted the German surrender; highly critical of the Versailles Treaty for being too lenient on Germany; advised the Polish army during its invasion of Russia in 1920.

GLADSTONE, William Ewart (1809-1898) – Liberal leader and Prime Minister of merchant origin. First a Tory, then supporter of Peel and Free Trade, eventually joining the Liberal Party whose leader he became in 1866.

GREY, Edward (Lord Grey) (1862-1933) – British Liberal politician, Foreign Secretary 1905-16.

GROVES, Reginald (1908-1988) – British Trotskyist. Member of the Westminster ILP in the 1920s, but later joined the CP. Developed opposition to the policies of the third period on the grounds that they gave poor practical results. Expelled from the CP in August 1932. Within the Trotskyist movement after 1932 he opposed the entry into the ILP. On the collapse of his own 'independent' group he joined the Labour Party in 1935.

GUEST, Haden Leslie (1877-1960) – Extreme right-wing Labourite.

HARDING, Warren (1865-1923) – American Republican politician, president of the US (1921-1923).

HENDERSON, Arthur (1863-1935) – Right-wing Labour politician; leader of the Party who rallied the party to support the First World War and became a government minister. He later served as Home Secretary in the first Labour government (1924) and Foreign Secretary in the second Labour government (1929-1931). A devout Wesleyan Methodist throughout his life. Left an estate of £23,000.

HOOVER, Herbert (1874-1964) – Republican President of the United States, 1929-32. A Quaker, Hoover was identified with the laissez-faire, less protectionist wing of American capitalism which was held in retrospect to have contributed to the Wall Street crash and the development of the slump.

HYNDMAN, Henry Mayers (1842-1921) – A founder of the British Marxist movement. The son of a colonial merchant, he qualified as a barrister and became a City businessman. Converted to socialism by reading *Capital* on a transatlantic voyage in 1880. In 1881 wrote *England for All*, drawing on many of Marx's ideas without acknowledgement. Set up the Democratic Federation, later Social Democratic Federation, the first organisation in Britain at the time claiming adherence to Marxism. Hyndman also led the British Socialist Party into which his movement merged, but led a pro-war minority which left the 1916 conference to set up a National Socialist Party. Despite his role in the propagation of Marxist ideas in Britain, Hyndman was always an extreme chauvinist, who never lost his airs as a city gentleman or gained an adequate grasp of Marxism.

JAMES, Cyril Lionel Robert (1901-1989) – Trinidadian Marxist who was active in the Trotskyist movements of both Britain and the United States. He came to Britain around 1933 and joined the Marxist Group in the ILP in 1935 and refused to support entry to the Labour Party. After this he went to the United States to join James P. Cannon in 1938 and was in the SWP until he left in 1940, together with Shachtman. He rejoined in 1947, but split again in 1950 during the Korean War. He wrote a book on the decline of the Comintern, *World Revolution* (1937), and another on the Haitian Revolution called *The Black Jacobins* (1938).

JOHNSTON, Thomas (1881-1965) – Labour MP. Elected to Parliament in 1922 as one of the Clydeside group of 'left' Labour MPs. Began to take an interest in the affairs of the British Empire which he thought "could be made the greatest lever for human emancipation the world has ever known". Remained closely identified with MacDonald.

JOYNSON-HICKS, William (1865-1932) – Extreme right-wing authoritarian Conservative politician; Home Secretary from 1924 to 1929. As such, he was responsible for the prosecution and jailing of the leaders of the CPGB for sedition during the run-up to the General Strike, and during the strike itself he was one of the most hawkish members of the government.

KANT, Immanuel (1724-1804) – German philosopher and cosmologist regarded as the last great philosopher of the Enlightenment.

KAUTSKY, Karl (1854-1938) – One of the leading theoreticians of the German Social Democratic Party and the Second International. By the outbreak of the First World War, he had abandoned revolutionary Marxism and took up an indecisive position between revolutionary opposition to the war and patriotic support for the German bourgeoisie. As such he became the theorist of 'centrism' in the socialist movement and strongly opposed the Russian Revolution.

KERENSKY, Alexander (1881-1970) – Russian lawyer with a reputation for defending radicals and revolutionaries. With the outbreak of the 1917 February Revolution, he entered the Provisional Government as a representative of the Socialist Revolutionaries. Head of the provisional government from July. Overthrown by the Bolsheviks in the October Revolution. After briefly attempting to retake Petrograd, he fled to France.

KEYNES, John Maynard (1883-1946) – British economist who advocated government intervention in the economy to mitigate the negative aspects of the business cycle (what later became known as Keynesianism); a member of the British delegation to the negotiations leading to the Versailles Treaty, he published a devastating critique called *The Economic Consequences of the Peace*.

KIRKWOOD, David (1872-1955) – Scottish politician and trade unionist. In 1914 he joined the Socialist Labour Party but soon after moved to the ILP being influenced by MacDonald's half-baked pacifism.

KITCHENER, Horatio Herbert (1850-1916) – Irish-born British soldier who commanded British imperialist forces in Egypt and Sudan. In 1900 he succeeded Lord Roberts as commander of the British forces in South Africa during the Second Boer War. Served as Secretary of State for War from 1914 until his death in 1916.

KOLCHAK, Alexander (1874-1920) – Russian admiral and leader of the counter-revolutionary White forces in Siberia; captured and executed in 1920.

LANSBURY, George (1858-1940) – Labour leader. In 1912 he helped in the foundation of the *Daily Herald* and was its editor from 1919 to 1922. After its move to the right for a short time he ran a paper called *Lansbury's Labour Weekly* (1925-26). MP from 1922 until his death. Commissioner for Works in the 1929-31 Government, and as the most prominent Labour leader to retain his seat in the 1931 landslide, he found himself at the head of the Party. He handed this position over to Attlee in 1935 after a vitriolic attack on him by Ernest Bevin for opposing on pacifist grounds the policy of the League of Nations sanctions against Italy after her bloody seizure of Abyssinia. He then toured Europe in an attempt to influence political leaders in favour of peace and disarmament.

LAW, Andrew Bonar (1858-1923) – Conservative MP from 1900 and leader from 1911-21 and 1922-23. Particularly active in support of army mutinies in opposition to Irish Home Rule before 1914. Chancellor of the Exchequer and Leader of the House of Commons under Lloyd George.

LLOYD GEORGE, David (1863-1945) – Liberal politician and arch-imperialist. Minister of Munitions 1915. In 1916 succeeded Asquith as Prime Minister forming his 'War Cabinet' with the Tories, lasting until 1922. Dictated the vindictive Versailles Treaty, together with French Prime Minister Clemenceau. Backed the White Guards in the Russian Civil War and every form of terrorism against the Irish people, but in both cases was forced to retreat. More successful in dealing with the leaders of the trade unions, notably the miners. Abandoned by the Tories at 1922 General Election in favour of Law's Tory cabinet. His subsequent position oscillated between his earlier reformism and extreme reaction as he fought in a rapidly declining and hopelessly split Liberal

Party. Returned to parliament in 1931 at the head of a party with only four seats. At different times intrigued with Labour leaders, expressed admiration for Hitler (1936), and supported Keynesian policies, but never regained his previous influence.

LOCKE, John (1632-1704) – English philosopher, first of the British empiricists.

LOCKHART, Robert Hamilton Bruce (1887-1970) – British diplomat and secret agent. British envoy in Russia from January 1918; implicated in a plot to assassinate Lenin; jailed and condemned to death, but was spared and released in exchange for the Soviet diplomat, Maxim Litvinov. He later wrote about his experiences in an autobiographical book, Memoirs of a British Agent (1934).

LONGUET, Jean (1876-1938) – French lawyer and socialist who held a pacifist position in the First World War but invariably voted for war credits.

LOVESTONE, Jay (1898-1990) – American communist. Occupied various leading positions in the CPUSA in the 1920s, was expelled in 1929 and ran various organisations supporting his views in the 1930s. Later he moved to the extreme right and became a pillar of American imperialism through his work in the labour movement and the building of CIA-backed anti-communist union organisations in various countries.

MACDONALD, James Ramsay (1886-1938) – Scottish Labour politician; member of ILP; adopted pacifist position during the First World War, Prime Minister in the first (1924) and second (1929-1931) Labour governments, defected in 1931 with Philip Snowden and James Henry Thomas to form National Government with the Conservatives after the Labour government split on the question of cutting unemployment benefits; served as Prime Minister until 1935.

MACLEAN, John (1879-1923) – Scottish revolutionary socialist and opponent of First World War; leading influence on the movement known as Red Clydeside; jailed in 1916 for his anti-war activities, but released again in 1917; supported October Revolution and appointed Soviet consul in Scotland, but never joined the Communist Party.

MARTOV, Julius (1873-1923) – Russian Social Democrat, leader of the Mensheviks.

MAXTON, James (1885-1946) – ILP leader much admired by Winston Churchill. Generally considered the leader of the 'Clydeside group' of left Labour MPs. After the disaffiliation of the ILP in 1932 he was its main political leader. He became associated with the Popular Front and in a notorious speech in 1938 expressed support for Chamberlain's appeasement of Hitler.

MCGOVERN, John (1887-1968) – A leader of the ILP in the 1930s, leaving it in 1947. He visited Spain as a supporter of the POUM. Participated in some of the hunger marches of the 1930s, but in later life became virulently anti-communist and joined Moral Re-Armament in 1954.

MILL, John Stuart (1806-1873) – British philosopher, political economist and politician. He was a leading liberal thinker of the nineteenth century and an advocate of utilitarianism. Son of James Mill.

MILLERAND, Alexandre (1859-1943) – French socialist politician; his membership of the Waldeck-Rousseau cabinet in 1899 alongside Gallifet, the butcher of the Paris Commune, provoked a heated debate within the international socialist movement about 'ministerialism'; expelled from the Socialist Party in 1903 he moved to the right, becoming Prime Minister for eight months in 1920 and president of the French Republic from 1920-24.

MILYUKOV, Pavel Nikolayevich (1858-1943) – Historian and liberal politician in pre-revolutionary Russia; founder of the Constitutional Democratic (Cadet) Party; member of first Provisional government in 1917; forced by mass movement to resign; after the October Revolution he supported and advised the counter-revolutionary White forces during the Civil War.

MORRISON, Herbert (1888-1965) – Right-wing Labour politician; held posts in the wartime coalition including Home Secretary 1940-5, showing his anti-communism by banning the *Daily Worker* and imprisoning Trotskyists. Leader of the House of Commons in 1945-51 and Foreign Secretary in 1951.

MOSLEY, Cynthia Blanche (1898-1933) – Daughter of Lord Curzon. She married Oswald Mosley in 1920; in 1931, along with her husband, she left the Labour Party to set up the 'New' Party, which soon became the British Union of Fascists.

MOSLEY, Sir Oswald Ernald (1896-1980) – Leader of British fascism in the 1930s. Conservative MP from 1918-24 and Labour MP from 1924-31. Husband of Cynthia Mosley. As Chancellor of the Duchy of Lancaster in MacDonald's 1929 Labour government, he tried to put forward various radical capitalist solutions to unemployment. When the Labour leaders would not accept them, he set up a 'New' Party, which became the British Union of Fascists in 1932.

MUSSOLINI, Benito (1883-1945) – Italian fascist and dictator of Italy from 1922 -43.

OWEN, Robert (1771-1858) – British utopian socialist.

PATON, John (1886-1976) – Secretary of the ILP 1927-33.

PEPPER, John (1886-1939) – Hungarian communist, associated with Bukharin in the International Right Opposition. Ultra-left at the time of the Third Congress of the Communist International; described by Trotsky in the late 1920s as "a political parasite".

PITT, William, 'The Elder' (Lord Chatham) (1708-1778) – Secretary of State from 1756 and effective Prime Minister who led the war with France, raised the militia and reinforced sea power.

PITT, William, 'The Younger' (1759-1806) – MP from 1781 and Prime Minister from 1783. In 1794 he raised the forces among the European powers to fight the armies of the French Revolution. He repressed the Irish Rising of 1798 and forced through the Act of Union of 1801. He introduced various other pieces of repressive legislation, notably the anti-union Combination Acts of 1799 and 1800. He resigned in 1801, but became Prime Minister again in 1804 when once more he had to rally the forces of European reaction to fight the French republic.

PLEKHANOV, Georgi (1856-1918) – Founder of Russian Marxism. Degenerated into social patriotism on the outbreak of war, and was bitterly hostile to the Bolshevik revolution.

POINCARÉ, Raymond (1860-1934) – French Prime Minister from 1922-24.

POLLITT, Henry (1890-1960) – British Stalinist leader.

PURCELL, Albert Arthur (1872-1935) – Trade union leader; a member of virtually every left-wing organisation that existed during his lifetime, but remained through a left trade unionist who for a time expressed an admiration for the achievements of the Soviet Union.

RAKOVSKY, Christian (1873-1941) – Bulgarian-born Romanian socialist and Soviet diplomat; Soviet diplomatic representative in London 1923-24 and Ambassador to France 1925-27.

RENAUDEL, Pierre (1871-1935) – French socialist leader, right-wing social patriot during the war.

RHODES, Cecil (1853-1902) – British imperialist active in Southern Africa. Founder of the colony of Rhodesia, today Zambia and Zimbabwe.

ROBERTS, Frederick Sleigh (Lord Roberts) (1832-1914) – Anglo-Irish soldier who was a leading commander of the British Army during the Victorian period. He served in many military campaigns in Afghanistan, Abyssinia and India. He was commander of the British forces in South Africa during the first phase of the Second Boer War in 1899-1900.

ROBERTSON – The name used by a prominent member of the Marxist Group of Trotskyists within the ILP. He visited Trotsky in November 1935 and reported fully to the Group on his discussions about leaving the ILP.

ROUSSEAU, Jean-Jacques (1712-1788) – Geneva-born philosopher of the Enlightenment whose political ideas had a great effect on the French Revolution and subsequent political developments.

RUSSELL, Bertrand (1872-1970) – British empiricist philosopher of aristocratic background and radical views. Active in various pacifist movements throughout his life. Fined during the First World War as a conscientious objector and imprisoned in the 1960s as an opponent of the H-bomb. At the end of his life, he associated himself with protest movements against Vietnam war. Always hostile to Marxism and Communism, Russell visited the Soviet Union soon after the Revolution and condemned it in *The Practice and Theory of Bolshevism* published in 1920. A member of the Labour Party from the 1920s, he left it in the 1960s.

SCHEIDEMANN, Philipp (1865-1939) – German journalist and Social Democratic politician; during the First World War he was a leader of the Majority Social Democrats, who continued to vote for war credits; a leader of the provisional government that emerged from the 1918 November Revolution; became Chancellor after the convening of the National Assembly in February 1919; resigned in June 1919 but remained influential in the SPD.

SHAUMYAN, Stepan (1878-1918) – Armenian Bolshevik, member of the Bolshevik Central Committee, leader of the Baku Commune until July 1918; captured by the British occupation forces in Krasnovodsk in September 1918 and executed without trial.

SHAW, George Bernard (1856-1950) – Fabian and playwright.

SMILLIE, Robert (1857-1940) – Scottish trade unionist; Labour MP (1923-1929); refused government office in the first Labour government (1924).

SMITH, Dr. Charles Andrew (1895-1984) – ILP leader; became associated with the policies of Maxton and Brockway. Visited Trotsky in 1933 on behalf of the ILP. By 1939 he had become a social patriot.

SNOWDEN, Ethel (1881-1951) – Active in the Labour, feminist, and temperance movements and a member of the Executives of the Fabian Society, Labour Party, and the National Union of Women's Suffrage Societies. Married to Philip Snowden.

SNOWDEN, Philip (1864-1937) – Joined the ILP and was one of its most active propagandists; Chancellor of the Exchequer in MacDonald's 1924 and 1929 cabinets and pursued policies of the strictest capitalist orthodoxy, favouring free trade and balanced budgets and thus proved quite incapable of arresting the growth of mass unemployment and the economic collapse of 1931. In that year he joined MacDonald in alliance with the Tories and became a member of the 'National' government and the House of Lords. Married to Ethel Snowden.

STEPHEN, Campbell (1884-1947) – ILP member and MP. One of the Clydeside group of 'left' Labour MP.

TEAGUE-JONES, Reginald (1889-1988) – British intelligence officer accused of ordering the execution of the twenty-six Baku Bolsheviks.

THOMAS, James Henry (1874-1949) – Labour and trade union leader. Favoured Labour participation in Lloyd George's coalition government and broke wartime strikes of railwaymen. For most of the period 1919-29 he played an active part in negotiations between government and unions.

TOLSTOY, Leo (1828-1910) – Russian author, widely regarded as one of the greatest in history. From the 1880s onwards he was famed in Russia as the proponent of a highly individualistic philosophy of Christian anarchism, renouncing property, the Church, and all forms of violence.

TOMSKY, Mikhail (1886-1936) – Old Bolshevik and a trade unionist. Always on the right wing of the Party, he opposed the 1917 insurrection and was closely involved in Stalin's policies in the mid-1920s, particularly on the Anglo-Russian Trade Union Committee. He opposed the left turn in 1928 along with Bukharin and Rykov and committed suicide after the first of the Moscow Trials.

VANDERVELDE, Emil (1866-1938) – Belgian right-wing socialist and one of the leaders of the Second International. During the First World War he was one of the most extreme social-chauvinists, becoming Prime Minister, and was extremely hostile to Soviet Russia.

WEBB, Beatrice (1858-1943) – Prominent Fabian. Married to Sidney Webb, with whom she collaborated in all his literary and political activities and shared his admiration for the Soviet Union of the Stalinist period.

WEBB, Sidney James (1859-1947) – Principal Fabian theoretician and Minister in two Labour governments between the wars. Wrote authoritative empirical studies on the *History of Trade Unionism* (1894) and *Industrial Democracy* (1897) with his wife Beatrice. They also wrote a multi-volumed work on *English Local Government* (1906-29), set up the London School of Economics, and began the *New Statesman* in 1913 as the journal of petty-bourgeois reformism.

WELLS, Herbert George (1866-1946) – British writer and journalist; had vague socialistic views; was a member of the Fabian Society for a short period.

WHEATLEY, John (1869-1930) – Labour MP; joined the Independent Labour Party in 1908; Minister of Health in MacDonald's first government in 1924. With the defeat of the Labour Government he went over to the left wing of the parliamentary party.

WILLIAMS, Robert (1881-1936) – Trade union leader; an architect of the Triple Alliance; leading member of the Labour Party and a member of the delegation to Russia in 1920. A member of the British Socialist Party and a founding member of the CP, from which he was expelled in 1921 for his role in the events of 'Black Friday'.

WILSON, Woodrow (1856-1924) – President of the United States 1913-1921; re-elected on an anti-war platform in 1916, Wilson brought the US into the war in April 1917; architect of the Versailles Treaty and the League of Nations.

WRANGEL, Pyotr Nikolayevich (1878-1928) – Tsarist officer and White Guard leader who regrouped the remnants of Denikin's defeated Volunteer Army in the Crimean Peninsula, and with substantial aid from Britain and France, attacked Soviet Russia from the south. His army was defeated by the end of 1920.

YUDENICH, Nikolai Nikolaevich (1862-1933) – Tsarist general during the First World War, commander of the counter-revolutionary White Army in the Baltic area of Russia, which was poised to take Petrograd in August and September 1919.

ZHORDANIA, Noe (1868-1953) – Georgian journalist and Menshevik politician; adopted social-chauvinist position during the First World War working closely with Plekhanov; head of Georgian government from July 1918 to March 1921, when Georgia was occupied by Soviet troops; headed Georgian government-in-exile until his death.

Index

C

M

List of Titles by Wellred Books

Wellred Books is a publishing house specialising in works of Marxist theory. A sister publisher and bookseller is based in the USA. Among the titles published by Wellred Books are:

Anti-Dühring, Friedrich Engels

Bolshevism: The Road to Revolution, Alan Woods

Chartist Revolution, Rob Sewell

China: From Permanent Revolution to Counter-Revolution, John Roberts

The Civil War in France, Karl Marx

The Class Struggles in France, 1848-1850, Karl Marx

The Classics of Marxism: Volume One, Various authors

The Classics of Marxism: Volume Two, Various authors

Dialectics of Nature, Friedrich Engels

The Eighteenth Brumaire of Louis Bonaparte, Karl Marx

The First Five Years of the Communist International, Leon Trotsky

The First World War: A Marxist Analysis of the Great Slaughter, Alan Woods

Germany: From Revolution to Counter-Revolution, Rob Sewell

Germany 1918-1933: Socialism or Barbarism, Rob Sewell

History of British Trotskyism, Ted Grant

The History of Philosophy, Alan Woods

The History of the Russian Revolution: Volumes One to Three, Leon Trotsky

The History of the Russian Revolution to Brest-Litovsk, Leon Trotsky

The Ideas of Karl Marx, Alan Woods

Imperialism: The Highest Stage of Capitalism, V. I. Lenin

In Defence of Marxism, Leon Trotsky

In the Cause of Labour, Rob Sewell

Ireland: Republicanism and Revolution, Alan Woods

Lenin and Trotsky: What They Really Stood For, Alan Woods & Ted Grant

Lenin, Trotsky & the Theory of the Permanent Revolution, John Roberts

Marxism and Anarchism, Various authors

Marxism and the USA, Alan Woods

Materialism and Empirio-criticism, V. I. Lenin

My Life, Leon Trotsky

Not Guilty, Dewey Commission Report

The Origin of the Family, Private Property & the State, Friedrich Engels

The Permanent Revolution and Results & Prospects, Leon Trotsky

Permanent Revolution in Latin America, John Roberts & Jorge Martin

Reason in Revolt, Alan Woods & Ted Grant

Reformism or Revolution, Alan Woods

Revolution and Counter-Revolution in Spain, Felix Morrow

The Revolution Betrayed, Leon Trotsky

The Revolutionary Legacy of Rosa Luxemburg, Marie Frederiksen

The Revolutionary Philosophy of Marxism, John Peterson [Ed.]

Russia: From Revolution to Counter-Revolution, Ted Grant

Spain's Revolution Against Franco, Alan Woods

Stalin, Leon Trotsky

The State and Revolution, V. I. Lenin

Ted Grant: The Permanent Revolutionary, Alan Woods

Ted Grant Writings: Volumes One and Two, Ted Grant

Thawra hatta'l nasr! - Revolution until Victory!, Alan Woods & others

What Is Marxism?, Rob Sewell & Alan Woods

What Is to Be Done?, V. I. Lenin

Women, Family & the Russian Revolution, John Roberts & Fred Weston

Writings on Britain, Leon Trotsky

To make an order or for more information, visit wellred-books.com, email books@wellred-books.com or write to Wellred Books, 152-160 Kemp House, City Road, London, EC1V 2NX, United Kingdom.